MS	mean square
n	the number of scores in a category
N	the total number of scores in an analysis
0	observed frequency (used in chi-square)
P or p	probability
r	a Pearson product-moment correlation coefficient
r^2	the coefficient of determination
s	the standard deviation of a sample
s^2	the variance of a sample
s_D	the standard deviation of the differences in paired scores
$s_{\overline{D}}$	the standard error of the difference between paired means
$s_{\overline{x}}$	the standard error of the mean of a sample
$s_{\overline{X}_1 - \overline{X}_2}$	the standard error of the difference in means
$s_{Y \cdot X}$	the standard error of estimate for Y
SS	sum of squares
t	a ratio of the difference between two means to the standard error of the difference in the means
T	a standard score equal to $10z + 50$; also the sum of all raw scores in an ANOVA
t_α	the critical value for t at the α-level of significance
UL	the upper limit of a class interval or a confidence interval
X	a raw score on variable X
x	a deviation score, $X - \overline{X}$
$\overline{X}$	the mean of a sample
Y	a raw score on variable Y
Y' or $\hat{Y}$	a predicted score on variable Y
z	a standard score equal to $(X - \overline{X})/s$ or $(X - \mu)/\sigma$
$>$	greater than
$<$	less than

Basic Statistics for Behavioral Science Research

Second Edition

Mary B. Harris
University of New Mexico

Allyn and Bacon

Boston   London   Toronto   Sydney   Tokyo   Singapore

Senior Vice President and Publisher, Education: *Nancy Forsyth*
Editorial Assistant: *Cheryl Ouellette*
Marketing Manager: *Kris Farnsworth*
Editorial-Production Service: *Maes Associates*
Manufacturing Buyer: *Megan Cochran*
Cover Administrator: *Linda Knowles*

Copyright © 1998, 1995 by Allyn & Bacon
A Viacom Company
Needham Heights, Mass. 02194

Internet: www.abacon.com
America Online: keyword: College Online

Library of Congress Cataloging-in-Publication Data
Harris, Mary B. (Mary Bierman)
    Basic statistics for behavioral science research / Mary B. Harris.
  —2nd ed.
      p.   cm.
    Includes bibliographical references and index.
    ISBN 0-205-26889-7
    1. Statistics.   I. Title.
QA276.12.H365 1998
001.4'22—dc21   97-7403
                                                                        CIP

Printed in the United States of America

10   9   8   7   6   5   4   3   2   02   01   00   99   98

Contents

Preface   xiii

1 Introduction   1

Why Study Statistics?   1
   Statistics and Research   1
What Are the Uses of Statistics?   6
   Descriptive Versus Inferential Statistics   6
   Populations Versus Samples   8
   Parameters Versus Statistics   10
   Summary of Uses of Statistics   11
What Are the Characteristics of Variables?   12
   Constants Versus Variables   12
   Qualitative Versus Quantitative Variables   12
   Scales or Levels of Measurement   15
   Relationships Among the Levels of Measurement   18
   Why Does Level of Measurement Matter?   19
What Are Parametric and Nonparametric Tests?   20
   Disadvantages and Advantages of Parametric Tests   21
What Symbols and Procedures Are Used in Statistics?   22
   Symbols for Scores   23
   Symbols for Mathematical Procedures   24
   Other Mathematical Procedures   27
   Formulas and Equations   31
What Is the Role of Calculators and Computers?   32
What Is the Best Way to Study Statistics?   33
Chapter Summary   35
Chapter Review   36
   Multiple-Choice Questions   36

Problems   *37*
Study Questions   *40*

2   Introduction to Research Design   42

What Is Scientific Research?   42
   Role of Observation   *43*
   Role of Hypotheses   *43*
   Research and Causality   *45*
What Are Some Approaches to Research?   46
   Types of Research   *46*
   Purposes of Research   *56*
   Research Setting   *57*
How Are Extraneous Variables Controlled?   58
   Methods of Control   *58*
   Internal and External Validity   *63*
What Are Some Guidelines for Using Statistics?   64
   Consider the Meaning of the Numbers   *64*
   Consider How the Numbers Will Be Interpreted   *64*
   Consider Whether Assumptions Are Met   *65*
   Estimate the Results That Would Be Reasonable   *65*
Chapter Summary   66
Chapter Review   67
   Multiple-Choice Questions   *67*
   Problems   *68*
   Study Questions   *71*

3   Describing Data: Tables and Graphs   73

How Should Scores Be Organized?   73
How Are Tables of Frequency Distributions Used?   74
   Simple Frequency Distributions   *74*
   Grouped Frequency Distributions   *75*
   Stem-and-Leaf Displays   *78*
   Cumulative Frequency Distributions   *78*
   Relative Frequency Distributions   *80*
   Cumulative Relative Frequency Distributions   *80*
What Are Percentiles?   81
   Percentile Rank   *82*
   Guidelines for Computing Percentile Ranks   *83*
How Are Graphs of Frequency Distributions Used?   84
   Ordinate and Abscissa   *84*
   Graphing Qualitative Data   *85*
   Graphing Quantitative Data   *87*

Shapes of Frequency Distributions   88
Graphs Showing the Relationship Between Variables   91
Misleading Graphs   93
What Is the Best Way to Present Data?   95
Tables   95
Graphs   96
Chapter Summary   98
Chapter Review   99
Multiple-Choice Questions   99
Problems   100
Study Questions   104

4 Describing Data: Central Tendency, Variability, and Standard Scores   106

What Is a Measure of Central Tendency?   106
Mode   106
Median   107
Mean   109
Selecting the Most Appropriate Measure of Central Tendency   113
Estimating Measures of Central Tendency from Grouped Data   115
Reporting Measures of Central Tendency in APA Style   115
What Is a Measure of Variability?   115
Range   116
Mean Absolute Deviation   118
Standard Deviation   119
Variance   126
Selecting the Most Appropriate Measure of Variability   128
Estimating Variability from Grouped Data   130
Reporting Measures of Variability in APA Style   131
What Are Standard Scores?   131
z-Scores   131
Other Standard Scores   134
When Should You Use the Techniques?   137
Chapter Summary   138
Chapter Review   138
Multiple-Choice Questions   138
Problems   140
Study Questions   143

5 Probability and the Normal Curve   145

What Are Empirical and Theoretical Distributions?   145
Types of Theoretical Distributions   145

What Is Probability?   146
    Combining Probabilities   147
What Is the Binomial Distribution?   151
What Is the Normal Distribution?   154
    Graphing a Normal Distribution: The Normal Curve   154
    Relationship Between the Normal Curve and Probability   155
    Dividing the Area Under the Normal Curve   156
What Is a Normal Curve Table?   157
    Probability and the Normal Curve Table   158
    Different Types of Normal Curve Problems   160
What Are Some General Guidelines for Solving Normal
Curve Problems?   172
    Deciding When to Use the Technique   174
Chapter Summary   174
Chapter Review   175
    Multiple-Choice Questions   175
    Problems   176
    Study Questions   178

6   Correlation   180

What Is Correlation?   180
    Use of Scattergraphs   181
What Is the Pearson *r* Statistic?   184
    Range of Values of r   185
    Assumptions of Pearson r   185
    Restriction of Range   187
    Formulas for Pearson r   187
What Is a Significant Pearson *r*?   195
    Characteristics of a Statistically Significant r   196
    Using a Table of the Significance of r   196
    What to Do If r Is Not Significant   198
    How to Interpret a Significant r   200
    Describing a Significant Correlation   203
    Reporting a Significant Correlation in APA Style   203
Are There Other Types of Correlation?   204
    Spearman Rho   204
    Partial and Multiple Correlations   207
When Are Correlation Techniques Used?   208
    Nature of the Research   208
    Characteristics of the Data   208
    Cautions   209
Chapter Summary   209
Chapter Review   210

Multiple-Choice Questions   210
Problems   212
Study Questions   216

7   Regression   217

What Is Regression?   217
Predicted Values   217
Relationship of Regression to Correlation   218
What Are the Formulas for Regression?   219
z-Score Formula for Regression   219
Computational Formula   220
Using the Regression Equations   223
How Are Regression Lines Plotted and Used?   227
Plotting the Regression Line   228
Using the Regression Line   229
What Is Regression Toward the Mean?   230
Conceptual Examples   231
Research Examples   231
What Is a Standard Error of Estimate?   236
Formulas   236
Interpretation   237
What Is Multiple Regression?   238
When Is Regression Used?   240
Chapter Summary   240
Chapter Review   241
Multiple-Choice Questions   241
Problems   242
Study Questions   247

8   The Logic of Inferential Statistics   249

How Are Samples Used in Inferential Statistics?   249
Random Sampling   250
Stratified Sampling   253
Quota Sampling   255
Systematic Sampling   255
Cluster Sampling   256
Convenience or Haphazard Sampling   257
Clearly Biased Sampling   257
Generalizing to a Population   258
What Are Sampling Distributions and How Are They Used?   259
Expected Value and Standard Error of a Sampling Distribution   260
Central Limit Theorem   260

What Are z-Tests and How Are They Used?   263
  General Procedure   *264*
  Using a z-Test with a Single Sample   *266*
  Using a z-Test to Compare Two Sample Means   *267*
What Are the Uses of Inferential Statistics?   270
  Parameter Estimation   *270*
  Hypothesis Testing   *272*
How Are Hypotheses Tested?   273
  Null Versus Alternative Hypotheses   *273*
  Significance Levels   *276*
  Types of Errors   *279*
  Power   *281*
  Effect Size   *282*
  One-Tailed Versus Two-Tailed Significance Tests   *282*
  Statistical Significance Versus Meaningfulness   *285*
Chapter Summary   286
Chapter Review   287
  Multiple-Choice Questions   *287*
  Problems   *289*
  Study Questions   *292*

9   *t*-Tests and Confidence Intervals About Means   294

How Are *t*-Tests Used to Test Hypotheses About Means?   294
  z-Tests Versus t-Tests   *294*
  Characteristics of t-Tests   *295*
Why Are There Different Types of *t*-Tests?   298
  Single-Sample t-Test   *298*
  Independent-Samples t-Test   *303*
  Dependent-Samples t-Test   *309*
How Are Confidence Intervals Used?   316
  Formulas   *317*
When Should These Techniques Be Used?   321
  Choosing the Appropriate Technique   *322*
Chapter Summary   325
Chapter Review   325
  Multiple-Choice Questions   *325*
  Problems   *328*
  Study Questions   *332*

10   One-Way Analysis of Variance   334

What Is the *F*-Distribution?   334
  Characteristics of the F-Distribution   *334*

Uses of F   335
What Is an Analysis of Variance?   341
    Relationship of F and t   341
    Assumptions   342
    ANOVA Versus Multiple t-Tests   343
    Formulas for the Analysis of Variance   344
    Analysis of Variance Summary Table   349
    Examples of One-Way ANOVAs   349
    Interpretation of F from ANOVA   356
How Do You Decide Which Analysis to Use?   357
    One-Way ANOVA Versus t-Test   357
    Other Analysis of Variance Procedures   357
    ANOVA Versus Multiple Regression   359
Chapter Summary   361
Chapter Review   362
    Multiple-Choice Questions   362
    Problems   364
    Study Questions   369

11   Comparisons Among Means   371

What Is a Comparison?   371
    Ways of Testing Differences in Means   371
    Advantages of a Comparison   372
    A Priori Versus Post Hoc Comparisons   373
    Weights   375
What Is the Scheffé Comparison Procedure?   376
    Formulas   377
    Computing the Critical Value   378
    Examples of Scheffé Comparisons   380
    Orthogonality   384
    Advantages and Disadvantages of the Scheffé Procedure   388
What Is the Tukey HSD Procedure?   389
    Formulas   390
    Examples of Tukey's HSD   391
    Advantages and Disadvantages of the Tukey HSD Procedure   393
What Are Some Other Comparison Procedures?   394
How Do You Select the Appropriate Procedure?   395
    Questions to Consider   395
    Other Issues   396
Chapter Summary   397
Chapter Review   398
    Multiple-Choice Questions   398

Problems   400
Study Questions   405

12 Two-Way Analysis of Variance   407

What Is a Two-Way Analysis of Variance?   407
   Types of Factorial Designs   408
   Assumptions of the Two-Way ANOVA   410
   Overview of the Two-Way ANOVA   411
What Are the Formulas for the Two-Way Analysis of Variance?   412
   Notation   412
   Partitioning of Sums of Squares   413
   Logic of the Analysis   414
   Computational Formulas   415
How Is a Two-Way ANOVA Used?   418
   Advantages of a Factorial Design   418
   Interpreting Significant Main Effects and Interactions   419
   Computational Example of a 2×2 ANOVA   423
   Computational Example of a 3×2 ANOVA   427
   Next Steps   434
Chapter Summary   436
Chapter Review   437
   Multiple-Choice Questions   437
   Problems   440
   Study Questions   445

13 Chi-Square   447

What Is a Chi-Square Test?   447
   χ^2 Distribution   447
   Assumptions   448
What Is a χ^2 Goodness-of-Fit Test?   449
   Formula   450
   Examples of Goodness-of-Fit Tests   452
   Deciding on the Hypothesis to Test   454
What Is a χ^2 Test of Independence?   456
   Contingency Tables   456
   Formulas   457
   Examples of χ^2 Tests   459
   Strength of the Relationship   465
How Can You Correct for Small Expected Frequencies?   466
   Collapse Across Categories   466
   Yates' Correction   467
   Fisher's Exact Probability Test   467

How Are Results of χ^2 Tests Reported?   467
  APA Style   467
  Describing the Finding   468
When Should χ^2 Tests Be Used?   468
  Goodness of Fit Versus Test of Independence   469
  χ^2 Versus r or ρ   469
  χ^2 Versus t or ANOVA   469
Chapter Summary   470
Chapter Review   470
  Multiple-Choice Questions   470
  Problems   472
  Study Questions   476

14   Selecting Appropriate Statistical Tests   478

What Is the Nature of Your Data?   478
  Scale of Measurement   478
  Shape, Variance, and Other Characteristics   479
What Is Your Purpose?   480
  Describing Data   480
  Predicting Scores   480
  Relating Variables   481
  Comparing Means   482
  Comparing Medians   482
  Differences in Frequencies or Proportions   483
  Multiple Independent and Dependent Variables   483
  Multiple Significance Tests   484
How Do Your Questions and Hypotheses Influence the Choice
of Analysis?   484
  Questions and Hypotheses   484
  Examples of Research Situations   485
What Are Some Issues in Reporting Research Results?   489
  What to Omit   489
  What to Include   490
  APA Style   490
  Significance   490
What Next?   491
  Take More Statistics Courses   491
  Learn About Computers   491
  Know When and How to Seek Help   492
  Get Involved in Research   492
Chapter Summary   493
Chapter Review   493
  Multiple-Choice Questions   493

Problems   *495*
Study Questions   *500*

References   503

Appendix Tables   507

Glossary   527

Answers and Solutions   539

Index   571

Preface

In this second edition of *Basic Statistics for Behavioral Science Research* I have made a number of changes.

First, I have added a chapter dealing with two-way analysis of variance (Chapter 12).

Second, I have added additional material dealing with such topics as research and causality, considering how numbers are interpreted, advantages of relative and cumulative relative frequency distributions, misleading graphs, box-and-whisker plots, further advantages of z-scores, restriction of range, multiple regression, power, effect size, and the debate about the importance and value of statistical significance testing.

Third, I have added a number of references from 1996 and 1997.

Fourth, I have added additional problems to each chapter.

Fifth, in this edition I have provided solutions to only the odd-numbered problems. The solutions to the even-numbered problems are provided in the *Instructor's Manual,* so the problems can be assigned as homework.

Sixth, I have relabeled the tables of critical values for Pearson r and Student's t to clearly identify one-tailed critical values.

Seventh, I have changed the language to conform with the 1994 edition of the American Psychological Association Publication Manual.

Eighth, I have deleted some of the less essential and more intimidating information on how to carry out interpolation.

Ninth, I have corrected the minor errors and clarified the ambiguities that somehow insinuated themselves into the first edition.

In spite of these changes, the focus and purpose of the book remain the same as in the first edition.

Most statistics textbooks are written for people who teach statistics. After all, these are the people who know the material; who decide what belongs in the course; who make up the lectures, problems, and tests that form the heart of the course; and, of course, who pick the textbook. I, too, hope that statistics instructors will like this book and want to use it. To this end, I have tried to be accurate and current in describing the way in which statistical procedures are used by researchers who publish the results of their analyses. However, I have really written this book not for those who already understand statistics but for those of you who want to (or have to) learn to use statistics in order to read, understand, and conduct research.

In writing this book, I have tried to accomplish several things.

1. First I have attempted to write a book that you, the reader, can understand. I remember my misery in my first statistics class, in which the instructor assumed a knowledge of calculus that I didn't possess. In this book, I've avoided the assumption that you have any particular background or expertise. I don't assume that you know more than elementary school mathematics. In case you don't, Chapter 1 reviews and explains all the mathematics that you will need. I do assume that you will make mistakes in computation. Everyone does. What I try to do is to show you how to identify mistakes and learn from them.

I don't assume that you are familiar with the statistics or research literature in any particular field, although most of my examples come from education and the social sciences. To help you become familiar with the research literature in your field, I have a number of study questions that encourage you to go to the library and to look for relevant research articles that you can use to understand statistics.

I don't assume that you can see a formula and immediately recognize the necessary steps to be carried out in solving it. Instead, I have provided step-by-step descriptions of how to carry out computations and arrive at the correct answer.

I don't assume that you know what kinds of statistical tests to conduct. Nor do I assume that you know how to interpret the numbers that you get when you've solved a statistical equation. Instead, this book teaches you how to select the appropriate analyses to do, how to understand the results of your analyses, and how to explain these results to others.

2. As the title implies, I have tried to keep a consistent focus on the use of statistics as a tool for conducting research. My decisions about what to include and to exclude have been determined by consideration of what researchers in psychology, education, and other areas of social science need to know about statistics. To achieve this goal, I have done several things.

I have included an entire chapter on research methodology, Chapter 2. Most of the decisions that researchers make about how to analyze their data are guided by their research questions or hypotheses and by the nature of the data they collect. I have tried to show the intimate connection between research design and statistical analysis not only in this chapter but throughout the book.

Rather than discussing how each statistical technique relates to probability theory and mathematics, I have stressed their usefulness for understanding and interpreting research data. Not only do I discuss relevant research issues as each technique is presented, but throughout the book I emphasize the differences between the statistical procedures in terms of the kinds of research questions they can answer. Indeed, the last chapter of the book is concerned primarily with how to select the appropriate technique to answer a particular research question.

I have described and given examples of the appropriate use of the American Psychological Association style for reporting research results. The book itself is written in APA style. Beyond this, I have emphasized the importance of describing and reporting results clearly and accurately, in a way that relates them to the purpose of the research study from which they come.

3. I have tried to be interesting. Most statistics books are dull. My students tell me that this book is reasonably entertaining. Would they lie to me—even anonymously?

4. I have used a number of pedagogical devices in the book.
- Throughout every chapter of the book, there are a number of *Tips* that identify things to look out for, mistakes to avoid, suggestions that can make your life (as a user of statistics) simpler, and/or information about what researchers really do. Some of my students (the same ones who say that the book is interesting) say that the *Tips* are helpful.
- Throughout the book summary tables present the major aspects of important concepts.
- In the first chapter, I have listed a number of suggestions about how to study statistics. Try them. They work for most people.
- New terms are boldfaced and defined in a glossary.
- The book also contains a list of symbols and a list of formulas inside the front and back covers.
- Each chapter includes a summary of the major points.
- Each chapter includes multiple-choice questions and conceptual and computational problems. Answers to odd-numbered questions and problems are provided. Many of the answers include detailed explanations not only of why the right answers are correct but of why the other alternatives are wrong.
- Each chapter includes four or five Study Questions. These are not problems that have single correct answers that you can look up. These are exercises that you can do to help you understand the meaning and use of the material in the chapter.
- Although it is unrealistic to think that you can learn all you need to know about every possible use of statistics from one book, it is realistic to assume that you can learn enough so that from now on you will know what to do or where to go next. Therefore, I have pointed out situations in which you might need to use statistical procedures

not covered in this textbook or to seek more expert statistical advice. I have also described several more advanced statistical techniques that you may encounter in your reading.

- Wherever possible, the Appendix tables give critical values to the .05, .01, and .001 α-levels. When you've finished the course, you will be glad to have these tables so that you can report your significance levels accurately.

I hope that this book will be useful not only to students taking a class but also to other people who want to do research. As a psychologist who teaches in a college of education and who has friends from teaching, nursing, social work, management, and other professions, I know a number of professional people who are interested in doing research but who may not have had much statistical training as part of their formal education. If you are such a person, I have tried to include in this book everything that you need to know in order to understand enough statistics to be able to conduct research and interpret your results.

Acknowledgments

I owe a great debt to Richard J. Harris, who taught me much of what I know about statistics and who reviewed an earlier version of this book. I am also very grateful to the following reviewers who read and commented on an earlier draft of the manuscript for the first edition; Ralph De Ayla, University of Maryland, College Park; Barbara Anderson Lounsbury; Walena Morse, West Chester University; Stephen Olejnik, University of Georgia; and Bruce Thompson, Texas A & M University. I am also very grateful to the following reviewers for the second edition: Timothy N. Ansley, University of Iowa; Thomas T. Frantz, State University of New York at Buffalo; Gary Greer, University of Houston-Downtown; Susan E. Harris, Michigan State University; Richard L. Marsh, University of Georgia; and Michael Wogan, Rutgers University. A number of students gave me helpful feedback on the previous edition of this book. Unfortunately, I can't blame any of these people for any mistakes that remain.

I am grateful to friends who supplied encouraging words, inspiration, and occasional diversions. Nancy Forsyth, whose title at Allyn & Bacon keeps getting more exalted but whose suggestions remain down to earth, provided support and helpful advice throughout the process of writing and rewriting. Dick, Jennifer, Christopher, Alexander, David, and Ryan have enriched my life in many ways. Special thanks to Alexander, who suggested the popcorn and soap examples and who did some of the cooking while I worked on the book.

Introduction

Why Study Statistics?

Statistics—close your eyes and think of the word. Does it conjure up the sound of romantic violin music, the smell of fragrant flowers, the vision of a sunset over the ocean? No? How about your heart beating faster, your palms getting sweaty, your hands shaking and butterflies in the stomach as you think about trying to deal with a bunch of arbitrary numbers after you thought you were through with math forever? Or does it cause your eyelids to droop and your chin to sink onto your hand as you try to stifle a yawn? Relatively few people beginning to study statistics see it as a topic that elicits passionate excitement. More common is either fear, often grounded in unhappy experiences with mathematics in the past, or boredom, based on the anticipation of a lot of rote memorization of arbitrary, useless formulas, due to be forgotten as soon as the course is over.

Many people, perhaps most, enter the study of statistics reluctantly. They recognize that it's something that they have to do, but view it as an ordeal more than an opportunity. If you are one of these students, this book may change your mind. A number of students report that learning statistics can go beyond being interesting to being exciting, once they see that they can indeed learn to do it and that knowledge of statistics is something to be used often, even outside of the classroom, rather than something to be forgotten.

Statistics and Research

Why Bother? Why should someone in the behavioral and social sciences know statistics? Although statistics is an important branch of mathematics in its own right, statistics for most social and behavioral scientists is primarily a useful tool for doing and understanding their research. Statistics is a vehicle that researchers can use to investigate research questions and interpret the **data**—facts, observations, information—that come from such investigations.

TIP ▬▬▬▬▬▬▬▬▬▬▬▬▬▬▬▬▬▬▬▬▬

> The word *data* is plural, with *datum* being the singular term used to refer to a single piece of data. However, it's certainly easy to think of "data" as a singular noun that is a synonym for "information." To entertain yourself in reading this book, you might want to look for the instances in which "data" has mistakenly been treated as singular.

This book focuses on the use of statistics to answer research questions, rather than on the derivations or mathematical implications of specific statistical tests. Whenever we deal with data, we need to evaluate and interpret those data so that we can understand what they mean and draw conclusions from them about the issues that led us to collect the data. For most kinds of data, the use of statistics is an essential contribution to that understanding.

There is even evidence that training in statistics can help people think and reason more logically about real-world problems. The title of a research-based article by Schaller, Asp, Rosell, and Heim (1996) makes this clear: "Training in Statistical Reasoning Inhibits the Formation of Erroneous Group Stereotypes." Learning about statistics can have a positive impact even if you don't plan to use this knowledge.

Statistics for Whom?   Future classroom teachers, nurses, counselors, and others who are focusing on professional careers in the helping professions may wonder at first why they have to study statistics as part of their program, if they don't intend to conduct research once they graduate. There are two answers to this question. First, you may become one of the many people who didn't plan to use statistics and do research when they first started studying statistics, but who came to see the importance of research as they got deeper into their field. For example, finding out whether or not counseling is having any effect, or knowing whether first-grade children who use invented spelling become better or poorer spellers, usually requires statistical analysis.

Second, even people who don't intend to do research should be able to read and evaluate the research of others, rather than relying on second- or third-hand summaries and judgments, which may well be inaccurate. Every teacher who wants students to think for themselves, or every health care worker who wants patients to be responsible for their own health, could model decision making and responsibility by reading and evaluating the research literature for herself or himself.

Examples of Research Questions.   The kinds of questions that lead researchers to gather data for which statistical analysis is appropriate are almost as varied as the questions children ask parents or people who are getting to know each other ask about their ideas and their past experiences.

- What are the effects of spanking children on their behaviors towards other children?
- Do teachers who correct all the errors on written papers have students who subsequently do better work or worse?
- Is it the case that using the keyword method of memorizing works better than trying to remember something in your own fashion?
- Do opposites attract or do birds of a feather flock together?
- Do personnel officers react differently to resumes submitted by males and females, if the only thing that differs is the gender of the name on the resume?
- Do people of different cultural groups report different experiences of parental treatment concerning such things as bedtime, rules, and expectations?
- Does patient education for people who are about to undergo surgery lead to a shorter hospital stay?
- What factors of a community (number of parks, population size, lighting, museums, or whatever you care to measure) predict the crime rate best, singly or in combination?
- Do countries with more restrictive gun control laws have more or fewer deaths by firearms?

These are just a few of the kinds of questions for which researchers use statistical inference and techniques to provide answers.

Examples of Nonresearch Questions.   Not all interesting questions can be answered by research, and not all research questions lend themselves to obvious statistical analysis.

Inherently Unresearchable Questions. Questions about what ought to be or about issues of faith or morality, for example, cannot be directly answered by research, although research studies can provide some information that might make such questions easier to answer.

- Should schools teach values or citizenship?
- Should they require a foreign language?
- Should teachers be paid as much as physicians or attorneys or plumbers?

No data can be observed or retrieved to provide definitive answers to these questions, any more than there are data that would persuade almost all people that the death penalty is right or wrong, or that God does or does not exist. Research can, however, answer questions about the effects of teaching a values clarification curriculum on student attitudes and behavior, or about factors that are associated with people's tendency to believe that the death penalty is or is not a good idea. Generally, if something that answers the question can be observed, it is a research question; if the question can be answered only by resorting to personal value systems or to logical (or illogical) thinking that is not dependent on data, then it is not a research question.

Currently Unresearchable Questions. In addition to questions that are inherently outside the realm of scientific research, others are currently impossible to study but might eventually be researchable once tools are available. In the social sciences, some questions about relationships among some personality and situational variables (like whether or not people who have high ego strength are more likely to survive emotionally traumatic situations) await, perhaps eternally, the development of valid and reliable measures of characteristics of individuals and situations. In the natural sciences, development of physical, chemical, and biological techniques—from cyclotrons to gene splicing—makes more and more topics researchable. Although ethical constraints on what can be studied exist, social science researchers recognize that to some extent research topics are dependent on the availability of methods to study them and that the list of research problems will change as more sophisticated methods become available. Indeed, the existence of advanced statistical methods such as structural equation modeling, which are beyond the scope of this book, has made it possible to study certain questions that would otherwise have been answered primarily by intuition.

Research Questions and Hypotheses. Although it is possible to ask a research question without having any ideas about what the answer to the question might be, most researchers go beyond asking questions to formulate some **hypotheses**, or predictions, about them. A research question is a query that you hope a research study will be able to answer, whereas a research hypothesis is a statement of the anticipated answer to the question. Although statistical procedures are sometimes used to provide *direct* answers to research questions, they are more commonly used as *indirect* ways to test the correctness of your research hypotheses. For instance, suppose that you have mileages per gallon of ten cars from the 1970s and ten cars from the 1990s. You can't use this information to *prove* that the mileage per gallon of cars has improved over the years, but you can decide that this hypothesis is likely to be correct, based on the results of a statistical analysis of the data. Information about how certain statistical procedures are used to test research hypotheses is presented in depth in Chapter 8.

Nonstatistical Research Questions. A final point to be considered is that a number of research methods do not utilize and do not obviously lend themselves to statistical analysis. Such methodologies, often termed *qualitative* or *ethnographic* by those who use them, include intensive case studies, participant observation, some historical research, and some political or theory-driven research that deliberately rejects the approach of attempting to objectify and categorize observations. Studies of the way in which a bilingual child learns to read, of the interactions on a psychiatric ward, or of the civil rights movement in America may be conducted in such a way as to make statistical analysis inappropriate. Moreover, questions that are extremely limited in scope, dealing with only one person at one point in time under one set of circumstances, rarely lead to the use of statistical procedures.

EXAMPLE

Birth Order and Social Skills Study. In order to see how statistics can be used as part of the process of understanding research, let's take an example of a particular research question. Suppose you are interested in the effects of having older or younger siblings (i.e., of being a first or a second child) upon children's skills at interacting with others. In your study, you are able to look at two sets of four-year old children: one group of 20 children with a brother or sister two or three years older and one group of 20 children with a brother or sister two or three years younger. You decide to bring the children into a laboratory setting, where you can measure their social skills. The research question that you wish to answer in this study is whether firstborn or secondborn children are more likely to understand another child's point of view and to recognize effective strategies for getting what they want from another child. Two approaches to this question are possible.

1. One way in which you might approach this question is to interview children individually and get a score on a measure in which you give a child a series of ten choices. Each choice is between a strategy you have previously determined to be more effective and/or more mature (e.g., saying "Let's take turns") and a strategy you have previously determined to be less effective and/or less mature (e.g., screaming). Each child would thus obtain a score from 0 to 10, representing the number of mature choices made.

2. A second approach is to use an observational measure that involves randomly pairing children who have an older or a younger sibling with other children who have an older or a younger sibling. Each pair of children would be introduced and given a single desirable toy for either or both of them to play with. They would then be left together for ten minutes in a room with a one-way mirror, so that other people can see them but they don't know that they're being observed. Two independent observers could then measure how long each child plays with the toy (including how long they play with it together). The score for each child would then be some number between 0 and 600 seconds. Presumably, a more socially adept child, who has the skills to get what he or she wants from another child, would spend a larger amount of time playing with the toy (either alone or together with the other child).

The question of the influence of birth order upon children's social skills is an example of one that can be studied by research and that will generate data that can be statistically analyzed. On the other hand, questions like "Should parents have only one child?" or "Should they treat the first child differently after a second child comes?" are not really research questions, although knowing the results of research might be useful to parents who wish to answer such questions. Similarly, while a question like "Why is Bobby so mean to his younger sister?" does not lend itself to statistical analysis, case study research might shed some light on its answer.

What Are the Uses of Statistics?

Thus far, we have seen that not all questions can potentially be answered by research, that ethical and practical concerns prevent us from gathering research data on some topics, and that some research studies do not utilize statistical techniques. What, then, is left for us to discuss in this book? Plenty. Many, probably most, of the questions that people ask are answerable by scientific research that uses statistical procedures as a part of the process. The next chapter will focus on research design and its relevance to statistics; the rest of this chapter focuses on statistics as a tool in doing research.

Descriptive Versus Inferential Statistics

The statistical procedures that we will be discussing in this book can be broadly categorized into two general categories reflecting the uses to which they are put: summarizing a set of data and drawing inferences.

Descriptive Statistics. The terms *data* and *scores* are used to refer to the numbers or information that you gather in your research study: hat size, eye color, number of freckles on one's nose, or length of ear from tip to lobe can all be considered scores or data. If you are a researcher specializing in Above-the-Neck Studies (soon to be the latest interdisciplinary major), you might wish to summarize and to describe the scores on all four of these measures. This general category of statistics, **descriptive statistics**, is used in instances when simply reciting or writing down the scores is too cumbersome to remember or too confusing to interpret; instead, you would summarize or describe a set of scores. For instance, you wouldn't want to list the exact number of freckles found on each of 97 persons' noses; you might prefer to give some kind of average or range of scores. As another example, imagine that someone were to ask you what the weather had been like over the past month. To answer this question, you could quote the hourly temperature over the previous 30 days. Although this procedure provides the relevant information, it can be less useful than even the single word "hot" or, more informatively, some description of the range of temperatures or the average temperatures at particular times of day, as illustrated in Table 1.1.

TABLE 1.1   Describing Weather

Bad Idea	Good Ideas (Using Descriptive Statistics)
February 1 1:00 A.M. 18° F 2:00 A.M. 17° F 3:00 A.M. 17° F 4:00 A.M. 16° F 5:00 A.M. 16° F 6:00 A.M. 17° F ⋮	"The lows ranged from 8° to 35° and the highs ranged from 21° to 53°." or "The average temperatures were 24° at 8 A.M. and 39° at 5 P.M." or

February 28
  6:00 P.M. 44° F
  7:00 P.M. 43° F
  8:00 P.M. 41° F
  9:00 P.M. 41° F
 10:00 P.M. 40° F
 11:00 P.M. 40° F
 Midnight 39° F

Note that the complete listing of the Bad Idea will take 672 lines—24 hourly temperatures for each of 28 days. Leap years will be even worse!

Descriptive statistics include both specific numbers and ways of presenting data in tabular and graphical form in order to make the information succinct but clear to the reader. When people refer to such government statistics as per capita income and number of registered voters per state, they are generally discussing descriptive statistics.

EXAMPLE

Descriptive Statistics from the Birth-Order Study. In the example of the study on siblings, there are some basic descriptive statistics that you could report. For example, you might want to describe the average number of minutes that a child with an older sibling plays with the toy when interacting with a child who has a younger sibling. You might also want to report the average number of mature/correct answers to the items about ways to get what you want given by the two groups of children. ■

Inferential Statistics.   The other general use of statistics is to draw inferences that go beyond the scores one actually has. **Inferential statistics** involves drawing conclusions about a broader group of people or scores than the ones available. Pharmacists who want to know the effects of a particular procedure on lowering blood pressure, sociologists who are interested in the relationship between some measure of social status and voting patterns, psychologists who study the effects of behavioral approaches to relieving children's fears, and educators who want to know if a constructivist curriculum leads to better understanding of material learned than a data-focused one—all are interested in generalizing beyond the particular scores they have in order to draw inferences about other people measured at other times in other places. Researchers who study human behavior, teachers who want to know what children are like, and indeed scientists of all kinds are interested in generalizations—that is, in going beyond the specific data collected to make predictions about what will be found in other situations. The *testing* of such predictions or hypotheses is a major function of inferential statistics.

EXAMPLE

Inferential Statistics in the Birth-Order Study. In the sibling example, you might want to draw some inferences about what type of child is likely to spend more time playing with the toy. You might, for example, think that secondborn children would be more socially adept, having had an older sibling to serve as a role model and skilled rival. This belief would lead to the prediction that secondborn children spend more time with the toy than firstborn children. Inferential statistical techniques provide the tools to tell you whether or not your data clearly support this prediction.

Populations Versus Samples

One of the important distinctions that researchers make is the contrast between a population and a sample. The scores that are studied, and the people or other entities providing these scores, are always categorized as either a population or only a sample.

Populations.   Sometimes a researcher is able to gather data on every person or score of interest. In that case, the researcher studies an entire **population**, which is the group of scores or people in whom the researcher is interested or about whom the researcher wishes to generalize. A population is an entire or complete group of scores, but is not necessarily an obvious group to someone other than the researcher. If someone studies introductory psychology students at Universal University, what is the population: the students studied, all introductory psychology students at Universal University, all psychology students, all college students, all young adults, or all human beings? We don't know the answer to this question unless the author tells us what population she was interested in. A researcher is responsible for identifying the population of interest and for acknowledging when the entire population has or has not been studied.

TIP

> In case you forget the meaning of a term, you don't have to try to figure out the place where it was first introduced. Just turn to the glossary in the back of the book.

Samples.   In contrast to the population, the **sample** in a research study consists of the scores that the researcher actually has or the people for whom scores are available. Ordinarily the sample is a subset of the population, a group of scores that comes from the population, but does not include all elements of it. Occasionally, however, the sample includes everyone in the population; in other words, the sample and the population are identical. In such cases, the sample is also called a **census**, and the results obtained from the sample describe the population exactly. In the great majority of research studies, however, the sample is only a part of the population, and the researcher attempts to draw inferences about the population based on the sample.

Research using samples instead of entire populations can save a great deal of time and money while permitting the researcher to come to correct and accurate conclusions (but only when the sample is reasonably typical of the population and large enough so that it can represent the population). When data are collected from a sample rather than an entire population, the researcher uses inferential statistical procedures by testing hypotheses or by making estimates about the population based on the data collected from the sample. Chapter 8 will discuss sampling procedures and the logic behind the techniques that researchers use to generalize from data collected on a sample to the population from which it comes.

EXAMPLE

Population and Sample in the Birth-Order Study. In the example of the study on siblings, the 40 children who actually participate in your study constitute the sample. The population is somewhat more problematic. Do you want to generalize to all children of any age who have older or younger siblings? Do you want to generalize only to four-year-old children who are separated by a two- or three-year age gap from their siblings? Do you want to generalize only to middle-class American children, like those in your sample, who might be socialized to be reasonably responsive to their siblings but not to be responsible for their care, as children in some cultures are?

TIP

> If you're not really sure how to answer these questions, you're not alone. Researchers studying issues like birth order rarely explicitly identify the population of interest but almost always describe the sampling procedures and discuss their limitations.

Parameters Versus Statistics

A third important distinction that researchers make is the distinction between two different terms that refer to numerical characteristics: a parameter and a statistic. A numerical characteristic is anything that can be expressed as a number, such as the largest score in a group or set of scores, some kind of average or typical score, or a measure of how spread out the scores are.

Parameter. A numerical characteristic of a population is called a **parameter**. Parameters are generally symbolized by Greek letters like

μ (mu) or σ (sigma)

Sometimes a Greek letter (like μ) is used to stand for an actual parameter, computed from a population. Sometimes it is used in a formula to stand for a hypothetical value of a parameter, such as a hypothesis that the mean (average) IQ score in a population is 100.

For example, if we have a population of three children in a family, ages 4, 6, and 8, we could use μ to stand for the mean age of these children, which turns out to be 6. On the other hand, if we didn't know what the ages of the children were, but formulated a hypothesis about them based on our knowledge of their mother's age, we could use the letter μ to stand for our guess or hypothesis about the mean age of this woman's children.

Statistic. A numerical characteristic of a sample is called a **statistic**. As you can see, this use of the term *statistic* or *statistics* is narrower than the use in the title of this book or the course you are taking, where it is more broadly used to refer to a set of procedures for describing and interpreting data. Statistics are symbolized by English letters like

$\overline{X}$ or s,

which, as you'll note, are usually italicized when reported.

In inferential statistics, researchers measure a sample of people, calculate one or more statistics based on this sample, and use these statistics to draw inferences about the population from which the sample came. One common kind of inference is to estimate a value of a population parameter. For instance, suppose that you could know the ages of two of a woman's three children. You could calculate the mean of these two ages and use this value as a statistic to draw an inference about the mean age of all three children in her family.

Researchers generally use a statistic as an estimate or estimator of a parameter, rather than as a number of interest in its own right, even though statistics are not perfect estimators of parameters. For instance, suppose that the population of interest is the three children in a family and that their ages are 15, 17, and 1. You know the ages of the two older children but not that of their baby brother. If you were to estimate the mean age of all three children (a parameter) from the mean age of the two older children (a statistic), the actual parameter (11 years) would be quite a bit lower than the value of the statistic (16 years).

TIP

> To take into account possible errors in estimation, sometimes the numerical formula for calculating a statistic is a little different from the formula for the parameter that it is intended to estimate. In other words, the formula that best describes a complete set of scores might not be precisely the same as the one that best estimates what would be typical of the complete set based on a sample of only some of the scores.

EXAMPLE

Parameter and Statistic in the Birth-Order Study. In the sibling study, a population of interest might be all firstborn children. An example of a parameter that you might wish to know is the percentage of time a firstborn child will play with a toy when she or he is interacting with a child who has an older sibling. A statistic that you could calculate would be the average number of minutes of the ten-minute interaction during which the firstborn children in the sample played with the toy when paired with a child who had an older sibling. If this average were 7 minutes, you could use this statistic to help you draw inferences about the relevant parameter, perhaps concluding that firstborn children tend to get more than their share of resources. ■

Summary of Uses of Statistics

To summarize, researchers sometimes measure an entire population, calculate one or more parameters from their scores, and use them to describe the population. More commonly, researchers are able to study only a sample from the population, calculate a statistic based on that sample, and use this statistic to draw inferences about the population. Because we cannot be sure that any particular sample of scores exactly reflects the population, we need to use inferential statistics to let us test hypotheses about the population and estimate its parameters.

Estimates and other inferences based on statistical analyses are likely but not guaranteed to be correct. Unfortunately, there is no way to ensure that our answers will be precisely accurate and our conclusions will all be correct, even with the use of the most appropriate and sophisticated statistical procedures.

What Are the Characteristics of Variables?

When a researcher makes an observation and assigns a score to a person, object, or event, she or he is using this score to represent a value on an underlying dimension or characteristic. The process of assigning scores according to rules is called **measurement**. Both the rules and the score assigned depend on the underlying characteristic that is being measured.

Constants Versus Variables

Every characteristic that is measured can be classified as either a constant or a variable in a particular research study.

Constants. Sometimes what is being measured is something that does not change. A characteristic that has the same value for every person or object is called a **constant**. For example, if you are studying only boys, then sex is a constant in your research study; if you are studying Americans, then nationality is a constant. In the study on siblings, the age of the child is a constant. Some constants are physical ones, such as the speed of light; others are arbitrary ones, such as the relationship between an ounce and a pound; and some apply to a particular research study (such as the age of the participants in the birth-order study) but might not be a constant in another study.

Variables. Although every research study has some things that are held constant, ordinarily they are not the things that are subject to statistical analysis. Instead, statistical analysis focuses primarily on **variables**, or characteristics that can and do take on more than one value. In other words, they vary, at least across the individual persons or other entities being measured. Almost anything interesting about people can be a variable: demographic characteristics, such as age; personality characteristics, such as shyness; cognitive qualities, such as spatial ability; or attitudes, aptitudes, and anything else you can conceive of measuring.

Qualitative Versus Quantitative Variables

Since anything whatsoever that can take on more than one value can be considered a variable, statisticians have identified numerous types of variables and devised numerous ways of categorizing or classifying them. One of the most useful ways of categorizing variables for researchers is as either qualitative, or categorical, variables or as quantitative, or numerical, variables.

Qualitative Variables.   A **qualitative variable** is one in which the different scores on the variable represent differences in quality, character, or type—but not in amount. Different values on qualitative variables may be represented by names—for example, purple, blue, and chartreuse for colors—or by numbers—for example, different code numbers for different individuals to access a mainframe computer. Even though the scores may be coded as numbers, such as scoring males as 1 and females as 2, the different numbers assigned to a qualitative variable do not reflect differences in the size or extent of what is being measured. In that sense, they are arbitrary; males could have been coded as 43 and females as 999, for example, with no loss of information.

Quantitative Variables.   A **quantitative variable** is one for which the actual number assigned is not arbitrary, but rather means something about the variable being measured. A score on a quantitative variable tells you something about the amount of the characteristic that the person or other entity being measured possesses. Generally, a larger numerical score means more of the variable, and if people are arranged in order of their numerical scores, they are also arranged in order of whatever the number represents.

TIP ▬▬▬▬▬▬▬▬▬▬▬▬▬▬▬▬▬▬▬▬▬▬▬▬▬▬▬▬▬▬▬▬▬▬▬▬

> A good rule of thumb in trying to decide whether a variable is qualitative or quantitative is to ask whether or not it would make sense to switch the numerical values around. If different numbers mean simply that the scores are different but say nothing about the relationship among them, then the variable is qualitative rather than quantitative.

Discrete Versus Continuous Quantitative Variables. If the scores on a variable come in whole units or if you count something to arrive at the score, then the variable is **discrete**. For example, family size (excluding pregnancies), number of cars one owns, and number of students in classrooms are all discrete quantitative variables. When something is measured accurately on a discrete quantitative variable, we can be assured that the value we get is exactly, precisely correct.

On the other hand, **continuous** variables cannot be measured precisely, because as we increase the accuracy of the measure, we get a finer and finer scoring system. Although we might say a person weighs 150 pounds, we know that with a more precise scale, he might weigh 149.7 pounds, or even

149.73 pounds. A continuous variable does not come packaged in units; instead, measures on a continuous variable represent arbitrary degrees of precision, with a recognition that they are rounded off to some extent. Thus, when we hear that a person weighs 150 pounds, we know that he weighs approximately 150 pounds. Personality and ability variables, height and weight, even temperature, are all examples of continuous quantitative variables.

TIP

If you had to learn the distinction between mass nouns and count nouns in high school English class, you know the distinction between continuous and discrete quantitative variables. Pain, for example, is a mass noun (and a continuous variable), as it cannot be counted; pills to relieve pain constitute a count noun (and a discrete variable) as the number of pills can be counted.

EXAMPLE

Variables in the Birth-Order Study. The variable of time spent with the toy in the sibling study is clearly a continuous quantitative variable. If you report the time as 180 seconds, you would not be guaranteeing that the exact number of seconds was not 179.6 or 180.231. The recorded value, in short, is only an approximation of the precise amount of time. At first thought, the score on the interview measure asking about social influence strategies might seem to be a discrete one, as the possible scores would be only the integers from 0 to 10, reflecting the number of correct/mature responses. However, more thought would indicate that these scores really are attempts to measure an underlying continuous variable, knowledge of social skills, which is only approximated by the actual test scores. Thus, in the birth-order example, both measures are really continuous variables. ■

Upper and Lower Limits.   As we have seen, continuous quantitative variables cannot be measured precisely; rather, each score represents an approximation of a true value that falls within a range of scores. If we say that someone has an IQ score of 120, we mean that his score is somewhere between 119.5 and 120.5. These boundaries to the values that a score represents are its **lower** and **upper limits**. Whenever we measure something approximately, we should acknowledge the fact that the score we assign actually represents a range of possibilities falling between two limits. A number of statistical procedures, especially those used when we group scores into categories, acknowledge the presence of the upper and lower boundaries of scores.

Constants and Variables

Constant: A characteristic or value that does not change and has the same value for everyone in a particular research study.

Common examples: sex (all males), grade (all first graders), university attended by subjects (all attend State U)

Variable: A characteristic that takes on more than one value, which varies across individuals.

1. Qualitative variable: A variable in which the different scores on the variable represent differences in quality, character, or kind but not in amount. Also called a nominal-level variable.

   Common examples: sex, religion, birthplace

2. Quantitative variable: A variable for which different scores represent different amounts of the property being measured.

   Common examples: height, age, test scores, speed

   - *Continuous quantitative variable:* A quantitative variable that can assume an infinite number of values
     Common examples: weight, age, time

   - *Discrete quantitative variable:* A quantitative variable that can take on only a limited number of values
     Common examples: number of children in a classroom, number of cars owned, number of English classes taken

Scales or Levels of Measurement

If we think of measurement as the process of using rules to assign scores or values to observations, we can see that variables are measured by researchers when people are given scores on them. A *scale* or *level of measurement* relates to the rules used to assign scores and is an indication of the kind of information that the scores provide. In fact there are four different levels or scales of measurement that researchers use to determine scores: nominal, ordinal, interval, and ratio scales.

The **level** of measurement depends largely on the nature of the variable that is being measured but also on the measurement procedure. The level of measurement underlies how informative the values or scores are. For example, depending upon the level of measurement, a score of 2 could mean that two of something were counted or that there was a category coded 2 or that the value of a 2 represented less of something than a value of 3 would. Depending on the level of measurement, the variable of age could be coded as "child" or "adult"; as "teens," "twenties," "thirties," and so on; or as the number of years since birth. Since the kinds of statistical procedures that can be used meaningfully depend to some extent upon the way in which variables are measured, it is important to be aware of some of the distinctions among different scales of measurement.

Nominal-Level Variables.   When a variable is measured on a **nominal scale**, different numbers simply represent different categories of the variable. All qualitative variables are measured on a nominal scale. Although New Mexico could be assigned number 1, Massachusetts number 2, and Oregon number 3, it would make no sense to say that these numbers reflect some underlying dimension of which New Mexico has the least and Oregon the most. Other examples of nominal-level variables include gender, major field of study, name of university attended, diagnosis, or brand of potato chips purchased.

Although nominal scales are used primarily to describe qualitative variables, occasionally a quantitative variable could be measured on a nominal scale in a particular study. For example, people could be classified as normal weight or abnormal weight, thereby combining people with high and low weights into the abnormal weight category and treating weight as if it represented two discrete categories, instead of an underlying continuous variable.

EXAMPLE

A nominal-level variable from the birth-order study would be the gender of the child (male or female).   ■

Ordinal-Level Variables.   A variable measured on an **ordinal scale** is one for which larger numbers represent larger amounts of the variable. Most commonly, the numbers represent ranks; for example, first through ninetieth place in a law school class or prizes in an art show. When the original scores are ranks, you don't know that the difference between, for example, first and second place represents the same distance in the underlying characteristic as the difference between ninth and tenth place. Other variables that are measured on an ordinal scale are positions in a spelling bee, social class, ordering of movies by preference, and responses to items on an instrument in which the responses are "never," "sometimes," "usually," and "always."

EXAMPLE

In the birth-order study, it would seem that birth order (first- or second-born) would be an ordinal-level variable. This is true; yet, we could also consider it a nominal variable, with first-borns and second-borns simply reflecting two different categories. An example of a clearly ordinal variable in the study is hard to find. However, you could look at the order in which the parents of the children signed them up to participate in the study, which would be an ordinal variable.   ◼

Interval-Level Variables.   When a variable is measured on an **interval scale**, the distance between two numbers or scores is a reflection of the distance between the values of the characteristic being measured. The Celsius and Fahrenheit temperature scales are examples of interval-level variables; a 10° increase in temperature reflects the same amount of heat, regardless of whether it represents a change from 10° to 20° or a change from 60° to 70°. A number of standardized achievement or aptitude tests probably represent interval scale variables. Scholastic Assessment Test (SAT) scores exemplify one such variable. The lowest score that you can get on the test is 200, not zero. However, answering the same several questions correctly will add 50 points to your SAT score, regardless of whether this gain raises the score from 400 to 450 or from 650 to 700. The assumption is that a 50-point difference in scores represents the same difference in magnitude of achievement or aptitude regardless of its location on the continuum.

EXAMPLE

Scores on the interview measure of social skills knowledge in the birth-order study can be considered to be measured on an interval scale. A zero on the test would not necessarily mean that the child knows nothing whatsoever about social skills. On the other hand, answering two questions correctly would increase a child's score by the same number of points, regardless of whether that increase was from 0 to 2 or from 3 to 5.   ◼

Ratio-Level Variables.   A variable measured on a **ratio scale** is one that has interval scale properties plus a true zero point.

TIP

> Remember that a ratio consists of one number divided by another. If one variable is three times as large as another, the ratio of the first to the second variable would be 3:1 or 3.

Whereas the value of zero is an arbitrary one on other scales, a zero on a ratio scale means a total absence of what is being measured. It follows from this property that the ratio of two scores measured on a ratio scale represents the actual ratio of the amounts of the characteristic being measured. For example, 4 pounds of flour is exactly twice 2 pounds; similarly 10 dollars is exactly half of 20 dollars. Many physical qualities—like height, weight, and area—are usually measured on ratio scales.

EXAMPLE

The measure of time in the birth-order study is a ratio scale measure, since 80 seconds is exactly twice as long as 40 seconds. ■

Relationships Among the Levels of Measurement

Ordering the Levels.   If we consider the properties of the different scales of measurement, we can see that they themselves form an ordinal scale. In general, each level of measurement possesses the basic characteristics of the preceding level, plus some additional properties. An ordinal-level variable has the basic property of a nominal scale—that different scores represent differences—plus the additional property that the order of the numbers from smaller to larger reflects the order of the amounts of the variable being measured. Sometimes this kind of scale is called **monotonic**, where a larger number represents an increase but not necessarily by any consistent amount. Scores on an interval-level variable also represent differences, with larger numbers representing more of the variable, but in addition, the differences between the scores represent differences between the values on the variable. Finally, all of the above qualities are true for a ratio-level variable, but the numbers reflect more than distances along the characteristic being measured; ratios of the numbers reflect ratios of the magnitude of the variable, with zero indicating an absence of the variable.

Identifying the Level of Measurement.   Although it is usually easy to identify a nominal-level variable or an ordinal one that is measured by the use of ranks, two difficulties frequently arise in trying to identify the scale of measurement used to classify a particular variable.

Ordinal Versus Interval Scales. In some instances, something may be measured in such a way that it falls between an ordinal and an interval scale. Scores on many attitudinal or opinion measures, in which responses may be coded on a five- or seven-point scale ranging from "strongly agree" to "strongly disagree," come to mind. Although we cannot be sure that the distance between "strongly agree" and "agree" is the same as the distance between "agree" and "probably agree," it seems reasonable to assume that there is a fairly close relationship between the spacing of the possible responses and the underlying attitudes they are attempting to measure.

TIP

These measures are called Likert scales, after the psychologist who developed the technique. They are widely used by social psychologists and pollsters.

Letter grades represent another example of a scale that seems to be somewhat more than ordinal but less than interval. Is the difference between a D and a C really the same as the difference between a B and an A? Probably not; yet it seems as if these grades do provide more information than simply the fact that one is better than another. The solution that most researchers take in such cases is to treat these in-between scales as if they were interval-level variables; they use the same statistical procedures they would use on interval scale data, but acknowledge that in fact they are really not measured on a true interval scale. Such scales are sometimes called *equal-appearing interval scales.*

Interval Versus Ratio Scales. Another problem that researchers often face is deciding whether a particular variable represents an interval or a ratio scale. If you give an achievement test in beginning Urdu, does a score of zero really represent a total lack of knowledge of Urdu? Maybe so, but what if the language were Spanish and your test omitted the word "taco"? Luckily, a researcher who cares only about using the correct statistical procedures does not have to worry about making a decision as to whether a particular variable was measured on an interval or ratio scale. Almost all the statistical procedures that are appropriate for interval-level data are also appropriate for ratio-level data and vice versa. In fact researchers often talk about "I/R data" (short for "data measured on an interval or ratio scale") as a prerequisite for the use of a particular statistical procedure.

Why Does Level of Measurement Matter?

Theoretical interest is not the primary reason why researchers and statisticians consider the level of measurement of a variable. Level of measurement is important because the kinds of statistical procedures that can be appropriately used depend on the level of measurement of the variable studied. As an obvious example, calculating the mean (average) telephone number of a group of people would be possible but ridiculous, since telephone number is a nominal level variable. Whenever we talk about a statistical technique, we'll be discussing the level of measurement that it implies.

Scales or Levels of Measurement ▰▰▰▰▰▰▰▰▰▰▰▰▰▰▰

Nominal scale: A scale or level of measurement in which scores represent names only but not differences in amount.

- A nominal-scale variable is a qualitative variable.
- It must be analyzed by nonparametric tests.
  Examples: telephone numbers, species of flower, preferred hobby

Ordinal scale: A measurement scale in which scores indicate only relative amounts or rank order.

- An ordinal-scale variable is the crudest type of quantitative variable.
- It must be analyzed by nonparametric tests.
  Examples: street number (usually some possible addresses are missing), position in a spelling bee, seedings of tennis players

Note: Some variables fall between ordinal and interval levels. The values imply something about relative distances between them but the spacing is not perfect. They are frequently analyzed by parametric tests.

  Examples: attitude scales, rating scales, letter grades

Interval scale: A scale of measurement for which equal differences in scores represent equal differences in amount of the property measured, but with an arbitrary zero point.

- An interval-scale variable is a quantitative variable.
- It may be analyzed by parametric tests.
  Examples: Fahrenheit temperature, score on an advanced Spanish test as a measure of knowledge of Spanish, many aptitude test scores

Ratio scale: A scale having interval properties except that a score of zero indicates a total absence of the quality being measured.

- Statements about ratios of scores are meaningful: Twice as big a number means twice as much of the variable.
- A ratio-scale variable is a quantitative variable.
- It may be analyzed by parametric tests.
  Examples: distance, duration, volume

What Are Parametric and Nonparametric Tests?

A major part of inferential statistics involves the computation of *statistical tests*, or procedures designed to permit you to answer certain questions about the data. However, not all statistical procedures can be used with all types of data.

In order to decide which statistical test to use, you need to understand yet another discrimination that statisticians make: the distinction between tests that make certain assumptions about the nature of the data to which they apply and tests that make far fewer assumptions. The tests that assume a number of characteristics about the parameters of the population from which the scores come are **parametric tests**. The tests that can be used for purely ordinal or nominal data are **nonparametric tests**.

One of the most important assumptions of parametric tests is that the data are measured on an interval or ratio scale. If the data are nominal or ordinal, so that it makes no sense to talk about a mean or average score, then parametric tests cannot be used. With the exception of some highly sophisticated procedures such as log-linear analysis, parametric tests can't be used to compare people's favorite brand of jeans; their ownership of IBM, IBM-clone, or Macintosh computers; or their choice of colleges to attend.

Disadvantages and Advantages of Parametric Tests

Disadvantages.   As implied in the previous paragraph, the major disadvantage of parametric tests is that they cannot be used in all circumstances; they don't lead to meaningful interpretations of nominal or rank-order data, and they must be used with caution when a number of other assumptions are not met.

Another disadvantage of parametric tests is that, computationally, they tend to be more complex than nonparametric procedures. Many nonparametric tests are (relatively) easy to perform with paper and pencil and downright simple with a hand calculator, at least when the sample size is reasonably small. Depending on the size of the numbers involved, parametric tests may be much more time consuming. Sometimes even when a parametric test is appropriate, a researcher may perform a nonparametric test first, just to get a quick picture of what the pattern of results is. For instance, if you want to compare the earnings of people in two occupations, and you can see that all but one person in one occupation makes more money than everyone in the second occupation, you can do a very quick nonparametric test called a *sign test*, rather than having to add up all these four-, five-, and six-figure incomes. Thus nonparametric tests have two advantages: fewer assumptions and (usually) greater ease of computation. Moreover, the results of nonparametric tests may be easier for people with no statistical training to understand than the results of some parametric procedures.

Advantages.   Given the advantages of nonparametric tests, why would anyone use parametric tests? In fact, there are three reasons, which together are important enough that the great majority of statistical analyses involve parametric tests. First, when their assumptions are met, parametric tests are usually more *powerful*, meaning that they are generally more likely than nonparametric tests to identify a difference in population parameters or a relationship among variables in the population. (When these assumptions are not met, nonparametric tests may be more powerful.) Second, they are also more *versatile* in the sense that some complex interactions and relationships can be investigated only by parametric techniques.

Finally, parametric techniques are usually *robust* to violations of most of their assumptions, meaning that they are likely to give you the correct results even if the assumptions under which they were derived are not fully met. The major exception to this statement is the assumption of level of measurement; if it does not make sense to calculate a mean (or arithmetic average), then it does not make sense to do a parametric test on the data. However, almost all researchers feel that it is appropriate to calculate a mean on the kind of questionnaire items that fall between ordinal and interval scales and thus use parametric procedures to analyze such data. Both the measure of number of correct answers and the measure of time spent playing with the toy in the birth-order study would be analyzed with parametric techniques.

This textbook, then, like most other statistics books, will focus primarily on parametric techniques for data analysis. However, two nonparametric procedures, Spearman's rho and chi-square, will be considered in some detail, and instances in which parametric procedures would be inappropriate will be discussed as they appear.

Parametric and Nonparametric Tests

Parametric Tests	*Nonparametric Tests*
Definition:	
Statistical tests that assume a number of characteristics about the parameters of the population from which the scores come	Statistical tests that make fewer assumptions about the population and can be used with nominal or ordinal data
Assumptions:	
• Interval- or ratio-scale data	• Independent or random sampling
• Independent or random sampling	
• Normal distribution of scores in the population	
• Equal variances of the scores in the populations from which the samples come	
Advantages:	
• Usually more powerful	• Fewer assumptions
• More versatile	• Computationally simpler
• Robust to violations of assumptions	

What Symbols and Procedures Are Used in Statistics?

Whenever you study a new field, learning a new vocabulary and symbol system can be a hurdle to overcome. The study of statistics is no exception. Some of the symbols described in this section may be familiar from previous mathematics courses you have taken, whereas others may be new. A few new symbols will be introduced later in the book, but the rest of this chapter includes most of the symbols and all of the mathematical procedures that you will have to know.

TIP ██

A list of symbols appears inside the front cover of the book, so you don't
have to hunt through this chapter if you can't remember the meaning of
a particular symbol.

Symbols for Scores

Raw and Transformed Scores.   The term **raw score** refers to a score just as
the researcher collects it, without "cooking" or changing it in any way. If
people are weighed on a scale, the reading in pounds is their raw score; if
they are given a test, the number of items correct is the raw score; if they are
asked what color their car is, the response "blue" or "silver" is the raw score.
Raw scores are most useful when the values on the variable being measured
are meaningful to the researcher or reader, as would be the case with weights
but would not usually be the case with number of items correct on a test. In
the latter case, the researcher usually transforms or changes the score in some
way in order to make the score more meaningful and interpretable to the
reader. For example, if a child answers 32 questions correctly on a reading
test, the raw score of 32 may not be very informative.

- Did the child get all the questions correct or miss most of them?
- Did the child do better or worse than the other children in the class or
  than other children of the same age?
- Was the test easy or hard?

A raw score alone won't answer such questions.

   A **transformed score**, like a grade-equivalent score indicating that the
child is reading at the fourth-grade reading level, might be much more meaningful. One common type of transformed score is a **deviation score**, which
relates a raw score to the mean (arithmetic average) of the distribution from
which it comes. For instance if your score on a test was 10 points above the
mean, your deviation score would be +10.

   Raw scores are usually symbolized by a capital letter, typically X if only
one variable is being considered, with Y usually used to represent a second
variable. For instance, if a researcher is measuring number of spoonfuls of
sugar people put into their coffee, then X would equal 0 for someone who
puts no sugar in her coffee, 1 for someone who uses one spoonful, and 3 for
someone who uses three spoonfuls.

Summation, Number, and Means.   The symbol Σ, uppercase Greek letter
sigma, means "the sum of" and indicates that the scores represented by the
letter(s) to its right should be added together. ΣX stands for "the sum of the
raw scores on variable X" and means that all of the individual scores on variable X should be added together.

The letter N is never used to stand for a raw score on a variable. Instead it represents the number of scores in a sample, not the number in a population, unless every score in the population is sampled. Thus, $\Sigma X \div N$ (or $\Sigma X/N$) stands for the sum of all the raw scores divided by the number of scores.

This formula, $\Sigma X/N$, is called the *mean* of a set of scores. When the scores reflect a sample, the mean is represented by a capital X with a line over it, $\overline{X}$; when the scores reflect an entire population, the mean is represented by the Greek letter μ (mu). As a numerical characteristic of a sample, $\overline{X}$ represents a statistic; as a numerical characteristic of a population, μ is a parameter.

For example, if the raw scores in a sample are 0, 1, and 3, ΣX would be 4, N would be 3, and $\overline{X}$ would be 4/3 or 1.33 (to two decimal places).

Symbols for Mathematical Procedures

Multiplication. In algebra, you may have learned several ways to represent multiplication: 2×2, $2 \cdot 2$ or $(2)(2)$ might all represent 2 multiplied by 2. In statistics, usually multiplication is indicated by parentheses rather than by an $\times$ or a dot. When two variables represented by letters are to be multiplied together, often the parentheses are omitted; either XY or $(X)(Y)$ represents X multiplied by Y. Thus, the term ΣXY means that, for each of N pairs of scores on variables X and Y, you multiply X times Y and then sum these N products (often called *cross-products*).

For example, if X represents the height and Y represents the weight of N people, ΣXY means that each person's height should be multiplied by his or her weight and that these N products should be added together, as illustrated in the following table.

Person	X (height)	Y (weight)	XY
1	60	120	7,200
2	65	150	9,750
3	68	160	10,880
	$\Sigma X = 193$	$\Sigma Y = 430$	$\Sigma XY = 27,830$

$\Sigma X \Sigma Y = 193(430) = 82,990$

Note that the term ΣXY means something very different from the expression $\Sigma X \Sigma Y$. This latter expression indicates that the raw scores on X should be summed, the raw scores on Y should be summed, and the two sums should then be multiplied together. It might seem clearer to represent the latter procedure by $(\Sigma X)(\Sigma Y)$, which would mean the same thing, but in the interest of brevity, statisticians usually omit the parentheses. Both of these terms, ΣXY and $\Sigma X \Sigma Y$, are used in statistical formulas. It's important to keep them straight.

Squares and Square Roots.   Many statistical procedures involve squaring many numbers and adding these squared scores together. To *square* a number means to multiply it by itself; it is represented by a superscript or exponent ^{2} after the number to be squared. For example 4^2 means 4(4), or 16; X^2 means X multiplied by X.

Many statistical procedures involve squaring each raw score (or each deviation score) and then summing these squared scores. The formula ΣX^2 means that each raw score should be squared and that these squares should then be summed. In other words, the summation is done last, after each of the raw scores has been squared. The expression $(\Sigma X)^2$ means something quite different; it says that the scores are first summed and then the sum of all N scores is squared. For example, if your raw scores are 1, 2, 3, and 4,

$$\Sigma X^2 = 1^2 + 2^2 + 3^2 + 4^2 = 1 + 4 + 9 + 16 = 30$$

On the other hand,

$$(\Sigma X)^2 = (1 + 2 + 3 + 4)^2 = 10^2 = 100$$

The following table gives additional examples of squares and their sums.

X	X^2
4	16
50	2500
18	324
$\Sigma X = 72$	$\Sigma X^2 = 2840$

$$(\Sigma X)^2 = 72(72) = 5184$$

It is very important to keep the difference between ΣX^2 and $(\Sigma X)^2$ clear, as many statistical formulas use one or both of these expressions.

TIP

Remember that $(\Sigma X)^2$ will always be larger than ΣX^2 if all the X's are positive, as most scores are. Also remember that, in statistics, the computations within a set of parentheses are always done first to get a single value before multiplying or squaring that value.

Statistics also requires the use of square roots. The *square root* of a number, symbolized by $\sqrt{}$, is a number that, when multiplied by itself, gives the original number. Thus, $\sqrt{9} = 3$, because 3(3) = 9. Other examples of square roots are

$$\sqrt{4} = 2$$
$$\sqrt{50} = 7.071$$
$$\sqrt{18} = 4.243$$

Since the advent of inexpensive calculators with a square root key, the use of square root tables and of formulas for calculating square roots has almost disappeared. We won't discuss them in this book.

Positive and Negative Numbers.   Up until now, our examples have been of positive numbers, which are symbolized by the number either alone or preceded by a + symbol. Thus, "5" stands for positive 5 or +5, in contrast to "–5," which stands for negative 5, also called minus 5. Although most of the raw scores and other numbers that you will be working with in statistics problems will be positive, not all will be. For instance, if you are studying the effects of a new multimedia program designed to increase scores in science, you may find that some people show lower scores on the posttest than on the pretest. (Even an excellent program may not lead to gains for everybody.) If you are dealing with winter temperatures you may also encounter negative numbers, depending on where you live, whether you are using °F or °C, and whether or not you are referring to the wind chill factor. Thus, it is important to know how to deal with negative as well as positive numbers.

When the numbers to be summed in working statistical problems include both positive numbers and negative numbers such as –1 or –15, the easiest way to proceed is to sum all the positive numbers, sum all the negative numbers, and subtract the smaller sum from the larger one. If the sum of the positive numbers is larger, the total sum will be positive; if the sum of the negative numbers is larger, the total sum will be negative. Thus, the sum of 2 + (–1) + (–3) is –2.

When multiplying or dividing positive and negative numbers, the important thing to remember is that the product (or quotient) of two positive numbers or of *two negative numbers* is *positive*; the product or quotient of one positive number and one negative number is negative. Thus, two like signs make a positive; two unlike signs lead to a negative product or quotient.

Two pieces of information are important to keep in mind when doing statistical analyses using square roots. First, in statistics only the positive square root is used. For example, earlier 3 was named as a square root of 9. It is also true that –3 is a square root of 9, since (–3)(–3) = 9, but negative square roots are not used in statistical formulas. Second, although mathematicians deal with imaginary numbers, which represent the square roots of negative numbers, researchers who use statistics do not have to do so. You will never be taking the square root of a negative number in any statistical procedure.

Occasionally, researchers talk about the **absolute value** of a number, meaning its value while ignoring a negative sign. The absolute value of 23 is 23; the absolute value of –8 is 8. The symbol for absolute value is a pair of straight lines on either side of the number, like |–6|, which equals 6.

TIP ▆▆▆▆▆▆▆▆▆▆▆▆▆▆▆▆▆▆▆▆▆▆▆▆▆▆▆▆▆▆▆▆▆▆▆▆

> Remember that a negative number does not have a real square root, as there is no number that, when multiplied by itself, will give a negative product. If you work through a formula and find that you apparently need to take the square root of a negative number, you have made a mistake in arithmetic. So, whenever you calculate that you need to take the square root of a negative number, stop and check your calculations. Somewhere there's a mistake in the arithmetic (or in copying values into the formula).

Subscripts. Another kind of mathematical symbol that statisticians use is the subscript. Unlike the exponent ^{2}, which is the only superscript encountered in this textbook and which tells you to do something (i.e., to square the number), a subscript is used solely for purpose of identification and clarity, not as an instruction. If there are two groups, for example, they might be identified by subscripts, with X_A standing for any raw score in group A and X_B standing for any raw score in group B. In the research study of siblings, $\overline{X}_F$ might stand for the mean score of the firstborn children and $\overline{X}_S$ for the mean of the secondborn children. As another example, n_1 frequently stands for the number of scores in group 1 and n_2 stands for the number of scores in group 2.

Other Mathematical Procedures

Proportions and Percentages. Frequently, researchers wish to report how many scores fall into various categories. For example, if they are measuring scores on a qualitative variable with relatively few levels, such as what type of beverage people drink with breakfast, they may choose to report some indication of the likelihood that scores fall into each category. One way to do this would be to report the subgroup sizes or frequencies, usually symbolized by n or f with a subscript. Thus n_c might stand for the number or frequency of people who drink coffee, or f_m might stand for the number or frequency of people who drink milk.

However, frequently researchers prefer to report not the raw numbers in each category but the proportions or percentages that fall into the categories. A **proportion**, usually symbolized by P, is a ratio of the number in a category to the total sample size or n_c/N. If three out of thirty people sampled drink tea for breakfast, then the proportion who drink tea is $3/30$ or, expressed as a decimal fraction, .1.

EXAMPLE ▆▆▆▆▆▆▆▆▆▆▆▆▆▆▆▆▆▆▆▆▆▆▆▆▆▆▆▆▆▆▆▆▆▆▆▆

In the birth-order study, you might want to calculate the proportion of the 600-second interaction that each child spent playing with the toy. A child who spent 120 seconds with the toy would then have spent 120/600 or .20 of the time playing with the toy. ∎

TIP

> It is important to remember that a proportion can never be smaller than 0 (which is the proportion in a category that has no scores) nor larger than 1 (which is the proportion in the category into which all scores fall). The sum of the proportions in all the categories will always equal 1; thus, $\Sigma P = 1.00$.

Although statisticians frequently deal with proportions, most people are more familiar with the use of percentages. A **percentage**, represented by a % sign, is simply a proportion multiplied by 100—that is, the percentage in category t is $P_t(100)$ or $(n_t/N)(100)$. Percentages present exactly the same information as proportions but the values are 100 times as large. The sum of the percentages in all the different categories therefore equals 100%.

TIP

> When dealing with percentages, especially percentage increases, it is important to remember the base or total from which the percentage was created. Humorist Dave Barry (1992) has a column in which he reports a frightening "infinity percent increase" in the number of articles about "giant toilet snakes" sent to him from 1991 to 1992—that is, an increase from 0 to 1. An increase from 1 to 2 represents a 100% increase, since $2 - 1$ (the increase) divided by 1 (the base) = 1, and $1(100) = 100\%$. On the other hand, an increase from 4 to 5 represents only a 25% increase, since $(5 - 4)/4 = 1/4 = .25$ and $.25(100) = 25\%$.

Fractions. Proportion is an example of a *fraction*, or ratio of one number to another, which is one number divided by another. The number that is divided by the other is placed above the line and called the numerator or dividend; the number below the line is the denominator or divisor. Some statistical equations require the addition of fractions, and many end up with a number being divided by another.

Adding Fractions. In order to add fractions, you must reduce them to a common denominator; then you simply add the numerators. For example, to add 1/4 and 1/8, you could convert 1/4 to 2/8 by multiplying both the numerator and the denominator by 2, and then add the 1/8 + 2/8 to get 3/8.

However, the most convenient way to combine fractions is to convert all numbers to decimals as the common denominator. For example, dividing 1 by 4 gives .25; dividing 1 by 8 gives .125; adding these together gives .375, which is 3/8. Thus, instead of worrying about what the lowest common denominator might be, it is typically easier to convert all fractions to decimals and then add the decimals.

Rounding Off.   When doing calculations, especially if you use a calculator, you will often find that the values you get are approximate rather than exact. For example, if you were to divide 2 by 3, you would get a value of 0.66666666, with an infinite number of 6's following. In order to round off the number, you can follow the rule of thumb that if the digit that you intend to drop is between 0 and 4, you round down, dropping the extra digit; if the extra digit is 5 through 9, you round up, increasing the digit to the left, which becomes the final digit after rounding. Thus, 3.346 would round up to 3.35, if you were rounding to two decimal places; and 4.84 would round down to 4.8, if you were rounding to one decimal place.

TIP ▬▬▬▬▬▬▬▬▬▬▬▬▬▬▬▬▬▬▬▬▬▬▬▬▬▬▬▬▬▬▬▬▬▬▬▬

Suppose that you wanted to round 3.346 to a single decimal place. It would round to 3.3, not 3.4, since 3.346 is closer to 3.300 than it is to 3.400. Remember that the goal of rounding is to arrive at the rounded number that most closely approximates the original number.

Interpolation.   Statistics sometimes involves the use of tables, in which raw scores or calculated statistics are related to or compared with certain values in the table. A number of tables are presented in an appendix to this book. Such tables frequently list some numbers along the top and left-hand side of the page and then present a value corresponding to these numbers in the center of the table. When the scores that you have are listed in the table, it is usually no trouble to locate the corresponding value that you need. However, sometimes in using tables, or even in doing calculations, you will find it impossible to find a table value that corresponds to the precise numbers or scores that you have. For example, you might see table values associated with the numbers 50 and 55, but the actual score you have is 52.

One way to get the answer that you need is to use the procedure called *interpolation*, in which you calculate a value in between the table values, that represents the same distance between the table values that the score you have represents between the corresponding scores. An easy way to interpolate, which is approximately (but not always precisely) correct is to calculate the proportion of the distance between the table scores represented by your raw score. For example, 52 is 2/5 of the distance between 50 and 55. Then you can take 2/5 of the difference between the table values corresponding to the raw scores of 50 and 55 and add that to the table value corresponding to 50.

An alternative to interpolation is to use the more conservative value from the table as your guideline. Thus, given a choice, you select the value that reduces your chance of mistakenly thinking that you have found a real difference when you have not. Although this description may seem confusing now, when you study each statistical procedure and learn what the conservative choice is, it will make more sense to you.

If you are using a computer to analyze your data, interpolation will not be necessary, since the computer will compute exact values for you.

Significant Digits and Decimal Places. One question that arises when computing the results of statistical analyses is the issue of the precision to which you report the results. It may seem obvious that rounding off numbers to the nearest million or reporting scores to 10 decimal places would be extreme, but how do you know how precise to be? Generally, people follow three guidelines in reporting their results.

1. The nature of the data and how much precision is meaningful are the primary considerations. To report weights to a hundredth of a pound when your scale is accurate only to the nearest pound is clearly inappropriate.

TIP

> Often, looking at the degree of precision utilized by other people studying the same topic or using the same measure will give you a clue as to how many significant digits to use. If you are reporting scores on an index of economic growth, for instance, look at some other studies or reports that have used the same index and follow their lead.

2. People often report the mean (or other descriptive statistics applying to an entire sample or population) to one or two significant digits more than the original raw scores. Thus, if the raw scores are in pounds, the mean may be reported to the nearest tenth or even hundredth of a pound.

3. The results of most statistical tests, such as r, t, F, or χ^2 (all of which will be covered later in this book), are typically reported to two decimal places. Unless you have a reason to do otherwise, it is reasonable to report the results of any statistical test to two decimal places.

These guidelines are only rules of thumb rather than absolute requirements, and they may not be applicable all of the time. The purpose of reporting numbers is to convey maximum information to the reader without giving a misleading impression of precision. It is up to you to decide the best way to accomplish this goal. For instance, if you were to report the mean scores on the social skills interview measure in the sibling study to four decimal places, people might assume that the measure was more accurate than it actually was.

TIP

> Remember that it is a good idea to *calculate* the number you want to present to one decimal place or significant digit more than you wish to report. If you calculate the value of r, for example, to 3 decimal places, then you can be sure that you are correctly reporting it to 2 decimal places after rounding off.

Formulas and Equations

Elementary statistical procedures involve only basic arithmetic and algebra—no geometry, trigonometry, or calculus. However, when statistical symbols and expressions are arranged into formulas or equations, they may look relatively daunting to someone who hasn't used any math in a long while. The guidelines that follow will help make such formulas and equations more manageable.

Guidelines for Solving Equations and Working Through Formulas. When working with equations (which contain equals signs) or formulas (which do not), it is helpful to follow a systematic, step-by-step procedure.

Step 1: Copy out the entire formula and double check to be sure that it is copied exactly.

Step 2: Calculate each of the specific quantities mentioned in the equation. For example, sum the individual X scores in order to get ΣX; square each individual X to get ΣX^2; multiply each X score by its corresponding Y score to get ΣXY; and count the scores to get the N for all the scores and/or the n's for each subgroup.

Step 3: Check all of your calculations, since if you mistakenly write that $3^2 = 6$, everything from there on, including your conclusion, may be completely incorrect.

Step 4: Substitute these values into the formula—that is, rewrite it with the numbers in place of the symbols like X.

Step 5: If the formula contains parentheses, calculate what is inside each set of parentheses first, reducing it to a single value, before adding, subtracting, multiplying, or dividing between parentheses.

Step 6: Remember that multiplication or division precedes addition; thus, $4(5) + X$ means that you add 20 to X.

Step 7: In order to remember in what order you should do mathematical operations, you may wish to use the heuristic "Please Excuse My Dear Aunt Sarah" to remind you to do the operations in the following order:

Parentheses, Exponents (e.g., squaring),

Multiplication, Division, Addition, Subtraction

Step 8: Reduce everything under a square root sign to a single number and then take the square root of that number.

Step 9: A number of formulas are really ratios, with a numerator and a denominator. In such cases, the very last step in calculating is to divide the numerator by the denominator.

What Is the Role of Calculators and Computers?

An issue that frequently arises in teaching statistics is the extent to which students should be encouraged to use calculators and/or computers. The use of a calculator is almost essential to save time in calculations, particularly in extracting square roots. For an introductory statistics class, the only qualities that are essential in a calculator are a memory (so that you can sum squares of numbers and cross-products of pairs of numbers) and a square root key. It is helpful, but not necessary, to have a statistical calculator that can calculate standard deviations and correlation coefficients as well. Most important is to have a calculator that is simple enough that you understand how to use it; an expensive programmable one is probably a waste of money in terms of doing statistics. When it comes to computers, most instructors try to strike a balance between the educational advantages of doing computations by hand versus the ability to work conveniently with much larger data sets, versus the classroom time required for students to learn how to use statistical software packages. The decision is not always simple.

You may have difficulty getting a "feel" for what the numbers mean and for what kinds of answers are reasonable if your first experience with them is via computer output. For this reason, many of the examples and problems in this book involve both small samples and small scores, so that you can do many of the calculations in your head and can see where the numbers come from. After working through problems by hand (which will be holding a calculator much of the time), it should be easy to recognize when computer output makes no sense, which is something that can happen due to a number being in the wrong column, one letter entered incorrectly, or even selection of the wrong procedure.

Once a person feels comfortable in interpreting statistical significance tests and in recognizing what kinds of results should be expected, then it is time to learn one or more of the major statistical software packages, such as SPSS, SAS, SYSTAT, Minitab, Mystat, or others. Remember that a computer only computes; it is up to the user to decide what to ask it to do and to interpret the results that it provides.

What Is the Best Way to Study Statistics?

Most people who have been in college or graduate school for a while have worked out ways of studying that work effectively for them. For some people, these ways transfer well to the study of statistics, but others may need to take a different approach to learning this topic. Because the material is so linear, with later material dependent on earlier material, it is very difficult to do well in the latter part of the class unless the basics have been mastered in the beginning of it. Moreover, many people find the material difficult on first reading or listening and have to return to it over and over, finding it clearer each time. Statistics definitely does not lend itself to heroic all-nighters the last day of the semester, even for those known to write brilliant papers in a 24-hour burst of inspiration. Accordingly, here are some suggestions for ways to study that seem to have worked well for many students over the years.

1. Study often. It's best if you can set aside some time every day to work on statistics, but several times a week is a minimum. Going to class is not enough; separate study time is important, since most people can absorb only so much statistics at once.

2. Read over the relevant material in the textbook before going to class, then go to class, and then reread the textbook. Hearing and seeing the material several times is often necessary for real comprehension.

3. In working problems, try not to look at the answers first. If you need to look at the answer for one problem, because you can't figure out how to get started on it, try to do the next one on your own. Although it's much easier to retrace someone's solution than to discover it for yourself, you need to learn to solve problems without any clues.

4. Before you do a problem, think about what kind of answer is reasonable. Try to estimate what range of answers might make sense. For instance, if you're calculating a mean or other average, you should never get a value smaller than the smallest score or larger than the largest score. With certain statistics, only a certain range of values is possible; a value outside that range must represent an error in arithmetic. For instance, the square of a number can never be negative, so the sum of a group of squared numbers must be positive. If you're trying to see how many people scored over 90, and it's clear that this group was a small minority, then the number must be less than half the total sample size. If you're calculating proportions, the numbers cannot exceed 1.

Remember that when doing statistical calculations, everybody makes mistakes. I do; you will; your instructor does; all the famous statisticians mentioned in this book do or did. One test of a thoughtful researcher is the ability to recognize impossible or silly wrong answers—in other words, to identify answers which are almost surely wrong and to correct them.

5. If possible, try studying with someone else. It can be a big help to look over someone else's notes, in case you wrote down different things; to ask someone else about material you find unclear; and especially to try to explain it to someone else. Teaching someone else can be an excellent way to learn. (If you don't believe this statement, ask your statistics instructor how much she or he has learned as a result of teaching the course.)

6. Try to make up problems and examples of the material that relate to your own experiences and share them with others. As you discuss the content with someone else, you may find it becoming clearer to you. Also, as you read the book, write examples related to your own experience in the margins next to the explanations. That way, when you study or when you use the book after the course is over, the explanations will come back to you through the experiences.

7. Keep a list of your mistakes and/or of the things that you seem to forget or find difficult. Everyone who studies statistics has his or her own idiosyncratic group of difficult topics. One person may confuse ΣX^2 and $(\Sigma X)^2$; another may confuse a correlated t-test and a correlation coefficient; another may let numbers drift in copying a formula, so that a $3 - 4/2$ becomes $(3 - 4)/2$. Even if you can't use your list on tests, it will be helpful in working problems and in doing analyses of your own research data. Of course you will make mistakes in statistics (like everyone else); but by keeping track of your mistakes, you can avoid making the same ones over and over. In this book, there will be frequent references to mistakes that are commonly made or to impossible answers that serve as a clue that something is wrong. Take advantage of them.

8. Every few weeks in the class, start over. Go back to the beginning of the textbook (and your notes) and reread the material. One thing this practice will do is relieve the dreadful feeling of always being just a step behind in understanding the material, which is so common in statistics. You may be amazed to discover how much you now understand of what was confusing before. The other thing that reviewing will do is to remind you of how much the later material depends on the earlier content; for example, analysis of variance (Chapter 10) depends on the idea of variance (Chapter 4); which, in turn relates to the symbol system discussed in this chapter.

9. Work problems. Work all the problems in the book, all the problems the instructor gives, and all the problems anyone else poses to you. Focus on understanding the meaning of the findings and on clearly stating your conclusions, not only on getting the correct number. Someday it may be possible to hire someone else or get a computer to do the computations for you, but only you can decide what it is that you want to find out and how to go about it. Working problems helps you recognize the complex relationship among research design, data, and conclusions, which is the most important thing that statistics can tell you.

10. Ask for help. Volunteer help. One of the most frustrating aspects of statistics (indeed, of math in general) is to know that you've made a mistake but be unable to find it. It is much easier to catch someone else's arithmetic mistake than your own. Don't spend hours agonizing over a minor error; put it aside and ask someone else to look over your calculations and try to catch it. Do the same for them. Of course, if it's a question of understanding content, it's even more important to ask for help—from your instructor, a more experienced student, or a tutor, if available. Remember that even experts in statistics seek help from other experts when they encounter problems to which they don't know the answer. This book will point out some situations in which the right solution is to ask for help, either because the answer is not clearcut or because the way to solve the problem is not covered in this book.

CHAPTER SUMMARY

Although some people study statistics as a branch of mathematics that is interesting in its own right, this book will focus on statistics as a tool for conducting and understanding research. Some questions cannot be answered by research, either because they deal with values rather than information, or because there are no tools to answer them. However, scientific research and statistical analysis are essential to investigating a number of practical and theoretical questions.

As part of the research process, statistics can be used to describe data (scores) that have been collected from a sample. Statistics can also be used to draw inferences about the population from which the sample has been selected. A parameter is an actual or hypothetical numerical characteristic of a population, whereas a statistic is a numerical characteristic of a sample.

Although researchers occasionally deal with constants, which do not change, most statistical analyses focus on variables, which take on different values for different people or objects. Qualitative variables differ only in kind or quality; quantitative variables differ in amount as well. Discrete quantitative variables yield precise values that cannot be further subdivided; scores on continuous quantitative variables are really approximations that reflect a true score between a lower and an upper limit. Variables may be measured on several types of scales or at several levels. Nominal-level variables have numbers reflecting only differences in type or kind; ordinal-scale variables indicate ranks, with larger numbers signifying larger quantities. Interval-level variables have the additional property that a difference of a given size between numbers reflects a distance of a consistent size in the trait being measured, and ratio scale variables also have a true zero point.

Some statistical procedures are called parametric procedures because they make certain assumptions about population parameters, including the assumption that the scores reflect a variable measured on an interval or ratio scale. These procedures are widely used because they are frequently robust enough to yield the correct answers even when some of the assumptions are violated and because they are usually more powerful than nonparametric tests.

Scores that are collected in a research project are called raw scores and usually symbolized by a capital letter such as X. Mathematical manipulations of scores are described by various symbols, which may reflect their use in formulas and equations. For example, a proportion, P, reflects the ratio of the number of scores in a category to the total number of scores, and a percentage equals a proportion multiplied by 100. Practice in dealing with numbers and statistical symbols, coupled with thinking about what kinds of answers to problems would be reasonable, is an important aspect of learning statistics.

CHAPTER REVIEW

Multiple-Choice Questions

Answers to odd-numbered Multiple-Choice Questions and Problems can be found at the back of the book. Try not to rely too much on the answers and remember that in some cases there may be more than one correct answer.

1. An example of a continuous quantitative variable would be

   a. the number of ounces in a pound

   b. the number of square inches in a square foot

   c. the number of houses on each of 30 streets

   d. the primary material used in building each of 20 houses—stucco, adobe, brick, or wood

   e. the number of square feet in each of 20 houses

2. If Alice gets a score of 0 on variable X and 5 on variable Y and Bob gets a score of 2 on variable X and 3 on variable Y, what is ΣXY?

   a. 6   **b.** 10   **c.** 15   **d.** 16   **e.** 30   **f.** none of the above

3. Parameters are usually symbolized by

   a. English letters   **b.** Greek letters

   c. Greek numbers   **d.** measures of central tendency

   e. parametric tests

4. A nonparametric statistical test is

   a. the most common kind

   b. robust to violations of assumptions

   c. one that makes few assumptions about the nature of the data

   d. one that must be used whenever the data are ratio level

   e. used only to describe data, not to draw inferences

5. Which level(s) of measurement is (are) considered quantitative?

   a. interval   **b.** nominal   **c.** ordinal   **d.** ratio

   e. both a and b   **f.** a, b, and c   **g.** a, c, and d   **h.** all of the above

   i. none of the above

6. A person's position in a beauty contest (first place, second place, and so on) is an example of what kind of variable?

   a. an interval-level variable   **b.** an ordinal-level variable

   c. a ratio-level variable   **d.** a nominal-level variable

   e. a qualitative variable   **f.** Both d and e are true.

7. The species of grass that people have in their yards (or the dominant species in each yard, omitting the weeds) is an example of what kind of variable?

   a. an interval-level variable   **b.** an ordinal-level variable

   c. a ratio-level variable   **d.** a nominal-level variable

   e. a qualitative variable   **f.** Both d and e are true.

8. $\sqrt{9^2} =$

   a. 1.732   **b.** 3   **c.** 9   **d.** 27   **e.** 81   **f.** none of the above

Problems

9. For each of the following say whether it is or is not an example of a research question. How can you tell?

   a. Should advertisements for condoms be permitted on television?

   b. Which type of reading instruction works better: the whole language approach or the phonics approach?

   c. Do cities with larger populations have larger crime rates?

   d. Can children reared without human contact learn to speak?

   e. What is the best method of teaching statistics?

10. For each of the following descriptions of a use of statistics, first tell whether it is descriptive or inferential, then identify the population or sample used and say whether it is a sample or population, and finally identify a parameter or statistic that might be calculated.

   a. A union leader measures the attitudes of the 248 steelworkers in his union chapter towards the proposition that unemployment benefits be extended, by asking them if they approve or disapprove of extending such benefits.

   b. A clinical psychologist analyzes the dreams of 10 children who have been physically abused to see whether or not images of the abuse appear in their dreams.

   c. An economist attempts to measure the quality of life in America's 100 largest metropolitan areas by combining several indices of cost of living, crime, employment, and so on.

    d. A teacher wants to see how her 27 students compare with the national norms on the Iowa Test of Basic Skills.

    e. A researcher is interested in the issue of whether men and women are paid equal amounts for equal work. Accordingly, he surveys 39 companies and compares the pay of male and female workers at these companies, after statistically equating for the company, years of experience, and job classification.

11. For each of the following characteristics, tell whether it is a variable or a constant. If it is a variable, say whether it is a qualitative variable, a discrete quantitative variable, or a continuous quantitative variable.

    a. the number of square feet in a square yard

    b. the number of square feet in each room of a house, where N is the number of rooms

    c. the number of houses on each city block in Petuniatown, with N being the number of blocks

    d. the occupations of the fathers of the children in a third-grade class

    e. the type of drinks ordered by 7 people at a bar

    f. the number of shirts in people's closets

    g. the scores that students got on a standardized test

    h. people's ages

    i. the species of cockroaches found in people's homes

12. For each of the following descriptions of a variable, identify the level of measurement that it represents.

    a. grades on an oral exam scored as distinguished, pass, marginal, and failing

    b. area of kitchen floors

    c. area of the country in which people live (Pacific Northwest, Midwest, Deep South, and so on)

    d. scores on a test of advanced physics

    e. rankings of the Big Ten football teams

    f. favorite flavors of ice cream

    g. number of gallons sold for each of 15 flavors of ice cream

    h. number of calories per 4 ounce portion of ice cream for 15 different brands

13. Name two reasons why nonparametric tests may be preferable to parametric tests and two reasons why parametric tests are preferred to nonparametric ones.

14. Find the numerical values for each of the following expressions:

    a. $|-3| + 9(12) - (-3)$ **b.** $\sqrt{[8^2 + (-2)^2] / 6}$ **c.** $(1/4 + 2/5)(4 + 3/8)$

15. In which of the following cases has someone made a mistake? How can you tell?

    a. $\Sigma X^2 = 3$ **b.** $(\Sigma X)^2 = -6$ **c.** $t = 1/\sqrt{-4}$

    d. $P_a + P_b = 1.4$, where each score is in either category a or category b

    e. $\Sigma(n_1 + n_2) = \Sigma(f_1 + f_2)$

16. For the following set of numbers,

    > X: 1 2 3 4
    >
    > Y: 4 2 1 0

    a. What is ΣX?   **b.** What is ΣY^2?   **c.** What is ΣXY?

    d. What is $\Sigma X \Sigma Y$?   **e.** What is $\Sigma X^2 - (\Sigma X)^2/n_x$?

17. Give the following set of numbers:

    466

    321

    87

    502

    100

    56

    612

    a. What is ΣX?

    b. What is N?

    c. What is $(\Sigma X)^2$?

    d. What is X^2 for the first score?

    e. What is ΣX^2?

    f. What is $\Sigma X^2/N$?

18. By asking children to describe their reactions to other children, you have been able to classify all the children in the seventh grade at Mediocre Middle School as popular ($n = 48$), rejected ($n = 24$), ignored ($n = 32$), or average ($n = 254$). You call this variable "sociometric status."

    a. What level of measurement is this?

    b. John is classified as "rejected." What is his raw score on the variable of sociometric status?

    c. Are you dealing with a population or a sample?

    d. What is the N for this study?

    e. What proportion of the students in the school are classified as rejected?

    f. If you wanted to do parametric tests on these data, could you?

19. Suppose that you have the following scores:

School	No. of Classes	No. of Teachers
A	17	32
B	15	15
C	18	22

a. Name one qualitative variable and one quantitative variable.

b. On what scale is the variable "number of teachers" measured?

c. What is ΣX if X is number of classes?

d. What is $(\Sigma Y)^2$ if Y is number of teachers?

e. Is $\Sigma X > \Sigma Y$?

f. What is ΣXY?

g. Is $\Sigma X \Sigma Y < \Sigma XY$?

20. Take the following formula and reduce it to a single number.

$$\frac{(73 - 69)^2 / 4 + (88 - 83)^2 / 5 - 25^2 / 3}{\sqrt{81} + 66}$$

Study Questions

Study questions are questions, issues, or problems for you to think about or sometimes to answer. Answers to study questions are not provided in the book, as the responses will differ for each individual. They provide a good basis for discussion with other students in the class and represent the kind of open-ended questions that some instructors like to use on tests to ensure that students understand the material and can apply it to real-life situations.

1. Consider five (or more) questions that you encounter or think about in your work, school, or other parts of your life. For each question, try to decide whether it is a research question and whether there are any data, any observations, that could conceivably provide an answer to it.

2. Go to the library and locate a journal in a field of interest to you that publishes research articles. Find an article with a results section that contains some reference to the use of statistics. Photocopy the section, highlight the statistical information, and try to describe what you do (if anything) and don't understand about it. Save this photocopy for the last week of the semester, when you'll look at it again.

3. Think about some things you encounter that are measured; perhaps you wear a size 10 shoe or would rate a movie as 4 on a ten-point scale. For each, try to identify the level of measurement that it represents. Could it have been measured differently, using a different scale?

4. Go to a newspaper or magazine and look for articles that seem to reflect some dependence on statistical analysis. Perhaps you'll read that people had 23% fewer cavities or that Americans today eat less beef than ever before. Try to identify what might be the sample and the population used for that analysis. If it isn't clear, imagine that you were going to do some research on that topic, and think about what sample you might use and what population might be of interest to you. Make up an example of a statistic and parameter that might be relevant to your study.

Introduction to Research Design

What Is Scientific Research?

Scientific research is a type of investigation used to answer a question or solve a problem. In its strictest form, it uses the scientific method, which consists of a series of steps:

1. Formulation of a **theory**, or a network of propositions about relationships among variables, with the purpose of explaining and predicting phenomena
2. Refinement of that theory into one or more hypotheses, or predictions, about what will happen under certain conditions
3. Design of a study that will permit the collection of data relevant to the hypotheses
4. Collection of the appropriate data
5. Analysis of the data
6. Formulation of conclusions relevant to the original theory

Although this textbook deals primarily with step 5, analysis of the data, it is important to realize that data analysis is only part of an entire process—a process whose purpose is answering a question or solving a problem.

Scientific research is not the same thing as library research, which involves finding out what others have done or discovered. Reviewing the literature is a part of scientific research, since it may influence the formation of theories and hypotheses, assist in designing the study, and aid in the interpretation of the findings. In other words, library research might be a part of steps 1, 2, 3, and even 6, but it is not considered to be original research unless the library materials themselves constitute the data for subsequent analysis.

Scientific research, of course, is not the only way to answer questions. Indeed, as was pointed out in Chapter 1, some questions cannot be answered by research, either because they deal with moral issues that are not dependent on data, or because they cannot be investigated for practical or theoretical reasons. People may prefer to resort to prayer, human authority, personal biases or feelings, pure logic, or other ways of answering questions rather than the scientific method, particularly when the questions are very personal ones.

Only a very unusual person would choose a partner for life based on a statistical analysis of those variables that best seem to predict marital satisfaction and a careful scrutiny of all potential candidates to see which one best fits the statistical model. However, researchers do formulate theories about what leads to happy (or, alternatively, stable) marriages, design studies, gather data, formulate conclusions, and do a better-than-chance job of predicting which marriages are more and less likely to succeed. Thus, the scientific method can be used to study even topics of great personal interest and importance.

Role of Observation

One thing that distinguishes research (which will be used from now on as a synonym for *scientific research*) from many other ways of answering questions is that it depends in part on original observations. In other words, it is **empirical**, which means based on data or observations. Research data can be gathered in many ways. Among these are

- Direct observations of behavior, which might be transcribed or coded in some way, such as a rating scale used to classify children as "hyperactive" or not
- Viewing and evaluation of videotapes, audiotapes, writing, drawings, homework problems, or other products that result from people's behavior
- Administration of tests of some kind, like ones given in classrooms or by personnel managers
- Use of physical or physiological measures, like the time taken to run a mile, or blood pressure
- Coding of records made by others, such as salary data, school registration data, or data available from public or private sources

Statistical analyses, when they are used, are applied to the data obtained from the observations. If there are no data, then a paper or project is not an empirical one and not a research study.

Role of Hypotheses

In order to test a theory or a model, which is a relatively narrow theory that applies only under certain constraints and in limited circumstances, it is necessary for the researcher to formulate hypotheses. A *hypothesis*, as stated earlier, is a prediction, a supposition about what will happen "if." Indeed, hypotheses are frequently stated in *if . . . then* form: If such-and-such is done or certain circumstances are met, then certain effects should follow and lead to certain observable consequences.

Theoretical Versus Operational Hypotheses.   Often the original hypotheses that follow from the theory are stated in general or theoretical terms. However, in order for research to be carried out, an **operational**, or testable, **hypothesis** has to be formulated—that is, the hypothesis is stated so specifically and clearly that exactly what is to be done and what is to be observed are spelled out in precise detail. An example of a theoretical hypothesis might be "Providing children with positive reinforcement contingent on good performance will improve their self-concept." An operational version of this hypothesis would be "If a random half of the fifth-grade children in Alexander Harris's class are given a gold star for every workbook problem they get correct, they will score higher on the Bandelier self-esteem scale than the children who did not get gold stars for correct answers."

If an analysis of the data gathered is consistent with the operational hypothesis, this confirmation provides support for the theory or model that generated it. If the results of the analysis contradict the hypothesis, then either the theory needs to be reformulated or the network of reasoning that led from the theory to the specific hypothesis has to be reconsidered.

Research Versus Statistical Hypotheses.   The hypothesis that the researcher formulates based on both theory and a knowledge of the subject matter is called the **research hypothesis**, whether stated generally or operationally. However, the research hypothesis is not the one that is usually tested statistically.

Null Hypothesis. As Chapter 8 will outline in more detail, the statistical hypothesis that is tested is the hypothesis of no difference between groups or no relationship between variables, and is typically called the *null hypothesis*. The null hypothesis for the positive reinforcement example is that there would be no difference in self-esteem scores for children who do and do not receive gold stars. Occasionally, a researcher may hypothesize that groups will not differ, particularly if other people have found a difference and he thinks that he has found a circumstance under which this difference will not appear. However, in most research studies, the researcher has a *directional hypothesis*—that is, a prediction that one particular group will have higher scores than another group or that high scores on one variable will be associated with high scores on another variable.

The relationship between the research hypothesis guiding the study and the null hypothesis that is directly tested by a statistical procedure is a somewhat indirect one: Researchers draw inferences about their research hypothesis by considering what the results of their statistical test imply about the likelihood of their hypothesis being correct. For example, if the results of the study suggest that it is extremely unlikely that the children given gold stars and those not given gold stars have equivalent self-concept scores, since those with the stars have much higher scores than the other children, you would conclude that your hypothesis that giving gold stars would increase self-concept was supported.

The important thing to remember at this point is that researchers should describe the reasoning that led them to their research hypothesis and should state that hypothesis clearly. It is not necessary or usual to describe the null hypothesis, as it should be obvious to the reader.

Research Without Hypotheses. Although most scientific research, particularly that which uses statistical analysis, involves the testing of theories or at least of hypotheses, there are several types of research studies that do not test hypotheses.

1. Some exploratory research studies do not test any specific hypotheses—for example, studies of what the effects of a new curriculum or drug might be, when there are no clear reasons to make predictions about its effects.

2. Sometimes there are studies in which a prediction is not made because two different theories lead to different predictions, and the researcher is interested in seeing which one the data support. In these cases, even though the researcher does not formulate a specific hypothesis, a statistical test of the null hypothesis is still conducted in order to draw inferences about the effects of the procedures or the relative merits of the contrasting theories.

3. Some qualitative or ethnographic research is deliberately carried out without hypotheses, ideally so that the researcher's preconceptions will not bias the results.

4. Some research is purely descriptive, using no inferential statistics at all. Census data on a population might be gathered, for example, by someone who is interested only in the data themselves and not in drawing any broader implications from them.

Research and Causality

One of the major uses of research is to study issues of cause and effect and to draw inferences about what factors cause certain outcomes and what variables influence other variables. Deriving such inferences is a complex issue, which is heavily influenced by the research design. Even if the researcher has hypotheses about a causal pathway, it is not always possible to test these hypotheses, because the appropriate data cannot be gathered.

For example, if the researcher compares groups of individuals who have had different experiences, such as having survived the death of a child or not, the researcher cannot be sure that differences between them are due to the experience, rather than to some other factor that made them different before the particular experience. Continuing the example, people who live in countries ravaged by war, who live in neighborhoods with a high crime rate, or who have little money for medical care may be more likely to lose a child than those who live in different circumstances.

Some types of research, like experimental research, and some statistical procedures, like structural equation modeling, are designed to test causal theories and models. Other types of research, like descriptive and correlational research, are far less likely to provide information that answers questions about cause and effect. It is important to remember that even the most carefully designed study can only suggest causal mechanisms and provide evidence consistent with a theory of how these mechanisms operate. Research cannot *prove* that something causes something else.

What Are Some Approaches to Research?

Researchers do not all agree on the best way to divide up the variety of research methods that have been used by behavioral and social scientists. Although some terms, like "experimental research," have very precise meanings, others, like "quasi-experimental research," mean somewhat different things to different people. Moreover, some ways of dividing up the research universe overlap with others so that a particular study could be both basic and developmental or applied and correlational. (These terms will be discussed a little later in the chapter.) Nevertheless, there is a reasonable amount of commonality in how most researchers classify different research methods.

Types of Research

This section will attempt to identify the most frequently used research methodologies or types of research and the terms commonly used to describe them.

Historical Research.   **Historical research** is designed to explain or interpret a particular event that happened in the past. It distinguishes between two types of data: **primary sources**, records made by a witness or participant in the event, and **secondary sources**, those written later by someone who did not experience it directly. Historical research is typically bound to a particular time and place and frequently relies on relatively subjective interpretations rather than on the use of statistical procedures. When statistical techniques are used, they are likely to be descriptive rather than inferential, as the focus is usually on understanding a particular situation rather than on deriving general laws or principles that are broadly applicable to human behavior.

EXAMPLE

A historical research project might be a study of textbooks used in the 1870s and how their content related to the political goals and philosophy of the period.

Qualitative Research.   Research that does not follow the traditional scientific model of theory formulation, hypothesis generation, data gathering, analysis, and conclusions is **qualitative research**, some of which is also called *ethnographic research*. Qualitative research uses a somewhat different vocabulary and methodology from the kind of research that will be emphasized in this book. Many qualitative researchers would consider all research designs discussed in this book as belonging to one general category called *quantitative research* and would emphasize the ways in which qualitative research differs from this approach:

- Qualitative research is based on an anthropological rather than a psychological model.
- The purpose of qualitative research tends to be the collection and subjective interpretation of data rather than the testing of theory.
- Qualitative research focuses on the specific context and setting of interactions, rather than on abstract constructs considered independently from any context.
- Qualitative researchers strive for completeness of description rather than isolation of variables.
- They prefer to consider the subjective quality of an interpretation of the data rather than to utilize statistical methods to draw inferences and generalizations. Although some qualitative researchers explicitly avoid the use of any statistical procedures, others may use descriptive statistics or even inferential ones as an adjunct to their approach.

TIP ▬▬▬▬▬▬▬▬▬▬▬▬▬▬▬▬▬▬▬▬▬▬▬▬▬▬▬▬▬▬▬

It should be emphasized that the term *qualitative research* does not imply that only qualitative variables are studied. Qualitative researchers may study processes such as learning to read or ways in which people react to illness along with more clearly qualitative variables such as kinship relationships. However, most qualitative researchers are not interested in measurement (i.e., in assigning numbers to observations) and in that sense are focusing on qualitative variables.

EXAMPLE ▬▬▬▬▬▬▬▬▬▬▬▬▬▬▬▬▬▬▬▬▬▬▬▬▬▬▬▬▬

A qualitative research project might be a study of a board of directors of a charitable institution using participant observation and interpretation by one of the members. To carry out such a project, the researcher might attend meetings and take notes on (or tape) what occurs, interview all of the board members, try to identify general themes derived from the transcripts of the meetings and their comments, and even photograph and describe the physical setting in which the meeting takes place. Documents describing the purpose of the board, minutes of meetings over the years, and references to the board in local newspapers could also constitute sources of data for the qualitative researcher. From all this information, the researcher would attempt to construct a description of the board that provides a rich and meaningful picture of how the board operates and of how its proceedings are viewed by the participants and by the researcher. ■

Case Studies.   A **case study** is a research project that involves the intensive investigation of a single individual or group. Case study research is very common in special education, clinical psychology, psychiatry, and other fields that emphasize individual differences rather than commonalities. Case study research is subject to biases due to the facts that unusual rather than typical cases are likely to be reported and that hypothesis testing and replication are unlikely. Nevertheless, case studies may be very useful when they serve to disprove a theory, when they illustrate a more general principle, and when they are the only way to study a topic. It is rare for case study research to utilize statistical analyses, but some case studies of treatment techniques use statistical procedures to measure changes that have occurred over time.

EXAMPLE

A case study might be a description of a person with manic depressive psychosis and of her struggles with her disease throughout her lifetime. ■

Descriptive Research.   **Descriptive research** is a very broad category that includes research in which the purpose is to describe or report scores on some variables, without an intention of explaining them or relating them to something else. Descriptive research may involve observation of behavior, sometimes using formal coding sheets or observation schedules, or measurement of scores on formal or informal tests. It often includes the reporting of norms or typical scores, such as scores on standardized tests like the Scholastic Assessment Test (SAT). More than most research projects, descriptive studies frequently utilize large samples, natural settings, and behaviors or scores that are of general interest. Descriptive research often, but not invariably, uses only descriptive statistics; however, it may use inferential statistics if there is an interest in comparing subgroups or in generalizing to a population from a sample.

EXAMPLE

A descriptive research study might be an analysis of interactions between floor managers and salespersons, with codes for the managerial styles used and the responses to them. ■

Developmental Research.   One subtype of descriptive research is called **developmental research**, because it deals with changes that occur as a result of maturation or development. Although occasionally such research focuses on the development of an organization or institution, almost always it has as its purpose the identification of principles of human development. There are two general research methods of studying development: the longitudinal method and the cross-sectional method.

Longitudinal Versus Cross-Sectional Research. As the syllable "long" indicates, **longitudinal research** is distinguished by the fact that it takes a relatively long time to conduct, since it involves measuring the same individuals at various times as they grow older. In a longitudinal study, the researcher looks at the same people when they are of different ages, meaning that the pattern of changes from age to age can be seen on an individual level. In contrast, **cross-sectional research** involves studying people who differ in age at the same point in time, meaning that age is confounded (or mixed up, entangled) with the year in which people were born. In a longitudinal study of changes in memory with aging, the same individuals would be studied at ages 60, 70, and 80; in a cross-sectional study, a group of 60-year-olds would be compared with groups of 70-year-olds and 80-year-olds.

Each of the two developmental research methods has some advantages for studying the processes of development. Longitudinal research looks at actual changes in individuals, rather than just average differences between people of different ages, and makes it possible to assess how well behavior at one point in time predicts behavior later on. For example, researchers who want to see whether children who are aggressive at age 2 are likely to become aggressive adults at age 22 or 62 would use the longitudinal research method. On the other hand, the cross-sectional research method is typically much faster, can use the same researchers without them dropping out of the study, and often has a larger, more representative sample since people are more willing to agree to participate in a one-shot study than to say that they will serve in a longitudinal project that might require their participation for the next 20 or so years.

TIP

The statistical techniques used to analyze results of the two developmental methods may differ, since the longitudinal method relies on procedures that acknowledge that the same individuals are being measured repeatedly. The cross-sectional method, on the other hand, compares different groups of individuals who have frequently been randomly selected as representative of their age groups, using statistical procedures that assume each person is measured only once.

As you can guess from these descriptions, cross-sectional research is much more common than longitudinal, since the time and expense of the latter preclude casual explorations. Most longitudinal studies are large-scale, well-funded ones, such as the Terman study of high IQ children begun in the 1920s and continuing until the subjects were elderly.

EXAMPLE ▬▬▬▬▬▬▬▬▬▬▬▬▬▬▬▬▬▬▬▬▬▬▬▬▬▬

A longitudinal developmental research study might be a study of the changes in moral judgments in individuals as they aged from 5 until 25. A cross-sectional developmental study might be a comparison of the amount of helping behavior shown to a crying child by people aged 5, 10, 15, or 20 years. ■

Survey Research.   One of the most common approaches to research used by social and behavioral scientists, **survey research**, can also be considered as a subcategory of descriptive research. Survey research, in brief, is research in which people are asked questions and their answers are analyzed. Political polls, consumer surveys, magazine questionnaires, and opinion polls are examples of survey research.

Questionnaire Versus Interview Research. Like developmental research, survey research is of two basic types. **Questionnaire research** involves asking people questions in written form and having them write down their answers; **interview research** is conducted by posing the questions orally (usually in person, although telephone interviews are possible) and having the researcher or interviewer record the responses. Either method can be relatively *structured*, meaning that the respondent selects from among a number of alternatives, or *unstructured*, meaning that the respondent constructs a response to an open-ended question. Questionnaires have the advantage of being relatively cheap, convenient, and potentially anonymous; interviews make it possible to survey people who do not read or write comfortably, to explain the study and increase rapport with potential respondents, and to eliminate people who are obviously confused or lying. Survey research uses a great variety of statistical measures depending on the nature of the data and the questions asked.

EXAMPLE ▬▬▬▬▬▬▬▬▬▬▬▬▬▬▬▬▬▬▬▬▬▬▬▬▬▬

A questionnaire study could use an anonymous questionnaire given to high school students asking about their use of alcohol and other drugs. An example of an interview study is the famous Kinsey survey, in which large numbers of people were asked about their sexual behaviors by trained interviewers. ■

Correlational Research.   A **correlational research** study is one that considers more than one variable and attempts to look at the relationships between two or more variables. In correlational research, each person is measured or assessed or observed on two or more dimensions, and through statistical procedures, some inferences are drawn about the relationship between those dimensions.

The essence of correlational research is that the researcher does not manipulate or change the individuals or their position on any variable but merely observes and measures. Because of this lack of control, it is rarely legitimate to draw inferences about the effect of one variable on another based on a correlational design. A particular correlational research study may lead to excellent descriptions and accurate predictions but reveal almost nothing about the causal influence of any particular experience or variable. When a researcher cannot randomly assign people to conditions or decide who will or will not receive particular experiences, correlational research may be the best way to see how these experiences are related to other variables. Some sciences are inherently correlational, like paleontology or astronomy, since researchers cannot directly affect the organisms that were fossilized nor the stars or other astronomical entities.

TIP

Correlational research can use a number of statistical procedures, including but not limited to correlation coefficients. Moreover, other research designs might involve the computation of a correlation coefficient. Remember that correlational research designs and correlation coefficients do not necessarily go together.

Causal–Comparative Research. Some authors use the term *ex post facto* or **causal–comparative research** for correlational research that attempts to draw inferences about cause and effect by looking at differences between groups of people who have and have not been exposed to some experience or other variable. For example, scores of athletes who have experienced one or another training regimen might be compared. However, since the researcher did not randomly assign the athletes to the training regimen, it is likely that differences in their scores after training reflect not only the effects of the training regimens but a host of other influences that led them to receive one or the other training program in the first place.

As another example, people who have their health needs served by a health maintenance organization might be compared with those who have individual insurance in terms of their satisfaction with their insurance and the number of visits to a physician they make. Although the researcher would like to conclude that the type of insurance contributes to their satisfaction and decision about visiting the doctor, the fact that the people who possess one of the two types of insurance may differ in other ways makes any such causal conclusion problematic.

EXAMPLE ▬▬

Correlational research might involve a comparison of people who voted for a Republican or Democratic candidate to see how their vote related to their opinions on other matters and to various demographic characteristics. ■

Quasi-Experimental Research. One of the least clearly defined types of research is referred to as **quasi-experimental**. In general, this type of research is intended to draw inferences about causality and has some built-in controls that make it reasonable to draw some tentative conclusions about cause and effect. Although quasi-experimental research has tighter controls than correlational research, it lacks the control of true experimental research and thus is generally more susceptible to criticisms and to alternative explanations of the findings.

Beyond this general description, there is little agreement on exactly what constitutes quasi-experimental research. Thus, a particular researcher might call her study quasi-experimental while someone else would label it merely correlational. Often quasi-experimental research involves manipulation but not random assignment, or control over the time of measurement but not over exposure to the variable of interest.

EXAMPLE ▬▬

A quasi-experimental study might be an attempt to find out the effects of year-round schooling upon academic performance of students at 6 schools by looking at standardized test scores of the students at the schools for a year before and 2 years after 3 of the schools began year-round schooling. ■

Experimental Research. It is generally accepted by scientists that **experimental research**, where appropriate, is the best method available for coming to conclusions about cause and effect. Experimental research is distinguished from other research in three ways.

 • *Independent and dependent variables:* First, experimental research includes at least one independent variable and one dependent variable. The **independent variable**, often called a *factor*, is the one whose effects the researcher is studying and is the one that the researcher manipulates. The independent variable, usually a qualitative variable, has at least two **levels**, or separate conditions, groups, or treatments. For instance, if a researcher is looking at the effects of three different diets on the weight of rats, the three diets constitute the three levels of the independent variable. The **dependent variable**, also called the **dependent measure**, is the one that is presumed to be affected by the independent variable and that is used to measure its effects. Usually, but not always, the dependent variable is a continuous, quantitative variable. In the rat diet example, for instance, the dependent variable would be the weight of the rats.

It is possible, indeed very common, for a research study to have more than one independent variable or factor, in which case it is called a **factorial design**. An experiment can also have more than one dependent variable, in which case statistical procedures called *multivariate techniques* would be used to analyze it.

- *Experimental and control groups:* A second characteristic of experimental research is that it has at least two conditions or groups of respondents: in its simplest form, an experimental group and a control group. The **experimental group** comprises those individuals who receive the special manipulation, procedure, or experience, which is usually called the *experimental treatment*. The **control group** consists of those who receive the ordinary, usual, common procedures to which the experimental procedure is being compared. A particular experiment could have more than one experimental group and, less commonly, more than one control group. For example, in a study comparing the effectiveness of three different procedures for reducing public speaking anxiety (behavioral therapy, psychoanalytic therapy, and exhortations to relax), the people receiving the two types of formal therapy would be considered the experimental groups and those just told to relax would constitute the control group.

- *Random assignment:* The third distinguishing characteristic of true experimental research is that it involves random assignment of participants in the research (formerly called *subjects*) to the experimental and control groups. The process of random assignment insures that no systematic error or **bias** (a four-letter word to researchers) enters into the procedure. Random assignment can be done by flipping a coin, by some other physical process, or by the use of a random number table, which will be explained in detail in Chapter 8. When subjects have been randomly assigned to conditions, it is possible to estimate the likelihood that the mean scores of people in the groups will differ by any given amount.

Reasoning Behind Experimental Research. The logic of experimental research is based on the idea that random assignment to groups makes it likely that the groups are equivalent at the start of the study—not that they are identical, but that any differences between them are due only to chance. Thus, on the average, if people are randomly assigned to conditions, the smart people, tall people, motivated people, uneducated people, pimply people, bearded people, and any other type of people you can identify will be equally likely to be in the experimental and control conditions. If the groups are equivalent before they are exposed or not exposed to the experimental manipulation—in other words, to the different levels of the independent variable—then any differences between them after this exposure must be due to the effects of the independent variable, the experimental treatment. Differences in mean scores on the dependent variable, therefore, should truly depend on the individuals' positions on the independent variable, since the random assignment should have assured that everything else would be equivalent.

It is important to realize that the logic of considering the independent variable as the cause depends on the assumption that the experimental and control groups would have been equal on the dependent measure if they had not been exposed to the independent variable. It also depends on the assumption that the cause precedes the effect, since the manipulation of the independent variable must precede the assessment of its effect by measuring the dependent variable.

Although this description of experimental research may make it appear to be the best kind of research, this is not always the case. Sometimes the constraints that would be necessary if one were to conduct experimental research make it almost impossible to generalize the results to real-life settings. Frequently, ethical and practical considerations preclude the use of experimental designs. For example, studies on the effects of child-rearing practices are almost always correlational, since it would rarely be possible to randomly assign people to rear their children in certain ways. Similarly, studies of the effects of attending college are always correlational or quasi-experimental, since it would be impossible in our society to assign people to attend college or not. School administrators frequently require that all children in a classroom or in a school receive the same experiences, rather than being randomly assigned to experimental and control groups. And, of course, researchers who wish to study genetic influences on behavior and development cannot randomly assign people to mate with others.

Types of Research

- **Applied research:** Research designed to solve a practical problem or to answer an immediate question
- **Basic research:** Research designed to test and evaluate theories or to contribute to a body of knowledge
- **Case study research:** A research project that involves the intensive investigation of a single individual or group
- **Causal–comparative research:** Correlational research that attempts to draw inferences about cause and effect by looking at differences between groups of people who have and have not been exposed to some experience or other variable
- **Correlational research:** A type of research in which two or more variables are measured but not manipulated and the relationship between the variables is assessed
- **Cross-sectional research:** A type of developmental research that involves studying people who differ in age at the same point in time
- **Descriptive research:** Research in which the purpose is to describe or report scores on some variables

- **Developmental research:** Research that deals with changes that occur as a result of maturation or development
- **Experimental research:** Research in which participants are randomly assigned to experimental and control groups, an independent variable is manipulated, and scores on a dependent variable are measured, leading to conclusions about the effect of the independent variable upon the dependent variable
- **Field research:** Research conducted in the real world or a natural setting
- **Historical research:** Research designed to explain or interpret a particular event that happened in the past
- **Interview research:** A type of survey research in which people are asked questions orally and their responses are recorded by the researcher
- **Laboratory research:** Research conducted in a setting specifically designed for research
- **Longitudinal research:** A type of developmental research that involves measuring the same individuals at various times as they grow older
- **Qualitative research:** Research that does not follow the scientific model and that focuses on the collection and subjective interpretation of data rather than on the testing of theory
- **Quasi-experimental research:** A loosely defined type of research that is intended to draw inferences about causality and that has some built-in methodological controls
- **Questionnaire research:** A type of survey research in which people are asked written questions and respond to them in writing
- **Survey research:** Research in which people are asked questions and their answers are analyzed

TIP

The assumption that research is experimental is so pervasive in statistical research that some second-level statistics textbooks have the words "experimental design" in the title, even though the statistical procedures that they describe (almost always analysis of variance procedures) can be used with other research methods as well as with experimental designs.

Examples of Experimental Research. Examples of experimental research are widespread in psychology and, to a somewhat lesser extent, in education and the health sciences. A study of the effects of different types of provocation upon college students' tendencies to retaliate aggressively, a project comparing the effects of two different approaches to teaching fifth-grade social studies on students' scores on a standardized test, and a test of the comparative effectiveness of two drugs designed to lower blood pressure might all be experimental studies, if participants are randomly assigned to conditions, then exposed to the different levels of the independent variable, and then measured on the relevant dependent measure.

Purposes of Research

The classification of research approaches into the methods described in the previous section is only one way in which to divide up the universe of behavioral and social science research projects. A different approach, which cuts across the prior one, is to categorize research studies according to their purpose, or generally into the categories of basic and applied research.

Basic and Applied Research.   Research designed to test and evaluate theories or, more generally, to contribute to a body of knowledge is known as **basic research**. Biologists who study the transmission of chemicals across cell membranes or psychologists who study the learning of nonsense syllables with a hope of understanding basic memory processes are doing basic research.

   Applied research, on the other hand, is designed to solve a practical problem or to answer an immediate question. Applied research is often stimulated by real-world issues, sometimes crises, such as the AIDS epidemic or the "crisis" in American education. Sometimes the term *action research* is used as a synonym for applied research, although some people use "action research" more narrowly to refer to research that is oriented to reaching and implementing a decision by taking some identifiable action. An applied research project might be carried out by a human resources manager who wishes to know whether or not to continue with an employee assistance program; another applied research study might be done at a shopping center by a manager who wishes to decide during what hours to open the store.

   The distinction between applied and basic research is not one of method, since any method could be used for basic research and almost any method for applied research. (It is hard to think of an applied longitudinal study, I must admit, but if you are selling a product that you advertise will fit people from cradle to grave, I suppose that it might be done.) Nor is it a distinction of quality, since both basic research studies and applied research studies can be designed well or badly. In general, basic research probably tends to be of higher quality, since few people with no training or interest in research per se do basic research, whereas almost anyone with a question to answer might find himself or herself doing an applied research study. It is probably also true that basic research is likely to be undervalued by people who are not scientists or researchers, since they may be less aware of the value of a good theory.

Nevertheless, both kinds of research can make important contributions to knowledge and to practice, and it is not rare for an applied study to add to theoretical knowledge and for a basic research project to spin off all kinds of useful applications (Snyder, 1993). Thus the distinction between basic and applied research is really in the mind and label of the researcher, and perhaps the funding agency, rather than in the procedures. However, some highly sophisticated statistical procedures, such as path analysis and structural equation modeling, that are used to test or confirm theories would be used primarily in basic theoretical research.

Research Setting

A final distinction among research studies, which researchers sometimes make, cuts across all of the previous categorizations. This distinction is between field research and laboratory research.

Field and Laboratory Research.   A **field research** project is set in the "real world" or in a "naturalistic" setting. Field research may take place in a classroom, an office, a national park, or any other place where people live their lives. Participants in a field research study may or may not know that they are being studied.

Laboratory research, on the other hand, is conducted in a setting specifically designed for research, with people who know that they are participating in a research study. The great majority of laboratory research in psychology is done with college sophomores, although white rats and pigeons are also popular subjects.

Although there is not a tight correspondence between the research setting and the research method, it is probably the case that field research studies are more likely to be descriptive, developmental, correlational, and survey in design than they are to be experimental. Similarly, laboratory studies are somewhat more likely to represent a true experimental design, reflecting the greater control that researchers are generally able to exert in a laboratory setting than in a naturalistic one. Nevertheless, field experiments have been frequently staged by social psychologists, who are interested in such topics as seeing how people respond to requests when the dress or language of the requester is varied. Laboratory studies have involved observations of even such intimate behaviors as sexual intercourse.

Because field research studies represent a greater variety of situations and environments that people experience, they have the advantage of leading to greater generalizability to real-life contexts. Laboratory studies have the advantage of greater control of irrelevant variables that might otherwise influence the results and thus of clearer clues as to the causes of the behavior being observed. Both types of studies have real limitations (as do all studies), and neither type of setting is necessarily associated with any particular statistical approach to data analysis.

How Are Extraneous Variables Controlled?

When individuals do research, even if their purpose is purely applied, they are almost always interested in understanding and explaining what is going on and what is affecting what. Because no two human beings are alike and because people are so complex, it is impossible to ever be sure of fully understanding the meaning and implication of any result based on research with human beings. Almost always, there are a number of possible alternative explanations of any given finding, and all a researcher can do is to say that a particular explanation seems to be more or less (or, perhaps even "extremely") likely. To come to such conclusions, it is necessary to eliminate other plausible interpretations of the data in order to say that a particular one is relatively likely to be correct.

The major way to eliminate alternative explanations is to control for nuisance or **extraneous variables**, meaning variables in which the researcher has no interest, at least for the purposes of that particular research project, but which might conceivably influence the results. Control of extraneous variables is sometimes discussed within the context of experimental design, but it is equally important for all methods of research. Regardless of the research design employed, there are a number of methods that have been used to control for extraneous variables in research.

Methods of Control

A variety of methods for controlling for extraneous variables in research studies have been developed.

Holding the Variable Constant.   One way to prevent a potential nuisance variable from confounding the results of a study is to hold it constant, which means to ensure that everyone in the study is at the same level of that variable. For example, gender might be held constant by using only males, or grade level might be held constant by using only sophomores. By turning a variable into a constant within a particular research study, the researcher guarantees that it cannot be responsible for differences between groups or cause people in the study to have different scores on some other variable.

Almost all research studies hold some variables constant, even if they do not explicitly state that they are doing so. Usually they sample people from only one geographic location, of a limited range of ages and cultures, and with enough similarity to the researcher to be willing and able to participate in the study. Of course, to the extent that a variable has been held constant, or at least limited to a narrow range of levels, the researcher has to be cautious in generalizing the findings to levels of or scores on the variable that have not been studied in this context.

Random Selection and Assignment.   Another way in which researchers reduce the chance of extraneous variables influencing their results is through the use of random selection and assignment.

Random Selection. Random selection, or **random sampling**, refers to an unbiased way of picking the participants for a research study. With random selection, every one in the population has an equal chance of being in the research study, meaning that the researcher can generalize from the research participants to the general population with confidence. You will learn how to carry out random selection procedures in Chapter 8 of this book.

Random Assignment. **Random assignment** of participants to conditions implies that the individuals in the different groups are equivalent and thus that major differences between them are due to the manipulation or treatment rather than to chance. The use of random assignment can go beyond assignment of participants to assignment of times, materials, evaluators, or anything else that might be varied in a research study and over which the researcher has control.

TIP ▓▓▓

> A good rule of thumb in doing research is that whenever a choice has to be made, unless there is a good theoretical reason for making a particular decision in a specific direction, it should be made randomly.

Factorial Designs.   A third way of controlling for extraneous variables is to include them as factors in the research design, forming a factorial design. For example, if sex might affect the scores on a (dependent) measure of physical strength that is used to estimate the effects of a strength training program, then both males and females could be used in the study, with each sex separately assigned randomly to the treatment (strength training) conditions. Such a design has more than one independent variable: Both training condition and gender are now considered to be factors in the design.

Even though gender is not a manipulated variable, since individuals were not compelled to be male or female, the study is still considered to be an experiment and gender would be called an independent variable by most people, as long as there is one true independent variable that is actually manipulated by the researcher in the study. However, factorial analyses are not limited to experimental designs. They can also be used with correlational research studies in which participants are classified on two qualitative variables and their scores on a third variable are compared. For example, the mean incomes of male and female United States Senators and Representatives could be compared.

Labeling a Factorial Design. In describing a factorial design, the researcher usually reports the number of levels of each factor separated from the number of levels of the next factor by an × (or sometimes by the word "by"), so that the total number of groups can be identified by multiplying the number of levels together. A study comparing the effects of three types of reinforcement on the job performance of interns who were or were not given an orientation to the job would thus be described as a 3 (reinforcement strategy) × 2 (orientation) factorial design. A study comparing the sex role stereotypes of male and female students in first, third, and fifth grades who had male and female teachers would constitute a 2 (sex of student) by 3 (grade level) by 2 (sex of teacher) factorial design. This latter study would not, however, be an experiment, since none of the variables was manipulated (unless children were randomly assigned to teacher); instead it would be a correlational study.

Advantages of Factorial Designs. A major advantage of a factorial design is that such a design makes it possible to directly investigate the effects of a variable that otherwise would have been only a nuisance, possibly influencing the results in unknown ways. Another advantage is that it makes it possible to look at interactions between variables. An **interaction** occurs when the effects of one variable or factor are different for different levels of another factor. For example, if the movie that is rated most highly by women receives the lowest ratings from men, there is an interaction between movie and gender of the participant. When there is an interaction between variables, it means that conclusions about the effects or correlates of one variable must be limited to individuals with a particular position on another variable. Only a factorial design is equipped to permit the identification and assessment of interactions.

Analyses of Factorial Designs. Studies utilizing factorial designs are almost always analyzed by a factorial analysis of variance procedure, as long as the scores on the dependent measure come close to an interval scale, so that it makes sense to talk about a mean. However, occasionally a factorial design will be associated with a nominal-level dependent variable; for instance, one could look at the effects of several different campaign procedures intended to get registered Republicans and Independents to vote for a candidate. In that case, campaign procedure and party affiliation would be the factors and candidate for whom one votes would be the dependent variable. For such a study a chi-square procedure would probably be the statistical procedure of choice.

Between-participants and Within-participants Factors. Although there are numerous ways to classify independent variables or factors, perhaps the most important one from a statistical point of view is into *between-participants factors* and *within-participants factors*, because they require different procedures for analysis. A **between-participants factor** (or between-participants variable) is one for which each participant is exposed to one and only one level of the variable. For example, if each person receives only one drug, which might or might not be effective in reducing acne, then drug is a between-participants factor. Individual differences and demographic characteristics are almost always between-participants factors, as the same person could not be both a Texan and an Alaskan or both a fifth-grade dropout and a Ph.D. except under extremely unusual circumstances.

A **within-participants factor** is one for which each person receives more than one level of the variable. For example, if a researcher comparing two drugs gave each individual one drug, noted its effects, and then at a later time gave each individual another drug, drug would be a within-participants factor. Similarly, if children are asked to draw a picture of Santa Claus on December 23rd and then again on January 3rd, date of drawing would constitute a within-participants factor.

Between-participants factors are the more common kind in research, partly because it is often impossible to make a particular variable a within-participants one, and partly because it may be more complex to design a study with one or more within-participants variables. Between-participants variables also make it possible to generalize to individuals who would be exposed to only one level of the independent variable, which would probably be the case for most variables of interest. However, within-participants variables do have the advantage that the same people are measured at all levels of the variable, so that the effects of the variable are not confused or confounded with individual differences. They may also be more powerful—that is, more likely to pick up a real but small effect of the variable. Different statistical techniques must be used to analyze the effects of between-participants and within-participants factors, as a within-participants variable necessitates the use of procedures that take into account that each person is being measured more than once.

TIP

Almost all statistics books and journal articles published before the mid-1990s refer to the people who participate in research studies as "subjects." The American Psychological Association Publication Manual (1994) recommends that the term "subject" be replaced by other terms, such as "participant," "respondent," or "student." However, you will find that many statistics and design books talk about "between-subjects" and "within-subjects" variables.

Statistical Controls.   The types of controls that have been mentioned up to this point are considered *design controls*, or controls that are built into the design of the study. As desirable as such controls are, sometimes they cannot be used or are not enough. Various statistical procedures have been devised to control for certain types of extraneous variables, as an adjunct to design controls. For example, in a study designed to get people to lose weight, the researcher might analyze a change score, in this case the difference between pretest and posttest weight, or the number of pounds lost. An alternative procedure for comparing groups of individuals who differ on some pretest measure, in order to see the effects of an experimental treatment on a dependent measure, is to use analysis of covariance, a procedure that attempts to statistically equate groups on the pretest measure, making it possible to view their posttest scores as reflecting only the effects of the independent variable. Partial correlation is a statistical procedure that makes it possible to look at the relationship between two variables—for instance, two measures of cognitive processing—while statistically controlling for differences related to scores on a third variable, such as chronological age.

Combinations of Methods.   The previous discussion of approaches to controlling extraneous variables has considered them in isolation, as if a particular research study would utilize one or another. In fact, it is not only common but typical for research studies to use several, sometimes all, of the above methods. For example, a project could use parents arrested for child abuse for the first time as participants, holding severity of the charge and previous arrest record constant; it could include type of treatment or punishment, sex of the parent, and sex of the child as variables in a factorial design; it could involve random assignment to treatment or punishment condition; and it could use educational level of the parent as a covariate.

Holding some variables constant serves to eliminate the chance that they might differentially affect scores on the dependent variable; using a factorial design makes it possible to see any interactions—for example, whether or not a particular treatment works better for mothers or fathers; random assignment serves to control for all kinds of variables you may never have thought of or considered at all; and the use of a covariate allows you to get rid of possible differences on the dependent measure caused by differences in education. Controlling for extraneous variables and thus reducing alternative explanations for the results is one of the most important and sometimes the most difficult aspects of research design.

Methods of Controlling Extraneous Variables

Design Controls
  Holding the variable constant
  Random selection
  Random assignment
  Factorial designs
    Between-participants factors
    Within-participants factors

> **Statistical Controls**
>   Change scores
>   Analysis of covariance
>   Partial correlation
>
> **Combinations of Methods**

Internal and External Validity

In conducting research, a distinction is sometimes made between **internal validity**, the ability to conclude that a result is indeed due to the variable that is believed to be its cause, and **external validity**, the generalizability of the findings (Campbell & Stanley, 1963). Experimental research usually possesses a high degree of internal validity, since it controls for most reasonable alternative explanations of the results. However, if a study is done in a laboratory setting, as is true of most experimental research, it might lack external validity, and the researcher might have little confidence that its findings would apply to another group of people tested under somewhat different conditions at another time and place. Field research, because it is conducted with people in their usual environment, is usually relatively high in external validity.

For example, a study of the effects of punishment (receiving an electric shock) on subsequent aggression (shocking someone else) in a laboratory setting using males enrolled in introductory psychology classes as participants might be internally valid and lead to very clear conclusions, such as that those who were shocked were more likely to shock someone else. However, its external validity might be low—in other settings, people who are the recipients of aggression could become more fearful or more empathetic rather than more aggressive. Similarly, a correlational field study conducted by interviewing 1200 randomly selected adults from Tennessee to study the relationship between being a target and an instigator of aggression might suggest a strong relationship between the two variables and be high in external validity. However, you could not conclude from such a study that being the recipient of aggression *caused* people to be more aggressive toward others: Poverty, modeling, cultural values, or some other third variable could be affecting both types of aggression.

To summarize the distinction between the two types of validity, internal validity refers to the confidence you can have in the causal relationships implied by the data—high in the experimental example and low in the survey described. Randomly assigning subjects to conditions increases the internal validity of a research study. External validity refers to the confidence you can have that the same results would be found under other circumstances and particularly with other participants—higher in the survey and lower in the experiment on aggression. Randomly selecting the participants for a research study from the population of interest increases its external validity.

What Are Some Guidelines for Using Statistics?

Research design is, in a sense, more important than statistical analysis, since it is much easier to reanalyze data that have been incorrectly analyzed than it is to redesign and conduct the study all over again, using new participants and collecting new data. However, if the statistical analyses are incorrect, then the interpretation of the findings will be just as wrong as if they had been based on a faulty design (Kromrey, 1993). Hence it is worth taking the time to think about several issues when doing statistical analyses of research data.

Consider the Meaning of the Numbers

Statistical procedures can be computed on any set of numbers, not just on the results of a research study. It would be possible to pick page numbers casually from the *Congressional Record* or the Pittsburgh telephone book and to put those numbers into a statistical formula. It would not be possible, however, to make any sense out of an analysis of such meaningless numbers, no matter how sophisticated the statistical procedure used. Unless the numbers entered into a formula make sense, the results of the calculations will not make sense either. Thus one of the first things to consider in analyzing data is what the actual numbers or scores mean.

For example, if people's attitudes are being measured on a number of five-point scales, is it the case that on some of the items a 5 means a negative attitude and on others it means a positive attitude? If so, values on some of the items would have to be reversed before they are added to form a total score. If responses to several different questions are being coded in the same study, is "no" always coded as 0 and "yes" as 1, or is a "no" coded as 1 in some instances and as 0 in other cases? Is a high score on something desirable, as it would be for items correct on a test, or less desirable, as it would be for minutes taken to cover a given distance in a race? Are you blindly averaging telephone numbers or their equivalent? Unless you fully understand the scoring procedures and what every possible score implies about the variable being measured, you cannot be confident that your choice of statistical procedures and your interpretations of the results will be correct.

Consider How the Numbers Will Be Interpreted

Even if your statistical analyses are technically correct, it is important to be sure that you report them in a way that will not be misinterpreted. Lind (1996) discusses an example from the political realm. Conservatives reported an enormous increase in the proportion of out-of-wedlock births among African American women, from 23% in the 1960s to over 60% in the 1990s. Although this information is correct, Lind points out that the increase in the *proportion* of illegitimate births is primarily due to a decrease in the number of children that married American women are having, paralleling the smaller family sizes for married women in most Western societies. The actual birth rate for unmarried Black teenagers has been relatively stable for approximately 70 years.

This example reiterates a tip from the previous chapter: When you are dealing with proportions or percentages, it is important to consider the base from which the proportion is taken. More generally, whenever you present statistical data, you want to be sure that you are depicting it in a way that gives an accurate and realistic picture of the situation that you are describing.

Consider Whether Assumptions Are Met

As mentioned in the discussion of parametric and nonparametric tests in Chapter 1, some statistical procedures cannot be used appropriately unless certain assumptions are met. Trying to carry out a procedure when the assumptions governing its use are not met will sometimes lead to incorrect inferences. (As you can figure out for yourself, this is called a *mistake*.) Alternatively, sometimes statistical procedures lead to approximately correct conclusions even if the assumptions that should guide their use are violated. (As you may recall, these procedures are called *robust*.) The conditions under which each statistical procedure can generally be used with confidence will be spelled out in this textbook as the procedure is discussed. When deciding to use a statistical procedure, it is important to look at the data to see whether or not the technique is appropriate in the circumstances and to seek assistance from an experienced researcher or statistician if it appears that the test you had planned might not be correct in that situation.

Estimate the Results That Would Be Reasonable

A final general guideline to consider when using statistics is to think about what results you might expect before you analyze the data. Writing down a very rough estimate of the range of possible results is a useful tool to save you from misinterpreting conclusions based on arithmetical errors as reflecting the real state of affairs. The "eyeball" test of data—can you see the pattern of results clearly by looking over the raw scores?—is not a definitive one or it wouldn't be necessary to use statistical analyses at all. Nevertheless, often the general pattern can be seen by glancing at the scores: whether high scores on one variable seem to be associated with high or low scores on another, or whether the scores for one group seem to be higher or lower than the scores for another. If the findings of your analyses don't seem to fit with those hypothesized or those which you expected from your perusal of the raw scores, stop and recheck all your calculations and analyses. Even if they do fit, it's not a bad idea to recheck your calculations anyway.

Besides saving you from possibly making a foolish mistake, there is another advantage to estimating the findings you should get before doing your analyses. If predictions are made in advance, then sometimes statistical tests that take advantage of these research hypotheses can be used. These planned tests or **a priori comparisons** may be more powerful—that is, more likely to discover a real difference between groups or relationship between variables in the predicted direction—than would a **post hoc test**, which is based on considering what comparisons to make only after the data have been collected.

In summary, it should be emphasized that research design and statistical analysis usually work together to achieve the goal of understanding a phenomenon and sometimes the applied goal of making the best decision. No research design or statistical procedure can guarantee that your conclusions and interpretations will always be correct. However, by careful planning of the study and of the statistical analyses used, you can substantially increase your chances of coming to valid conclusions and of adding to scientific knowledge, if not your chances of achieving fame and fortune.

CHAPTER SUMMARY Scientific research is a way of answering questions and testing theories by formulating hypotheses, gathering relevant data through observations, and using analysis (usually statistical) to draw inferences about whether or not the theory is correct. Common types of research include historical, qualitative, case study, descriptive, developmental, survey, correlational, quasi-experimental, and experimental research designs. Experimental research, the best way to test hypotheses about cause and effect, involves independent and dependent variables, experimental and control groups, and random assignment of participants to experimental conditions. By randomly assigning individuals to experimental and control groups and then measuring them on the dependent variable, inferences can be drawn about the probable effects of the independent variable upon the dependent measure. However, ethical and practical considerations often preclude the use of experimental designs.

Research can also be classified as relatively basic or theoretical as contrasted with applied or decision-oriented research. It can be conducted in a laboratory setting with participants who know that they are participating in a research study or in a field setting, also known as the "real world."

Researchers try to control extraneous variables by holding them constant, using random selection and assignment, incorporating them into the study by the use of factorial designs, and using statistical controls. Most research studies use more than one method of control. Experimental and laboratory research approaches are usually higher in internal validity, or the ability to draw causal inferences; field research is usually higher in external validity, or the ability to generalize beyond the particular setting and individuals tested.

Statistical analysis is a tool that can be used to interpret the results of a research study. To use statistics wisely, it is useful to think about the meaning of the numbers, consider how the numbers will be interpreted, consider whether or not the assumptions for particular statistical procedures have been met, and estimate the kinds of results that would be reasonable. Although neither a good research design nor appropriate statistical analysis can guarantee that your conclusions will be correct, they can greatly increase the likelihood of this happening.

CHAPTER REVIEW

Multiple-Choice Questions

1. A study to assess the effects of note-taking on learning had students hear one lecture on which they took notes and another lecture on a different topic of equal difficulty on which they did not take notes. Their performance under the two conditions (note-taking versus no note-taking) was compared by means of scores on two multiple-choice tests, matched for difficulty. What type of design did this study use?

   a. a within-participants design   **b.** a between-participants design

   c. a qualitative design   **d.** a cross-sectional design

   e. a statistical design

2. Questionnaire and interview research are both subcategories of:

   a. developmental research   **b.** experimental research

   c. quasi-experimental research   **d.** survey research

   e. historical research

3. Research that has two or more independent variables utilizes what kind of design?

   a. a multivariate design   **b.** a factorial design

   c. a repeated measures design   **d.** a nonparametric design

   e. a negatively skewed design   **f.** a quasi-experimental design

4. If I assign a random half of the people in my study to give an oral report on a topic and assign the other half to give a written report and I then compare the two groups on a test of knowledge about the topic, the test score is

   a. a constant   **b.** a dependent variable

   c. an independent variable   **d.** an experimental manipulation

   e. Both c and d are true.

5. The type of research that is opposite to field research is

   a. experimental research   **b.** case study research

   c. laboratory research   **d.** applied research

   e. survey research

6. The two types of developmental research are

   a. correlational and causal–comparative

   b. longitudinal and cross-sectional

c. field and case study

d. applied and basic

e. questionnaire and interview

7. An experiment *must* have more than one
   a. independent variable
   b. dependent variable
   c. experimental group
   d. control group
   e. level of the independent variable
   f. all of the above
   g. none of the above

8. Another name for a nuisance variable is a(n)
   a. extraneous variable
   b. independent variable
   c. dependent variable
   d. controlling variable
   e. hypothetical variable

9. Which type of research is essentially the same as action research?
   a. applied research
   b. basic research
   c. hypothetical research
   d. developmental research
   e. historical research

10. Which of the following is an essential part of descriptive research?
    a. random assignment
    b. a longitudinal approach
    c. a sample
    d. an independent variable
    e. a between-participants design

Problems

11. For each of the following titles, try to identify the type of research that it represents.
    a. "Consistency in temperament over the life span"
    b. "The effects of steroids on weight lifting performance"
    c. "The effects of sex on mental spatial rotation ability"
    d. "The effects of Sputnik on the American space program"
    e. "Teaching a two-year-old to read: The case of Johnny"
    f. "The meaning of illness: A study of a pediatric ward"

12. In order to investigate the stereotypes that people hold of individuals who wear eyeglasses, I showed each of 217 adults either a picture of a person wearing eyeglasses or a picture of the same person in the same pose without eyeglasses (Harris, 1991). Whether a participant saw a person with or without glasses was randomly determined. The participants were then asked to rate the pictured person on a number of dimensions, including attractiveness and intelligence.

a. What type of research study was this?

b. What was/were the independent variable(s)? How many levels did it/they have?

c. What was/were the dependent variable(s)?

d. What was a constant in this study?

e. What was a hypothesis of this study?

13. Name at least three methods that a researcher might use to control for the effects of an extraneous variable, and give an example of the use of each method that might be found in a research study.

14. For each of the following examples, say whether it is a within-participants or a between-participants variable.

a. Each person is tested once under quiet conditions and once with loud music blaring.

b. Half of the people are tested while listening to "Row, row, row your boat" and half are tested while listening to "Mary had a little lamb."

c. Some people are given small gifts as rewards for good work; others are given cash.

d. Blood sugar levels are tested for each person both before and after eating breakfast.

e. Absentee rates in 47 classrooms are compared for a Monday and a Wednesday.

15. For each of the following research studies say whether it was apparently an applied or a basic research project and whether it was a laboratory or a field research study.

a. In order to decide whether or not to discuss Santa Claus in his classroom, Mr. Ken DerGarten interviews the parents of his 22 kindergarten children about their wishes.

b. In order to discover whether children are able to understand increasingly abstract concepts as they grow older, a researcher gives a test of conceptual complexity to first through fifth graders in their classrooms.

c. In order to discover how the human immune system works, a researcher tests the effects of several potential drugs on human immune system cells, checking the results on an electron microscope.

d. In order to decide which abbreviated description of the proposed amendments to place on the ballot, an elections clerk brings in a sample of 50 registered voters and has them read and react to alternative versions of the wording.

e. In order to discover how people cope with adversity, a researcher attends meetings of support groups for people with close relatives who have mental illness.

f. In order to investigate the factors leading people to disclose more or less intimate information about themselves, a social psychologist brings people into a room, two at a time, and asks them to hold a discussion either with or without a third person present.

16. Distinguish between each of the following pairs of terms:

a. longitudinal and cross-sectional research

b. quasi-experimental and experimental research

c. historical research and qualitative research

d. survey research and questionnaire research

e. descriptive research and correlational research

17. For each of the following research hypotheses, state the relevant null hypothesis.

a. As people age, their ability to hear high-pitched tones declines.

b. Americans are more likely to vote in national elections than are Venezuelans.

c. Eating a vegetarian diet is good for your health.

d. Men and women who enter medical school are equally likely to finish in 4 years.

e. People who floss their teeth daily have less gum disease than people who do not use dental floss.

18. In a study entitled "Aggressive Experiences and Aggressiveness: Relationship to Ethnicity, Gender and Age," I had 363 university students in their classrooms fill out a questionnaire about their experiences as an aggressor and as a victim of aggression. I used statistical procedures to compare the experiences of males and females, Anglos and Hispanics, and people of different ages.

a. What type of research study was this?

b. Was this research conducted in a field or laboratory setting?

c. I investigated the relationship between variable A and variable B in this study. What actual variables might be substituted for variable A and variable B in this sentence?

d. What was a constant in this study?

e. Name a qualitative variable and a quantitative variable from this study.

f. What might be a threat to the external validity of this study?

19. Suppose that a physician is interested in studying the effects of a new long-lasting drug on the outcomes of people who are infected with the HIV virus. Of her next 90 patients who carry the HIV virus but who do not have the symptoms of AIDS, she gives a random 1/3 an injection of the drug, a random 1/3 an injection of water, and a random 1/3 no injection. She then examines each patient every 6 months and to see whether they have developed

the symptoms of AIDS. Her hope is to find out whether the drug retards or prevents the development of AIDS.

a. What type of research study was this?

b. Was this research conducted in a field or laboratory setting?

c. Was this basic or applied research?

d. Was this a factorial design or not? What was (were) the factors in the study?

e. What is a dependent measure in this study?

20. A researcher has spent 2 years interviewing a serial murderer, the people who know him, relatives and friends of the victims, law enforcement and legal officials involved in the case, and psychiatrists who have attempted to treat him. The researcher wants to find out about the factors causing someone to become a serial killer. He has the hypothesis that serial killers all have endured abnormal child-rearing experiences that would qualify as abuse.

a. What type of research is this?

b. Is it basic or applied?

c. Was the setting field or laboratory?

d. Is external validity likely to be a big problem in this study?

e. Is there any evidence this study could provide that would prove that the author's hypothesis is correct?

f. Is there any evidence this study could provide that would prove that the author's hypothesis is incorrect?

Study Questions

1. Think of a question that should be answerable by scientific research. Then try to formulate a theoretical research hypothesis that describes what you would expect to observe. Now try to translate this general hypothesis into an operational one, thinking about what you would actually do to gather the data. How would the data that you get be coded or scored? If they are not originally numerical data, could you turn them into numbers? What pattern of scores would you expect to get if your hypothesis is correct?

2. Go (back) to the library and look for a journal that publishes research articles of interest to you. Alternatively, you may already have a research article handed out in a course or from a book of readings. Read over the introduction section and see if you can identify the purposes of the study. Then read the methods section (usually divided into sections dealing with the participants, measuring instruments, and procedures), and see if you can identify the type of research design used. Questions to consider include whether or not the study looked at more than a few participants; if so, it's not a case study. Were participants randomly assigned to conditions? If not, it's not an experiment. Were the authors seeking to explain a particular event? If so, it

may be historical. Were they looking at people of different ages? If yes, did they do so longitudinally or cross-sectionally? Were they asking people questions? Considering the context and avoiding objectifying the data? Coding behaviors with formal systems? Administering standardized tests to large groups of individuals? Measuring people on a number of variables? Treating people differently depending on the group to which they were assigned? Thinking about such questions should help you to decide what category of research the study best fits.

3. Try to think of three questions, ideally one from work, one from school, and one from home, that would best be answered by applied research. Then for each of the questions or issues you identified, see if you can think of a basic or theoretical research question, the answer to which might shed light on your applied question. For example, an applied research question might be "What kind of study regimen would get me the best grades in this class?" A related basic research question would be "What are the effects of studying in large blocks of time versus studying for smaller, more frequent periods, while keeping total study time constant?"

4. For the next hour that you spend in one or more public places other than a classroom—possibly driving, eating at a restaurant, shopping, or studying in the library—imagine that someone is conducting a field research study. What could it be? Might someone be watching how much food you take in the cafeteria line and comparing it with the amount of food taken by people who appear to be much heavier? Could the person jaywalking in front of you be part of a study to see if observers are more likely to cross the street against the light if they see someone else doing so? Is the sale on frozen turkeys designed to increase overall customer spending, and is someone comparing sales receipts from this week with those of last week? Am I (MBH) using you as the subject of a field study to see whether or not thinking about questions like the preceding ones increases students' paranoia? Are there any field research studies that you might like to conduct in such settings? (We'll assume of course, that you are concerned about the well-being of your potential participants and will have your research proposal approved by a review board concerned about ethical issues.)

Describing Data

Tables and Graphs

How Should Scores Be Organized?

After a researcher has designed a study and collected some data, the question of what to do with the data arises. In order to see what the pattern of findings might reveal, it is necessary to organize the scores in some way. If there are very few, and the numbers are very small, it might suffice to simply present the scores as they are gathered. However, there are two reasons why this approach will not work for most research studies.

- First, original data rarely appear in an organized form, since you usually can't expect the person with the highest score to be measured first and the person with the lowest score to be measured last. For example, if you hand out a test to a class, the test you collect first will belong to the first person to finish or the first person in the left-hand row of seats, not necessarily the person with the most extreme score on the test.

- Second, there are usually too many scores for a reader to assimilate. Trying to remember hundreds or even dozens of unorganized scores is usually both frustrating and futile.

Thus, most of the time it is necessary to organize and perhaps tabulate the scores in some way. The purpose of doing so is not to learn something new or to gain new information but to make some sense of the mass of information already collected by describing it in a way that a reader can understand and interpret (Aron & Aron, 1997; Hartley, 1992; Wainer, 1992). This chapter focuses on ways of organizing the entire set or distribution of scores in order to present them to the reader in an informative way via the use of tables or graphs.

How Are Tables of Frequency Distributions Used?

One of the most common ways to represent scores that have been collected is to put them into some kind of table. A table consists of a fully labeled summary of scores or other information. An arrangement of the scores collected in a research study that indicates how often each possible score occurred is called a **frequency distribution**.

Simple Frequency Distributions

The least complicated table of a frequency distribution, appropriately called a **simple frequency distribution**, simply lists each possible or actual score, along with the number of times that score appeared, which is also called its *frequency, f.* To create a simple frequency distribution, you record, in order, every possible score from the lowest score to the highest one. Then the number of times each score appears is counted and listed next to the raw score. Sometimes, to save space, scores that did not actually occur in the distribution are omitted, rather than being listed with a frequency of zero. Usually, the largest score is at the top of the list and the smallest score at the bottom, but occasionally the order is reversed.

A simple frequency distribution is frequently the most useful way to present data when the dependent measure is a nominal-level variable. For example, if people were asked to name their favorite type of reading material, the data might be recorded as follows:

Reading Material	f
Fiction	31
Comic Books	10
Newsmagazines	21
Biographies	5
Self-help Books	18
Statistics Books	1
TV Guide	25

Because nominal-level variables are not ordered by magnitude, a simple frequency distribution for such data might be ordered either arbitrarily, alphabetically, or from the most frequent to the least frequent category. Regardless of how the scores are ordered, the sum of the frequencies in a frequency distribution equals the number of scores, or N.

EXAMPLE

High School Memory Study. Suppose that you have been invited to a high school reunion. Embarrassingly, you are having a lot of trouble remembering names of your classmates and teachers. Are you the only person who feels the onset of premature senility or is this a typical phenomenon? To find out, you survey a group of adults attending a high school basketball game, asking them to list all the names of their high school classmates and teachers that they can remember.

You collect the data and assign the following scores according to the number of names remembered by each of the subjects in your sample:

63	49	98	22	56	87	98	34	23	65	87	65	44	46
47	83	76	67	34	56	53	65	47	85	32	98	54	37
48	64	49	74	69	75	57	84	38	37	85	45	65	54

A simple frequency distribution for the scores is given in Table 3.1.

When all the scores are counted, it is clear that there is a total of 42 scores. This total is, of course, the same as the sum of the frequencies.

TABLE 3.1   Simple Frequency Distribution of Scores in High School Memory Example

Score	f	Score	f	Score	f
98	3	65	4	46	1
87	2	64	1	45	1
85	2	63	1	44	1
84	1	57	1	38	1
83	1	56	2	37	2
76	1	54	2	34	2
75	1	53	1	32	1
74	1	49	2	23	1
69	1	48	1	22	1
67	1	47	2	Total 42	

Note that the scores are in three columns to save space and that scores with a frequency of zero are not given for the same reason.

Grouped Frequency Distributions

When there are a large number of different scores in the distribution, presenting the scores in a simple frequency distribution can be extremely unwieldy. For example, if you were going to present the annual earnings for a large sample of people, you would need tens of thousands of lines to present every individual income, with separate lines for $23,112 and $23,113. Instead, you would be likely to present the data in the form of a **grouped frequency distribution**, one in which ranges of scores, called *class intervals*, are presented rather than individual scores. If earnings were your measure, for example, you might use the ranges $0–$999.99, $1,000–$1,999.99, if you wanted to report incomes in thousand-dollar class intervals.

Advantages and Disadvantages of Grouped Frequency Distributions.   An advantage of using a grouped frequency distribution is that it presents the data in a condensed format that makes it easy for the researcher or reader to understand. A disadvantage is that some information is necessarily lost. For example, a score in the category $1000–$1999 might represent an income of $1233 or of $1876; there is no way of telling from a grouped frequency distribution. Thus, the use of such a distribution sacrifices detail for economy of presentation.

Class Intervals.   In a grouped frequency distribution, each **class interval** or category into which the scores are put represents a certain range of scores. Each class interval has a lower limit, ordinarily half a point below the lowest score that could be in the interval, and an upper limit, usually half a point above the highest score that could be in the interval. Sometimes these limits are called the *exact lower limit* and the *exact upper limit*. Some people report the interval as stretching from the lower limit to the upper limit (e.g., from 9.5 to 19.5), whereas others report it as the distance between the lowest whole score and the highest whole score (e.g., from 10 to 19). Since the lower and upper limits are described more precisely than any actual score, each score should fit into one and only one class interval.

Guidelines for Constructing Grouped Frequency Distributions.   There is no single correct way to present data in a grouped frequency distribution, but there are a number of guidelines that people follow in deciding what interval width to use and where to begin and end the intervals.

1. As indicated in the previous paragraph, each score should fit into one and only one interval.
2. Each interval should be the same size or width.
3. It is important to have enough intervals to convey the important pattern of the data but not so many that the reader cannot assimilate all the information. Generally, 6 to 15 class intervals will let you achieve this goal, with more intervals used when the number of different raw scores is very large.
4. Researchers often use multiples of 5 or 10 as their interval width. What categories to use, however, depends most importantly upon the nature of the data; for example, in reporting ages, classification into the teens, the twenties, the thirties, etc., is probably going to be most familiar and thus most useful to the reader.
5. Another guideline agreed on by researchers is that it is generally a bad idea to use open-ended intervals (e.g., <10 or 60+). If such intervals are used, it becomes impossible to estimate what the mean score might be, and some important information might be lost. Occasionally, researchers do use an open-ended interval in order to avoid a large number of empty categories; for example, if almost all the scores are evenly distributed between 40 and 100, but there is one

score of 200. When deciding how best to present such data, the simplicity of the table has to be balanced against the loss of information.

Two other rules of thumb are less important and less generally followed:

- It is desirable to have the interval width be an odd number, so that the midpoint of the interval is a whole number; for example, if you wish to estimate a mean of a distribution, it is easier to do so when the midpoints of the intervals are whole numbers. (Note that this guideline may conflict with the fourth one.)
- Some statisticians have suggested that it is a good idea to have each class interval begin with a multiple of the interval width (e.g., using 20–29 ($2 \times 10 = 20$), rather than 21–30 as a class interval).

EXAMPLE

Grouped Frequency Distribution for the High School Memory Study. As an example of a grouped frequency distribution, we can look at the data from the simple frequency distribution for the high school memory study. Although there are several ways in which the data could be presented, it seems reasonable to have categories with an interval width of 10 and to begin with the category of 20–29, or 19.5–29.5. In this case, the distribution appears as shown in Table 3.2.

TABLE 3.2 Grouped Frequency Distribution of Scores in High School Memory Example

Class Interval	f
90–99	3
80–89	6
70–79	3
60–69	8
50–59	6
40–49	8
30–39	6
20–29	2

TIP

Note that the grouped frequency distribution in Table 3.2 is much shorter than the simple frequency distribution given in Table 3.1 and that it sacrifices some information to achieve this brevity.

Stem-and-Leaf Displays

A stem-and-leaf display or diagram is an alternative way of presenting the data that both groups the data into categories and retains all of the original information that a grouped frequency distribution loses. In a **stem-and-leaf display**, each raw score is viewed as having two parts: a stem, consisting of all but the last digit, and the leaf, the last digit of the number. (When the numbers are decimals, this procedure may be altered somewhat.) For example, the number 125 would have 12 as the stem and 5 as the leaf. To construct a stem-and-leaf display, the stems of the numbers are written in one column and the leaves are written in another column, with each leaf written by the stem of the number from which it came.

EXAMPLE

Stem-and-Leaf Display for the High School Memory Study. To illustrate a stem-and-leaf display, let's take the scores from the high school memory study. The first raw score, 63, would have a stem of 6 and a leaf of 3; the next score, 49, would have a stem of 4 and a leaf of 9.

By putting the stems in a column and the leaves next to them, we get the pattern shown in Table 3.3. The first 8 in the Leaves column represents one score of 98; the next two 8's represent two additional scores of 98. The 3 and 2 at the bottom of the Leaves column, which are opposite the stem of 2, represent scores of 23 and 22, respectively. A stem-and-leaf display enables you to see every raw score and gives you a visual picture of the entire distribution, making it a simple but informative way of presenting complete data about a frequency distribution (Cohen, 1990; Wang, Haertel & Walberg, 1993). However, it is not very useful for large data sets with many different values for raw scores and a large sample size. Perhaps for this reason, such displays are not in common use.

TABLE 3.3   Stem-and-Leaf Display for High School Memory Example

Stem	Leaves
9	888
8	775543
7	654
6	97555543
5	766443
4	99877654
3	877442
2	32

Cumulative Frequency Distributions

Sometimes, instead of reporting the number of times each raw score occurs or the number of scores in each category, an investigator may wish to report the number of scores that fall below some value. This kind of frequency distribution, which gives the number of scores less than some value, is called a **cumulative frequency distribution**. For instance, a coach might want to know how many students could do at least 5 situps, at least 10, at least 15, etc. In this case, the frequency by a given raw score or class interval is not the frequency of that score or interval but the total number of scores below the upper limit of that category. In other words, to report the cumulative frequency, it is necessary to add the frequencies for all the categories below the upper limit of the category.

Cumulative frequency distributions can be used only with data measured on an ordinal, interval, or ratio scale; constructing such a distribution implies that the scores can be ordered from low to high.

EXAMPLE

Cumulative Frequency Distribution for the High School Memory Study. Let's repeat the grouped frequency distribution from the high school memory study given in Table 3.2, but add another column to represent the cumulative frequency, as shown in Table 3.4. If you keep in mind the definition of cumulative frequency as the total number of scores below the exact upper limit of a category, you can see that there were 8 scores below 39.5, 30 scores below 69.5, and 42 scores in all.

TABLE 3.4   Cumulative Frequency Distribution for High School Memory Example

Class Interval	f	Cum f
90–99	3	42
80–89	6	39
70–79	3	33
60–69	8	30
50–59	6	22
40–49	8	16
30–39	6	8
20–29	2	2

TIP

As can be seen from Table 3.4, the sum of the frequencies equals the sample size or N. Using symbols, we write $\Sigma f_i = \Sigma n_i = N$. With a cumulative frequency distribution, the cumulative frequency for the class interval containing the highest score is also equal to N, the total number of scores.

Relative Frequency Distributions

The frequency distributions discussed thus far have listed actual numbers or frequencies by each category, whether raw or cumulative frequencies. An alternative approach is to report the proportions or percentages of scores falling into each category (or, for a simple frequency distribution, the proportions of people with each raw score). This kind of frequency distribution, called a **relative frequency distribution**, uses proportions or percentages. In Chapter 1, we saw that to get the proportion of scores in a category, it is necessary to divide the number, or frequency, of scores in the category by the total number of scores. Thus, if there are 8 scores in some category or class interval out of a total of 40 scores, the proportion of scores in that category is $8/40 = .2$, and the percentage is $.2(100) = 20\%$. Relative frequency distributions can be reported for the scores on any kind of variable, including a nominal-level variable. For example, the percentages of students majoring in each of a number of fields could be reported.

The advantage of a relative frequency distribution is that it can be used to compare frequency distributions based on different sizes. For example, if 10% of Americans and 10% of Canadians go to the movies at least twice a week, a relative frequency distribution will make it easy to see that the percentages are comparable, even though the absolute numbers are very different.

EXAMPLE

Relative Frequency Distribution for the High School Memory Study. As an example of a relative frequency distribution, let's consider the same scores for the high school memory study given in Table 3.2, but with a column added for proportions, as shown in Table 3.5. To get the proportion in the category 50–59, the number in that category, 6, was divided by 42, the total N. As can be seen from the table, the sum of the proportions will equal 1.00, with a possible discrepancy in the last digit due to rounding.

TABLE 3.5   Relative Frequency Distribution for High School Memory Example

Class Interval	f	P
90–99	3	.071
80–89	6	.143
70–79	3	.071
60–69	8	.190
50–59	6	.143
40–49	8	.190
30–39	6	.143
20–29	2	.048

TIP ▰▰▰▰▰▰▰▰▰▰▰▰▰▰▰▰▰▰▰▰▰▰▰▰▰▰▰▰▰▰▰▰▰

> If we want to report percentages, the proportions would be multiplied by 100, indicating, for example, that 19% of the scores fell between 40 and 49.

Cumulative Relative Frequency Distributions

Finally, for the curious and/or courageous, it should be recognized that it is possible to construct a cumulative relative frequency distribution using percentages or proportions. A **cumulative relative frequency distribution** reports the proportions or percentages of scores falling below certain values.

The advantage of a cumulative relative frequency distribution is that it makes it possible to see the proportion or percentage of people who score below various points. For example, if you were trying to decide what cutoff point to use on a test for admission into a program or for certification, a cumulative relative frequency distribution would let you know what proportion of the people you would be excluding if you used various possible minimum scores.

EXAMPLE ▰▰▰▰▰▰▰▰▰▰▰▰▰▰▰▰▰▰▰▰▰▰▰▰▰▰▰▰▰▰▰▰▰▰▰▰▰

A cumulative relative frequency distribution for our familiar high school memory data is given in Table 3.6. To get the cumulative percentage for the category of 60–69, we divide the number of scores below 69.5, 30, by the N of 42 and multiply by 100 to get 71.4%. The cumulative percentage for the category with the highest score should be 100%, subject to rounding errors in the last digit, which we see from Table 3.6 is the case for our data.

TABLE 3.6 Cumulative Relative Frequency Distribution for High School Memory Example

Class Interval	Cum %	Class Interval	Cum %
90–99	100%	50–59	52.4%
80–89	92.9%	40–49	38.1%
70–79	78.6%	30–39	19.0%
60–69	71.4%	20–29	4.8%

What Are Percentiles?

It is only a short step from a cumulative relative frequency distribution using percentages to a distribution based on percentiles. A **percentile**, or percentile point, is a number or hypothetical score at or below which a given percentage of the scores fall. The 18th percentile, for example, is that number or score below which 18% of the scores in the distribution fall (and above which 82% of the scores are found). A percentile does not have to be an actual raw score; most percentile points, in fact, do not correspond precisely to raw scores, because they are computed to several decimal places more than actual scores.

Percentile Rank

Although percentiles are not the same as raw scores, every raw score in a distribution has a corresponding **percentile rank**—that is, a corresponding percentage of scores that it exceeds. If a raw score of 65 exceeds 43% of the scores in a distribution, then the percentile rank of 65 is 43%; that is, the score of 65 is at the 43rd percentile. A percentile rank is an example of a transformed score, which (you may remember from Chapter 1) is a score that has been changed in some way so that it gives somewhat different information than the original raw score.

TIP

Percentiles and percentile ranks are ordinarily calculated only for distributions with large sample sizes—that is, with N's at least in the hundreds or thousands. The reason for this restriction is that it makes sense to discuss percentiles only when they can be unambiguously interpreted. When you have thousands of scores, each score represents a fraction of one percentile, so your assignment to the nearest whole percentile is going to be precise. The 879th score of 1000 exceeds 878 of the scores and is exceeded by 121 scores, making it reasonable to say that it is at the 87.8th percentile. Suppose, however, that there are only three scores in a distribution. In that case, the highest score exceeds 66.7% of the scores, but no scores fall above it. One could argue that assigning it any percentile rank between 66 and 99 would make some sense. No single percentile rank is obviously correct.

In thinking about a what a percentile rank means, it may seem confusing to consider a score at the 88th percentile as larger than 88% of the scores but smaller than 12% of the scores. What about the raw score itself? The way in which statisticians deal with this issue is to recognize that any particular percentile point represents not a real score but an ideal score carried out to many more decimal places than any actual score. Thus, if the 62nd percentile point is 123.0143, a raw score of 123 exceeds more than 61% of the scores and is exceeded by more than 38% of the scores. It is unlikely that a raw score will fall exactly at a whole percentile point (i.e., the 44.000000 percentile) unless the sample size is very large, in which case the reported percentile rank of that score will be accurate.

The other assumption that statisticians make is that a particular raw score is only an approximation and that any scores that are apparently tied (because they're all called 39, for example) would not be tied if they were carried out to more decimal places. Thus it is assumed for the purposes of calculating percentile ranks that any particular score is higher than all the scores below it plus half of the scores tied with it. In other words, if you have a raw score of 183, it is assumed that you have a true score higher than anyone who got a score of 182 or below and also higher than half of the other people who got a score of 183.

Guidelines for Computing Percentile Ranks

Although there are formulas for computing percentiles and percentile ranks from grouped frequency distributions or from distributions with tied scores, they are outside the scope of this book. However, the percentile rank of a score can be approximated from a simple frequency distribution by a few simple steps.

Step 1: Construct a cumulative frequency distribution from the simple frequency distribution.

Step 2: Find the cumulative frequency of the score.

Step 3: Divide the cumulative frequency by N.

Step 4: Multiply this quotient by 100.

EXAMPLE

For the 32nd score out of 256 scores, the percentile rank is

$$\frac{32}{256}(100) = .125(100) = 12.5$$

With percentiles, it is necessary to round down, so that you could conclude that this score was higher than 12% of the scores.

TIP

It is unlikely that you will be computing percentiles or percentile ranks, unless you work with large data sets and are presenting descriptive or normative data. However, it is very useful to be able to understand percentiles reported by others and to read tables of percentiles. Sometimes such a table is set up like a cumulative relative frequency distribution, with each raw score listed and its corresponding percentile rank reported beside it. Alternatively, or even as an adjunct, a distribution of percentiles may be set up, with each percentile rank from 1 to 99 listed and the corresponding percentile point or score listed alongside.

Ways of Presenting Data in Tables

- **Simple frequency distribution:** Lists each possible or actual score and its frequency; can be used for qualitative data
- **Grouped frequency distribution:** Lists class intervals and frequencies within each interval
- **Stem-and-leaf display:** Lists stems (all but last digit of scores) in one column and leaves (last digits) in another column
- **Cumulative frequency distribution:** Lists scores or class intervals and frequencies below the upper limits of the scores or intervals
- **Relative frequency distribution:** Lists proportions or percentages for each score or class interval; can be used for qualitative data
- **Cumulative relative frequency distribution:** Lists proportions or percentages below the upper limit of each class interval
- **Percentile distribution:** Lists scores and the percentages falling below each score

How Are Graphs of Frequency Distributions Used?

Up until now, the discussion has focused on reporting a frequency distribution in the form of a table. Such a table almost always identifies the score (or the class interval) and the frequency (or cumulative frequency or relative frequency) with which that score occurs. An alternative mode to presenting the distribution of the frequencies of scores is in the form of a graph. Depending on the way in which the graph is set up, a graphical representation may convey somewhat more or less information than the table on which it is based. Moreover, a well-constructed graph may be easier to understand and a more effective way of communicating information than a table (Wainer, 1992) or a summary statistic (Cohen, 1990).

Ordinate and Abscissa

A graph is a way of representing scores in two dimensions, almost always on a grid formed by two lines intersecting at a value of 0. Frequency distributions are graphed in the upper right-hand quadrant (unless some of the scores are negative), with the intersection of the two lines in the lower left-hand corner. The vertical line of a graph is called the y-axis or the **ordinate**; the horizontal line is called the x-axis or the **abscissa**. As shown in Figure 3.1, when graphing a distribution of scores, the scores are reported along the abscissa, increasing in value from left to right, and the frequencies are reported along the ordinate, increasing in value from bottom to top.

In order to represent scores and frequencies in a graph of a frequency distribution, equal distances on the axes should represent equal distances of the

FIGURE 3.1   Axes for a Graph of Frequency Distribution

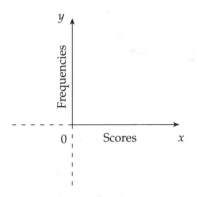

scores or frequencies. An axis line might be marked off as 0 10 20 30 but not as 0 70 80 90.

   If there is a big gap between zero and the first scores or frequencies, then a squiggle or a double slash is usually drawn to indicate that something is missing. For example, the graph shown in Figure 3.2 indicates that there is a gap in the values of both the frequencies and the scores shown on the graph.

Graphing Qualitative Data

The kind of graph that can be drawn to represent a frequency distribution depends to some extent on the nature of the data. When the data are measured on a nominal scale, there is no logical way to order the scores along the *x*-axis, except alphabetically or in terms of frequencies.

Bar Graphs.   One way of graphing nominal scale data is to use what is called a **bar graph**, with the scores or categories along the *x*-axis and their frequencies on the *y*-axis. Because the scores are not ordered, they do not touch

FIGURE 3.2   Graph of a Frequency Distribution with Gaps in Scores and Frequencies

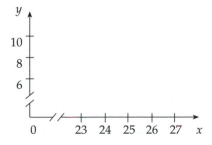

FIGURE 3.3   Bar Graph of a Distribution of Preferred Colors

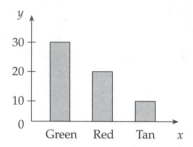

and their frequencies are represented by bars, the heights of which correspond to the number of times that score occurs. Consider the example of a bar graph shown in Figure 3.3. It shows that 30 people picked green, 20 people picked red, and 10 people picked tan as their favorite color of M&M candy. Notice that it would be possible to put tan or red first; the order of the values on the x-axis is arbitrary.

Pie Graphs.   The other common way of graphing qualitative or nominal-level data is in the form of a **pie graph**, which looks just like its name: a circle divided into segments (or pieces of the pie). Each segment represents one value or score and has an area that corresponds to the proportion of the total sample size that this score represents. For example, the pie graph pictured in Figure 3.4 represents the same data as the bar graph in Figure 3.3: 30 of 60 people (.5) picked green, 20 of 60 (.33) picked red, and 10 of 60 (.17) picked tan. Pie graphs seem to be quite common in some social sciences, such as economics, and less common in other fields, like psychology.

FIGURE 3.4   Pie Graph of a Distribution of Preferred Colors

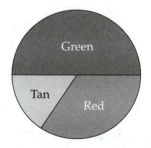

Graphing Quantitative Data

When the data are ordinal, interval, or ratio level, both bar graphs and pie graphs are rarely used to represent frequencies. Instead the data are usually graphed in the form of a frequency polygon or, alternatively, a frequency histogram. In either a **frequency polygon** or a **frequency histogram**, the scores are ordered along the x-axis from 0 at the left to the largest score at the right. Although occasionally frequencies of raw scores may be graphed, it is much more common to graph the results of a grouped frequency distribution, with each score listed on the abscissa representing a class interval or range of scores.

Frequency Polygons.   In a frequency polygon, a dot is placed over the midpoint of each class interval or score, with the height corresponding to the frequency of that score. It is a common practice to include the class interval below the one containing the lowest score and the class interval above the one containing the highest score. When these dots are connected by straight lines, the result is a frequency polygon. As an example, consider a frequency polygon showing the grouped frequency distribution from the high school memory study given in Table 3.2. Notice that the x-axis is labeled by the midpoints of the class interval, which is typical for a frequency polygon or frequency histogram. For example, 4.5 is the midpoint of the interval 0–9 and 14.5 is the midpoint of the interval 10–19. As can be seen from the graph in Figure 3.5, there were no scores between 0 and 9 or between 10 and 19 and eight scores between 40 and 49.

Frequency Histograms.   A frequency histogram is almost identical to a frequency polygon, except that horizontal lines are drawn across the tops of the class intervals, and these lines are connected by vertical ones. Each horizontal line goes from the lower limit of the class interval that it represents to the upper limit of the class interval. A frequency histogram therefore looks like a bar graph with the bars touching or connected. Figure 3.6 shows the same data from Table 3.2 represented in a frequency histogram.

FIGURE 3.5   Frequency Polygon for High School Memory Example

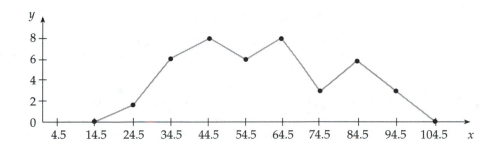

FIGURE 3.6   Frequency Histogram for High School Memory Example

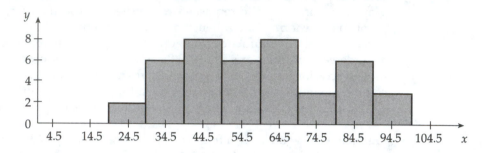

TIP

In graphing a frequency polygon or histogram it is usual to pick a scale for the x-axis so that the height of the graph is about 2/3 of the width; otherwise stated, the width is 1.5 times the height. It is also reasonably common to close off a frequency polygon by graphing the frequencies of zero for the class intervals below and above the ones that contain the scores. Thus, a frequency polygon is drawn to intersect the x-axis on each end, which represents a frequency of zero.

Graphing Cumulative Frequency Distributions.   Occasionally, a researcher wants to present the data from a cumulative frequency distribution in graphical form. In this case, the abscissa represents scores, as it would for a frequency polygon or histogram, but the upper limits of the class intervals are usually plotted rather than the midpoints. Instead of raw frequencies, cumulative frequencies appear along the ordinate. Because a cumulative frequency for a class interval can never be lower than the cumulative frequency for the previous (lower) class interval, the cumulative frequency polygon reaches what is called an *asymptote*, or highest level, once the class interval with the highest score has been reached, and it looks like a straight line stretching to the right after that. An example of a cumulative frequency distribution for the data previously graphed is shown in Figure 3.7.

Shapes of Frequency Distributions

When a frequency polygon is plotted, the graph can take a number of different shapes. Some of these shapes are so common that they have well-known names.

Normal Distribution.   Perhaps the most common type of frequency polygon is bell shaped and symmetric around the middle, as shown in Figure 3.8. Such a graph represents a member of a family of theoretical frequency distri-

FIGURE 3.7   Cumulative Frequency Distribution for High School Memory Example

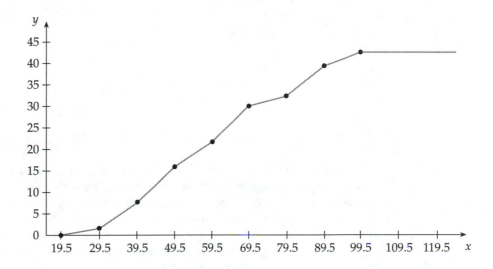

FIGURE 3.8   Normal Distribution

butions collectively titled the **normal distribution**, or normal curve. Note that it is fairly common in presenting shapes of frequency distributions to omit the y-axis. Scores on many interval and ratio-level variables tend to be approximately normally distributed: test scores, heights and weights, running speeds, and probably even number of hairs on peoples' heads.

Bimodal Distribution.   A second type of frequency distribution that you may encounter fairly often is a bimodal distribution. The mode is the most frequent score in a distribution; if a distribution has two "most frequent" scores, it is called a **bimodal distribution**. As illustrated in Figure 3.9, a bimodal distribution resembles a Bactrian camel rather than a dromedary; it has two humps. In fact, any distribution that has two peaks separated by some score or scores occurring less often is often informally called *bimodal*, even if it does not meet the strict definition of having two modes, as in the example presented here.

FIGURE 3.9   A Bimodal Distribution

TIP

A bimodal distribution of scores often results when a frequency distribution is based on samples from two different populations. For instance, if an achievement test reveals a bimodal distribution, it is likely that the scores represent two populations: those who know the material and those who do not. A bimodal distribution of hours spent exercising might also represent two populations: those who make a formal attempt to exercise and those who do not. Heights of a sample of adults are usually bimodally distributed, representing the populations of men and women.

Skewness.   One characteristic frequently used to describe frequency distributions is *skewness*, which refers to a lack of symmetry. A **positively skewed distribution** has many low scores and few high ones; in other words, as shown in Figure 3.10, the "tail" of the distribution or the point of the skewer is at the right. A **negatively skewed distribution** has the opposite shape, with many high scores, relatively few low ones, and its "tail" on the left.

An example of a positively skewed variable is income. Most people have incomes near the low end, but a small number of millionaires and a tiny number of billionaires lead to a tail at the high end. When a distribution of scores on an achievement test is positively skewed, most people did poorly, with only a few doing well, suggesting that the test may be a difficult one. Al-

FIGURE 3.10   Skewed Distributions

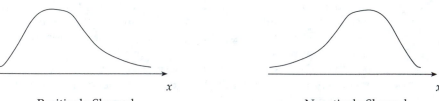

Positively Skewed   Negatively Skewed

ternatively, a negatively skewed distribution of test scores might imply that the test has a relatively low ceiling, not permitting the assessment of fine distinctions among people who know the content well. Such a distribution might be very appropriate for a competency-based test, such as the examination to receive a driver's license, where it is assumed that most people should possess the basic competencies measured.

Graphs Showing the Relationship Between Variables

Besides graphing frequency distributions, researchers use graphs to present data in different ways. You may wish to present mean scores of several groups or scores of individuals on more than one variable. Relationships between variables can be presented graphically in several formats.

Bar Graphs of Mean Scores of Groups.   In addition to the use of a bar graph to present the frequency distribution of a qualitative variable, researchers use a different kind of bar graph to present mean scores of various groups of subjects. Often these groups represent different levels of the independent variable; for example, special education students receiving one of three types of classroom placements. As is true of a bar graph of a frequency distribution, a bar graph of mean scores presents the scores on the x-axis. The y-axis, instead of representing frequencies, is labeled to indicate scores on the dependent variable, so that the height of the bar represents the mean score for the group. As can be seen on the graph in Figure 3.11, bars representing the variables on the x-axis, such as males and females from a group, may touch each other, although such a graph should not be confused with a frequency histogram.

Line Graphs.   A second way of presenting scores of groups is by the use of a line graph. A **line graph** typically has class intervals for scores on a variable along the x-axis and mean scores for each class interval along the y-axis.

FIGURE 3.11   Bar Graph of Mean Pretest and Posttest Scores of Boys and Girls

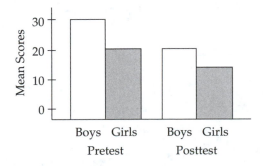

(Occasionally, some summary statistic other than the mean may be used.) The midpoint of each class interval is indicated by a point with a height representing the mean score on a second variable, which is coded along the y-axis. Although a line graph may look like a frequency polygon, it is different in two ways:

1. The ordinate presents mean scores rather than frequencies.
2. The abscissa does not list class intervals with no scores.

Thus, a line on a line graph that touches the x-axis indicates that the mean score for that class interval is 0, not that there are no scores in that interval. A line graph thus represents a relationship between two variables, with each point representing the intersection of a middle or midpoint score for a group on one variable with a mean score for a group on another variable. An example of a line graph is presented in Figure 3.12, with the x-axis giving age and the y-axis representing time spent caring for family members each week.

Scattergraphs. A third form of graph for representing scores on two variables is called a *scattergram*, *scattergraph*, or *scatterplot*. A **scattergraph** is similar to a line graph in that it has scores on two quantitative variables represented on the x- and y-axes. However, unlike a line graph, a scattergraph does not present means. Instead it consists of a series of points or dots, with each dot representing the intersection of an individual's score on both variables. Thus, if a scatterplot were to present height along the abscissa and weight along the ordinate, as illustrated in Figure 3.13, each dot would represent the height and weight of a single individual. If, as is sometimes the case, two individuals have the same scores on both variables, two dots can be positioned very close together or a (2) can be placed beside a single dot to indicate that it represents two scores. Scattergraphs are often used to represent data that are described by a statistic called a *correlation coefficient*, which will be discussed in more detail in Chapter 6.

FIGURE 3.12 Line Graph Relating Age and Time Spent Caring for Family Members

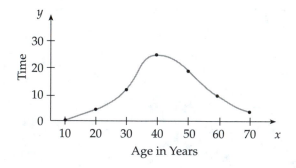

FIGURE 3.13   Scattergraph of the Relationship Between Height and Weight

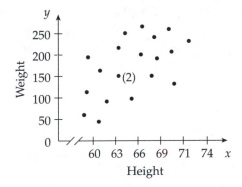

Misleading Graphs

Although graphs can be a very useful way of presenting data, they can also be misleading. The most common type of misleading graph gives a wrong impression by adjusting the scale of the ordinate or, less commonly, the abscissa. For example, Figure 3.14 gives the impression that the mean IQ varies importantly with hours spent studying vocabulary words; yet the difference in IQ scores is almost meaningless, and the numbers of hours studied are very large. Figure 3.15 gives the impression that the percentages of people favoring candidates A, B, and C in an election are very different; yet the actual differences are only a couple of percentage points.

Graphs can also give a misleading impression if they (mis)use shapes, colors, or widths of bars or other elements of the graph to emphasize one aspect of the results, without giving a realistic overall picture. The title or labels of the axes can also be confusing, as can a graph that tries to include too

FIGURE 3.14   Relationship Between Hours Studying Vocabulary and IQ Scores in Tenth-Grade Students

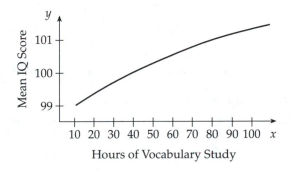

FIGURE 3.15 Percentages Preferring Candidates *A*, *B*, and *C*

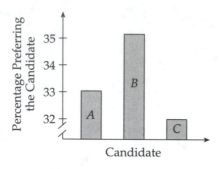

much data. To avoid being misled by a graph, be sure that you understand the labels, and look at the actual numbers along the axes to see what the drawings represent.

Ways of Presenting Data in Graphs

- **Bar graph of frequency distribution:** Lists each raw score on the *x*-axis and its frequency on the *y*-axis; can be used for qualitative data
- **Pie graph:** Forms a circle divided into segments proportional to frequencies of each score; can be used for qualitative data
- **Frequency polygon:** Lists class intervals on the *x*-axis and frequencies on the *y*-axis, with frequencies of midpoints of class intervals connected by straight lines
- **Frequency histogram:** Lists class intervals on the *x*-axis and frequencies on the *y*-axis, with horizontal lines representing frequencies drawn across the tops of class intervals and connected by vertical lines
- **Cumulative frequency polygon:** Lists class intervals on the *x*-axis and cumulative frequencies on the *y*-axis, with cumulative frequencies of upper limits of class intervals connected by straight lines
- **Bar graph of mean scores of groups:** Lists groups or levels of the independent variable on the *x*-axis and mean scores on the *y*-axis, usually a qualitative variable on the *x*-axis and a quantitative one on the *y*-axis
- **Line graph:** Has class intervals on the *x*-axis and mean scores for each class interval on the *y*-axis; relates scores on two quantitative variables
- **Scattergraph, scattergram, or scatterplot:** Has raw scores on a quantitative variable on each axis, with each pair of scores being represented by a dot; relates scores on two quantitative variables

What Is the Best Way to Present Data?

The decision about how to present a large mass of data is not always an easy one. If you want to summarize a large group of scores by presenting them in the form of a frequency distribution, a basic choice is whether to present them in the form of a table or as a graph. Generally, a table provides more detailed information, but a graph may convey the overall picture in a way that is easier to grasp and remember.

Tables

Once you have decided to present a frequency distribution in tabular form, you still have other decisions to make.

• A first choice is whether to use a simple or a grouped frequency distribution. A simple frequency distribution, or a stem-and-leaf diagram, will provide the most information, but the amount of data is likely to be unwieldy if there are more than 20 or 30 different values to be presented. With a stem-and-leaf diagram, the sample size matters, too; it would be difficult to fit a stem-and-leaf diagram with thousands of scores on a normal-sized piece of paper. A grouped frequency distribution is often the method of choice, but it necessitates thinking carefully about what class intervals to select in order to make them meaningful to the reader. Of course, a grouped frequency distribution does not make sense with nominal data, although two or more small categories can certainly be combined or grouped to make a larger one.

• A second choice when constructing a table to represent a frequency distribution is whether to use raw frequencies or a relative frequency distribution presenting proportions or percentages. Raw frequencies immediately inform the reader about the sample size but may not be as intuitively interpretable or as comparable across samples of different sizes as percentages are.

TIP

If you choose to present relative frequencies, be sure to mention the sample size in the text, as 20% of 5 clearly is a less representative statistic from which to generalize to a larger population than 20% of a sample of 200. Note that it is generally a better idea to report percentages than proportions, unless the intended audience is a mathematically sophisticated one, as most people are more familiar with percentages.

• A third decision to make when constructing a table of a frequency distribution is whether to present the frequencies (or relative frequencies) for each class interval or to present the cumulative frequencies. Generally, cumulative frequencies are presented only when readers are likely to be interested in the numbers or proportions falling below certain values, as might be the case with a test that measures level of ability or competence.

• Finally, there may be circumstances in which you wish to present tables of percentiles and percentile ranks. Typically, this is done only when the purpose of a study was to gather descriptive or normative data on a large, representative sample or population of individuals. If that is the case, it is common to present both a table of raw scores with the corresponding percentile rank of each and a table listing the percentile ranks from 1 to 99 (sometimes with the addition of 99.9) with the corresponding percentiles or scores alongside them. Tables of percentiles and of cumulative frequencies are presented only when the variable measured is a quantitative one.

TIP

Regardless of the type of table used, the table should have a title that describes it clearly and should have all columns clearly labeled. Ideally, the table should be interpretable on its own, without recourse to the text. It is a good idea to show a table to someone else before using it to be sure that it is easy to understand.

Graphs

Frequency Distributions.   If the data from a frequency distribution are to be presented graphically, the nature of the variable should be considered first. The frequency distribution of a qualitative variable is most commonly presented in the form of a bar graph, but if there is a reason to expect a pie graph to be more interesting or more comprehensible to the audience, it is an acceptable alternative.

When the data are quantitative, a frequency histogram or frequency polygon is the usual way to graph a frequency distribution. Since frequency polygons and frequency histograms present the same data and look virtually identical when the sample size is large and the class interval width is small, the choice of which to use is a personal one, although frequency polygons appear to be both more common and easier to construct. If you intend to present the data from more than one distribution on the same axes, using frequency polygons, perhaps coding them by color or in another way, is preferable to using histograms.

The use of a cumulative frequency polygon is less common, as there are relatively few situations in which you want to display graphically the proportion of responses below some value. However, for admissions or personnel officers looking at standardized test scores, a cumulative frequency polygon may be quite common.

TIP

> The size of a class interval for a frequency polygon or frequency histogram is something to consider carefully, since too large an interval width may obscure details of the pattern and too small an interval may produce a jagged-looking graph resembling the smile of a jack-o-lantern with frequencies of almost all 0's and 1's, as illustrated in Figure 3.16.

Graphing Scores on Two Variables. When you wish to present the relationship between two variables in graphical form, a bar graph is the correct method when one of the variables is a nominal one. Very frequently, the nominal-level variable represents levels of the independent variable in an experiment. In almost all cases, this variable is presented along the abscissa and the quantitative variable along the ordinate, so that the bars are vertical.

If the variables are both quantitative ones, you have two choices. Mean scores on variable y for the individuals falling into various class intervals on variable x can be presented in the form of a line graph. Alternatively, you can represent each individual pair of scores by a point in a scattergraph. The scattergraph presents more information and is frequently constructed prior to calculating a correlation coefficient or a regression equation, but if there are a large number of scores the density of the information may make it less useful for seeing the pattern of scores than a line graph. Additionally, a scattergraph usually takes more time to construct.

TIP

> As with tables, graphs should be carefully titled, and both axes should be clearly labeled. Every graph, called a figure in this book and in most journal articles, should ideally be readable and understandable on its own without resorting to the accompanying text.

FIGURE 3.16 Frequency Polygon with a Narrow Interval Width

CHAPTER SUMMARY

When there is a large number of scores to be described, it is both useful and usual to present them in some kind of organized and summarized form, in order to make it easier for someone to see the overall pattern of scores. A simple frequency distribution presents each actual or possible raw score and lists the number of times that it occurs. A grouped frequency distribution presents ranges or class intervals of possible scores and lists how many scores fall into each class interval. Each class interval has a lower limit and an upper limit, with all actual scores falling between these limits. A stem-and-leaf diagram provides each individual score in a pattern that combines the information from simple and grouped frequency distributions.

Relative frequency distributions provide the proportion or percentage of times each score occurs or the proportion or percentage of scores falling into each class interval. Cumulative frequency distributions provide the numbers or percentages of scores that fall below the upper limit of each class interval or score. Percentiles describe the scores at or below which a certain percentage of the scores in a distribution fall.

Frequency distributions can be presented in pictorial or graphical form as well as in the form of tables. Ordinarily, scores are presented along the x-axis, or abscissa, and frequencies along the y-axis, or ordinate. Frequency polygons have lines connecting the frequencies over the midpoints of the class intervals; frequency histograms have horizontal lines representing the frequency over the entire interval. Bar graphs, frequently used for nominal-level data, have scores along the x-axis but do not have the bars touching. Pie graphs are circular figures, with the segments of the pie proportionate to the frequencies of scores in the different categories. Line graphs and scattergraphs both represent relationships between two variables rather than frequency distributions.

The shape of the graph represents the shape of the frequency distribution. A normal distribution is symmetric and bell shaped, with most scores piled up in the middle. Positively skewed distributions have many low scores and few high ones, whereas negatively skewed distributions have the "tail" at the low end. Bimodal distributions have two most frequent scores with a region of less frequent scores between them.

The decision of how to best describe a set of data should be made by considering the nature of the data, including the level of measurement, the number of scores, the range of scores, and the amount of information that you want the reader to comprehend.

This chapter has focused on selecting an appropriate way of presenting the distribution of scores in a sample. The following chapter will consider ways of further summarizing these scores to arrive at a few numbers that can in some sense represent the distribution. Remember that the purpose of presenting such descriptive data is to provide the reader with information. Your selection of how best to do so should be based on your judgment of how much the reader needs and wants to know, as well as on the way of presenting the data that will be most useful and comprehensible to your audience.

CHAPTER REVIEW

Multiple-Choice Questions

1. In a simple frequency distribution, the sum of all the frequencies is equal to
   a. the sum of the raw scores   **b.** 1   **c.** the sample size   **d.** N
   e. Both c and d are correct.   **f.** None of the above is necessarily correct.

2. In a positively skewed distribution, which of the following is very likely to be true?
   a. The distribution is symmetric.   **b.** The distribution is bimodal.
   c. The scores are normally distributed.   **d.** There are few very low scores.
   e. The scores are concentrated at the low end.

3. Which of the following types of graph is the most appropriate for graphing a frequency distribution of a nominal-level variable?
   a. a bar graph   **b.** a frequency histogram
   c. a frequency polygon   **d.** a cumulative frequency polygon
   e. a line graph

4. Which type of graph plots points representing pairs of scores on two variables?
   a. a point graph   **b.** a stem-and-leaf graph   **c.** a frequency polygon
   d. a line graph   **e.** a scattergraph

5. In a stem-and-leaf display, the leaf is
   a. the first digit of the raw score
   b. the last digit of the raw score
   c. the number of scores between the lower and upper limit of the category
   d. the proportion of scores between the lower and upper limit of the category
   e. the interval width

6. If you are constructing a cumulative frequency distribution, the cumulative frequency for the class interval containing the highest score will be equal to
   a. the sum of the raw scores
   b. N
   c. the number of scores in that interval
   d. the percentage of scores in that interval
   e. the proportion of scores in that interval

7. Which of the following kinds of frequency distribution retain(s) all of the information from the raw scores?

   a. a percentile distribution

   b. a simple frequency distribution

   c. a stem-and-leaf distribution

   d. a grouped frequency distribution

   e. a cumulative relative grouped frequency distribution

   f. Both b and c are correct.

8. If 40% of all 80 scores in a distribution fall below 70, and .3 of the scores lie between 70 and 60, how many scores are equal to 70 or above?

   a. 24 scores   b. 30 scores   c. 32 scores   d. 48 scores   e. 56 scores

   f. It is impossible to determine from the above information.

9. If you have decided to graph children's temperament types in a pie chart, and you have 30 easy children, 12 difficult children, and 20 slow-to-warm-up children, how many different segments will you need for the chart?

   a. 3   b. 12   c. 30   d. 62   e. 100

10. If a cumulative relative frequency distribution reveals that the cumulative percentage for scores in the class interval from 50 to 59 is 40%, which of the following do you know to be true?

   a. 40% of the scores in the distribution fall between 50 and 59.

   b. 40% of the scores in the distribution fall between 49.5 and 59.5.

   c. 40% of the scores in the distribution are lower than 59.5.

   d. 40% of the scores in the distribution are higher than 59.5.

   e. The median is below 59.5.

Problems

11. Imagine that you have been soliciting for charity and have collected the following donations: 30 people gave nothing, 1 person gave 10 cents, 4 people gave a quarter each, five people gave 50 cents each, 40 people gave a dollar each, 20 people gave $2 apiece, 3 people gave $3, 4 people gave $4, 8 people gave $5, 1 person gave $7, 1 person gave $8, 2 people gave $10, and 1 person each gave $12, $15, $20, $25 and $40.

   a. What would be the best way of presenting the data (keeping in mind that it has already been organized for you)? If a grouped frequency distribution, what different groupings would make most sense?

   b. What type of distribution would this be considered? Normal? Bimodal? Positively or negatively skewed?

12. Answer the questions for the frequency distribution given in the following table:

Class Interval	f
75+	1
60–74	2
50–59	2
40–49	4
30–39	5
20–29	5
10–19	0
0–9	1

a. What is the real upper limit of the interval containing the raw score of 32?

b. What is the N for this sample?

c. What interval contains the 50th percentile?

d. What percentage of the scores are lower than 59.5?

e. What is the cumulative frequency for the category of 20–29?

f. What is one mistake that was made in constructing this frequency distribution?

13. What is a synonym (in statistical usage, at any rate) for each of the following terms?

a. percentile point   b. rank   c. nominal-level variable

d. ordinate   e. n f. scattergram

14. Lulu got a score of 67, which placed her at the 33rd percentile. Which of the following statements are true?

a. Lulu got a higher score than 33 people.

b. Lulu got 67% of the items correct.

c. Lulu got 33% of the items correct.

d. Lulu did better than 33% of the people who took the test.

e. The percentile rank of a score of 67 was 33.

15. Suppose that you have surveyed people as they stood in line for the latest Disney movie. The ages of the people in line were as follows:

7	4	6	37	2	5	5	7	39	4	7	8	26
10	12	31	4	6	6	65	3	6	27	29	5	7
9	36	8	6	22	13	15	34	7	17	22	9	32

a. Put the data into a simple frequency distribution.

b. (Parts b through d can be done right next to each other.) Now put the data into a grouped frequency distribution. Discuss your reasons for using the class intervals that you did.

c. Now put the data into a relative frequency distribution using percentages.

    d. Next add a column reading "cumulative %," thus constructing a cumulative relative frequency distribution.

    e. Finally, graph your results in a frequency polygon.

16. Identify or describe each of the graphs in Figure 3.17, using one or more of the following descriptors: bar graph, bimodal distribution, cumulative frequency polygon, frequency histogram, frequency polygon, negatively skewed distribution, normal distribution, pie graph, positively skewed distribution, scattergraph.

FIGURE 3.17 Graphs for Problem 16

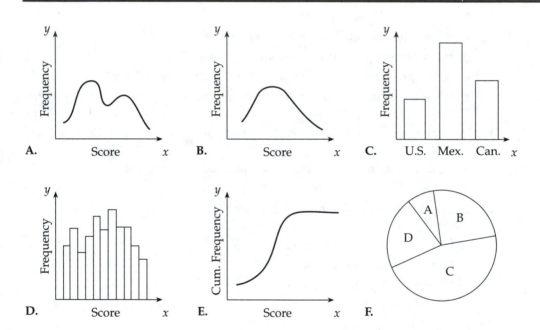

17. According to police records, the number of apparent suicides in Dystopia was 10 for January, 6 for February, 6 for March, 8 for April, 9 for May, 10 for June, 12 for July, 10 for August, 8 for September, 6 for October, 7 for November, and 15 for December.

    a. Put these findings into a frequency distribution.

    b. Now put them into a cumulative frequency distribution.

    c. Is it reasonable to present these frequencies in a frequency polygon? If so, do so. If not, present them in some other graphical form.

    d. Based on the above data, can you say anything about the pattern of suicides over the year?

18. Answer the following questions about these frequency distributions for a sample of males and females.

Age Categories	f_{males}	$f_{females}$
70–79	3	8
60–69	8	10
50–59	12	12
40–49	20	15
30–39	15	18
20–29	10	8
10–19	5	0

a. Were there more males or females in the sample?

b. Was the youngest person in the sample male or female?

c. Was the oldest person in the sample male or female?

d. Would you call the distribution of males' ages approximately normal, bimodal, positively skewed, or negatively skewed?

e. What proportion of the males in the sample were younger than 50 years?

f. What percentage of the females in the sample were younger than 50 years?

g. What percentage of all the people in the sample were younger than 50 years?

19. Answer the questions below based on Figure 3.18, which graphs fictitious data about reasons given by men and women for selecting a best friend.

FIGURE 3.18 Men's and Women's Primary Reasons for Choosing a Best Friend

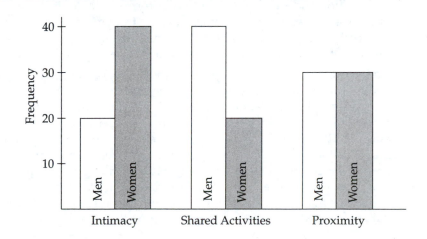

    a. How many men were in the study?

    b. Which type of reason was preferred by the women in the study?

    c. Which type of reason was preferred overall by the people in the study?

    d. What proportion of the women chose "shared activities" as a reason for selecting a best friend?

    e. What type of graph is this?

20. What would be the best kind of (1) tabular and (2) graphic presentation to use for each of the following types of data?

    a. Marital status: scored as currently married, divorced, widowed, never married, other

    b. Age

    c. Political affiliation: scored as Democrat, Republican, or other

    d. The relationship between age and political affiliation

Study Questions

1. Try to think of an instance in which you might gather some data—perhaps handing out a test or questionnaire to a class you are attending or teaching. Imagine yourself collecting the tests. What would be the score on the first test? the second? the last? What would the data look like if you simply reported all the scores as they come in? Now imagine that you repeat the process until you have collected ten times as many scores. How would you want to present them so that someone else could get a picture of the overall pattern of scores?

2. For this problem, you need to locate a journal, newspaper, or popular magazine that presents some data in the form of a table or graph. See if you can find a table or graph of a frequency distribution. Imagine what steps the author went through to put the information into that form. Now take the same information and put it into a different form—a table, if it was a graph; a graph (or perhaps a relative or cumulative frequency distribution), if it was originally a table of a simple or grouped frequency distribution. Which method of presentation seems most informative or easiest to understand?

3. Go to your bookshelf (or in a pinch to the library) and count the colors of the books you see. Stop at one hundred, if necessary. Lump the colors into broad categories—blues, reds, etc.—and use a category called "other" to include books that are not easily classified. Now construct a simple frequency distribution of the colors. Based on this information, draw a bar graph and a pie graph of the same data. If you have several pens, you can color code the graphs, especially the pie graph. Be sure that all three are adequately labeled. Now describe in a sentence what the data look like—that is, which colors seem to be more or less common. Which of your three ways of presenting the data seems to do the best job of representing the overall pattern?

4. Turn on the television and watch a news show. Think about the information reported and how the data might be put into a frequency distribution. For example, if there's a reported crime wave, what kind of table would best report the numbers of crimes committed per month? Would a different kind of table be used to report the different types of crimes committed? If the news concerns a political campaign, what kinds of polls might be taken and how would the results best be reported? Would a table or a graph be better? Which kind? Imagine that you have to write up information on the items reported in the news, expanding the scope if necessary, and think about the best way to report each item.

Describing Data

Central Tendency, Variability, and Standard Scores

What Is a Measure of Central Tendency?

In the previous chapter, we considered two general approaches to presenting the data from a frequency distribution: tables and graphs. Both of these methods are excellent for describing the entire pattern and picture (literally, in the case of a graph) of the scores in a distribution. Sometimes, however, a researcher wants to present just one or two numbers that summarize a group of scores. In that case, she or he often begins by selecting or computing a number to represent a score that is considered typical or average or central to the distribution. Such a measure of a central point in a distribution of scores is called a **measure of central tendency**.

A number of measures of central tendency, some of which have exotic names like the geometric mean, harmonic mean, and contraharmonic mean, can be used to represent a distribution. Although such measures may be used occasionally, social and behavioral scientists almost always report one of the three most common measures of central tendency: the mode, the median, and the mean.

Mode

The **mode** of a frequency distribution is the score that occurs most often; it is the most frequent score. Thus if there are ten scores of 5, five 3's, and 45 2's, 2 is the mode, since there are more scores of 2 than any other value.

TIP ▰▰▰▰▰▰▰▰▰▰▰▰▰▰▰▰▰▰▰▰▰▰▰▰▰▰

> Note that the mode is the score itself, not the number of times it occurs; in other words, be careful not to confuse the mode with its frequency. Of course, when the data reflect a nominal-scale variable that has not been coded with numbers, there is no trouble in identifying the mode; for example, if more people vote for Candidate Cutup than for Candidate Catchup, Candidate Cutup is not only the winner but the *modal choice*.

It is possible for a frequency distribution to have two modes, in which case it is called *bimodal*. A frequency distribution can also have more than two modes, in which case it would be called a *multimodal distribution*.

Mode of a Grouped Frequency Distribution. It is not possible to determine the mode from a grouped frequency distribution, since every score in a class interval could represent any raw score between the lower and upper limit of the interval. Thus, if the interval 8–10 has a frequency of 33 and the interval 14–16 has a frequency of 14, with all other intervals having frequencies of less than 5, we cannot tell which score is the mode. About the most that one can say about the mode from a grouped frequency distribution is that the "modal category" or the category with the largest frequency can be identified, recognizing that the actual mode will not always be in the modal category. In short, it is necessary to look at the simple or relative frequency distribution of the raw scores in order to identify the mode.

Median

The **median** of a distribution is the score in the middle when the scores are arranged in order from the smallest to the largest. Another name for the median is the *50th percentile*, or the score at or below which 50% of the scores fall and above which 50% of the scores fall. If there is an odd number of scores, the median is the middle score, counting from either end; if there is an even number of scores, the median is, by convention, halfway between the two middle scores.

Figuring out the Middle Score. In order to figure out which score is the middle one, you can count from the top and the bottom until you have reached the score that is the same rank counting from either end. More precisely, if the sample size, N, is an odd number,

Step 1: Add 1 to N.

Step 2: Divide $N + 1$ by 2 to get the location or rank of the middle score or median.

If the sample size is even,

Step 1: Add 1 to N.

Step 2: Divide $N + 1$ by 2 to get the average rank of the two middle scores.

EXAMPLE

Find the median when there are 37 scores in a distribution, and when there are 38 scores in the distribution.

Solution: For 37 scores, the median is

$$\frac{37 + 1}{2} = 19$$

Thus the median is the 19th score from either the top or bottom. If there are 38 scores in a distribution,

$$\frac{38 + 1}{2} = 19.5$$

So the median is halfway between the 19th and the 20th score.

Hints for Computing the Median.   Although the median is usually easy to identify, several cautions should be kept in mind when computing it.

   1. Remember to arrange the scores *in order*. The median is the score with the middle rank, not the one that just happens to be in the middle of the pile of answer sheets.

   2. Remember that the median is not ordinarily halfway between the largest and the smallest scores; it's the score that has the middle location. In a skewed distribution, it could be closer to the largest or smallest score than to the midpoint of those two scores.

   3. When scores are tied, one of which is the median, some statisticians think that it is important to use a formula that takes into account the fact that the median is the second of 7 tied scores, for example. Most computer packages use such a formula. However, when calculating the median by hand, researchers usually consider the median to be the middle score (or halfway between the two middle scores) regardless of whether the score is tied with others or not. This procedure has the advantage of both simplicity and comprehensibility.

Median of a Grouped Frequency Distribution.   Like the mode, the median cannot be computed precisely from a grouped frequency distribution, because such a table does not provide information on what the raw scores were. The formula for estimating the median from a grouped frequency distribution is based on the assumption that all the scores are evenly distributed between the lower limit and the upper limit of the class interval. This formula is identical to the formula for calculating the median when several raw scores are tied and is a variant of the formula for calculating any percentile point, adjusted to specify the 50th percentile. It is presented in more advanced statistics texts.

Property of the Median.   The median has the property of minimizing the average absolute deviation of the raw scores. That is, if you subtracted the median from every raw score, and added those deviations while ignoring their signs, you would get a smaller value than if you averaged the absolute deviations from any other point. If you were going to estimate the number of points scored by the average player in a basketball game and you had to pay a penny for every point your estimate differed from the score of each player, the median would be your best guess.

Mean

The most common measure of central tendency, the one you probably learned about in grade school or junior high school, is called the *arithmetic average*, the *arithmetic mean*, or just the *mean*. As you may recall from Chapter 1, when a score on a variable is symbolized by X, the formula for the **mean** of the scores on that variable is $\Sigma X / N$, which is the sum of the raw scores divided by N. The mean of a population is called μ (mu). Thus,

$$\mu = \frac{\Sigma X}{N}$$

The mean of a sample of scores on variable X is called $\overline{X}$ (X-bar) or M (in APA style). When researchers can measure μ, they ordinarily do so; however, much of the time researchers are forced to estimate μ from $\overline{X}$, since they cannot measure every score in the population.

Properties of the Mean.   The mean has several properties that make it a particularly useful measure of central tendency.

   1. The sum of the deviations around the mean is 0. Thus, if the mean is subtracted from every raw score, producing a discrepancy or deviation score symbolized by $X - \overline{X}$, or x, the sum of these deviation scores will equal 0.

TIP ▬▬▬▬▬▬▬▬▬▬▬▬▬▬▬▬▬▬▬▬▬▬▬▬▬▬▬▬▬

> This property makes it possible to check to see whether the mean has been computed correctly; if so, the sum of the deviation scores will be 0.

2. The sum of the *squared* deviations of the raw scores from the mean will be smaller than the sum of the squared deviations about (or from) any other number. In other words, the mean minimizes the squares of the deviation scores compared to the squares of the deviations of the raw scores from any other value. This kind of approach, called a *least-squares estimate*, is used in a number of more sophisticated statistical procedures, like the analysis of variance discussed in Chapter 10.

3. The mean can be viewed as the amount that each person would get if the total amount (not frequency) of the variable being measured were divided up equally. This property gives us a useful way to think of some variables like money; for example, the mean amount of money possessed by people in a sample is the amount that each person would get if the total money were pooled and an equal amount given to each person. On the other hand, the mean score on an attitude scale is not as easily visualized as each person's share of the total attitude and might be thought of more sensibly as the score from which the sum of the deviations is 0 and from which the sum of the squared deviations is minimal.

Computing the Mean from Subgroup Means.   Occasionally you will read a report of a research study in which the means for two or more subgroups are given but not the mean for the entire sample. If you should wish to get the mean of the combined scores of people in different subgroups, there is a formula that can be used. If the means are from subsets or subgroups of a sample, the formula is

$$\overline{X}_t = \frac{\Sigma f_i \overline{X}_i}{N}$$

where the subscript t refers to the total mean of all the scores and the subscript i refers to any frequency and any subgroup mean. This formula states the procedure for getting the mean of all the scores:

- Each subgroup mean must be multiplied by the frequency or number of scores in that subgroup.
- These products must then be summed.
- This sum must be divided by the total number of scores.

EXAMPLE

Suppose that the mean score for the 8 boys in a class is 22 and the mean score for the 12 girls in the class is 26. What is the mean score of all the children in the class?

Solution: We begin by writing the problem another way:

Boys	*Girls*
$n = 8,$ $\overline{X} = 22$	$n = 12,$ $\overline{X} = 26$

Step 1: Estimate what kind of answer would be reasonable. Clearly, the mean for the entire class should be somewhere between 22 and 26; moreover, since there are more girls than boys in the class, it should be somewhat closer to the mean for the girls, 26, than to the mean for the boys, 22.

Step 2: Add the individual frequencies (which can be symbolized by either f or n) in order to get N, the total sample size:

$$8 + 12 = 20$$

which in this case is the total number in the class.

Step 3: Multiply the mean for each subgroup by the frequency for the subgroup:

$$8 \times 22 = 176$$
$$12 \times 26 = 312$$

Step 4: Sum these two products:

$$176 + 312 = 488$$

Step 5: Divide this sum by the total number of scores to find the mean:

$$488 \div 20 = 24.4$$

TIP

> Most calculators can do these operations in a fashion that makes it unnecessary to write down the products of 176 and 312. Try solving the problem on yours.

Notice in Step 5 that the value for the mean is *not* equal to the mean of 22 and 26, the two means for boys and girls. Instead, it is closer to 26, reflecting the fact that the mean of 26 was based on a larger subgroup size, or n. ∎

TIP

> Remember that the mean of a group consisting of two (or more) subgroups will not be equal to the mean of the group means, unless each of the groups has the same sample size.

Characteristics of Mean, Median, and Mode

Mean

- Includes precise information from every score and thus is affected by a change in any score.
- Gives extra weight to extreme scores (by minimizing the average squared distance between each score and the mean), which makes it a least-squares estimate.

Median

- Minimizes the average distance between itself and the raw scores. In other words, if you subtract each score from the median, ignore the sign of the difference, and take the average of these distances, this average will be less than the average deviation from any other value.
- Considers the relative position of each score but not the distances between scores. (The median is less sensitive to an extreme individual score than is the mean.)

Mode

- Provides no information about the distribution, except for the fact that every other score occurred less frequently than the mode.
- Maximizes the probability of being exactly correct. If you can make only one guess, which is judged as either "right" or "wrong," the mode would be the best choice.

Relationship Among the Measures.   If a distribution of scores is normal, the mean, median, and mode will coincide. As illustrated in Figure 4.1, if the distribution is positively skewed, the mean will be higher than the median, with the mode usually being the smallest of the three measures of central tendency; a negatively skewed distribution will usually have a higher mode than median, which in turn will exceed the mean.

FIGURE 4.1   Positively and Negatively Skewed Distributions

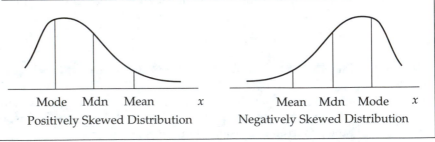

Mode   Mdn   Mean x Mean   Mdn   Mode x
Positively Skewed Distribution   Negatively Skewed Distribution

Selecting the Most Appropriate Measure of Central Tendency

Each of the measures of central tendency has its own relative advantages and disadvantages. Although the mean is the most frequently reported measure of central tendency, it is not an appropriate measure in all instances. In order to decide which measure of central tendency is the best one to use and to report in a particular situation, the researcher must consider several issues.

Level of Measurement.   One of the factors to take into account when deciding which measure of central tendency to report is the type of variable being measured. Computing a mean on a nominal level variable is likely to lead to a meaningless number. For example, if you code breeds of dog as 1, 2, 3, etc., it makes no sense to average across Airedales, poodles, and German shepherds to come up with a mean breed. Similarly, mean football jersey number (or telephone number), mean favorite food, or mean brand of computer is unlikely to lead to any meaningful interpretation, no matter how accurately you compute it. Means should be computed and reported only with data that are measured on an interval or ratio scale or on one of the Likert-type scales that fall in between ordinal and interval scales.

TIP

> Remember that if the numbers assigned are arbitrary, the mean of those numbers will not ordinarily be interpretable.

As implied in the previous paragraph, when the data are qualitative, neither a mean nor a median will be comprehensible. Only a mode will make sense. However, with ordinal-level data, a median can be reported and often will be more informative than the mode. For example, in a large athletic meet in which all the athletes from many schools are seeded or ranked, the median rank of the athletes from School A might be compared with the median rank of the athletes from School B. With interval- or ratio-level data all three of the major measures of central tendency could be reported, so the choice of which to use will depend on other considerations.

Shape of the Distribution.   When a distribution of scores is highly skewed, then the mean may not be the most appropriate measure of central tendency to use.

For example, if we were to calculate the mean income of 42 public school teachers, one of whom had a trust fund that netted him seven million dollars a year, the mean income of these 42 teachers is likely to be higher than the income of 41 of them. Think about it:

- If the 41 teachers averaged $30,000 a year, they would earn a total of 41($30,000) = $1,230,000.
- Add the $7,000,000 (we'll assume that the wealthy teacher donates his salary to charity) to get a total income of $8,230,000.
- Divide by 42 to get the mean income. $8,230,000 ÷ 42 = $195,952.

Clearly this mean is not very representative of the typical earnings of the 42 teachers, although a school board member who's trying to hold the line on teacher salaries might think that it would be a good statistic to report. The median income might be better than the mean in such a case, or perhaps reporting both might be necessary to fully inform the reader. The mode is unlikely to be a useful measure of central tendency for income, as it is unlikely that more than a few people will have identical incomes.

Similarly, if a distribution is clearly bimodal, the mean may be somewhat misleading. Imagine a university where most students are aged between 17 and 22 but which has a large enrollment of senior citizens whose education is heavily subsidized by the state. If a substantial percentage, say 15%, of the student body is in their 60's and 70's, the mean age might be typical of nobody—older than the young students, who are in the majority, but much younger than the minority group of older students. In such a case, with a bimodal distribution, it might be useful to report two or more measures of central tendency, but probably the most informative thing to do would be to present the entire frequency distribution, as no single measure would do an adequate job of describing the distribution.

Purpose of the Study.   Sometimes the most important thing to consider in deciding which measure of central tendency to report is the purpose of the study or your reasons for measuring the dependent variable.

- If you are a clothing manufacturer and you want to know (and make) the size that will fit the greatest number of people, you would seek the modal size, even if size were a normally distributed variable.
- If you were an agricultural economist and wanted to convey the point that there are sufficient food supplies available to sustain life and good health for all people on earth, you might report the mean number of calories eaten per person, implying that if we all ate the same number of calories, there would be enough food to go around.
- A politician wishing to convey the fact that many people go hungry might report the modal caloric intake, a value proving that many people have insufficient food to eat.
- Someone wanting to report a middle value for a positively skewed distribution like caloric intake would probably choose the median as a measure.

Estimating Measures of Central Tendency from Grouped Data

When data are presented in the form of a grouped frequency distribution, it is generally impossible to know the exact value of the mode, median, or mean. Although there are formulas for estimating these measures from a grouped frequency distribution, it should be remembered that they are only estimates, not precise values. Whenever you have collected some data, it is important to calculate the measure(s) of central tendency that you wish to report directly from the raw data, not from a grouped frequency distribution that you may have constructed.

Reporting Measures of Central Tendency in APA Style

Almost all scholarly journals in psychology and the majority of those in education, medicine, and many other fields use a particular style of reporting research study results that is described in the *American Psychological Association Publication Manual* (1994). The mean of a sample is typically represented by an italic capitalized *M* (typed as an underlined M, M); the median is represented by an italic *Mdn*, typed Mdn, and the mode is just called the mode. Thus $\overline{X}$ in statistics is usually written *M* in a journal article, which is one of life's arbitrary mysteries.

What Is a Measure of Variability?

As was stated earlier, if you had to pick a single number to represent an entire distribution of scores, most people would pick a measure of central tendency to represent some kind of typical score. However, an issue that arises when you consider such measures is just how typical they really are. If all the scores in a distribution are very similar to each other, then a measure of central tendency will be very representative of them all. If the scores are very spread out or dispersed, then the typical score will be less typical. In fact, it may not be very representative of any single score in the distribution.

Thus, a second kind of measure that is very helpful for a researcher to report is a measure of how spread out or bunched together the scores in a distribution are. A measure of how much the scores in a distribution differ from each other is called a **measure of variability,** dispersion, or spread. When descriptive statistics are presented, there is usually at least one measure of central tendency and at least one measure of variability reported. Like measures of central tendency, several measures of variability are commonly computed, and each has its relative advantages and disadvantages. These measures include the range, the mean absolute deviation, the standard deviation, and the variance.

Range

The measure of variability that is best known to people not schooled in statistics is the **range**, a measure of the distance between the highest and lowest score in the distribution.

Inclusive Range. Researchers sometimes use the term **inclusive range** to indicate that they are measuring the distance between the upper limit of the highest score and the lower limit of the lowest score. If the raw scores are whole numbers, then the highest score reported will be .5 below its upper limit and the lowest score reported will be .5 above its lower limit. Thus,

Inclusive range = (highest score − lowest score) + 1.

TIP

> Usually, when researchers use the term *range*, they mean and compute the inclusive range, which is what you should do when computing the range of a group of scores. However, sometimes the word range is used loosely to refer to the distance between the reported highest and lowest scores, without adding the extra distance to the upper and lower limits, so you should not be startled if you encounter this definition.

Advantages. The range has several advantages as a measure of variability:

- It is very easy to compute.
- It is equally easy to understand.
- When the scores are approximately normally distributed, the range is related to another measure of variability, the standard deviation, which is more informative but much more tedious to compute.

TIP

> With sample sizes in the twenties, the range may be roughly four times the standard deviation; with samples in the hundreds, the range would be roughly six standard deviations; and with sample sizes in the tens of thousands, the range may be seven or eight standard deviations. Thus, the range can be used to give a "quick and dirty" approximation to the standard deviation; it is a convenient procedure when you have to estimate the standard deviation in a hurry or when you want a check on your computations.

Disadvantages. In spite of these advantages, the range has two serious problems that reduce its usefulness to statisticians.

- First, it depends on only the two most extreme scores. If one score in a distribution is very far from all the others, which tend to cluster together, the range may not give a very good picture of how variable the scores really are. For example, the ranges of the following two distributions are the same even though the pattern of scores is quite different.

| A: | 1 | 90 | 210 | 280 | 390 | 470 | 580 | 700 | 810 | 920 | 1001 |
| B: | 1 | 2 | 2 | 4 | 4 | 5 | 5 | 6 | 6 | 1001 | |

In distribution A, the scores are spaced out reasonably evenly over the range, and the range without the score of 1001 would be 920. In distribution B, the score of 1001 is completely anomalous, with all the other scores having a range of 6 (6.5 – 0.5). Such a score is called an *outlier*.

TIP

> Sometimes an outlier is changed to another value or even omitted before further analyses are conducted, especially if the researcher has reason to think that it might not be accurate.

Generally, a measure of variability that depends on all of the scores is preferable to one that uses only two scores. The fact that the two scores used to calculate the range are the most extreme ones makes it even less likely that the range will represent all scores well.

- The second major disadvantage of the range is that it is likely to increase as the sample size increases. As you add a score to your sample, you have the possibility of increasing the range but no possibility of decreasing it. Thus, the larger the sample size, the larger is its possible range. This property makes the range of a sample a poor estimate of the range of the population from which it comes, since small samples are likely to underestimate the range of the population. It is also difficult to appropriately compare ranges of distributions based on different sample sizes.

TIP

> In practice, it is much less common to *compute* the range than it is to simply *report* the highest and lowest scores of a distribution. If the highest raw score in a distribution of ages was 65 and the lowest was 22, most researchers would say that the ages ranged from 22 to 65, neither subtracting to calculate the value of the range nor reporting the lower and upper limits of the scores.

Interquartile Range.   A measure of variability that attempts to correct for the problems caused by the use of extreme scores in computation is the **interquartile range**, which is the distance between the 25th and 75th percentiles. The interquartile range, in other words, is the range of the middle 50% of the scores. Although it is an easily understandable statistic, it is not widely used.

   Box-and-Whisker Plots. The most common use of the interquartile range is as part of a graph called a *box-and-whisker plot*, or sometimes just a box plot. This type of graph presents the median, the 25th and 75th percentiles, and the range of scores for a single variable. The values are presented along the *y*-axis. The box extends from the 25th to the 75th percentile, and the whiskers usually represent the lowest and highest scores. Figure 4.2 presents an example of a box-and-whisker plot of the number of dollars a sample of people were carrying in their wallets. In it you can see that the range goes from $0 to $60, the interquartile range goes from $5 to $30, and the median is approximately $12. Because a number of computer programs provide box-and-whisker plots, their use is becoming more common.

Mean Absolute Deviation

If you were going to construct a new measure of variability—one that would be based on all the scores in a distribution—a good place to start might be the deviations or distances of each raw score from the mean. Clearly, a distribution in which the deviations from the mean are large is more spread out, more variable, than a distribution in which the distances of all the scores from the mean are small. As the definition of the mean implies, the sum of all

FIGURE 4.2   Box-and-Whisker Plot of Dollars in Wallets

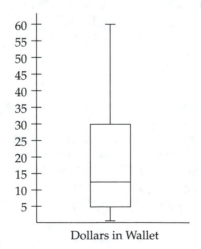

Dollars in Wallet

the deviations of the raw scores from the mean is 0, so neither the total nor the average of the deviation scores would be a useful measure of variability. However, the sum of the absolute values of the deviations from the mean, the **mean absolute deviation**, would make sense as a measure of how far the raw scores deviate from the mean. Although easily interpretable, this measure is rarely used, nor is the mean absolute deviation from the median, which would also make some intuitive sense. Instead, two measures based on the squares of the deviation scores are more frequently reported: the standard deviation and the variance.

Standard Deviation

Statisticians prefer the standard deviation to the mean absolute deviation because it does not require dealing with absolute values. It is also closely related to the concepts of sums of squares and variance, which are used in a number of advanced statistical procedures.

The **standard deviation** of a group of scores is, more or less, the square root of the average squared deviation. The basic procedure for finding the standard deviation follows:

- The deviation of each raw score from the mean is computed.
- These deviation scores are squared and then summed.
- The sum is divided by either the number of scores or one less than N.
- The square root of the sum is then computed.

Squaring and then taking the square root assures that the standard deviation is in the same units as the original scores and, like the range, can be interpreted as reflecting a distance in the same units as the raw scores.

However, the standard deviation is somewhat more complicated than the basic procedure implies because there are different formulas for the standard deviation, depending on whether you are dealing with a population or a sample. To complicate matters even further, there are two formulas for the standard deviation of a population and two for the standard deviation of a sample; one is based on raw scores and one is based on deviation scores, but both yield the same numerical value.

Standard Deviation of a Population.   When a researcher has measured all the scores of interest, then these scores constitute a population, and the formula for the standard deviation of a population, symbolized by the Greek letter sigma, σ, should be used to describe them.

Deviation Score Formula. The deviation score formula for σ, also called the *definitional formula*, is

$$\sigma = \sqrt{\frac{\Sigma(X - \mu)^2}{N}}$$

The use of this formula requires several steps.

Step 1: Calculate the mean using the formula:

$$\mu = \frac{\Sigma X}{N}$$

Summing the raw scores and dividing this sum by N gives us the mean.

Step 2: Subtract each of the N raw scores from the mean, which means that there will be N deviation scores. Remember that each deviation score is symbolized by $X - \mu$, or x.

Step 3: This step is optional, but a good check on your arithmetic. Sum the deviation scores. If the sum is not equal to 0, except in the last decimal place, you have made a mistake in arithmetic.

Step 4: Square each of these deviation scores.

Step 5: Sum the squared deviation scores.

Step 6: Divide the sum by N, the sample size. Since every score in the population was in the sample, N in this case also equals the population size and the number of deviation scores you just added. This step gives you the average squared deviation.

Step 7: Take the square root of the value calculated in step 6 to get the standard deviation of the population.

TIP

Notice that in step 5 you summed a number of squared deviations. This sum is called a *sum of squares*, *SS*. (In Chapters 10 and 12, you will find that sums of squares are used frequently in a procedure called analysis of variance.) A sum of squares must always be positive, since the square of any number other than 0 is positive. (The square of 0 is 0, neither positive nor negative.) Since N is also positive, the next step of the formula involves dividing a positive number by a positive number, leading to a positive quotient. In the last step of the formula, the positive square root of this positive number is taken. Thus, the standard deviation is always positive, since it is based on the positive square root of a sum of positive numbers, perhaps with an occasional 0 added to the sum.

Raw Score Formula. If you compute the standard deviations of a number of sets of data using the deviation score formula, you will find that using this formula can be very tedious. If the mean and the raw scores are all whole numbers, then the deviation scores and their squares will also be whole numbers. However, if the mean is not a whole number, as is often the case, then calculating and squaring each deviation score can be extremely time consuming. For this reason, another formula for the standard deviation uses only the raw scores and does not require the computation of deviation scores. For obvious reasons, this formula is called the raw score formula for the standard deviation of a population. The formula is

$$\sigma = \sqrt{\frac{\Sigma X^2 - (\Sigma X)^2/N}{N}}$$

Looking at this formula, you can see that the difference between it and the deviation score formula is in the numerator. Instead of summing the squared deviation scores, the raw score formula subtracts the squared sum of the raw scores divided by N from the sum of the squared raw scores. These two numerators lead to identical values, as you will see if you use both formulas with the same data.

Use of the raw score formula for σ requires the following steps.

Step 1: Square each raw score.

Step 2: Sum these squared raw scores.

Step 3: Sum all the raw scores.

Step 4: Square the sum of the raw scores.

Step 5: Divide this squared sum of the raw scores by N.

Step 6: Subtract this quotient from the sum of the squared raw scores.

Step 7: Divide this difference by N.

Step 8: Take the square root of this quotient.

TIP

As with the case of the deviation score formula, the value for σ will be positive. In particular, the sum of the squared raw scores will always be larger than the squared sum of the raw scores divided by N. If you don't have a positive number in the numerator of the formula, stop and check your arithmetic before proceeding; you have made a mistake in computation.

EXAMPLE

Computing a Standard Deviation Using the Deviation Score Formula. As an example of how to compute the standard deviation of a population using the deviation score formula, let's look at some data. Suppose that these numbers represent the number of meals that a population of elderly adults report having eaten in the last 24 hours. Perhaps this population consists of the members of a World War I veterans association. The total population is 9 people, who have eaten a total of 20 meals. The scores are

> 3 2 0 3 4 3 2 1 2

The range of the number of meals eaten could be called 4 or 5, or even 4.5; although 5 is technically the inclusive range, some people would feel that the true lower limit of a score of 0 meals is 0, since it makes no sense to consider a negative number of meals (we'll ignore severe cases of indigestion and intestinal flu).

Solution: We use the deviation score formula for the standard deviation of a population:

$$\sigma = \sqrt{\frac{\Sigma(X - \mu)^2}{N}}$$

Step 1: Begin by calculating the mean of the scores:

$$\mu = \frac{\Sigma X}{N} = \frac{20}{9} = 2.22$$

Step 2: Calculate the deviation scores $(X - \mu)$ for each member of the population. These results and the squares calculated in the next step are given in Table 4.1.

Step 3: Square the deviation scores. As shown in Table 4.1, the first raw score is 3 and its corresponding deviation score is 3 – 2.22, or .78, so the square of the deviation score is .61.

TIP

Notice that all numbers in Table 4.1 have been rounded off to two decimal places. If your calculator has sufficient memory, you may wish to carry out all calculations to more decimal places. Notice too that, because we will be using both formulas, the table also includes the squares of the raw scores. In practice, you would not, of course, calculate the squares of both the raw scores and the deviation scores; however, both are presented here so that you can see the relationship between them.

Step 4: Sum the deviation scores. Looking at the table numbers, you can see that the sum of the deviation scores is .02, although this sum is not actually used in the formula for the standard deviation.

TIP ▰▰▰▰▰▰▰▰▰▰▰▰▰▰▰▰▰▰▰▰▰▰▰▰▰▰▰

> If it seems wrong to you that the sum of the deviation scores should be .02 rather than 0, you are thinking sensibly. The reason for the discrepancy is the fact that the scores were rounded off to two decimal places and thus will be completely accurate to only one decimal place.

TABLE 4.1   Values for the Standard Deviation Examples

Scores		Deviations	
X	X^2	$X - \mu$	$(X - \mu)^2$
3	9	.78	.61
2	4	−.22	.05
0	0	−2.22	4.93
3	9	.78	.61
4	16	1.78	3.17
3	9	.78	.61
2	4	−.22	.05
1	1	−1.22	1.49
2	4	−.22	.05
$\Sigma = 20$	56	.02	11.57

$N = 9$

$\mu = 20/9 = 2.22$

Step 5: Compute the sum of the squared deviation scores. As you can see from the table, this sum is 11.57.

Step 6: Divide the sum of squares by N:

$$11.57 \div 9 = 1.286$$

Step 7: Solve the formula by taking the square root of 1.286:

$$\sigma = \sqrt{\frac{\Sigma(X - \mu)^2}{N}} = \sqrt{1.286} = 1.13$$

TIP ▰▰▰▰▰▰▰▰▰▰▰▰▰▰▰▰▰▰▰▰▰▰▰▰▰▰▰

> As a rough check on whether or not this answer is in the right ballpark, we can see that it is approximately 1/3 to 1/4 of the range. For such a small sample size, such a value for the standard deviation is reasonable.

EXAMPLE

Computing a Standard Deviation Using the Raw Score Formula. To see how the raw score formula works, let's use it with the data on meals eaten by elderly adults in the previous example.

Solution: The formula is

$$\sigma = \sqrt{\frac{\Sigma X^2 - (\Sigma X)^2 / N}{N}}$$

Step 1: Square each raw score (see Table 4.1).

Step 2: Sum the squared raw scores to obtain a total of 56.

Step 3: Find the sum of the raw scores, which is 20.

Step 4: Square the sum of the raw scores:

$$20^2 = 400$$

Step 5: Divide this sum by N:

$$400 \div 9 = 44.44$$

Step 6: Subtract this quotient from the sum of the squared raw scores:

$$56 - 44.44 = 11.56$$

Step 7: Divide this difference by N:

$$11.56 \div 9 = 1.284$$

Step 8: Take the square root of this quotient:

$$\sqrt{1.284} = 1.13$$

Note that the discrepancy between the raw score formula and the deviation score formula is due to rounding off. If the numbers were carried out to more significant digits before rounding, the values would be identical to more significant digits. ▣

TIP

As was said before, the raw and deviation score formulas are algebraically identical. The choice of which to use should be made on the basis of convenience—and usually it is most convenient to use the raw score formula.

Standard Deviation of a Sample. The preceding formulas for finding a standard deviation are to be used when describing the standard deviation of an entire population. Although measuring an entire population is sometimes an aim of a research study, more commonly a researcher measures a sample of scores and wishes to estimate the standard deviation of a population based on the standard deviation of the sample. Another common occurrence is that a researcher has measured two samples—perhaps males and females, or people from the experimental and control groups—and wishes to know whether or not they are likely to be random samples from the same population. In such instances, the researcher is interested in generalizing or drawing inferences beyond the particular scores measured and thus is going to be using inferential statistics. In such cases, the formula for the standard deviation of a sample, s, should be used, rather than σ.

Formulas for **s.** Like the formulas for σ, there are two formulas for s, a deviation score or definitional formula and a raw score formula. The only difference between the formulas for σ and the formulas for s is that the formulas for s use $N-1$ in the denominator of the fraction (and $\overline{X}$ in the numerator of the deviation score formula), whereas the formulas for σ use N in the denominator (and μ in the numerator of the deviation score formula). Dividing by a smaller number has the effect of making the quotient somewhat larger. This effect might be quite noticeable when N is small, but will be minimal when N is large.

Using the formula for s when estimating the standard deviation of a population based on a sample provides an unbiased or accurate estimate of the population parameter. Using a formula that involves dividing by N would produce an estimate that would be slightly too small. There are two ways to think about this issue. First, you can recognize that the sample might not include the most extreme scores from the population, although those scores contribute disproportionately to the sum of squares and thus to the value of the standard deviation. Alternatively, you can consider the fact that $\Sigma(X - \overline{X})^2$ for any sample is less than any other number, including $\Sigma(X - \mu)^2$, so the formula based on the former would slightly underestimate the standard deviation of the population if N rather than $N-1$ were used in the denominator.

The deviation score formula for s is thus

$$s = \sqrt{\frac{\Sigma\left(X - \overline{X}\right)^2}{N - 1}}$$

and the raw score formula for s is

$$s = \sqrt{\frac{\Sigma X^2 - (\Sigma X)^2 / N}{N - 1}}$$

Examples Using the Formulas for **s.** In order to see how these formulas are used, let's assume that we have collected the same data on meals eaten by elderly adults, but that these nine scores represent only a sample from a larger group. Perhaps these nine people are the members of a local chapter of an organization and we want to generalize to other chapters and members. In this case, we use the formulas for s, not σ.

• With the deviation score formula for s, the numerator under the radical is still 11.57. However, this number must be divided by $N - 1$ rather than N:

$$s = \sqrt{\frac{11.57}{N - 1}} = \sqrt{\frac{11.57}{8}} = \sqrt{1.45}$$

Taking the square root gives the standard deviation for the sample:

$$s = \sqrt{1.45} = 1.20$$

• With the raw score formula for s, the numerator still reduces to $56 - 44.44 = 11.56$:

$$s = \sqrt{\frac{11.56}{8}} = \sqrt{1.45}$$

Taking the square root gives

$$s = \sqrt{1.45} = 1.20$$

Thus s, the standard deviation of a sample used to estimate the standard deviation of the population from which these nine scores came, is a little larger than σ, the standard deviation of a population consisting of the identical nine scores.

Variance

Although the standard deviation is probably the most commonly reported measure of variability in research articles, with the possible exception of the range, a closely related measure of variability, the **variance**, is frequently discussed by researchers as an indicator of how much variability there is in an entire distribution of scores. The variance forms a part of some major analytic techniques called analysis of variance procedures and enters into various analysis of variance formulas. Even though the variance is not commonly reported as a descriptive statistic, researchers talk about explaining or accounting for or partitioning (dividing up) the variance of a group of scores. The formula for the variance enters into a number of other formulas to be considered later on in this book and other statistics texts.

In fact, the variance is simply the square of the standard deviation. As you should be able to guess from this description, there are therefore four formulas for the variance:

1. A deviation score formula for the variance of a population, σ^2
2. A raw score formula for σ^2
3. A deviation score formula for the variance of a sample, s^2
4. A raw score formula for s^2

These formulas look exactly like the corresponding formulas for the standard deviation with the square root sign removed. Thus, the deviation score formula for the variance of a population, symbolized by σ^2, is

$$\sigma^2 = \frac{\Sigma(X - \mu)^2}{N}$$

The raw score formula for σ^2 is

$$\sigma^2 = \frac{\Sigma X^2 - (\Sigma X)^2/N}{N}$$

Note that the value of the variance (σ^2) for the data on meals eaten by elderly adults was calculated in a previous example before the square root was taken: it is 1.28.

The deviation score formula for the variance of a sample used to estimate the variance of a population, symbolized by s^2, is

$$s^2 = \frac{\Sigma(X - \overline{X})^2}{N - 1}$$

Similarly, the raw score formula for the variance of a sample is

$$s^2 = \frac{\Sigma X^2 - (\Sigma X)^2/N}{N - 1}$$

For the number of meals example, s^2 has been previously calculated to be 1.45.

Characteristics of Measures of Variability

Range

- Is easy to compute and understand.
- Includes information from only the most extreme scores.
- Is frequently not calculated, with highest and lowest scores being reported instead.
- Increases as the sample size increases.

Interquartile Range

- Does not depend on extreme scores.
- Is not commonly reported.

Mean Absolute Deviation

- Shows the average distance of individual scores from the mean.
- Is not commonly reported.

Population Standard Deviation, σ

- Uses data from every score.
- Is not meaningful to someone without background in statistics.
- Is widely used in research.
- Describes an entire set of data.

Sample Standard Deviation, s

- Uses data from every score.
- Is not meaningful to someone without background in statistics.
- Is widely used in research.
- Is used in drawing inferences from samples to populations.

Population, σ^2, and Sample, s^2, Variances

- Use data from every score.
- Are not meaningful to someone without background in statistics.
- Are not widely reported but used in other analyses.

Selecting the Most Appropriate Measure of Variability

The choice of the most appropriate measure of variability to report is a dilemma comparable to the selection of the most appropriate measure of central tendency—that is, intermediate in difficulty between choosing between chunky and creamy peanut butter and deciding on your lifelong career. The researcher must consider several issues when deciding which one to report.

Level of Measurement.   One of the issues to consider in deciding on a measure of variability to use is the nature of the dependent variable.

   Nominal-Level Data. When the data are qualitative, there is no decision to be made; no commonly used measure of variability exists to be reported.

   Ordinal-Level Data. When the raw data are ranks, so that the scores tell you nothing at all about the distance between them, then no measure of variability makes much sense. However, with ordinal scales for which distances between numbers are somewhat related to the size of the number (like responses of "rarely," "sometimes," "usually," or "always"), then either the range or the interquartile range could be reported, with the range a much more common choice.

Interval- or Ratio-Level Data. With interval or ratio data (including Likert scales and other rating scales that really fall in between the ordinal and interval level of measurement), several alternatives are possible.

- It is very common to report the highest and lowest scores in the form of "The scores ranged from X to Y," but much less usual to actually compute the range and report its value.

TIP ▬▬▬▬▬▬▬▬▬▬▬▬▬▬▬▬▬▬▬▬▬▬▬▬▬▬▬▬▬▬▬▬

> Generally, it is a good idea to report the lowest and highest values if you can think of any reason why the reader might be interested in them, which would usually be the case. It is also a good idea to compute (but not report) the range if you want to estimate the standard deviation of the distribution of scores. Remember that the range will be from 3 (for very small samples) to 8 (for enormous samples) times the standard deviation.

- The interquartile range is not reported, unless there are one or a couple of extreme scores that make the range very unrepresentative of the entire distribution and there is reason to expect the reader will be interested in the middle half of the scores; for instance, if test scores were being reported.

- The mean absolute deviation is not ordinarily reported either, but it might be meaningful to an audience that has no statistical expertise but can understand a statement that "The average person was 10 points away from the average score of 54." For example, if you were explaining to a parent whose child scored 3 standard deviations below the mean that the child's score was very low, in some cases comparing the child's score to the mean absolute deviation might be useful. However, presenting the child's percentile rank might be even more helpful.

- The standard deviation is typically reported whenever the scores are measured on close to an interval scale and the audience can be expected to have some knowledge of statistics. The question is usually not *whether* to report a standard deviation, but *which* standard deviation to report, s or σ. To make this decision, you have to think about the purpose of your research and the data you have gathered. If you have gathered all the scores in which you are interested, and if you do not wish to generalize beyond these scores, then you can consider that you have measured the population and report σ as your measure of variability. These are the identical instances in which you would report μ as your mean.

TIP

> The choice of which formula you use to calculate σ is irrelevant, as the raw score and deviation score formulas will give you the same value.

Descriptions Versus Inferences. Most of the time, researchers are not interested in simply describing the scores that they have; most of the time they are interested in drawing some inferences based on their data. Therefore, most of the time they use the formulas for s rather than σ. Whenever you have measured only a sample of the scores (or people) of interest, you should be calculating and reporting s. If you are in doubt about whether σ or s is more appropriate for your data, chances are that you should be reporting s; however, it is a good idea to discuss the purpose and methodology of your research with an expert to be sure that you have made the right decision.

TIP

> As stated earlier, it is unusual for researchers to report the value of the variance as a descriptive statistic, even though they might discuss some aspects of it in their report. Therefore, I don't recommend that you report either σ^2 or s^2 unless there is some compelling reason to do so (such as a comparison with another research study in which the variance was reported).

Estimating Variability from Grouped Data

As is the case for measures of central tendency, there are formulas that permit the estimation of the standard deviation and the variance from grouped data. However, these formulas are bound to be inaccurate and should not be used unless you do not have access to the raw data (and do have access to a grouped frequency distribution). This situation would be highly unusual, since most researchers who would present a grouped frequency distribution would also report the value of at least one measure of central tendency and one measure of variability. The only such instance that you might encounter with your own data would occur if you gathered your raw data by asking for categorical membership rather than actual scores—for example, if you asked people to indicate their age as in their twenties, thirties, forties, and so on, rather than asking for their exact age. This generally poor technique makes it impossible to compute a mean age or the standard deviation of the ages, thereby making it impossible to compare the mean ages of two groups using parametric (i.e., more powerful) statistical tests.

> **TIP** ▬▬▬▬▬▬▬▬▬▬▬▬▬▬▬▬▬▬▬▬▬▬▬▬▬▬▬▬▬▬▬▬
>
> It is always better to collect your raw data in a form that is as accurate and detailed as feasible. Scores can later be combined into categories when appropriate, but you will not lose the opportunity to use more powerful statistical techniques.

Reporting Measures of Variability in APA Style

In most psychology and education journals, almost all of the measures of variability are referred to exactly as they are in this textbook and other statistics textbooks. There is no common abbreviation for the range; and σ and σ^2 are used to represent, respectively, the standard deviation and variance of a population. However, the symbol for what is probably the most commonly reported measure of variability, the standard deviation of a sample, is *SD* rather than *s*.

What Are Standard Scores?

The term **standard score** refers to a kind of transformed score that relates a raw score to the mean and standard deviation of the distribution from which it comes. A standard score is therefore a score, not a characteristic of a distribution like a mean or a standard deviation. Every raw score in a distribution has a corresponding standard score, depending on which kind of standard score is being calculated. It is possible to compute the standard score for every raw score and the raw score for every standard score as long as you know the mean and the standard deviation of the distribution of the raw scores. However, standard scores would not be computed for distributions that reflect a purely ordinal or nominal scale of measurement, as there would be no way to interpret these scores, since the mean and standard deviation would themselves be meaningless.

z-Scores

The most common kind of standard score is the z-score; in fact, sometimes people use the terms as synonyms. A z-score is simply a deviation score, $X - \mu$ or $X - \overline{X}$, divided by the standard deviation, σ or *s*, depending on whether you are dealing with a population or a sample. A z-score represents the number of standard deviations a score is above (if z is positive) or below (if z is negative) the mean of its distribution.

Formulas. The formulas for finding z-scores are

$$z = \frac{X - \mu}{\sigma} \qquad z = \frac{X - \overline{X}}{s}$$

Computing a z-score corresponding to a particular raw score requires the following steps.

Step 1: Compute the mean of the distribution from which the raw score comes.

Step 2: Compute the standard deviation of the distribution.

Step 3: Subtract the mean from the raw score.

Step 4: Divide this difference by the standard deviation.

The hardest part of the procedure is computing the standard deviation, not computing the actual z-score.

Although in your own research you would be collecting raw scores and transforming them to z scores, sometimes you may see a reported z-score and wish to transform it to a raw score. The formulas for doing so are

$$X = z\sigma + \mu \text{ for a population}$$
$$X = zs + \overline{X} \text{ for a sample}$$

The steps in using this formula follow.

Step 1: Calculate the mean of the scores.

Step 2: Calculate the standard deviation of the scores.

Step 3: Multiply the z-score by the standard deviation.

Step 4: Add this product to the mean. The sum will equal X.

TIP

It doesn't matter if you multiply z times σ or σ times z; just remember to do the multiplication before adding the mean to the product. For example, since a z-score of +1.2 represents a raw score 1.2 standard deviations above the mean, to convert this z-score to a raw score, you would just multiply the standard deviation of the distribution by 1.2 and add it to the mean.

Advantages. There are a number of reasons for computing z-scores that extend beyond the goal of increasing the misery of statistics students. A z-score provides a substantial amount of information that a raw score may not.

1. The sign of the z-score tells you something. If the z-score is positive, you know that the raw score was above the mean. Since the denominator of the formula, σ, must always be positive, the numerator of the formula, $X - \mu$, must also have been positive for the z-score to be positive, meaning that the raw score was above the mean. Moreover, a z-score of 0 means that the raw score was exactly equal to the mean, since $X - \mu$ must have equaled 0 in order for the quotient of the formula to be 0. Similarly, a negative z-score means that the corresponding raw score was below the mean.

2. Not only the sign but also the size of the z-score is informative, particularly when the distribution of the scores is approximately normal. As will be discussed in more detail in the next chapter, approximately two-thirds of all the scores in a normal distribution fall between the z-scores of -1 and $+1$; approximately 95% of the scores fall between the z-scores of -2 and $+2$. Thus, a man with a z-score of -2 not only was below the mean, but he did better than only about 2% or so of the population from which his score came. Someone with a z-score of $+1$ in a roughly normal distribution did better than approximately 5/6 of the population or sample—that is, better than the 2/3 with z-scores between -1 and $+1$, and the half of the remaining 1/3 who had z-scores below -1. In the next chapter you will learn to compute more precisely the percentage of scores falling above and below any particular z-score coming from a normal distribution. Indeed, when a distribution is normal, percentile scores can be directly transformed to z-scores and vice versa.

3. Another major advantage of z-scores is that they permit comparisons across distributions that may have different means and standard deviations. For example, suppose that you got a 45 on a statistics test with a total of 50 possible points, a mean of 40, and a standard deviation of 5 points. Your friend Sylvester was taking a different statistics class; he got a score of 70 on a 100-point test with a mean of 70 and a standard deviation of 10 points. Who did better? To compare raw scores and say that Sylvester did better because he got 70 points and you got only 45 points seems ridiculous, since the maximum number of points you could possibly have received would be 50. You might think that it would be fair to conclude that you did better because you got 90% correct and he got only 70% correct, but it could have been the case that his test was much more difficult than yours.

On the other hand, you could try comparing z-scores. Your z-score of $(45 - 40)/5 = +1$ means that you did better than the majority of the people who took your test. In fact, you did better than about 84% of those who took the test with you. Sylvester's z-score of 70 (his raw score) -70 (the mean) divided by $10 = 0$ means that he was exactly at the mean for his class. Thus, you could reasonably conclude that you did better than Sylvester on your corresponding tests, based on a comparison of your z-scores.

TIP

Of course, comparing z-scores on different measures is fair only if one can assume that the samples or populations being compared were roughly equivalent. If Sylvester were taking honors statistics and you were taking developmental statistics, then a comparison of your z-scores might not be valid.

4. A fourth advantage of z-scores is that they permit the creation of new measures. By adding z-scores on several variables, a new, composite measure can be created that gives equal weight to each variable, rather than emphasizing those with larger standard deviations. For example, Anderson and Anderson (1996) were interested in the relationship between violent crime and temperature in a large sample of cities. They created a violent crime index by adding together the z-scores on several measures of violent crime for each city and a temperature index by summing z-scores on several measures of temperature for each city.

TIP

If you want to create a composite measure in which one variable is more important than the other ones, you could choose to multiply the z-scores on this variable by a number larger than 1 before adding them to the z-scores on the other variables.

Other Standard Scores

Although z-scores are by far the most common kind of standard scores, a number of *standardized tests* (tests that are manufactured by large companies and given to large groups of people to provide typical scores called norms) provide standard scores that are based on z-scores but are not identical to them. As was stated earlier, when a distribution of scores is normal, then percentile scores can be converted directly to z-scores and vice versa; for example, a percentile score of 50 is equal to a z-score of 0, since they represent the median and mean of a distribution, which are identical in a normal distribution. Two other types of standard scores will be briefly mentioned below: *T*-scores and SAT scores.

T-Scores. A **T-score** (not to be confused with a *t*-test, which will be discussed in Chapter 9) is a standard score based on a mean of 50 and a standard deviation of 10. More formally,

$$T = 10z + 50$$

To compute a *T*-score, you multiply the z-score by 10 and add 50. Thus, a z-score of $-.5$ corresponds to a *T*-score of 45:

$$(-.5)(10) = -5$$

$$-5 + 50 = 45$$

To transform a *T*-score into a z-score, the formula is

$$z = \frac{T - 50}{10}$$

In other words, to find the z-score corresponding to a given T-score, you must subtract 50 from the T-score and divide this difference by 10. Thus, a T-score of 65 corresponds to a z-score of 1.5:

$$\frac{65 - 50}{10} = \frac{15}{10} = 1.5$$

TIP

A raw score at the mean corresponds to a T-score of 50 and a z-score of 0.

T-scores are used to report the results of several personality tests, including the famous Minnesota Multiphasic Personality Inventory, more commonly called the MMPI. They have the advantage of almost always being positive, since it is extremely rare for scores in a distribution to be as many as five standard deviations below the mean or correspond to z-scores as low as –5. For people who find it difficult to deal with negative numbers and who might confuse a z-score of 0 with a raw score of 0, T-scores may be more comprehensible than z-scores and are sometimes used for that reason (Wang, Haertel & Walberg, 1993).

SAT Scores.   One kind of standard score familiar to most students who have been admitted to a college or university is the Scholastic Assessment Test (formerly called the Scholastic Aptitude Test) score or *SAT score*. (The ACT test, which is used in a number of universities in the western United States, is also based on standard scores, but the means and standard deviations vary across the different subtests, so it is not as easy to interpret unless you know the means and standard deviations of all the subtests.)

The SAT test was originally set up to have a mean of 500 and a standard deviation of 100 for each of its two sections (quantitative and verbal), based on a large standardization sample of roughly a million testtakers. However, the mean scores have declined over the years and vary significantly by sex.

To compensate for this decline, SAT scores were recalibrated in 1995 to again have a mean of 500 and a standard deviation of 100, making the scores from year to year no longer directly equivalent. At any rate, the scores reported on the SAT are not raw scores but rather standard scores; a 650 does not mean that someone got 650 correct answers. A student with a score of 650 on the verbal SAT test has a z-score equal to his or her raw score minus the mean divided by the standard deviation, or

$$\frac{650 - 500}{100} = \frac{150}{100} = 1.50$$

compared to the standardization sample for the SAT.

There are a number of other commercial standardized tests that also report standard scores, particularly those used for admission to postgraduate programs: the Graduate Record Examination, the Law School Admission Test, the Graduate Management Admission Test, and the Medical College Admission Test. Remember that with any such test, you can turn your standard score into a z-score if you know the mean and standard deviation of the distribution, and you can compare your performance with those of others taking the test by considering these standard scores.

Standard Scores

Definition: A standard score is a type of transformed score that relates a raw score to the mean and standard deviation of the population or sample from which it comes.

z-score: A type of standard score equal to a raw score minus the mean divided by the standard deviation.

Formulas: $z = \dfrac{X - \mu}{\sigma}$ $z = \dfrac{X - \overline{X}}{s}$ $X = z\sigma + \mu$ $X = zs + \overline{X}$

Advantages:

- The sign of a z-score indicates whether the raw score is above the mean (if z is positive) or below it (if z is negative).
- When a distribution is normal, a z-score can be directly transformed to a percentile score and vice versa.
- z-scores permit comparisons across distributions with different means and standard deviations.

T-score: A type of standard score based on a mean of 50 and standard deviation of 10.

Formulas: $T = 10z + 50$ $z = \dfrac{T - 50}{10}$

Advantages:

- Values are almost always positive.
- Used for the MMPI and some other personality tests.

Other Standard Scores: Scores on the SAT, GRE, LSAT, MCAT, GMAT, and some other standardized tests.

When Should You Use the Techniques?

Chapters 3 and 4 have discussed a number of different ways in which researchers might present their data. The choice among the various kinds of frequency distributions, graphs, and measures of central tendency and variability should be made based primarily on the needs of the reader and secondly on such practical considerations as available space and what the publication outlet would expect. For instance, in a dissertation there are typically no space limitations, and tables of simple frequency distributions of the raw scores or of the percentile rank or z-score of each raw score could be presented in an appendix if they might be of interest to a reader. In a professional journal, there are likely to be severe restrictions on space and a premium on conciseness; thus a grouped frequency distribution, perhaps giving percentages, or a graph, would probably be preferred to a list of the raw scores.

- For qualitative data the percentages of people picking each category are reported, along with the total N; if there are many categories with small frequencies and percentages, they might all be combined into a category labeled "other." A bar graph or pie graph would be an alternative; or if only the mode is of interest, that might be reported (along with the percentage of people with that score) instead of the entire frequency distribution.

- For ordinal data (such as type of belt earned in karate), a grouped frequency distribution, a cumulative frequency distribution, or a frequency polygon are probably most commonly reported; an alternative would be to present a percentile distribution. If only a general picture is desired, then the median and the range may be the only statistics reported.

- When the data are close to interval or ratio data (including attitude scales), there are far more options and less consensus about which to select. If the data are approximately normally distributed, it is common to report only the mean and standard deviation, perhaps adding the lowest and highest scores. If the data are skewed, the median is typically added. When the distribution is bimodal or oddly shaped, either a frequency polygon or a grouped frequency distribution, using either raw frequencies or percentages, is commonly presented. If the data are test scores which are intended for use as a normative (comparative) sample for the reader, then a distribution of percentiles would ordinarily be expected.

TIP

The choice between presenting complete information and being succinct is not always an easy one, but it is probably better to err on the side of being comprehensive when describing your data.

CHAPTER SUMMARY

Data from a frequency distribution can be summarized in a number of ways. A measure of central tendency is a number that in some way represents a typical or central score in a group. The mode is that score with the highest frequency (i.e., the score that occurs most often). The median, or 50th percentile, is the score that is in the middle when the scores are ordered from highest to lowest. The mean or arithmetic average is the sum of the raw scores divided by the number of scores.

Measures of variability reflect how different the scores in a distribution are from one another. The range measures the distance between the highest and lowest score in the distribution. The variance of a population is equal to the sum of the squared deviations about the mean divided by the number of scores, and the standard deviation is equal to the square root of the variance. When the scores from a sample are used to estimate the variance and standard deviation of a population, the divisor in the formulas is $N - 1$ rather than N. Although measures of central tendency and variability can be estimated from grouped frequency distributions, it is always better to calculate them directly from the raw data.

The choice of the most appropriate summary measures to use to represent a distribution should be made based upon the level of measurement, the shape of the distribution, and your purpose.

When the mean and standard deviation of a distribution are known, then individual scores can be transformed into standard scores, which relate the raw scores to the mean and standard deviation of their distribution. The most common kind of standard score is a z-score, which is computed by taking the raw score minus the mean and dividing the difference by the standard deviation. Positive z-scores represent scores above the mean, a z-score of 0 equals the mean, and negative z-scores represent scores below the mean. Other commonly used standard scores are T-scores and SAT scores. Standard scores facilitate comparisons across different distributions.

CHAPTER REVIEW

Multiple-Choice Questions

1. Which would be the most appropriate measure of central tendency if you are measuring people's preference for brand of computer? (The raw scores are things like "Mac," "IBM," "Compaq," etc.)

   a. the mean   **b.** the median   **c.** the mode   **d.** the harmonic mean

   e. Any of the above might be the most appropriate, depending on the distribution of scores.

2. Which of the following is *not* a standard score?

   a. a deviation score   **b.** a z-score   **c.** a T-score   **d.** an SAT score

   e. All of the above *are* standard scores.

3. In his first sociology class, Don got a score on a quiz that was 8 points above the mean of 14 in a distribution with a standard deviation of 4. Which of the following do you know to be true?

  a. Don had a *T*-score of 22.

  b. Don had a *z*-score of 8.

  c. Don's score was higher than 99% of the other scores in the distribution.

  d. Don's score was half a standard deviation above the mean.

  e. Don had a *z*-score of 2.

  f. None of the above is necessarily true.

4. Tom got a *z*-score of .75 on a test, whereas Mark got a score of 90, when the mean was 80 and the standard deviation was 15. What can you say about their scores?

  a. Tom did better on the test than Mark.

  b. Mark did better on the test than Tom.

  c. Mark and Tom got the same score on the test.

  d. Mark scored below the mean on the test.

  e. Both a and d are true.

5. Which of the following statements about measures of variability *must* always be true if the standard deviation is larger than 1?

  a. The standard deviation is larger than the range.

  b. The standard deviation is larger than the variance.

  c. The range is larger than the variance.

  d. The variance is larger than the standard deviation.

  e. The standard deviation is larger than the mean.

6. Which measure of variability would be a good one to use with nominal-level data?

  a. the standard deviation

  b. the range

  c. the variance

  d. the semi-interquartile range

  e. All of the above might be appropriate with qualitative data.

  f. None of the above are true.

7. If the range of scores in a normal distribution of 400 scores is from 50 to 350, which of the following is most likely to be the standard deviation?

  a. 50   b. 100   c. 150   d. 200   e. 350

8. If you were going to describe the findings of a survey about what the annual income is for the people of Manhattan (New York City, although the findings

for Manhattan, Kansas, might be similar), in which you have both extremely wealthy and extremely poor people, which two measures would you use?

a. the mean and the mode

b. the mean and the standard deviation

c. the median and the range

d. the standard deviation and the range

e. the mode and the standard deviation

9. If the range of scores in a distribution goes from 56 to 92, which of the following must be true?

a. There is no score of 54 in the distribution.

b. The standard deviation must be between 6 and 7.

c. The mean must be 74.

d. The median must be 74.

e. Both a and d must be true.

10. The standard deviation of 25 scores was 10, and the mean was 81. What was the variance?

a. 5   b. 3.162   c. 2.5   d. 9   e. 100   f. none of the above

Problems

11. For each of the following statistics, say whether or not it could possibly be a negative number.

a. the mean   b. the mode   c. the variance

d. the range   e. σ f. s

12. What are the relationships among the relative sizes of the mean, range, s, σ, and σ^2?

13. For the following set of scores,

0 0 1 5 3 2 6 3 6 3 4 3 2 1 6

a. What is the mean?

b. What is the median?

c. What is the mode?

d. Assuming that the scores represent a population, what is σ^2?

e. Suppose that the same raw scores represented a sample rather than a population. What is the value of s^2?

14. If a sample of 101 scores had a mean of 66 and a standard deviation of 15,

a. What would be the z-score of a person with a raw score of 60?

b. What would be the T-score of a person with a raw score of 70?

c. What is the variance of the sample?

d. Suppose that these scores were from a population rather than a sample. What would the population variance have been?

15. For the second quiz in his sociology class, Don got a score that was 18 points above the mean of 44 in a distribution with a standard deviation of 12. Which of the following must be correct?

a. Don had a T-score of 62.

b. Don had a z-score of 1.8.

c. Don's score was 1.5 standard deviations above the mean.

d. Don's score was higher than 18 other scores in the distribution.

e. Don scored at the 50th percentile.

16. What measures of central tendency and variability would be most reasonable for reporting each of the following?

a. The preferred beach for a sample of 86 scuba divers.

b. The number of movies seen per year by 666 college students.

c. The international rankings of tennis players from four different countries (used to see which country has better players).

d. The number of hours of sleep per night for 100 lawyers, 100 doctors, and 100 artists.

e. The scores on a scale of attitudes toward providing economic aid to Cuba, coded 1 = approve, 2 = not sure, and 3 = disapprove.

17. Given the following sample of numbers:

15

25

5

15

10

20

25

30

15

5

0

a. What is the mean?

b. What is the median?

c. What is the mode?

d. What is the inclusive range?

e. What is the mean absolute deviation?

f. What is the variance?

g. What is the standard deviation?

18. On a test of flexibility, the mean of a group of 49 high school gymnasts is 99, with a variance of 225. The mean of a group of 49 high school swimmers is 77, with a standard deviation of 10.

   a. Which group appears to be more flexible?

   b. Which group appears to be more variable in flexibility?

   c. Which group has a higher median?

   d. Tanya got a flexibility score of 88. What is her z-score compared to the gymnasts?

   e. What is Tanya's z-score compared to the swimmers?

   f. What is Tanya's T-score compared to the swimmers?

19. Look at the box-and-whisker plot given in Figure 4.3. It represents scores on a 100-point examination to get a driver's license.

   a. What is the range of scores?

   b. What is the 75th percentile?

   c. What is the median?

   d. What is the mean?

   e. Is the distribution symmetric, positively skewed, or negatively skewed?

   f. John got a score of 65 on the test. What can you say about his score?

FIGURE 4.3   Box-and-Whisker Plot of Driver's License Test Scores

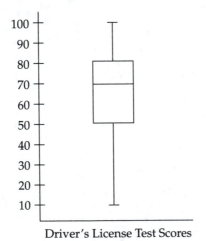

Driver's License Test Scores

20. Consider the following information, gathered from six 12-month-old children. Each child was classified as walking or not, and the number of words in his or her spoken vocabulary was measured.

Child	Walking Status	Vocabulary Size
Roy	Yes	1
Rita	No	2
Ralph	Yes	0
Robbie	No	0
Ruthie	Yes	3
Ryan	Yes	15

a. What would be the most appropriate measure of central tendency to use for walking status? for vocabulary size?

b. What is the modal score on walking status? on vocabulary size?

c. What measure of variability would you use for each of the dependent variables?

d. What is the mean vocabulary size for the children who are walking?

e. Would it be useful to compute z-scores for the children on walking status? on vocabulary size?

Study Questions

1. Try to think of ten different examples in which you or someone else uses a term such as "typical," "usual," or "average." What do you or they really mean by the term in each instance? Try to think of how you would actually measure the quality to which it refers and about what the appropriate measure of central tendency would be. For example, if an advice columnist reported that the "typical" American woman would rather cuddle than have sexual intercourse, what does that mean? Probably, the data were qualitative: a choice between alternatives not ordered in any way. If so, presumably "cuddle" was the modal response. On the other hand, perhaps there was an ordinal scale of activity, ranging from holding hands (or talking? or gazing into each other's eyes?) to sexual intercourse (or ???). In that case, perhaps the median response would be the most representative of what is "typical," particularly if the distribution is skewed. Or perhaps both the mode and median should be reported.

2. Suppose that you are going to be teaching a high school English class. There are two classes available: one with a mean of 45 and a standard deviation of 20 on the High School English Proficiency Exam, and one with a mean of 45 and a standard deviation of 5 on the same exam. Which class would you prefer to teach and why?

3. Suppose that you are the assistant personnel director at a large corporation and that you have been given the assignment of selecting a test of motivation to be administered to all potential employees. What kind of statistical information would you want the test company to provide? What would be most useful to you? What kind of information would you give to potential employees and to their potential supervisors about individual scores?

4. In the course of several years working in the city parks and recreation department, you have gathered a lot of information about how widely used the different recreational facilities are, the demographic characteristics (age, sex, race, occupation) of the people using them, and the amount of money that they bring in. Now you want to present the information in such a way as to convince the taxpayers that supporting the parks and recreation department is worthwhile. You know that most taxpayers have not had the inestimable delight of taking a statistics class. How would you present the various types of data in order to inform the public without confusing them? (Just go ahead and make up the data.)

Probability and the Normal Curve

What Are Empirical and Theoretical Distributions?

Up until this point, we have been discussing distributions of actual scores that were gathered in the course of a research study. Such an **empirical frequency distribution** is an essential element of research and depends upon the collection and interpretation of actual data. However, in order to draw inferences from an empirical distribution, researchers often compare the results that they have collected with the results to be expected if in fact the data fit some particular theoretical frequency distribution. A theoretical distribution is not a distribution of real scores or even the distribution that a researcher truly expects to find. Instead it is a hypothetical distribution that would appear only under certain unusual circumstances that may or may not actually exist. In other words, a **theoretical frequency distribution** is a mathematical distribution based on a theoretical model of the relative frequencies of different scores in a population.

Although an empirical frequency distribution will rarely, if ever, be identical to a theoretical one, often an empirical distribution will be similar enough to a theoretical distribution for the researcher to assume that the empirical distribution corresponds to the theoretical one and to draw conclusions based on that assumption. When this is the case, it is possible to solve a number of practical problems such as estimating how likely it is that certain events will happen or the percentages of individuals who will make certain scores.

Types of Theoretical Distributions

Among the theoretical distributions with which statisticians deal are the normal distribution, the t-distribution, the F distribution, the chi-square distribution, and the binomial distribution. In fact, most of these distributions are not single distributions but rather families or sets of distributions.

We will not spend much time discussing these theoretical distributions in this book, except for mentioning how they are used to make inferences about data that have been collected. Other theoretical distributions, such as the Poisson distribution, will not be discussed in this book at all. However, you should recognize that researchers sometimes describe their data *as if* they fit one of the above distributions, while recognizing that they do not. By making such (incorrect but useful) assumptions, researchers can draw some conclusions about the likelihood or probability of certain outcomes. Given that theoretical distributions provide the assumptions that help to determine the probabilities of events and that these probabilities help us understand the implications of our data, it is useful to examine the concept of probability more closely.

What Is Probability?

The **probability** or likelihood of a particular outcome occurring is the proportion of times that it will occur. This proportion is usually expressed as a fraction consisting of the number of specific events that are classified as instances of that particular outcome, which we could call A, divided by the total number of possible events, t.

Formula.   The formula for the probability of a specific event A is thus

$$P_A = \frac{n_A}{t}$$

In order to compute the probability of a specific event, you must use the following procedure:

- Count the number of instances of that specific event, n_A.
- Count the total number of events, t.
- Divide the number in step 1 by the number in step 2.

EXAMPLE

Suppose that you want to calculate the probability that a particular person selected from a population will be female. This problem is equivalent to finding the proportion of persons in that population who are classified as females—that is, the number of females divided by the total number of individuals in the population. Imagine that there are 14 females and 7 males in the class. What is the probability that any student selected would be female?

Solution: There are 14 instances of the event "female" and a total of 14 + 7 or 21 possible events (people). The probability that a selected student will be female is

$$P_{\text{female}} = \frac{14}{21}$$

$$= \frac{2}{3} = .667 \quad \text{(in decimal form)}$$

TIP ▮▮▮▮▮▮▮▮▮▮▮▮▮▮▮▮▮▮▮▮▮▮▮▮▮▮▮▮▮▮▮▮▮▮▮▮

> The definition of probability depends on the assumption that each possible event is equally likely. When the events are characteristics of people, this assumption amounts to assuming that each person is equally likely to be selected, which is the essence of random sampling. Random sampling and other sampling procedures will be discussed in more detail in Chapter 8.

Combining Probabilities

Sometimes a researcher is interested in determining the probability that more than one event will occur.

Probability That at Least One of Two Events Will Occur.   The likelihood that one or the other (or both) of two events will occur is equal to the likelihood of the first one occurring, plus the likelihood of the second one occurring, minus the likelihood of both of them occurring. In other words, when you want to know the likelihood of one *or* another event occurring, you should *add* the probability of one event to the probability of the other event and then *subtract* the probability that both events will occur.

   Formula. If the probability of the first event is called P_A, the probability of the second event is called P_B, and the probability of both events is called P_{A+B}, then

$$P_{A \text{ or } B} = P_A + P_B - P_{A+B}$$

EXAMPLE ▮▮▮▮▮▮▮▮▮▮▮▮▮▮▮▮▮▮▮▮▮▮▮▮▮▮▮▮▮▮▮▮▮▮▮▮

Suppose that you are observing people shopping in a drugstore. You notice the following:

- 2 of 10 people are buying only aspirin.
- 1 of 10 is buying only toothpaste.
- 4 of 10 are buying both aspirin and toothpaste.
- 3 of 10 are buying only candy bars.

What is the probability that a particular shopper is buying either aspirin or toothpaste?

Solution: To answer this question, we can use the formula:

$$P_{A \text{ or } B} = P_A + P_B - P_{A+B}$$

Step 1: Find the probability that a person is buying aspirin (P_A):

$$\frac{2 + 4}{10} = .6$$

Step 2: Find the probability that a person is buying toothpaste (P_B):

$$\frac{1 + 4}{10} = .5$$

Step 3: Find the probability that a person is buying both aspirin and toothpaste (P_{A+B}):

$$\frac{4}{10} = .4$$

Step 4: To get the probability that someone is buying either aspirin or toothpaste, substitute these values into the formula:

$$P_{\text{aspirin or toothpaste}} = .6 + .5 - .4 = .7$$

You can see that this result is correct by noticing that only 3 of the 10 shoppers (.3) were buying neither aspirin nor toothpaste. In other words, the likelihood that a particular person shopping in a drugstore will be buying either aspirin or toothpaste is equal to the proportion of people who are buying aspirin, plus the proportion of people who are buying toothpaste, minus the proportion of people who are buying both aspirin and toothpaste (because otherwise you would be counting these efficient shoppers twice). ∎

As another example, you might decide to bring a raincoat if the probability either of rain or of a temperature under 40° or of both is greater than .7. To make your decision, you would add the probability of rain (e.g., .6) to the probability of a temperature under 40° (e.g., .5) and subtract the probability of both (e.g., .4). The probability of either rain or cold occurring would be $(.6 + .5) - .4 = .7$, so you would not take your raincoat.

Mutually Exclusive Events. When two events are what is called *mutually exclusive events*, then only one of them can occur and the likelihood of both of them occurring is 0. When you use the formula for finding the probability that at least one of two mutually exclusive events will occur, the P_{A+B} term disappears, since the probability of both of them occurring is 0. Thus, to get the probability that either event A or event B will occur, you add:

$$P_{A \text{ and } B} = P_A + P_B$$

For example, the mean of a population might be between 5 and 9.99999 or between 10.00000 and 14.99999, but it could not be both of those values. Therefore, the probability that the mean of a population is between 5 and

14.99999 is equal to the sum of the probability that the mean is between 5 and 9.99999 and the probability that the mean is between 10.00000 and 14.99999.

Most of the uses of probability in this book will involve combining the probabilities of two or more mutually exclusive events, which means that all that needs to be done is to add the probabilities of the events that are associated with the outcome of interest. However, occasionally, you might wish to consider the probability that one or the other or both of two events that are not mutually exclusive might occur.

Probability That Two Events Will Both Occur. Besides estimating the likelihood that at least *one* of two events will occur, a second use of probability that you may encounter is to estimate the likelihood that *both* of two (or more) events will occur. For purposes of calculation, it does not matter whether the events occur successively or simultaneously, as long as they are independent.

Independent Events. Two events are **independent events** when they are unrelated to each other; whether or not one occurs tells you nothing about the likelihood that the other event will occur. The responses of four different people in the same household to the question "What kind of animal is your favorite pet?" are probably not independent, as you would expect all of them to be affected similarly by the presence of a pet in the household. On the other hand, the outcomes of two different tosses of a fair coin should be independent; whether the coin came up heads or tails on one trial has nothing to do with whether or not it will come up heads on any other trial. Each time a fair coin is flipped, the chance that it will come up heads is .5, no matter what happened the last time it was flipped or the 99 times before that. Even though a person may remember that a coin has come up heads 10 times in a row, the coin does not.

Gamblers who believe in a lucky streak or, alternatively, that if they've been losing for a while, they're due for a win, are denying that they are dealing with independent events. On the other hand, baseball players who are in a slump or on a hitting streak are probably not dealing with independent events; their likelihood of getting a hit does depend on how well they have been hitting in the recent past.

Formula. The probability of two independent events both occurring is equal to the probability of one occurring times the probability of the other occurring. In other words, if you want to know if a first event *and* a second event will *both* occur, then you *multiply* the probability of the first event times the probability of the second event. The formula for the probability of both events occurring is

$$P_{A+B} = (P_A)(P_B)$$

EXAMPLE

Suppose you want to know the likelihood of throwing two sixes when two dice are tossed.

Solution: The probability of throwing a 6 on the first die is (1/6); the probability of throwing a 6 on the other die is (1/6). Thus,

$$\left(\frac{1}{6}\right)\left(\frac{1}{6}\right) = \frac{1}{36}$$

As a slightly more complicated example, imagine that 54% of the students at some university are female and 12% are African-American. What is the probability that any particular student is a male African-American? To answer this question you need to find the proportion of students who are male, which is 1.00 − .54 = .46. Multiplying .46 by the proportion of African-American students, we get (.46)(.12) = .0552 as the proportion of male African-American students at the university. Note that this example assumes that gender and ethnicity are independent. If, for example, a greater percentage of males than females are black, then this calculation will be wrong.

TIP

> This example gives you information about the percentage of students who were female but asks a question about the proportion of males. When you are dealing with real data, it won't always be presented in the way that best fits your questions, so look at both the data and the question you need to answer very carefully. (This advice applies to tests, too.)

Nonindependent Events. When the probability of an outcome occurring is contingent or dependent on the previous outcome (i.e., when the events are not independent), then more sophisticated equations for calculating the probability of both outcomes happening have to be used. For example, when the two events discussed are scores sampled from the same population, then it is necessary to consider whether the procedure used was sampling with replacement or sampling without replacement. **Sampling with replacement** refers to a procedure in which a given individual or unit can be sampled more than once. **Sampling without replacement** occurs when each individual can appear only once in the sample.

As an illustration of a more complex situation in which we might want to estimate probabilities, if we sample a card from a deck of cards, the probability of getting the ace of spades on the first try is 1/52. If we replace the first card drawn, reshuffle, and draw another card—sample with replacement—then the probability of getting the ace of spades on the second draw is also

1/52. However, if we do not replace the first card—sample without replacement—then the probability of getting the ace of spades on the second draw is either 1/51 (if it was not drawn originally) or 0 (if it was drawn on the first try). Generally, in statistics we either assume that the sampling was done with replacement or we have such large samples that there is very little difference between sampling with replacement and sampling without replacement.

Probability

Probability of a particular outcome or event occurring: The probability or likelihood of a particular outcome occurring is the proportion of times that it will occur.

Formula: $P_A = \dfrac{n_A}{t}$

Probability that at least one of two events will occur: The likelihood that one or the other (or both) of two events will occur is equal to the likelihood of the first one occurring, plus the likelihood of the second one occurring, minus the likelihood of both of them occurring.

Formula: $P_{A \text{ or } B} = P_A + P_B - P_{A+B}$

Mutually exclusive events: When two events are mutually exclusive, then only one of them can occur and the likelihood of both of them occurring is 0.

Formula: $P_{A \text{ or } B} = P_A + P_B$

Probability that two independent events will both occur: The probability of two independent events both occurring is equal to the probability of one occurring times the probability of the other occurring.

Formula: $P_{A+B} = (P_A)(P_B)$

Probability that two nonindependent events will both occur: When the probability of an outcome occurring is dependent on a previous outcome, then more sophisticated equations for calculating the probability of both outcomes happening have to be used.

What Is the Binomial Distribution?

In order to illustrate some of the uses of probability theory, let's consider the family of frequency distributions called the *binomial distribution*. From the term *binomial*, which comes from the Latin words for *two* and *name*, it is reasonably easy to remember that **binomial distribution** refers to the distribution of events that have only two possible outcomes. Another way to think of it is that it refers to the distribution of scores on a nominal-level variable that has only two possible values. These values or outcomes could be "yes" and "no," "on" and "off," or "heads" and "tails." It is not necessary that the two outcomes be equally likely (as heads and tails presumably are for a coin) in order for a distribution to be binomial, only that there be only two possible outcomes.

In order to discuss the binomial distribution somewhat generally, we can call the first outcome (say, heads) A and the second (say, tails) B. When a distribution is binomial, the two outcomes of each event are *mutually exclusive*, and one or the other of them must occur. Thus, the probability of outcome A (heads) plus the probability of outcome B (tails) must equal one:

$$P_A + P_B = 1.00$$

In the case where there is only one score (one person saying "yes" or "no" or one coin being tossed), the binomial distribution is very straightforward. If both outcomes are equally likely, the probability of A and the probability of B are each equal to .5. However, where the number of scores or trials is greater than one (several people making choices or several coin tosses), the binomial distribution becomes more interesting. Assuming that the events (trials) are independent, you can use the rules of probability mentioned above to calculate the likelihood of each of several outcomes.

EXAMPLE

Suppose that a coin is tossed three times. For each toss, the probability of getting heads is .5. As the following table shows, there are eight possible outcomes of three tosses.

Outcome	Probability
Heads, Heads, Heads	1/8 = .125
Heads, Heads, Tails	1/8 = .125
Heads, Tails, Heads	1/8 = .125
Heads, Tails, Tails	1/8 = .125
Tails, Heads, Heads	1/8 = .125
Tails, Heads, Tails	1/8 = .125
Tails, Tails, Heads	1/8 = .125
Tails, Tails, Tails	1/8 = .125

Each of these outcomes has a 1/8 chance of happening. For example, the probability of getting 3 heads (HHH) is equal to the probability of heads on the first toss times the probability of heads on the second toss times the probability of heads on the third toss, or

$$\left(\frac{1}{2}\right)\left(\frac{1}{2}\right)\left(\frac{1}{2}\right) = \frac{1}{8}$$

The probability that one of these outcomes will occur is

$$\frac{1}{8} + \frac{1}{8} + \frac{1}{8} + \frac{1}{8} + \frac{1}{8} + \frac{1}{8} + \frac{1}{8} + \frac{1}{8} = \frac{8}{8} = 1.00$$

As another example, suppose that you want to know what the probability of getting two tails and one head is when a coin is tossed three times. To find out, you have to add up the probabilities of all the different events that can lead to that outcome—that is, the probabilities of HTT (1/8) + TTH (1/8) + THT (1/8) for a total of 3/8. More formally, we can say that if events A, B, and C are mutually exclusive,

$$P_{A \text{ or } B \text{ or } C} = P_A + P_B + P_C$$

An alternative way of looking at the binomial distribution is to consider the probability of getting each possible number of heads. With three tosses, the probability of four or more heads is 0 (of course); of three heads, 1/8; of two heads, 3/8; of one head, 3/8; and of no heads, 1/8. As Figure 5.1 indicates, with five tosses, the probability of five heads is 1/32; of four heads, 5/32; of three heads, 10/32; of two heads, 10/32; of one head, 5/32; and of no heads, 1/32.

If these probabilities aren't obvious (if they are, shouldn't you be taking a more advanced statistics class?), try writing down all the possibilities starting with HHHHH and calculate the probabilities for yourself. As you should be able to see if you put the number of heads (or "yes" answers) on the x-axis, as the number of events or scores (or the sample size, N) gets larger, the binomial distribution begins to look more and more like the normal distribution, with most of the scores bunched up in the middle and fewer and fewer scores as you get farther away from the mode.

FIGURE 5.1   Binomial Distribution for Coin Tosses

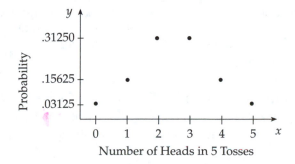

Number of Heads in 5 Tosses

TIP

> In fact, with a large enough sample size, it is possible to consider a binomial distribution as if it were a normal distribution. However, it is important to remember that the assumptions that we make about the binomial distribution are based upon the more basic assumption that we are dealing with independent events. If the probability that one person's answer is "no" depends on another person's answer, then the calculations made above would be incorrect.

What Is the Normal Distribution?

Although the binomial distribution is often used to provide relatively simple demonstrations of probability and is an important component of the general field of probability theory, the most useful distribution for social science researchers is the normal distribution. Many statistical tests depend on the assumption that scores are normally distributed in the population from which the sample was selected. Moreover, if an empirical distribution is close enough to the normal distribution, then it is possible to solve a lot of problems simply by knowing the mean and standard deviation of the raw scores and by having access to a table that describes the normal distribution in some detail.

TIP

> People often use the terms *normal curve* and *normal distribution* interchangeably.

As was discussed in Chapter 3, the **normal distribution** is a symmetrical, bell-shaped distribution of scores, in which the scores are bunched up in the middle and the mean, median, and mode coincide. The normal distribution is really a family of distributions, each with its own mean and standard deviation. A special case of the normal distribution is called the *unit normal distribution*, which is a normal distribution with a mean equal to 0 and a standard deviation (and therefore variance) equal to 1. Unlike most empirical distributions, therefore, the unit normal distribution has negative scores as well as positive ones.

Graphing a Normal Distribution: The Normal Curve

The graph of a theoretical normal distribution is called a *normal curve*. The tails of a normal curve never touch the x-axis, meaning that there is always a

FIGURE 5.2   Normally Distributed Scores: The Normal Curve

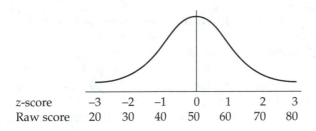

z-score	−3	−2	−1	0	1	2	3
Raw score	20	30	40	50	60	70	80

slight probability that a score very far away from the mean can occur. In contrast, an empirical distribution that is very close to normal typically has a range of 6 to 8 standard deviations, depending upon the sample size. Ordinarily, the normal distribution is graphed with z-scores along the x-axis, ranging from $z = -3$ or -4 to $z = +3$ or $+4$. When the distribution is an empirical one, it is both useful and common to double label the x-axis in both z-scores and raw scores, so that the relationship between the two can easily be seen. An example of a nearly normal empirical distribution with a mean equal to 50 and a standard deviation of 10 is shown in Figure 5.2.

Relationship Between the Normal Curve and Probability

If a score is selected from a normal distribution, there is a definite and known probability of that score falling within any given limits. For example, Figure 5.3 shows that the probability of getting a score below the mean (which, of course, is equal to the median and mode) is .5000, exactly the same as the likelihood of getting a score above the mean.

FIGURE 5.3   Proportions of Scores Above and Below the Mean in a Normal Distribution

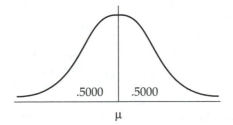

.5000   .5000

μ

Assumptions. When using the normal curve to solve problems, we make a number of assumptions:

- We are dealing with a continuous quantitative variable (as discussed in Chapter 1).
- With a continuous variable, any reported score is only an approximation to the true value; therefore, the probability of getting a score exactly equal to the true value of the mean (or to any other exact value) would be 0, if we were to measure it precisely enough.
- If you divide up the normal curve into mutually exclusive ranges, the probabilities of all of the mutually exclusive ranges of scores will add up to 1.00. In other words, if the y-axis is viewed as representing probabilities (which, you will remember, are frequencies divided by the total frequency, and so are equivalent to proportions) of getting particular scores, then the entire area under the normal curve from the smallest value of X (or the smallest possible z-score) to the largest will equal 1.00.
- Since the scores are mutually exclusive (a score cannot be both +2 and +3.1), it makes sense to add the probabilities of scores within different nonoverlapping categories (or ranges or limits) in order to get the probability of getting a score that falls anywhere within those limits.

Dividing the Area Under the Normal Curve

Mutually Exclusive Areas. As stated previously, if the entire area under the normal curve has a probability of 1.00, it is possible to divide up this area into mutually exclusive parts that, when added together, will have a total probability equal to 1.00. By dividing the area in different ways, it is possible to solve a number of problems that are based on the assumption that scores are normally distributed.

z-Scores and the Normal Curve. Most of these problems involve z-scores. Remember that a z-score is a transformed score obtained by the formulas

$$z = \frac{X - \overline{X}}{s} \qquad z = \frac{X - \mu}{\sigma}$$

A z-score indicates how many standard deviation units a score is above or below the mean. With a normal curve, the proportion of scores between $z = -1$ and the mean, or between $z = -2$ and $z = -1$, or between any other two z-scores is known. Thus, if a particular distribution of scores (test scores, for example) is known to be normal, it is possible to identify exactly what proportion of the scores fell between any two numbers, such as 65 and 70, or above or below any particular score.

When a distribution is normal, it is also possible to translate raw scores into z-scores and percentile scores or vice versa without having to compute a table of percentile ranks or z-score equivalents of each raw score.

For example, knowing that .5000 of the scores in a normal distribution lie below the median, we could subdivide this .5000 into three parts:

- The proportion lying below a z-score of –3
- The proportion between a z-score of –3 and one of –2
- The proportion between a z-score of –2 and one of 0

Alternatively, we could divide up the scores in a distribution into the bottom 25% (or those below the 25th percentile), the middle 50%, and the top 25%, if we wished. By using a normal curve table, we can easily identify the cutoff points to divide up the total distribution into whatever subgroups we wish, including percentiles.

What Is a Normal Curve Table?

In order to identify the proportion of the scores in a normal distribution that falls between certain limits, it is necessary to use a normal curve table (see Appendix Table 1). A **normal curve table** is a table that lists the proportions of scores falling between any z-score and the mean of a distribution. The first part of a normal curve table is shown in Table 5.1.

TABLE 5.1   Sample Portion of Appendix Table 1: Areas Under Unit Normal Curve

z	Area Between z and Mean	Area Beyond z
0.00	0.0000	0.5000
0.01	0.0040	0.4960
0.02	0.0080	0.4920
0.03	0.0120	0.4880
0.04	0.0160	0.4840
0.05	0.0199	0.4801
0.06	0.0239	0.4761
0.07	0.0279	0.4721
0.08	0.0319	0.4681
0.09	0.0359	0.4641
0.10	0.0398	0.4602

Looking at Table 5.1, you can see that a normal curve table consists of three columns. The first column represents z-scores beginning with 0.00.

TIP

> Appendix Table 1 has a range of z-scores from 0.00 to 4.00. The choice of this degree of precision, to two decimal places, and of the fact that the z-scores extend only to 4.00 is somewhat arbitrary; other tables might provide somewhat more or less information. The fact that only positive z-scores are presented is not arbitrary; since the normal curve is symmetric, the proportion of scores between a z-score of .68 and the mean will be exactly identical to the proportion of scores between a z-score of −.68 and the mean. Thus, you can ignore the sign of z and use its absolute value when looking up the proportion of scores between a particular z-score and the mean.

As the heading implies, the second column in the normal curve table gives the proportion of scores in a normal distribution that lie between the corresponding value of z and the mean (or median, or mode, or a z-score of 0). The third column gives the proportion of scores that lie farther away from the mean than that particular value of z. As you can see, the numbers in columns 2 and 3 corresponding to any particular z-score in column 1 add up to .5000, which is the proportion of scores that fall between the mean and a z-score of infinity, the highest theoretically possible z-score.

TIP

> Column 3 is redundant, as you could compute it by subtracting the values in column 2 from .5000, were you energetic enough to want to do so.

Probability and the Normal Curve Table

Finding z-Scores. The normal curve table gives the probabilities of getting a score between any value of z and the mean but not the probability of getting any particular value of z. In fact, the probability of getting any single specific z-score in a normal distribution is 0.

The reason that there is a probability of 0 associated with any particular z-score is the assumption that if you were to measure a score precisely enough it would be a minuscule bit either above or below that particular z-score. To reiterate, the normal curve table deals only with probabilities of scores that fall between certain limits, based on the assumption that the probability of finding a score exactly identical to any given value measured infinitely precisely would be 0.

Solving Probability Problems.   Although the normal curve table is based on the theoretical unit normal distribution, it can be used to solve a number of probability problems based on empirical distributions.

EXAMPLE

Let's consider the question of the proportion of scores lying between a z-score of 1.00 and a z-score of –1.00. You may remember that, in the previous chapter, I stated that approximately 2/3 of all the scores in a normal distribution fall between a z-score of –1 and a z-score of +1. Suppose that you fear that I made up these numbers out of thin air, just like some of my problems, and want to check the values for yourself. How would you know whether or not I was right?

Solution: To solve this problem, first of all you should draw a graph of what you want to know. Figure 5.4 shows such a graph, and you can see that you need to know the proportion of scores between a z-score of –1 and the mean and the proportion between a z-score of +1 and the mean. To get these proportions requires a number of steps:

Step 1: Look in column 1 of Appendix Table 1 for a z-score of 1.00.

Step 2: Look over to the corresponding value in column 2. Column 2 shows that .3413 of all the scores fall between a z-score of 1 and the mean.

Step 3: Use the knowledge that the normal curve is symmetric to deduce that .3413 of all the scores lie between a z-score of –1 and the mean.

Step 4: Add the .3413 of the scores that fall between a z-score of –1 and the mean to the .3413 that fall between the mean and +1 for a total of .6826.

Depending on whether or not you feel that .6826 is an adequate approximation to 2/3 (.6667), you can decide whether my statement that 2/3 of the

FIGURE 5.4   Finding the Proportion of Scores Between $z = -1$ and $z = +1$

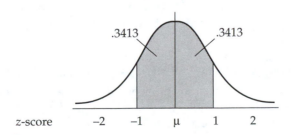

scores in a normal distribution fall between z-scores of –1 and +1 is correct or not.

Suppose that you wish to know the percentage of scores that lie outside the z-scores of –1 and +1. In order to do so, you would have to look at column 3, which gives you the proportions falling below a z of –1 or above a z of +1. Adding the proportion of .1587 below –1 to the proportion of .1587 above +1 gives a total of .3174 of the scores outside those limits. As expected, the sum of .6826 and .3174 = 1.000.   ∎

There's nothing magic about a z-score of 1. For example, suppose that you wanted to get the proportion of scores between a z-score of –2 and a z-score of +2. To do this, you would need to look in column 2 of Appendix Table 1 to see that .4772 of the scores lie between each one of those z-scores and the mean. By adding these numbers, you can see that .4772 + .4772 or .9544 (roughly 95%) of all the scores in a normal distribution lie between those values.

Converting Raw Scores to z-Scores.   Although the normal curve table presents only probabilities corresponding to particular z-scores, it is easy to solve problems about the proportions of scores between particular raw scores by converting these raw scores to z-scores, using the formula $z = (X - \overline{X})/s$ when the scores constitute a sample, as they usually do. A problem about the number or frequency of scores rather than the proportion can also be solved if the proportion is converted to a frequency by multiplying it by the sample size. Thus, a question worded in terms of "How many scores fall below 45?" can be reworded as "What proportion of scores fall below a z-score of –1.2?" (or whatever z-score corresponds to a raw score of 45) and answered by multiplying the appropriate proportion by the total number of scores in the sample.

Different Types of Normal Curve Problems

A number of types of problems can be solved by using the normal curve table when scores are appropriately distributed. They can be grouped into several different categories.

Finding Proportions Above or Below Certain Scores.   One type of problem concerns the proportions of scores that exceed (or fall below) certain values.

EXAMPLE

Suppose that you are a special education coordinator for a school district that mandates that all children with an IQ score below 70 be placed in a special education classroom. What proportion of children would that be?

Solution: To answer the question, you need to know the mean and standard deviation of the distribution of IQ scores. For most IQ tests and most normal populations, IQ scores have a mean of 100 and a standard deviation of 15.

Step 1: Draw a graph of the normal curve and double label its abscissa in both z-score units and in raw score units. Figure 5.5 shows such a graph with the x-axis labeled in both z-scores and raw scores. The part of the curve that is the solution to the problem is shaded. By looking at Figure 5.5 it should be easy to see that what is wanted is the proportion of scores that lie below the z-score corresponding to the raw score of 70.

Step 2: Calculate the z-score that corresponds to a raw score of 70 using the formula

$$z = \frac{X - \overline{X}}{s}$$

Substituting the values of X, $\overline{X}$, and s into the equation, we get

$$z = \frac{70 - 100}{15} = \frac{-30}{15} = -2$$

Step 3: Decide whether you need to use column 2 or column 3 in Appendix Table 1. By looking at the diagram of the problem in Figure 5.5, you should be able to see that the proportion below a negative z-score is equal to the proportion farther away from the mean. To solve the problem, then, you need to look in column 3 parallel to the z-score of 2 (or –2, in this case) in column 1.

Step 4: Find the correct value in column 3, which is .0228.

This value indicates that .0228 of the scores in a normal distribution lie below a z-score of –2; therefore, .0228 is the proportion of scores in a normal distribution of IQ scores that lie below 70. ■

FIGURE 5.5   Finding the Proportion of IQ Scores Below 70

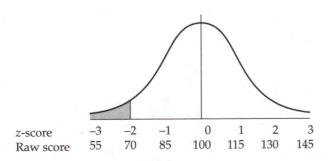

z-score	–3	–2	–1	0	1	2	3
Raw score	55	70	85	100	115	130	145

When solving problems about the proportions above or below certain scores, a diagram of what is being requested (or a mental diagram for some people) is necessary in order to decide whether column 2 or column 3 is the one to use. A graph is also needed to ascertain whether or not the value in the table needs to be added to the .5000 of the scores on the other side of the mean.

EXAMPLE

Suppose that you are giving a driver's license test to applicants, and you know that 72 is the cutoff for passing. The mean score on the test is 84, the standard deviation is 5, and the scores are normally distributed. What proportion of people pass the test?

Solution: In order to answer this question, you will need to draw a graph similar to the one shown in Figure 5.6. From this figure, you can see that the answer requires both the people who scored between 72 and the mean of 84 and the people who scored above the mean of 84.

- To solve the problem, you must convert the raw score of 72 to a z-score:

$$\frac{72 - 84}{5} = \frac{-12}{5} = -2.40$$

- Using Appendix Table 1, you can see that .4918 of all the scores in a distribution lie between a z-score of –2.40 and the mean.
- When this proportion is added to the .5000 of the scores that are above the mean, you get .9918 as the proportion of people who pass the test. ■

Finding Proportions Between Two Scores.   A second kind of normal curve problem involves finding the proportion of the scores that lie between two values.

FIGURE 5.6   Finding the Proportion of Scores Above 72

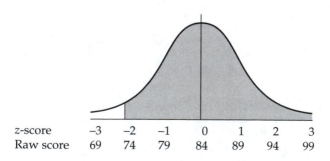

| z-score | –3 | –2 | –1 | 0 | 1 | 2 | 3 |
| Raw score | 69 | 74 | 79 | 84 | 89 | 94 | 99 |

EXAMPLE

A teacher wants to know what proportion of her students are reading no more than one grade level below or two grade levels above the norm, assuming that she will have to devise special materials for those students who are farther away from the norm. (The reason for the asymmetry is that higher-achieving students can read texts at a lower level, but lower-achieving students may not be able to read texts written at a higher level.) If the mean grade level equivalent on a reading test for a fifth-grade class is 5.5 and the standard deviation is 1.5, what proportion of students are reading at a grade level between 4.5 and 7.5?

Solution

Step 1: Draw a graph similar to the one shown in Figure 5.7. From this figure you can see that you will need to add the number of students who score between 4.5 and the mean of 5.5 to the number falling between the mean and 7.5.

Step 2: Calculate the z-score corresponding to the raw score of 4.5:

$$\frac{4.5 - 5.5}{1.5} = \frac{-1}{1.5} = -.67$$

Step 3: Look at column 2 of Appendix Table 1 to find the proportion of scores between a z-score of −.67 and the mean, which is .2486.

Step 4: Calculate the z-score corresponding to the raw score of 7.5:

$$\frac{7.5 - 5.5}{1.5} = \frac{2.0}{1.5} = 1.33$$

Step 5: Use column 2 of Appendix Table 1, which indicates that .4082 of the scores fall between a z-score of 1.33 and the mean.

Step 6: Add the values from steps 3 and 5.

FIGURE 5.7   Finding the Proportion of Scores Between 4.5 and 7.5

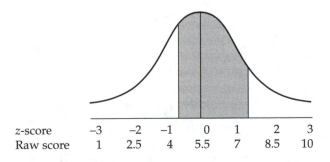

z-score	−3	−2	−1	0	1	2	3
Raw score	1	2.5	4	5.5	7	8.5	10

Thus a total proportion of .2486 + .4082 = .6568 of all the reading test scores lie between the grade level equivalents of 4.5 and 7.5. ∎

Although the previous example was straightforward, finding the proportion of scores falling between two values that both lie above or both lie below the mean is somewhat trickier, particularly in the absence of a diagram.

EXAMPLE

Suppose that you are running a marketing survey and want to know the proportion of your respondents who have family incomes between $50,000 and $75,000 per year. The mean family income of your sample is $40,000, and the standard deviation is $12,000.

Solution: The very first thing to do in this case is to consider whether or not income is approximately normally distributed in your sample, since it would be incorrect to use the normal curve table to draw inferences about a distribution that was grossly abnormal. Assuming that income turns out to be roughly normally distributed, you would draw your graph similar to the one shown in Figure 5.8, noting that all of the people of interest had incomes above average. As it happens, several different approaches can be used to solve this problem.

1. One way is to look at the proportion of scores between the mean and the more extreme score of interest and to subtract from that the proportion of scores between the mean and the less extreme score. In this sample, $75,000 is more extreme (i.e., farther from the mean) than $50,000. The z-score corresponding to a raw score of $50,000 = (50 – 40)/12 = .83. According to column 2 of Appendix Table 1, .2967 of the scores lie between $40,000 and $50,000. Using the same procedures, you can see that the z-score corresponding to an income of $75,000 = (75 – 40)/12 = 2.92; .4982 of all the scores lie between a z-score of 2.92 and the mean. To get the proportion of incomes between $75,000 and $50,000, you subtract .2967 from .4982 to get .2015.

FIGURE 5.8   Finding the Proportion of Incomes Between 50K and 75K

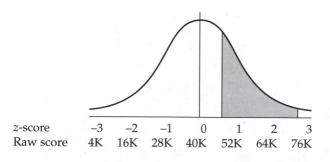

| z-score | –3 | –2 | –1 | 0 | 1 | 2 | 3 |
| Raw score | 4K | 16K | 28K | 40K | 52K | 64K | 76K |

2. An alternative way to solve the problem involves focusing on the scores farther away from the mean than the scores of interest. In this sample, .2033 of all the scores are farther from the mean than a z-score of .83, and .0018 of all the scores are farther from the mean than a z-score of 2.92. Subtracting, you again get .2015 as the proportion of scores between those two values.

3. A final way to solve the problem is to remember that .5000 of the scores are above the mean. Of these, .2967 fall between the mean and $50,000. An additional .0018 of the scores are more extreme than $75,000, leaving .5000 −.2967 −.0018 or .2015 of the scores between $50,000 and $75,000. ▪

Finding Percentages or Numbers of Scores Within Certain Limits. A variant on the types of problems considered thus far has a question about the percentages or numbers of scores rather than the proportions that fall into certain ranges. Such questions are solved like the previous ones with the addition of an extra step. Once the desired proportion has been obtained from the table, this proportion must be converted either to a percentage or, for other questions, to a number or frequency. You already know from Chapter 1 that to convert a proportion to a percentage you simply multiply the proportion by 100, a procedure equivalent to moving the decimal place two places to the right. Although this step is easy to do, it is also easy to forget; so take the time to see whether the answer requested is a proportion or a percentage.

In order to convert the proportion to a frequency or number of scores, it is necessary to multiply it by the total sample size, N. Thus, in the previous example, if the family incomes of 300 individuals had been sampled, the proportion of .2015 would correspond to .2015(300) or 60.45 individuals. Looking at this response, it is obvious that it can be only an approximation, as it is impossible to have .45 of a person (we'll exclude pregnancies, multiple personalities, and people who are half-asleep).

TIP ▬▬▬▬▬▬▬▬▬▬▬▬▬▬▬▬▬▬▬▬

> Whether to report the exact number computed or to round it off to the nearest whole person is a matter of personal preference. However, when the answer requested is a percentage or proportion, researchers do not round it off to a proportion that would correspond to a whole number of individuals.

Finding Scores That Cut Off Certain Percentages. Another type of problem that can be solved by using a normal curve table concerns finding scores that cut off certain percentages of a distribution or, in other words, finding certain percentile points.

EXAMPLE

Suppose you are running a training program for highly skilled athletes and wish to limit your participants to the top 2% of all athletes, as measured by a score on a test of athletic ability. You know that the test of athletic ability had a mean of 40 points and a standard deviation of 10 points. You want to find the raw score that corresponds to the 98th percentile and thus cuts off the top 2% of the scores.

Solution

Step 1: As always, draw a graph, which in this case will look like the one shown in Figure 5.9. From the figure, you can see that you need to find the score that has .02 of the scores above it (or farther away from the mean).

Step 2: Find this score by going to column 3 of Appendix Table 1 and looking for .0200, which represents 2% of the scores beyond the corresponding z-value.

Step 3: Move to column 1 of the table, which reveals that the z-value that cuts off the top 2% of the scores is between 2.05 and 2.06. Since .0202, which corresponds to a z-score of 2.05, is closer to .0200 than is .0197, which corresponds to a z-score of 2.06, use 2.05 as the z-score.

Step 4: Find the raw score that corresponds to a z-score of 2.05. To do that, first multiply the z-score by the standard deviation:

$2.05(10) = 20.5$

Step 5: Add the 20.5 to the mean of 40 to obtain the score that cuts off the top 2% of the distribution:

$20.5 + 40 = 60.5$ ■

A somewhat more complicated version of this type of problem occurs when you want a score that necessitates considering scores on the other side of the mean to arrive at the appropriate cutoff. Suppose, for example, that you wanted to identify the 70th percentile, as illustrated in Figure 5.10.

FIGURE 5.9   Finding the 98th Percentile

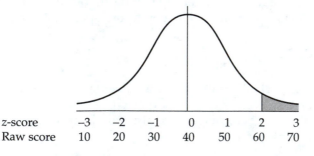

| | z-score | −3 | −2 | −1 | 0 | 1 | 2 | 3 |
| | Raw score | 10 | 20 | 30 | 40 | 50 | 60 | 70 |

FIGURE 5.10   Finding the 70th Percentile

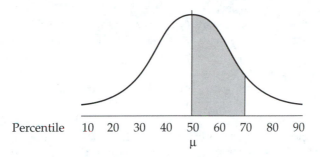

Percentile   10   20   30   40   50   60   70   80   90
                            μ

- First, you would have to convert 70% to .7000.
- Then you would subtract .5000 to get .2000, which is the proportion of scores between the z-score you need and the mean.
- Looking in Appendix Table 1, you should see that a proportion of .2000 in column 2 corresponds to a z-score between .52 and .53, but a little closer to .52. Alternatively, you could have used column 3 and looked for the z-score that was associated with a proportion of .3000 farther away from the mean. This z-score is, of course, .52.
- Once this z-score was found, you could find the corresponding raw score by using the formula $X = z(s) + \overline{X}$.

Suppose that you had wanted the 30th percentile instead of the 70th percentile. In this case, you could have used the same column from Appendix Table 1, but you would have had to recognize that in this case your z-value would be negative and the corresponding raw score would therefore be below the mean.

TIP ▬▬▬▬▬▬▬▬▬▬▬▬▬▬▬▬▬▬▬▬▬▬▬▬

> Remember that any percentile rank below 50 corresponds to a negative z-score and a raw score below the mean.

Inclusion and Exclusion Problems.   Still another related type of problem involves finding the values that identify the middle X% of all the scores. A private school might want to report, for example, that 95% of its students score between X and Y on a standardized test, or a public school might want to assign the top 3% and the bottom 3% to special education classes. In these cases, and in most problems of this type, the researcher is searching for a symmetric pair of cutoff scores, which cut off equal percentages at each end. However, there is no logical reason why someone could not want to know the scores that cut off the bottom 7% and the top 3%, if this information would be useful.

Example of an Inclusion Problem. As an example of an inclusion problem, suppose that you decide that you want to manufacture shoes that will fit 98% of the male population, leaving the 1% with the biggest feet and the 1% with the smallest feet to go barefoot or weave their own sandals. You want to know what sizes to manufacture, recognizing that shoes come in sizes measured to the nearest half unit (e.g., you can get a size 8 1/2 shoe but not a size 8.7 shoe). We'll assume that the mean shoe size is 10, that the standard deviation is 1.2, and that shoe size is normally distributed. This latter assumption must be literally wrong, since measured shoe size is a discrete quantitative variable. However, foot size is probably normally distributed, and shoe size is probably close enough to permit use of the normal curve table. The problem, therefore, is to find the shoe sizes that cut off the middle 98% of the population. From the graph in Figure 5.11, you can see that you need to find the absolute value of z that has .4900 of the scores between it and the mean.

You need to determine the raw scores that correspond both to the corresponding negative z-score and to the positive z-score. The value of z that has .4900 of the scores between it and the mean, as seen in column 2 of Appendix Table 1, and that has .0100 of the scores farther away from the mean than it, as seen in column 3, is 2.33, which is seen in column 1 of the table. Therefore, the raw score corresponding to a z of –2.33 for this distribution is

$$(-2.33)(1.2) + 10 = -2.796 + 10 = 7.204$$

The raw score corresponding to a z of 2.33 is

$$2.796 + 10 = 12.796$$

Thus, to be sure of making shoes to fit the middle 98% of all men's feet, the manufacturer could make sizes 7 to 13, thus fitting more than 98% of all men.

This example illustrates that inclusion problems are worded in terms of scores that include a certain percentage or proportion of the distribution. Confidence intervals, which will be discussed in Chapters 8 and 9, can be viewed as a type of inclusion problem.

FIGURE 5.11 Finding the Middle 98% of Scores

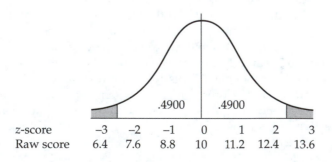

z-score	–3	–2	–1	0	1	2	3
Raw score	6.4	7.6	8.8	10	11.2	12.4	13.6

Example of an Exclusion Problem. Sometimes problems are worded in terms of excluding a certain proportion of the scores. An example of an exclusion problem would be to find the scores that identify the most extreme percentages, perhaps the cutoffs for the top and bottom 5%.

If you were a physician, for instance, you might want to identify children who are in the bottom 5% of weight for height, given their sex and age, and also children who are in the top 5% of weight for height. Some members of the former group may be at risk for malnutrition or undernutrition, and members of the latter group may suffer from overnutrition or obesity. Indeed, growth charts for physicians are available that identify these and other cutoff points.

If, for example, the mean weight for 10-year-old girls 56″ tall is 80 pounds, with a standard deviation of 10 pounds, then you can see from the graph in Figure 5.12 that the 5th percentile is somewhere around 60 pounds or so and the 95th percentile is somewhere around 100 pounds.

- To find the 95th percentile, you would look in column 3 of Appendix Table 1 for the value of .0500. Although there is no value of .0500 in column 3, values of .0505 and .0495 are listed. To be conservative and to be sure that you are including everyone in the top 5%, you might decide to use the value of .0505.
- Looking across to column 1 of the table, you can see that the corresponding z-score is 1.64. Similarly, the corresponding z-score for the 5th percentile is −1.64.
- Using the formula for finding the raw score at the 95th percentile, you would have $X = (1.64)(10) + 80$, or 96.4 pounds.
- To find the weight at the 5th percentile, you would use $X = (−1.64)(10) + 80$, which equals 63.6 pounds.

Finding Scores That Cut Off Certain Numbers.   Sometimes a researcher wants to find the raw scores that will identify a certain number of scores at one end of a distribution.

FIGURE 5.12   Finding the 5th and 95th Percentiles

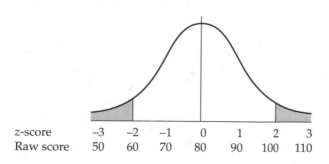

| z-score | −3 | −2 | −1 | 0 | 1 | 2 | 3 |
| Raw score | 50 | 60 | 70 | 80 | 90 | 100 | 110 |

EXAMPLE ▬▬▬▬▬▬▬▬▬▬▬▬▬▬▬▬▬▬▬▬▬▬▬▬▬▬▬▬

Suppose that you are director of admissions for a law school and that you can admit only 120 out of 802 applicants. You have managed, by certain devious processes that shall remain unspecified, to assign every applicant a numerical value between 32 and 165. These scores have a mean of 99 and a standard deviation of 11. What is the cutoff point for accepting the top 120 candidates?

TIP ▬▬▬▬▬▬▬▬▬▬▬▬▬▬▬▬▬▬▬▬▬▬▬▬▬▬▬▬

> You might object to calculating this point from a normal curve table by saying that you could simply rank all the scores and count off the top 120. This is certainly true, although whether or not that is an easier process is not clear. However, we'll go on to solve this problem, recognizing that the same procedures could be used to identify any kind of cutoff score, not just the top 120.

Solution: To solve this problem, you first draw a graph, as shown in Figure 5.13, and then translate the frequency or number to be cut off into a proportion so that you can use Appendix Table 1.

- Divide 120 by the population size of 802, getting .1496, the proportion of scores that are more extreme than the projected cutoff point.
- Look in column 3 of the table to find the closest value to .1496, which seems to be .1492. This value corresponds to a z-score of 1.04 in column 1.
- Convert the z-score of 1.04 to a raw score by multiplying it by the standard deviation and adding it to the mean. Thus the correct cutoff score is

$$1.04(11) + 99 = 11.44 + 99 = 110.44$$

FIGURE 5.13 Finding the Top 120 of 802 Scores

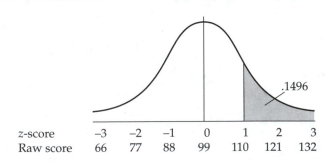

| z-score | −3 | −2 | −1 | 0 | 1 | 2 | 3 |
| Raw score | 66 | 77 | 88 | 99 | 110 | 121 | 132 |

Deciding If a Distribution Is Close to Normal. A final kind of problem that requires the use of a normal curve table involves deciding whether or not a particular distribution is close to normal. Suppose, for example, that you are assigning letter grades and have been told that these grades should fit a normal curve. Before doing so, you want to look at the distribution of total points earned in the class, in order to see whether that distribution is close to normal. If you calculate the mean and standard deviation of the distribution of points, you can then use Appendix Table 1 to calculate what proportion of the scores should lie between any two values if the distribution is truly normal.

For instance, we can use Appendix Table 1 to see that .1915 of the scores in a normal distribution should lie between a z-score of −.5 and the mean, and .1915 of the scores in a normal distribution should lie between a z-score of +.5 and the mean. If the distribution were vastly different from this, one might conclude that it was nowhere near normal.

Of course, the distribution of letter grades can never be exactly normal, as letter grades are discrete categories and cannot ordinarily exceed A or be below F. However, if the mean is considered to be 2.00 (a C), you could have a distribution that was reasonably close to normal, depending on what you identified as the standard deviation. At the very least, you would want a nearly normal distribution to be symmetric, with all of the scores falling between F and A (or perhaps F− and A+ at some schools).

Using the Normal Curve to Solve Problems

General purpose: To draw inferences about values, numbers, or proportions of scores that fit certain parameters.

Assumptions:

- A continuous quantitative variable
- Approximately normally distributed scores
- A known mean and standard deviation

Types of problems:

- Finding the proportions or numbers above or below certain scores
- Finding the proportions or numbers between two scores
- Finding the percentages or numbers of scores within certain limits
- Finding the values that cut off certain percentages
- Finding the values that identify the middle X% of all the scores
- Finding the scores that cut off certain frequencies
- Deciding if a distribution is close to normal

What Are Some General Guidelines for Solving Normal Curve Problems?

Unlike some formulas that will be covered in this book, there is no algorithm or rigid set of rules that can be blindly applied to arrive at the correct numerical solution for all normal curve problems. No computer can automatically solve these problems, as it takes a human being to figure out what kind of response is being requested. However, the guidelines given in this section can help you think through the problem and decide on the steps to take in answering it. Observing these guidelines should help you in solving such problems.

Decide Whether or Not the Normal Curve Can Be Used.   You need to consider the nature of the data and to look at the shape of the distribution. If the dependent measure is a qualitative variable, such as preferred brand of canned creamed corn, these responses (e.g., brand names) cannot be logically ordered along a quantitative dimension, and the normal curve cannot be used. If the distribution of the population or sample is obviously bimodal or skewed, then the normal curve would not be appropriate. The normal curve table is used when the problem deals with the proportions, numbers, probabilities, or percentages of scores falling between certain values, when the sample size is reasonably large and when the distribution is roughly bell shaped.

Draw a Graph.   It is certainly possible to solve normal curve problems without drawing a graph if you are completely clear as to what the problem entails. However, almost everyone who deals with such problems finds it beneficial to draw a graph first, in order to identify exactly what is being asked. By marking off the area that is relevant to the solution, you can see whether you need to use column 2 or column 3 of the normal curve table, and whether or not you need to consider the scores on the other side of the mean. You will also be reminded of whether you are dealing with a negative z-score (i.e., a raw score below the mean) or with a positive z-score. Labeling the x-axis in both z-scores and raw scores, although it may take an extra minute, can save many more minutes in puzzling out what steps to take in solving the problem.

Estimate What Would Be a Reasonable Answer.   One of the most important reasons to draw a graph is that it can help you estimate what would be a reasonable answer to the problem. Common sense is another important aid. To decide what kind of answer is reasonable, you have to consider what is being sought—percentages, frequencies, proportions, or scores? For instance, if the question concerns the proportion of people scoring below some value that is itself below the mean, you should recognize that the only reasonable answers will be numbers between .0001 and .5000. If the question concerns the number of scores falling between certain values, the response will be some positive number that is less than the sample size. If a score that cuts off the top several percent is being requested, the response should be a score that would be considered high with respect to the distribution of raw scores.

Some people find it helpful to think in terms of a distribution of percentiles when conceptualizing normal curve problems and trying to estimate what a reasonable answer would be. Many people need to be particularly careful to keep in mind the distinction between proportions and percentages when the problem asks for the percentage or proportion falling above some extreme value; a proportion of .04 is not the same as .04%, even though both are small values.

By estimating, even within very broad limits, what kind of answer would be reasonable, you can sometimes identify instances in which you must have used the wrong procedure or made a serious computational error. Taking the time to make (and write down) such an estimate can save a lot of time and frustration in actually solving the problem.

Decide on the Steps to Follow.   Once you have seen from the graph what is being requested and have estimated what kind of answer would be reasonable, it should be relatively easy to decide on the appropriate steps to follow. Usually, you can follow one of the examples described in this chapter. However, there are a few general tricks that usually work when you are stuck on a problem.

1. If you begin with a raw score, convert it to a z-score.
2. Think about whether you want the area between the z-score and the mean (column 2 of Appendix Table 1) or farther away from the mean than the z-score (column 3 of the table).
3. If you begin with a percentage, convert it to a proportion and then look for the corresponding z-score. Remember that you have to think about whether the relevant proportion is more extreme than z or between z and the mean.
4. Check to see whether the answer requested is a proportion, percentage, or frequency. If necessary, convert the proportion from the table to a percentage or frequency.

General Guidelines for Solving Normal Curve Problems

1. Decide whether the normal curve can be used.
2. Draw a graph.
3. Estimate what would be a reasonable answer.
4. Decide on the steps to follow, based on the type of problem.

5. Similarly, check to see whether the answer requested is a *z*-score or a raw score. If the latter, be sure to convert your *z*-score to a raw score. If you're dealing with a score below the mean, don't forget that your *z*-score is negative.

6. If you wish to identify the middle X% (e.g., the middle 95%), remember that you want to find the *z*-scores and then the raw scores that cut off half of X% (e.g., 2½%) at either end.

Deciding When to Use the Technique

The normal curve table is used to solve problems in which you want to find the percentages or proportions or frequencies falling within certain limits or to find the scores that cut off certain percentages, proportions, or numbers in an approximately normal distribution of scores. If the mean and standard deviation of a large, approximately normal distribution of scores are known, regardless of whether the distribution is of a sample or an entire population, the use of the normal curve table can be very helpful. It is most commonly used with standardized tests or other instruments that have been given to large normative samples of individuals, as is the case in both educational and business settings. To a large extent, the information used to solve these problems overlaps with the information contained in a percentile distribution, so the use of both procedures is rarely necessary.

CHAPTER SUMMARY

Unlike previous chapters, which have focused on empirical distributions of actual data, this chapter focused on theoretical distributions, which are mathematical distributions useful in drawing inferences about the likelihood or probability of certain outcomes. The probability of an event is the proportion of times that it will occur. It can be calculated when you know all of the possible outcomes and which ones of those will be considered instances of the event. Probabilities that both of two events or either of two events will occur can also be calculated. Much of inferential statistics deals with estimating the probability of various outcomes.

The binomial distribution is the distribution of events that have only two possible outcomes, like "yes" or "no." The binomial distribution is often used to estimate the likelihood of various independent events, like getting three heads in a row when tossing a coin.

The normal distribution is the one that underlies much of inferential statistics. If a score is selected randomly from a normal distribution, there is a known probability that the score will fall within certain limits. The area under the normal curve can be divided up into mutually exclusive parts, with the probabilities of all of these parts summing to 1.00. With a normal distribution, *z*-scores can be directly converted to percentiles and vice versa.

A normal curve table, which gives the probabilities that a score will fall between the mean and any possible z-score, can be used to solve a number of possible problems involving scores believed to be normally distributed. For example, you can find the proportion of scores above or below certain scores, the proportion between two scores, the percentages or numbers of scores within certain limits, the scores that cut off certain proportions, the scores that include or exclude certain proportions, and the scores that cut off certain numbers. In order to solve such problems, it is useful to consider using interpolation, to draw a graph of the distribution and the problem, to estimate what would be a reasonable answer, and to think through the steps to follow.

CHAPTER REVIEW

Multiple-Choice Questions

1. What percentage of the scores in a normal distribution lie below a z-score of 1.65?

   a. 1.65%   **b.** 15%   **c.** 45%   **d.** 60%   **e.** 75%   **f.** 90%   **g.** 95%

2. Suppose that the probability of a kitten being a female is .5 and that the probability of any one kitten being born female is unrelated to the probability of any other kitten being born female. What is the probability that in a litter of 3 kittens, all 3 will be born female?

   a. .037   **b.** .125   **c.** .250   **d.** .333   **e.** .500

3. What percentage of the scores in a normal distribution lie below a z-score of 0.50?

   a. 5%   **b.** 30.85%   **c.** 50%   **d.** 55%   **e.** 69.15%   **f.** 80.85%

   g. none of the above

4. What is your chance of flipping 4 heads *or* 4 tails in a row with a fair coin (i.e., one that comes up heads 50% of the time)?

   a. .0625   **b.** .125   **c.** .250   **d.** .375   **e.** .500

5. What percentage of the scores in a normal distribution lie below a z-score of −1.8?

   a. −1.8%   **b.** 1.8%   **c.** 3.6%   **d.** 46.4%

   e. 48.2%   **f.** 53.6%   **g.** 98.2%

6. On a standardized test of flexibility, the average score for 2000 14-year-olds was 35, $\sigma = 7$. The students in your school had a mean score of 28. How many of the 2000 students in the national survey did better than the mean score of the students in your school?

   a. 16   **b.** 168   **c.** 683   **d.** 1168   **e.** 1683

7. Which of the following is true of the normal distribution?

   a. It is an empirical distribution.

b. It is a theoretical distribution.

c. It is a skewed distribution.

d. It applies to both quantitative and qualitative data.

e. Both b and d are true.

f. It can take any shape, depending on the nature of the data.

8. What percentage of the scores in a normal distribution lie below a z-score of −.75?

   a. −.75   b. .75%   c. 7.5%   d. 22.66%   e. 27.34%   f. 72.66%

   g. none of the above

9. If a distribution is normal, what values cut off the middle 30% of the scores?

   a. the 35th and 65th percentiles

   b. z-scores of −.30 and +.30

   c. a z-score of −.84 and the mean

   d. z-scores of −.84 and +.84

   e. none of the above

Problems

10. Suppose that exactly half of the students in a class are male, and you independently select 3 students from the class.

    a. What is the probability that all of them will be male? Assume that you have sampled with replacement, so that the probability of getting a male remains .5 for each choice.

    b. What is the probability of selecting at least 2 males?

11. In a normal distribution, what proportion of the scores fall between a z-score of −1.5 and

    a. the mean?   b. a z-score of +.25?   c. a z-score of −.25?

12. Researchers with the Allergy Association questioned a random sample of 2000 adults about the number of times they sneezed per day. They found a roughly normal distribution of sneezes, with a mean of 14 per day and a standard deviation of 3.

    a. Al sneezes 10 times per day. What percentage of people sneeze less frequently than Al?

    b. Based on the above data, how many of the 2000 people surveyed sneezed between 10 and 12 times per day?

13. Your best friend, Alberta, seems very depressed to you and starts attending a program for depressed people in the community. The 100 people in the program are given the Depression Energy Profile Rating (DEPR) test, and their mean score is 85, with a standard deviation of 15. For the standardization sample of 1000 nondepressed individuals who took the test to standardize it,

the mean score was 50 with a standard deviation of 20. Alberta's score on the DEPR test was 80.

a. What was Alberta's z-score compared to the standardization sample?

b. What was Alberta's z-score compared to the other people in her program?

c. What percentage of the standardization sample was more depressed (or at least scored higher on the test) than Alberta?

d. How many people in the standardization sample got higher scores than Alberta?

e. How many people in her program were more depressed than Alberta?

f. Based on the above data, what would you say to someone who wanted to know whether or not Alberta was depressed?

14. Assume that a sample of 400 school districts indicated that the mean per-pupil expenditure was $1600, $s = \$300$.

a. How many school districts spent between $1000 and $1800 per pupil?

b. Cacophony County is ranked 360th of the 400 schools in per-pupil expenditure. How much money does it spend per pupil?

c. The federal government has decided to sue all school districts in the sample that spend less than $900 per pupil. How many districts will it sue?

d. If you were to pick one school district at random, what is the probability that it spends between $1700 and $2000 per pupil?

15. If you draw a card from a deck of 52 cards, what is the probability

a. that it is either an ace or a king?

b. that it is a spade or a club?

c. that it is the king of clubs?

16. Joe got a raw score of 69 on a test on which the mean was 90. His z-score was −3. What was the standard deviation of the test scores?

17. Suppose that there are 40 girls and 45 boys in kindergarten, 60 girls and 60 boys in first grade, 65 girls and 60 boys in second grade, and 70 girls and 70 boys in third grade in a particular elementary school.

a. What is the probability that a child picked at random from the above population will be a boy?

b. What is the probability that a child picked at random will be a kindergarten boy?

c. What is the probability that two children picked at random will both be boys?

d. What is the probability that two children picked at random will both be first graders?

e. If two children are picked at random, what is the probability that at least one of them will be a boy?

18. A researcher has developed a test that measures the ability of middle school students to understand grammatically complex sentences. A nationally normed sample produced a mean score of 58 with a standard deviation of 7.

   a. What are the 25th, 50th, and 75th percentiles on this test?

   b. What is the interquartile range?

   c. What is the 99.9th percentile?

19. A rubber band manufacturer wants to be sure that the rubber bands produced are within certain limits. When a sample of 500 three-inch rubber bands is taken and measured, it turns out to have a mean of 3.01 inches and a standard deviation of .100 inch.

   a. What proportion of the rubber bands are longer than 3 inches?

   b. How many rubber bands are shorter than 2.85 inches?

   c. The manufacturer wants to discard all rubber bands that are outside the limits of 2.85 to 3.15 inches. What proportion of the rubber bands will be discarded?

   d. How many of the 500 rubber bands will not be discarded?

20. A national sample of social workers employed full time indicated that their mean annual salary was $48,770, $s = \$8000$. A sample of social workers in Louisiana indicated that their mean annual salary was $40,225, $s = \$5000$.

   a. Arlene has been offered a beginning social work position for $30,000 in Baton Rouge, Louisiana. What is the z-score for this job compared with the national sample?

   b. What is the z-score for the job offered Arlene compared to the Louisiana sample?

   c. Why are these z-scores negative?

   d. Why are they different from each other?

   e. What would Arlene's percentile rank be compared to other social workers in Louisiana if she took the job?

Study Questions

1. Imagine that you are in charge of special education for a large school district. You need to estimate the numbers of children who will be in various special education classes; you need to decide on cutoff points for entry into such classes; you need to make decisions about allocating funds based on the numbers of children in special education programs. You have access to various tests that have been given to children in your school district. Try to describe some ways in which you might use the normal curve table to solve problems you would encounter.

2. See if you can think of ten (yes, 10) variables that seem to fit a binomial distribution. For each of them, think of a question that someone might ask about the probability of some event occurring.

3. Why do you think that the procedures for computing probabilities are easier when the events to be considered are independent? Try to think of some examples of two events that are not independent. How would you compute the likelihood of (both or either of) such events occurring? Similarly, suppose that you had sampling without replacement. For example, you might pick one of 10 children in a class and then plan to pick another. How would the probability of your selecting a male (for example) as the second child in your sample be affected if one child has already been withdrawn from the population?

4. The phrases "probability of an event," "relative frequency of an event," "likelihood of an event," or "proportion of times an event will occur" all refer to the same thing. Do they have the same connotations in everyday speech? Take a problem dealing with the probability of something occurring and see how many different ways you can word it in order to have it be the same problem.

5. Try to teach someone else to solve some kind of problem with probability—probably a problem dealing with either the binomial distribution or the normal curve. You can try to explain the theory behind it or simply show them how to do it, step by step. What difficulties do you encounter? What questions do they have? Do they raise issues that make you think more carefully about the concept of probability?

Correlation

What Is Correlation?

Up until this point, we have been focusing primarily on research dealing with a single dependent measure or variable and on the ways to describe the scores on that variable. Quite frequently, however, a researcher wants to look not at only one variable, or even at the effects of one independent variable on a single dependent measure, but at the **correlation**, or statistical relationship between two variables, which are usually symbolized by X and Y.

In order to study the relationship between two variables, it is necessary to consider the distribution of scores on two variables, which is sometimes called a **bivariate distribution**. Such a distribution implies that each individual or unit has a score on each of two variables, or that the basic data can be viewed as pairs of scores rather than individual scores.

EXAMPLE

Friendship Study. Suppose you are interested in learning about the relationship between number of friends people have (which we could call X) and average depth of friendship (Y). You could measure the number of friends by asking each subject to name all of his or her friends. Depth of friendship could be measured by asking each of the friends named to indicate how close their relationship to the subject is on a seven-point scale and taking the mean rating across all of each subject's friends. Each person would then have a score on two variables: number of friends and average depth of friendship.

You would then be in a position to see whether people with more friends have stronger friendships (based on the theory that some people are more sociable and some are relative loners) or whether people with more friends have more superficial relationships and those with fewer friends have deeper ones (based on the theory that you have only so much emotion and time to invest in friendships and that it can either be spread thin or concentrated). Of course, it could also be the case that number of friends and average depth of friendship are completely unrelated. How could you tell?   ■

Correlation Coefficient.   One way of assessing a relationship such as the one in the preceding example is by using a numerical measure of association known as a correlation coefficient. A **correlation coefficient** is a way of describing some aspects of a bivariate distribution. In the example, each person's number of friends (X) and average depth of friendship as rated by those friends (Y) would serve as the two scores of one pair.

Use of Scattergraphs

One way of viewing a bivariate distribution is by considering the type of graphical representation known as a scattergram, scattergraph, or scatterplot, which was described in Chapter 3. A *scattergraph* represents individual pairs of scores on two variables, with one variable listed along the x-axis and the other along the y-axis. Each point on the scattergraph indicates an individual's score on both dimensions or variables. By looking at the pattern of scores on the scattergraph, both a visual and a conceptual picture of the relationship between the variables can be obtained. A scattergraph is a pictorial representation of the relationship represented numerically by a correlation coefficient.

Direction of the Relationship.   The pattern of the points on the scattergraph provides a clue to the direction of the relationship between the variables.

Positive Correlations. Since a point near the left-hand side of the graph represents a low score on X and a point near the bottom of the graph represents a low score on Y, a point in the lower left-hand corner would represent a low score on both X and Y. Similarly, a point in the upper right-hand corner would represent a high score on both variables. Thus, a scattergraph in which the points are scattered from lower left to upper right, such as the one shown in Figure 6.1, indicates that low scores on one variable tend to be paired with low scores on the other variable and, conversely, that high scores on one variable are associated with high scores on the other. Such a relationship reflects a **positive correlation**, or direct relationship. If number of friends were listed along the x-axis and depth of friendship along the y-axis, such a pattern would indicate that people with more friends have deeper friendships.

Negative Correlations. Alternatively, a scattergraph in which the points go from upper left, reflecting high scores on Y and low scores on X, to lower right, reflecting low scores on Y and high scores on X, indicates that high scores on one variable are associated with low scores on the other variable and vice versa. Such a relationship, which is shown in Figure 6.2, reflects a **negative correlation**, or inverse relationship. If people with fewer friends had the deepest relationships, such a pattern would be found.

FIGURE 6.1   Scattergraph of a Positive Relationship Between X and Y

An example of a positive correlation would be the relationship between achievement test scores and any of a number of variables: score on another achievement test, score on an aptitude test, grades in school, and interest in the subject matter, to name a few. An example of a negative correlation would be between jockeys' weights and the number of races they win (or perhaps the number of commercials they are hired to do selling diet products).

Curvilinear Relationships. Another pattern of relationship that can be reflected in a scattergraph is what is called a curvilinear relationship. In a **curvilinear relationship**, there is a pattern of scores, but it does not fit a straight line. Instead, typically, low scores on one of the variables, usually graphed on the y-axis, are associated with both high and low scores on the x-axis, as in the graph in Figure 6.3. It is clear from looking at the data that scores on X and Y are related; someone with a moderate score on X is likely to have a high score on Y, whereas a person with either a very low score or a very high score on X is likely to have a low score on Y. However, it is equally clear that the relationship is not a linear one; you cannot say that scores on Y increase or decrease consistently as scores on X increase.

An example of a curvilinear relationship is the association between weight and health; people with moderate weights are healthier than those with either extremely high or extremely low weights. If the relationship

FIGURE 6.2   Scattergraph of a Negative Relationship Between X and Y

FIGURE 6.3   Scattergraph of a Curvilinear Relationship Between X and Y

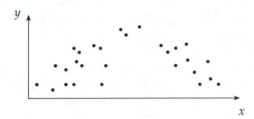

between number of friends and depth of friendship were curvilinear, it would suggest that both people with many friends and those with very few friends are likely to have relationships that are more superficial than those with an intermediate number of friends.

Near-Zero Relationship. A final pattern of scores that can be seen on a scattergraph is a big "blob"—that is, as illustrated in Figure 6.4, the points seem to be all over the place. In such a case, there is no obvious relationship between scores on X and Y, since a high, medium, or low score on either variable seems equally likely to be associated with a high, medium, or low score on the other. In such cases, it appears that knowing someone's score on variable X tells you nothing about that person's score on variable Y and vice versa. Presumably, the correlation between annual rainfall in Spain and annual sales of the recording of "My Fair Lady" in Albuquerque over several decades is near zero.

Strength of the Relationship.   Besides giving a literal picture of the relationship between two variables, a scattergraph also gives a clue to the strength of the relationship. If the two variables are perfectly correlated, meaning that it is possible to predict score on Y exactly from knowing score on X, then all of the points reflecting pairs of scores on X and Y will fall on a line. If the relationship is weaker, then fewer of the points will fall on the line and many of them will fall far from the line. Finally, if there is no relationship

FIGURE 6.4   Scattergraph of a Near-Zero Relationship Between X and Y

between scores on the two variables, then the points will fall all over the graph, forming a big blob.

Regression Line.   When there is a perfect linear or straight-line relationship between two variables, then all of the points representing pairs of scores on the two variables will fall on a straight line known as the regression line. The **regression line** for predicting Y is the straight line that minimizes the sum of the squared deviations between the predicted values on Y and the actual values; the equation for the regression line is called the *regression equation*. If there are no deviations—that is, if the predicted scores and the actual scores coincide—then all the points will lie exactly on the regression line. The farther the points are from the regression line, the weaker is the linear relationship between the two variables and the less accurate the prediction from one variable to another based on a regression equation.

If the regression line goes from lower left to upper right, then the relationship between the variables is positive; if the regression line goes from upper left to lower right, then the relationship is negative. The regression line will be discussed in more detail in Chapter 7, as part of the general topic of regression.

Characteristics of Correlations

Characteristics of a positive correlation:

- High scores on X go with high scores on Y and low with low.
- Points on the scattergraph go from lower left to upper right.
- Also called a direct relationship.

Characteristics of a negative correlation:

- High scores on X go with low scores on Y and low with high.
- Points on the scattergraph go from upper left to lower right.
- Also called an inverse relationship.

Characteristics of a zero correlation:

- Reflects a lack of a linear relationship between X and Y.
- May reflect a curvilinear relationship.

What Is the Pearson *r* Statistic?

The **Pearson product-moment correlation coefficient,** or Pearson *r*, invented by Karl Pearson, is a measure of the degree of linear relationship between two interval- or ratio-level variables. The value of *r* gives information about both the strength and the direction of the relationship.

FIGURE 6.5   Range of Values for Pearson *r*

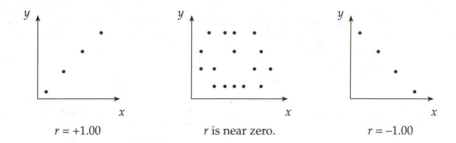

r = +1.00   r is near zero.   r = −1.00

Range of Values of *r*

Pearson *r*, or indeed any correlation coefficient, can take on values only between −1 and +1. As illustrated in Figure 6.5, a value of +1 indicates a perfect positive linear relationship, reflecting the fact that the higher the score on *X*, the higher the score on *Y* and vice versa. Conversely, a negative value of Pearson *r* indicates that low scores on *X* go with high scores on *Y*. An *r* of either +1 or −1 indicates perfect prediction, as well as the direction of the relationship; there will be no errors in predicting scores on *X* or on *Y* if *r* is +1 or −1. An *r* of zero, on the other hand, means that there is no linear relationship between *X* and *Y* and that the points representing scores on both variables do not lie close to a straight line. In other words, unless there is some curvilinear or other complex relationship between *X* and *Y*, a person's score on *X* tells you nothing about his score on *Y* and vice versa.

Assumptions of Pearson *r*

Before any statistical procedure can be appropriately used, it is important that certain assumptions be met. Some procedures are robust to violations of certain assumptions—that is, you will come to the correct conclusions even if some of the assumptions are not met. Pearson *r* is a parametric procedure and, like other statistical techniques, has certain assumptions that should be satisfied for it to be used.

Interval/Ratio-Scale Data.   One of the usual assumptions underlying the use of the Pearson product-moment correlation coefficient is that the variables under consideration have been measured on an interval or ratio scale. Since the formula involves deviations from mean scores on the variables, it does not make sense to calculate a Pearson *r* if it does not make sense to calculate a mean of the raw scores on each variable. Almost all researchers agree that variables measured on equal-appearing interval scales, such as the seven-point scale measuring perceived depth of friendship, are close enough to a true interval scale to make it reasonable to compute a mean and to use parametric procedures such as Pearson r. It is true that some correlation coefficients based on Pearson r can be calculated between two variables, each consisting of only two levels (dichotomous or dichotomized variables). However, computing a correlation between a qualitative variable with more than two levels and another variable, or between raw scores on two ordinal variables when the raw scores are not ranks, will lead to a value that is uninterpretable.

TIP ▰▰▰▰▰▰▰▰▰▰▰▰▰▰▰▰▰▰▰▰▰▰▰▰▰▰▰▰

> There are other correlation coefficients that can be used to assess the relationship between two ordinal-level variables, including Spearman's rho, which will be discussed later in this chapter. Similarly, a statistical procedure called a *chi-square (χ^2) test of independence* can be used to assess whether or not there is an association or relationship between two nominal-level variables; it will be described in Chapter 13.

Linearity.   A second assumption of Pearson r is that it is to be used to assess the degree of linear relationship between the two variables. Pearson r gives an accurate measure of the linear relationship but does not directly assess the curvilinear relationship between the variables. An r of $+1$ or -1 means that there is no curvilinear relationship between the variables, because the linear trend accounts for the entire relationship between them. An r near zero could mean that the two variables are unconnected, but it could also mean that there is a strong curvilinear relationship between the variables.

Whenever you think that there is a possibility that two variables have a curvilinear relationship, it is important to draw a scattergraph to see whether or not there is such a relationship. For example, as illustrated in Figure 6.6, the relationship between arousal level and test score performance is usually determined to be curvilinear. That is, the best performance on a test is usually evidenced by someone who is neither so relaxed as to be asleep nor so panicky as to be unable to function. A Pearson r would be the wrong procedure to use to assess such a relationship, as it would (correctly) indicate that the linear relationship is zero, which is not what you would want to discover. A measure called the *correlation ratio*, η (eta), which is covered in more advanced texts, would be the appropriate one to assess a curvilinear relationship.

Random Sampling.   A third assumption for Pearson r is that the scores have been randomly sampled from the population. In other words, all individuals in the population had the same chance of being selected for the sample. If you violate this assumption, which is often done by researchers, you will have to be more cautious in generalizing your results.

FIGURE 6.6 Scattergraph of the Relationship Between Arousal Level and Test Performance

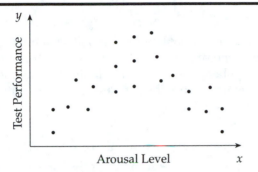

Normality of Distributions. Finally, when inferences are going to be drawn from a Pearson r, it is assumed that the distributions from which the scores have been sampled are normal. Violations of this assumption rarely lead to serious misinterpretations.

Restriction of Range

Although this is not an assumption for Pearson r, an important issue to consider in using Pearson r is whether the range of scores on both variables includes the entire range of scores to which you want to generalize. If you have a limited (or restricted) range of scores on one variable, then the value of the r that you correlate between that variable and a related variable will probably be lower than r would be if you had the entire range of scores in your sample.

For example, suppose that reading ability is highly positively correlated with knowledge of history in a population of seventh graders whose reading ability varies from second-grade level to twelfth-grade level. If you limit your sample to seventh graders whose reading ability ranges only from seventh-grade level to eighth-grade level, then the correlation coefficient between the reading scores of this sample and their knowledge of history is likely to be noticeably lower than the correlation for the entire population.

Formulas for Pearson r

There are a number of formulas for Pearson r, all yielding the same numerical answer, but varying in their ease of use and in the information that is necessary in order to use them. The formula that gives the best intuitive picture of what a correlation coefficient means, but that is the least convenient to compute from raw data, is the definitional formula or the z-score formula.

The z-Score Formula. The z-score formula is simple enough:

$$r = \frac{\Sigma z_X z_Y}{N}$$

where the z-scores have been calculated using both σ_X and σ_Y. It indicates that r equals the sum of the products of the pairs of z-scores on variables X and Y divided by the number of pairs of scores. In this formula, as in all of the formulas for r, N stands for the number of pairs of scores or the number of individuals having scores on X and Y. Use of the z-score formula requires several steps.

Step 1: Compute each person's z-score on X and z-score on Y.

Step 2: Multiply each person's z-score on X by his or her corresponding z-score on Y.

Step 3: Sum these N products.

Step 4: Divide this sum by N.

The only difficulty in using this formula arises from the inconvenience of calculating z-scores, which necessitates computing the mean and the standard deviation of the raw scores and then converting each raw score to a z-score. What's more, this has to be done twice, once for the distribution of the scores on variable X and once for the distribution of the scores on variable Y.

TIP

Unless you have access to z-scores or are planning to compute them anyway, as might be the case if you are planning to report test scores, this formula is too time consuming to be widely used.

Interpreting the Formula. Looking at the z-score formula for Pearson r can provide some insight into the meaning of a correlation coefficient. Suppose, for instance, that people who score above the mean on variable X are also above the mean on variable Y. These people will have positive z-scores on both variables and their cross products will be positive. Similarly, people who are below the mean on both variables will have negative z-scores on both and the products of their z-scores will also be positive. Thus, where there is a direct or positive correlation between the variables, the numerator of the formula for Pearson r will be positive. Since the denominator of the formula, N, is always a positive number, the value of r will be positive.

When scores are above the mean on one variable, leading to a positive z-score, and below the mean on the other variable, leading to a negative z-score, then the product of the z-scores on the two variables will be negative. If a bivariate distribution has scores above the mean on one variable associated with scores below the mean on the other and vice versa for most of the scores, then the numerator of the formula for r will be negative and r will be a negative number. Finally, if scores above the mean on one variable are approximately equally likely to be associated with scores above and below the mean on the other variable, then some of the cross products of the z-scores on X and Y will be negative and some will be positive, leading to a numerator and a value for r near zero.

TIP

> Notice that the product of two scores that are both very far from the mean contributes more to the value of r than does the product of two scores that are both very close to the mean. Pairs of extreme scores will have a major impact upon the value of r.

Another advantage of the z-score formula is that it makes it clearer that the values of the means and standard deviations of the original scores are removed from the correlation coefficient. In other words, it doesn't matter if the original units for X and Y are very different from each other; we can still calculate and interpret a correlation between them.

Formula Using Means. A far more convenient formula for computing the value of r uses the means and the standard deviations of the scores on both variables (using the formulas for σ, not s). This formula is

$$r = \frac{\dfrac{\Sigma XY}{N} - (\overline{X})(\overline{Y})}{\sigma_X \sigma_Y}$$

Using this formula requires the following steps:

Step 1: Multiply each person's raw score on X by his or her raw score on Y.

Step 2: Sum these products.

Step 3: Divide this sum by the sample size.

Step 4: Compute the means of X and Y.

Step 5: Multiply these means.

Step 6: Subtract this product from the quotient in step 2 to obtain the numerator of the formula.

Step 7: To get the denominator, compute the standard deviation of the scores on X and on Y, in both cases using the formulas with N rather than $N - 1$ in the denominator. In other words, you want to compute σ_X and σ_Y.

Step 8: Multiply these standard deviations.

Step 9: Divide the numerator from step 4 by this product to get r.

In situations in which you will be calculating the means and standard deviations of the scores on the variables, this formula is the easiest one to use, as long as you remember that it is σ, not s, in the denominator.

Raw Score Formula. The longest and most horrendous-looking formula for Pearson r, the raw score formula, is also the easiest to use in most circumstances. The raw score formula for r is

$$r = \frac{N\Sigma XY - \Sigma X\Sigma Y}{\sqrt{\left(N\Sigma X^2 - (\Sigma X)^2\right)\left(N\Sigma Y^2 - (\Sigma Y)^2\right)}}$$

To get the numerator of this formula, you proceed as follows:

Step 1: Multiply each raw score on X by the corresponding raw score on Y.

Step 2: Sum these products.

Step 3: Multiply the sum by N.

Step 4: Multiply the sum of all the raw scores on X by the sum of the raw scores on Y.

Step 5: Subtract this product from the product in step 3.

The denominator, which is the square root of the product of two numbers, is found as follows:

Step 6: To get the first number in the denominator, square the raw scores on X.

Step 7: Sum these squares.

Step 8: Multiply this sum by N.

Step 9: Square the sum of the raw scores on X.

Step 10: Subtract this number from the product in step 8.

Step 11: To get the second number in the denominator, square the raw scores on Y.

Step 12: Sum these squares.

Step 13: Multiply this sum by N.

Step 14: Square the number of the raw scores on Y.

Step 15: Subtract this number from the product in step 13.

Step 16: To get the denominator, multiply the numbers from steps 10 and 15 and take the square root of the product.

Step 17: To get r, you then divide the numerator in step 5 by the denominator in step 16.

Comparing the Formulas.   In order to see how the formulas for Pearson *r* work, let's take some data and use all the formulas with the same data.

EXAMPLE

Pet Ownership Study. Suppose you are interested in testing two opposing theories of pet ownership: one saying that people are either dog lovers or cat lovers, and the other saying that people are either animal lovers or not animal lovers. The first theory would predict a negative correlation between the number of cats and dogs that individuals own, and the second would predict a positive correlation. Having surveyed a small sample of people at a large shopping center, you have collected the data in the following table.

Person	Number of of Cats Owned	Number of Dogs Owned
Arnie	0	0
Bubba	1	2
Callie	2	1
Donnie	0	0
Eunice	3	3
Fannie	3	2
Gil1	0	

In order to use the formulas, we need to calculate some basic information. If the number of cats owned is considered X, then

$$\Sigma X = 10$$
$$\Sigma X^2 = 0 + 1 + 4 + 0 + 9 + 9 + 1 = 24$$

If the number of dogs owned is Y, then

$$\Sigma Y = 8$$
$$\Sigma Y^2 = 0 + 4 + 1 + 0 + 9 + 4 + 0 = 18$$

Since N, the number of pairs of scores, is 7, the mean of the raw scores on $X = 10/7 = 1.43$, and the mean of the raw scores on $Y = 8/7 = 1.14$. The sum of the cross products of the raw scores on X and Y is

$$(0)(0) + (1)(2) + (2)(1) + (0)(0) + (3)(3) + (3)(2) + (1)(0) =$$
$$0 + 2 + 2 + 0 + 9 + 6 + 0 = 19$$

We can put all of this information into an expanded version of the original table, as shown in Table 6.1.

TABLE 6.1 Data for the Pet Ownership Study Example

Person	X	X²	Y	Y²	XY
Arnie	0	0	0	0	0
Bubba	1	1	2	4	2
Callie	2	4	1	1	2
Donnie	0	0	0	0	0
Eunice	3	9	3	9	9
Fannie	3	9	2	4	6
Gil	1	1	0	0	0
Σ	10	24	8	18	19
	$\overline{X}=1.43$		$\overline{Y}=1.14$		

Solution with the Raw Score Formula: The numbers in Table 6.1 are all that we need to know in order to use the raw score formula for r.

- Find the numerator of the formula:

$$[(7)(19)] - [(10)(8)] = 133 - 80 = 53$$

- Find the denominator:

$$\sqrt{[(7)(24) - 10^2][7(18) - 8^2]} = \sqrt{(168 - 100)(126 - 64)}$$
$$= \sqrt{(68)(62)}$$
$$= \sqrt{4216} = 64.93$$

- The value of r is then

$$\frac{53}{64.93} = .816$$

Solution with the z-Score Formula: In order to use the z-score formula for r, it is helpful to calculate the deviation scores from the means of X and Y. These scores can be seen in Table 6.2, along with the squared deviations from the means of variables X and Y and their sums. As you know from Chapter 3, the sum of the deviation scores around the mean is zero. The fact that the sum of the deviation scores around the mean for Y appears to be 0.02 is due to rounding off.

Based on the information in Table 6.2, we can calculate σ_X and σ_Y, using the deviation score formulas:

$$\sigma_X = \sqrt{\frac{\Sigma(X - \mu)^2}{N}} = \sqrt{\frac{9.68}{7}} = \sqrt{1.38} = 1.18$$

TABLE 6.2 Deviation Scores for the Pet Ownership Study

Person	$X - \bar{X}$	$(X - \bar{X})^2$	$Y - \bar{Y}$	$(Y - \bar{Y})^2$
Arnie	−1.43	2.04	−1.14	1.30
Bubba	−0.43	0.18	0.86	0.74
Callie	0.57	0.32	−0.14	0.02
Donnie	−1.43	2.04	−1.14	1.30
Eunice	1.57	2.46	1.86	3.46
Fannie	1.57	2.46	0.86	0.74
Gil	−0.43	0.18	−1.14	1.30
Σ	0.00	9.68	0.02	8.86

Since the sum of the squared deviation scores for $Y = 8.86$,

$$\sigma_Y = \sqrt{\frac{8.86}{7}} = \sqrt{1.27} = 1.13$$

Now that we have the means and standard deviations of all the scores, we can calculate the z-scores corresponding to the raw scores on variables X and Y. The fact that we have already computed the deviation scores has saved us a step; all we need to do to get each z-score is to divide the deviation score by σ. Person A's z-score on X is therefore

$$\frac{-1.43}{1.18} = -1.22$$

and Person A's z-score on Y is

$$\frac{-1.14}{1.13} = -1.01$$

The z-scores of each person on X and Y, as well as the products of those z-scores, are given in Table 6.3. The sum of the cross products of the people's z-scores on X and Y equals 5.69. Substituting that into the z-score formula gives

$$r = \frac{\Sigma z_X z_Y}{N} = \frac{5.69}{7} = .812$$

TIP

The difference between the .812 above and the value of .816 from the raw score formula is due to rounding off.

TABLE 6.3   z-Scores for the Pet Ownership Study

Person	z_X		z_Y		$z_X z_Y$
A	$\dfrac{-1.43}{1.18} = -1.22$		$\dfrac{-1.14}{1.13} = -1.01$		1.23
B	$\dfrac{-.43}{1.18} = -.36$		$\dfrac{.86}{1.13} = .76$		−.27
C	$\dfrac{.57}{1.18} = .48$		$\dfrac{-.14}{1.13} = -.12$		−.06
D	$\dfrac{-1.43}{1.18} = -1.22$		$\dfrac{-1.14}{1.13} = -1.01$		1.23
E	$\dfrac{1.57}{1.18} = 1.33$		$\dfrac{1.86}{1.13} = 1.65$		2.19
F	$\dfrac{1.57}{1.18} = 1.33$		$\dfrac{.86}{1.13} = .76$		1.01
G	$\dfrac{-.43}{1.18} = -.36$		$\dfrac{-1.14}{1.13} = -1.01$		.36
Σ	−.02		.02		5.69

Solution with the Formula Using Means: The formula with the means of the scores on variables X and Y is

$$\frac{\dfrac{\Sigma XY}{N} - (\overline{X})(\overline{Y})}{\sigma_X \sigma_Y}$$

- Calculating the numerator gives

$$\frac{19}{7} - [(1.43)(1.14)] = 2.71 - 1.63 = 1.08$$

- The denominator is $(1.18)(1.13) = 1.33$
- Dividing yields

$$\frac{1.08}{1.33} = .812$$

Several things are worth noting from comparing all of these formulas.

- First, the raw score formula is definitely the easiest if all that you have are the raw scores. Moreover, it is likely to be the most accurate, since it involves less rounding off than the other formulas.

- Second, each one of the formulas has in the numerator a term that represents the sum of the cross products of the individuals' scores on both variables. Thus, it is impossible to calculate a Pearson r (or any other correlation coefficient) unless each score on variable X comes paired with one and only one score on variable Y.

- Finally, no one but a masochist, an obsessive-compulsive neurotic, or a person writing a statistics book (which implies one or both of the previous categories) would really use all of these formulas on the same data. ◼

What Is a Significant Pearson *r*?*

Suppose that you have (laboriously, joyously, or both) calculated the value of Pearson r. What do you do next? What you generally do next is look at the value of r to see whether or not it is reasonable and matches the pattern of your data. For instance, if high scores on X are paired with high scores on Y and low with low, then r should be high and positive. Above all, if r is not between –1 and +1, you know that you have made a mistake in your arithmetic. Even if the value of r seems correct, it is a good idea to check your calculations, perhaps by using a different formula.

Once you're sure that your calculations are correct, you have to decide whether your scores refer to a population or a sample before you can interpret the meaning of r. If your scores come from a population and you have no interest in generalizing beyond them to any other scores, then you can proceed directly to interpret the meaning of r. However, in most of the instances when researchers calculate correlation coefficients, they are dealing with a sample and are interested in the question of the general relationship between the measured variables, not just in the relationship for the particular individuals studied. When this is the case, before you can interpret the importance of r, you have to decide whether or not the value of r is statistically significant.

Statistical significance is a complex concept that will be discussed in much more depth in Chapter 8. For the present, it is enough to know that a *statistically significant* result is one that is likely to represent the actual state in the population rather than being due to chance (Harris, 1997; but see Shaver, 1993). Calling a finding statistically significant implies that it is large enough that you would expect a similar result with a different sample. When you refer to a correlation coefficient as statistically significant, you are implying that it reflects a true positive or negative correlation in the population, rather than a correlation of zero. In other words, if the correlation between number of friends and depth of friendship for our sample was positive and statistically significant, we could make some tentative generalizations and do some

_____

*You may want to skip this section until after you have read Chapter 8.

theorizing about the relationship between these variables. If it was not statistically significant, we would have to restrain ourselves and acknowledge that with a different sample the Pearson *r* might have been negative or near zero.

Characteristics of a Statistically Significant *r*

In order for a correlation coefficient to be statistically significant, it must possess two characteristics:

- It has to be reasonably far from zero.
- It has to be based on a reasonably large sample size.

To some extent these characteristics can compensate for each other; a small absolute value for *r* will be statistically significant if *N* is huge, and a value of *r* that is very close to 1 or –1 may be significant with a quite small sample size. However, too small a sample size, such as an *N* of 1 or 2, can never lead to a statistically significant correlation, and it is unusual to find statistically significant *r*'s with *N*'s less than 10.

Using a Table of the Significance of *r*

Appendix Table 2 presents the minimal values, called **critical values**, of *r* that are needed to achieve statistical significance for any given sample size. A portion of the appendix table is reproduced as Table 6.4. Use the numbers under the label "Level of Significance for Two-tailed Test." These numbers are called *two-tailed critical values*. You will almost always be using these kinds of values, although later on you will learn to use one-tailed critical values as well.

Degrees of Freedom.   The first column in Table 6.4 lists the *degrees of freedom* (*df*). The concept of degrees of freedom is a difficult one and will be considered in Chapter 9. It is always related to the number of observations or scores that you are analyzing minus the number of parameters that have to be estimated from these observations. Almost every statistical procedure has its associated degrees of freedom, and $N - 2$ is the degrees of freedom for Pearson *r*.

Critical Values for Different Significance Levels.   The second, fourth, and sixth columns of Table 6.4 give the minimal values that *r* must reach to be considered statistically significant at three increasingly stringent or rigorous alpha (α) levels: the .05 α-level, the .01 α-level, and the .001 α-level of significance (sometimes called the *p* level). If the absolute value of *r* is as large as the table value or larger, then *r* would be considered statistically significant at the relevant alpha level. If the value of *r* is closer to zero than the table value, then *r* would not be considered statistically significant at that level.

TABLE 6.4   Portion of Appendix Table 2: Critical Values for Pearson *r*

	Alpha Level					
df	*.10*	*.05*	*.02*	*.01*	*.002*	*.001*
1	0.988	0.997	1.000	1.000	1.000	1.000
2	0.900	0.950	0.980	0.990	0.998	0.999
3	0.805	0.878	0.934	0.959	0.986	0.991
4	0.729	0.811	0.882	0.917	0.963	0.974
5	0.669	0.754	0.833	0.875	0.935	0.951
6	0.621	0.707	0.789	0.834	0.905	0.925
7	0.582	0.666	0.750	0.798	0.875	0.898
8	0.549	0.632	0.715	0.765	0.847	0.872
9	0.521	0.602	0.685	0.735	0.820	0.847
10	0.497	0.576	0.658	0.708	0.795	0.823

TIP

> Ordinarily, an *r* that reaches the critical value needed for significance at the .05 α-level would be considered statistically significant, and any *r* with a smaller absolute value would not. However, if a value for *r* also reaches significance at the .01 or .001 significance levels, then the most stringent level that it reaches would be reported.

As you can see, you need a larger and larger value for *r* to reach significance as the significance level gets smaller or more stringent. This reflects the fact that the significance level is the probability of getting a sample value of *r* that far away from zero when you take a sample of size *N* from a population where the true correlation between the variables is zero (i.e., when they are unrelated). Thus, if you sample 12 pairs of scores on variables *X* and *Y* from a population where *X* and *Y* are uncorrelated, which means that you have 12 – 2 or 10 degrees of freedom, you have less than a 5% probability (often written $p < .05$) of finding a correlation coefficient as large as .576 or as small as –.576, and you have less than a 1% probability of finding a correlation coefficient as large as .708 or as small as –.708.

Values Not in the Table.   If you want to find a critical value for a value of degrees of freedom that is not in the table, you have two alternatives.

1. One alternative is that you can use the more conservative (or larger) critical value, which will be associated with the smaller number of degrees of freedom in the table. Thus, if your *N* is 55, you would look for the critical value with 50 degrees of freedom, which is .273 at the .05 α-level. If your *r* is significant by this criterion, it is significant for your sample. Correspondingly, if your calculated r would not be significant with a larger number of degrees of freedom than you have, such as 60, it would not be significant for your sample.

2. The other alternative is that you could interpolate, calculating the critical value that would be proportionate to the distance between the actual degrees of freedom and the table values. If you want to find the .05 critical value for 53 degrees of freedom, it must be .7 of the distance between the upper limit of the critical value for 50 degrees of freedom and the lower limit of the critical value for 60 degrees of freedom added to the lower limit of the value for 60 degrees of freedom.

$$.7(.2735 - .2495) + .2495 = (.7)(.0240) + .2495$$
$$= .0168 + .2495 = .266 \text{ to 3 decimal places}$$

EXAMPLE

Let's check out the significance of the correlation coefficient that we calculated between the numbers of dogs and cats owned by a sample of seven people. The value calculated from the raw score formula, .816, is likely to be the most accurate, so we will use it. The degrees of freedom for $r = 5$, and the critical value at the .05 α-level is .754. The critical value for 5 degrees of freedom at the .01 α-level is .875. We can then say that the correlation of .816 between number of dogs owned and number of cats owned is statistically significant at the .05 level but not at the .01 α-level. ∎

Steps in Using the Table.   The steps in using a table of the significance of r follow.

Step 1: Calculate the value of r.

Step 2: Subtract 2 from N to get your degrees of freedom.

Step 3: Look at the .05 column of the table to see whether your computed value is at least that large, ignoring the sign. If yes, your r will be considered statistically significant. If no, it will not.

Step 4: If your r is significant at the .05 α-level, look at the .01 column to see if it also reaches significance at that level. If it does, then check out the .001 column to see if it also reaches significance at that level. When reporting or discussing the significance of r, report the most stringent level at which r reaches statistical significance, remembering that .05 is the least stringent level.

What to Do If r Is Not Significant

Acknowledge That r Was Not Significant.   Stop. Do not pass "go." Do not collect $200. Rant. Rave. Swear. Complain. Or, possibly, gloat, if the value of *r* is near zero and you had predicted that the variables would not be correlated with each other. It is true that a number of sophisticated researchers and theoreticians have indicated concern about rigid adherence to the sacred dividing line between statistically significant and not significant (Abelson, 1997; Carver, 1993; Cohen, 1990, 1992a, 1992b; Greenwald, 1975; Harlow, 1997; Huberty, 1987; Hunter, 1997; Kupfersmid, 1988; Meehl, 1978; Rosenthal, 1979; Rosnow & Rosenthal, 1989; Schneider & Darcy, 1984; Shaver, 1985, 1993; Thompson, 1989a, 1989b, 1993). However, I am presuming that you aren't one of them—yet. So unless you are describing a population and not interested in drawing any inferences about how the variables relate to each other in any other instances, you have to simply quit and say that the correlation was not statistically significant. Period.

Consider How to Interpret the Nonsignificant *r*. Of course, you are free to think and speculate about the meaning of the fact that the Pearson *r* was nonsignificant. The most likely interpretation, of course, is that there is not a strong (or, perhaps, any) linear relationship between the two variables in the population. On the other hand, if your sample size is small, then even a reasonably large correlation coefficient will not be statistically significant (Cohen, 1992a; Hunter, 1997; Shaver, 1985; Thompson, 1989).

If you had good theoretical reasons for expecting a relationship, there are several things that you can do.

- Certainly, you would want to look at other research studies that have assessed at the relationship between these two variables, to see whether or not your value of *r* is similar to those reported in the literature.
- It would definitely make sense to look at a scattergraph of the scores, to see if perhaps the variables were related in a curvilinear fashion.
- If the value for *r* was in the expected direction and the sample size was small, you might want to repeat the research project with a larger sample.
- If your measures of *X* and *Y* were not very accurate, you might want to choose more precise measures next time.
- If the range of scores on either or both variables in your sample was small, you might want to use a sample with a wider range of scores on both variables, as a limited (or truncated) range will reduce the possible value of the *r* that you could obtain from a sample, thus leading to an underestimate of the value of *r* in the population.

All of these possibilities can be raised and mentioned in the discussion section of a research report. However, the bottom line is that you should not go further and try to interpret a nonsignificant correlation but should acknowledge that there is a reasonable probability that the real correlation coefficient in the population is near zero.

How to Interpret a Significant r

If your value for r was statistically significant, or if you have measured the entire population of interest, then you can consider what this value of r means. There are several different ways in which an r may be interpreted, some or all of which may be appropriate in a given situation.

Causality. One of the most important reasons why people do research is to draw some inferences about causes and effects. Whether or not it is legitimate to come to conclusions about causality depends more upon the research design than upon the statistical procedure used to analyze it (Shaver, 1993). In general, only a true experimental design or a quasi-experimental design that manages to control for almost all alternative interpretations of the results can be used to draw firm inferences about cause and effect. A statistically significant correlation coefficient can tell you that two variables are associated and vary together, but it cannot let you conclude that one of them causes the other. Of course, you can state that the significant positive correlation between X and Y (e.g., hours since last meal and self-reported hunger) is consistent with your theory that X causes Y, but it may also be consistent with Y causing X or with some third variable causing both X and Y.

No Causal Relationship. It is possible to devise examples of correlations in which it is clear that neither variable causes a particular score on the other. For example, there is a positive correlation between amount of money people spend on housing and amount of money they spend on food. Does eating more expensive food cause the rent to rise (because the landlord sees lobster tails in the garbage and figures you can afford it)? Does buying a more expensive house cause your food bills to rise (because you have spent so much money on the house you would hardly notice the cost of caviar)? Both possibilities seem extremely unlikely. Much more likely is the fact that income or wealth affects both the amount that people can afford to spend for housing and the amount that they can afford to spend for food.

Multiple Causation. A more typical example of a correlation coefficient is one in which there may be several causal pathways operating. For example, there is doubtless a positive correlation between education achieved and annual income (although those of you who are studying for your Ph.D. in education should recognize that this correlation is by no means perfect). To some extent, this correlation may reflect the fact that, in some cases, getting more education will increase income level. For example, some jobs are limited to people with a high school diploma, a college degree, or an M.D. However, it is also the case that, for some people, having an insufficient income prevents them from continuing their education. I frequently have students in my classes who had been unable to afford to go back to school until their income reached a high enough level. Another possibility is that certain factors such as intelligence, motivation, and coming from an upper-middle-class family may cause people both to earn more money and to continue their education (not necessarily simultaneously, of course).

TIP ▬▬▬▬▬▬▬▬▬▬▬▬▬▬▬▬▬▬▬▬▬▬▬▬▬▬▬▬▬▬▬▬▬▬▬▬▬▬

> The point to remember is that a significant correlation almost always indicates that something causal is going on. However, it does not tell you the direction of the causal relationship, except in those rare instances in which one of the variables was manipulated in an experimental design (perhaps drug dosage or study time, for instance). The reason that these instances are so uncommon is not that true experimental research is rare, but that it is unusual to have enough levels (at least three or four) of a manipulated interval-scale independent variable that you would calculate the correlation between level and score on the dependent variable. So, in general, you should avoid making any statements that indicate that one variable has an effect upon another based solely on a correlation coefficient.

Concomitant Variation. One conclusion that can definitely be drawn from a significant correlation coefficient is that the scores on the variables tend to change or vary together. When r is positive, you can justifiably say that a larger value of X is associated with a larger value of Y and vice versa. Similarly, if r is negative, you can say that lower scores on X are associated with higher scores on Y and vice versa. In fact, you can be more precise than the preceding statements; the value of r is a measure of how much larger a score (in terms of z-score units) you can expect for one variable when the score on the other variable is one standard deviation larger. For example, if $r = -.65$, you can expect the value of scores on variable Y to be .65 of a standard deviation lower, on the average, for every increase of one standard deviation on variable X.

If you prefer to think in terms of raw scores, $r(\sigma_Y/\sigma_X)$ is a measure of how much larger you could expect a person's raw score on Y to be if that person's score on X were one point higher. This value is also called the *slope of the regression line* for predicting Y and will be discussed in more detail in the next chapter. Similarly, $r(\sigma_X/\sigma_Y)$ is a measure of how much people who differ by one point on Y can be expected to differ in their scores on X.

EXAMPLE ▬▬▬▬▬▬▬▬▬▬▬▬▬▬▬▬▬▬▬▬▬▬▬▬▬▬▬▬▬▬▬▬▬▬▬▬▬▬

Suppose that the standard deviation of the scores on X is 2, the standard deviation of the scores on Y is 4, and the correlation between X and Y is .6. You could then predict that for every one-point difference on X, there would be a .6(4/2) or 1.2 point difference on Y. For every one-point difference on Y, there would be a .6(2/4) or .3 difference on X. Thus, the correlation coefficient can be interpreted as indicating the average difference in scores on one variable associated with a given amount of difference in scores on the other. ∎

Accuracy of Prediction. Another way in which to interpret a correlation coefficient is in terms of accuracy of prediction of scores on one variable from scores on the other. Although the next chapter will consider how to compute a regression equation and actually carry out such predictions, it should be recognized now that the larger the absolute magnitude of r (or, to be more precise, of r^2), the more precisely a score on one variable can be predicted from the score on the other. If two variables are significantly correlated, then it can be said that knowing a person's score on one variable will improve someone's ability to predict that person's score on the other variable.

Proportion of Common Variance. Another way to interpret Pearson r is in terms of the amount of overlap in the variance of scores on the two variables. The square of r reflects the proportion of variance on one variable predictable from or attributable to or due to the other variable. Remember, though, that this communality in variance does not imply that one variable is the cause of the other.

Coefficient of Determination. The term **coefficient of determination** is used to refer to r^2; it serves as a measure of the strength of the relationship between the variables. In fact r^2 multiplied by 100 can be thought of as the percentage of the information in Y that is contained in X. Thus, if variable X is correlated .40 with variable Q and .80 with variable W, the coefficient of determination between variables X and Q equals .16, and the correlation with variable Q accounts for 16% of the variance in the scores on X. Because $.80^2 = .64$, variable W accounts for 64% (or four times as much) of the variance in the scores on variable X.

In order to assess the relative strength of two correlation coefficients, researchers compare their respective coefficients of determination rather than the r's themselves. Thus, a correlation that is three times as large as another actually is nine times as important and accounts for nine times the variance that the weaker correlation coefficient does. It also leads to only one-ninth the error in prediction.

Proportion of Common Elements. A variant on the preceding approach to interpreting a correlation coefficient is to view r^2 as representing the proportion of elements common to both X and Y, as opposed to those elements that are unique to X or Y. Sometimes this makes sense, as when X and Y are both tests that are measuring the same or overlapping constructs. Sometimes it makes no sense, as when X is number of football games won by schools and Y is number of meals served in the school cafeterias. (What do these have to do with each other? Not much, but if school size affects both the chance of finding good football players and the number of meals served daily, these variables could be positively correlated.) If you are talking about the correlation between some physical characteristic of fathers and sons, for example, you may want to interpret this r as reflecting a common genetic inheritance.

Describing a Significant Correlation

Which interpretation to use to describe a particular relationship depends partly on common sense and partly on personal preference. There are often several possible ways to describe a significant r, all of which have some validity.

EXAMPLE

If time since taking a painkiller is significantly negatively correlated (−.54) with how much pain people report feeling, you could say that "People feel better and better as the time since taking the medicine increases," "Time since taking the painkiller accounts for .29 of the variance in experienced pain," or "If you wait longer after they've taken the painkiller to ask how they feel, people will report feeling less pain." It would not be correct to conclude that "Time since taking the painkiller causes people to feel better," even if you systematically manipulated time between taking the painkiller and measuring their pain in an experimental design, since it is probably some physiological process that occurs over time rather than time itself that is causing the reduction in pain.

Reporting a Significant Correlation in APA Style

The way in which any statistic is reported in American Psychological Association style is more or less standard. The author reports the name of the statistic, the degrees of freedom in parentheses, the value of the statistic, and the most stringent level at which it reaches statistical significance.

For example, you might say "$r(20) = .54, p < .01$," meaning that a Pearson r calculated on 22 pairs of scores was equal to .54 and reached significance at the .01 level. Ordinarily, this information would be reported as part of the sentence describing the meaning of the correlation coefficient. Thus, you might say something like "The correlation between the number of tomatoes thrown and the number of eggs thrown at 17 political candidates was not statistically significant, $r(15) = .12, p > .05$."

Or, for another study, you might report, "The correlation between dollars spent on advertising and number of cars sold by a sample of car dealers was statistically significant, $r(35) = .33, p < .05$, but accounted for only 11% of the variance, suggesting that other factors may contribute more than does the cost of advertising to car sales."

Are There Other Types of Correlations?

In addition to the Pearson product-moment correlation coefficient, several other types of correlations are in common use. The *point biserial* (a special case of Pearson *r*) and *biserial correlation coefficients* are used to assess the relationship between an interval- or ratio-scale variable and a variable that is dichotomous or artificially dichotomized (divided into two categories). The *phi coefficient* and *tetrachoric correlation coefficient* are used to assess the degree of correlation between two dichotomous or dichotomized variables. As mentioned earlier, eta (η), also called the correlation ratio, is used to assess the degree of nonlinear relationship between two interval- or ratio-scale variables. The results of such correlations can be interpreted much like a Pearson *r*. The procedures for computing such statistics are shown in more advanced texts, although most can be computed by applying the formula for Pearson *r* to ranks or to scores of zero or one.

Spearman Rho

When you wish to calculate the correlation between two variables that are measured on an ordinal scale or that have been converted to ranks, either *Kendall's tau* or the **Spearman correlation coefficient** called **rho** (ρ), are appropriate procedures. Because rho is much easier to calculate, it is the only one that will be discussed here. In fact, Spearman rho can be viewed as a special case of Pearson *r*, if *r* were to be calculated on the ranks rather than on the raw scores. However, the computation of rho is substantially easier than the computation of *r* when there are no ties. The formula for rho is as follows:

$$\rho = 1 - \frac{6\Sigma D^2}{N(N^2 - 1)}$$

Using the Formula.   In order to use the formula, you have to have pairs of ranks—that is, each person must be ranked on both variables *X* and *Y*. The steps for using the formula follow.

Step 1: To get the numerator of the formula, subtract each person's rank on variable *Y* from his or her rank on variable *X*.

Step 2: Square these differences, symbolized by the letter *D*.

Step 3: Sum these squares.

Step 4: Multiply the total by 6.

Step 5: To get the denominator, square the sample size.

Step 6: Subtract 1 from this square.

Step 7: Multiply this difference by *N*.

Step 8: Divide the numerator by the denominator.

Step 9: Subtract this quotient from 1 to get Spearman rho.

EXAMPLE

Art Contest Entrants. In order to see how the formula works, let's imagine that two judges have each ranked the entries in an art contest. Judge A ranked the entries as follows: first prize to Alan, second to Beth, third to Carl, fourth to Don, fifth to Edgar, sixth to Frances, and last place to Gertrude. Judge B gave first prize to Beth, second to Alan, third to Don, fourth to Carl, fifth to Gertrude, sixth to Edgar, and seventh to Frances. Before the formula can be used, each person has to be ranked on the two variables identified.

Solution: As shown in Table 6.5, we reorganize the data by person, indicating his or her rank on each variable.

The sum of the squared difference scores is 10. Substituting in the formula for ρ, we get

$$1 - \frac{6(10)}{(7)(49 - 1)} = 1 - \frac{60}{(7)(48)} = 1 - \frac{60}{336} = 1 - .179 = .821$$

TABLE 6.5   Data for the Art Contest Example

Person	Judge A's Ranking	Judge B's Ranking	D	D²
Alan	1	2	−1	1
Beth	2	1	1	1
Carl	3	4	−1	1
Don	4	3	1	1
Edgar	5	6	−1	1
Frances	6	7	−1	1
Gertrude	7	5	2	4
Σ	28	28	0	10

Two cautions should be kept in mind when using the formula for Spearman rho.

1. Remember that the part of the formula that involves multiplying and dividing is subtracted from the number 1. Don't let the 1 creep up into the numerator as you copy the formula, or you may end up with some very odd (not to mention incorrect) results.

2. When there are tied ranks, you must be careful to give each of the tied scores the average of the tied ranks. For example, if two people are tied for rank 6, they should each be given the rank of 6.5, and the next person should be given rank 8. If there is a three-way tie for third place, this represents ranks 3–5, and each of the three should be assigned the rank of 4. The person after them, of course, gets rank 6, reflecting the fact that five persons scored higher.

TIP

If there are many tied ranks, a correction factor can be applied to the formula for Spearman rho, but this is rarely used. It can be found in more advanced texts on nonparametric statistics. An alternative is to use the formula for Pearson r on the ranks. This may seem to contradict previous statements that Pearson r applies only to interval or ratio data, but the result of applying the formula for Pearson r to the ranks will be identical to applying the formula for Spearman rho and will represent ρ, not r. This procedure is generally more tedious than using the formula for ρ but less complicated than correcting for ties.

Interpreting Rho. To interpret a Spearman rho, we must first decide whether or not it is statistically significant, just as with a Pearson r. The only exception would be the case in which you have measured the entire population of interest and are not interested in generalizing beyond those scores that you have.

Appendix Table 3 presents the critical values for the statistical significance of Spearman rho. To use this table, you should again concentrate on the two-tailed values and should look at the number of pairs of scores in the first column or the degrees of freedom in the second column. The next three columns give the minimum values necessary for statistical significance at the .05, .02, and .01 α-levels. If the calculated value for ρ is at least as large as the value in the table at the .05 α-level, then it is considered to be statistically significant.

Once you have identified a significant ρ, you can interpret it more or less as you would a value of r; a positive ρ means that higher ranks on one variable are associated with higher ranks on the other, and larger absolute values of ρ indicate a stronger relationship between the variables.

TIP

Spearman rho is the first nonparametric test to be described in this book and, as you will discover if you practice using the formulas for r and ρ, it is a lot simpler to compute than Pearson r. Because it is so much easier, sometimes researchers will turn their raw data into ranks and compute a Spearman rho, rather than going through the more tedious procedures of computing Pearson r. If ρ is nowhere near significant, then r is unlikely to be significant either, even though it is a more powerful test. If you are planning to use ρ, be sure to remember that you need to do your calculations on ranks, not on raw scores.

Pearson *r* Versus Spearman Rho

Pearson r	Spearman Rho

Computational formula:

$$r = \frac{N\Sigma\ XY - \Sigma X\Sigma Y}{\sqrt{\left(N\Sigma\ X^2 - (\Sigma X)^2\right)\left(N\Sigma\ Y^2 - (\Sigma Y)^2\right)}} \qquad \rho = 1 - \frac{6\Sigma D^2}{N\left(N^2 - 1\right)}$$

Assumptions:

- Pairs of scores are available.
- Both variables are measured on (close to) an interval or ratio scale.
- You want to assess the linear relationship between the variables.
- Scores have been randomly sampled from the population.
- The distributions of scores on variables X and Y are normal.

- Pairs of scores are available.
- Both variables are measured on at least an ordinal scale.
- Scores have been randomly sampled from the population.

Advantages:

- When assumptions are met, it is more powerful than Spearman rho.
- It is reasonably robust to violations of the assumptions.

- It can be used with ordinal data.
- It is relatively easy to compute.

Similarities:

The formulas for Pearson *r* and for Spearman rho will lead to the same numerical value when used on the same set or ranks.

Partial and Multiple Correlations

There are two other types of correlations that you may encounter or that you might wish to use in analyzing your research. **Partial correlation**, symbolized by $r_{XY\cdot Z}$, gives the relationship between two variables with the effect of a third variable statistically removed or "partialled out." For instance, if you were interested in the relationship between a measure of quantitative ability and a measure of verbal ability in a sample of children, you would probably want to partial out, or get rid of, the effect of age.

Multiple correlation, symbolized by R, depicts a correlation between a group or combination of variables and another variable. For example, the multiple correlation could be computed between several measures of performance in high school (e.g., grades, test scores, and teacher evaluations) and grade point average in college. A multiple R can be interpreted like a Pearson r, in the sense that R^2 reflects the proportion of variance in the single variable predictable from scores on the best linear combination of the other (predictor) variables. It is most commonly discussed in the context of multiple regression, in which an equation for predicting scores on one variable from scores on others is developed.

When Are Correlation Techniques Used?

A correlation coefficient is used when you are interested in assessing the linear relationship between two variables or, in other words, when you are interested in the degree to which pairs of scores on the variables can be plotted on a straight line. Assuming that you have scores on two variables, the decision about whether or not to use a correlation coefficient depends on both the nature of your research and the characteristics of the data you have gathered.

Nature of the Research

A correlation coefficient is commonly used to test hypotheses about the relationship between variables, such as the hypothesis that one causes the other or that a third factor causes both. Usually correlation coefficients are computed as part of correlational research studies, but a developmental study might look at the correlation between age and various measures, a survey might correlate demographic characteristics with various responses, and almost any type of research could generate examples where correlation coefficients have been computed.

Characteristics of the Data

Formal Assumptions.   As stated earlier, a Pearson r is supposed to be used when the assumptions of an interval/ratio scale, random sampling, linearity, and normality have been met. Pearson r, like other statistical techniques, is sometimes used when sampling has not been random, recognizing that generalizing to the population from the sample may not be completely valid. However, if the hypothesized or actual relationship between the variables to be correlated is strongly curvilinear, then Pearson r may simply indicate that there is no linear relationship, and the correlation ratio, η (eta), should be used instead of r.

Level of Measurement.   Like other parametric procedures, Pearson r is often used with measures, like attitude scales, that fall between the ordinal and interval level of measurement. However, if the data are ordinal, Spearman rho (or Kendall's tau) should be used instead, and if one or more of the variables is a true or artificial dichotomy, one of the alternative correlational techniques mentioned above would be more appropriate. If the question asked concerns whether or not two nominal-level variables are associated, then a chi-square test of independence, to be covered in Chapter 13, would be the correct procedure to use for testing the statistical significance of the relationship.

Cautions

There are several cautions to keep in mind when you are deciding whether or not to use a correlation coefficient to analyze some data.

1. Remember that it is possible for a question to be worded in a way that sounds as if you are looking for a correlation coefficient when you really want to know the size of a difference in means. For example, although you might say that you are looking for the correlation between gender and income, you may really want to know whether or not there is a difference in the mean income of males and females. Although it would be possible to answer this question by coding males as zero and females as one (or vice versa) on the variable of gender and computing the correlation between gender and income, this approach would be unusual. Much more common would be to do a direct test of the difference in the mean income levels of males and females, such as an independent-samples *t*-test, which is discussed in Chapter 9.

2. Remember, too, that if you do not have each person's score on both variables, you cannot compute a correlation coefficient between the variables. You cannot relate height to weight without measuring both for everyone. You could not calculate the correlation between depth of friendship and number of friends if you had not measured the mean depth of friendship for some of the subjects (unless you excluded them from the study, thereby raising questions about the representativeness of your sample).

3. Remember that a correlation coefficient assesses a relationship between variables, meaning that you have a minimum of several scores on each variable. If you don't have enough pairs of scores in your sample to represent the population, then you won't be able to draw inferences about the relationship between the variables in the population. For example, if you have only two pairs of scores, the correlation between them will be +1 or –1, regardless of what the scores are. It does not make sense to talk about how *my* intelligence and *my* test score are correlated, or how the warm sunshine you feel right now is correlated with the beautiful pattern of shadows in front of you, since in each of these examples you have just one score on each variable.

CHAPTER
SUMMARY   When a researcher wants to consider the relationship between pairs of scores on two quantitative variables, correlation is the technique usually used. A scattergraph gives a visual picture of the relationship, and a corre-

lation coefficient gives a numerical representation of it. When higher scores on one variable are associated with higher scores on the other, then the points on the scattergraph go from lower left to upper right and the correlation coefficient is direct or positive. When higher scores on one variable are associated with lower scores on the other, the points on the scattergraph go from upper left to lower right, and the correlation coefficient is negative or inverse. A zero correlation coefficient represents a lack of linear relationship between the variables.

A Pearson product-moment correlation coefficient, symbolized by r, assumes that the variables are measured on an interval or ratio scale, that you are interested in the linear relationship between them, that the scores were randomly sampled from the population, and that the distributions from which the scores came were normal. Several formulas can be used to compute Pearson r.

If the r is large enough in absolute magnitude, given the sample size, then it is called statistically significant, meaning that it is unlikely that the real correlation in the population from which the sample is drawn is either zero or in the opposite direction from the r calculated for the sample. If the r for a sample is not statistically significant, you must acknowledge that it could represent a sample from a population with a true r near zero; if it is significant, you can conclude that it is likely that larger values of X are associated with larger (if r is positive) or smaller (if r is negative) values of Y in the population. However, you cannot conclude that X necessarily causes Y (or vice versa).

The square of the correlation coefficient, called the coefficient of determination, is a measure of the strength of a relationship and also is related to the accuracy of predicting scores on one variable from scores on the other.

Another type of correlation coefficient, Spearman rho, can be used when the scores on the two variables are or have been converted into ranks. This technique is a nonparametric test. Other types of correlation procedures, including biserial and point biserial correlations, partial correlation, and multiple correlation, may be used in other situations.

CHAPTER REVIEW

Multiple-Choice Questions

1. Suppose that you have calculated that the correlation between number of hours spent studying for a statistics test and grade on the test is 1.25. Which of the following do you know to be true?

   a. People who studied longer got higher grades on the test.

   b. Studying longer caused people to do better on the test.

   c. The coefficient of determination is 1.5625.

    d. Both a and b are true.

    e. All of the above are true.

    f. You have made a mistake.

2. What is the critical value for the correlation coefficient between height and weight for 20 first-grade children at the .01 level, two-tailed?

    a. .492   **b.** .503   **c.** .516   **d.** .537   **e.** .561   **f.** none of the above

3. If the correlation between the number of times 32 people brush their teeth per day and the number of cavities in their mouths is –.20, which of the following is a correct inference?

    a. People with fewer cavities need to brush more.

    b. Brushing teeth helps to reduce cavities.

    c. Brushing teeth and having cavities are significantly inversely related.

    d. The majority of people with cavities brush their teeth.

    e. None of the above is necessarily true.

4. Grade-point average (GPA) for a sample of 100 people is correlated .65 with score on test A, –.44 with score on test B, and –.26 with score on test C. Which of the following is true?

    a. Score on test A is the best predictor of GPA.

    b. Score on test B is the best predictor of GPA.

    c. Score on test C is the best predictor of GPA.

    d. People with lower scores on test B have higher GPAs.

    e. Both a and d are true.

    f. Both b and d are true.

    g. Both c and d are true.

5. Suppose that you have calculated Spearman's rho between the ranks assigned by Mr. and Mrs. J to ten houses that they had just viewed, trying to decide which one to buy. The value for rho was .56. What should you conclude?

    a. Mr. and Mrs. J. do not agree significantly in their rankings of the houses.

    b. Mr. J. liked the houses significantly better than his wife liked them.

    c. Mr. and Mrs. J. agreed at the .05 α-level but not at the .01 α-level in their rankings.

    d. Mr. and Mrs. J. agreed at the .01 α-level but not at the .05 α-level in their rankings.

    e. Mr. and Mrs. J agreed significantly in their rankings of the houses.

6. If the correlation between family size and family income is –.5, what is the coefficient of determination?

    a. –25   **b.** –.5   **c.** –.25   **d.** .25   **e.** .7071

    f. None of the above, because income doesn't determine family size.

7. How large a sample size do you need to find a correlation coefficient of .600 statistically significant at the .05 α-level?

   a. 7   **b.** 8   **c.** 9   **d.** 10   **e.** 11   **f.** 12

8. If 49% of the total variability in Y is accounted for by X, which of the following could be the value of r?

   a. −.70   **b.** .2401   **c.** .49   **d.** .51

   e. It could be any of the above values.

   f. It could not be any of the above values.

Problems

9. What is the Pearson product-moment correlation coefficient likely to be between length of big toe (yes, on your foot) and score on a reading achievement test for a large sample of people—positive, negative, or near zero? Why?

10. What are the critical values for each of the following?

    a. Pearson r at the .05 level, two-tailed, with 26 degrees of freedom

    b. Spearman rho at the .05 level, two-tailed, with 26 degrees of freedom

    c. the correlation between the ages and weights of 62 runners at the .01 level

    d. the minimum value necessary to call the relationship between the UPI and AP rankings of the same 20 football teams statistically significant

    e. the critical value at the .01 level for correlating scores on two measures of bilingualism for a sample of 100 students

11. Can people really agree on what a great performance is? You and theater critic Frederick Fierce have watched several people audition for the part of Hamlet. You ranked them as follows from best to worst: Perry, Parry, Peter, Paul, Percival, and Popeye. Mr. Fierce ranked them in the following order: Perry, Peter, Parry, and Paul, with Popeye and Percival tied for last.

    a. What is the proper test to use to measure the extent to which your ranking of the actors and Mr. Fierce's rankings agree? Why should you use this procedure?

    b. Compute the value of this statistic.

    c. Is the result statistically significant or not?

    d. Report your conclusion about how much you and Frederick Fierce agree in your evaluations of the actors in a sentence.

12. A recent research study was conducted by surveying the five individuals who received their Ph.D. degrees from Serenity University College of Education. They were each asked to indicate how many statistics courses they had taken in their graduate program (X) and how happy they were on a five-point scale (Y), where 1 = unhappy and 5 = ecstatic. The data are given in the following table:

Person	Courses (X)	Happiness (Y)
Josie	0	2
Arthur	5	5
Marvin	4	4
Tammy	2	3
Ralph	3	2

    a. What is the correlation between the number of statistics courses taken and the self-rated happiness of the subjects?

    b. Is this correlation statistically significant or not?

    c. Report your conclusion about the relationship between the number of statistics classes taken and self-rated happiness in a sentence or two, based on the data above.

13. Suppose that you have evidence that the Pearson product-moment correlation coefficient between number of hours spent reading and number of hours spent watching television for a sample of 200 adults was −.60. Which of the following conclusions would be correct?

    a. There is no significant relationship between hours spent reading and hours spent watching television.

    b. People who watch more television read more.

    c. You can predict the amount of reading someone does to a greater-than-chance extent by knowing the amount of time that person spends watching television.

    d. Watching more television causes people to become less interested in reading.

    e. Because there are only so many hours in a day, spending time reading means that you will have to devote less time to watching television.

14. Based on a sample of 40 homes in Albuquerque, a researcher concluded that the correlation between the number of rooms in the house and the monthly heating bill was 1.2. What can you correctly conclude from the above information?

15. You are interested in predicting students' performance in introductory Russian. Based on a group of 100 students who took two tests, A and B, and then took introductory Russian, you discovered that the correlation between scores on test A and grades in the course was .3. The correlation between scores on test B and grades in the class was .6. Which of the following conclusions can be correctly drawn from the above information?

    a. Test A and test B have 18% of their variance in common.

    b. Test A and test B are significantly positively correlated.

    c. Test A accounts for 30% of the variance in introductory Russian grades.

d. Test A accounts for four times as much of the variance in introductory Russian grades as test B.

e. Knowing someone's grade in introductory Russian enables you to predict that person's score on test B at a level above chance.

16. Draw a picture of a scattergraph to represent each of the following relationships:

   a. X = number of correct answers on the GRE exam and Y = number of errors on the exam.

   b. X = weight and Y = rated attractiveness.

   c. X = amount of annual rainfall and Y = amount of mildew in buildings for a sample of 50 U.S. cities.

17. **a.** Given the following set of data, calculate the Pearson r between X and Y using the z-score formula.

X	Y
8	4
6	5
4	3
3	5
1	6
0	10

   b. Now calculate the same correlation with the formula using means.

   c. Now calculate the same correlation using the raw score formula.

18. Professor Plum is interested in testing two contrasting theories about the relationship between number of times one logs on to the Internet per day and the amount of time spent at each logon. One theory, the Computer Nerd theory, says that people who love computers log on a lot and spend a lot of time at each logon; other computer users use it infrequently and only for brief moments. A second theory, the Total Time theory, says that individuals spend only a limited amount of time on the Internet; those who log on less often spend more time at each logon; those who log on more frequently spend less time at each logon. To test this theory, he has gathered some clues from the following people.

Person	Logons per Day	Minutes per Logon
Colonel Mustard	1	10
Miss Scarlett	2	20
Miss White	2	30
Dr. Green	6	80
Miss Peacock	8	90

a. Compute the correlation coefficient for the relationship between logons per day and minutes per logon.

b. Is this relationship statistically significant?

c. Describe the relationship between logons per day and minutes per logon in words.

d. Do these data tend to support either one of the theories? If so, which one?

19. A sample of 330 men has revealed a correlation between their heights and their annual earnings of .32.

a. Is this relationship statistically significant?

b. Based on this sample, what proportion of the variance of annual earnings can be predicted from knowing a man's height? Is this an important amount?

c. If you were to draw a scattergraph of the relationship, where would the points fall?

d. What can you say about causal relationships based on this information?

20. After reading the above study, you decide to collect your own data relating annual salaries to height in women. Therefore, you collect the following data on a sample of women:

Person	Height (inches)	Annual Salary (dollars)
Margaret	65	33,988
Maria	60	12,776
Matilda	68	49,999
Madonna	66	1,412,593
Marlene	62	19,472
Melissa	67	45,000
Maxine	62	31,300
Margo	64	30,000
Minerva	65	78,650

a. After looking at the data, you recognize that the salary data are very skewed, and you decide to perform a Spearman rho on the data. Calculate the value of rho.

b. Is this value statistically significant?

c. What can you conclude about the relationship of height to salary for the women in this sample?

d. What would have happened if you had put the raw scores from the table above into the formula for rho?

e. Finally, plug the values for the ranks into the formula for Pearson r. Compute r on the ranks.

Study Questions

1. Try to formulate some hypotheses or questions about relationships between two variables. For each of these relationships, consider whether or not a Pearson r would be the appropriate way of assessing the degree of relationship. To do this, you have to think about how the variables are measured—that is, about what kinds of scores people might get on the variables. For example, is there a relationship between amount of money lobbyists spend to persuade legislators and the votes on issues?

2. Try to think of an example of a question for which a correlation coefficient would be calculated from each of the following kinds of research design: correlational, experimental, developmental, and survey. Can you think of an example of a historical research question or a question arising from a case study that would be answered by a correlation coefficient? [*Hint:* I can.]

3. Go to the library, browse through some journals to find relevant articles, and look in the results section to see examples of reported correlation coefficients. Go back to the methods section of each article and read about how the variables were measured. Then reread the sentence in which the correlation coefficient was reported and see whether you could rewrite it in another way that would also be correct.

4. As you can see from this chapter, the term *correlation* has a very specific meaning in statistics. See if you can find some ways in which the word was incorrectly used in the popular press or in other discussions of research (maybe your old term papers?) to imply something other than the calculation of a correlation coefficient. Vow that you will use the term *correlation* precisely from now on whenever you are talking about research or statistics.

Regression

What Is Regression?

Those of you who have studied clinical or developmental psychology may think of regression as a defense mechanism, a reversion to an earlier way of thinking, feeling, or behaving. In statistics, *regression* has a very different meaning: It is a synonym for *prediction*.

Predicted Values

A **regression equation** is an equation that gives a predicted value on one variable for every value of the other variable. The regression equation for predicting weight in pounds from height in inches will not necessarily be the same as the regression equation for predicting height from weight or the regression equation for predicting weight from both height and sex. However, if you have scores for a number of people on each of at least two variables, then you can compute a regression equation for predicting people's scores on either one of these variables from their scores on the other.

A regression equation is a formula for a straight line, and the *regression line* is the line described by the equation. The regression line for predicting Y provides what is called a *least-squares estimate* of Y. In other words, it is the line that minimizes the sum of the squared deviations between the actual scores that people have on Y and their predicted values of Y. If it is possible to predict the scores on Y perfectly from knowing the scores on X, then all of the points on a scattergraph will fall on the regression line. If you were to draw a scattergraph and then draw in the straight line that appears to come closest to minimizing the sum of squared deviations between the height of the points and the line, you would come very close to drawing the regression line shown in Figure 7.1. The type of regression that relates scores on two variables is referred to as *bivariate* (two variables) *linear* (straight line) *regression*.

FIGURE 7.1   A Regression Line

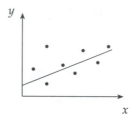

Notation for Predicted Scores.   Since a regression equation is a formula for generating predicted scores, there has to be a way of representing predicted scores that differentiates them from actual scores. There are two common ways to represent predicted scores: a caret or "hat," as in $\hat{Y}$, and a prime symbol, as in Y'. The discrepancy between an actual score and the score that is predicted by the regression equation (or the point on the regression line corresponding to the value of X paired with that of Y) would therefore be $Y - Y'$. Such a discrepancy is occasionally symbolized by an e for error.

Relationship of Regression to Correlation

Similarities.   There is a very close relationship between the topic of correlation and the topic of regression, as well as between r and the regression equation. As discussed in the previous chapter, if two variables are significantly correlated, then it is possible to predict the score on one from the score on the other. If you have calculated r, then there is a relatively simple formula to use in calculating the slope of the regression line, although it is also possible to calculate it directly from the raw scores.

Differences.   Regression and correlation are not identical concepts, however.

   1. Researchers often calculate correlation coefficients for theoretical reasons; they have theories or at least hypotheses about relationships between variables. Although some experimental psychologists do calculate regression equations in order to test the parameters derived from a theory, researchers are more likely to compute regression equations for practical reasons; they may want to predict such behaviors as job performance or test performance in order to make appropriate decisions about hiring or admittance to institutions. Thus, the use of correlation coefficients is relatively more likely to be associated with basic research studies, while the use of regression equations is somewhat more likely to form part of applied research projects.

   2. Another common difference between the concepts of regression and correlation is the sample size of the studies that use them. Although neither correlation coefficients nor regression equations are commonly calculated with very small sample sizes (i.e., <10), correlation coefficients are often calculated with moderate sample sizes of 30 or so, whereas regression equations are usually based on quite large samples, typically in the hundreds. The reason for the use of large samples to calculate regression equations is to be reasonably sure that the equation is accurate, since poor predictions (or rather poor decisions based on inaccurate predictions) may be costly.

3. Regression equations are calculated only for interval/ratio-scale variables; there is no equivalent formula corresponding to Spearman rho. (There are some complex procedures, such as discriminant analysis, that allow the prediction of group membership from scores on other variables, but they are not called regression equations and will not be covered in this book.)

TIP

In spite of their differences, the two concepts remain closely related; unless two variables are correlated, there is no sense in developing a regression equation to predict the score on one from the score on the other. Conversely, if score on one variable can be used to accurately predict score on the other, then you know that they are correlated. And, as you will see, the formulas for regression are related to the formulas for correlation.

What Are the Formulas for Regression?

Although there are formulas for predicting scores on variable X from scores on variable Y, they will not be dealt with in this chapter. In this chapter, we will assume that the variable you wish to predict is labeled variable Y and that your predictor variable is labeled variable X.

z-Score Formula for Regression

As was true for Pearson r, the z-score formula for regression is simpler and easier to remember than the raw score or computational formula. And, as was true for r, this formula requires the computation of z-scores and is therefore quite tedious to use. The z-score regression equation for predicting Y from X is

$$z_Y' = r_{XY} z_X$$

where: z_Y' stands for the predicted z-score on variable Y
  r_{XY} stands for the correlation between variables X and Y
  z_X stands for the actual z-score on variable X

There are two things worth noting about the z-score regression equation.

1. Notice that when r is positive, the z-score on X will be multiplied by a positive number, and the predicted z-score on Y will be positive if z_X is positive and negative if z_X is negative. In other words, when r is positive, then the predicted z-score on Y will have the same sign as the z-score on X; high scores (i.e., positive z-scores) will go with high scores and low scores with low. When r is negative, the sign of the predicted z-score will be the opposite of the sign of the z-score on the predictor variable; low scores will be predicted to go with high scores and high scores with low ones.

2. A second thing to notice about the formula for z_Y' is that, when $r = 1$, the predicted z-score on Y is exactly the same as the z-score on X. However, when the absolute magnitude of r is less than 1, which is almost always the case with real data, then the predicted z-score will be closer to zero than the z-score on the predictor variable. Since a z-score closer to zero represents a raw score closer to the mean, the implication is that the predicted score will always be closer to the mean than the raw score on which the prediction was based. The extreme case occurs when the value of r is zero. In that case, the z-score in the regression equation is multiplied by zero and the predicted z-score is zero, or the mean of the distribution.

TIP

When two variables are uncorrelated, your best prediction of a person's score on one variable is the mean on that variable. That is indeed correct; as you may remember from Chapter 4, the mean is the score that minimizes the sum of squared deviations around it, just as the regression equation minimizes the sum of squared errors in prediction. If X and Y are correlated, you can minimize your errors in prediction by using the regression equation; otherwise, your best guess as to someone's score is the mean (which is the predicted value of X or Y when the correlation between X and Y is zero).

Computational Formula

The computational formula for predicting the value of Y from the value of X and for predicting X from Y is a regression equation that uses the slope of the regression line and its intercept with the x-axis. The formula uses raw scores instead of z-scores and looks simple:

$$Y' = a + bX$$

The letters a and b are constants and are sometimes called the *regression coefficients* (Freund & Simon, 1991; Spatz & Johnson, 1989), with a standing for

FIGURE 7.2   Slope of a Regression Line

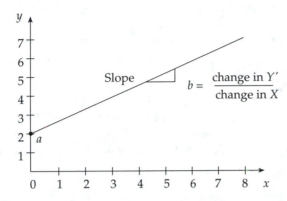

the Y-intercept and b standing for the slope of the regression line. As illustrated in Figure 7.2, the **Y-intercept** (a) is the value of Y' when the regression line crosses the y-axis—that is, the predicted value of Y when $X = 0$. The **slope of the regression line** (b), as mentioned in the previous chapter, is a fraction equal to the amount of difference in the predicted values of Y for a one-unit difference in the values of X. In other words,

$$b = \frac{\text{change in } Y'}{\text{change in } X}$$

TIP

> Unless the standard deviations for X and Y are the same, which is unlikely, the slope of the regression line for predicting Y from X will not be the same as the slope of the regression line for predicting X from Y. It is even less likely that the intercepts of the two regression equations will be the same. Thus, when computing and using a regression equation, it is essential to keep in mind which variable you are predicting from which.

Computing the predicted value of Y using the regression equation, $Y' = a + bX$, is easy: Just multiply the raw score on X by b and add the product to a. Any value of X at all can be substituted into the equation, although presumably you would concentrate on values that might represent realistic raw scores. The only difficult part of the process is computing the values of the regression coefficients, a and b. To do this, you have to start by computing b.

Computing the Slope. There are three formulas for computing the slope of the regression line, b, in order to predict Y from X. Two require a correlation coefficient and one uses raw scores.

Slope Formulas Using r. Two of the slope formulas involve Pearson r:

$$b = r\left(\frac{\sigma_Y}{\sigma_X}\right) \quad b = r\left(\frac{s_Y}{s_X}\right)$$

Both formulas indicate that the slope of the regression line for predicting Y is equal to the correlation between X and Y multiplied by the standard deviation of the scores on variable Y divided by the standard deviation of variable X.

TIP

> There are two things to keep in mind when using these formulas. First, remember that the standard deviation for the variable that you want to predict is in the numerator and the standard deviation of the predictor variable is in the denominator. Second, remember that the same type of standard deviation must be in both numerator and denominator: either σ or s. If you have already calculated r and the standard deviations for both variables, then these are the easiest formulas to use.

Slope Formula Using Raw Scores. The other formula for calculating the slope of the regression line, like all raw score formulas, looks more complicated than the formulas using r but is actually easier to calculate. The raw score formula for b is

$$b = \frac{N\Sigma XY - [(\Sigma X)(\Sigma Y)]}{N\Sigma X^2 - (\Sigma X)^2}$$

This formula involves the following steps.

Step 1: Multiply each person's scores on X and Y.

Step 2: Sum these cross products.

Step 3: Multiply the sum by the sample size.

Step 4: Sum the scores on X.

Step 5: Sum the scores on Y.

Step 6: Multiply these sums.

Step 7: Subtract this product from the product in step 3 to get the numerator.

Step 8: To get the denominator, sum the squared raw scores on variable X.

Step 9: Multiply this sum by N.

Step 10: Sum the raw scores on variable X.

Step 11: Square this sum.

Step 12: Subtract this square from the sum in step 8, which gives you the denominator.

Step 13: Divide the numerator by the denominator to get the value for b.

TIP

> Two features of the raw score formula are worth noticing. First, the denominator involves calculations based on scores on the predictor variable, not the one that you want to predict. Second, both the numerator and the denominator are used in the raw score formula for Pearson r. The numerators of the two formulas are identical, and the denominator of the regression equation is the first term under the square root sign in the denominator of the raw score formula for r.

Computing the Intercept. After the slope (b) of the regression equation ($Y' = a + bX$) has been determined, the next step is to calculate the Y-intercept (a). The formula for calculating a is

$$a = \overline{Y} - b\,\overline{X}$$

which is the mean on Y minus the slope of the regression line for predicting Y times the mean on X.

TIP

> If this formula seems arbitrary to you, try to remember that, when using it, you subtract something from (not add to) the mean on the variable that you want to predict. Remember, also, that it is set up so that when $X = \overline{X}$, then $Y' = \overline{Y}$.

Using the Regression Equations

Slope Formula Using r. To begin with, let's start with an example in which the correlation between the variables and the standard deviations of scores on both variables have already been determined.

EXAMPLE

Predicting Thrill Seeking from Analytical Problem Solving. Suppose that you have given a group of 30 people a test of thrill seeking, T, and a test of analytical problem solving, A. The mean on the T test was 40, $s_T = 3$. The mean on the A test was 20, $s_A = 2$. The two tests were correlated, with $r = -.60$. Those of you (are there any?) who find analytical problem solving to be one of life's greater thrills can ponder what this negative value of r implies. Meanwhile, we want to predict thrill seeking (T) from scores on analytical problem solving (A) using our data, which may be summarized as follows:

$\overline{T}$	s_T	$\overline{A}$	s_A	r
40	3	20	2	−.60

Solution: We must first determine the regression equation for predicting T from A. Since we are replacing Y and X with the variables T and A, we know that it will take the form

$$T' = a + bA$$

and that we need to find the values of the regression coefficients, a and b.

- To calculate b, which equals $r(s_Y/s_X)$, we substitute into the formula:

$$b = r\left(\frac{s_T}{s_A}\right) = -.60\left(\frac{3}{2}\right) = -.90$$

- To calculate a, which equals $\overline{Y} - b\,\overline{X}$, we substitute into the formula:

$$a = \overline{Y} - b\overline{X}$$

$$= 40 - (-.90)20 = 40 + 18 = 58$$

- Using the values we have calculated for a and b, we can now substitute into the regression equation:

$$T' = a + bA = 58 - .90A$$

To see how the regression equation is used, let's predict the score on T for someone who had a score of 15 on A. Using the formula, we get

$$T' = 58 - .90A$$
$$= 58 - .90(15) = 58 - 13.5 = 44.5$$

Now suppose that we want to predict T for someone who had a score of 20 on A, which is the mean of the analytical problem-solving test scores. The predicted score on T for someone with a score of 20 on A is

$$T' = 58 - .90A$$
$$= 58 - .90(20) = 40$$

which is also the mean on T. In fact, the predicted score on one variable for a person with a score at the mean on another variable will always be the mean. ▪

EXAMPLE

Predicting Analytical Problem Solving from Thrill Seeking. Suppose, in the previous example, that we had wanted to predict scores on A from scores on T.

Solution: We have to consider T as X and A as Y in the regression equation. To make clear that the values for b and a would be different in this case than in the case where we were predicting score on T, we use A as a subscript so that we will use a_A and b_A in the formulas for computing the regression coefficients.

- We begin our calculations by computing the value of b_A:

$$b_A = r\left(\frac{s_A}{s_T}\right) = -.60\left(\frac{2}{3}\right) = -.40$$

- We now compute a_A, which is $\overline{Y} - b_A\overline{X}$, by substituting:

$$a_A = \overline{A} - b_A\overline{T} = 20 - (-.40)40 = 20 - (-16) = 36$$

- The regression equation for predicting scores on A is, therefore,

$$A' = a_A + b_AT = 36 - .40T$$

Suppose that we know someone who scored 50 on the thrill-seeking test. What is his predicted problem-solving score? Substituting into the equation, we get

$$A' = 36 - .40(50) = 36 - 20 = 16$$

For someone with a score of 40 (the mean) on T, the predicted score is

$$A' = 36 - .40(40) = 20.$$

Note that 20 is the mean on A. ▪

Slope Formula Using Raw Scores. As another example of the use of regression equations, let's consider a situation in which the standard deviation and r have not been calculated. In this case, we have to use the raw scores to predict Y from X.

EXAMPLE

Marital Happiness. Suppose that Dr. D. Vorce has been studying the marital happiness of couples and attempting to relate it to the number of

TABLE 7.1   Data for Marital Happiness Example

Subject	Years Married X	X^2	Happiness Y	Y_2	XY
Ted	1	1	1	1	1
Red	1	1	1	1	1
Ned	3	9	2	4	6
Fred	4	16	1	1	4
Ed	5	25	2	4	10
Jed	5	25	2	4	10
Joe	7	49	4	16	28
Mo	7	49	3	9	21
Bo	8	64	4	16	32
Beau	9	81	5	25	45
Σ	50	320	25	81	158

$$N = 10 \qquad \overline{X} = \frac{50}{10} = 5.0 \qquad \overline{Y} = \frac{25}{10} = 2.5$$

$$(\Sigma X)^2 = (50)(50) = 2500 \qquad (\Sigma Y)^2 = (25)(25) = 625$$

years of marriage. Using the Vorce scale of happiness, ranging from 1 (mild) to 5 (extreme), he has gathered the data in Table 7.1 based on a sample of married men.

Solution

• To calculate the regression equation for predicting happiness from length of marriage, use the formula

$$b = \frac{10(158) - 50(25)}{10(320) - (2500)} = \frac{1580 - 1250}{3200 - 2500} = \frac{330}{700} = .471$$

$$a = 2.5 - .471(5.0) = 2.5 - 2.355 = .145$$

• Substitute into the regression equation for predicting happiness from years of marriage:

$$Y' = a + bX = .145 + .471X$$

• Use several values for X to see if the predictions seem reasonable. When $X = 1$,

$$Y' = .145 + .471(1) = .616$$

When $X = 5$, the mean on X,

$$Y' = .145 + .471(5) = 2.5 \text{ (the mean on } Y)$$

When $X = 10$,

$$Y' = .145 + 4.71 \text{ or } 4.855$$

When $X = 20$,

$$Y' = .145 + .471(20) = 9.565$$

which is an impossible value on a five-point scale.

TIP

The example when $X = 20$ illustrates that the predictions based on a regression equation may produce unlikely values when you are dealing with scores on one variable that are outside the range of your data. It is also true that this extreme predicted value would not have occurred were there not such a high correlation between X and Y. (In fact, $r_{XY} = .917$; check it out.) If the correlation had been substantially lower, then the predicted value of Y would have been much closer to the mean of the raw scores on Y and therefore would have been a much more typical value.

How Are Regression Lines Plotted and Used?

As noted at the beginning of this chapter, the best-fitting line to all the points on a scattergraph is the regression line, when "best fitting" means minimizing the sum of the squared errors of prediction. As is evidenced by the fact that there are separate regression equations for predicting score on Y and score on X, there are *two* regression lines for any scattergraph that reflects a less-than-perfect correlation. When it is the case that the variables are uncorrelated, then the regression equation for predicting Y is $Y' = \overline{Y}$, and the regression line is a horizontal line parallel to the x-axis with a value equal to the mean of the Y scores for every value of X. Similarly, when $r_{XY} = 0$, the regression equation for predicting X is $X' = \overline{X}$, which is a vertical line giving a value of the mean on X for every value of Y. These lines intersect at the point ($\overline{X}, \overline{Y}$), the intersection of the means of the two variables. This point will always be on both regression lines, regardless of the value of the correlation between X and Y.

When X and Y are imperfectly correlated but to an extent >0, then the two regression lines will intersect each other at less than a 90° angle. The line for predicting Y will minimize the sum of the squares of the vertical distances between the actual points and the regression line; the line for predicting X will minimize the sum of the squared horizontal discrepancies. If both lines are plotted on the same scattergraph, they will look like a tilted X. However, in most practical situations, you are interested in predicting in only one direction and therefore would plot only one of the regression lines.

Regression

> **Purpose:** To predict scores on one variable from scores on another.
>
> **Definition:** Regression is the use of an equation that gives a predicted value on one variable for every value of the other variable. This equation describes a straight line called the *regression line*.
>
> **Assumptions:**
>
> - Variables X and Y are measured on an interval or ratio scale.
> - Scores have been randomly sampled from the population.
> - The distributions of scores on variables X and Y are normal.
> - There is a linear relationship between variables X and Y in the population.
> - The distribution possesses *homoscedasticity*, which means equal variances on Y for all values of X.
>
> **Computational Formula:** $Y' = a + bX$
>
> $$\text{Slope formulas:} \quad b = r\left(\frac{\sigma_Y}{\sigma_X}\right)$$
>
> $$b = \frac{N\Sigma XY - [(\Sigma X)(\Sigma Y)]}{N\Sigma X^2 - (\Sigma X)^2}$$
>
> $$\text{Intercept formula:} \quad a = \overline{Y} - b\overline{X}$$
>
> **Predicting X from Y:** The regression equations and the regression line for predicting values of X from scores on variable Y will almost always be numerically different from those for predicting Y from X.

Plotting the Regression Line

To plot the regression line, it is necessary to identify any two points that fit the equation and connect them by a straight line. As mentioned before, one point on the regression line for Y' will always be $(\overline{X}, \overline{Y})$ and another will always be $(0, a)$, the Y-intercept. You could simply plot and connect these two points to get a picture of the regression line. However, I would suggest plotting an additional point as well, substituting in a value of X that is reasonably far from the mean and from zero, just to guard against the possibility of making an error. If all three points lie on the same straight line, as they should, you have wasted a little time; if not, you know that you need to search for a mistake in computation or drawing.

Using the Regression Line

The reason that people plot the regression line, aside from the exhilaration of seeing it fall neatly in the middle of the scattergraph, is that sometimes a very carefully plotted regression line, especially if it is drawn on fine graph paper, can substitute for actually calculating the predicted Y' for every value of X. If you are making decisions based on predicted scores, it may be that the plotted regression line will give the predicted values in fine enough detail for your purposes and save you from needing to use the formula.

EXAMPLE

Talking in School. Suppose the following scores represent the number of times that six children in a classroom spoke up during the first week of the school year (X) and during the tenth week (Y):

X	X^2	Y	Y^2	XY
3	9	7	49	21
1	1	2	4	2
1	1	4	16	4
2	4	5	25	10
2	4	6	36	12
3	9	5	25	15
Σ 12	28	29	155	64

We want to plot the regression line for predicting Y (talking in week 10) from X (talking in week 1).

Solution: We must first derive the regression equation.

Step 1: Calculate the slope:

$$b = \frac{N\Sigma XY - [(\Sigma X)(\Sigma Y)]}{N\Sigma X^2 - (\Sigma X)^2}$$

by substituting the appropriate sums and sums of squares:

$$b = \frac{6(64) - 12(29)}{6(28) - 12^2} = \frac{384 - 348}{168 - 144} = \frac{36}{24} = 1.50$$

Step 2: To get a, calculate $\overline{X}$, which $= 12/6$ or 2.000, and $\overline{Y}$, which $= 29/6$ or 4.833.

Step 3: Use the formula for the intercept, $a = \overline{Y} - b\overline{X}$:

$$a = 4.833 - 1.50(2.000) = 4.833 - 3.000 = 1.833$$

FIGURE 7.3   The Regression Line for Prediction in the Talking in School Example

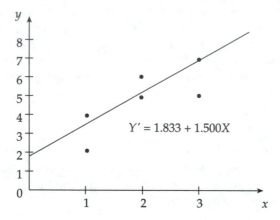

Step 4: Substitute into the regression equation:

$$Y' = 1.833 + 1.500X$$

Now, let's plot both the scattergraph of the original data points and the regression line on the same axes, as shown in Figure 7.3. You can see from the scattergraph (and from the preceding table) that the relationship between the two variables is positive. You can also tell that one point on the regression line will be (0, 1.833), the Y-intercept, and that another point will be (2.00, 4.83), the means on X and Y. We can also calculate a predicted value for $X = 1$, which would be 1.833 + 1.5(1) or 3.333, and plot it as well. The predicted value for $X = 3$ would be 1.833 + 4.500 = 6.333. On this graph, you can see an example of a discrepancy or error in prediction, $Y - Y'$, reflecting the fact that the predicted scores differ from the actual ones. ■

What Is Regression Toward the Mean?

The term **regression toward the mean**, or statistical regression, refers to the tendency for predicted scores to be closer to the mean on the predicted variable than the raw scores are on the predictor variable. The regression equation provides an explicit statement of the amount of regression toward the mean to be expected, with the z-score equation showing the amount of regression most clearly.

Whenever r is positive but imperfect, the predicted z-score on one variable lies somewhere between the mean on that variable and the corresponding z-score on the predictor variable. The range of predicted z-scores, therefore, is always somewhat less than the range of the z-scores on the predictor variable, unless $|r| = 1$. If $r = 0$, then the predicted z-score is, of course, zero (the mean), regardless of the score on the predictor variable. The fact that the range of *predicted* z-scores on Y is less than the range of z-scores on X does not indicate that the range of *actual* z-scores (or raw scores) on Y is necessarily less than the range of scores on X.

Conceptual Examples

Although the concept of regression toward the mean may seem rather abstract, most people have an intuitive idea of what it means. For example, if you were told that Sue got a z-score of 2 on the first of several tests in a class and were asked to predict what her z-score on the second test was, you would probably recognize that scores on two tests in the same course are likely to be positively but not perfectly correlated. If your prediction of Sue's score on the second test is that she did better than the average student in the class but not quite as well as she did on the first test, you are showing an implicit belief in regression toward the mean. Similarly, if you were told that Joe got a z-score of −1.5 on the second test and were asked to estimate his score on the first test, would you guess that he did worse than average, but maybe not quite so badly as he did on the second test? If so, your judgment is again reflecting the effects of regression toward the mean.

Regression Toward the Mean and Test Scores.   When thinking about predicting a score on one test from a score on another, whether the tests are two closely related measures or perhaps the same test administered twice, it may help to think of a test score as composed of both a true score and a certain amount of error. A person who receives an extremely low score probably is truly below average but may also have had some bad luck, such as guessing wrong on everything, feeling sick, and in general having all the random factors influencing performance come out in the direction of a low score. Upon a retest, or upon taking a related test, this person will still have a true score below average but might have better luck in guessing; in other words, all the errors in measurement won't be in the same direction, and his or her score on the retest may come out somewhat higher.

Keep in mind that regression toward the mean does not reflect any actual change in a person's behavior or performance, such as trying harder if he or she gets a low test score. Instead it reflects only the statistical relationship between actual scores and predicted scores. Remember that if a test measures perfectly, then the correlation between the score on the test and a retest would be perfect (unless the people being measured had changed by different amounts in the meantime on the variable being measured). Regression toward the mean operates only when two variables are not perfectly correlated, such as when a test has some error in measurement.

Research Examples

The importance of regression toward the mean is that it can frequently lead one to mistaken conclusions when doing research, unless it is taken into account. There are many occasions in which regression toward the mean can be a *threat to validity*—that is, it can cause someone to form incorrect interpretations about the meaning of the data.

Treatment Programs.   One instance in which regression toward the mean may operate is in the case in which students or other individuals are chosen to be in remedial or treatment programs on the basis of their low test scores. If people are chosen because their scores are far below the mean and then they are retested on the same or a correlated test, you would expect their scores on a retest to be higher regardless of whether they participated in the program or not and regardless of whether or not such a program was effective. In the fields of education and social services, people are often chosen to participate in programs because their scores are low and because it is assumed that individuals with low scores are those most in need of educational or social service programs. Depending on the methodology, regression toward the mean may be a threat to validity in studies that attempt to assess the effects of such programs.

Experimental Versus Nonexperimental Designs. If there is an experimental design, with participants randomly assigned to receive the remedial program or some alternative, then statistical regression will not threaten the validity of the conclusions. Although regression toward the mean will be operating, it will be equally potent in the experimental and control groups; the difference in gains between the groups should reflect only the effects of the experimental treatment. However, if there is no control group, some of the gains in scores shown by a group selected on the basis of low pretest scores will be due to regression toward the mean. If the correlation between pretest and posttest scores and the standard deviations of scores on both measures are known, perhaps based on data from earlier samples, then it is possible to estimate how much of the gain in scores is due to statistical regression and how much is due to other causes (such as the program). However, without such information and without a control group, regression toward the mean is *confounded*, or mixed up, with the effects of the treatment program. For example, statistical regression may account for part of the apparent gains of some bilingual education programs (Willig, 1985).

Social Programs. A related situation is the case of social programs that are instigated when some variable that normally vacillates—crime rates, accident rates, interest rates, or some such sociological or economic variable—is at its peak. One would predict that the frequency or value of the variable would be closer to the mean when remeasured, without knowing anything about what specific events might have occurred in the interim. However, if a social program is begun at the time when the variable is at an extreme, some people might assume that the program is solely responsible for the fact that the score on the variable is closer to average when retested at a later date.

Examples of Treatment Programs. One example of a treatment program is the situation in which children are selected for the WIC (Women, Infants, and Children) Supplemental Nutrition Program because their scores on pretest measures of height, weight, and blood iron content are just low enough to meet the criteria for selection. Since these values fluctuate naturally, it may appear that the WIC program caused improvements in these values, whereas the changes from pretest to posttest were due to regression toward the mean (Devaney, 1991).

Another instance in which regression toward the mean can account for some portion of seeming improvements is in the case of psychotherapy. Suppose that people have normal ups and downs in mood, for instance, but that they are particularly likely to seek therapy when their mood is at its nadir. One would predict an improvement in mood with or without treatment. Without a control group, it is difficult to know what proportion of any improvement should be attributed to regression toward the mean.

Enrichment Programs. Of course, regression toward the mean is not a possible explanation of a change in scores when the change is in the direction opposite to the mean. If a group of high-scoring individuals is given a special enrichment program, such as a class for the gifted or a training program for superior athletes, then an improvement in scores that is greater than the gains that would be expected due to maturation alone could not be due to statistical regression. However, it is possible that regression toward the mean might obscure the effects of such a program by making them appear weaker than they really are.

It is important to be cautious if you read a report of a new program or curriculum stating that it appears to be particularly effective for the low-achieving or low-scoring individuals but that it does not seem to aid the performance of the high achievers. Such a result is exactly what one would predict if regression toward the mean is operating. Of course, this does not mean that there are no programs well suited to people on the low end of the continuum and poorly suited to high performers. Indeed, if the low and high scorers on the pretest had been randomly assigned to experimental and control groups, it would be quite possible to come to valid conclusions about aptitude-treatment interactions, or the relative effects of the program for high- and low-scoring individuals.

Matched Groups. Another instance in which regression toward the mean may operate is when matched groups are used for purposes of comparison in such a way that the lowest scoring children from one group are selected along with the highest scoring children from the other group.

Bilingual Education Example. One instance when regression toward the mean may lead to false conclusions is found in the area of bilingual education. Children selected to receive a bilingual program in the United States may come from the lower end of a population with respect to English language proficiency. The children from the comparison groups, on the other hand, are likely to come from a population with higher average scores on a measure of English language proficiency. If the group of children who are receiving bilingual education and the comparison group from other classrooms are matched based on their scores, then those in the comparison group are likely to come from the lower end of their population and to regress toward the mean of their distribution, showing an improvement in scores from pretest to posttest. Their matched counterparts in the bilingual program, who have higher scores than the average of their population, are likely to regress toward the mean of their population and show a decline in scores from pretest to posttest. Such changes would be due purely to regression toward the mean and in no way reflect the effects of the bilingual or other educational program. Regression toward the mean would have the effect of reducing the apparent effects of the bilingual program (Willig, 1985).

Other Examples of Matching. Similar examples could come from many instances in which two curricula or medical treatments or programs are being compared for samples of people from different populations. If individuals were randomly assigned to the treatments, there would be no confounding of the changes in scores due to statistical regression with the changes due to the treatment. However, whenever naturally occurring populations with different means are compared, you can expect that groups that are matched on pretest scores will each show changes in the direction of their population mean, thus giving the false impression that the program was more effective for those people selected from the population with the higher mean.

TIP

> In short, matching of groups on pretest scores is not an adequate way to control for group differences. Although no way, short of random assignment, is ideal, an analysis of covariance, which takes pretest scores into account, can be helpful in reducing the potentially confounding effects of regression toward the mean. The use of very precise measures is even better; if true scores could be measured exactly, then regression toward the mean would not be a problem in such situations.

To summarize, whenever people are selected on the basis of extreme scores and their scores change in the direction of the mean, regression toward the mean is likely to be operating. You should be cautious in assuming that any or all changes are due to some program or treatment intervening between pretest and posttest, unless there is a randomly assigned control group that did not receive the treatment.

Regression Toward the Mean

What is it? Statistical regression is the tendency for predicted scores to be closer to the mean (in standard deviation units) on the predicted variable than are the raw scores on the predictor variable.

When does it occur? Regression toward the mean operates only when two variables are not perfectly correlated, such as when a test has some error in measurement.

When is it a threat to validity? Regression toward the mean is a problem when it leads to incorrect interpretations about the meaning of the data.

Examples:

1. Treatment programs. If individuals are chosen to be in remedial or treatment programs on the basis of their low test scores and then they are retested on the same test or a correlated measure, regression toward the mean, not necessarily the treatment, would lead their scores to improve.

2. Social programs. If a social program is instigated when a variable is at an extreme, regression toward the mean, not necessarily the treatment, would lead to scores on the variable getting closer to the mean.

3. Matched groups. When groups that are to have different experiences are matched on pretest scores for purposes of comparison in such a way that the lowest scoring from one group are selected along with the highest scoring from the other group, the posttest scores may regress toward the means of their respective groups, leading to a difference in posttest means that is not caused by any subsequent experience.

When is it not a threat to validity? Statistical regression is generally not a problem if it does not lead you to mistakenly conclude that a treatment or program had an effect.

Examples:

1. True experiments. When subjects are randomly assigned to conditions, regression toward the mean will affect all groups equally and will not lead to misleading conclusions.

2. Scores getting farther from the mean. If posttest scores of a group receiving a treatment are farther from the mean than pretest scores, regression toward the mean can lead to an underestimate of the effects of the treatment but not to an overestimate. It would not lead to the mistaken conclusion that a treatment is effective.

What Is a Standard Error of Estimate?

A **standard error of estimate** is a measure of the average amount of error in estimating scores on one variable from scores on another. In fact, several types of standard errors are associated with regression, such as the error in estimating the slope and the error in estimating the intercept, but we will discuss only the standard error of estimate for predicting scores on Y.

The standard error of estimate for predicting Y from X is symbolized as $s_{Y \cdot X}$. If this symbol looks similar to the symbol for standard deviation, that is not a coincidence. The standard error of estimate is essentially the standard deviation of the errors in estimating Y from X.

As was mentioned in the previous chapter, the standard error of estimate is closely related to the correlation coefficient and, in particular, to the coefficient of determination. When two variables are perfectly correlated, with $r = 1$ or -1, then there will be no error at all in predicting the value of Y or X. As the correlation coefficient gets closer to zero, the value of Y' gets closer to $\overline{Y}$ and the value of X' gets closer to $\overline{X}$, indicating an increased amount of regression toward the mean. This relationship between r and $s_{Y \cdot X}$ is easier to see when we examine the formulas for $s_{Y \cdot X}$.

Formulas

Formula Using r. The formula for the standard error of estimate for estimating Y from X is

$$s_{Y \cdot X} = s_Y \sqrt{1 - r^2}$$

Strictly speaking, this formula should be multiplied by $\sqrt{N/(N-2)}$ (Cohen & Cohen, 1983; Evans, 1996). Because $N/(N-2)$ will be close to 1 unless N is quite small, this correction term can usually be ignored. In other words, the standard error of estimate equals the standard deviation of the scores on variable Y times the square root of $1 - r^2$.

Looking at the formula, you can see that if r equals either $+1$ or -1, then r^2 will equal 1; the number under the square root sign will be zero, and the standard error of estimate will be zero. In other words, there will be no errors in estimation. If r gets close to zero, on the other hand, the standard error of estimate will get close to the standard deviation of the Y scores. Since your estimate of every score would be the mean in this case, the deviations from your estimates would be exactly the same as the deviations of the raw scores from the mean and $s_{Y \cdot X}$ would equal s_Y.

Formula Using Deviations. The other formula for the standard error of estimate does not involve calculating r but does require calculating the predicted value of Y for every set of scores. The discrepancy or error score, symbolized by $Y - Y'$ or e, is then calculated for each raw score. The formula for the standard error of estimate, $s_{Y \cdot X}$ (which is sometimes written s_e in this formula) is

$$s_{Y \cdot X} = \sqrt{\frac{\Sigma(Y - Y')^2}{N - 2}}$$

This formula is sometimes abbreviated $\sqrt{\Sigma e^2/(N - 2)}$. As you can see, it is very similar to the formula for the standard deviation of a sample, except that the deviation scores are deviations from Y' instead of $\overline{Y}$, and it has $N - 2$ in the denominator, rather than $N - 1$.

Interpretation

Accuracy of Prediction. Since the standard error of estimate is a kind of standard deviation, albeit of errors rather than of raw scores, you can use the normal curve table to calculate the likelihood that the true score is any particular distance from Y' or X'. For example, 68% of the time the true score will be within one standard error of estimate of the predicted score, and 95% of the time the true score will be within 1.96 standard errors of estimate of the predicted score.

In other words, the standard error of estimate is a measure of how accurate your estimates are. The lower the error in prediction, the more confidence you can have that your predictions are correct. If you are predicting something important, such as job performance or college grades, you would hope to find a predictor with a small standard error of estimate.

Homoscedasticity. Strictly speaking, these conclusions about the standard error of estimate are true only when the population possesses the quality of **homoscedasticity**, which is a term that can be broken down into two parts: *homo*, which means *same*, and *scedasticity*, which refers to variance or spread. As illustrated by the scattergraph in Figure 7.4, a bivariate distribution that possesses homoscedasticity is one in which the variance (or standard deviation or range) of the scores on Y is the same for any value of X. The range of scores on Y in the first scattergraph is about 20 points for every value of X.

The alternative to homoscedasticity is **heteroscedasticity**, a condition in which the scores on Y vary in differing amounts at different levels of X. An example of heteroscedasticity can be seen in the second scattergraph in Figure 7.4. The range of scores on Y for some values of X is 40 points; the range of scores on Y for other values of X is 0 points. Another way of thinking about homoscedasticity is that it refers to the situation when the standard deviation of the errors of estimate is approximately the same for every value of X (or, alternatively, of Y). Homoscedasticity is important because it would not be particularly useful to calculate an overall standard error of estimate if the errors in estimating Y varied greatly depending on the value of X.

FIGURE 7.4   Variance in a Bivariate Distribution

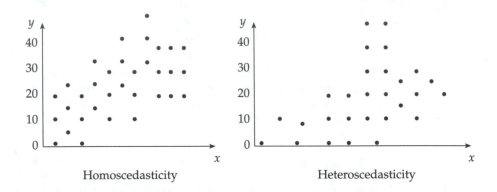

Homoscedasticity   Heteroscedasticity

Standard Error of Estimate

Definition: The standard error of estimate is a measure of the average amount of error in estimating scores on one variable from scores on another.

Symbols: $s_{Y \cdot X}$ or s_e

Formulas: $s_{Y \cdot X} = s_Y \sqrt{1 - r^2}$ $s_{Y \cdot X} = \sqrt{\dfrac{\Sigma (Y - Y')^2}{N - 2}}$

Interpretation: The standard error of estimate is a measure of how accurate your estimates are. The lower the standard error of estimate, the more accurate your prediction.

Use: Since the standard error of estimate for predicting Y is a kind of standard deviation of the errors in estimating Y, you can use the normal curve table to calculate the likelihood that the true score is any particular distance from Y'.

Range of possible values: The standard error of estimate can range from zero (if there is no error in prediction) to s_Y (if variables X and Y are uncorrelated).

What Is Multiple Regression?

This chapter has dealt with the use of scores on one variable to predict scores on another. Although bivariate distributions are common, leading to the use of regression equations involving only one predictor, an even more common procedure is the use of multiple predictors, a technique called **multiple regression**. The symbol R stands for both multiple regression and multiple correlation, although multiple regression is the more common technique. Multiple regression is used to predict the score on a single dependent measure from a weighted combination of predictor variables.

A multiple regression equation looks a lot like a bivariate linear regression equation, except that it has more coefficients than a and b; a separate coefficient is included for each of the predictors. For example, a multiple regression equation for predicting scores on Y from scores on variables G, E, and F might look like

$$Y' = 3 + 2.5G - 1.6E + 8.9F$$

This kind of multiple regression equation uses raw scores on the predictor variable and is almost as easy to use as a bivariate regression equation—just plug in the raw scores, multiply by their corresponding coefficients, and add them. The sum you get is the predicted score on Y. The correlation between these predicted values and the actual scores on Y, R, is called the *multiple correlation*.

For theoretical purposes, multiple regression equations are sometimes written with special coefficients called beta weights or standardized regression coefficients (Aron & Aron, 1997) that are multiplied by z-scores on the different predictor variables, rather than by raw scores. This form of multiple regression equation makes it easier to see the relative contributions of the predictors in the equation than does the form using weights for raw scores. Essentially, the larger the absolute value of the beta weight is, the larger the contribution to the regression equation.

Multiple regression is, in fact, substantially more complicated than bivariate regression. For one thing, deriving the formula is much more complex, particularly if there are many predictors. Deciding on which predictors to enter at what point in the equation and on whether to include measures of the interactions between different predictors can turn out to be difficult. (The interaction between predictors refers to the extent to which the effect of one predictor variable on Y depends on the level of the other predictor.) Interpreting a multiple regression equation requires the knowledge that how much a factor contributes to a multiple regression equation depends on the other variables in the equation, not just on its correlation with the dependent measure. In short, multiple regression is a complex statistical technique that requires informed decisions about the best procedure to use in any particular case. Many universities, including my own, offer entire courses covering multiple regression.

Although the details of how to carry out a multiple regression are complex and the use of a computer is essential, it is a useful and important technique. Multiple regression equations are widely used for screening decisions, such as deciding who qualifies for a risky medical procedure, and for making predictions about outcomes ranging from grade-point averages to life expectancies.

When Is Regression Used?

If you remember that regression is a synonym for *prediction*, you will consider using it any time you want to predict scores on one variable from scores on another. Regression is used when both variables are measured on an interval or ratio scale, and when you have data on a representative sample, so that you can formulate a regression equation that can be generalized to other samples from the same population.

TIP

> Of course, there is no point in using the regression equation to predict Y' for people whose scores on variable Y have already been measured. The purpose of a regression equation is not to make predictions about the original sample but to be able to make predictions about new individuals whose performance is unknown.

If you could predict the degree of success an individual would be likely to experience as a football player, violinist, parent, cook, or physician, based on scores of people who did and did not subsequently excel at one of these activities, then you could use these predictions to advise in career selection or to develop programs to help individuals who might need assistance to excel in some area. If these possibilities seem a bit far-fetched, think about the usefulness of predicting who will do well in an advanced German class by giving a pretest or who will be likely to benefit from chemotherapy or to develop hypertension based on a screening measure. Regression equations could be used in all these areas.

CHAPTER SUMMARY   In statistics, the term *regression* means *prediction*. A regression equation is a formula for predicting scores on Y from scores on X (or vice versa); it describes the line that best fits the points on the scattergraph. This line is the regression line. The simplest regression equation states that the predicted z-score on Y is equal to the corresponding z-score on X times the correlation between X and Y. The computational formula, which uses raw scores, for predicting Y from X is $Y' = a + bX$.

The letter a in the regression equation for predicting Y denotes the Y-intercept, and b denotes the slope. The Y-intercept is the predicted value of Y when $X = 0$, and the slope is the amount of difference in the predicted values of Y for a one unit difference in the value of X. By computing the predicted value of Y for any two values of X, the regression line for predicting Y can be plotted. It will be the same as the regression line for predicting X only if $r = 0$, in which case all the points on the scattergraph will fall on the regression line.

When two variables are not perfectly correlated, regression toward the mean will lead the predicted scores on either variable to be closer to the mean than the actual scores usually are. This characteristic can lead to misinterpretations of research (e.g., if a gain in scores by people who were far below average is assumed to be due solely to some intervention).

The standard error of estimate is a measure of the average amount of error in estimating scores on one variable from scores on another. When r is 1 or –1, the standard error of estimate is zero, and there is no error in prediction. When r is close to zero, the standard error of estimate is close to the standard deviation of the distribution of scores on the variable being predicted.

Multiple regression is a widely used but computationally complex technique for predicting scores on one variable from scores on a combination of other variables.

CHAPTER REVIEW

Multiple-Choice Questions

1. The regression equation for predicting shoe size, S, from glove size, G, is $S = 1.2G + 1$. The mean glove size is 6, and the mean shoe size is 8.2. Alice wears a size 5 glove. What is her predicted shoe size?

   a. 5   **b.** 6   **c.** 6.2   **d.** 7   **e.** 7.2   **f.** 8.2

2. Which of the following is an example of regression toward the mean possibly leading a researcher to mistaken conclusions?

   a. Bill tries out a remedial program with learning-disabled children and their scores decline.

   b. In an experimental study, the scores of a randomly assigned experimental group improve more than the scores of the control group.

   c. A program for children chosen because they were gifted in math shows huge gains.

   d. Boys selected because they scored poorly on a reading readiness test showed huge gains in reading after a new program.

   e. After watching a violent movie, children got more violent.

3. The best measure of the amount of variability in the errors of prediction when using a regression equation is

   a. the standard deviation

   b. the standard error of estimate

   c. the variance

d. the sum of the errors

e. the regression coefficients

4. The regression equation for predicting SAT math score, M, from SAT verbal score, V, is $M = .8V + 136$. The mean on M is 474, and the mean on V is 422. Della got a 600 on the verbal SAT. What is her predicted math SAT score?

   a. 474   **b.** 515   **c.** 600   **d.** 616   **e.** 674   **f.** 736

   g. none of the above

5. If the correlation between two variables is −1.00 and Laura got a score 1.3 standard deviations below the mean on the first variable, what score would you predict for Laura on the second variable?

   a. a raw score of 1.3   **b.** a raw score of −1.3   **c.** a raw score of −.65

   d. a z-score of 0   **e.** a z-score of 1.3   **f.** a z-score of −1.3

6. If the standard deviation of the scores on $X = 3.2$, the standard deviation of the scores on $Y = .8$, and $r = .6$, what will the value of b for predicting Y be?

   a. .125   **b.** .15   **c.** .25   **d.** .6   **e.** 1.5   **f.** 2.4   **g.** 4

   h. none of the above

7. If the correlation between variables X and Y is .4, the standard deviation of the scores on variable X is 10, and the standard deviation of the scores on variable Y is 8, what is the slope of the regression line for predicting scores on X from scores on Y?

   a. .32   **b.** .4   **c.** .5   **d.** 4   **e.** 40   **f.** 50   **g.** none of the above

8. The regression equation for predicting property taxes, P, from sales taxes, S, in a locality is $P = 1000 - 3S$. The sales tax in Poplarville is 6. What is the predicted property tax?

   a. 982   **b.** 997   **c.** 1018   **d.** 2994   **e.** 3006   **f.** 5000

9. The slope of the regression line for predicting Y from X is 6 and the Y-intercept is 4. What is the formula for the regression line?

   a. $Y' = 4 + 6X$ **b.** $Y' = 24$ **c.** $Y' = 4Y + 6X$

   d. $Y' = 6Y + 4X$ **e.** $Y' = 6 + 4X$

10. The mean of the scores on diastolic heart rate, D, for a sample of 900 patients is 100, $s_D = 19$. The mean systolic heart rate, S, is 150, $s_S = 26$. The correlation between S and D is .9. What is the standard error of estimate for predicting D from S?

    a. 3.61   **b.** 8.28   **c.** 11.34   **d.** 43.6   **e.** 65.40   **f.** none of the above

Problems

11. As the head of a new manufacturing plant that is going to open in Greensboro in August, you have decided to give the Assembly Line Accuracy Test

(ALAT) to all job applicants and use it to predict job performance. You gave this test to a sample of applicants at the old plant and related it to the number of errors they made in working on the assembly line there. You compile the following table of data:

Worker	ALAT Score	Errors per Day on the Job
Fran	14	0
Frank	8	2
Frances	6	4
Frieda	4	6
Fred	1	10

a. Compute the regression equation for predicting the number of errors per day on the job from a person's ALAT score.

b. Fay got a score of 12 on the ALAT. How many errors per day would she be predicted to make?

c. Do you think that it makes sense to use the ALAT as a screening test, assuming that errors per day is the crucial measure of performance? Why or why not?

12. The regression equation for predicting the average size of a middle school in a school district from the average size of the elementary schools in the district is $M = 2.2E + 100$. Across a large sample of school districts, the mean elementary school size is 300 students.

a. Typicaltown, USA, has an average of 200 students in its elementary schools. What is the predicted size of its middle schools, according to the equation?

b. What is the size of the average middle school in the sample?

c. Is the correlation between elementary school size and middle school size positive or negative? How can you tell?

13. You have given a group of 38 people a measure of creativity, C, and a test of neuroticism, N. The two tests were correlated with $r_{CN} = .4$. The mean score on the creativity test was 30, $s_C = 4$. The mean on neuroticism was 20, with $s_N = 2$. Use this information to answer the following questions.

a. Was the correlation between creativity and neuroticism statistically significant?

b. What is $s_{N \cdot C}$, the standard error of estimate for predicting N from C?

c. What is the regression equation for predicting C from N?

d. Goofy got a score of 25 on the neuroticism test. What is his predicted creativity score?

14. In which of the following conditions is statistical regression likely to lead a naive researcher to mistaken conclusions—that is, to be a possible cause of some findings that could be misinterpreted as due to the treatment or program?

   a. A random sample of 30 children from the sixth grade at Solicitude School are given a program to increase aerobic fitness. They all improve.

   b. Students at Artesano Elementary School are given a test of artistic ability. The top 25% are selected for a special art education program. When those who had the program are retested, they all show higher scores.

   c. The lowest 20% of the class at Harrison High School is randomly split into two groups, one of which receives a special study skills program. Their grades improve more than those of the control group, who don't receive the program.

   d. The poorest ten students in the Okefenokee Orchestra, as judged by a two-minute rendition of "Twinkle, Twinkle, Little Star," are given seven hours of individual lessons. When they play the tune again after the lessons, their performance has improved.

   e. Kids in school B have higher average spelling test scores than kids in school A. The bottom 10% of the kids in school B have a mean score of 30 on a pretest, as do the top 10% of kids in school A. You decide to compare these two groups of students with mean scores of 30 after they have had one of the spelling programs. After school B gets the Superific Spelling Series and school A gets Dull Old Drill, the kids are retested. The kids who were in the bottom 10% at school B before the lesson now have a mean of 30 (still), while the ones who were in the top 10% at school A now have a mean of 50 on the spelling test. So you conclude that Dull Old Drill is better than the Superific Spelling Series.

15. If $s_H = 6$, $s_P = 8$, $N = 10$, $\overline{H} = 20$, $\overline{P} = 30$, and $r_{HP} = -.5$,

   a. What is the slope of the regression line for predicting H from P?

   b. What is the slope of the regression line for predicting P from H?

   c. What is the standard error of estimate for predicting H from P?

   d. What is the coefficient of determination?

   e. What percentage of the variance in the scores on Y can be predicted from knowing people's scores on X?

16. You are interested in seeing whether or not you can predict musical abilities from mathematical abilities and vice versa. Therefore, you give a sample of adults the Mozart Test of Musical Talent and the Newton Mathematical Aptitude Test. Their scores are as follows:

Name	MTMT Score	NMAT Score
Marlene	4	8
Norman	6	6
Omar	2	4
Phil	1	5
Quentin	3	7
Ron	0	4
Sharon	6	10

a. What is the correlation between MTMT score and NMAT score?

b. Is this correlation statistically significant?

c. Describe this relationship in a sentence.

d. What is the regression equation for predicting NMAT score from MTMT score?

e. What is the regression equation for predicting MTMT score from NMAT score?

f. Susan got a score of 4 on the MTMT. What score would you predict for her on the NMAT?

g. Carlos got a score of 4 on the NMAT. What would be his predicted score on the MTMT?

17. You are interested in knowing how stable children's interest in reading is. Therefore, you ask children in your class to count the number of books that they read during the month of October and again during the month of January. The data look like this:

	October	January
Linda	0	0
Larry	2	1
Laurie	3	4
Landra	5	6
Louis	6	8
Lionel	3	4
Luisa	3	3
Lola	1	1

a. What is the correlation between the number of books read during the month of October and the number read during January?

b. Based on the correlation coefficient, will the slope of the regression line for predicting the number of books read in January from the number of books read in October be positive or negative? Now compute the slope.

c. Compute and write out the regression equation for predicting the number of books read in January from the number of books read in October.

d. Lulu read 4 books in October. How many books is she predicted to read in January?

18. You are interested in predicting the number of times a worker asks for help from the number of times he or she is asked for help. In other words, do people who help others a lot also receive more help from others, as a theory of reciprocity or mutual friendship might suggest, or do they receive less help, as a theory of unequal expertise might imply? To study this, you observe salesclerks serving customers in a department store for a day and note how many times each person is asked to help another salesclerk and how many times he or she asks another clerk for help. The data look like this:

	Requested to Help	Requests Help
Joe	3	4
Jackie	0	0
José	5	4
John	2	1
Jessica	6	6
Jake	2	3

a. From looking at the data, can you guess whether the slope of the regression line for predicting how often someone requests help is likely to be positive or negative?

b. Compute the slope of the regression line.

c. Now compute the regression equation for predicting the number of times someone will request help from the number of times he or she is asked to help.

d. Jennifer has been asked to help someone else an average of 6 times per day. How often would you predict that she would ask another salesclerk to help her?

e. Notice that Jessica was asked to help someone else six times, just like Jennifer. How do you explain the discrepancy between Y' for Jennifer and the actual value of Y for Jessica?

19. For each of the following situations, suggest the most appropriate statistical procedure to use (from the ones covered in the textbook so far, even if you don't know how to compute them).

a. You want to predict Masculinity scores on a measure of gender roles from number of older brothers a person has.

b. You want to predict Femininity scores on a measure of gender roles from number of older brothers, number of older sisters, and Masculinity scores.

   c. You want to see what is the relationship between Masculinity scores and Femininity scores on a multidimensional measure of gender roles.

   d. You want to see what is the relationship between Masculinity scores and Femininity scores while controlling for number of sisters and brothers.

   e. You want to know how much increase (or decrease) in predicted Masculinity score you could expect for every additional brother that a person has.

   f. You want to know how far off you are likely to be if you predict Masculinity scores for people using a regression equation based on a sample of individuals.

20. For a sample of 52 people, the correlation between a measure of dullness and a measure of originality turned out to be $-.500$. The mean score on the Dullness scale was 25, $s = 5$, and the mean score on the Originality index was 75, $s = 15$.

   a. Was the correlation between Dullness and Originality statistically significant?

   b. What is the regression equation for predicting Dullness from Originality?

   c. Tom got a score of 50 on the Originality scale. What is his predicted Dullness score?

   d. What is the standard error of estimate for predicting Dullness score from Originality?

   e. What is the standard error of estimate for predicting Originality score from Dullness?

Study Questions

1. Try to think of five situations in which you would want to predict scores on one interval/ratio variable from scores on another. Are there any instances in which you might want to predict in both directions? In each of these situations, would it be feasible to measure a sample of people on both variables? If so, would it be possible to develop a regression equation to predict people's scores on one of the variables?

2. Think about all the information you had to submit when you applied to college—such things as test scores, teachers' recommendations, grades, essays, and letters of reference from your babysitter and your dog. For each piece of data, think about how it was scored or how it might have been coded by the college admissions committee (e.g., reference from your dog on a five-bark scale). Then try to make up coefficients for the slope and intercept that would allow you to plug in reasonable values on this variable and predict a student's grade-point average. For instance, you could say, if five barks is the best and one bark the worst, that the regression equation for predicting GPA from barks would be $Y' = .5 + .6X$, where $Y = $ GPA and $X = $ barks. If the mean

GPA is 2.3, for instance, the possible range of GPAs based on this formula would seem reasonable. Note that I'm not asking you to compute a regression equation, just to think about what kind of regression equation would predict reasonable values on variable Y (GPA) from variable X (your predictor variable).

3. Try to find some instances in which regression equations have been used. You can look in professional journals, talk to people who work in personnel or admissions offices, or even look through newspapers and magazines. In which of these situations, if any, is there a reference to the standard error of estimate?

4. Try to locate and read about at least three examples of situations in which regression toward the mean could have been operating and could have affected the interpretations of some research. Your best bet would be to search professional journals, particularly in education, counseling, and psychology, but you will probably also find some examples in the popular press, if you look for reports of new programs or treatments. In each case, see if you can come up with some ideas about how regression to the mean could have been eliminated as a threat to validity.

The Logic of Inferential Statistics

How Are Samples Used in Inferential Statistics?

As stated in Chapters 1 and 2 of this text, behavioral researchers are interested in looking for relationships and explanations that apply to populations, usually composed of people but sometimes of cities, hospitals, schools, or other units. Whenever possible, researchers try to study everyone (or every unit) in the population, so that they can be sure that their results will be accurate and apply to the whole population. When an entire population cannot be studied, inferential statistics are used to draw inferences from a sample that can be applied or generalized to the population from which the sample came.

This chapter outlines the logic of statistical reasoning in several sections. The first major section discusses sampling procedures; the next discusses how a single sample can be considered to represent many possible samples; the third considers a statistic, the z-test, which uses sample means to draw inferences about population means; and the last sections discuss the uses of inferential statistical procedures and how hypotheses are tested.

As noted in Chapter 1, if every unit in the population has been measured, so that the data are based on the entire population, then the scores or the individuals generating the scores are referred to as a *census*. Organizations that have a complete list of all their members and that have enough control over the members to compel or induce them to participate in a research study may be able to actually conduct a census. The U.S. government attempts to do so every ten years but fails to achieve this goal completely, as is evident from the many complaints made by representatives of groups who feel that their constituency has been undercounted.

Although conducting a census and gathering descriptive data on the participants is always the most desirable procedure for selecting subjects if your goal is to produce clearly interpretable data, it is frequently impossible (and even more frequently, inconvenient) to do so. Most of the time when we do research we are unable to measure the entire population of interest. We are therefore forced to rely on a less inclusive sample and to generalize from the statistics gathered on the sample to the entire population.

Random Sampling

The next best thing to doing a census, if your purpose is to use a sample to draw inferences about a population, is to use a random selection or sampling procedure. Although no sampling procedure, even random sampling, can guarantee that the sample will precisely reflect the population (Shaver, 1983, 1985), random sampling makes it possible to generalize from the sample to the population from which it was randomly selected with a high degree of confidence.

As defined in Chapter 2, *random sampling* is a procedure by which scores (or elements or individuals) are selected from a population in such a way that each sample of size N is equally likely to be chosen. A slightly less precise but perhaps clearer statement is that random sampling is a procedure that guarantees that each element in the population has an equal chance of being selected for the sample. Random sampling is a procedure conducted without *bias* (the bad four-letter word to a statistician or researcher), meaning that no systematic error has entered into the process.

Methods of Random Sampling. There are two general approaches to obtaining a random sample, both of which require that you have some way to identify each element of the population, although it doesn't have to be by name. One of these approaches is based on the use of a physical mixing process, and the other is based on the use of a random number table.

Physical Mixing Process. In order to use a physical mixing process, you need access to a procedure that produces randomly ordered outcomes. One such procedure is tossing a coin; heads and tails are equally likely to appear on each flip, and the outcome of one coin toss is independent of the outcome of the previous toss. If you wanted to have half of the people in a population serving in your sample, you could toss a coin for each person to decide whether or not he would be in the sample. A related procedure would be throwing one or more dice. Yet another physical mixing process would be to write all the names or identification numbers of the people in the population on identical-sized pieces of paper, or on cards, or on ping-pong balls; mix or shuffle well, and then draw out as many as you need for your sample. If your mixing process is thorough, then each element in the population has an equal chance of being selected and your sampling procedure is random.

Random Number Table. The use of a random number table, somewhat more formally called a table of random digits, is a more efficient procedure than a physical mixing process when the population is large. A **random number table** is a table that consists of numbers generated by a random or unbiased process. When using a table of random digits, it is important to remember that at any location in the table each of the digits from 0 through 9 is equally likely to appear. Similarly, all two-digit pairs from 00 to 99, and indeed all possible digit strings of any given length, are equally probable.

Table 8.1 presents a part of the random number table in this book, which is Appendix Table 4. To use this table, you can begin by noting that the columns and rows are numbered and that the digits are clustered into blocks of three columns of single digit numbers with spaces between each block.

TIP

> The only reason for these labels and clustering is to help you keep straight where you are in the table. A different random number table might have a different spacing of the digits, as the arrangement is purely arbitrary.

When you wish to select a random sample from a population using a table of random numbers, you proceed as follows.

- **Step 1:** Begin by deciding on your sample size.
- **Step 2:** Assign each person or element in the population an identification number with the same number of digits. Use zeros to precede other digits when necessary. For example, if there are from 11 to 99 people in the population, you would assign the number 01 to the first person and some number between 11 and 99 to the last.

TABLE 8.1   Portion of Appendix Table 4: Table of Random Numbers

Row	Columns									
	1–3	4–6	7–9	10–12	13–15	16–18	19–21	22–24	25–27	28–30
1	318	627	204	014	302	833	519	776	969	017
2	989	953	621	950	703	395	318	887	920	450
3	292	001	125	919	351	167	872	447	257	508
4	572	080	091	638	502	966	876	692	455	253
5	804	305	226	990	758	928	618	782	321	929
6	741	026	148	109	433	053	130	719	520	310
7	550	696	174	503	107	625	729	244	977	353
8	373	374	252	896	781	701	886	378	562	369
9	254	035	974	487	089	846	373	333	532	866
10	866	893	607	299	995	325	608	436	136	294

TIP

> If there are ten or fewer elements in the population you probably would do a census rather than take a sample.

If there are between 100 and 999 elements in the population, you would begin with the ID number 001. If we had 548 elements in our sample, they would be numbered 001, 002, ... 548, each with three digits.

Step 3: Find a starting place in the table. Once you have used the table for sampling or assignment, you can simply mark where you left off and begin with the next digit the next time you need to randomly sample. However, to begin to use the table for the first time, the closed-eyes-and-pencil-point method will do—that is, close your eyes and stab at the page with a pencil and where you land is your starting point. As an example, let's suppose that we landed in row 1, column 4.

Step 4: After identifying your starting point, identify the first q-digit number, where q is the number of digits needed to identify every element in the population (e.g., three digits for a population of 548 elements). Starting in row 1, column 4, the first three-digit number we identify is 627.

Step 5: Use the number in Step 4 if it corresponds to a number you assigned in Step 2—that is, to an element in your population. The person (or other unit) whose number it is will be in the sample. If the q-digit number does not correspond, skip the number and continue down the column of q-digit numbers until you find a number that refers to someone in the population. That person will be in your sample. In the example of a population of 548 individuals, since neither 627 nor the next number in the column, 953, corresponds to the number of a person in the sample, the first person to be in your sample will be person 001 and the next one will be person 080.

Step 6: When you reach the end of a column, begin at the top of the next column that you have not used.

Step 7: Once you have identified as many individuals as you want for your sample, stop the selection process.

Random Selection Versus Assignment.   The procedure described here for random selection can easily be adjusted to apply to random assignment. You can select those to be in the experimental group and then select those to be in the control group, or, if the n's in the two groups are to be equal, you can assign the person whose number is first selected to be in the experimental group, the next person selected to be in the control group, and so forth. Since any three-digit number is equally likely to appear at any point in the table, both of the processes are random.

When to Use Randomization. Because a random sampling or assignment procedure increases your ability to generalize to a population and reduces the chances of extraneous variables affecting your results, a basic principle of research design is that randomization should be used whenever possible. If you have to make a decision and there is no logical a priori reason to make a particular selection, then make the decision randomly—whether it be the assignment of subjects to treatment conditions, the ordering of questionnaire items, the assignment of observers or researchers to subjects, the assignment of coders or scorers to data, or any other choice that you must make. This use of random assignment or selection means that selection bias will not be a possible interpretation of your results and that you can therefore learn more about the variables in which you are interested.

Stratified Sampling

Stratified sampling is a selection procedure that can be used when the population of interest is divided up into mutually exclusive subgroups or strata. The strata frequently reflect demographic variables, such as gender, grade level, or ethnicity, but sampling can be stratified with respect to any variable or variables for which you have the relevant information. To conduct stratified sampling, you simply sample from each stratum within the population. For example, you might stratify on age and gender, selecting separately from women in their twenties, men in their twenties, women in their thirties, and so on. Stratified sampling is used when you have reason to believe that the variable(s) on which you stratify might be related to the dependent measure(s). It therefore is a way of controlling for extraneous variables by permitting the use of a factorial design, as discussed in Chapter 2.

Stratified Random Sampling. It would certainly be possible to obtain a stratified sample nonrandomly, by picking the people from each stratum in some haphazard fashion. However, this approach is definitely inferior to *stratified random sampling*, in which the individuals are selected randomly from within each stratum. Occasionally, you might be in a situation in which you have access to different strata—perhaps different hospitals—and have the opportunity to sample from each stratum but for some reason are prevented from doing so randomly. In that case, you might have to use a sample that is stratified but not random. However, it is typical in stratified sampling for you to have the opportunity to select randomly from each stratum; when you do, stratified random sampling is the procedure of choice.

Stratified Random Sampling Versus Simple Random Sampling. Stratified random sampling can be contrasted with random sampling from the population as a whole, which is sometimes called *simple random sampling*. Generally, simple random sampling has the advantage of being faster and easier, as you have to go through only one set of sampling procedures. Stratified random sampling is more time consuming but permits you to achieve an equal degree of accuracy with a smaller sample size. If you have a choice between simple random sampling and stratified random sampling, you would want to consider the relative costs of identifying the sample (cheaper for simple random sampling) versus obtaining data from a larger or smaller sample (cheaper for stratified random sampling). Particularly when each individual in the study will be experiencing lengthy or repeated interviews or other measurement sessions, stratified random selection is usually the sampling procedure of choice.

Proportional Versus Equal *n*'s.   One decision that you must make when using stratified sampling is the choice of how many individuals to include from each stratum.

   *When to Use Proportional *n*'s.*   Most of the time, you want your sample to reflect the population and therefore will want to have the same proportion from each stratum in your sample as there is in the population. Thus, if 3% of the patients in the general population of hospitalized patients are females with breast cancer, you would want 3% of the patients in your sample to be females with breast cancer.

TIP

> The easiest way to achieve this goal is to take the same percentage of each stratum in the population for your sample. If you can have a sample of 200 and the population is 4000, then the sample is .05 of the population, and you would (randomly) select 5% of each stratum to be in your sample.

   *When to Use Equal *n*'s.*   Occasionally, the purpose of your study is not to draw inferences about the entire population but to compare the responses of two subgroups. In this case, you may wish to use equal-sized samples from each subgroup.

   For example, you might be interested in comparing the intended areas of specialization of male and female nursing students. Suppose that only 12.5% of nursing students are male. If you were to take an equal percentage of male and female nursing students, you would end up with seven times as many females as males in your sample. This procedure would be appropriate if you wanted to generalize to all nursing students, but less powerful for comparing males and females than would be using more equal numbers from the two groups. In that case, you might want to take all of the male nursing students and 1/7 of the females (or maybe 20% of them) for your sample.

TIP

> It is important to keep in mind that overrepresentation or oversampling of any subgroup means that your sample may not accurately reflect the population as a whole. Of course, it would be possible to adjust your predictions by taking the differential proportions in your sample into account, but this would be more complicated than simply selecting the same proportion from each subgroup in the population for your sample in the first place.

Quota Sampling

Quota sampling is a kind of sampling procedure used by large polling organizations and is closely related to stratified sampling. **Quota sampling involves stratifying on a large number of demographic variables to end up with target numbers of respondents from very precisely specified subgroups.** For example, the assignment may be to get three African-American women who are registered Democrats between the ages of 20 and 29 living in this precinct; six Caucasian women Democrats of the same age and precinct; and so forth. The numbers needed for each subgroup are determined from census data on the population (or occasionally from estimates), including such information as the proportion of adults in each precinct who are registered voters and the proportion who vote.

By using prior information and stratifying on a large number of variables believed or shown to be related to the dependent measure, professional polling organizations may be able to arrive at highly representative samples even though the sampling within each subgroup typically is not done randomly. On the other hand, quota sampling may systematically underrepresent certain individuals within each stratum—for example, those who are poorer, less accessible, or less cooperative. Regardless of whether or not it leads to a representative sample, quota sampling is usually too difficult for an individual researcher to undertake and so is not ordinarily a choice to consider when designing a study.

Systematic Sampling

Systematic sampling refers to a procedure in which every nth person on a list or in a line or whose responses are available is sampled. Depending on the size of the population, it could be every other person, every thousandth person, or anything in between.

TIP

> Since both systematic and random sampling procedures require the same information about the population, whenever you could do systematic sampling, you could also do random sampling. Even though random sampling may be more tedious and time consuming, the extra time is only a tiny fraction of the total time spent on a research project. Yet it might make the difference between a sample from which you can generalize and a nonrepresentative sample. The bottom line: Don't use systematic sampling; use random sampling instead.

Systematic sampling is a very easy procedure to use for anyone who can count. However, it raises the possibility of ending up with a nonrepresentative sample whenever the list or ordering of the population is not random (which is almost always the case). For example, if you have students in your class count off "1," "2," "3," "4" and you pick all the 4's as your sample, you might end up with the entire back row—either those with good vision and hearing or those who prefer to sleep through class in peace. When you take every tenth name from an alphabetical list, if people from certain ethnic groups are likely to have the same or similar last names, you may increase the chance of over- or underrepresenting people from those groups as compared with a random sampling procedure.

Cluster Sampling

Cluster sampling is a procedure in which individuals or other elements in the population are not sampled independently but rather in clusters or groups. Within each cluster, all or almost all of the elements or people serve in the sample. For example, you may sample households or classrooms or law offices and include all of the residents or students or attorneys in your sample.

If the clusters are chosen randomly, then they should be representative of the entire population, as long as the number of clusters is large enough. For instance, if you were to sample 100 households from a town, this sample might be large enough to represent the attitudes of people in the community. However, if you were to sample three classrooms with a total of 90 students to represent a school district, even if the three classrooms were chosen randomly, this sample would be less representative than a sample in which the 90 students had randomly been selected from the population of all students in the district.

Statistical Analysis.   When cluster sampling has been used, appropriate statistical procedures should be used to reflect the fact that the elements in the sample were not selected independently. One possibility is to use the cluster as your unit and the means for the clusters as your raw scores. This procedure is appropriate and powerful *if* (but only if) the number of clusters is large enough, since it is the number of clusters rather than the number of original scores that will serve as the *N* in subsequent analyses. A second approach is to use a statistical procedure that acknowledges that you have what is called a nested design, with individual scores nested within clusters. These procedures are more complex and are covered in more advanced textbooks. At a minimum, you should describe your methodology accurately and identify the fact that you have used cluster sampling.

Convenience or Haphazard Sampling

Convenience sampling, sometimes called *haphazard sampling*, refers to a sampling process in which the researcher selects a sample primarily because it is accessible and reasonably representative of the population of interest. Although randomly sampling from the population of interest, with or without stratifying, is the ideal, much of the time researchers have no list of the population and therefore cannot use random or stratified sampling. At other times, random sampling is impossible because permission cannot be obtained or for other practical or ethical reasons.

Under such circumstances, researchers do the best that they can. If the intent is to generalize to a population, then they make an effort to include in their sample people who are as representative of the population as possible. If the intent is not so much to represent a population as to examine the relationships among variables, then researchers often look for a sample that represents the full range of values on each of the variables of interest. In these situations, researchers may go to shopping centers, student union buildings, restaurants, flea markets, schools or other institutions that give permission, or any other place where they can get a sample. Such a procedure is convenience or haphazard sampling, not because the sample was necessarily easy to obtain but because it does not fit any of the other patterns.

Clearly Biased Sampling

Although any nonrandom sample is biased to some extent, a convenience or haphazard sample is not the same as a clearly biased sample. A clearly biased sample is one which the researcher or a knowledgeable observer can recognize would give misleading and inappropriate results. For example, picking people as they exit Democratic Party headquarters for a political poll would constitute a clearly biased sampling procedure. A sample of only teenagers for a marketing survey of which prime time television shows to air would also be clearly biased. Such a sample should, of course, be avoided, unless your intent is to report clearly biased results.

Different Types of Samples

- **Biased sampling** A procedure leading to a sample that clearly is not representative of the population
- **Census** A sample that includes each unit or score in the population
- **Cluster sampling** A sampling procedure in which entire groups of scores are sampled and each person in the group then serves in the sample
- **Convenience or haphazard sampling** A sampling process in which the researcher selects a sample primarily because it is accessible and reasonably representative of the population of interest
- **Quota sampling** A sampling procedure that involves stratifying on a large number of demographic variables to end up with target numbers of respondents from very precisely specified subgroups
- **Random sampling** An unbiased procedure by which all members of a population have an equal chance of being selected and all samples of a given size have the same chance of being selected
- **Stratified sampling** A sampling procedure in which participants are drawn from each of a number of mutually exclusive subgroups (stratified random sampling is preferred)
- **Systematic sampling** A sampling procedure in which every nth score or person is sampled

Generalizing to a Population

When generalizing the results of your research from your sample to a population, there are two major questions that you need to consider.

- The most obvious question concerns the way in which you chose your sample from the population: To what extent do your sampling procedures enable you to legitimately generalize to the population from which you sampled? The prior discussion of sampling techniques has illustrated some of the advantages and disadvantages of various sampling procedures and should help you answer this question.

- The more subtle question concerns the population from which you sampled: Were you able to sample from the entire population to which you would really wish to generalize?

The Accessible Population.   Although books on statistics and research design often describe an ideal sampling procedure in which the population is clearly identified and the sample is selected from it, researchers often have access only to a limited population from which they can select their sample. The telephone book, city directory, list of children in a school, list of hospital patients, list of registered voters or vehicle owners, or other limited populations from which one might sample may not represent the intended population of all adult Americans or all children. Sometimes the nature of the accessible population limits the type of sampling procedure you can use. For instance, if a list of the elements of the population is not available, then random sampling is not possible and convenience sampling may be the most feasible procedure.

TIP

> It is legitimate to generalize with a substantial degree of confidence only to the population from which a sample was randomly selected. When attempting to generalize to a different population, the researcher should be cautious and temper any generalization with an acknowledgment of the known differences between the sample and the population of interest. In other words, you can cautiously generalize from research done with 45 schoolchildren in one school to all children who might be experiencing the same curriculum materials; but, before doing so, you need to describe the limitations of the sample and recognize that your results are likely to be much more appropriate for similar populations than for ones that are very different from your sample.

What Are Sampling Distributions and How Are They Used?

Up until this point, with the exception of the discussion of theoretical frequency distributions in Chapter 5, this book has focused primarily on *empirical* distributions of real scores, like the scores from samples selected according to the procedures just described. In this section, we are going to discuss how a particular kind of *theoretical* frequency distribution helps us to draw inferences about characteristics of populations. A **sampling distribution** is a frequency distribution of a statistic calculated from many different samples, all of the same size and all randomly drawn from the same population. A sampling distribution is not the same as a distribution of raw scores.

The primary reason that researchers discuss sampling distributions is that knowing the shape, mean, and standard deviation of a sampling distribution makes it possible to draw some inferences about the population from which the samples that constitute the sampling distribution come. Imagine, for example, that we were to draw 50 samples, each consisting of 100 dental patients, in order to see how often they brush their teeth. For each sample, we compute a mean of the 100 scores. Then we put the means of the 50 samples into a frequency distribution. That frequency distribution would be called a *sampling distribution of the mean*, which means exactly the same thing as a distribution of sample means.

Expected Value and Standard Error of a Sampling Distribution

Every sampling distribution, whether it be based on sample means, sample variances, sample proportions, or any other sample statistic, consists of a number of scores, each of which is a statistic calculated from a random sample of size N. The mean of all the scores in a sampling distribution is called the **expected value** of the statistic for that distribution. In other words, the mean of a distribution of sample means is the expected value of the sampling distribution of the mean.

As you might have guessed, there is also a special name for the standard deviation of a sampling distribution. The standard deviation of a distribution of a statistic is called the **standard error** of that statistic. The standard deviation of the sampling distribution of the mean is, therefore, the standard error of the mean, symbolized by $\sigma_{\bar{X}}$.

TIP

Notice that this symbol is different from σ_X, the standard deviation of a population. The bar over the X symbolizes the fact that this is a standard error of the mean—that is, a standard deviation of sample means rather than of raw scores.

Central Limit Theorem

The Central Limit Theorem is a theorem that describes the characteristics of a sampling distribution of the mean that is based on a reasonably large sample size. In other words, it describes the characteristics of a distribution of sample means when each mean is based on a sample of size N, and N is a relatively large number. Many inferential statistical procedures are based on the assumption that the Central Limit Theorem applies to the data.

The **Central Limit Theorem** states that as the size of the sample, N, gets infinitely large, the shape of the sampling distribution of the mean approaches a normal distribution with a mean equal to μ, the mean of the population, and a standard deviation equal to $\sigma/\sqrt{N}$. In other words, as N approaches infinity, a graph of the distribution of the sample means approaches a normal curve with an expected value of μ and a standard error of $\sigma/\sqrt{N}$. Thus, the larger the sample size is, the smaller will be the standard error of the mean, and the closer all the sample means will be to the population mean.

Notice what the Central Limit Theorem does not say. It does not say that the shape of the population needs to be normal or close to normal, as long as N is large, roughly 30 or so scores. This implies that a distribution of sample means will be a normal distribution even if these means come from a popu-

FIGURE 8.1   Effects of Increasing the Sample Size on $\sigma_{\overline{X}}$

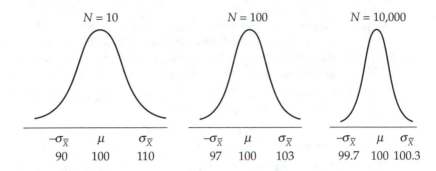

lation that is not itself normally distributed. The Central Limit Theorem applies to all populations and can therefore be used to estimate the mean of any population from which reasonably large samples can be drawn. Moreover, if the population from which you are sampling is normally distributed, then the distribution of means from even very small samples will be normal.

Figure 8.1 illustrates how the sample means cluster together and how the standard error of the mean decreases as the sample size gets larger.

EXAMPLE

In order to see how the Central Limit Theorem works, I find it helpful to look at a distribution of scores that come from a known population: the cards in a deck of playing cards. Consider aces as equal to 1, jacks as 11, queens as 12, and kings as 13. Ignore the suits. The 52 cards in the deck constitute a population with a rectangular distribution of four 1's, four 2's, and so on, up to four 13's. In this example, we will compute the population mean and standard deviation; draw 20 samples each for $N = 2$, $N = 5$, and $N = 10$; calculate the means of the samples; graph the sampling distribution of the mean for each group of 20 samples; and calculate the standard error of the mean. By doing so, we should be able to see whether or not the Central Limit Theorem accurately describes our data for a relatively small population that is not normally distributed.

Solution

Step 1: Considering the value of each of the 52 cards to be a raw score, X, calculate the mean of the population, μ:

$$\frac{\Sigma X}{N} = \frac{364}{52} = 7.0$$

Step 2: Calculate the standard deviation of the population, σ:

$$\sqrt{\frac{3,276 - (132,496\,/\,52)}{52}} = \sqrt{\frac{3,276 - 2,548}{52}} = \sqrt{14} = 3.74$$

Step 3: Gather your empirical data by using a deck of playing cards with the jokers removed. Shuffle the cards well and deal out two cards, thus obtaining a random sample with $N = 2$. Write down the values of the two cards. Consider these values as raw scores.

Step 4: Return these cards to the deck, reshuffle, and deal another sample with $N = 2$. Write down these two values.

Step 5: Repeat this procedure 18 more times until you have 20 samples of 2 cards each.

Step 6: Now compute the means of each of the 20 samples. Each mean will be based on two raw scores. These 20 means constitute a sampling distribution of the mean.

Step 7: Group these means into a grouped frequency distribution with class intervals going from 0.50–1.499, 1.50–2.499, and so forth.

Step 8: Plot this frequency distribution as a frequency polygon.

Step 9: Now repeat the entire procedure, except that this time you should obtain 20 random samples, each with $N = 5$.

Step 10: Graph this sampling distribution on the same axes as the other one, using a dotted line or a different colored pen or pencil.

Step 11: Repeat the procedure with samples based on an N of 10. Again, plot the frequency distribution of these 20 sample means on the same graph, using a dashed line or a different color marker. As illustrated in Figure 8.2, the graph now shows three lines that represent sampling distributions based on increasingly large N's. If the Central

FIGURE 8.2 Distribution of Sample Means for Three Sample Sizes

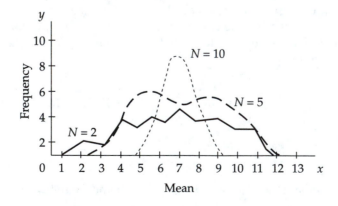

Limit Theorem is true, then the graph based on the samples of size 10 should be closest to a normal curve in shape, should have a mean of the 20 means that is closest to the population mean of 7, and should have a standard deviation that is close to the population standard deviation of 3.74 divided by the square root of 10.

Step 12: Compute the standard error of the mean expected for samples of $N = 2$. It should equal $\sigma/\sqrt{2} = 3.74/1.414 = 2.64$. You can compare this with the standard deviation based on your 20 means, if you want to calculate it.

- The standard error of the mean for N's of 5 = 1.67
- The standard error of the mean for N's of 10 = 1.18.

TIP

> Your distributions probably will not look exactly normal and the standard deviations of your sampling distributions will not be identical to the computed values. However, you should see your means getting closer together as the sample size increases, like the illustration in Figure 8.2. Whereas you might have some means as low as 1 or as high as 13 based on an N of 2, your means from larger samples will be much closer to 7. If you can get together with others who have done the same exercise and pool your values, you should see that the standard errors should cluster around the values calculated by $\sigma/\sqrt{N}$ and that the means should increasingly cluster around 7 as N increases.

The demonstration of a sampling distribution in the previous example does not reflect the way in which research is usually conducted. Although in theory it would be possible to collect multiple random samples from a population, to compute the sample means, and to plot their distribution, in practice researchers typically gather only one sample in a given research study and attempt to draw inferences from that one sample about the population from which it was drawn. In order to make such inferences, it is helpful to recognize that the Central Limit Theorem makes it possible to assess how likely it is that a random sample would yield a value for the sample mean, $\overline{X}$, that is any given distance from the population mean μ.

What Are z-Tests and How Are They Used?

One kind of statistical procedure that is based on the Central Limit Theorem is called the z-test. A *z-test* is a statistical procedure used to test hypotheses about population parameters based on samples gathered from populations whose standard deviations are known. The usual reason for doing a z-test is to test a hypothesis about one or more means.

Sometimes the hypothesis is that the mean of a population is equal to some particular value. For example, if you have a class of children, you might want to know if their IQ differs from the average value of 100—that is, to test the hypothesis that they represent a sample from a population with a mean IQ of 100. Sometimes the hypothesis is that the means of two populations are the same. If you want to know whether children who eat breakfast get higher grades in school than children who eat no breakfast, you are interested in testing the hypothesis that the difference in the mean grade-point averages of the children who do and do not eat breakfast is zero. Following the generally accepted procedure of symbolizing statistics by English letters and parameters by Greek letters, we will use $\overline{X}$ to symbolize the mean of a sample and μ to symbolize the (hypothesized) value of the mean of the population.

General Procedure

The general procedure for the z-test is similar to the calculation of a z-score. Remember that a z-score from a population is a transformed score that is equal to $(X - \mu)/\sigma$. The difference between a sample mean and a hypothesized value for the population mean, $\overline{X} - \mu$, divided by the standard error of the mean, $\sigma_{\overline{X}}$, is equivalent to a z-score.

After computing a value for z, you can use the normal curve table (Appendix Table 1) to look up the probability of getting a value of z that extreme. This probability can be used to draw inferences about how likely it is that the sample mean really did come from a distribution of scores where the hypothesized value for μ is the value of the population mean. If the sample mean yields a value for z that would be extremely unlikely if the mean of the population were equal to the hypothesized value for μ, then you come to the conclusion that the mean of the population probably is not equal to that hypothetical value. More specifically, you state that there is a statistically significant difference between the sample mean and the hypothesized value.

TIP ▰▰▰▰▰▰▰▰▰▰▰▰▰▰▰▰

> When the population standard deviation is not known, instead of using a z-test, you should use a related procedure called a t-test, which will be described in the next chapter.

More specifically, the procedure for conducting a z-test follows.

1. Hypothesize a value for some population parameter. For example, you might want to test the hypothesis that the means of two populations are equal;

in that case your hypothetical parameter would be $\mu_1 - \mu_2$ and its hypothetical value would be zero. If you wanted to compare your basketball team with the average basketball player's height of 78" to see if your team is shorter than average, then your hypothetical value for the parameter μ would be 78".

TIP

> The parameter in which you are interested does not have to be a mean. You could test a hypothesis about a proportion, for example, although hypotheses about means are by far the most common. However, if you do not have any hypothesis in mind, then it makes no sense (and is impossible) to use hypothesis-testing statistics (like the z-test).

2. Draw a sample from the population, and calculate the relevant statistic from your sample. If your sample size is reasonably large—say 30 or so—then the statistic from your sample should be reasonably close to the corresponding population parameter.

3. Compare your sample statistic to the hypothetical parameter by

$$z = \frac{\text{Statistic} - \text{parameter}}{\text{Standard error of the statistic}}$$

4. Use the normal curve table in the appendix to see how likely (or, more precisely, how unlikely) it is that you would draw a sample yielding that large an absolute value of z from a population where your hypothesized value is the true value of that parameter.

TIP

> The use of this table follows from the assumption of the Central Limit Theorem that the sampling distribution of the mean is a normal curve. For example, if you were to sample randomly from a population in which the mean is equal to your hypothesized value of μ, you would draw a sample yielding a value of z that is less than −1.96 or greater than 1.96 less than 5% of the time. Thus, if your absolute value of z from the z-test is as large as 1.96 (or larger), the chance that this sample came from a population with a mean equal to your hypothetical μ is less than 5%. Based on such evidence, you would conclude that your sample did not come from such a population and that the mean for the population is unlikely to equal μ.

Using a z-Test with a Single Sample

A single-sample z-test involves the use of only one sample. As an example of this use of a z-test, let's take the situation in which you wish to know if the kind of students who are in the high school classes that you are teaching have significantly higher IQ scores than average. Knowing that the mean IQ test score in normal or unselected populations of schoolchildren is 100, you decide to test the hypothesis that your students are a random sample from a population with a mean IQ of 100. In other words, your hypothesis is that μ = 100. You may believe that your students are significantly above average in IQ (after all, they have devised fiendishly adult and ingenious ways to torment you), but you still compare their mean to the value of 100, because you want to be able to rule out the conclusion that they constitute a random sample from a population where μ = 100.

EXAMPLE

Suppose that the mean IQ of the students in your classes is 110, the sample size is 100, and you know that the standard deviation of IQ scores in the population of schoolchildren is 15. How likely is it that this mean of 110 reflects a random sample from a population with a mean of 100?

Solution: Substitute into the formula

$$ z = \frac{\overline{X} - \mu}{\sigma_{\overline{X}}} $$

The value of z would equal

$$ \frac{110 - 100}{15/\sqrt{100}} = \frac{10}{15/10} = \frac{10}{1.5} = 6.67 $$

Note that this result is an extremely large z, so large that it is not even listed in Appendix Table 1. The chance of getting a z value this large is far less than .001. Therefore, we would infer that it is extremely unlikely that your students constitute a random sample from a population with a mean IQ equal to 100 and would conclude that your students were indeed significantly above average in IQ. ∎

Comparing a Single Score with a Mean. Let's look at a related situation. Suppose that you have a student, Joe, who gets an IQ score of 125. You want to know how likely it is that Joe is really different from other schoolchildren.

Joe's z-score is (125 − 100)/15 or 1.67. A z-score that far away from the mean would happen 2(.0475) or .095 of the time. Thus it is much, much more likely that you would get a single raw score of 125 from a population with a mean of 100 than it is that you would get a mean of 110 for a sample of size 100 from a population with a mean of 100.

TIP ▰▰▰▰▰▰▰▰▰▰▰▰▰▰▰▰▰▰▰▰▰▰▰▰▰▰▰

> This example illustrates the Central Limit Theorem: The larger the sample size, the closer the sample mean should be to the population mean.

Using a z-Test to Compare Two Sample Means

As a second instance of the use of a z-test, consider the situation in which you want to compare the means of two samples. You want to know whether these samples come from populations with different means or whether they come from populations with the same mean. For instance, if you had test scores from a sample of boys and a sample of girls from the same classroom, you might want to know if the difference in these sample means reflects a difference in the mean test scores of the populations of boys and girls who might be tested.

In this case, the parameter of interest is the difference between the means of two populations. If you want to know whether or not the population means are different, then you would hypothesize that the value of the difference in the means, $\mu_1 - \mu_2$, would be zero. If the samples are from populations with identical means, then the difference in the population means would be zero and the difference in the sample means, $\overline{X}_1 - \overline{X}_2$, should be very small. The numerator of the formula for z would therefore be $\overline{X}_1 - \overline{X}_2 - 0$ (the hypothetical value of the difference in the means) and the denominator would be the standard error of the difference in the means.

The standard error of the difference between two means is the standard deviation of the differences in the means of each pair, if you were to sample many pairs of means from the same population.

Formula.   There are several formulas for the standard error of the difference in the means, $\sigma_{\overline{X}_1 - \overline{X}_2}$, but, for purposes of this discussion, we can use a formula based on the standard deviations of the populations from which the samples come. This formula states that the standard error of the difference in the means equals the square root of the sum of the square of the standard error of the mean for group 1 and the square of the standard error of the mean for group 2. It is written as

$$\sigma_{\overline{X}_1 - \overline{X}_2} = \sqrt{\sigma_{\overline{X}_1}^2 + \sigma_{\overline{X}_2}^2}$$

The formula for z is

$$z = \frac{\overline{X}_1 - \overline{X}_2 - 0}{\sqrt{\sigma_{\overline{X}_1}^2 + \sigma_{\overline{X}_2}^2}}$$

To use the formula for z, you need to proceed as follows.

Step 1: Find the means of both samples.

Step 2: Calculate the difference in the means to get the numerator of the formula for z.

Step 3: Find the standard error of the mean for both X_1 and X_2.

Step 4: Square these standard errors.

Step 5: Sum these squares.

Step 6: Take the square root of the sum to get the denominator of the formula for z.

Step 7: Divide the numerator by the denominator to get the value of z.

EXAMPLE

Asthma Treatment. Suppose that we have randomly assigned 288 patients with asthma to an experimental or a control group of 144 patients each. The experimental group received a new drug, whereas the control group received the conventional medication. Over the last six days, the patients in the experimental group had a mean of 7.5 asthma attacks, whereas those in the control group had a mean of 8.2 attacks. We know that the standard deviation of the number of asthma attacks in the population is 3 for the control condition and 2 for the experimental condition. How likely is it that the experimental and control groups represent random samples from the same population (in other words, that the experimental treatment had no effect)?

Solution: To solve this problem, we will need to know the standard error of the mean for each group. For the experimental group, it is

$$\frac{2}{\sqrt{144}} = \frac{2}{12} = .1667$$

$$.1667^2 = .0278$$

The standard error of the mean for the control group is

$$\frac{3}{\sqrt{144}} = \frac{3}{12} = .250$$

$$.25^2 = .0625$$

The standard error of the difference in the means is therefore

$$\sqrt{.0278 + .0625} = \sqrt{.0903} = .300$$

Substituting into the formula for z, we get

$$z = \frac{7.5 - 8.2}{.300} = \frac{-.7}{.300} = -2.33$$

Looking in Appendix Table 1, we can see that .0099 of the scores are lower than this value and another .0099 are higher than a z of 2.33, making .0198 of all the scores more extreme than our computed value of z. We can conclude, therefore, that there is less than a 2% chance that the experimental and control group means are equal or that they might represent random samples from the same population. We would therefore probably conclude that the experimental treatment appears to be effective and state that the difference in the means of the experimental and control groups is statistically significant. ∎

If the z value that we calculate is so large that it is unlikely to occur by chance, we call the difference in means a statistically significant one, which does not necessarily mean that the difference was a large or important one. In order to see the difference between statistical significance and importance, let's take another example of a situation in which we might do a z-test.

EXAMPLE

IQs by Zip Code.[*] Suppose that the mean IQ test score of the 12,000 students in one zip code of the Houston school district is 99.85 and the mean IQ of the 188,000 other students in the district is 100.15. We would like to know whether or not the mean IQ of the students in the area represented by the first zip code (whom we'll call group Z) is statistically significantly lower than the mean IQ of the students in the rest of the city (group R). We already know that the standard deviation of IQ scores in a typical population is approximately 15; let's assume that this is true for these samples as well.

Solution: To solve the problem we need to calculate the standard error of the mean for each group. For the students in group Z, the standard error of the mean would be

$$\frac{15}{\sqrt{12,000}} = \frac{15}{109.545} = .137$$

For the other students, the standard error of the mean would be

$$\frac{15}{\sqrt{188,000}} = \frac{15}{433.590} = .035$$

The standard error of the difference in the means would be

$$\sqrt{.137^2 + .035^2} = \sqrt{.0188 + .0012} = \sqrt{.0200} = .141$$

---

[*]This example was suggested by Bruce Thompson of Texas A & M University, who reviewed an early draft of this book. It is adapted from Thompson (1993). Used with permission.

The difference in the means of the two groups of students can now be tested by a z-test:

$$z = \frac{\overline{Z} - \overline{R}}{\sigma_{\overline{Z}-\overline{R}}} = \frac{99.85 - 100.15}{.141} = \frac{-.30}{.141} = -2.13$$

The absolute value of –2.13 exceeds the critical value of 1.96, meaning that the difference in the means would be statistically significant. But is it meaningful? I am positive that no one, no one, who uses IQ scores for any purpose would attempt to say that there is any meaning to a difference of .30 IQ points. There is no way that you could recognize a difference that small (or even a difference ten times that large) by observing any behavior or performance of the individuals involved. In short, this example should serve to indicate that when you have a very large sample a totally trivial difference in means can be statistically significant. Similarly, a quite large difference in means can fail to reach statistical significance if the sample size is very small.

TIP

You can use this somewhat silly example to remind yourself that statistical significance depends on the sample size as well as on the size of the difference in the means (Carter, 1993; Shaver, 1993; Thompson, 1993).

What Are the Uses of Inferential Statistics?

The use of a z-test is one example of a use of inferential statistics. In general, as indicated previously, *inferential statistics* is used to draw conclusions or form inferences about characteristics of a population based on characteristics of a sample. These uses can be classified into two general categories: parameter estimation and hypothesis testing.

Parameter Estimation

At first glance, and perhaps upon later reflection as well, parameter estimation seems like the most logical kind of inferential statistics. In **parameter estimation**, a sample is drawn from a population, a statistic is calculated from the sample, and an estimate of the corresponding parameter is formulated based on the statistic. For example, the mean age of the 12 children in a particular Cub Scout pack could be used as an estimate of the mean age of all

Cub Scouts. In fact, there are two general types of parameter estimation, differing in the kind of estimate that is made from the statistic.

Point Estimation.   Point estimation is the easiest kind of inference to understand. In **point estimation**, the relevant statistic is simply used as the best estimate of the population parameter. In order to estimate the population mean μ, you use the sample mean $\overline{X}$; in order to estimate σ, you use s; in order to estimate σ^2, you use s^2; and in order to estimate r for a population (which some people refer to as ρ, not to be confused with Spearman's rho), you use r calculated from the sample. Such a procedure is easy both to compute and to understand. Moreover, most point estimates have the desirable characteristic of being unbiased. An *unbiased point estimate* is one that, on the average, will not be too low or too high but will provide you with the single number that is closest to the population parameter. So why not use point estimation all the time?

Problems with Point Estimation.   Point estimates are not used more frequently because they are almost always wrong. Recall the example in which you drew 60 samples from a deck of cards. The mean of each sample was an unbiased point estimate of the population mean. Yet it is quite possible that some of your samples, particularly those based on the N's of 2, had means that were extremely far from the population mean of 7. It is also possible that none of your samples had means that were equal to 7.

In fact, it is common to get samples that are not highly representative of the population when the sample size is small. Small samples may yield means that are a substantial distance from μ. If the population from which the samples are drawn is normally distributed, then approximately 5% of the time a sample mean will be as far as 1.96 standard errors of the mean from the population mean. Estimates of other parameters from samples may also be some distance from the actual parameter.

Confidence Intervals.   Because point estimates can be so inaccurate, researchers often use another kind of estimate instead of a point estimate. This alternative kind of estimate, which is a confidence interval, gives a more accurate impression of the degree of confidence that you can have in your estimate.

Unlike a point estimate, a confidence interval is not a single number. Instead, a **confidence interval** is a range of scores selected according to a procedure that provides a certain probability that such intervals will "capture" or include the population parameter. In order to convey a more realistic picture of what a sample statistic tells about the population parameter, researchers often report a 95% or 99% confidence interval. If you calculate one hundred 95% confidence intervals, each one based on a different sample, approximately 95% of them will include the parameter (and 5% will not).

TIP

> Some statisticians do not like to say that any particular 95% confidence interval has a 95% probability of including the parameter, since an individual confidence interval either does or does not include the relevant parameter from that population. So, to be precise, it is better to think of the degree of confidence as representing the percentage of such intervals that will include the parameter rather than the probability that a particular interval includes a particular parameter.

Characteristics of Confidence Intervals. Since the single best estimate of a population mean is the mean of the sample and since the distribution of sample means is symmetric, a confidence interval for a mean will be symmetric around the sample mean. When the sample size is reasonably large, or when you know the standard deviation of the population, then the normal curve table can be used to identify the limits of any given confidence interval. For example, the 95% confidence interval around a sample mean for which σ is known will range from a lower limit of $\overline{X} - 1.96\sigma_{\overline{x}}$ to an upper limit of $\overline{X} + 1.96\sigma_{\overline{x}}$, since slightly less than 5% of the scores in a normal distribution lie outside of these limits. Similarly, the 99% confidence interval for the mean of a population with a known standard deviation will range from a lower limit of $\overline{X} - 2.58\sigma_{\overline{x}}$ to an upper limit of $\overline{X} + 2.58\sigma_{\overline{x}}$, and the 99.9% confidence interval will go from $\overline{X} - 3.30\sigma_{\overline{x}}$ to $\overline{X} + 3.30\sigma_{\overline{x}}$. The 95% confidence interval for a difference between two means from populations with known σ's will range from $(\overline{X}_1 - \overline{X}_2) - 1.96\sigma_{\overline{x}_1 - \overline{x}_2}$ to $(\overline{X}_1 - \overline{X}_2) + 1.96\sigma_{\overline{x}_1 - \overline{x}_2}$.

Two other points about confidence intervals should be made. First, confidence intervals can be computed for other statistics, such as a correlation coefficient. Second, when the population standard deviation is not known and the sample size is less than 120, then the values of 1.96, 2.58, and 3.30 are not used. Instead, the values used to multiply the standard error come from the table of critical values for the *t*-distribution, which will be discussed in the next chapter.

Hypothesis Testing

The other use of inferential statistics besides parameter estimation is hypothesis testing. The focus of this approach is not on estimating the actual value of the parameter in the population. Instead, a hypothesis about the value of this parameter is formulated, a sample is drawn, and the likelihood that the hypothesis is correct is calculated based on one or more statistics calculated from the sample. Hypothesis testing could really be subsumed under confidence interval estimation; for example, if your hypothesized value for a parameter is outside the 95% confidence interval, then there is less than a 5% chance that this hypothetical value is the correct one. However, for reasons that have more to do with custom than logic, hypothesis testing remains a much more widely used approach to inferential statistics, and the rest of this chapter will focus on its use and ramifications.

How Are Hypotheses Tested?

When conducting a research study, most of the time you will have one or more research hypotheses that you want to test. As stated in Chapter 2, a research hypothesis is a prediction about what results you expect to find—for example, this mean will be larger than that mean, or these two variables will be positively correlated. You have already seen examples of two types of hypothesis tests—a single-sample z-test and a z-test to compare two sample means.

Null Versus Alternative Hypotheses

Conventional statistical hypothesis testing does not directly consider the research hypothesis and evaluate the probability that it is correct. Instead it sets up a "straw man," the *null hypothesis*, symbolized by H_0, and estimates the likelihood that the empirical data that were collected would have been obtained if the null hypothesis were true (Harlow, 1997; Harris, 1997). If it seems very unlikely that such scores would have been found if the null hypothesis were true, then a decision is made to reject the null hypothesis and to accept an alternative hypothesis (either the directional research hypothesis or its opposite) as a reasonable probability. Of course, it must be recognized that there may be other reasons why the results turn out in the direction of the research hypothesis than the theory that led the researcher to formulate the hypothesis. A finding that is statistically significant and consistent with the researcher's prediction could still be due to some other factor in the study that the researcher had not considered.

Null Hypothesis.   The **null hypothesis** is generally the hypothesis that the results are due to random sampling from a population with the hypothesized parameter and that any differences in means or any difference between a correlation coefficient and the hypothesized value (usually zero) or any apparent relationship between variables is due to chance. In actuality, the null hypothesis is unlikely to be precisely true, since there is likely to be some small difference between population means, some small effect of an experimental variable, or some small deviation of a correlation coefficient from zero (Hunter, 1997). However, if the differences are so small as to be trivial, then the null hypothesis is retained (some even say "accepted," although that implies that H_0 is true) as a reasonable description of the population.

Occasionally, the research hypothesis will be the same as the null hypothesis—that is, the researcher will predict no difference in population means or a zero correlation between two variables in the population. Such a prediction is most interesting when other people have found such a difference or relationship and the researcher thinks that there are certain circumstances in which it will not be found. Support for such a hypothesis would be provided by a very narrow confidence interval that includes only values very near zero.

In testing hypotheses about means, the Central Limit Theorem is used to describe what the sampling distribution of the mean would be if the null hypothesis is true. It allows us to estimate the likelihood of getting a difference in sample means as large as any particular value *if the null hypothesis is true*—that is, if the population means do not differ. By comparing the data with the sampling distribution of the mean, we can see how probable it is that such a mean could come from the hypothetical sampling distribution—that is, the distribution to be expected if H_0 is true.

Alternative Hypothesis.   The statistical **alternative hypothesis**, symbolized by H_a, is the hypothesis that would be true if the null hypothesis is false. If the null hypothesis is that the means of two populations do not differ, the alternative hypothesis that is tested is typically the hypothesis that the means do differ. Some statisticians (Harris, 1994, 1997) prefer to think of two alternative hypotheses: $\mu_A > \mu_B$ and $\mu_A < \mu_B$.

Directional Alternative Hypothesis.   A *directional alternative hypothesis* is a hypothesis that the means differ in a particular direction. It is true that a directional research hypothesis could be associated with a directional alternative hypothesis: The research hypothesis that mean *A* will be higher than mean *B* could be associated with the alternative hypothesis that $\mu_A > \mu_B$ and the corresponding null hypothesis that $\mu_A \leq \mu_B$. However, testing this directional alternative statistical hypothesis is usually not a good idea.

TIP

Even though you conduct a study expecting your research hypotheses to be confirmed, every experienced researcher knows of instances in which the results of a study turned out in the opposite direction from the one predicted. For this reason, it is generally inappropriate to statistically test a directional null (and alternative) hypothesis, even when your research hypothesis is directional (Abelson, 1995). When you test a nondirectional hypothesis, if the results turn out in the direction of your research hypothesis, you can conclude that it has been supported. If, on the other hand, they should unexpectedly appear in the opposite direction, improbably far away from what would be found if the null hypothesis were true, you must conclude that, under the present conditions, the opposite of your hypothesis appears to be true.

The directional alternative/null hypothesis pair for $\mu_A > \mu_B$ makes it impossible to distinguish between the situation in which the means do not differ and the situation in which $\mu_A < \mu_B$. If you had conducted a research study with this directional statistical hypothesis and $\overline{X}_A$ came out many stan-

Uses of Inferential Statistics

Parameter Estimation: Estimating the value of a parameter from a statistic calculated from a sample.

1. *Point estimation:* The relevant statistic is used as the best single estimate of the parameter.

   Advantage: It is easy to compute and understand.

   Disadvantage: The estimate is almost certainly wrong.

2. *Confidence intervals:* A range of scores is computed according to a procedure that provides a certain probability that such intervals will include the population parameter.

   Advantage: It gives a realistic picture of the accuracy of the estimate of the population parameter.

   Disadvantage: There is no guarantee that the confidence interval contains the value of the parameter.

Hypothesis Testing: Testing the likelihood that a hypothesis about the value of the parameter is correct, based on one or more statistics calculated from the sample.

1. *Research hypothesis:* The hypothesis postulated by the researcher states what he or she expects to find; it usually states the direction of the expected results.

2. *Null hypothesis:* The hypothesis that indicates that the results reflect random sampling from a population with the hypothesized parameter and that any difference in sample means or any apparent relationship between variables is due to chance.

3. *Alternative hypothesis:* The hypothesis that would be true if the null hypothesis were false.

   Directional alternative hypothesis: The hypothesis that specifies the direction of the difference in the size of two population means or the sign of a correlation coefficient in the population.

   Nondirectional alternative hypothesis: The hypothesis that indicates that the difference in the population means or the size of a correlation coefficient is not equal to zero; it does not specify the direction of the difference or correlation.

dard deviations below $\overline{X}_B$, you would have to conclude that the means did not differ significantly, even if such an interpretation seems clearly wrong.

Contrary to what some people think, it is impossible to prove statistically that a particular hypothesis, either the null or the alternative hypothesis, is or is not true. Instead the null hypothesis is subjected to a test and, depending on the results, is either retained as a possibility or rejected. The decision about whether to retain the null hypothesis or to reject it and decide that the alternative hypothesis is likely to be correct depends primarily on the data and the value of the statistic computed to test its significance. It also depends on the statistical significance level that you have decided to use.

Significance Levels

Carver (1978, 1993) has stated that "statistical significance simply means rareness." More specifically, a statistical significance level is a value that relates to the probability of getting scores from a sample drawn from a population with a parameter equal to that of the null hypothesis. The level of statistical significance at which a decision is made is the likelihood that such results would be found if the null hypothesis is true. When you conclude that a finding is statistically significant, you are concluding that it is unlikely or rare that such a finding would occur if the null hypothesis were true.

The more stringent, or lower, the significance level, the less likely it is that a sample that is called statistically significant at that level would be drawn from a population with the hypothesized parameter. A significance level of .001 is considered more stringent than one of .05, for example, because results are 1/50th as likely to reach the .001 level as the .05 level if the null hypothesis is true. Another term that is frequently used as a synonym for significance level is alpha level, often symbolized as α-level.

TIP

It would, of course, be possible to select some other level as the appropriate cutoff for statistical significance. However, this is rarely done because it raises the issue of whether or not the researcher was being arbitrary in his or her decision. If you choose to use some other alpha level than the conventional ones, you should be able to justify it. In particular, use of a less stringent level, such as .10 or .15, is almost never considered acceptable practice, except perhaps in a preliminary screening to be sure that no promising possibilities get overlooked.

Conventional Significance Levels. Three levels of significance are much more commonly used than any other ones: the .05 level, the .01 level, and the

.001 level. As was mentioned in Chapter 6, most of the time the .05 α-level is considered to be the minimum level necessary for significance. If the findings are also significant at the .01 or .001 α-levels, then the most stringent level is the one reported. Sometimes researchers will report exact probability levels rather than indicating only whether or not the findings are significant at the $p < .05$ level, the $p < .01$ level, or the $p < .001$ level.

Critical Values.   In order to make a decision about whether or not a finding is statistically significant, it is convenient to have some value to which you can compare your test statistic—that is, the value of z, t, F, r, or whatever statistic you have computed to test your hypothesis. As discussed in Chapter 6, these values are called *critical values*. As shown in Figure 8.3, when a graph is drawn of the sampling distribution, then the critical values appear as the cutoff points that distinguish statistically significant results from nonsignificant results. If the sampling distribution is normal, then the cutoff points for the .05 level will be –1.96 and +1.96, those values that cut off .025 of the scores at either end.

    The region of the sampling distribution that would lead to rejection of the null hypothesis—that is, the region associated with a value of the statistic that is at least as large in absolute magnitude as the critical value—is the **critical region** or the **region of rejection**. The region of the sampling distribution that would lead to retention of the null hypothesis is called the **region of retention**. If the null hypothesis is true, then the test statistic will yield a value in the region of rejection alpha (e.g., .05 or .001) of the time. If the null hypothesis is false, then obtaining a value in the critical region is much more likely.

    So far, the process of assessing statistical significance seems pretty straightforward.

- Use the .05 α-level unless there is reason to be more conservative, but check out the .01 and .001 levels in any case.

FIGURE 8.3   Critical Values and the Critical Region of a Normal Distribution

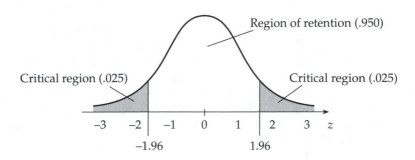

- Look up the relevant critical values (+ and –) in the appropriate table, compute the test statistic from your data, and compare the value of this statistic with the critical values.
- If the test statistic falls into the critical region, reject the null hypothesis and conclude that the larger of your two means is really larger (or the correlation in the population is really in the direction of the sample *r*).
- If not, retain the null hypothesis as a possibility.

If you are doing only one statistical test, this procedure is perfectly appropriate. Suppose, however, that you have computed 20 correlation coefficients and wish to test the significance of each. If each *r* is tested at the .05 level, your chance of finding *at least one* of the 20 to be statistically significant is far greater than .05, even if the null hypothesis is true. (It's about .64, in fact.) In other words, 5% of your correlations (1 out of 20) would probably be called statistically significant, even if all the correlations in the population were equal to zero.

In order to keep your overall probability of finding a statistically significant result at .05 (or whatever you select as your *p*-level), when the null hypothesis is true, you need to control the **experimentwise error rate**, or your chance of (mistakenly) calling some finding in your research study statistically significant. (By convention, people use the awkward term "experimentwise error rate" even when the research study is not an experiment.)

Bonferroni Adjustment. One way to control the experimentwise error rate is to use the **Bonferroni critical value procedure**, which adjusts for the number of statistical significance tests being performed. The easy way to do this is to divide your desired alpha level by the number of significance tests that you intend to conduct and then compare the results of each of the tests to the critical value at the new, more stringent, alpha level. For example, if you are going to be computing 20 correlation coefficients, test each one at the .05/20 or the .0025 significance level. This will achieve your goal of keeping the overall chance of finding anything statistically significant at .05, assuming that the null hypothesis is true.

Other ways of controlling the error rate in addition to the Bonferroni procedure will be discussed in later chapters, particularly in Chapter 11.

TIP

The Bonferroni procedure, aside from having a glamorous name that any sports car manufacturer would envy, is a correct and conservative procedure that will protect you from some instances in which you would otherwise make the error of rejecting the null hypothesis when it is true (Harris, 1994). This error, and others, will be discussed further in the next section.

Types of Errors

When testing statistical hypotheses, eventually a decision has to be made about whether to retain or reject the null hypothesis, H_0. Whatever decision you make, some of the time you will be wrong. Statisticians like to put the possible decisions into a table as follows:

	Actual Situation	
Decision	**H_0 true**	**H_0 false**
Reject H_0	Type I error	Correct
Retain H_0	Correct	Type II error

Type I Error. If the null hypothesis is true (or true enough for all practical purposes), then if you reject it and decide that there is a difference in the direction of your sample means, you have made a Type I error. In other words, a **Type I error** involves rejecting the null hypothesis when it is true. The probability of making a Type I error is exactly α; in other words, you get to select your chance of making such an error. Of course, if the null hypothesis is correct and you retain it, you are making a correct decision.

Figure 8.4 shows the probability of making a correct decision and of making a Type I error when the null hypothesis is true and you are doing a one-tailed test.

Type II Error. At first thought, you might decide to use a more stringent alpha level and thereby reduce your chance of making a Type I error. Indeed, you could reduce it to zero by always retaining H_0 as a possibility. Alas, however, if you were to do this, you would be increasing your chance of making a Type II error; namely, failing to identify a real difference or relationship in

FIGURE 8.4   Probability of a Type I Error When the Null Hypothesis Is True

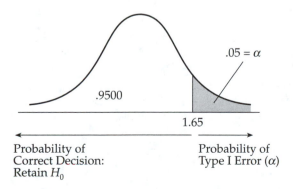

the population. In other words, a **Type II error** consists of retaining the null hypothesis when it is false. Although this kind of error is generally considered less serious than a Type I error (since presumably some other dedicated soul will eventually discover a relationship between variables that does exist in the population), you still don't want to miss such a finding if at all possible. Indeed, it has been argued that many psychologists are too concerned about Type I errors and not enough about Type II errors (Berkowitz, 1992). Ideally, you want to decrease your chance of making a Type II error while also keeping your likelihood of making a Type I error quite small. In other words, you want to increase your chance of finding a real difference or relationship without increasing your chance of crying "wolf," or mistakenly rejecting the null hypothesis.

The probability of making a Type II error is symbolized by β (beta), and it is less easy to select or to manipulate than is alpha. To identify beta you must know the minimum size of the difference in means (or the value of r) in the population that you wish to detect, as well as the variance or standard deviation of the scores in the population. However, even if you don't know the exact value of beta, there are things that you can do to reduce beta without increasing alpha. Another way of stating this is to say that it is possible to increase your *power*, your likelihood of finding a real difference or relationship or of correctly rejecting a false null hypothesis (Cohen, 1988, 1992a, 1992b; Leventhal & Huynh, 1996).

Figure 8.5 shows the probability of making a correct decision (power) and of a Type II error when the null hypothesis is false and you are doing a one-tailed test.

FIGURE 8.5   Probability of a Type II Error When the Null Hypothesis Is False

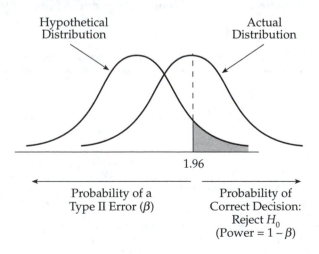

Power

The power of a statistical test is equal to $1 - \beta$ or 1 minus the chance of making a Type II error. In other words, **power** is the likelihood that you will correctly reject the null hypothesis when it is false and therefore conclude that there is a real difference in means or relationship among variables in the population (Benjafield, 1994; Cohen, 1992a). The power of any statistical procedure is greatly dependent upon the sample size (Aron & Aron, 1997; Benjafield, 1994; Carver, 1978, 1993; Cohen, 1992a; Shaver, 1993; Thompson, 1993).

Power is a particularly important concept, since a number of statisticians and psychologists have suggested that the null hypothesis is almost never true, so Type I errors are almost never made. Unfortunately, the average power of statistical significance tests in many areas of research is less than .5, so the majority of such tests lead to the wrong conclusion when they fail to reject the null hypothesis (Hunter, 1997). Other psychologists have suggested that the real issue is not whether there is sufficient power to reject the null hypothesis but whether there is enough information to come to a valid conclusion about the direction of the difference or relationship in the population (Abelson, 1997; Harris, 1997; Leventhal & Huynh, 1996; Scarr, 1997).

Tables of the power of various statistical procedures for different sample sizes are available in more advanced statistics books and articles (Aron & Aron, 1997; Cohen & Cohen, 1983; Cohen, 1988; Cohen, 1990).

Ways to Increase Power.   There are several approaches that researchers use to increase the power of their analyses, even when they are unable to measure it precisely. In order to increase your power without also increasing your chance of making a Type I error (i.e., while holding your alpha level constant), you can do the following.

1. Increase your sample size. Increasing the sample size is often the easiest and the best way to increase power. Estimates based on larger samples are more accurate, have less error, and lead to more correct conclusions. Increasing the sample size is particularly important when sample sizes are small. If your sample is less than 100, and particularly if it is less than 30, your analyses may not be powerful enough to pick up a small or moderate difference in population means (Cohen, 1992). Increasing your sample from 10 to 100 would have a much bigger effect on your power than increasing your sample size from 1000 to 3000.

2. Use parametric tests where appropriate, and consider using either nonparametric tests or alternative procedures—such as "trimming" the mean (Wilcox, 1992)—when the assumptions are not met. Parametric tests are generally more powerful than nonparametric tests. However, if their assumptions are not met, sometimes these tests will have low power or will not yield meaningful results (Wilcox, 1992).

3. Increase the accuracy of your dependent measures, if possible. If your measure is imprecise, then some of the differences in raw (and mean) scores will reflect error in measurement rather than actual differences in the variable of interest. Such measurement error will inflate the standard deviations, the standard error of the mean, and your chance of making a Type II error (Zuckerman, Hodgins, Zuckerman & Rosenthal, 1993).

4. Increase the sensitivity of your design, if possible, by using some of the ways of controlling for extraneous variables outlined in Chapter 2. If some variables that are related to your dependent measure are held constant and others are incorporated into a factorial design, then the error variance (the variability in the scores due to something other than the variable in which you are interested) will be reduced and your power will be increased.

Effect Size

One of the reasons why researchers are interested in the idea of power is that they want to know how small a difference in means their statistical procedures will detect. The term **effect size** is usually applied to experimental research by researchers who wish to estimate how large a difference there really is between the experimental and control groups. Since the difference in the means of the raw scores depends on the unit of measurement, researchers usually standardize such a difference by transforming it to what is called an effect size (Cohen, 1992a, 1992b).

An effect size for a difference in means, symbolized by d, equals the difference between the means of the experimental and control groups divided by the standard deviation of the control group. In other words, an effect size is a measure of the amount of difference there is between the experimental and control groups in standard deviation units. An effect size can also be calculated for a correlation coefficient or for a difference in means from a non-experimental study (Abelson, 1995).

For a given sample size, a more powerful statistical procedure will be able to detect a smaller effect size. Similarly, a more powerful test is one that will be more likely to detect a difference of any given effect size. An effect size of .2 is generally considered small, one of .5 medium, and one of .8 large (Cohen, 1988, 1992b). Ideally, a researcher wants a design and statistical analysis procedure that will be powerful enough to pick up the smallest effect size that would be of interest. On the other hand, a huge sample size could lead to such a powerful test that it would find a difference that is so small as to be of no scientific importance to be statistically significant (Carver, 1978, 1993; Thompson, 1993).

One-Tailed Versus Two-Tailed Significance Tests

Until this point, all the examples of significance tests that have been discussed have been instances of two-tailed tests. A **two-tailed significance test**

FIGURE 8.6   Example of a Two-Tailed z-Test

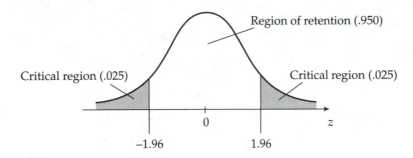

is one that divides up the critical region into two areas, each cutting off half of the alpha level. With a two-tailed test, you have two critical values, two critical regions, and three possible conclusions that you could reach:

1. $\mu_A > \mu_B$
2. $\mu_A < \mu_B$
3. There is not enough evidence to reject the null hypothesis that $\mu_A = \mu_B$.

Figure 8.6 presents an example of a two-tailed z-test.

A **one-tailed significance test** is one that has only one critical value and one critical region, the direction of which depends upon your research hypothesis, as illustrated in Figure 8.7. A one-tailed test is more powerful if the results are in the predicted direction but far less powerful if they are in the opposite direction. If you are doing a one-tailed test and the direction of the results is contrary to your hypothesis, all that you can do is retain the null hypothesis. Since this decision to retain H_0 can be extremely misleading and lead to incorrect interpretations of the true state of affairs, the use of one-tailed tests is generally not recommended (Harris, 1997; Leventhal & Huynh, 1996).

Decision Rules for One- and Two-Tailed Tests

- *Rule 1:* Always use two-tailed tests. This is a fine rule. No one will criticize you, journal editors will approve, and other researchers will have confidence in your findings.

- *Rule 2:* Use a one-tailed test *only* when you would be willing to retain the null hypothesis if the results came out very, very far in the opposite direction. When might that be?

As Abelson (1995) suggests, it is hard to think of realistic examples, because most intellectually curious people would want to consider the meaning of very strong findings, no matter how unexpected they might be.

FIGURE 8.7   Examples of One-Tailed z-Tests in Both Directions

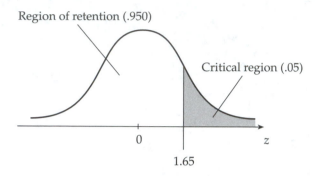

Region of retention (.950)

Critical region (.05)

0

1.65

z

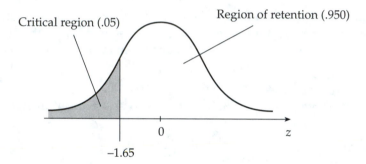

Critical region (.05)

Region of retention (.950)

0

−1.65

z

However, if you were a dietitian trying to see if a new recipe for rutabaga casserole should be substituted for the old tried-and-true one so beloved of dormitory students, you might be interested only in one direction of the results: whether or not the new recipe is preferred to the old one. For your purposes it is immaterial whether it is liked less or not preferred, since you would switch only if it is liked better. For similar decisions about whether or not a more expensive new treatment is more effective than the less costly older one, or whether a new curriculum is so much better that it merits changing, the use of a one-tailed test might be justified. However, be honest: If you would be interested in discussing the results if it turned out that the old curriculum or treatment or recipe was better than the new one, then you should be using a two-tailed test.

• *Rule 3:* Divide up your alpha level and use an uneven two-tailed test. Braver (1975), Harris (1994; 1997), and Leventhal & Huynh (1996) recommend splitting your alpha level to have perhaps .04 in one tail of the distribution and .01 in the other tail. This procedure, called a "lopsided test" by Abelson (1995), has the advantages of keeping your overall alpha level at .05 (or whatever you choose), providing some protection against an extremely large difference in the direction opposite from prediction, and increasing your power for finding a significant difference in the predicted direction over that which a conventional two-tailed test would provide. It is not widely used, however, perhaps because researchers are reluctant to use a relatively unconventional procedure and perhaps because there are no clear guidelines as to how best to split the alpha level.

Statistical Significance Versus Meaningfulness

The extended discussion of hypothesis testing and statistical significance in this chapter should not blind you to the distinction between statistical significance and meaningfulness or importance, a topic that has even made it into the pages of *Newsweek* in an article about what constitutes good science (Begley, 1993). A statistically significant result is one that is likely to represent a real difference or correlation in the population, a result that is unlikely to be due to sampling error. If a result is not statistically significant, then you cannot have confidence in it, since there is a reasonable possibility that the findings would be different if the study were repeated. Thus, you could say that statistical significance is a necessary condition for a result to be considered an important one.

Statistical significance is no guarantee of importance, however. It is certainly possible for a statistically significant result to be so tiny, so trivial, that it is of little or no practical importance (Carver, 1978, 1993; Shaver, 1985, 1993; Thompson, 1993). A study with thousands of subjects can reveal statistically significant correlations or differences in means that are so minuscule as to account for less than 1% of the variance in the scores. Even though such a difference may reflect a difference in the population, it may be so small as to have no use or practical impact at all. For example, in early 1993, the Environmental Protection Agency implied that the 1958 Delaney law, which banned the use of cancer-causing chemicals in processed foods, was obsolete, since it was now possible to identify traces of chemicals that were present in such small amounts as to have no impact on health. (I don't know whether statistical significance tests were actually used in this research or not). As another example of a totally trivial statistically significant difference, remember the earlier example of how a difference of .30 of an IQ point was significant with a sample size of 200,000.

On the other hand, even a minuscule difference may have some theoretical importance, if it is consistently found and provides support for a theory. Prentice and Miller (1992) argue that even a small effect is important if it is produced by a minimal manipulation of an independent variable or holds for a seemingly unlikely dependent variable. The thing to keep in mind when interpreting and discussing the results of your analyses is that the size of a statistically significant difference or relationship is usually the key to how important or meaningful it is.

To complicate things even further, some psychologists and statisticians have questioned the value of statistical significance testing (Harlow, 1997).

Recognizing that there is usually at least a minuscule difference or relation-ship in the population, making the null hypothesis literally false, many psy-chologists feel that the real question is whether the difference or relationship in the population is large enough to matter, either theoretically or practically. It is not clear to what extent statistical significance tests are helpful in answer-ing that question.

In an extended and somewhat heated debate (Abelson, 1997; Estes, 1997; Harris, 1997; Hunter, 1997; Scarr, 1997; Shrout, 1997; Wilkinson, 1996), such issues as low power, misuse of tests, and mistaken inferences have led some researchers to suggest that statistical significance tests should be banned in psychology journals, perhaps to be replaced with confidence intervals. This issue is still unresolved (Harlow, 1997), but it does suggest that researchers should be cautious about overinterpreting the importance of statistical sig-nificance and confusing it with effect size or importance.

CHAPTER SUMMARY The sample for a research study is a very important factor in its design. A census is a sample comprising the entire population. The next best type of sample, a random sample, is selected so that every possible sample of size N has an equal chance of being selected from the population. Random selection can be done through a physical mixing process or by the use of a random number table.

Stratified sampling involves selecting within mutually exclusive sub-groups; it is usually done randomly, with subgroup sizes proportional to those in the population. Quota sampling, often used by professional poll-sters, is similar to stratified sampling but involves stratifying on a large num-ber of demographic variables and nonrandom selection within precisely specified subgroups. Systematic sampling involves picking every nth score. Cluster sampling uses entire groups or clusters, like classrooms, as the unit. Convenience or haphazard sampling occurs when the researcher makes an effort to describe the characteristics of the sample and to get a reasonably rep-resentative sample, but does not use any of the above approaches. A clearly biased sample is obviously not representative of the population of interest.

Inferential statistics involves generalizing from a sample to a population, based on assumptions about sampling distributions, which are distributions of statistics calculated from randomly drawn samples. The standard error of the mean is the standard deviation of a distribution of sample means. The Central Limit Theorem, which provides the basis for most inferential statisti-cal tests about means, states that as the sample size gets infinitely large, the sampling distribution of the mean approaches a normal distribution with a mean equal to the population mean, μ, and a standard deviation equal to the standard deviation of the population, σ, divided by the square root of N.

A z-test can be done to compare a sample mean with a hypothetical mean drawn from a distribution with a known σ or to compare two sample means from distributions with known σ's.

The two major types of inferential statistics are parameter estimation and hypothesis testing. Parameter estimates can be either point estimates, the single best estimate of the population parameter, or confidence intervals, a range of scores with a certain probability of including the parameter. Since point estimates are almost always wrong, confidence intervals give a more meaningful picture of the population parameter.

Hypothesis testing usually involves estimating the probability that a hypothesis about the value of a parameter in the population, called the null hypothesis, is correct. If this probability is very small, the researcher decides to reject the null hypothesis and accept the alternative hypothesis, which is typically the hypothesis that two population means differ or that the correlation coefficient in a population is unequal to zero. Ordinarily, people reject the null hypothesis if the likelihood that it is true is less than .05, .01, or .001, which are called the alpha levels or significance levels.

Rejecting the null hypothesis when it is correct is called a Type I error; retaining it when it is false is called a Type II error. The probability of making a Type I error is called alpha, and the probability of making a Type II error is called beta. Power, the likelihood of correctly rejecting a false null hypothesis, is equal to $1 - \beta$. The larger the sample size, the greater the power of a test.

In order to decide whether to reject or retain the null hypothesis, it is necessary to compute a value of a statistic and to compare it with a critical value. Critical values are based on theoretical distributions and are found in tables like the normal curve table. Many statistical tests can be either one-tailed, in which only a difference or correlation in a predicted direction is called statistically significant, or two-tailed, in which a large enough difference or correlation in either direction is called significant. The critical values for one-tailed and two-tailed tests will be different. Generally, researchers make directional predictions, but use two-tailed tests to guard against the possibility that their predictions are in error.

A statistically significant finding is one that is unlikely to be due to chance and likely to represent a true difference or relationship in the population. However, the statistical significance of a finding is not the same as its importance, as a trivial difference may be statistically significant with a large sample size and a moderate one may not be statistically significant if the sample size is small.

CHAPTER REVIEW

Multiple-Choice Questions

1. If you are doing a statistical test with $\alpha = .05$ and $\beta = .10$, what is your power?

   a. .99   **b.** .95   **c.** .90   **d.** .10   **e.** .09   **f.** .05   **g.** .01

2. If the mean from one sample is 37 and the mean from another sample is 3, what can we conclude?

   a. We can conclude nothing until we do a statistical significance test.

   b. They come from the same population.

   c. They come from different populations.

   d. The difference between them is due to sampling error.

   e. Both b and d are true.

3. Sally has concluded that the difference between the means of sophomores and freshmen is not significant, when in fact the null hypothesis is true. What type of error has she committed?

   a. a Type I error

   b. a Type II error

   c. the standard error of the mean

   d. the standard error of estimate

   e. none of the above

4. If you never make a mistake in your arithmetic and you do 200 statistical significance tests comparing random samples from the same population, each one at the .05 α-level, about how many times can you expect to make a Type I error?

   a. none

   b. less than 1

   c. approximately 5 times

   d. approximately 10 times

   e. approximately 40 times

   f. approximately 200 times

5. Which of the following terms has a very different statistical meaning from the others?

   a. alpha level

   b. level of the independent variable

   c. level of significance

   d. p-level

   e. probability level

6. For a population with a mean of 60 and a standard deviation of 12, if you take a random sample of size 100, which of the following is true?

   a. The standard error of the mean will be 60.

   b. The standard error of the mean will be 6.

   c. The standard error of the mean will be 10.

   d. The standard error of the mean will be 12.

    e. The expected value of the mean will be 60.

    f. None of the above is true.

7. If you are doing a z-test and your computed value of z falls into the critical region, what should you do?

    a. Retain the null hypothesis.

    b. Reexamine your calculations, as you must have made a mistake in computation.

    c. Conclude that there is a significant difference in the means.

    d. Conclude that there is not a significant difference in the means.

    e. Both a and d are correct.

8. In order to increase your power while holding your alpha level constant, which of the following would be most effective?

    a. Switch to a nonparametric test.

    b. Decrease your sample size.

    c. Increase your sample size.

    d. Use less sensitive dependent measures.

    e. Use a two-tailed test instead of a one-tailed test.

9. If the 99% confidence interval for the difference in two means runs from 2 to 7, what must be true?

    a. The 95% confidence interval for the difference in the means equals 95% of the distance from 2 to 7.

    b. The 95% confidence interval for the difference in the means equals 95% of the distance from 1.5 to 7.5.

    c. The two means differ significantly at the $p < .01$ level.

    d. The two means do not differ significantly at the $p < .01$ level.

    e. The sample means differ by exactly 5 points.

10. According to the Central Limit Theorem, as the sample size increases,

    a. the standard deviation of the sample increases.

    b. the standard deviation of the sample decreases.

    c. the standard deviation of the population decreases.

    d. the standard error of the mean decreases.

    e. the mean of the sample decreases.

    f. none of the above is necessarily true.

Problems

11. The mayor's Commission on Clean, Healthy Living is conducting a survey of students' attitudes toward drugs. For each of the descriptions listed, identify the kind of sampling procedure that it represents.

a. Six classrooms are chosen, and every student in these classrooms is in the sample.

b. Every high school student in the city is in the sample.

c. Students who belong to NORML, an organization dedicated to legalizing the use of marijuana, are selected for the sample.

d. Every 10th student on the school district's list of students enrolled in high school is selected for the sample.

e. All the names of the students at Mellow Middle School are written on separate pieces of paper, which are then put in a hat and well shuffled; 10% of the names are then drawn and included in the sample. This procedure is repeated at Methadone Middle School, Maybelline Middle School, and every other middle school in the school district, until 10% of the students at each school have been selected.

f. Ten students are selected from each school in the city to be in the sample.

12. Name a statistical synonym for (or at least define) each of the following terms:

a. critical region   b. significance level   c. regression   d. $X - \overline{X}$

e. dependent variable   f. power   g. H_0

h. the mean of a sampling distribution of the mean

13. The 400 new employees of your company have taken the New Employees Suffering Test (NEST), a widely used measure of how quickly new employees are expected to adapt to their job. In the national population of new employees, the mean on this test is 48 and the standard deviation is 12. Your sample of employees has a mean of 50 and a standard deviation of 10. Is this significantly higher than the national mean?

14. Identify each of the following errors—that is, for each situation described, say what kind of error it represents.

a. You conclude that age and memory are significantly negatively correlated when they are unrelated in the population.

b. You take the standard deviation for a population and divide it by the square root of the sample size.

c. Based on a z-test, you conclude that the null hypothesis is false when the mean for group A in the population is higher than the mean for group B.

d. Based on a z-test, you conclude that the mean for group A in the population is higher than the mean for group B when the two sample means really come from the same population.

e. After computing a correlation coefficient, you take the square root of $(1 - r^2)$ and multiply that by the standard deviation of the scores on Y.

f. You conclude that the difference in two sample means is small enough so that it might represent a difference of zero in the population. The real difference in the population is 1.

15. According to the Central Limit Theorem, which of the following is true?

   a. As N gets large, the shape of a sampling distribution approximates the shape of the frequency distribution of the population from which the sample was drawn.

   b. As N gets large, the standard deviation of a sampling distribution approximates the standard deviation of the population from which the sample was drawn.

   c. As N gets large, the mean of a sampling distribution approximates the mean of the population from which the sample was drawn.

   d. As N gets large, the N of a sampling distribution approximates the number of scores in the population from which the sample was drawn.

16. Suppose that some canine psychologists (a deliberately ambiguous term) have measured a sample of 225 dogs and found that they ate a mean of 300 grams of dog food daily. The standard deviation of the number of grams eaten was 50 grams, which you know is also true for the population of dogs at the pound. What is the 99% confidence interval for the mean number of grams of dog food eaten daily? Why would you want to know this? Maybe you're planning on adopting a dog and want to know how much an average dog eats.

17. Suppose that a very inexperienced researcher wants to get a sample that will represent all women in Kansas City as part of a study of Midwestern women. Like many large cities, Kansas City has a substantial amount of stratification by ethnicity and income. Give an example of each of the following procedures:

   a. clearly biased sampling

   b. cluster sampling

   c. census

   d. convenience sampling

   e. quota sampling

   f. simple random sampling

   g. stratified random sampling

   h. stratified nonrandom sampling

   i. systematic sampling

18. The 300 children at Cuddles Childcare Center range in age from 2 to 72 months, with a mean of 36 months and a standard deviation of 15 months. They are divided into smaller groups of 9, each with a caretaker and an aide, in order to provide a more familylike atmosphere. Supposedly, the children are randomly assigned to groups. You are responsible for a group of 9 children whose ages are as follows: 2, 4, 15, 18, 22, 32, 36, 38, and 54 months. You are suspicious that these children do not constitute a random sample of the Cuddles Childcare population. (For one thing, only one of them is toilet trained.)

a. What kind of test would you perform to discover whether it is likely that your children represent a random sample from the population?

b. Perform this test and report the value of the statistic.

c. What can you conclude about the likelihood that your children represent a random sample from the Cuddles Childcare population?

19. You are interested in comparing a problem-based curriculum with a traditional curriculum for teaching ninth-grade science. School P uses the new curriculum, and School T uses the traditional one. You have measured all the students in both schools on the Basic Science Test in May, after they have had 8 months of one or the other curriculum. At School P, the 100 freshman students have a mean of 80 on the test and a standard deviation of 15; at School T, the 81 freshmen have a mean of 75 and a standard deviation of 12.

a. How likely is it that the students in the schools represent random samples from the same population?

b. How likely is it that the problem-based curriculum caused an improvement in test scores?

20. Nurse Nectarine has done a study comparing the amount of weight that undernourished hospital patients gain when they are served a diet high in fresh fruit as compared to one high in fat. Based on this study, describe, identify, or give an example of each of the following terms.

a. power

b. Type I error

c. Type II error

d. directional hypothesis

e. null hypothesis

f. effect size

g. a statistically significant difference

Study Questions

1. Imagine that you are trying to survey American citizens to measure their opinions on whether or not persons with mental retardation who commit serious crimes like rape or murder ought to be subject to the death penalty. Try to think of an example of how you might use each of the following: simple random sampling, stratified random sampling, stratified nonrandom sampling, cluster sampling, quota sampling, systematic sampling, convenience sampling, and clearly biased sampling. Of course, you cannot use all of these procedures to sample from all American citizens, so you will have to limit the populations from which you sample for some of these examples.

2. Identify a limited population with which you have some contact, preferably one with between 50 and 100 elements. This could be coworkers, all the friends and relatives you can think of and write down on a piece of paper,

everyone who sent you a Christmas card last year, or (in a pinch) the names of the 50 states. Then identify some way in which the members of this population could be stratified—gender, occupation, relationship to you, geographical region; the variable doesn't matter. Now use the random number table (Appendix Table 4) to select a stratified random sample, assuming that you have a potential sample size of approximately 20. [Hint: You'll have to divide 20 by the size of the population to get the proportion of the population that is in the sample, and you'll have to round off your anticipated sample sizes from each stratum to the nearest whole person.] Do the units in your sample appear to be representative of the population? If not, why not?

3. Think of a research study that you might wish to conduct that would involve comparing the mean scores of two groups on some variable. First, imagine what your dependent measure might be and what you would predict would be the mean scores on the two variables. State your research hypothesis: The mean of group A would be > (or <) the mean of group B. Then think about the minimum difference that would be of interest to you—that is, the smallest effect size that you would wish to detect. Would you be at all interested in detecting a difference in the opposite direction? If not, why not?

4. Yet again, go to the library and browse through journals that interest you and look for some that involve parameter estimation. See if you can find several instances in which the researchers constructed confidence intervals or even one instance in which a point estimate was used. Why do you think that they used this procedure rather than hypothesis testing? Conversely, try to locate an example of a research study in which hypothesis testing was used for which parameter estimation would have been equally or more appropriate.

t-Tests and Confidence Intervals About Means

How Are *t*-Tests Used to Test Hypotheses About Means?

Of all of the uses that researchers find for statistics, the one that is probably most common is to test some hypotheses or answer some questions about means. Do mothers play more (or less) with their infants than do fathers? How many (supply some nonoffensive name) does it take, on the average, to screw in a light bulb? How long does the average light bulb last? How many children does the average American family have? Does Soggytown really get significantly more rain per year than Dryville? Do blondes have more fun than brunettes? If relevant data can be gathered and a relevant null hypothesis formulated, then each of these questions can be answered by a statistical procedure designed to test a hypothesis about means, either a *z*-test or a *t*-test.

z-Tests Versus *t*-Tests

You have already been introduced to one of the procedures that can be used to test hypotheses about one or two means: a *z*-test. This chapter focuses on a similar but more common procedure: Student's *t*-test. A Student's *t*-test, usually just called a **t-test**, is a statistical significance test used to test hypotheses about one or two means when the population standard deviation is unknown. Although the formulas for *z*-tests and *t*-tests look almost identical, there are some differences between the two procedures.

Differences Between *z*-Tests and *t*-Tests. A *z*-test can be used to test for differences between means when the standard deviation of scores in the population is known. One kind of instance in which it is likely that σ is known is that in which the dependent measure is the score on a standardized test that has been tried out with many different populations and has a known value of

σ, such as studies comparing IQ test scores of different groups. Another type of situation in which σ would be known occurs when you wish to compare the mean of a sample to the population from which it came, in order to assess whether or not the sample was truly random. For example, you might want to see whether or not the patients on ward D remain in the hospital longer than the patients on other wards or whether graduate students in the college of education at your university are older than the average graduate student. However, most of the time researchers know no more about σ than they do about μ. When the standard deviation in the population is unknown, then a *t*-test, rather than a *z*-test, is the procedure that must be used.

A *t*-test differs from a *z*-test in several ways.

1. A *t*-test uses an estimate of σ based on s to produce an estimate either of the standard error of the mean, symbolized by $s_{\bar{X}}$, or of the standard error of the difference between the means, symbolized by $s_{\bar{X}_1 - \bar{X}_2}$.
2. Unlike a *z*-test, each *t*-test has associated with it a certain number of degrees of freedom, which is related to the sample size and the number of parameters that must be estimated from the sample.
3. A *t*-test is based on the *t*-distribution (or family of distributions), whereas a *z*-test is based on the normal distribution.

Similarities Between *z*-Tests and *t*-Tests.   In spite of the above differences, the formulas for *z*-tests and *t*-tests are almost identical.

1. In the formulas for the two-sample case, the numerator consists of the difference in the sample means minus the hypothetical difference in the population means. The *z* and *t* formulas for the single-sample case have the difference between the sample mean and the hypothetical mean in the numerator.
2. The formulas for both *t* and *z* have in the denominator the standard error of the mean or the standard error of the difference in means. The only difference in the formulas is that the formula for *t* uses s where the formula for *z* uses σ.
3. Both the *z*-test and the *t*-test are used to test hypotheses about one or two sample means; neither is normally used to test hypotheses about more than two sample means.
4. The procedures are so similar that they are essentially identical when the sample size is large—indeed so similar that many researchers always do *t*-tests of hypotheses and report *t*-values, even when they could have done a *z*-test.

Characteristics of *t*-Tests

Absolute Value of *t*.   The absolute value of *t* is a measure of the relative size of the difference in the means, which is associated with the probability that this difference reflects a true difference in the population. A *t*-value of zero indicates that the means are identical, with larger absolute values indicating larger differences in the means. The sign of *t* signifies the direction of the difference, indicating which mean was larger than which other one. Researchers sometimes report the value of *t* as positive, even if they originally subtracted in the opposite direction; this is not generally considered a problem as long as the actual values of the means are reported or there is a clear statement indicating which mean was the larger.

Since the formula for *t* is the difference in the means divided by the standard error of the difference—that is, $(\overline{X} - \mu)/(s/\sqrt{N})$, the absolute value of *t* will be larger if

- The difference in the means is larger (because the numerator will be larger)
- The standard deviation is smaller (because the denominator will be smaller)

and/or

- The sample size is larger (also leading to a smaller denominator)

In other words, *t* is more likely to have a large absolute value if there is a big difference between the mean of the sample and the mean of the population, if the scores within the sample are very similar to each other, and if the sample mean is based on a large number of scores. All of these characteristics should indeed be associated with an increased likelihood that the null hypothesis is false.

Assumptions of *t*-Tests.   You may (or may not?) recall from Chapter 1 that parametric statistical tests make a number of assumptions about population parameters. Like any parametric technique, the *t*-test has a number of assumptions associated with it.

1. Its use assumes that the scores have been randomly sampled, or at least independently sampled (selected individually), from the population to which you wish to generalize.
2. It assumes that the population(s) from which the sample(s) comes is/are normally distributed.
3. It assumes that, if two independent samples are involved, the two samples come from populations with equal variances.
4. It assumes that the data are measured on a scale of measurement such that it makes sense to calculate and discuss a mean: either an interval- or ratio-level dependent measure or one with properties close to an interval scale, such as responses to attitude scale items.

Violations of the Assumptions. How could you know if these assumptions are true? What would you do if they were not? Consider the first assumption. Does it mean that you could not compare the scores of men and women who responded to a telephone survey asking them how many hours of television they watched per week, since they surely don't constitute a random sample of all people who own a television, all people who own a television and a phone, or even all people who own a television and a phone and who answered the phone when you called (Don't forget the three who hung up on you!)? Clearly, much less research would be done (or at least statistically analyzed) if this assumption were always followed. It is a common practice to perform a *t*-test on data that have not been randomly sampled; however, depending on the actual sampling procedure, you must be correspondingly cautious in your generalizations from the data.

The issue of nonindependence of sampling is a somewhat different one. If your data were sampled in clusters, as discussed in Chapter 8, it is not strictly appropriate to treat them as if they had been selected one by one. If the data come in natural pairs, father/son or husband/wife, for example, then there is a special kind of *t*-test used for comparing the scores of the pairs (husbands versus wives, for example). If you have a reason to expect that people within a cluster are more similar to each other on the dependent measure than they are to the general population, you should either use the cluster mean as your unit of analysis or seek help from a statistician so that you can use a nested analysis procedure.

The second assumption, that of a normal distribution in the population from which the sample comes, is almost impossible to check and almost certainly wrong in any case. Because the *t*-test is reasonably robust to violations of the assumptions, a *t*-test will generally lead to approximately correct conclusions for any distribution in which most of the scores are piled up in the middle and there are fewer as you get farther away from the middle. On the other hand, if 70% of the scores are 0, for example, with the rest reflecting various positive values, it would probably be best either to use a nonparametric test or to transform the scores in some way that makes their distribution closer to normal. Different transformations and their uses are discussed in more advanced statistics texts.

The *t*-test is also quite robust to violation of the assumption of equal variances. Even if the ratio is as high as 7 or 8 to 1, you ordinarily do not have to worry about this assumption. On the other hand, if you violate the assumption that the data must be measured in such a way that it makes sense to calculate the mean, there is nothing that will make the results of a *t*-test useful. Garbage in, garbage out is still a sensible rule.

Aside from asking yourself whether or not it is reasonable to calculate a mean on the dependent measure, the only time when you need to be seriously concerned about the assumptions of the *t*-test is when you are comparing two samples with very unequal *n*'s *and* their distributions are very far from normal *and* they have variances that differ by a factor of 10 to 1 or so. If all three violations are happening at once, then the *t*-test is not necessarily robust, and you will need to transform the data or use a nonparametric test (Coombs, Algina & Oltman, 1996).

The Family of *t*-Distributions.   The **t-distribution** is not a single distribution but rather a group of distributions, each symmetric around a mean of zero and each associated with a different number of degrees of freedom. When the sample size is very large, in the hundreds or more, then the shape of the *t*-distribution looks very much like that of the normal distribution. For smaller sample sizes, the shape of the associated *t*-distribution is symmetrical like the normal distribution but is more spread out, with less of a peak in the middle and more scores several standard deviations away from the mean.

Degrees of Freedom.   The shape of a *t*-distribution directly depends not on the sample size but on the **degrees of freedom**, which is the number of scores in a distribution that are free to take on any value. The degrees of freedom for a particular statistical test will equal the sample size minus the number of parameters that have to be estimated from the sample, or N minus the number of restrictions on the data. For instance, if you know that the mean of a sample is 40 and you have five scores, four of the scores can each have any value whatsoever. However, once the values for those four scores are known, the fifth score can have only one possible value in order for mean to be 40. The degrees of freedom for this situation is therefore 4, or $N - 1$.

As you learned in Chapter 6, the degrees of freedom for Pearson $r = N - 2$. We can think of the two "lost" degrees of freedom as needed to estimate the slope and intercept of the regression line that best fits the data. Each of the kinds of *t*-tests that we will be discussing in this chapter has an associated number of degrees of freedom. In order to know whether a value of t is statistically significant or not, you need not only to compute the value of t but to compare it with the critical value from the *t*-distribution with the appropriate number of degrees of freedom.

Why Are There Different Types of *t*-Tests?

Different hypotheses about means require different kinds of inferential statistical tests. Depending on the hypothesis to be tested and on the nature of the data, researchers may use one of three different types of *t*-tests to analyze their findings: single-sample *t*-tests, independent-samples *t*-tests, and dependent-samples *t*-tests.

Single-Sample *t*-Test

One type of *t*-test, appropriately named a **single-sample *t*-test**, has as its purpose to compare the mean of a (single) sample with some hypothesized value.

Formula.   The formula for a single-sample *t*-test has been presented before:

$$t = \frac{\overline{X} - \mu}{s_{\overline{X}}}$$

where $s_{\overline{X}} = s/\sqrt{N}$.

To use this formula, you must first determine the difference in means.

Step 1:   Sum the raw scores.

Step 2:   Divide this sum by *N* to get the mean of the sample, $\overline{X}$.

Step 3:   Decide on your hypothetical value for μ (usually zero) and subtract μ from $\overline{X}$ to get the difference in means.

You then compute the standard deviation of the sample.

Step 4:   Square each raw score.

Step 5:   Sum these squares.

Step 6:   Square the sum of the raw scores from step 1.

Step 7:   Divide this product by *N*.

Step 8:   Subtract this quotient from the sum in step 5.

Step 9:   Divide this difference by *N* – 1.

Step 10: Take the square root of this quotient to get the standard deviation.

Next, you need the standard error of the mean, $s_{\overline{X}}$.

Step 11: Take the square root of the sample size.

Step 12: Divide the standard deviation in step 10 by the square root in step 11.

The next step gives the value of *t*.

Step 13: Divide the numerator in step 3 by the denominator in step 12 to get *t*.

Statistical Significance.   When the value of *t* has been computed, the next step is to determine whether or not it is statistically significant. To decide this, it is necessary to look up the critical value of *t* with $N - 1$ degrees of freedom in Appendix Table 5, since a single-sample *t*-test has $N - 1$ degrees of freedom. A portion of that table is given in Table 9.1, where you can see that the labels across the top identify what the critical values are for the .10, .05, .02, .01, .002, and .001 two-tailed significance levels. Along the side, the labels for the rows represent the degrees of freedom. If you look at the last row, you can see that with infinite degrees of freedom, the critical values for *t* are identical to the critical values for the normal curve. Even with only 100 degrees of freedom, the critical values for the *t*-distribution are very close to the critical values for the normal curve.

TABLE 9.1   Portion of Appendix Table 5: Two-Tailed Critical Values for *t*-Ratios

df	.10	.05	.02	.01	.002	.001
1	6.314	12.706	31.820	63.657	318.309	636.619
2	2.920	4.303	6.965	9.925	22.327	31.599
3	2.353	3.182	4.541	5.841	10.215	12.924
⋮	⋮	⋮	⋮	⋮	⋮	⋮
30	1.697	2.042	2.457	2.750	3.385	3.646
50	1.676	2.009	2.403	2.678	3.261	3.496
100	1.660	1.984	2.364	2.626	3.174	3.390
∞	1.645	1.960	2.326	2.576	3.090	3.291

TIP

> The values in the *t*-table are two-tailed critical values, since these are the ones that you should be using almost all of the time. However, one-tailed critical values that you might wish to know are easy to get from the table, since the two-tailed .10 level corresponds to the one-tailed .05 level, the two-tailed .02 level corresponds to the one-tailed .01 level, and the two-tailed .002 level corresponds to the one-tailed .001 level (Abelson, 1995; Harris, 1997).

Interpretation.   Interpretation of a two-tailed single sample *t* is quite simple. If the absolute value of the computed value for *t*, also called the *test statistic*, is smaller than the critical value listed in Appendix Table 5, then retain H_0 and conclude that it is possible that the sample comes from a population with a mean equal to your hypothetical value of μ. If the value of *t* is positive and significant, implying that the sample mean is larger than the hypothesized μ, reject the null hypothesis and conclude that the sample mean is truly larger than μ. If *t* is negative and significant, reject H_0 and conclude that the sample comes from a population with a mean lower than μ.

TIP

> Remember the three rules for deciding whether to use one-tailed or two-tailed tests. Unless you have an extremely strong justification for doing otherwise, use the two-tailed critical values for *t*. If you were to use the one-tailed critical value, you would have to retain H_0 if the findings came out in the opposite direction from your prediction, regardless of how large the difference in the means might be.

Examples of Single-Sample *t*-Tests. One example of a single-sample *t*-test might be the instance in which you want to see whether or not certain scores exceed some well-known minimum standard.

EXAMPLE

Caloric Intake. Suppose you have been told that a mean of 1200 calories per day is necessary for healthy growth in boys of a certain age. A dietary recall measure revealed that the daily caloric intake for a random sample of 30 boys who receive free lunches in your school ranged from 700 to 1500 calories per day, with a mean of 1100 and a standard deviation of 200 calories. Is their mean daily caloric intake significantly below 1200 calories?

Solution

- To answer this question, we first compute $s_{\overline{X}}$. We have a sample of 30 boys, so

$$s_{\overline{X}} = \frac{200}{\sqrt{30}} = \frac{200}{5.477} = 36.52$$

- Using the formula, $t = (\overline{X} - \mu) / s_{\overline{X}}$, we get

$$t = \frac{1100 - 1200}{36.52} = \frac{-100}{36.52} = -2.74$$

- Looking up the two-tailed critical values for *t* with 29 degrees of freedom, we can see that this value just misses significance at the .01 level but is significant at the .05 level.

Since the sample mean is lower than the hypothetical value, leading to a negative value for *t*, we would conclude that the boys as a group did eat statistically significantly fewer calories than the minimum desirable amount, based on their daily intake over the last 30 days. ■

Two points related to this example are worthy of mention. First, this is one of the few instances in which you might be able to justify using a one-tailed test. Presumably you would be interested only in whether the boys' intake did or did not fall below the minimum, not in whether it exceeded the minimum recommendation, even by a huge amount. On the other hand, the use of a two-tailed test permits you to guard against the possibility that you might have been mistaken and the boys could have been eating more than the standard amount.

Second, you might be interested in reporting the data in APA style. One example of how to state this would be "A single-sample *t*-test revealed that the mean daily caloric intake ($M = 1100$, $S_D = 200$) of 30 boys on the free lunch program at this school was statistically significantly less than the minimum

recommended amount of 1200 calories, $t(29) = -2.74$, two-tailed $p < .05$."
Actually, people usually do not identify their t values as two-tailed because
of the assumption that two-tailed values would be used; however, the use of
a one-tailed t-test would need to be both identified and justified.

Another example of the use of a single-sample t-test might be the case in
which you have access to the scores of a group and want to know whether or
not they exceed some value of theoretical interest.

EXAMPLE

Geography Knowledge. Suppose that you have read that the average
high school senior can identify 32 out of 70 countries on a map of the world.
In this case, the null hypothesis would be that the mean score of the students
in your class on the same identification test does not differ significantly from
32. You give this test to the 16 students in your eighth grade geography class
and find that their scores are as follows:

32 26 61 38 45 29 55 35 27 44 48 52 38 44 34 40

Solution: The first steps in solving the problem are to compute some basic
statistics.

Step 1: Add the raw scores:

$\Sigma X = 648$

Step 2: Sum the squared scores:

$\Sigma X^2 = 27,790$

Step 3: Find the square of 648:

$(\Sigma X)^2 = 419,904$

Step 4: Divide by the number of scores:

$$\frac{(\Sigma X)^2}{N} = \frac{419,904}{16} = 26,244$$

Step 5: Find the mean of the raw scores:

$$\frac{648}{16} = 40.5$$

Step 6: Calculate s:

$$s = \sqrt{\frac{\Sigma X^2 - \left((\Sigma X)^2/N\right)}{N - 1}} = \sqrt{\frac{27,790 - 26,244}{15}} = \sqrt{\frac{1546}{15}}$$

$$= \sqrt{103.067} = 10.15$$

Step 7: Calculate $s_{\overline{X}}$:

$$s_{\overline{X}} = \frac{10.15}{\sqrt{16}} = \frac{10.15}{4} = 2.54$$

Step 8: Calculate *t*:

$$t = \frac{\overline{X} - \mu}{s_{\overline{X}}} = \frac{40.5 - 32}{2.54} = \frac{8.5}{2.54} = 3.35$$

With 15 degrees of freedom, a *t* of 2.947 is needed for significance at the .01 α-level and a *t* of 4.073 at the .001 α-level. The computed value of *t* falls in between these critical values. Therefore, you would reject the null hypothesis at the $p < .01$ level and conclude that (in APA style) "the students in the class had a statistically significantly higher mean score ($M = 40.5$, $S_D = 10.15$) than the norm of 32 correct for high school seniors, $t(15) = 3.35$, $p < .01$." ∎

TIP

> In this example, there would be no excuse for doing a one-tailed test, even though you had predicted that your students would exceed the norm, because if they had done worse than the norm, you should have been willing to report that fact.

Independent-Samples *t*-Test

An independent-samples *t*-test is the most commonly used type of *t*-test. The purpose of an **independent-samples *t*-test** is to compare the means of two different groups of scores when no particular score in one group is in any way paired with a particular score in the other group. Whenever individuals are randomly sampled from one population and other individuals are separately randomly sampled from another population, an independent-samples *t*-test would be an appropriate procedure to compare the means of those two samples. If a large number of people have been sampled from a population and they are then individually randomly assigned to an experimental or a control condition, an independent-samples *t*-test would be the appropriate procedure to compare the means of subjects in the experimental and control groups. Indeed, whenever you want to compare the means of two samples of unequal *N*'s (unless the scores are paired except for a few missing values), an independent-samples *t*-test is the procedure of choice.

Formulas.   The general formula for an independent-samples *t*-test is the difference in the sample means minus the hypothetical difference in the population means divided by the standard error of the difference in the means.

Because the hypothetical difference is almost always zero and therefore would not affect the computations, the "minus zero" term is omitted from the numerator of the formulas. There are two computational formulas that can be used for the independent-samples t-test—one that uses the standard deviations (or variances) of the two samples and one that uses the raw scores. The formula involving standard deviations is

$$t = \frac{\overline{X}_1 - \overline{X}_2}{\sqrt{\left[\frac{(n_1 - 1)(s_1^2) + (n_2 - 1)(s_2^2)}{n_1 + n_2 - 2}\right]\left(\frac{1}{n_1} + \frac{1}{n_2}\right)}}$$

To use this formula, you need to do the following.

Step 1: Compute the means of groups 1 and 2.

Step 2: Subtract the mean of group 2 from the mean of group 1 to get the numerator.

Step 3: Multiply the variance of group 1 by one less than the number of scores in group 1.

Step 4: Multiply the variance of group 2 by one less than the number of scores in group 2.

Step 5: Sum these products.

Step 6: Divide this sum by the total number of scores minus two.

Step 7: Divide one by the number of scores in group 1.

Step 8: Divide one by the number of scores in group 2.

Step 9: Sum these quotients.

Step 10: Multiply this sum by the quotient in step 6.

Step 11: Take the square root of this product to get the denominator of the formula.

Step 12: Divide the numerator by the denominator to get the value of t.

This formula is easy to use if you have already calculated the standard deviations or variances of the two samples, but it is less convenient than the following formula if you have not. The raw score formula for an independent-samples t-test is

$$t = \frac{\overline{X}_1 - \overline{X}_2}{\sqrt{\left[\frac{\Sigma X_1^2 - \left((\Sigma X_1)^2/n_1\right) + \Sigma X_2^2 - \left((\Sigma X_2)^2 / n_2\right)}{n_1 + n_2 - 2}\right]\left(\frac{1}{n_1} + \frac{1}{n_2}\right)}}$$

To use this formula, you need to do the following.

Step 1: Compute the numerator by subtracting the mean of group 2 from the mean of group 1, as in steps 1 and 2 of the previous formula.

Step 2: Sum the raw scores in group 1.

Step 3: Square this sum.

Step 4: Divide this square by the number of scores in group 1.

Step 5: Square each raw score in group 1.

Step 6: Sum these squares.

Step 7: Subtract the quotient in step 4 from the sum of the squared raw scores in step 6.

Step 8: Square the sum of the raw scores in group 2 and divide this square by the number of scores in group 2.

Step 9: Subtract this quotient from the sum of the squared raw scores in group 2.

Step 10: Add the two numbers from steps 7 and 9.

Step 11: Divide their sum by the total number of scores minus 2.

Step 12: Divide one by the number of scores in group 1.

Step 13: Divide one by the number of scores in group 2.

Step 14: Sum these quotients.

Step 15: Multiply this sum by the quotient in step 10.

Step 16: Take the square root of this product to get the denominator of the formula.

Step 17: Divide the numerator in step 1 by the denominator in step 16 to get the value of *t*.

Statistical Significance. When you have computed the value of an independent-samples *t*-test (often abbreviated to "an independent *t*"), you need to look up the corresponding critical value in Appendix Table 5 using $N - 2$ (or $n_1 + n_2 - 2$) degrees of freedom.

TIP

> If it helps you to remember it, you can think of the degrees of freedom as reflecting the fact that two means have to be estimated, making two restrictions on the data.

Interpretation. The interpretation of a two-tailed independent-samples *t*-test is reasonably straightforward. If the absolute value of the test statistic (i.e., the value of *t* computed from the data) is smaller than the critical value from Appendix Table 5, you retain H_0 and conclude that it is possible that the means represent random samples from the same population and that you don't have enough evidence to conclude anything about the sign of $\mu_1 - \mu_2$. If the value of *t* exceeds the critical value at the .05 level, you check to see whether or not it is significant at the $p < .01$ and $p < .001$ levels and report that it is significant at the most stringent level that it exceeds. You then conclude that the larger mean is significantly larger than the smaller mean—that is, that this difference is likely to reflect a difference in the population means.

Interpretation of a One-Tailed Test. Suppose, however, that you have conducted a one-tailed test instead of a two-tailed test. If the sample mean that you hypothesized to be higher is actually higher, then you have no problem; if t exceeds the critical value, you say that it was significantly higher than the other mean, and if t is less than the critical value, you say that it was not significantly higher. But what if the results turn out in the opposite direction from the predicted one (e.g., with a t-value of –6), representing the fact that the mean you expected to be lower is many standard errors higher than the other mean? All that you can say is that the means did not differ significantly. You cannot change your mind and do a two tailed-test (nor, of course, do a one-tailed test in the other direction, since that would be the equivalent of doing a test at the .10 level). If this interpretation seems incorrect to you, if you feel that other people reading your results would think that you have missed something that might be of importance, then use a two-tailed test in the first place.

Examples of Independent-Samples t-Tests. Independent-samples t-tests are often used to compare the mean scores of an experimental group and a control group.

EXAMPLE

Stopping Excessive Drinking. Suppose that you have designed an experimental program that you think will get alcoholics to stop drinking. You begin by doing a small pilot study with six participants, randomly assigning three of them to receive the program and three of them to be in a waiting list control group. After the three-week intensive program, you measure the number of drinks each person has in a two-day period. The three people in the experimental group drank 0, 0, and 2 drinks, respectively; the three people in the control group had 6, 8, and 10 drinks. What can you conclude about the effectiveness of the program, based on this small pilot sample?

The null hypothesis that you would be testing is that the sample means could come from the same population—that is, that $\mu_1 - \mu_2 = 0$. The alternative hypothesis would be that the population means are not equal—that is, $\mu_1 - \mu_2 \neq 0$.

Solution

• To test H_0, first we need to get the sums and means of the raw scores, sums of the squared raw scores, and squared sums of the raw scores for each group:

For group E (experimental),

$$\Sigma X_E = 2 \qquad \Sigma X_E^2 = 4 \qquad \overline{X}_E = .667 \qquad (\Sigma X_E)^2 = 4$$

For group C,

$$\Sigma X_C = 24 \qquad \Sigma X_C^2 = 200 \qquad \overline{X}_C = 8.000 \qquad (\Sigma X_C)^2 = 576$$

- Substituting into the equation

$$t = \frac{\overline{X}_1 - \overline{X}_2}{\sqrt{\left[\dfrac{\Sigma X_1^2 - \left((\Sigma X_1)^2/n_1\right) + \Sigma X_2^2 - \left((\Sigma X_2)^2/n_2\right)}{n_1 + n_2 - 2} \right]\left(\dfrac{1}{n_1} + \dfrac{1}{n_2}\right)}}$$

we have

$$t = \frac{.667 - 8.00}{\sqrt{\left[\dfrac{4 - (4/3) + 200 - (576/3)}{4} \right]\left(\dfrac{1}{3} + \dfrac{1}{3}\right)}}$$

$$= \frac{-7.33}{\sqrt{\left(\dfrac{4 - 1.33 + 200 - 192}{4} \right)\left(\dfrac{2}{3}\right)}}$$

$$= \frac{-7.33}{\sqrt{\left(\dfrac{10.67}{4} \right)(.667)}} = \frac{-7.33}{\sqrt{1.78}} = \frac{-7.33}{1.33} = -5.51$$

- Since $n_1 + n_2 = 6$, we look up the critical value of t with 4 degrees of freedom, which is 4.604 at the .01 α-level and 8.610 at the .001 α-level.
- We therefore reject H_0 at the .01 level and conclude that the means are unlikely to come from the same population.

In APA style, we might say that the people in the experimental group drank significantly fewer drinks ($M = .667$, $S_D = 1.15$) over a two-day period than the people in a waiting list control group ($M = 8.00$ drinks; $S_D = 2.00$), $t(4) = -5.51$, $p < .01$, suggesting that the treatment program was effective (at least in the short run). ∎

As a second example in which an independent-samples t-test might be used, let's take Simple Simon's research study on the preferences people have for types of pie.

EXAMPLE

Pie Preferences. Suppose Simon randomly assigned people to eat either pecan or cherry pie and noted the number of grams of pie that they ate. The data are given in Table 9.2.

TABLE 9.2   Data for Pie Preferences Example

Person	Pecan Pie (grams)	Person	Cherry Pie (grams)
Sally	40	Tom	50
Sue	30	Tim	40
Stan	100	Tommy	60
Steve	80	Terry	90
Stella	0	Tallulah	60
Saul	10	Travis	0
Sigmund	20	Toni	50
Sarah	10	Ted	30
Stuart	40	Truman	40

Solution: For this example, let's use the formula that involves the standard deviations.

• To get the standard deviation of group P (pecan), we need to calculate the following:

$$\Sigma X_P = 330 \qquad (\Sigma X_P)^2 = 108{,}900 \qquad \Sigma X_P^2 = 21{,}100$$

• Although we don't need it yet, we may as well calculate $\overline{X}_P$:

$$\overline{X}_P = \frac{330}{9} = 36.67$$

• Using the raw score formula for s_P, we get

$$s_P = \sqrt{\frac{21{,}100 - (108{,}900 / 9)}{8}} = \sqrt{\frac{21{,}100 - 12{,}100}{8}} = \sqrt{\frac{9000}{8}}$$

$$= \sqrt{1125} = 33.54 \text{ grams}$$

• For group C (cherry),

$$\Sigma X_C = 420 \qquad (\Sigma X_C)^2 = 176{,}400 \qquad \Sigma X_P^2 = 24{,}400$$

$$\overline{X}_C = \frac{420}{9} = 46.67$$

• Using the raw score formula for s_C gives

$$s_C = \sqrt{\frac{24{,}400 - (176{,}400 / 9)}{8}} = \sqrt{\frac{24{,}400 - 19{,}600}{8}} = \sqrt{\frac{4800}{8}}$$

$$= \sqrt{600} = 24.49 \text{ grams}$$

- The formula for *t* is

$$t = \frac{\overline{X}_1 - \overline{X}_2}{\sqrt{\left[\frac{(n_1 - 1)(s_1^2) + (n_2 - 1)(s_2^2)}{n_1 + n_2 - 2}\right]\left(\frac{1}{n_1} + \frac{1}{n_2}\right)}}$$

$$= \frac{(36.67 - 46.67)}{\sqrt{\left[\frac{(8)(1125) + (8)(600)}{16}\right]\left(\frac{1}{9} + \frac{1}{9}\right)}}$$

$$= \frac{-10}{\sqrt{\left(\frac{9000 + 4800}{16}\right)(.222)}} = \frac{-10}{\sqrt{\left(\frac{13{,}800}{16}\right)(.222)}} = \frac{-10}{\sqrt{191.48}}$$

$$= \frac{-10}{13.84} = -.72$$

From Appendix Table 5, you should be able to see that the critical value for a *t* with 16 (i.e., 9 + 9 – 2) degrees of freedom would be 2.12. The *t* of –.72 is not statistically significant at any level. In fact, if |*t*| is < 1.96, it will not be statistically significant by a two-tailed test even with infinite degrees of freedom.

The correct conclusion, therefore, is that there was no statistically significant difference in the amount of pie eaten, indicating that there is not enough evidence to conclude that there is a preference for one or the other type of pie in the population. ◼

Dependent-Samples *t*-Test

A dependent samples *t*-test is also called a *paired-samples t-test* or a *correlated-samples t-test*; some people even abbreviate the terms by leaving out the word "samples." Regardless of the terminology, a **dependent-samples *t*-test** is used to compare the means of two groups when individual scores in one group are paired with particular scores in the other groups. Such pairing would not occur if scores were individually randomly sampled from the two groups, as is the case for an independent-samples *t*-test.

There are three general ways in which scores may be paired in such a way that a dependent-samples *t*-test would be the appropriate procedure to compare the means of the two groups of scores.

1. Sometimes scores are naturally paired. Scores of wives and husbands, twins, pairs of siblings, or even the grip strength of persons' right and left hands constitute natural pairs of scores that the researcher needs only to recognize.

2. The same individual may be measured twice, usually in a before–after or pretest–posttest design. In such a case, time of measurement is a within-participants variable and each individual's score at one time is paired with his or her score at another time.

3. The pairing is performed by an experimenter, who creates matched pairs by equating participants with respect to some pretest variable or variables. For example, the two fastest runners could constitute one pair, the next two fastest would be a second pair, and so forth. The purpose of such matching is to reduce the *error variance*—that is, the variance in the scores on the dependent measure that would be due to individual differences. Such a procedure is effective only if the pairs are matched on a variable that is relevant to the dependent measure. Matching individuals on a pretest of running speed would be very appropriate if you are going to be assessing the effect of a program to improve running speed; it would probably be counterproductive if you are going to be evaluating the effect of a program to get people to buy more granola bars (unless you expect them to run to the store).

TIP

> If you are going to be using a matched pairs design, remember one important point: The individuals within each pair must be assigned randomly to the experimental and control group. To convince yourself of this, imagine the situation in which you had matched the top two runners, the next best two, and so on down to the worst two runners. If you were to put the first person on the list in the experimental group, the second in the control group, the third in the experimental group, and so on, you would almost guarantee that the experimental group would have higher scores, as the faster runner of each pair would be in the experimental group. If you match pairs, then, be sure to randomly assign; otherwise, you are running the risk of drawing mistaken inferences, just as can happen when matched groups are used without random selection.

Formulas.   There are two formulas for a correlated- or dependent-samples *t*-test, but one of them is far simpler to use than the other. The simpler formula, sometimes called the direct difference formula, is

$$t = \frac{\overline{D}}{s_{\overline{D}}}$$

To get $\overline{D}$, you have to get a difference score for each person, which consists of his or her raw score on variable X_1 minus his or her raw score on X_2. The mean of these differences scores equals $\overline{D}$, which is also $\overline{X}_1 - \overline{X}_2$.

To get $s_{\overline{D}}$, the standard error of the mean difference, you first need to get s_D, the standard deviation of the difference scores. The formula for s_D is identical to the formula for s, except that difference scores are used instead of raw scores. More precisely,

$$s_D = \sqrt{\frac{\Sigma D^2 - \left((\Sigma D)^2/N\right)}{N - 1}}$$

Dividing by $\sqrt{N}$ gives $s_{\overline{D}}$, the standard error of the mean difference.

The computational formula for the paired-samples *t*-test is, therefore,

$$t = \frac{\Sigma D/N}{\dfrac{\sqrt{\left[\Sigma D^2 - \left((\Sigma D)^2/N\right)\right]/(N - 1)}}{\sqrt{N}}}$$

The following steps are required to compute the numerator of this formula.

Step 1: For each pair of raw scores, X_1 and X_2, subtract the score on X_2 from that on X_1, to get a difference score, D.

Step 2: Sum these N difference scores to get ΣD.

Step 3: Divide this sum by N to get $\overline{D}$, the mean difference.

The next steps are required to compute the denominator.

Step 4: Square each difference score.

Step 5: Sum these squared difference scores.

Step 6: Square the sum of the difference scores from step 2.

Step 7: Divide this squared sum by N.

Step 8: Subtract this quotient from the sum in step 5.

Step 9: Divide this difference by $N - 1$.

Step 10: Take the square root of this quotient.

Step 11: Divide this number by $\sqrt{N}$.

You can now get the value of *t*.

Step 12: Divide the numerator in step 3 by the denominator in step 11.

A second formula for a correlated-samples *t*-test is much more complicated to compute because it requires computing both standard errors of the mean, as well as the correlation between X_1 and X_2. On the other hand, if you have already computed those statistics, then the formula is an easy one:

$$t = \frac{\overline{X}_1 - \overline{X}_2}{\sqrt{s_{\overline{X}_1}^2 + s_{\overline{X}_2}^2 - 2rs_{\overline{X}_1}s_{\overline{X}_2}}}$$

To use this formula, you proceed as follows.

Step 1: First compute the numerator either by subtracting the mean of X_2 from the mean of X_1 or by taking the mean of the difference scores, as in the previous formula.

Step 2: Compute the standard deviations for X_1 and X_2.

Step 3: Divide these standard deviations by $\sqrt{n_1}$ and $\sqrt{n_2}$, respectively, to get $s_{\bar{X}_1}$ and $s_{\bar{X}_2}$.

Step 4: Square the standard error of the mean for group 1 and add that to the square of the standard error of the mean for group 2.

Step 5: Compute the correlation, r, between X_1 and X_2.

Step 6: Multiply the correlation between X_1 and X_2 by two.

Step 7: Multiply this product by the standard error of the mean for group 1.

Step 8: Multiply this product by the standard error of the mean for group 2.

Step 9: Subtract this product from the sum of the squared standard errors of the mean in step 4.

Step 10: Take the square root of this difference to get the denominator of the formula.

Step 11: Divide the numerator in step 1 by the denominator in step 10 to get the value of t.

TIP

> If you look at this formula, you can see that when the correlation between X_1 and X_2 is close to +1, the denominator of the formula gets smaller and t gets larger. If the correlation between the variables is 0, then the formula reduces to the independent-samples formula. However, since the number of degrees of freedom for a correlated-samples t-test is only half the number of degrees of freedom for an independent-samples t-test, there is a disadvantage to using a matched pairs design (which would require a paired-samples t-test) when the variables X_1 and X_2 are uncorrelated.

Statistical Significance. To ascertain the statistical significance of a dependent-samples t-test, you look up the critical value in Appendix Table 5 with $N-1$ degrees of freedom, where N equals the number of *pairs* of scores, not the number of individual raw scores. If the computed value of t is at least as large as the critical value, you can reject the null hypothesis and conclude that the direction of the difference between the two population means is the same as the direction of the difference between the corresponding sample means.

Interpretation. As with other *t*-tests, you interpret a nonsignificant value of *t* as reflecting a reasonable possibility that the population means do not differ and a significant *t*-value as indicating a high likelihood that the population means differ in the same direction as the sample means did. Of course, if you were to do a one-tailed test, you would be forced to retain the null hypothesis unless the means were significantly different in the predicted direction.

Examples of Correlated-Samples *t*-Tests. As one example of the use of a dependent-samples *t*-test, let's take the pie-testing situation described earlier.

EXAMPLE

More Pie. Sophisticated Simone has decided to compare the popularity of pecan and cherry pies by using a within-participants design, assuming that some people eat more of all kinds of pie than others and that taking individual differences into account will therefore reduce error variance. Accordingly, she gets nine volunteers and serves each person pecan pie on one occasion and cherry pie on another. The data are given in Table 9.3.

TIP

If she were really doing this experiment, she would probably include the order of presentation as a factor in the design, so that satiation with pie would not affect the results. However, we'll assume that random assignment to which flavor was first eaten will take care of that.

TABLE 9.3 Data for More Pie Example

Person	Pecan Pie (grams)	Cherry Pie (grams)	D	D²
Bob	40	50	−10	100
Beth	30	40	−10	100
Babs	100	60	40	1600
Barney	80	90	−10	100
Bretta	0	60	−60	3600
Betty	10	0	10	100
Barbara	20	50	−30	900
Brendan	10	30	−20	400
Ben	40	40	0	0

Solution: The first step in analyzing the data is to get the difference between the scores on variables P and C for each individual, being careful to subtract in the same direction each time. Column D in the table provides these differences.

- Now calculate the sum of the differences and its square:

$$\Sigma D = -90 \qquad (\Sigma D)^2 = (-90)^2 = 8100$$

- The mean difference is

$$\frac{\Sigma D}{N} = \frac{-90}{9} = -10$$

- The squares of the differences are shown in the D^2 column in the table. The sum of the squares is 6900.

- The next step is to calculate s_D:

$$s_D = \sqrt{\frac{\Sigma D^2 - \left((\Sigma D)^2/N\right)}{N-1}} = \sqrt{\frac{6900 - (8100/9)}{8}} = \sqrt{\frac{6900 - 900}{8}}$$

$$= \sqrt{\frac{6000}{8}} = \sqrt{750} = 27.39$$

- The next step is to calculate $s_{\overline{D}}$:

$$s_{\overline{D}} = \frac{s_D}{\sqrt{N}} = \frac{27.39}{\sqrt{9}} = \frac{27.39}{3} = 9.13$$

- Dividing the mean difference by $s_{\overline{D}}$, we find that

$$t = \frac{-10}{9.13} = -1.095$$

This value is not significant with 8 (nor 8 billion) degrees of freedom, since the critical value at the .05 α-level is 2.308. Therefore, we retain the null hypothesis and conclude that there was not a significant preference for either type of pie:

$$t(8) = -1.10, \quad p > .05$$

EXAMPLE

Emotional Impact of Paintings. Let's imagine that Art Student wants to know if the flower paintings of Georgia O'Keeffe have more impact upon the viewer when they are seen in a larger size rather than in miniature. Since both large and small books of her flower paintings are available, he sets up a matched pairs design in which each painting is shown to one person in a miniature size and to another in a larger size. The ten viewers are randomly assigned to see one of the five paintings in either a large or small size. Each viewer is then asked to rate the painting on how much emotional impact it has upon him or her on a five-point scale ranging from 0 (none) to 5 (overwhelming). Here are the data, with columns added for D and D^2:

Painting	Miniature	Larger Size	D	D^2
Lily	0	2	−2	4
Morning glory	1	2	−1	1
Pansy	2	4	−2	4
Rose	3	4	−1	1
Peony	0	1	−1	1

Solution: As usual, you will need the values of D:

$$\Sigma D = -7 \qquad \Sigma D^2 = 11 \qquad (\Sigma D)^2 = 49 \qquad \frac{(\Sigma D)^2}{N} = 9.8 \qquad \overline{D} = -1.4$$

To get the standard deviation of the differences in the means, we have

$$\sqrt{\frac{11 - 9.8}{4}} = \sqrt{.300} = .548$$

The standard error of the difference in the means is

$$s_{\overline{D}} = \frac{.548}{\sqrt{5}} = \frac{.548}{2.236} = .245$$

The value of t is

$$t = \frac{-1.4}{.245} = -5.71$$

Even with only 4 degrees of freedom this t exceeds the critical value of 4.604 at the .01 α-level. We would therefore reject the null hypothesis and conclude that the paintings had more impact when seen in a larger size than when seen in miniature. ∎

TIP

The experiment in this example has a somewhat unusual design because the matching is on the basis of the stimulus rather than the individual. Moreover, the matching is done by the researcher and is not based on any preexisting qualities of the individual subjects. Nevertheless, it should be clear that each painting in the miniature size is paired with a particular painting in the larger size (the same picture) and therefore a paired-samples analysis must be used.

Characteristics and Types of *t*-Tests

General use: To test hypotheses about means of one or two samples

Assumptions:

- Independent sampling was used to gather the data.
- The population(s) from which the sample(s) came is/are normally distributed.
- If two independent samples are involved, the two samples come from populations with equal variances.
- The data are measured on (close to) an interval or ratio scale.

1. *Single-sample t-tests:* To compare the mean of a (single) sample with some hypothesized value

   Formula: $t = \dfrac{(\overline{X} - \mu)}{s_{\overline{X}}}$

2. *Independent-samples t-test:* To compare the means of two different groups of scores when no particular score in one group is in any way paired with a particular score in the other group.

   Formula: $t = \dfrac{\overline{X}_1 - \overline{X}_2}{\sqrt{\left[\dfrac{\Sigma X_1^2 - \left((\Sigma X_1)^2/n_1\right) + \Sigma X_2^2 - \left((\Sigma X_2)^2/n_2\right)}{n_1 + n_2 - 2}\right]\left(\dfrac{1}{n_1} + \dfrac{1}{n_2}\right)}}$

3. *Dependent-samples t-test:* To compare the means of two groups when individual scores in one group are paired with particular scores in the other groups

   Formula: $t = \dfrac{\Sigma D/N}{\dfrac{\sqrt{\left[\Sigma D^2 - \left((\Sigma D)^2/N\right)\right]/(N - 1)}}{\sqrt{N}}}$

How Are Confidence Intervals Used?

As you recall, a *confidence interval* is a way of estimating a parameter by constructing a pair of limits that have a certain probability of including the population parameter. For example, 99% of all 99% confidence intervals will contain the parameter they are estimating. Confidence intervals are very useful for several reasons.

1. The midpoint of the confidence interval provides a point estimate of the population parameter.
2. The range of the interval provides information about the accuracy of the estimate.
3. The confidence interval provides information about whether or not a statistical significance test would reach statistical significance at the corresponding alpha level. A 95% confidence interval that contains 0 would occur about 95% of the time when the null hypothesis is true. A 95% confidence interval that does not contain zero would occur less than 5% of the time when the null hypothesis is true.

Chapter 8 indicated that, when the standard deviation of the population is known, the standard error of the mean, $\sigma_{\bar{X}}$, or the standard error of the difference in the means, $\sigma_{\bar{X}_1 - \bar{X}_2}$, can be used to estimate a confidence interval. In such cases, the critical values from the normal curve table, such as 1.96 or 2.58, are used in the formula as well.

There are two differences between confidence intervals based on known population variances and those based on unknown population variances. These differences are similar to those between *z*- and *t*-tests. First, when σ is unknown, estimates of the standard error of the mean (or the standard error of the difference in the means) based on *s* are used, rather than the actual values based on known σ's. Second, the formulas when σ is unknown use the critical values based on the *t*-distribution with $N - 1$ or $N - 2$ degrees of freedom, depending on the test, rather than the critical values from the normal distribution.

Formulas

One Sample Mean.   When you wish to estimate the mean of a single sample with a certain degree of confidence, the formula is

$$\bar{X} \pm [t_a(N - 1)](s_{\bar{X}})$$

where $t_a(N - 1)$ stands for the critical value of *t* with $N - 1$ degrees of freedom. To use this formula, you proceed as follows.

- First calculate the mean of the raw scores.
- Then look up the two-tailed critical value for *t* at the appropriate alpha level with $N - 1$ degrees of freedom. The correct alpha level to use in locating the critical value is .05 for the 95% confidence interval, .01 for the 99% confidence interval, and .001 for the 99.9% confidence interval.
- Multiply this critical value by the standard error of the mean.
- Find the lower limit of the confidence interval by taking the sample mean and subtracting the product of the critical value and the standard error of the mean. Find the upper limit by adding the sample mean to the product of the critical value and the standard error.

Difference in the Means of Two Independent Samples. The formula for estimating the difference in the means of two independent samples is

$$\left(\overline{X}_1 - \overline{X}_2\right) \pm \left[t_\alpha(N - 2)\right]\left(s_{\overline{X}_1 - \overline{X}_2}\right)$$

In other words, the limits are the difference in the sample means, plus or minus the two-tailed critical value for t with $N - 2$ (or $n_1 + n_2 - 2$) degrees of freedom multiplied by the standard error of the difference in the means.

Difference in the Means of Two Correlated Samples. As you have probably guessed by now, the formula for estimating the difference in the means of two paired samples is

$$\left(\overline{X}_1 - \overline{X}_2\right) \pm \left[t_\alpha(N - 1)\right]\left(s_{\overline{D}}\right)$$

In other words, the limits are the difference in the sample means, plus or minus the two-tailed critical value for t with $N - 1$ degrees of freedom (where N equals the number of *pairs* of scores) multiplied by the standard error of the difference in the means.

Similarities in the Formulas. There are two similarities in these three formulas for confidence intervals that are worth noting. The first is their similarity to each other. In each case, the lower limit is the mean (or difference in means) minus the product of a critical value from the t-table and a standard error; the upper limit is the mean plus the product.

Second is the similarity between these formulas and the formulas for the corresponding t-tests. In each case, the critical value against which the test statistic for t would be compared is the critical value used in constructing the confidence interval, and the denominator of the formula for t is the standard error used in the formula for the confidence interval. In other words, you could say that the formula for a confidence interval is the numerator of the corresponding formula for t plus or minus the critical value times the denominator of the formula for t.

Examples. As an example of a correlated-samples design, we can look at the data from the large and small Georgia O'Keeffe paintings discussed earlier.

EXAMPLE

Emotional Impact of Paintings Revisited. Suppose that we want to know what the mean difference in emotional impact was between the larger-sized paintings and the smaller-sized paintings.

Solution: The formula for the 99% confidence interval is

$$\left(\overline{X}_1 - \overline{X}_2\right) \pm [t_{.01}(N - 1)](s_{\overline{D}})$$

Using the values calculated before and substituting into the equation, we get

$$-1.4 \pm (4.604)(.245)$$

The lower limit of the 99% confidence interval is therefore

$$-1.4 - 1.128 = -2.528$$

The upper limit is

$$-1.4 + 1.128 = -.272$$

There is thus a 99% chance that the emotional impact of the smaller reproduction minus the emotional impact of the larger one was between −2.528 and −.272; in other words, that the larger copies had more emotional impact than the smaller ones. This finding corresponds to the fact that the previous analysis of the data using a dependent samples *t*-test concluded that the difference between the two means was statistically significant at the .01 probability level.   ▨

Since the previous example dealt with a correlated-samples design, let's look at an example with a single-sample design.

EXAMPLE

Snow Days in St. Louis. Suppose that your entrepreneurial spirit has you looking ahead to the next winter Olympics and interested in estimating the mean number of days in which it snows in St. Louis. A sample of ten randomly chosen years in which snowfall records were kept reveals the following number of days of snow:

$$10 \quad 0 \quad 2 \quad 5 \quad 0 \quad 1 \quad 3 \quad 4 \quad 8 \quad 2$$

What is the 95% confidence interval for the number of days in which it snows in St. Louis?

Solution: To answer this question, we will need (as always) ΣX, $\Sigma X/N$, $(\Sigma X)^2$, and ΣX^2. Based on the above data,

$$\Sigma X = 35 \qquad \frac{\Sigma X}{N} = 3.5 \qquad (\Sigma X)^2 = 1225 \qquad \Sigma X^2 = 223$$

- The standard deviation of the scores is

$$s = \sqrt{\frac{223 - (1225 / 10)}{9}} = \sqrt{11.167} = 3.34$$

- The standard error of the mean is

$$s_{\overline{X}} = \frac{3.34}{\sqrt{10}} = 1.056$$

- The critical value for t with $N - 1 = 9$ degrees of freedom at the $p < .05$ level is 2.262.

  - The lower limit of the 95% confidence interval is therefore

$$3.5 - (2.262)(1.056) = 3.5 - 2.39 = 1.11$$

The upper limit is

$$3.5 + 2.39 = 5.89$$

The 95% confidence interval is therefore from 1.11 to 5.89 days of snow per year. ∎

We next consider an example of an independent-samples design.

EXAMPLE

Children's Sit-Ups. Suppose that we sampled children from Somnolent School and Pushup Prep and measured the number of sit-ups that the children at the two schools could do in one minute. What is the 99% confidence interval for the difference in the means of the two schools, based on the data given in Table 9.4?

TABLE 9.4 Data for the Children's Sit-Ups Example

SS (X_1)	X_1^2	PP (X_2)	X_2^2
0	0	1	1
0	0	5	25
1	1	6	36
0	0	9	81
0	0	8	64
2	4	5	25
3	9	4	16
4	16	2	4
1	1		
4	16		

Solution

- First we calculate the essential sums and other statistics we need. Based on the above data,

$$\Sigma X_1 = 15 \qquad \frac{\Sigma X_1}{n_1} = 1.5 \qquad (\Sigma X_1)^2 = 225 \qquad \Sigma X_1^2 = 47$$

$$\Sigma X_2 = 40 \qquad \frac{\Sigma X_2}{n_2} = 5.0 \qquad (\Sigma X_2)^2 = 1600 \qquad \Sigma X_2^2 = 252$$

- Next, let's calculate the standard error of the difference in the means, which is

$$s_{\bar{X}_1 - \bar{X}_2} = \sqrt{\left[\frac{47 - (225 / 10) + 252 - (1600 / 8)}{10 + 8 - 2}\right]\left(\frac{1}{10} + \frac{1}{8}\right)}$$

$$= \sqrt{\left[\frac{(47 - 22.5) + (252 - 200)}{16}\right](.225)} = \sqrt{1.076} = 1.037$$

- The two-tailed critical value for *t* with 16 degrees of freedom at the .01 α-level is 2.921.
- The difference in the means of the two numbers is 1.5 – 5 or –3.5.
- The 99% confidence interval is therefore –3.5 ± (2.921)(1.037) or –3.5 ± 3.03. The confidence interval therefore runs from –6.53 to –.47. ■

Notice that the confidence interval in this example includes only negative numbers. From it, you can conclude two things. First, the students at Somnolent School did fewer situps than the students at Pushup Prep.

Second, since this confidence interval did not contain the value of zero, there is less than a 1% chance that the true difference in the means is zero (or that the population mean for *SS* is greater than the population mean for *PP*). The difference in the means is therefore statistically significant at the *p* < .01 level. This illustrates the point made earlier: A confidence interval can be used for hypothesis testing, since an interval that does not contain zero implies that there is less than an α% chance (e.g., a 5% chance at the .05 level) that we would have obtained such extreme results if the null hypothesis were true.

As another example, Ito, Miller, & Pollock (1996) used a confidence interval that excluded 0 to reject the null hypothesis that intoxication would not increase aggression.

When Should These Techniques Be Used?

In order to decide whether or not you can use a parametric technique, like a *t*-test or a confidence interval, you must consider the purpose of your study and the nature of the data. Both of these techniques are used to compare one or two sample means. They can be used

- When the data are measured on (close to) an interval or ratio scale

and

- When the sample sizes are roughly equal

or

Confidence Intervals for Means

Purpose: To estimate a parameter by constructing a pair of limits that have a certain probability of including the population parameter

Assumptions:

- Random sampling was used to gather the data.
- The population(s) from which the sample(s) came is/are normally distributed.
- If two independent samples are involved, the two samples come from populations with equal variances.
- The data are measured on (close to) an interval or ratio scale.

1. *One sample mean:* To estimate the mean of a single sample with a certain degree of confidence

   Formula: $\overline{X} \pm [t_a(N-1)](s_{\overline{X}})$

2. *Two independent samples:* To estimate the difference in the means of two independent samples with a certain degree of confidence

   Formula: $(\overline{X}_1 - \overline{X}_2) \pm [t_a(N-2)](s_{\overline{X}_1 - \overline{X}_2})$

3. *Two paired samples:* To estimate the difference in the means of two dependent samples with a certain degree of confidence

   Formula: $(\overline{X}_1 - \overline{X}_2) \pm [t_a(N-1)](s_{\overline{D}})$

- When there are roughly equal variances

or

- When there are roughly normal distributions in the populations from which the samples come

These procedures are reasonably robust to violations of these latter three assumptions.

Choosing the Appropriate Technique

t **Versus** *r.* Both a correlated-samples *t*-test and a Pearson *r* can be computed for the same set of data: data in which you have paired scores on two interval- or ratio-level variables. However, these two statistics provide different information and answer different questions. A Pearson *r* describes the extent of the linear relationship between two variables and answers questions such as "Is the income of sons related to the income of their fathers?" A *t*-test describes the extent of a difference in means and answers questions such as "Do sons have a higher (or lower) income than their fathers?" It would be possible to have a significant correlation between two variables but no significant difference in means; for example, if the sons with richer fathers had higher incomes but overall the mean incomes of the two generations did not differ. Similarly, it would be possible to have a mean difference between the incomes of sons and fathers (maybe fathers make more money, due to their extra years of experience), but no significant correlation between the two variables, making it impossible to predict a son's income from his father's income.

There is indeed a relationship between a correlated *t*-test and Pearson *r*, as indicated both by the formula for a dependent-samples *t*-test, which incorporates *r*, and by the fact that the critical values for *r*, which are presented in Appendix Table 2, can be derived from the *t* table by using a formula for converting a correlation coefficient into a value of *t*:

$$t = \frac{(r)\sqrt{N - 2}}{\sqrt{1 - r^2}}$$

This *t*-value can then be compared with the critical value from the *t*-table and used to draw inferences about the significance of *r*. When would you do this? Only if you are marooned on a desert island with a *t*-table but without a table of critical values of *r*. Otherwise, enjoy the fact that someone else has already done the work for you and use Appendix Table 2.

In summary, even though the dependent-samples *t*-test and *r* are related, they measure different things. In general, you should use *r* when you wish to draw conclusions about the relationship between two variables. Use *t* when you wish to draw conclusions about a difference between means. As is generally true, the choice of the appropriate statistic depends upon the question you are asking.

Dependent Versus Independent t.   While there should be no problem in identifying instances in which to use a single-sample *t*-test, since there is only one sample, some students have trouble in deciding whether to use an independent-samples *t*-test or a dependent-samples *t*-test. The proper test to use depends upon the design of the study and the type of data collected. Generally, it should be clear whether or not the scores were paired or independent in any particular study. However, if you are having trouble deciding how to analyze some data that someone else collected, here are some general guidelines:

- If there are unequal *n*'s, you must use an independent-samples *t*-test.
- If you cannot tell which score in one sample would be paired with which score in the other sample—that is, if there are no natural pairs,

repeated measures, or pairings constructed by the researcher—use an independent-samples *t*-test.

- If you have separate random sampling from two populations, use an independent-samples *t*-test.
- Independent-samples *t*-tests are more commonly used, because a paired samples design (an example of a within-participants design) is harder to arrange.

t **Versus Confidence Interval.**   Sometimes you need to decide whether to perform a *t*-test or construct a confidence interval around the mean. In making this decision, you should consider two contradictory pieces of information:

1. Hypothesis testing via *t*-tests is by far the more commonly used procedure.
2. A confidence interval gives you all the information that you need in order to test the relevant hypothesis (i.e., the same information as a *t*-test) but also provides additional information about the likely value of the parameter.

The choice of procedure is yours.

Measuring Change.   One of the major uses of a dependent-samples *t*-test is to measure the amount of change from pretest to posttest (i.e., before or after some experience, such as exposure to a particular variable). The variable *D*, which is created in this procedure, is a direct measure of the amount of change. A dependent-samples *t*-test will test the null hypothesis that the mean amount of change is equal to 0.

Suppose that you want to compare two programs that are designed to change behavior, perhaps by conducting an experiment. In this case, you have four sets of scores: pretest and posttest scores for people in the experimental and the control groups. At first, you might think it impossible to perform a *t*-test, because a *t*-test can compare only two means. However, what you can do is create a new variable, a change or difference score, for each individual and then do a *t*-test on the change scores rather than on the raw scores. For example, if you want to compare the effects of two weight control programs, you can subtract each person's pretest weight from her posttest weight to create a new variable called pounds lost (or gained). You can then do an independent samples *t*-test comparing the amount of change (loss, we hope) experienced by people in the two conditions.

There are also some more complicated statistical procedures that can be used to analyze change, including analysis of covariance, repeated-measures analysis of variance, multivariate analysis of variance, and Hotelling's T^2. These topics are addressed in more advanced statistics books.

CHAPTER SUMMARY Although *z*-tests can be used to test hypotheses about means when the standard deviations in the population are known, *t*-tests are more widely used, since they do not require that σ be known. The use of a *t*-test assumes that random samples of scores on an interval- or ratio-level variable have been drawn from normally distributed populations (with equal variances, if there is more than one sample); however, the procedure is generally robust to violations of these assumptions. Because there are a series of *t*-distributions, each *t*-test has an associated degrees of freedom parameter that is closely related to the sample size and that determines the critical value for the test.

There are three different types of *t*-test. A single-sample *t*-test tests the null hypothesis that a sample mean is equal to some hypothetical value. An independent-samples *t*-test tests the null hypothesis that the difference in the means of the populations from which two separately selected samples come is equal to some particular value, usually zero. A paired- or dependent- or correlated-samples *t*-test also tests the null hypothesis that the difference in the means of two groups of scores is 0, but it is used when each score in one group is associated with a particular score in the other group. Although these tests can be one-tailed, two-tailed *t*-tests are almost always more appropriate, since they permit the conclusion that the larger mean is significantly larger than the smaller one, even if the difference is not in the predicted direction.

As an alternative to *t*-tests, it is possible to construct confidence intervals for a mean or for a difference in the means of two independent or paired samples. Confidence intervals are used to estimate the value of a parameter by constructing a pair of scores with a certain probability of including the parameter. For example, 95% of all 95% confidence intervals will include the parameter they are estimating.

Both confidence intervals for means and *t*-tests include the sample mean(s), the standard error of the mean, and the critical value for the mean in their formulas. If the 95% confidence interval for a difference in two means does not include 0, then you have a result that will occur less than 5% of the time when the null hypothesis is true—that is, you can reject the null hypothesis at the 5% level, two-tailed. However, even though confidence intervals provide more information than *t*-tests, they are less commonly used.

CHAPTER REVIEW ## Multiple-Choice Questions

1. Suppose that you have decided to do a one-tailed test of the hypothesis that people who have taken a music appreciation class will have more favorable attitudes toward classical music than those who have not. Using a test of liking for classical music, where 0 indicates hatred and 10 adoration, you find

that the mean score for those 40 people who have taken the course is 3, the mean score for a sample of 50 people who had not taken the course was 6, and the standard error of the difference in the means was 0.5. What should you conclude from this study?

a. Taking a music appreciation course caused people to dislike classical music.

b. People who took the course had significantly lower scores on a measure of liking classical music than did people who had not had the course.

c. People who took a music appreciation course liked classical music significantly more than people who had not had such a course.

d. There was no significant difference in liking for classical music between those who had or had not had the music appreciation course.

e. Both a and b are correct.

2. You have randomly sampled scores of 100 men and found that their mean score was 15, $s = 20$. What is the associated t-value for the appropriate statistical test of the null hypothesis that the population mean is 20?

    a. −.25   b. −.75   c. 1.0   d. −2.5   e. −5.0   f. none of the above

3. If you are doing a t-test and your computed value of t falls into the region of rejection, what should you do?

a. Reject the alternative hypothesis.

b. Recheck your calculations, since you must have made a mistake in computation.

c. Conclude that there is a significant difference in the means.

d. Conclude that there is not a significant difference in the means.

e. Both a and d are correct.

4. In order to find out whether sophomores have higher grades than freshmen, you take a random sample of UNM students who have just finished their sophomore year and compare their grades from their sophomore year with their grades from their freshman year. What kind of statistical test should you do?

a. a paired-samples t-test

b. a correlated-samples t-test

c. a single-sample t-test

d. an independent-samples t-test

e. a Pearson r

f. a Spearman rho

g. Both a and b are correct.

5. In order to find out whether sophomores have higher grades than freshmen, you take a random sample of UNM students who have just finished their

sophomore year and a random sample of students who have just finished their freshman year. You intend to compare the grades made by these two groups of students during the past year. What kind of statistical test should you do?

a. a paired-samples *t*-test

b. a correlated-samples *t*-test

c. a single-sample *t*-test

d. an independent-samples *t*-test

e. a Pearson *r*

f. a Spearman rho

g. Both a and b are correct.

6. In order to find out if people who get good grades their freshman year also get good grades their sophomore year, you take a random sample of UNM students who have completed their sophomore year, intending to see if the same people did well (or poorly) both freshman and sophomore year—that is, if freshman grades and sophomore grades are related. What kind of statistical test should you do?

a. a paired-samples *t*-test

b. a correlated-samples *t*-test

c. a single-sample *t*-test

d. an independent-samples *t*-test

e. a Pearson *r*

f. a Spearman rho

g. Both a and b are correct.

7. In order to find out if the mean grade point average of sophomore students is significantly higher than 2.00, you look at the grades of a random sample of students who have just completed their sophomore year. What kind of statistical test should you do?

a. a paired-samples *t*-test

b. a correlated-samples *t*-test

c. a single-sample *t*-test

d. an independent-samples *t*-test

e. a Pearson *r*

f. a Spearman rho

g. Both a and b are correct.

8. If the 95% confidence interval for the difference in two means runs from –3.4 to 1.6, what must be true?

a. The 99% confidence interval for the difference in the means equals 99% of the distance from –3.4 to 1.6.

b. One of the sample means was positive and one was negative.

c. The two means differ significantly at the .05 α-level.

d. The two means do not differ significantly at the .05 α-level.

e. The sample means differ by exactly 5 points.

9. You have (correctly) computed that the 99% confidence interval for the difference in two means runs from $-.5$ to 9.5. Only one of the following can possibly be the 95% confidence interval. Which is it?

    a. 1 to 8   **b.** -1.5 to 10.5   **c.** 10   **d.** 5 to 15   **e.** 3 to 7

10. Suppose that you compute a value for a t-test comparing a mean based on a sample of 30 with a hypothetical mean and get a t of -3.85. What should you conclude?

    a. The mean for the sample is statistically significantly smaller than the hypothesized mean at the .001 α-level.

    b. The mean for the sample is statistically significantly smaller than the hypothesized mean at the .05 α-level but not at the .01 level.

    c. Since the computed value of t is less than the critical value, the difference in the means is not significant.

    d. You must have made a mistake in computation.

    e. You should have used a z-test instead of a t-test.

    f. The sample mean is 3.85 less than the hypothetical mean.

Problems

11. Beth and Bertha were interested in the issue of whether students learn better at 7 A.M. or at 2 P.M. Accordingly, Beth took ten aspiring students and randomly assigned five of them to learn some vocabulary words at 7 A.M. and another five to learn some vocabulary words at 2 P.M. The scores on a vocabulary test were as follows:

7 A.M. Group		2 P.M. Group	
Joy	100	Jim	50
Joyce	80	Joel	40
Joan	60	Joseph	20
Jean	50	Julia	10
John	40	June	5

Bertha, instead, took only five students and taught them vocabulary words at 7 A.M. one day and at 2 P.M. another day. The scores on the vocabulary tests she gave her students follow:

Participants	7 A.M. Test	2 P.M. Test
Anne	100	50
Andy	80	40
Arnie	60	20
Alice	50	10
Art	40	5

a. Did Beth find a significant effect of the time of day on learning? Report your conclusions in a sentence.

b. Did Bertha find a significant effect of the time of day on learning? Report your conclusions in a sentence.

c. Using the data from Bertha's study, construct the 95% confidence interval for the difference in the means.

12. As a busy worker, you have nothing else to do but to count the number of interruptions to your work every day. For a sample of 31 days, you have calculated that the 95% confidence interval for the daily number of interruptions goes from 16.416 to 24.584.

a. What is the mean number of daily interruptions in the sample?

b. What is the 99% confidence interval for the number of daily interruptions?

13. For each of the following situations, indicate the correct statistical procedure to use.

a. You want to predict the running speed of a group of 50 seven-year-olds from their fathers' running speed.

b. You want to compare the mean running speed of a randomly chosen group of 25 seven-year-old girls with the mean running speed of a randomly chosen group of 25 seven-year-old boys.

c. You want to see if the mean running speed of a group of 200 seven-year-old children measured in May is faster or slower than their speed measured a month later, in June.

d. Based on a sample of 25 brother–sister pairs, you want to see what the relationship is between the running speed of sisters and that of their brothers.

e. Based on a group of 100 seven-year-old children, you want to estimate the mean running speed of seven-year-old children with no more than a 1% chance of being mistaken.

f. Based on a sample of 25 brothers, who competed for first through twenty-fifth place in a boys' race, and their sisters, who competed for first through twenty-fifth place in a girls' race, you want to know if the faster boys had faster sisters and vice versa.

14. You are interested in whether Democrats or Republicans contribute larger amounts to political campaigns. Based on the theory that Republicans are

richer, you predict that the mean donation given by Republicans will be higher than the mean donation given by Democrats. To get some relevant data, you stop ten people on the street, ask them their political affiliation, and ask them how much money they donated to political campaigns in the past year. The data are as follows:

Person	Affiliation	Donations	Person	Affiliation	Donations
1	D	$2	6	R	$50
2	D	$6	7	R	$80
3	D	$5	8	R	$ 0
4	D	$4	9	R	$60
5	D	$5	10	R	$60

a. Members of which political party, Democrats or Republicans, have the smaller standard deviation of donations? Members of which party have the larger sample mean? Don't compute the answers; you should be able to answer these questions by the eyeball test.

b. What would be the degrees of freedom and the critical values at the .05, .01, and .001 α-levels for the appropriate statistical significance test to see if your prediction that Republicans will donate more is correct?

c. Perform this test and report your conclusion.

15. Does training in critical thinking actually improve students' critical thinking skills? To find out, you give some students a measure of critical thinking skills, a training program, and then the critical thinking skills test again. The data are as follows:

Person	Pretest	Posttest
Barney	10	15
Bobby	8	12
Billy	6	7
Brandy	8	10
Betty	7	8

a. Perform the appropriate test of the null hypothesis that the critical thinking program has no effect.

b. Report your conclusion about the effect of the critical thinking program in a sentence.

c. What other factors besides the program might have been responsible for the change in the scores?

16. Which of the following statements are true and which are false?

a. On the average, about .001 of 99% confidence intervals will fail to capture the population mean.

b. The standard error of the mean decreases as the population mean decreases.

c. A between-participants design is an example of a correlated-samples design.

d. The sample mean is a point estimate of μ.

e. If two means, each based on a sample of 10, are not identical, you should reject the null hypothesis.

f. A one-tailed *t*-test and a two-tailed *t*-test differ from each other in the critical value used but not in the computation of *t*.

g. You can do a *z*-test whenever you want to test a hypothesis about means and you have approximately equal *n*'s, roughly normal distributions in the populations, and equal variances.

17. You have been offered a job by a marketing research company that is looking at people's ratings of two different formulas for a new soap. People are asked to use two bars of soap, one made with Formula A and one with Formula B, and to say how much they like each bar on a scale from 0 (strongly dislike) to 10 (prefer it to any other soap). Several different people have rated the two bars of soap, and their ratings look like this:

Rater	Bar A	Bar B
Stinky	0	3
Scruffy	5	5
Smelly	2	3
Snoozy	6	7
Snoopy	4	3
Spotty	5	6

a. What is the correct procedure to use to test the null hypothesis that the two formulas for soap are equally well liked?

b. Perform this procedure and report the value of the appropriate statistic.

c. How many degrees of freedom does this statistic have?

d. What conclusion can you draw from this study?

18. George has been experimenting with drying beef jerky. He has made it eight times and found that it took 7, 8, 5, 5, 6, 6, 7, and 8 hours to dry.

a. Based on George's data, what is the 95% confidence interval for the mean amount of time that it takes for beef jerky to dry?

b. George wants to be sure that he won't miss his plane if he starts to dry a load of jerky. What is the upper limit of the 99% confidence interval for the amount of time that it takes his jerky to dry?

c. George has a cookbook that says that jerky takes an average of 6 hours to dry. Did his jerky take significantly longer than the cookbook suggests?

19. You are interested in knowing whether parents have positive, negative, or neutral attitudes toward a curfew for teenagers. You survey a sample of 225 parents and measure their attitudes about a curfew on a scale of 1 (strongly opposed) through 2 (opposed), 3 (slightly opposed), 4 (neutral), 5 (slightly in favor), and 6 (in favor) to 7 (strongly favor). Their mean score is 4.32 and the standard deviation is 2.11. What, if anything, can you say about their opinion?

20. Veterinarians have been known to recommend that cats have their teeth cleaned periodically. But does this cleaning really extend the cat's life span? The Feline Foundation has funded an experiment to study this issue. The next 20 kittens adopted from the animal shelter were randomly assigned to two conditions: Control and Cleaning. Owners of cats in both groups were paid $25 per year to bring their cats in for a checkup. At that time, the cats in the Cleaning group had their teeth checked and cleaned, if needed. No owner in the Control group paid to have his or her cat's teeth cleaned. The major dependent variable was the age at which the cat died, rounded to the nearest year. A quarter-century after the study began, the last cat had passed away and the data looked like this:

Control	Cleaning
3	8
7	5
12	18
9	9
17	14
15	22
17	12
8	11
12	20
13	15

a. What is the proper test of the research hypothesis that the cats who had their teeth cleaned would live longer?

b. What will the degrees of freedom be for this test?

c. Perform the appropriate test.

d. Report your conclusions in a sentence in APA style.

Study Questions

1. Try to think of an example in which you might be testing a hypothesis about the difference in two means. Consider the participants whom you might use

and the dependent variable that you would measure. What kind of test would you use—a *z*-test, an independent-samples *t*-test, or a paired-samples *t*-test? Make up some imaginary data and decide what values for the two means, for *t*, and for your degrees of freedom would be reasonable.

2. Imagine that you have been asked to talk to a group of researchers on the relative advantages and disadvantages of parameter estimation versus hypothesis testing. What would you say?

3. Go to the library, browse through relevant journals, and identify an example of research studies using each of the following: a single-sample *t*-test, an independent-samples *t*-test, a paired-samples *t*-test, and a confidence interval. Which procedure was harder to locate?

4. Try to formulate three questions that could be answered only by a correlated-samples *t*-test and three that could be answered only by a correlation coefficient. Best of all, try to think of two questions pertaining to the same data that would be answered by the two different techniques.

5. To convince yourself that Appendix Table 2 was derived from Appendix Table 5, pick a correlation coefficient and sample size. Look up the significance of that *r* in Table 2. Then substitute into the formula that transforms *r* into a *t* and look up the significance level for the associated *t* in Table 5. They should be the same.

   Alternatively, pick a critical value for *r* from Table 2. Then compute the corresponding *t* for that critical value and compare it to the critical value for *t* from Table 5.

One-Way Analysis of Variance

What Is the *F*-Distribution?

After reading about the normal distribution, the binomial distribution (remember Chapter 5?), and the *t*-distribution, you are no doubt eager to learn about the next one. (If "eager" is the wrong term, how about "resigned"?) The **F-distribution**, named after Sir Ronald Fisher, is the distribution that underlies the statistical procedures collectively referred to as *analysis of variance*, sometimes abbreviated ANOVA. The analysis of variance, which will be discussed in detail in the next section of this chapter, is a procedure used for determining the statistical significance of differences among means. Because the analysis of variance, in all of its variations, is probably the most widely used inferential statistical technique, the *F*-test, based on the *F*-distribution, may be the most widely used statistical test.

The *F*-distribution is of particular interest because it is frequently used to test hypotheses about differences in the means of several groups of scores. For instance, if you wanted to know whether there was a difference in days spent in the hospital for patients who received one of three different surgical procedures, you could use an analysis of variance and an *F*-test to answer that question. However, the *F*-distribution has another use as well: It can be used to test hypotheses about the difference in two variances. Although this latter use is less common, perhaps because hypotheses about means are much more usual than hypotheses about variances, it will be discussed first, since it is simpler to compute and easier to understand.

Characteristics of the F-Distribution

Two major characteristics of the *F*-distribution will be discussed here: that *F* is a ratio of two variances and that it is really a series of distributions.

Ratio of Two Variances. The F-distribution is based on a ratio of two independent variances, one of which is in the numerator and one of which is in the denominator of the formula. The formula for F is therefore

$$\frac{s_1^2}{s_2^2}$$

This ratio gives the F-distribution certain properties. First, remember that a variance is based upon sums of squares. Since the square of a number is always positive, an F ratio will always be a ratio of two positive numbers. Thus, F will always be a positive number.

Second, when the F-test is used as part of an analysis of variance, it is based upon the ratio of two estimates of the same variance. If the null hypothesis is true, then these two estimates should be the same and F should equal 1.00 (except for sampling error). The estimate of variance that is theoretically expected to be larger if H_0 is false is always put in the numerator of the F-test based on an analysis of variance. Thus, if the null hypothesis is false, F is likely to be greater than 1, since the numerator of the fraction will be larger than the denominator. If the null hypothesis is true, F should be close to 1, since the numerator and denominator should be the same except for sampling error. In other words, a value for F between zero and one is relatively unlikely when the F-test is used as part of an analysis of variance. On the other hand, a value of F substantially greater than 1 will lead to the rejection of the null hypothesis.

F as a Series of Distributions. Like the t-distribution, the F-distribution is not a single distribution but rather a series of distributions, each with its associated number of degrees of freedom. Unlike the t-distribution, each F-distribution has not just one but two different degree of freedom parameters associated with it. The F-distributions are all positively skewed but are close to normal when the two degree of freedom parameters are both large.

Uses of F

Testing Hypotheses About Variances. Although the primary use of an F-test is as the final step in the analysis of variance procedure, an F-test can also be used to test the simple null hypothesis that the population variances of two groups are equal. Most of the time, researchers formulate hypotheses in terms of means; for example, the mean number of yawns will be greater when sitting through a showing of your father's slides of the buildings he saw on his last vacation than when sitting through a funny movie. Other hypotheses may have to do with frequencies or proportions; for example, the proportion of people who eat popcorn while watching a movie will be greater than the proportion who eat candy bars or the proportion who eat nothing. However, occasionally, a theory will lead to an hypothesis about differences in variability or variances.

For example, in a study I did on waiters and tipping, I predicted that people who worked as waiters would be more accurate at estimating what 15% of a bill would be than people who had never worked as waiters but who had been customers in restaurants (Harris, 1995). To test this theory, I had waiters and customers quickly estimate 15% of a particular amount. The mean estimates made by both the customers and the waiters were very close to the actual value of 15% of the bill and did not differ significantly. I used an F-test of the differences in variance to show that indeed waiters were more accurate in their estimates of the bill; the variance of their estimates was smaller than the variance of the customers' estimates.

EXAMPLE

Restrained Eaters. Researchers who study restrained eaters (people who continually watch what they eat and don't let themselves eat whatever they want) have noted that, after they have been induced to eat some high-calorie food (i.e., to blow their diet), some restrained eaters disinhibit or go on a binge, whereas others eat almost nothing. Nonrestrained eaters who have been induced to eat some high-calorie food show much less variability in how much they eat. Thus, you might hypothesize that the variance in the number of grams of ice cream eaten by a sample of restrained eaters who have been lured into eating a candy bar would be greater than the variance in the number of grams of ice cream eaten by a sample of nonrestrained eaters who have eaten a candy bar under similar circumstances.

To test this hypothesis, you could do an F-test. First, you would classify people as restrained or nonrestrained eaters, induce them all to eat a candy bar as part of a taste experiment, and then ask them all to eat and rate various samples of ice cream. The number of grams of ice cream eaten by each person would be your dependent measure. You would then calculate the variance of the number of grams eaten by the restrained eaters using the formula outlined in Chapter 4:

$$s_1^2 = \frac{\left(\Sigma X^2 - (\Sigma X)^2/N\right)}{N-1}$$

The reason that you use the formula for s^2 rather than for σ^2 is that it is unlikely, indeed almost impossible, that you could measure the entire populations of restrained and nonrestrained eaters.

Calculating the Variances. Suppose that your raw scores were

20   30   40   90   80   70   60   10

Table 10.1 presents these raw scores and their squares. The sum of the squared raw scores, ΣX^2, would then be 26,000, $(\Sigma X)^2$ would be 400^2, or

TABLE 10.1   Grams of Fat Eaten by Eight Restrained Eaters

X	X²
20	400
30	900
40	1600
90	8100
80	6400
70	4900
60	3600
10	100
$\Sigma = 400$	26,000

160,000, and $(\Sigma X)^2/N$ would be 20,000. Substituting into the equation for the variance, we get

$$s_1^2 = \frac{\Sigma X^2 - (\Sigma X)^2/N}{N - 1} = \frac{26,000 - 160,000/8}{7}$$

$$= \frac{26,000 - 20,000}{7} = \frac{6000}{7} = 857.14$$

Is this number a reasonable value for the variance of these scores?

One way to find out is to remember the relationships between the variance, the standard deviation, and the range that were discussed in Chapter 4. With an N of only 8, the standard deviation is likely to be roughly 1/3 or a somewhat smaller proportion of the range. Since the inclusive range of scores is 81 (that is, 90.5–9.5), you would expect a standard deviation between about 20 and 40. Recognizing that the square root of 857 is around 30 (actually 29.27), you can see that the calculated variance is in the right ballpark.

As the next step in solving the problem, you would calculate the variance of the number of grams eaten by the nonrestrained eaters. As shown in Table 10.2, if the numbers were

20   40   30   30   50   40   40   30

then the sum of the raw scores would be 280, $(\Sigma X)^2$ would be 78,400, and the sum of the squared raw scores would be 10,400. Substituting into the formula for variance, we get

$$s_2^2 = \frac{\Sigma X^2 - (\Sigma X)^2/N}{N - 1} = \frac{10,400 - 78,400/8}{7} = \frac{10,400 - 9800}{7}$$

$$= \frac{600}{7} = 85.71$$

TABLE 10.2   Grams of Fat Eaten by Eight Nonrestrained Eaters

X	X^2
20	400
40	1600
30	900
30	900
50	2500
40	1600
40	1600
30	900
$\Sigma = 280$	10,400

Given that the range of scores is 31, and that $\sqrt{85.71} = 9.26$, the value of this variance is reasonable, too.

Computing F. To do an F-test, you would divide the variance of the number of grams eaten by the restrained eaters by the variance of the number of grams eaten by the nonrestrained eaters:

$$F = \frac{s_1^2}{s_2^2} = \frac{857.14}{85.71} = 10.00$$

The fact that F turned out to be exactly 10 is due to the coincidence that the variance for the restrained eaters happened to be 10 times the variance for the nonrestrained eaters.

Testing for Statistical Significance. To discover whether or not the value of F is statistically significant, you need to go to Appendix Table 6, a portion of which is reproduced in Table 10.3. The degrees of freedom parameter for the numerator is equal to the N for the sample in the numerator minus 1, or 7. Similarly, the degrees of freedom for the denominator equals the N for the denominator minus 1, which is also 7, since the sample sizes of the two groups were the same. To use the table, you need to look at the intersection of the degrees of freedom for the numerator, marking the columns, and the degrees of freedom for the denominator, marking the rows. The three numbers at each intersection represent the .05, .01, and .001 alpha levels. However, you have to recognize that, for an F-test comparing the variances of two samples, the alpha levels listed in the table are one-tailed alpha levels and therefore are half the size of the alpha levels you need to use (e.g., the critical values listed as significant at .05 in the table are really significant at .10 for a two-tailed test).

The critical values listed in the F-table are based on the assumption that you have specified ahead of time which variance will go in the numerator.

TABLE 10.3 Sample Portion of Appendix Table 6: Critical Values for *F*-Ratios

		df for Numerator				
*df**	*p*	*1*	*2*	*3*	*4*	*5*
1	.05	161.447	199.500	215.707	224.583	230.162
	.01	4052.176	4999.492	5403.344	5624.574	5763.641
2	.05	18.513	19.000	19.164	19.247	19.296
	.01	98.502	99.000	99.166	99.249	99.299
	.001	998.500	999.000	999.166	999.250	999.299
3	.05	10.128	9.552	9.277	9.117	9.013
	.01	34.116	30.816	29.457	28.710	28.237
	.001	167.029	148.500	141.108	137.100	134.580
4	.05	7.709	6.944	6.591	6.388	6.256
	.01	21.198	18.000	16.694	15.977	15.522
	.001	74.137	61.246	56.177	53.436	51.712
5	.05	6.608	5.786	5.409	5.192	5.050
	.01	16.258	13.274	12.060	11.392	10.967
	.001	47.181	37.122	33.202	31.085	29.752
6	.05	5.987	5.143	4.757	4.534	4.387
	.01	13.745	10.925	9.780	9.148	8.746
	.001	35.507	27.000	23.703	21.924	20.803
7	.05	5.591	4.737	4.347	4.120	3.972
	.01	12.246	9.547	8.451	7.847	7.460
	.001	29.245	21.689	18.772	17.198	16.206

*For denominator.

When doing an analysis of variance, this assumption is valid. When doing an *F*-test to compare the variance of two groups, this assumption would be valid only in the instance in which you had decided to do a one-tailed test, considering only a difference in the predicted direction. Most of the time you would want to do a two-tailed test, placing whichever of the two sample variances is larger in the numerator. In that case, you would need to use the critical values of *F* listed as significant at the .025 and .005 *a*-levels to be sure that the results reach significance at the .05 and .01 levels, respectively. Although Appendix Table 6 doesn't show it, $F_{.005}(7, 7) = 8.89$. Since your computed value for *F*, 10.00, is greater than the critical value of 8.89, you would reject the null hypothesis that the samples came from populations with the same variance and conclude that the variance of the amount of ice cream eaten by the restrained eaters was significantly greater than the variance of the amount eaten by the nonrestrained eaters, $F(7, 7) = 10.00$, $p < .01$. ∎

To reiterate, an *F*-test is based on the *F*-distribution and can be used to test the null hypothesis that two variances are equal. When comparing two sample variances, it is a two-tailed test, as the larger variance is always placed in the numerator. If the value for F exceeds the critical value for F with $N_{\text{numerator}} - 1$ and $N_{\text{denominator}} - 1$ degrees of freedom, then you can reject the null hypothesis and conclude that the variance in the numerator is significantly greater than the variance in the denominator.

Testing Hypotheses About Means. Although the F-test directly tests hypotheses about variances, it can also be used to indirectly test the null hypothesis that the mean scores of different groups are equal. The analysis of variance procedure employs an F-test to draw inferences about the mean scores of different groups measured on the same dependent variable. The way in which this is done is to generate two different estimates of the variance of the scores. One estimate, the between-groups estimate, is based on how far the means of the various groups differ from the mean of all the scores. The other estimate, the within-groups estimate, is based on the deviations of the individual scores from the means of their groups. If the estimate of variance based on the deviation of the group means from the overall mean is significantly larger than the estimate based on the deviation of the raw scores from their group means, then the F-test will lead to the conclusion that the groups do not all come from populations with the same mean.

The *F*-Test for Comparing Two Variances

Purpose: To test the null hypothesis that the population variances of two groups are equal

Example: To test the hypothesis that weights of a sample of female college gymnasts will have a smaller variance than weights of a sample of nonathletic women attending the same university

Assumptions:

- The data are measured on an interval or ratio scale.
- The scores are randomly sampled.
- The distribution of the dependent measure is normal in the populations from which the data come.

Formula: $F = \dfrac{s_1^2}{s_2^2}$ where s_1^2 is the larger variance

Significance: The critical value at the .05 α-level is the value at the .025 level in the F table with $n_1 - 1$ and $n_2 - 1$ degrees of freedom. If F equals or exceeds this value, the variances differ significantly at the .05 level.

What Is an Analysis of Variance?

The **analysis of variance** procedure (often abbreviated as ANOVA) is used to draw inferences about differences in the means of two or more groups. More specifically, the analysis of variance tests the null hypothesis that the groups represent random samples from populations with the same means. An analysis of variance ends with the computation of an F-ratio that has a numerator reflecting differences among group means and a denominator reflecting only differences among scores within each group. If the numerator is sufficiently larger than the denominator—that is, if the value for F is significantly larger than 1.00—then the null hypothesis can be rejected and the conclusion drawn that the means of the groups differ significantly.

A **one-way analysis of variance** is a particular kind of analysis of variance that is used when there is only one independent variable. In this case, the purpose of the analysis is to compare the means for two or more levels of the independent variable, or to compare the means of several groups that can be viewed as differing with respect to some independent variable. Usually the variable on which the groups differ is a qualitative one such as experimental condition, group membership, or some nominal-level demographic variable, such as ethnicity, gender, or religion. However, it is possible to classify people into groups based on a quantitative variable—for example, aged under 30, from 30 to 50 years, or over 50—and to do an analysis of variance comparing people from the different age categories. The dependent measure for an analysis of variance always has to be an interval- or ratio-scale variable, however, or at least one for which it makes sense to calculate a mean.

Relationship of F and t

This description of the purpose of the analysis of variance may sound very similar to the purpose of the t-test. Indeed it is. In fact, when there are only two groups to be compared, either an independent-samples t-test or a one-way analysis of variance could be performed, and both would lead to the same conclusion. Why is this the case? The reason is based on the fact that the F-distribution, the normal distribution, and the t-distribution are all related to each other. In particular, the t-distribution with $N - 2$ degrees of freedom is equal to the square root of the F-distribution with 1 and $N - 2$ degrees of freedom. If you were to compute an independent-samples t-test comparing the means of two groups and then to compute an analysis of variance comparing the means of the same two groups, the value of t that you obtained from the t-test would be equal to the square root of the value of F obtained from the analysis of variance. Similarly, the critical value of F with 1 and any number (say $N - 2$) degrees of freedom is equal to the square of the critical value of t with $N - 2$ degrees of freedom.

TIP

> The relationship between the t- and the F-distributions means that if you were ever caught on a desert island with your F-table but without your t-table, you could use the first column of your F-table to get the critical values for t. For example, note that $1.96^2 = 3.84$, and that the critical value for t with 20 degrees of freedom, which is 2.086 at the .05 α-level, is equal to the square root of 4.35, the critical value of F with 1 and 20 degrees of freedom.

Since F is directly related to t, the same factors that are associated with a large value of t will also be associated with a large value of F. Specifically, the F from an analysis of variance will be *larger* if

1. The difference in the means is *larger*
2. The standard deviations (or variances) of the groups are *smaller*
3. The sample sizes (n's) are *larger*

Assumptions

Similarly, the assumptions underlying the use of the F-test as part of an analysis of variance are the same as the assumptions underlying the use of the t-test. More specifically, the F-test is appropriate when

1. The data are measured on an interval or ratio scale (or close enough to it for it to be reasonable to compute a mean).
2. The scores are randomly (or at least independently) sampled.
3. The distribution of the dependent measure is normal in the populations from which the data come.
4. The populations have equal variances.

As is true with t, you rarely know whether or not the latter two assumptions are true, but the analysis of variance is quite robust to violations of all but the assumption of independence. The exception occurs when you have greatly unequal sample sizes. If the n's are both small and unequal (one is several times another), the sample variances are greatly unequal (perhaps a 10-to-1 ratio), and the distribution of scores in the sample looks very far from normal (perhaps 80% are zero), then the analysis of variance is probably not a proper procedure to use on the data (Coombs, Algina & Oltman, 1996). Either the data need to be transformed in some way, such as by taking the logarithm or the square root of the raw scores, or a nonparametric test might be used as an alternative. At any rate, if it appears that the assumptions of normality and equal variances are being violated when the sample sizes are small and unequal, it is time to seek out some statistical advice.

A violation of one of the first two assumptions for the use of an ANOVA is as much a design problem as a statistical issue. If it is meaningless to talk about a mean, it is meaningless to do an analysis of variance or any other technique based on means. If the scores do not represent random samples from the population in which you are interested, then you cannot generalize from them to that population with a great deal of confidence.

ANOVA Versus Multiple *t*-Tests

I have already said that, when there are only two groups to be compared, the analysis of variance tests the exact same hypothesis as a two-tailed independent-samples *t*-test and will lead to the same conclusion. What if there are more than two means? You might conclude that it would be possible to discover whether or not they are all random samples from the same population simply by doing multiple *t*-tests, each test comparing one mean with another. In a sense, this is true. Suppose that you wanted to know whether the mean number of runs scored in a season by the Aardvarks, Buffalos, and Crocodiles differ significantly from each other. You could indeed compare the means of the Aardvarks and the Buffalos by one *t*-test, the means of the Buffalos and the Crocodiles by another, and the means of the Aardvarks and the Crocodiles by a third *t*-test.

However, if you were to do all three tests, each one at the .05 α-level, your chance of finding a significant result if the null hypothesis were true would be substantially larger than .05. In order to keep your chance of making a Type I error at .05, you would have to adjust your significance level for each test. The use of an analysis of variance procedure makes it possible to do only one test of the overall null hypothesis that the population means of all of the different groups are equal, while holding the alpha level at whatever value you choose.

Advantages of ANOVA. As compared with the use of multiple *t*-tests, the analysis of variance procedure has several important advantages. First, as mentioned in the previous paragraph, the one-way analysis of variance technique will test the null hypothesis that all the means come from the same population while keeping your chance of mistakenly rejecting this H_0 at whatever alpha level you choose. Second, the analysis of variance procedure requires only one test to do what might otherwise take a large number of *t*-tests. If you wanted to compare five groups by *t*-tests, for example, you would have to compare group A with group B, group C, group D and group E; group B additionally with groups C, D, and E; group C with groups D and E; and group D with group E for a total of ten *t*-tests. With 6 groups, you would need fifteen different *t*-tests to test the same null hypothesis that one analysis of variance could test.

There is a third relative advantage of the analysis of variance procedure which is a little less obvious. The denominator of the *t*-test consists of an estimate of the standard error of the difference in the means that is based on the standard deviations of the two groups being compared. The denominator of the analysis of variance consists of an estimate of variance (the square of the standard deviation) that is based on the scores from *all* of the groups. An estimate based on the standard deviations or variances of each of the groups in a study is called a *pooled error term*, meaning that the estimates of the variability or error within each of the groups are pooled or combined across all the groups. If the null hypothesis that the groups are random samples from the same population is true, then an estimate of the population standard deviation or variance that is based on the data from all of the groups should be more accurate than an estimate based on only two of the groups. Therefore, when there are more than two groups to be compared, an analysis of variance ordinarily should be a more powerful test of the overall null hypothesis than a series of individual *t*-tests.

Formulas for the Analysis of Variance

The formulas for analysis of variance use a number of new terms, some of which refer to quantities that you have encountered before. A **sum of squares**, abbreviated *SS*, stands for a sum of squared deviations around a mean. The numerator of the formulas for variance constitutes a sum of squares: either $\Sigma(X - \overline{X})^2$ in the deviation score formula or $\Sigma X^2 - (\Sigma X)^2/N$ in the raw score formula. A **mean square** equals a sum of squares divided by its corresponding degrees of freedom, making it an estimate of variance. When the sum of squares in the formula for the variance of a sample is divided by $N - 1$, the resulting quotient can be called a mean square. The term **grand mean** refers to the mean of all the scores in a sample (i.e., in a research study) without regard to the group from which they come. Finally, the symbol K stands for the number of groups or levels of an independent variable in a study. Thus, if you were comparing the mean number of rooms in houses sampled from four areas of a city, K would equal 4.

The **sum of squares total** (or total sum of squares), abbreviated SS_T, stands for the sum of the squared deviations of all the raw scores around the grand mean. In other words, it is identical to the numerator of the formula for the variance of a group of scores. The **sum of squares between groups**, SS_B (often called the *sum of squares between* or the *between sum of squares*) stands for the sum of the squared deviations of the group means from the grand mean, weighted by the size of the groups. (The weighting is necessary because the Central Limit Theorem shows that the variance of a group of means decreases as the size of the samples increases.) The farther apart the means of the groups are from each other, the farther most of these group means will be from the grand mean, and the larger will be the value of the sum of squares between groups. The **sum of squares within groups**, SS_W (also called the *sum of squares within*, the *within sum of squares*, or the *error sum of squares*) is equal to the sum of the squared deviations of each raw score from the mean of its group, summed across all the groups. If all of the scores within each group are very similar to each other, then the sum of squares within groups will be small; if the scores within each group are very different from each other, then the within sum of squares will be large.

Notice that the sum of squares total reflects the deviations of all the scores from the grand mean, the sum of squares between reflects the deviations of the group means from the grand mean, and the sum of squares within reflects the deviations of the raw scores from their group means. If you think about the implications of the above sentence, you may recognize that the

$$SS_T = SS_B + SS_W$$

The total of all the squared deviations can be divided or partitioned into two parts, one reflecting how much the groups differ from each other and one reflecting the amount of variability within the groups. In somewhat similar fashion, each individual score can be viewed as consisting of several components, one reflecting the grand mean, one representing the deviation of the mean of the group to which the score belongs from the grand mean, and one reflecting the deviation of the score from the mean of its group. This concept of breaking down an individual score into independent components that can be added together is called the *linear model*; it is discussed in detail in most intermediate statistics textbooks.

As previously noted, a mean square is a sum of squares divided by its corresponding degrees of freedom. What might these be? The degrees of freedom for the sum of squares total is equal to one less than the total sample size or $N - 1$. The degrees of freedom for the sum of squares between, usually called the degrees of freedom between, is equal to one less than the number of groups or $K - 1$. The degrees of freedom within groups is equal to $N - K$.

TIP

In each case, you can consider the degrees of freedom as equaling the number of scores you add up in the formula minus the number of means you have to estimate from these scores: one for df_T, one for df_B, and K (one for each group) for df_W. Notice that the total degrees of freedom is equal to df_B plus df_W; or

$$N - 1 = (K - 1) + (N - K)$$

The mean square total would equal the $SS_T/(N - 1)$ if you were to calculate it. However, perhaps because it serves no useful purpose, the mean square total is not calculated or reported as part of the analysis of variance procedure. The MS_B equals the $SS_B/(K - 1)$, and the MS_W is equal to $SS_W/(N - K)$. The F for the analysis of variance equals the MS_B divided by the MS_W, and its critical value at the .05 level is $F_{.05}(K - 1, N - K)$.

Partitioning of Variance.   It is possible to think of the total variance in the scores as composed of two parts, that due to the differences between the group means and that due to the differences of individual scores from the means of their groups. Dividing up the total variance into these components is often called partitioning of variance. The farther apart the means of the different groups are, the greater will be the SS_B and the MS_B, since the calculations are based on the difference of these means from the grand mean. The more similar the scores of people within a group are to each other, the smaller will be the SS_W and the MS_W.

If the mean square between groups is large, relative to the mean square within groups, then most of the variance in the scores is due to the differences in the means of the groups. When this is the case, there is relatively little overlap in the scores of the groups, and the ratio of the MS_B to the MS_W, as measured by F, will be large, leading to a conclusion that the means differ to a statistically significant degree. If the mean square between groups and the mean square within groups are approximately equal, then the F ratio will be near 1.00, and the difference in the means will not be statistically significant.

Notation System.   The formulas for the sums of squares in the analysis of variance are easier to compute than they may look. The problem is that there is not a single simple way of representing the steps to be taken in a formula that all statisticians agree upon. There are a number of different *notation systems*, or ways of representing the terms in the equation and the procedures that have to be carried out to compute the sums of squares. Unfortunately, there is no guarantee that the notation system used in this text will be the same as the one used in your next statistics course.

If reading through the formulas is confusing, don't give up. First, it is only the formulas for the sums of squares that look difficult. Once the sums of squares have been computed, dividing them by the degrees of freedom to get the mean squares and dividing the MS_B by the MS_W to get the value for F is easy. Second, once you have seen a clear example of the procedures to follow, you will realize that computing a one-way analysis of variance is relatively easy, no matter how daunting the formulas may look.

Formula for SS_T.   The formula for SS_T can be expressed in the deviation score form as

$$SS_T = \Sigma(X - \overline{X}_T)^2$$

where $\overline{X}_T$ equals the grand mean. However, as you know, the deviation score formulas are usually not convenient for computation. The computational formula for SS_T can be written most simply as

$$\Sigma X^2 - \frac{T^2}{N}$$

where X equals each raw score and T equals the sum or total of all the raw scores. The last part of the equation, the T^2/N, is usually called the correction term.

This formula tells you to proceed as follows.

Step 1: Square each raw score.

Step 2: Sum these squared raw scores.

Step 3: Sum all the raw scores.

Step 4: Square this sum.

Step 5: Divide this squared sum by N.

Step 6: Subtract this quotient from the sum of the squared raw scores.

Formula for SS_B. The deviation score formula for the between-groups sum of squares for a one-way analysis of variance can be written as

$$SS_B = \Sigma \left[n_j \left(\overline{X}_j - \overline{X}_T \right)^2 \right]$$

The computational formula can be written most concisely as

$$SS_B = \Sigma \frac{T_j^2}{n_j} - \frac{T^2}{N}$$

The subscript j is used to stand for each and any of the K groups; T_j therefore stands for the total of the scores in group j, whereas T without a subscript stands for the total of all the raw scores. The summation notation indicates that the scores are summed across all K groups, beginning with the first and ending with the Kth. To use the formula for the sum of squares between, you proceed as follows:

Step 1: For each group, sum the raw scores.

Step 2: Then square this sum.

Step 3: For each group, divide the squared sum of the raw scores by the number of scores in the group.

Step 4: Sum these K quotients.

Step 5: Compute the correction term by squaring the sum of all the raw scores and dividing this number by the total number of scores.

Step 6: Subtract the correction term from the sum in step 4.

Formula for SS_W. The deviation score formula for the sum of squares within can be written as

$$SS_W = \Sigma(X_1 - \overline{X}_1)^2 + \Sigma(X_2 - \overline{X}_2)^2 + \dots \Sigma(X_K - \overline{X}_K)^2$$

There are two different computational formulas for the SS_W. The slightly shorter one can be written as

$$SS_W = \Sigma \left[\Sigma X_j^2 - \frac{(\Sigma X_j)^2}{n_j} \right]$$

or, more simply, as

$$SS_W = \Sigma X^2 - \Sigma \frac{T_j^2}{n_j}$$

This formula requires the following steps.

Step 1: Square each raw score.

Step 2: Sum all the squared raw scores.

Step 3: Add up the scores in each group.

Step 4: For each group, square the sum of the scores.

Step 5: Divide this sum by the number in the group.

Step 6: Sum these quotients.

Step 7: Subtract this sum from the sum of the squared raw scores.

A slightly longer formula for the sum of squares within groups might be somewhat preferable to use, as it relates more obviously to the deviation score formula. This formula is

$$SS_W = \left(\Sigma X_1^2 - \frac{(\Sigma X_1)^2}{n_1} \right) + \left(\Sigma X_2^2 - \frac{(\Sigma X_2)^2}{n_2} \right) + \ldots \left(\Sigma X_K^2 - \frac{(\Sigma X_K)^2}{n_K} \right)$$

It says to do the following steps.

Step 1: For each group, square each raw score and sum the squared raw scores.

Step 2: For each group, sum the raw scores and square this sum.

Step 3: Divide this sum by the number in the group.

Step 4: Subtract this quotient from the sum of the squared raw scores in the group.

Step 5: Add these differences across all K groups.

The advantage of this formula is that it lets you see which of the K groups contributes the most to the sum of squares within.

Checks on Computation. Note that there are two built-in checks on your computation. First, as you doubtless remember, each sum of squares must be positive. If you get a negative number, you have made an error in computation. If you get a value of zero for a sum of squares, either all the scores are identical (in which case, why bother to compute anything?) or you have made an error.

Second, the SS_T must equal $SS_B + SS_W$. Of course, it is possible to get one of the latter two values by subtraction, instead of using the formula, but that is a good idea only for people who never make any errors in computation. The rest of us should work out the formulas for each of the sums of squares, step by step. However, these two checks do not protect against certain kinds of errors, such as making a mistake when adding up the raw scores in a group or saying that $3^2 = 6$ instead of 9. Because doing an analysis of variance can be fairly tedious if a lot of scores are involved, it is a good idea to double check your addition and squaring of the raw scores in each group before proceeding to compute the sums of squares.

Analysis of Variance Summary Table

Although the computation of the sums of squares is the hardest part of an analysis of variance, you are not through when you have done so. These computations are followed by the computations of the mean square within, the mean square between and, finally, the F-value. The value of F then has to be compared with the critical value from Appendix Table 6 and a decision made about its significance. Are you done then? Not quite. By convention, the results of an analysis of variance are usually reported not only in words but in the form of an *analysis of variance summary table*, which summarizes the numbers and conclusions of the analysis.

The ANOVA summary table takes a fairly simple form when it reports the data from a one-way ANOVA, the kind that we are discussing in this chapter. It begins with a column heading called Source, which includes the sources of the sums of squares: Between groups, Within groups and Total. More complex analysis of variance designs have more sources in the table; for example, there would be one for each factor in a factorial design as well as one for each interaction between factors. The next columns in an ANOVA summary table are for the sums of squares, the degrees of freedom (these can be in either order), the mean squares, the F, and the significance of F. Sometimes the level of significance is indicated not by a separate column but by asterisks next to the F-value and a note at the bottom of the table stating the meaning of the asterisks. The analysis of variance table provides an easy summary of what can be a series of complex analyses. The headings look like this:

Source   SS   df   MS   F   p

Examples of One-Way ANOVAs

As was said earlier, one-way analyses of variance are used when you want to compare the mean scores of various groups. Sometimes, ANOVAs are used to compare scores of pre-existing groups, usually but not always to test a theory that leads to predictions about how the group means will differ. Sometimes, ANOVAs are used to analyze the results of an experimental study in which participants have been randomly assigned to different treatment groups or conditions, and the researcher wishes to compare the effects of the different conditions. An example of each type of research will be presented.

EXAMPLE

Dentists and Leisure. Suppose that you are interested in the issue of whether male and female dentists have equal amounts of leisure time. Because women have not been widely represented in the field of dentistry until recently, almost all the older dentists are male. Therefore, you divide your sample into three groups: younger or novice female dentists (group 1), younger or novice male dentists (group 2), and older or more experienced male dentists (group 3). Each dentist is then asked to report the number of hours devoted to leisure time activities in a week. The three female dentists have 1, 2, and 3 hours of leisure time; the three younger male dentists have 4, 5, and 6 hours of leisure time per week: and the three older male dentists have 7, 8, and 9 hours of leisure time each week. Your problem is to determine whether these differences in leisure time between the three groups of dentists are statistically significant or are likely to be due to chance.

Solution: The first step in solving the problem is to put the data into the form of a table and to compute some basic information, including the sum of the raw scores for each group and the sum of the squared raw scores for each group:

Group 1		Group 2		Group 3	
X_1	X_1^2	X_2	X_2^2	X_3	X_3^2
1	1	4	16	7	49
2	4	5	25	8	64
3	9	6	36	9	81
$\Sigma = 6$	14	15	77	24	194

- The group n's and the overall N along with the sum of all the raw scores and of the squared raw scores also need to be calculated:

$$n_1 = 3 \qquad n_2 = 3 \qquad n_3 = 3 \qquad N = 9$$

$$\Sigma X = 6 + 15 + 24 = 45 = T$$

$$\Sigma X^2 = 14 + 77 + 194 = 285$$

$$T^2 = (\Sigma X)^2 = 45^2 = 2025 \qquad \frac{T^2}{N} = \frac{2025}{9} = 225$$

You now have all the information that is needed to compute a one-way analysis of variance.

- The next step is to compute the total sum of squares:

$$SS_T = \Sigma X^2 - \frac{T^2}{N} = 285 - 225 = 60.00$$

Even though in this case the sum of squares is an integer, it is still reported to two decimal places. The degrees of freedom for the total sum of squares is $N - 1$ or 8.

- Next we compute the sum of squares between:

$$SS_B = \Sigma \frac{T_j^2}{n_j} - \frac{T^2}{N} = \left(\frac{6^2}{3} + \frac{15^2}{3} + \frac{24^2}{3} \right) - 225$$

$$= \left(\frac{36}{3} + \frac{225}{3} + \frac{576}{3} \right) - 225 = (12 + 75 + 192) - 225$$

$$= 279 - 225 = 54.00$$

- The degrees of freedom between is equal to $K - 1$ or 2, since there are three groups. The mean square between is therefore

$$MS_B = \frac{SS_B}{df_B} = \frac{54.00}{2} = 27.00$$

- There are two different ways in which the sum of squares within can be calculated. The simpler formula is as follows:

$$SS_W = \Sigma X^2 - \Sigma \frac{T_j^2}{n_j} = 285 - \left(\frac{36}{3} + \frac{225}{3} + \frac{576}{3} \right) = 285 - 279 = 6.00$$

- Alternatively, you could use the formula that involves computing the SS_W group by group:

$$SS_W = \left(\Sigma X_1^2 - \frac{(\Sigma X_1)^2}{n_1} \right) + \left(\Sigma X_2^2 - \frac{(\Sigma X_2)^2}{n_2} \right) + \dots \left(\Sigma X_K^2 - \frac{(\Sigma X_K)^2}{n_K} \right)$$

$$= \left(14 - \frac{36}{3} \right) + \left(77 - \frac{225}{3} \right) + \left(194 - \frac{576}{3} \right)$$

$$= (14 - 12) + (77 - 75) + (194 - 192)$$

$$= 2 + 2 + 2 = 6.00$$

- Since the degrees of freedom within groups $= N - K$ or $9 - 3$ or 6, it happens that the $MS_W = 1.00$. Will you get such convenient numbers with real data? Don't count on it.

- To compute F, it is necessary to divide the MS_B by the MS_W:

$$F = \frac{MS_B}{MS_W} = \frac{27.00}{1.00} = 27.00$$

Statistical Significance. In order to decide whether or not this value is significant, it is necessary to look up the critical value for F with 2 and 6 degrees of freedom in Appendix Table 6. Since the actual value of F is equal to the critical value of 27.00 at the $p < .001$ level, you can reject the H_0 and conclude that the means are unlikely to represent random samples from the same population.

So how do you interpret this information? What does this significant difference represent? In APA style, your conclusion might read, "A one-way analysis of variance revealed that the numbers of hours spent on leisure activities by novice female dentists ($M = 2.00$, $SD = 1.00$), novice male dentists ($M = 5.00$, $SD = 1.00$), and experienced male dentists ($M = 8.00$, $SD = 1.00$) differed significantly at the $p < .001$ level." In other words, it is unlikely that less experienced female dentists, less experienced male dentists, and more experienced male dentists all spend about the same amount of time on leisure activities.

The final step in the analysis of variance process is to put your results into an analysis of variance summary table:

Source	SS	df	MS	F(2, 6)	p
Between	54.00	2	27.00	27.00	.001
Within	6.00	6	1.00		
Total	60.00	8			

EXAMPLE

Effects of Labels on Attitudes. Social psychologists, special educators, and people with disabilities are interested in the topic of how labels affect people's perceptions of the person to whom the label is applied. They would predict, for instance, that a term like "cripple" seems to define the individual and would lead the individual to be perceived differently than a term like "person with a disability," which implies that the person's disability is but one attribute of the individual.

In order to find out whether or not this prediction is true, you randomly assign four groups of 15 people each to read a vignette describing a person who has muscular dystrophy and is in a wheelchair. The vignettes are identical except for the term used to describe the individual: "cripple" (*C*), "handicapped person" (*HP*), "person who has a disability" (*PWHD*), and "person

TABLE 10.4   Data for the Effects of Labels Example

C	C^2	HP	HP^2	PWHD	$PWHD^2$	PWUW	$PWUW^2$
5	25	8	64	12	144	14	196
6	36	7	49	10	100	17	289
10	100	10	100	15	225	19	361
9	81	15	225	18	324	22	484
6	36	13	169	20	400	15	225
7	49	12	144	19	361	21	441
12	144	15	225	23	529	24	576
8	64	13	169	17	289	18	324
5	25	12	144	21	441	24	576
6	36	16	256	16	256	16	256
8	64	10	100	22	484	25	625
5	25	8	64	15	225	18	324
7	49	10	100	19	361	21	441
9	81	9	81	13	169	14	196
7	49	11	121	20	400	23	529
$\Sigma = 110$	864	169	2011	260	4708	291	5843
$(\Sigma)^2 = 12{,}100$		28,561		67,600		84,681	

who uses a wheelchair" (*PWUW*). The subjects are then asked to rate the individual on nine-point scales indicating how independent, powerful, and capable they think the person is. Since all three scales correlate highly with each other, with r's ranging from .87 to .94, you decide to simply add the three ratings to get one total score for each participant. Higher scores therefore reflect ratings of the person in the vignette as more independent, powerful, and capable. Your research hypothesis is that the two vignettes with "person who . . ." in the description will lead to higher ratings than the vignettes using "cripple" and "handicapped person." The null hypothesis, of course, is that the mean ratings of the four groups will represent random samples from the population and will not differ more than expected by chance. The raw data are presented in Table 10.4, along with their squares and the sums.

Solution:

- The first step in the analysis of variance is to compute the sum of squares total. To do that, we need to get ΣX^2:

$$\Sigma X^2 = 864 + 2011 + 4708 + 5843 = 13{,}426$$

- We also need the value of ΣX, which is called T in the formula:

$$\Sigma X = 110 + 169 + 260 + 291 = 830 = T$$
$$T^2 = (830)(830) = 688{,}900$$
$$N = 15 + 15 + 15 + 15 = 60$$

$$\frac{T^2}{N} = \frac{688,900}{60} = 11,481.67$$

- Once we have these values, we can use the formula for SS_T:

$$\Sigma X^2 - \frac{T^2}{N} = 13,426 - 11,481.67 = 1944.33$$

- Next we need to calculate SS_B:

$$SS_B = \Sigma \frac{T_j^2}{n_j} - \frac{T^2}{N} = \left(\frac{12,100}{15} + \frac{28,561}{15} + \frac{67,600}{15} + \frac{84,681}{15}\right) - \frac{688,900}{60}$$

$$= (806.67 + 1904.07 + 4506.67 + 5645.40) - 11,481.67$$

$$= 12,862.81 - 11,481.67 = 1381.14$$

- The third sum of squares to be calculated is the sum of squares within groups:

$$SS_W = \Sigma X^2 - \frac{T_j^2}{n_j}$$

$$= 13,426 - \left(\frac{12,100}{15} + \frac{28,561}{15} + \frac{67,600}{15} + \frac{84,681}{15}\right)$$

$$= 13,426 - (806.67 + 1904.07 + 4506.67 + 5645.40)$$

$$= 13,426 - 12,862.81 = 563.19$$

- As a check on your computations, you may wish to use the formula that involves computing the SS_W group by group:

$$SS_W = \left(\Sigma X_1^2 - \frac{(\Sigma X_1)^2}{n_1}\right) + \left(\Sigma X_2^2 - \frac{(\Sigma X_2)^2}{n_2}\right) + \ldots \left(\Sigma X_K - \frac{(\Sigma X_K)^2}{n_K}\right)$$

Substituting into this formula gives

$$SS_W = \left(864 - \frac{12,100}{15}\right) + \left(2011 - \frac{28,561}{15}\right) + \left(4708 - \frac{67,600}{15}\right) + \left(5843 - \frac{84,681}{15}\right)$$

$$= (864 - 806.67) + (2011 - 1904.07) + (4708 - 4506.67) + (5843 - 5645.40)$$

$$= 57.33 + 106.93 + 201.33 + 197.60 = 563.19$$

TIP ▓▓

As another a check on our computations, we can use the fact that the sum of squares total can be partitioned into the sum of squares between plus the sum of squares within. As we expected (well, hoped), 1944.33 = 1381.14 + 563.19.

- Now that we have computed the sums of squares, we can compute the mean squares. The degrees of freedom between equals $K - 1$ or 3. Therefore, $MS_B = SS_B/3$:

$$MS_B = \frac{1381.14}{3} = 460.38$$

- The degrees of freedom within equals $N - K$ or $60 - 4 = 56$. Therefore, the $MS_W = SS_W/56$:

$$MS_W = \frac{563.19}{56} = 10.06$$

- To get the value for F, we have to divide the MS_B by the MS_W:

$$\frac{460.38}{10.06} = 45.76$$

Statistical Significance. To know if this value is statistically significant, we have to compare it with the critical value for F with 3 and 56 degrees of freedom. Looking in Appendix Table 6, we see that the critical values for $F_{(3, 50)}$ at the .05, .01, and .001 α-levels are 2.790, 4.199, and 6.336, respectively. Since the calculated value for F far exceeds all of these critical values, we would reject the null hypothesis that all of the means came from the same population and conclude (in APA style) that "the label had a statistically significantly effect upon evaluation of a person described in a vignette, $F_{(3, 56)} = 45.76$, $p < .001$." The results of the analysis of variance are summarized in the following table:

Source	SS	df	MS	F(3, 56)	p
Between	1381.14	3	460.38	45.76	<.001
Within	563.19	56	10.06		
Total	1944.33	59			

Three points about the conclusion in this example are worth noting. First, the value for F is a very large one, relative to the critical value. This might cause you to check your calculations for a mistake; however, the fact that there is very little overlap in the raw scores for the four groups of people suggests that the value for *F* is a reasonable one. Second, because this was a true experiment, it is fair to talk about the "effect" of the label upon evaluations. If the design had been a correlational one, then any conclusions should be worded only in terms of differences or relationships, not in terms of causes or effects. Third, notice that the conclusion does not say which label(s) led to higher or lower scores than which other one(s). In other words, the ANOVA is not an exact *t*-test of your research hypothesis that the means for *PWHD* and *PWUW* would be higher than the means for *C* and *HP*. In order to draw conclusions about differences between particular means, you need to use a comparison, a procedure that will be outlined in the next chapter. ■

Interpretation of *F* from ANOVA

Nonsignificant *F*.   The interpretation of a nonsignificant *F* from an analysis of variance is very easy. If the computed value of *F* is less than the critical value, you have to retain the null hypothesis that it is possible that the population mean scores of the groups do not differ. In the discussion section of your paper, perhaps you could speculate that with a larger sample size, a more accurate dependent measure, or a more powerful design, you might have been able to reject the null hypothesis; however, a nonsignificant *F* does not allow you to say that the means of the populations from which the groups come are different.

Significant *F*.   A significant *F* from a one-way analysis of variance indicates that it is improbable that the means represent random samples from the same population. If there are only two means, then a significant *F* can be interpreted in only one way: The larger mean is significantly larger than the smaller one. If there are more than two means, however, the only conclusion that can be drawn is that they do not come from the same population: It is not legitimate to conclude that any particular mean (even the largest) is significantly larger than any other particular mean (even the smallest). In order to draw any conclusions about which specific mean or means differ from which other means, it is necessary to perform another type of statistical procedure, which is called a post hoc comparison. The details of when and how to use such procedures are spelled out in Chapter 11.

Relationship Between Independent and Dependent Variables.   Although the *F*-test is a measure of the statistical significance of the overall differences in means, two other measures are more directly related to the magnitude of the relationship between the independent and dependent variables. The sum of squares between groups divided by the sum of squares total is called *eta* *squared* (η^2), which you may remember from Chapter 6 is a measure of the degree of curvilinear relationship between the variables.

The formula for eta squared looks like this:

$$\eta^2 = \frac{SS_B}{SS_T}$$

Eta squared can be viewed as a descriptive statistic identifying the proportion of the variance in the dependent variable explained by the independent variable in the sample. However, to generalize to the population, you must use *omega squared* (ω^2), another measure of effect size, which has a more complicated formula.

$$\omega^2 = \frac{SS_B - (k - 1)MS_W}{SS_T + MS_W}$$

Omega squared is a measure of association between the independent and dependent variables that is an unbiased estimator of the proportion of variance in the dependent variable in the population that can be explained by the independent variable (Diekhoff, 1996; Evans, 1996; Hinkle, Wiersma & Jurs, 1994).

How Do You Decide Which Analysis to Use?

One-Way ANOVA Versus *t*-Test

Whenever you want to compare the means of two groups for which the scores are not paired, you can perform either an independent-samples *t*-test or a one-way analysis of variance. The former procedure is the more traditional choice, probably because most people feel that it is easier to compute. However, both tests provide exactly the same information in the two-group case, with the actual and critical values for F being the square of the actual and (two-tailed) critical values for t. The only thing to keep in mind is that it is important in either case to describe the direction of the difference in means to the reader.

Other Analysis of Variance Procedures

The one-way analysis of variance is the simplest of a large body of related techniques, all of which involve comparing means indirectly via the computation of relevant F-ratios. If there is only one dependent measure, if scores from the groups are not matched or paired with each other, and if the groups or means are classified along only one dimension, then a one-way ANOVA is used. However, there are a number of more complex analysis of variance designs that are more useful than the one-way ANOVA under certain circumstances.

Factorial Analysis of Variance.   A factorial analysis of variance is used when there are two or more independent variables or factors in the research design. Factorial analyses of variance will be discussed in more detail in Chapter 12.

Repeated Measures Analysis of Variance.   Just as a one-way analysis of variance can be viewed as an extension of an independent-samples *t*-test to the situation where there are more than two groups, a repeated measures analysis of variance can be viewed as an extension of a paired or dependent-samples *t*-test. When each person has been measured more than once, or when a particular score in one group has been matched with a particular score in each of the other groups, then a procedure that takes into account the fact that these scores are not independent must be used. Although other terms have sometimes been used, the most common name for such a procedure is a *repeated measures analysis of variance*. Such a procedure makes it possible to separate out the effect of individual differences from the effect of time of measurement or whatever variable serves to differentiate the groups. A repeated measures analysis of variance is used whenever the research design has a within-participants factor, to remove the effect of the differences among individuals from the overall differences among levels of the factor. A factorial research design that includes both within-participants and between-participants variables would be analyzed by a factorial analysis of variance that would involve a repeated measures analysis on some of the variables.

Multivariate Analysis of Variance.   With the exception of regression and correlation, which are usually considered bivariate, the kinds of analyses discussed so far in this book all fall under the categories of *univariate analyses*, or analyses of one dependent variable at a time. Sometimes, however, a researcher is interested in more than one dependent measure; for example, in scores on three subscales of a comprehensive personality inventory. Of course, it would be possible to perform three separate analyses of variance (or *t*-tests) in such a case, one for each of the subscales. However, this procedure leads to at least one difficulty: the potential problem of inflating the overall Type I error rate by doing each test at the .05 α-level.

This problem can be dealt with by using what is called the *Bonferroni critical value* procedure of adjusting the significance level of each individual test (in this case to the .05/3 or .0167 α-level) so as to keep the chance of finding anything significant at the desired alpha level. However, an extension of the analysis of variance procedure to deal with two or more dependent variables simultaneously is able both to keep the overall alpha level at .05 and to consider what combination of the dependent variables is best able to differentiate among the groups being compared. This type of procedure, a **multivariate analysis of variance**, is actually an extremely versatile approach to analysis that can deal with repeated measures and unequal sample sizes as well as with multiple dependent variables. However, the computational procedures are so complex that it is rare that anyone attempts to do a multivariate analysis of variance (MANOVA) by hand.

Analysis of Covariance.   Sometimes a researcher wishes to compare groups which are known to differ with respect to some variable. For example, a researcher might be unable to control for the age of children randomly assigned to one of three programs designed to stimulate creativity. In such an instance, if age is linearly related to the dependent measure, which might be score on a measure of creativity, it is possible that differences in age between the groups might be associated with differences in creativity test scores, regardless of the effects of the programs. An **analysis of covariance** procedure (sometimes abbreviated as ANCOVA) can be used to statistically remove the effects of the pre-existing variable, called the *covariate*, from the differences between groups. It is really a two-step procedure, combining both regression and analysis of variance. First, the scores on the covariate are used to predict what scores individuals would be expected to have on the dependent measure; then these adjusted scores are analyzed by a type of analysis of variance. Although an analysis of covariance may not completely correct for pre-existing differences in means on the covariate and can produce misleading conclusions when a quasi-experimental design has been used rather than a true experiment (Campbell & Erlebacher, 1975), it can often increase the power of your comparisons by removing some of the variance due to individual differences. Of course, an ANCOVA increases power only if the covariate is indeed related to the dependent variable; if it is unrelated, it will slightly decrease power, by decreasing the degrees of freedom for the analyses.

An analysis of covariance is most commonly used when the researcher wants to compare posttest scores for people assigned to various groups, while taking into account the fact that the individuals in the groups differed on some pretest. For example, two programs designed to get people to decrease their weight by making dietary changes might be compared to each other and to a control group by an analysis of covariance, using posttest weight as the dependent measure and pretest weight as the covariate. If weight, systolic blood pressure, and diastolic blood pressure were all used as variables, a multivariate analysis of covariance (MANCOVA) could be used with pretest scores on all three measures as covariates, posttest scores as the dependent variables, and type of program as the independent variable. Add in gender as another factor and you get a factorial MANCOVA. Add in a set of follow-up measures taken after two years and you have a factorial MANCOVA with repeated measures. You get the point.

ANOVA Versus Multiple Regression

An analysis of variance, as I have said, is designed to compare the mean scores of several groups. An underlying but usually unstated assumption is that the groups represent levels of a qualitative variable. However, as mentioned earlier, it is possible to divide up scores on a quantitative variable into categories and to treat these groups as if they represented different levels of a nominal variable. For example, men could be classified as high or low on masculinity based on a median split of the scores on a masculinity test and as older or younger than average based on the distribution of ages. A 2 (masculinity) × 2 (age) factorial ANOVA could then be done of the subjects' use of swear words. This procedure has the advantage of simplicity but the disadvantage of failing to use all the information from the masculinity scores. It treats an interval-scale variable as if it were dichotomous, which is a misrepresentation of the underlying distribution. Moreover, two different studies might have different medians, which would make it impossible to directly compare the analyses based on median splits.

One-Way Analysis of Variance

Purpose: To draw inferences about differences in the means of two or more groups by testing the null hypothesis that the groups represent random samples from populations with the same means

Assumptions:

- The data are measured on an interval or ratio scale.
- The scores are randomly sampled.
- The distribution of the dependent measure is normal in the populations from which the data come.
- The populations have equal variances.

Formulas:

$$F = \frac{MS_B}{MS_W} = \frac{SS_B/(K-1)}{SS_W/(N-K)} \qquad SS_B = \Sigma \frac{T_j^2}{n_j} - \frac{T^2}{N} \qquad SS_W = \Sigma X^2 - \frac{\Sigma T_j^2}{n_j}$$

Significance: If F equals or exceeds the critical value in the F table with $K-1$ and $N-K$ degrees of freedom, the means are unlikely to represent random samples from the same population.

Other Related Procedures:

- Multiple independent-samples t-tests
- Factorial analysis of variance
- Repeated measures analysis of variance
- Multivariate analysis of variance
- Analysis of covariance
- Multiple regression

An alternative procedure would be to use the actual masculinity test scores and the actual ages as predictors of swear words via a multiple regression equation. Using special ways of coding, even nominal-level variables can be entered as predictors in a multiple regression equation (MRA); terms corresponding to the interactions from an ANOVA can also be used in the MRA. Thus, a multiple regression equation can be used to test the same hypotheses as an analysis of variance, and the analysis of variance procedure can even be viewed as a special case of multiple regression. However, since multiple regression equations are usually far more difficult to calculate, analysis of variance remains the more popular procedure.

CHAPTER SUMMARY

The *F*-distribution is a series of distributions, each based on a ratio of two variances, each with its own degrees of freedom. Although it can be used to test a research hypothesis about the variances of two populations, an *F*-test is most commonly used as the final step in a procedure called the analysis of variance (ANOVA). By comparing a variance estimate based on the differences between the means of several groups with one based only on differences in the scores within each group, a one-way ANOVA can test the null hypothesis that the scores of several groups come from populations with the same mean.

The *F*-distribution is closely related to the *t*-distribution and has the same assumptions; the value for *F* from a one-way ANOVA with two groups will be the square of the value for an independent-samples *t*-test computed on the same scores. However, unlike a *t*-test, a one-way ANOVA can compare more than two means at once.

The analysis of variance formula includes sums of squares, which are sums of squared deviations about means, and mean squares, which are variance estimates constructed by dividing sums of squares by their corresponding degrees of freedom. Results of an analysis of variance are usually presented in a summary table.

A nonsignificant *F* from an ANOVA leads to retention of the null hypothesis that the means of the populations from which the groups come are equal. If the *F*-value exceeds the critical value, you can conclude that the group means differ significantly, but you cannot conclude that any particular mean differs significantly from any other mean, unless there are only two groups being compared.

More complex analysis of variance designs include factorial ANOVA, which looks at the effects of more than one independent variable and at their interactions; repeated measures ANOVA, which considers a variable for which individuals have been measured several times; multivariate ANOVA, which can analyze scores on several dependent measures simultaneously; and analysis of covariance, which controls for scores on pre-existing variables called covariates.

Multiple-Choice Questions

1. Which of the following depends most closely upon the difference in the *means* of the groups?

   a. the sum of squares within

   b. the sum of squares between

   c. the mean square within

   d. the degrees of freedom within

   e. the critical value for F

2. You have done an analysis of variance on three groups of nature lovers, with means of 10 (group A), 9 (group B), and 1 (group C) plants in their house. The value for F was 12.99, with 2 and 86 degrees of freedom. Based on the above information, what can you conclude?

   a. Group A had more plants in their house than group B.

   b. Group A had more plants in their house than group C.

   c. Group B had more plants in their house than group C.

   d. The groups did not have equal numbers of plants in their houses.

   e. b, c, and d are all true.

   f. All of the above are true.

   g. None of the above is true.

3. In doing an analysis of variance, a sum of squares is equal to

   a. a direct estimate of variance

   b. a sum of squared raw scores

   c. a sum of squared deviation scores

   d. the standard deviation of the raw scores

   e. the ratio of the group differences to the variability of the average group

4. Ann has done a t-test comparing the mean scores of 14 men and 13 women on a clerical test and has found a value for t of -3.00. Harry did an analysis of variance on the same data. What did he find?

   a. $F = -9.00$ **b.** $F = -3.00$ **c.** $F = 1.732$ **d.** $F = 3.00$ **e.** $F = 9.00$

5. An F-test consists of

   a. a ratio of two variances   **b.** a ratio of two means

   c. a ratio of two standard deviations   **d.** a ratio of two proportions

   e. a ratio of two frequencies

6. You have done an analysis of variance comparing the mean numbers of sneezes per day during allergy season for people treated by medicine A, medicine B, or no medicine. Group A had a mean of 8 sneezes, group B had

a mean of 10 sneezes, and group C had a mean of 23 sneezes. The value for F was 1.82 with 2 and 66 degrees of freedom. Based on the above information, what can you conclude?

a. Group A sneezed less than Group B.

b. Group A sneezed less than Group C.

c. Group B sneezed less than Group C.

d. The groups did not have equal numbers of sneezes.

e. b, c, and d are all true.

f. All of the above are true.

g. None of the above is true.

7. You have done an analysis of variance of people's test scores comparing 2 groups with 14 people in each. Your computed value of F was 4.00. Which of the following do you know to be true?

a. The means differ significantly at the $p < .01$ level.

b. The means differ significantly at the $p < .05$ level.

c. Both a and b are true.

d. If you had done an independent-samples t-test instead of an analysis of variance, t would have been -2.00 or $+2.00$.

e. Both b and d are true.

f. You must have done the wrong test; an ANOVA cannot be used in these circumstances.

8. Arlene has computed an analysis of variance comparing the mean number of pets owned by random samples of Americans ($\overline{X} = 2.3$) and Canadians ($\overline{X} = 1.3$), $F(1340) = 12.30$, $p < .001$. What should she conclude?

a. Americans and Canadians differ significantly in the number of pets they own.

b. Americans own significantly more pets than Canadians.

c. Canadians own significantly fewer pets than Americans.

d. Both a and b are correct.

e. All of the above are correct.

f. None of the above, until she does a Tukey HSD or other comparison.

9. In computing an analysis of variance for four groups of 12 people each, you have found that the $SS_T = 20$, the $SS_B = 9$, and the $SS_W = 11$. What is the F for the analysis of variance?

a. .27   b. .82   c. .92   d. 1.64   e. 3.26   f. 12.00

g. none of the above

10. Under what circumstance(s) would it be incorrect to use a one-way analysis of variance?

a. when you wish to compare the mean scores of two independent groups

b. when you wish to compare the mean scores of three independent groups

c. when you wish to compare pretest and posttest scores of individuals

d. when you wish to compare the proportions of people in three states voting for each of seven political candidates

e. Using a one-way ANOVA in situations a, b, or d would be incorrect.

f. Using a one-way ANOVA in situations c and d would be incorrect.

Problems

11. Suppose that you are interested in knowing whether movies that are classified as comedies do better at the box office than action movies featuring danger and violence. Since you work in the box office of a large multiscreen theater, you can easily collect data on the number of tickets sold for each kind of movie. Over a period of several months, you count the average number of tickets sold per week for each film that could be classified as either a comedy or an adventure film. (To satisfy the assumption of independence of sampling, we'll assume that each person saw only one movie.) The data are as follows:

Film	Classification	Tickets Sold
The Three Stooges Meet Groucho	C	600
Rambo Meets Godzilla	A	1200
Rambo Meets God	A	1000
Forward to the Past	C	800
Dad for a Day	C	900
202 Dachshunds	C	1000
Vietnam Victory	A	1100
Sam Samson, Private Eye	A	1500

a. Perform an analysis of variance on the data to test the null hypothesis that action films and comedies lead to equal ticket sales.

b. Report your conclusions in a sentence.

c. Now perform an independent-samples t-test on the same data. What similarities and differences do you notice between it and the analysis of variance?

12. You have done an analysis of variance of people's test scores comparing 2 groups with 26 people in each. Your computed value of F was 4.41. Which of the following do you know to be true?

a. The means differ significantly at the $p < .05$ level.

b. The means differ significantly at the $p < .01$ level.

    c. Assuming that your computations are correct, if you were to construct a 95% confidence interval for the difference in the means, it would include zero.

    d. Assuming that your computations are correct, if you had done an independent-samples t-test instead of an analysis of variance, t would have been –2.10 or +2.10.

    e. You cannot assume that your computations are correct; in fact, you must have made an error in arithmetic.

    f. You must have done the wrong test; an ANOVA cannot be used in these circumstances.

13. Is it really true that people with graduate degrees in certain fields earn substantially less money than people with graduate degrees in certain other fields? To answer this question, you look at data collected by Yuppie University on the mean salaries earned by recent graduate and professional students:

Engineering Ph.D.	Humanities Ph.D.	Education Ph.D.	J.D.	M.D.
$40,000	$22,000	$25,000	$40,000	$50,000
$28,000	$24,000	$27,000	$35,000	$43,000
$32,000	$28,000	$31,000	$33,000	$33,000
$36,000	$24,000	$24,000	$36,000	$39,000
$30,000		$27,000	$38,000	$50,000
			$32,000	

    a. Perform an appropriate statistical test of the null hypothesis that the populations from which these five groups of people come do not differ in their mean annual incomes.

    b. Report your conclusions in an ANOVA summary table and in a sentence.

    c. Looking at the data, what hypothesis about the difference in means would you want to test next? In other words, which means look as if they differ from which other means?

14. You have completed a one-way analysis of variance with 5 subjects in each of 3 groups. SS_B was 12, and SS_W was 24. What was the value of F? Was it statistically significant?

15. Which is the appropriate analysis procedure in each of the following situations?

    a. You have one independent variable with two levels and an interval-scale dependent measure.

    b. You have manipulated two independent variables in an experiment and have assessed their effects on a ratio-scale dependent measure.

c. You want to know whether people can recognize more aircraft from silhouettes after a training program than they could before the program.

d. You want to know whether people who have been through psychotherapy show greater variability in their scores on an overall measure of self-concept than do people who have not been through psychotherapy.

e. You want to know whether the mean neuroticism score of 200 people who are taking a community college class in self-awareness is higher than the normative mean of 40 reported to be typical of adults in the community.

f. You want to know whether people sleep better when they have had warm milk just before going to bed, have been read a bedtime story just before retiring, were sung a lullaby just before bedtime, or had none of the preceding experiences.

16. Which of the following statements about the analysis of variance procedure are true?

a. An F-statistic is an estimate of a population variance.

b. The MS_T in a one-way ANOVA always equals $MS_B + MS_W$.

c. The df_T in a one-way ANOVA will always equal $df_W + df_B$

d. The larger the sample size, the more likely you are to reject the null hypothesis based on an analysis of variance when the groups are really random samples from the same population.

e. The MS_B in an analysis of variance based on the results of an experiment is your most direct measure of the effects of the experimental treatment.

f. The less the overlap in the scores of different treatment groups, the larger will be the F from the analysis of variance comparing them.

g. A significant F for an ANOVA of four groups means that the largest of the four means is significantly higher than the smallest of the four means.

17. I am interested in the ways in which people evaluate others who differ in body weight. As part of a study, I have 20 single, male undergraduate students read a brief paragraph describing a fictitious female undergraduate student. All students read the same paragraph, but they are randomly assigned to three conditions. In one condition the paragraph is accompanied by a photograph of a thin woman, in the second condition they see a photograph of a normal-weight woman, and in the third condition they see a photograph of an overweight woman. I then ask them to rate, on a scale from 0 to 10, where 0 means "not at all" and 10 means "extremely," how much they would like to work together with this woman on a task of evaluating some Academy Award winning movies. My research hypothesis is that the respondents will be least likely to want to work with the overweight woman. The data look like this, with the numbers reflecting the ratings of how much they wanted to work with the pictured woman.

Thin Photo	Normal Photo	Fat Photo
5	8	3
4	10	2
5	7	4
7	7	5
3	6	0
5	9	1
4	10	

a. Perform an analysis of variance on the findings.

b. Report your results in an analysis of variance summary table.

c. Now report your conclusions in a sentence. Do participants have different attitudes toward (ratings of) the three photographs?

18. Is it the case that children who have digital watches will have more trouble learning to tell time from a normal (analogue) clock than children who do not have digital watches? To test this hypothesis, you give inexpensive digital watches to a random half of the children in your kindergarten class. Three months later, you teach a unit on telling time by reading an analogue clock and measure their score on a test. The data look like this:

	Digital Watch	Test Score
Donny	Yes	3
Davey	Yes	4
Darla	Yes	5
Demetra	Yes	6
Nancy	No	5
Norman	No	6
Nora	No	7
Nolan	No	8
Nicky	No	9

a. Perform an analysis of variance on the results.

b. Report your results in an analysis of variance summary table.

c. Report your conclusions in a sentence. Is there a difference in the test scores for children who were and were not given a digital watch?

d. Now perform an independent-samples t-test on the same data.

e. Report your conclusions in a sentence.

f. What similarities do you see between the analysis of variance and the independent-samples t-test?

19. You are interested in knowing whether people who have medical insurance use the emergency room more or less than people without medical insurance. You sample people in line to get driver's licenses in New Mexico, a state in which over 25% of the population have no medical insurance, and ask them how many visits to the emergency room they have made in the last 3 years. The data are as follows:

Insured	No Insurance
0	4
0	5
1	2
2	0
1	6
0	
0	
0	

a. Do your data meet the assumptions for performing a one-way analysis of variance?

b. Go ahead and perform an analysis of variance on these data.

c. Report your results in an analysis of variance summary table.

d. What conclusions can you reach from the above data?

20. You have heard that ginger might be effective in reducing motion sickness. To test this, you randomly assign three groups of people planning a cruise to either use a patch containing medicine, eat 15 gingersnap cookies daily, or do nothing special to prevent motion sickness. You have 10 people in each group, and each person rates his average queasiness on a scale from 1 (normal) to 7 (miserably seasick). After a few sums have been calculated, the data look like this:

Patch group (X_1): $\Sigma X_1 = 20$, $\Sigma X_1^2 = 60$

Ginger group (X_2): $\Sigma X_2 = 30$, $\Sigma X_2^2 = 150$

Control group (X_3): $\Sigma X_3 = 50$, $\Sigma X_3^2 = 340$

a. Perform an analysis of variance on the data.

b. Report your results in an analysis of variance summary table.

c. Report your conclusions in a sentence.

d. Can you conclude anything about the effect of eating gingersnap cookies on seasickness from these data?

Study Questions

1. Think about the difference between the central tendency of a group of scores and its variability. More specifically, first try to formulate a hypothesis about a difference in means of the scores of certain groups on some dependent variable. Then try to construct a hypothesis concerning differences in variability of scores on some related variable. For example, you could hypothesize that the mean head circumference of two-year-old children fed adequate diets would be greater than the mean head circumference of two-year-old children raised during a time of famine. You might also hypothesize that the variance in weight of children raised in circumstances in which only a small variety of foods is available would be less than the variance in weight of children raised in a place in which a huge variety of foods ranging from low calorie to high fat is available. Even though both of these hypotheses would be tested by an *F*-test, one of them would use the *F*-test as part of an analysis of variance and the other would use it to directly compare two sample variances. Which is which? Answer the same question for the hypotheses you generated.

2. Yet again (!), head for the library and look at some of the recent issues of journals in your field. Look for articles that use some type of analysis of variance. Keep a list of how many used a one-way ANOVA, how many used factorial ANOVAs, how many used repeated measures ANOVAs, and how many used other designs. Look at the summary tables from those analyses. (Not all may report them, but most will.) Can you figure out from the summary table what the different sources represent? You may have to read the description of the methods to understand the different treatments, conditions, or groups. Can you figure out which of the effects were statistically significant?

3. How is it that an analysis of *variance* can lead to conclusions about differences in *means*? One explanation is that the variance in sample means is an estimate of how different they are from each other. If they all came from the same population, the means of all the samples would be very close to each other and the population means would be identical (by definition), leading to a σ^2 of zero and an s^2 reflecting only sampling error. To help yourself see how an analysis of variance works, try fiddling with some very simple numbers. Make some changes in the scores and see how they affect the different sums of squares in an analysis of variance. For instance, start with two groups of scores: 3, 3, 4 in the first group and 6, 6, 7 in the second. Perform an analysis of variance on them. Now subtract one point from every score in group 1 and add one point to each score in group 2. Will this change the difference in the means of the two groups? If so, you should see this reflected in the sum of squares between (and later in the MS_B and *F*). Will this change the variance within either of the two groups? If not, the within-groups sum of squares shouldn't change. Repeat the analysis of variance with these new numbers and see if your predictions hold. Now make another change, one which you think should change the variance within groups but not between groups.

[*Hint:* Try subtracting 1 from the smallest score within each group and adding 1 to the largest score within each group. This should change the group variance but not the mean—or should it?] See if you can predict the effect of other changes you might make in the numbers and test your predictions by carrying out an analysis of variance for each one.

4. Sometimes, one of the hardest things for a beginning researcher to do is to describe your findings accurately in a sentence, so that both a statistically sophisticated authority like yourself and a reluctant reader like your friend who has so far avoided taking statistics can understand what was found. Try to think of several (say, five or so) examples of situations in which you might use an analysis of variance. For each one, imagine that you actually carried out such an analysis and did or did not find significant results. Then write out a sentence that you might use to describe your findings. If you are forced to conclude that the groups differ but are unable to say which means differ from which other means, then try to state one or more research hypotheses about which means seem to be, or theoretically should be, larger or smaller than which other means. In the next chapter, you will learn how to test such hypotheses by performing the type of procedure called a contrast or comparison.

Comparisons Among Means

What Is a Comparison?

Many, perhaps most, behavioral research studies involve some kind of hypothesis about differences between means. Do men talk more than women? Do people who are under stress stammer more than people who are relaxed? Do people who are diagnosed as visually impaired score higher or lower on measures of vocabulary than people with normal vision? Is there a difference between people living in urban, suburban, or rural areas in the amount of time they spend watching television? Differences in means are such an important topic in statistics that much of the last three chapters has focused upon them.

Ways of Testing Differences in Means

Chapter 7 mentioned the z-test, which can be used to compare the means of one or two groups to some hypothetical value when the standard deviation in the population is known. Chapter 9 discussed the various types of t-tests, which can be used to compare one mean with a hypothetical value or two means with each other and to come to some conclusions about whether or not one mean is significantly larger than another. Chapter 10 revealed that the analysis of variance technique can be used to test the null hypothesis that all the means being compared are random samples from the same population (or from populations with identical means). This chapter will discuss an additional type of procedure that can be used to examine differences in means: the **comparison**, or contrast.

In all of the procedures described in the previous chapters—that is, the z-test, t-test, and analysis of variance—a small value of z, t, or F (the test statistic) requires the researcher to continue to entertain the possibility that the null hypothesis may be true. When there are only two means being compared, a large enough test statistic permits the researcher to reject the null hypothesis and to conclude that the larger mean is statistically significantly larger than the smaller mean. (Of course, if the null hypothesis is true, your chance of being incorrect in rejecting it is equal to your alpha level.) However, if there are more than two means being compared in an analysis of variance, a significant value of F does not allow the researcher to conclude that any particular mean is significantly larger or smaller than any particular other mean. In order to come to such a conclusion, it is necessary to perform a comparison or contrast.

Advantages of a Comparison

Can Compare Sets of Means.   A comparison or contrast is a procedure that allows the researcher to test a particular hypothesis about how different means compare with each other. Unlike the t-test, which can compare at most two means, some comparison procedures can compare an entire group or set of means with another mean or set of means. This ability to compare combinations of means with other means can be a definite advantage, making it possible to test specific hypotheses that could not be directly tested by a t-test or the overall F from an analysis of variance.

In other words, it is possible to do either pairwise comparisons (which compare only two means at a time) or nonpairwise comparisons (which compare more than two means at a time), depending on the type of comparison procedure you select. Clearly, there are instances in which a nonpairwise comparison would be the most direct and appropriate way to test a particular hypothesis.

EXAMPLE

Nonpairwise Comparisons. It would be possible to do a comparison testing the hypothesis that the mean score of students attending the three schools that use a particular bilingual curriculum would be higher than the mean score of students at the four schools that use a second bilingual curriculum, and that the mean score of students at these four schools would be higher than the mean score of students at an eighth school that has only a monolingual curriculum. Or you could compare the mean scores of the three groups of girls in your study with the scores of the three groups of boys, in order to assess sex differences.   ■

More Efficient Than Multiple t-Tests.   Someone who already knows how to perform t-tests and who doesn't want to learn another statistical technique might decide that it should be possible to compare means with each other by doing a lot of t-tests. For example, if you predict that the mean for group 1 will be higher than the means for groups 2 through 5, you might compare the mean of group 1 versus group 2, group 1 versus group 3, group 1 versus group 4, and group 1 versus group 5. Of course, if you wanted to add to this hypothesis the prediction that group 2 would be the second highest, you would also have to compare group 2 with group 3, with group 4, and with group 5. In contrast, a comparison permits you to test a hypothesis about several means by carrying out only one procedure. Even if you love doing analyses, you can see that doing one contrast is more efficient than doing multiple t-tests to test the same hypothesis.

Uses a Pooled Estimate of Variance.   Using a comparison provides another advantage over the use of multiple t-tests. If you were to do the eight t-tests listed previously, each one would have a somewhat different denominator, depending on the two groups that you were comparing. If the homogeneity of variance hypothesis (that all the group means reflect random sampling from populations with equal variances) is true, then each of these denominators is an estimate of the same error term from this population, the standard error of the difference between the means or the within-groups variance (or mean square or error). The formula for the within-groups error term used in the analysis of variance procedure will be a more accurate estimate of the variability in the population than the denominator of any single t-test, because it is based on the scores of all the groups, not just the two that are being compared in any particular t-test. A comparison uses the error term from the analysis of variance, the mean square within. Such an estimate of variance, which is based on all of the groups, is a **pooled estimate of variance**, and it provides a more accurate test than a t-test if the assumption of homogeneity of variance is true.

Controls the Overall Alpha Level.   A fourth advantage of the use of a comparison, as compared to multiple t-tests, is that it keeps the overall significance level at alpha. If you were to perform eight t-tests, each one at the .05 α-level, your chance of finding one significant result would be greater than .05, since you can expect to find a statistically significant result for any one of the eight tests about .05 of the time when the null hypothesis is true. With a contrast or comparison, you can perform only one significance test, which will be approximately the equivalent of several t-tests, thus keeping your overall alpha level at .05 or whatever you choose (Hancock & Klockars, 1996).

A Priori Versus Post Hoc Comparisons

A contrast can be constructed to test any hypothesis that you formulate about group means. An *a priori hypothesis* is formulated prior to gathering the data; a research hypothesis is an a priori hypothesis. If you are interested in testing a hypothesis based on theory and/or previous research, rather than on the data actually collected, then an **a priori comparison**, or contrast, that corresponds to your research hypothesis can be computed.

TIP

> Another term for *a priori comparison* is *planned comparison* or *planned contrast*.

Almost all basic research, and much applied research as well, involves the formulation and testing of a priori research hypotheses. However, not all statistical procedures involve the use of a priori tests. Frequently, a researcher wishes to investigate a difference between means that was not formally predicted but that looks relatively large when the data are examined. Such a procedure is an a posteriori or **post hoc comparison**; it is also known by the descriptive term "data snooping."

The difference between an a priori and an a posteriori comparison is not in the computation of the test statistic but in the critical value against which it is compared. Because a less stringent critical value is used when an a priori hypothesis is tested, it might appear that your chances of finding an a priori hypothesis significant are greater than your chances of finding a post hoc hypothesis significant. This would be true if you were to do the same exact test; an a priori test of a particular comparison is more powerful than a post hoc test of the same comparison. However, when an a posteriori test is computed, the critical value takes into account the fact that you could be performing any or all possible comparisons and holds the chance that any one of them would be considered statistically significant at alpha if the null hypothesis is true.

For example, consider the situation in which there are six means. If a researcher predicts that mean 2 will be the highest and mean 5 the lowest of the six, this pattern of results would be a relatively unlikely finding if the null hypothesis were true. If, after the data are collected, a researcher wants to test the hypothesis that the mean that happened to be the highest (e.g., mean 2) is significantly higher than the other means and that the mean that happened to be the lowest (e.g., mean 5) is significantly lower than the other means, the post hoc procedure takes into account the fact that the pattern of having *some* mean higher and *some* mean lower than the others is much more likely than the pattern of having *a particular* mean highest and *a particular* mean lowest.

In short, planned comparisons (a priori contrasts) have two advantages over post hoc comparisons: They require you to think about your data in advance, and they are more powerful tests of particular hypotheses. On the other hand, post hoc comparisons can be used when you have no a priori hypotheses or when you discover patterns in your data that you had not anticipated.

Relationship to ANOVA. An a priori comparison may be performed instead of (or in addition to) an analysis of variance. If the only hypothesis that you wish to test is a comparison of certain means with certain others, it is not necessary to do an analysis of variance (Hancock & Klockars, 1996). Performing only an a priori contrast is perfectly acceptable, although not the usual procedure. On the other hand, a post hoc comparison is ordinarily performed only after an analysis of variance has resulted in a significant value for F. If the analysis of variance does not lead to rejection of the null hypothesis, then it is not correct to perform any post hoc contrasts, no matter how alluring they might be.

Weights

A comparison or contrast is sometimes defined as a weighted set of means or as the weights assigned to the means. The weights or coefficients that constitute a comparison are a direct reflection of the hypothesis that is being tested. If two means are hypothesized to have the same value, then they must be given the same weights. If one mean is hypothesized to be larger than another, then the first mean must have a larger weight assigned to it than the second one.

The weights themselves, like the hypotheses that they represent, can be based either on theory or on the actual data. If they were formulated based on theory and previous research, then they reflect an a priori hypothesis; if they were formulated after looking at the data, then they reflect data snooping.

Selection of Weights. Several points should be kept in mind when selecting weights to test a particular hypothesis.

1. The weights that constitute a comparison *must* sum to zero. That is the only constraint put on the weights, but it is an absolute one. It implies, of course, that some of the weights must be positive and some must be negative.

2. Every mean must have a weight, but the weight can equal zero. A weight of zero effectively means that the particular mean does not figure into the hypothesis (and, since it is multiplied by zero, will not enter into the equation for the comparison).

3. As stated previously, larger weights should represent larger hypothesized values, smaller weights should stand for smaller values, and equal weights should represent equal hypothesized values.

4. There are two alternative rules of thumb that people use in selecting their weights:

- Some researchers prefer to have all of the negative weights sum to -1 and all of the positive weights sum to $+1$. If you use this approach, you will find it easy to be sure that the coefficients add up to zero. However, you will have to use fractions as your weights, unless there are only two groups in a particular contrast.
- The other approach, which I prefer, is to use small whole numbers to represent the weights. For example, if you wanted to test the hypoth-

esis that the means of groups A, B, and C would be higher than the means of groups D and E, you would assign weights of +2, +2, +2, –3, and –3 to groups A through E, respectively.

TIP ▰▰▰

> Using the fractional approach, the corresponding weights would be +1/3, +1/3, +1/3, –1/2, and –1/2.

5. Multiplying (or dividing) every weight by the same value does not change the meaning of the comparison. Thus, by multiplying each term in the +2, +2, +2, –3, and –3 comparison by 1/6, we end up with the +1/3, +1/3, +1/3, –1/2, and –1/2 comparison that is exactly equivalent to it. Since a comparison of +4, +2, and –6 is identical to a comparison of +2, +1, and –3, there is no reason not to use the smaller numbers, which will make the computations simpler.

6. A final thing to keep in mind when choosing weights for a comparison is that the coefficients for a comparison involving only two means (i.e., a pairwise comparison) are always –1 for the mean hypothesized to be the smaller and +1 for the (presumably) larger mean.

TIP ▰▰▰

> If there are only two groups in the research study, then the formula for such a comparison will reduce to the formula for an analysis of variance for the two groups and the conclusion from such a single pairwise comparison will be the same as the conclusion from an analysis of variance or from an independent-samples *t*-test.

What Is the Scheffé Comparison Procedure?

A Scheffé post hoc comparison is a post hoc procedure for testing any hypothesis about differences in means after an analysis of variance has led to the conclusion that the means are unlikely to represent random samples from the same population. In other words, it is used to test a specific research hypothesis after the overall null hypothesis has already been rejected. In order to perform a Scheffé comparison, the following procedures are necessary.

- Decide on the weights that match your hypotheses.
- Compute the means for each group.
- Know the sample size for each group.
- Compute the mean square within term from the analysis of variance.

TIP ▬▬▬▬▬▬▬▬▬▬▬▬▬▬▬▬▬▬▬▬▬▬▬▬

Of course, both the individual n's and the MS_W will have already been computed as part of the analysis of variance.

- Substitute these numbers into a formula.
- Compare the resulting value with the appropriate critical value.

If the F value for the comparison is significant, you have evidence in favor of the hypothesis that led to the selection of the coefficients. A finding that the comparison is not significant suggests that the research hypothesis is unlikely to be correct.

TIP ▬▬▬▬▬▬▬▬▬▬▬▬▬▬▬▬▬▬▬▬▬▬▬▬

Although, strictly speaking, a Scheffé comparison is a post hoc procedure, the exact same formula and computations are used to test the significance of an a priori comparison. The difference between the two procedures lies in the critical value with which they are compared.

Formulas

Formula for F.   The most useful one-step formula for a comparison is

$$F_C = \frac{(\Sigma C_j \overline{X}_j)^2}{(MS_W)\left(\Sigma \dfrac{C_j^2}{n_j}\right)}$$

In this formula, the term C_j stands for the coefficient used for any group and the $\overline{X}_j$ stands for the mean of the corresponding group. Using words, rather than symbols, this equation says to perform the following steps.

Step 1: Select the weights for each mean and multiply each mean by its corresponding coefficient.

Step 2: Sum these K products.

Step 3: Square this sum to get the numerator of the equation.

Step 4: For each of the K groups, square the coefficient or weight.

Step 5: Divide the squared coefficient by the number of scores in the group.

Step 6: Sum these K quotients.

Step 7: Multiply this sum by the mean square within calculated from the analysis of variance.

Step 8: Divide the squared sum of the cross products from step 3 (i.e., the numerator) by the product calculated in step 7 (i.e., the denominator). This quotient is your F for the comparison.

Alternative Formulas. For those who like to see the source of this one-step formula, it can be broken down into three steps.

1. A sum of squares for the comparison, SS_C, is computed by using the formula

$$SS_C = \frac{(\Sigma C_j \overline{X}_j)^2}{\Sigma \dfrac{C_j^2}{n_j}}$$

In other words, the sum of squares for the comparison equals the squared sum of the products of the weights and their corresponding means divided by the sum of the squares of the weights divided by their corresponding sample sizes. This sum of squares, like the sum of squares for any comparison, has 1 degree of freedom.

2. Compute the mean square for the comparison, MS_C, which is $SS_C/1$, which equals SS_C. (A comparison has 1 degree of freedom.)

3. Compute the F for the comparison, F_C. Like any other F, F_C is a ratio of two variances or mean squares, specifically the MS_C/MS_W, which is the same formula given earlier:

$$F_C = \frac{(\Sigma C_j \overline{X}_j)^2}{(MS_W)\left(\Sigma \dfrac{C_j^2}{n_j} \right)}$$

TIP

There is also a formula for an a priori comparison that yields a value for t rather than F. It equals the square root of the formula for F_C given and is compared with a critical value for t, rather than F.

Computing the Critical Value

Critical Value for a Post Hoc Comparison. Unlike the other tests that we have considered, the Scheffé post hoc comparison does not have a critical value that can be directly copied from a table. Instead, the critical value has to be computed, by using both the F-table and the number of groups in the analysis of variance, symbolized by K. The formula for the critical value for a Scheffé post hoc comparison is

$$F_C = (K-1)[F_a(K-1, N-K)]$$

The following steps are necessary in order to compute the critical value for a post hoc Scheffé contrast.

Step 1: Look up the critical value for F at the desired alpha level with $K-1$ and $N-K$ degrees of freedom. Remember that K equals the number of groups in the *study*, which might be more than the number of groups having weights not equal to zero in the *comparison*.

TIP

> The value in step 1 is the same value used as the critical value for F in the analysis of variance.

Step 2: Subtract 1 from K.

Step 3: Multiply this difference by the critical value in step 1.

EXAMPLE

Suppose you had three groups and 83 scores in your research study. What is the critical value for a post hoc Scheffé comparison if $K-1 = 2$ and $N-K = 80$?

Solution: From Appendix Table 6 you can see that the critical value for $F(2, 80) = 3.11$ at the .05 α-level and 4.88 at the .01 α-level. The critical values for the Scheffé comparison are therefore (2)(3.11) or 6.22 at the .05 level and (2)(4.88) or 9.76 at the .01 level.

As you can see, the critical values in this example are quite a bit larger than the corresponding values from the analysis of variance; $K-1$ times as large, in fact. These values are large enough so that the chance of finding one or more significant comparisons is kept at .05 (or whatever α level you select), even if every possible comparison is tested.   ■

TIP

> Of course, you would really test only the ones that look the most likely to lead to statistical significance, but the Scheffé procedure is conservative enough to permit you to test any and all hypotheses that you wish while still holding your chance of making a Type I error at alpha (Hancock & Klockars, 1996).

Critical Value for an a Priori Comparison. The critical value for an a priori comparison is equal to the critical value for F with 1 and $N - K$ degrees of freedom. More formally,

$$F_C = F_\alpha(1, N - K)$$

Thus, for the situation in the preceding example where $K = 3$ and $N = 83$, the critical values would be 3.96 at the .05α-level and 6.96 at the .01 α-level.

TIP

> Note that these values are substantially smaller than the corresponding critical values for a post hoc comparison, reflecting the decreased likelihood that you are capitalizing on chance when you are testing only one a priori comparison (or a few), rather than simply picking out the largest apparent difference in means, as is done with a post hoc test. However, this critical value is slightly larger than the critical value for the overall test from the analysis of variance, since it has only 1 rather than $K - 1$ degrees of freedom in the numerator.

Degrees of Freedom. As was stated earlier in the discussion of the formulas for a comparison, each comparison has 1 degree of freedom, and the F-test for a comparison has 1 and $N - K$ degrees of freedom. This is true for both a priori and post hoc comparisons. With an a priori comparison, it is easy to remember the degrees of freedom, as they match up perfectly with the critical value from the F-table.

TIP

> Keep in mind that the F for a post hoc comparison also is reported as having 1 and $N - K$ degrees of freedom, even though the critical value is computed by multiplying the critical value for F with $K - 1$ and $N - K$ degrees of freedom by $K - 1$.

Examples of Scheffé Comparisons

As an example of the use of a Scheffé comparison, let's reconsider the example of 3 groups of dentists, each with 3 subjects, from the previous chapter.

EXAMPLE

Dentists and Leisure. The analysis of variance in Chapter 10 revealed that the MS_B was 27.00, the MS_W was 1.00, and $F(2, 6) = 27.00$, $p < .001$. The mean of the three scores in group 1 was 2.00; the mean for group 2 was 5.00; and the mean for group 3 was 8.00. Remember that the dependent measure was the number of hours of leisure that a person had per week and that group 1 comprised novice female dentists (those practicing for fewer than ten years), group 2 consisted of novice male dentists, and group 3 consisted of experienced male dentists (those with more than 20 years of experience). Because so few women went through dental school prior to 20 years ago, it was not possible to obtain a sample of experienced women dentists for the study. Suppose that you had an a priori hypothesis that the mean number of hours of free time would be greater for male than for female dentists, due to the fact that male dentists would have fewer domestic responsibilities to add to their professional hours. The corresponding coefficients for that hypothesis would be –2, +1, and +1 for groups 1, 2, and 3.

Solution: In order to test this hypothesis, you would substitute into the formula:

$$F = \frac{(\Sigma C_j \overline{X}_j)^2}{(MS_W)\left(\Sigma \dfrac{C_j^2}{n_j}\right)}$$

$$= \frac{\left[((-2)(2)) + ((1)(5)) + ((1)(8))\right]^2}{(1.00)\left(\dfrac{(-2)^2}{3} + \dfrac{1^2}{3} + \dfrac{1^2}{3}\right)} = \frac{(-4 + 5 + 8)^2}{(1)\left(\dfrac{4}{3} + \dfrac{1}{3} + \dfrac{1}{3}\right)}$$

$$= \frac{9^2}{2} = \frac{81}{2} = 40.50$$

The critical value at the .01 α-level for this a priori hypothesis would be $F_{.01}(1, 6) = 13.74$. Since the test statistic far exceeds this critical value, we would conclude (in APA style) that "the two groups of male dentists had significantly more leisure hours per week than did the female dentists, $F(1, 6) = 40.50, p < .01$."

Suppose that we decided to look further at our data and, after a bit of snooping, decided that the pattern of the means suggested that the more experienced dentists seemed to have more leisure time than the less experienced dentists. We could test the significance of this difference by a Scheffé post hoc comparison. The weights for this comparison would be –1, –1, and +2, and F would be

$$F = \frac{\left[((-1)(2)) + ((-1)(5)) + ((2)(8))\right]^2}{(1.00)\left(\dfrac{(-1)^2}{3} + \dfrac{(-1)^2}{3} + \dfrac{2^2}{3}\right)} = \frac{(-2 + (-5) + 16)^2}{(1)\left(\dfrac{1}{3} + \dfrac{1}{3} + \dfrac{4}{3}\right)}$$

$$= \frac{9^2}{2} = 40.50$$

as was true for the a priori comparison. The fact that these values are identical is only a coincidence—due to the fact that the three means were equally spaced and that the three n's were the same. Usually, two comparisons will lead to different values for F.

Because this comparison is post hoc, it is necessary to compute the critical value with which to compare it. For an F-test with $K = 3$ and $N = 9$, the critical value at the $p < .01$ α-level is $F_{.01}(2, 6) = 10.925$; the critical value at the .001 α-level is 27.000. Multiplying these by 2 (i.e., by $K - 1$), we get 21.850 and 54.000 as the critical values at the .01 and .001 levels, respectively, for the Scheffé post hoc comparison. Since the actual value for the comparison exceeded the .01 critical value, we would reject the null hypothesis and conclude that a Scheffé post hoc comparison revealed (in APA style) that "the mean number of leisure hours for the more experienced dentists was significantly higher than the mean number of leisure hours reported by the two groups of less experienced dentists, $F(1, 6) = 40.50$, $p < .01$."

Note that the number of degrees of freedom for the post hoc comparison is the same as the number of degrees of freedom for the a priori comparison; only the critical value is different.   ▪

As another example of a Scheffé comparison, we can consider the study dealing with the effects of labels on the perceptions of people with handicaps, as described in the previous chapter.

EXAMPLE

Effects of Labels. The sums, means, and sample sizes for the four groups of people who read a vignette about a person who was labeled a "cripple" (C), a "handicapped person" (HP), a "person who has a disability" (PWHD), and a "person who uses a wheelchair" (PWUW) are presented in the following table:

	C	HP	PWHD	PWUW
Σ	110	169	260	291
$\overline{X}$	7.33	11.27	17.33	19.40
n	15	15	15	15
$MS_W = 10.06$				

The first comparison that we would want to perform is one to test the hypothesis that the two groups who read the labels with "person who" in the label (*PWHD* and *PWUW*) will evaluate the protagonist more positively than the two groups reading the other two labels (*C* and *HP*).

Solution: Since this hypothesis was formulated prior to gathering the data, it is appropriate to test it by an a priori comparison. The critical value for such a comparison would be the critical value for F with 1 and 56 degrees of freedom, since 56 is the degrees of freedom for the MS_W from the analysis of variance. Looking at Appendix Table 6, we see that the critical values are 4.034, 7.171, and 12.222, respectively, for the .05, .01, and .001 α-levels for 1 and 50 degrees of freedom.

Before using the formula, we need to decide on the weights for the comparison. Based on the hypothesis, the weights would be −1, −1, +1, and +1, which sum to zero, as they should.

- We use the formula for a comparison:

$$F = \frac{\left(\Sigma C_j \overline{X}_j\right)^2}{(MS_W)\left(\Sigma \dfrac{C_j^2}{n_j}\right)}$$

- Substituting, we get

$$F = \frac{\left[((-1)(7.33)) + ((-1)(11.27)) + ((1)(17.33)) + ((1)(19.40))\right]^2}{(10.06)\left(\dfrac{(-1)^2}{15} + \dfrac{(-1)^2}{15} + \dfrac{(1)^2}{15} + \dfrac{(1)^2}{15}\right)}$$

- The numerator of the formula becomes 18.13^2, or 328.697.
- The denominator becomes

$$(10.06)(.067 + .067 + .067 + .067) = (10.06)(.267) = 2.683$$

- Finally, we have

$$F = \frac{328.697}{2.683} = 122.51$$

What can we conclude? Since this F far exceeds the critical value for an a priori comparison, we can conclude (in APA style) that, as predicted, "the two descriptions that labeled the protagonist as 'a person who' has certain characteristics led to more positive evaluations than did the descriptions that labeled the protagonist as a cripple or a handicapped person, $F(1, 56) = 122.51$, $p < .001$."

Since no other a priori hypotheses were formulated, this is the only a priori comparison that can legitimately be done on the data. However, looking at the responses may make us want to do a little data snooping and make a post hoc comparison. For instance, it looks as if the label "cripple" led to far more negative evaluations than did the other three labels. To test this hypothesis, we could do the relevant contrast, for which the appropriate weights would be −3, +1, +1, and +1.

- Substituting into the formula, we would get

$$F = \frac{[(-3)((7.33) + (1)(11.27) + (1)(17.33) + (1)(19.40))]^2}{(10.06)\left(\dfrac{(-3)^2}{15} + \dfrac{(1)^2}{15} + \dfrac{(1)^2}{15} + \dfrac{(1)^2}{15}\right)}$$

- As a next step, we get

$$F = \frac{(-21.99 + 11.27 + 17.33 + 19.40)^2}{(10.06)\left(\dfrac{9}{15} + \dfrac{1}{15} + \dfrac{1}{15} + \dfrac{1}{15}\right)}$$

- Next, we get

$$F = \frac{26.01^2}{(10.06)(.600 + .067 + .067 + .067)} = \frac{676.52}{(10.06)(.801)} = \frac{676.52}{8.06}$$

$$= 83.95$$

To know whether or not this value for F is statistically significant, we have to compute the appropriate critical value. To do so, we must multiply the critical values for $F(3, 56)$ by $K - 1$ or 3. From Appendix Table 6, we can see that the critical value at the .001 α-level for $F(3, 50) = 6.336$. Multiplying $(6.336)(3) = 19.01$, which is far less than our computed value for the F for the contrast. Therefore, we can say (in APA style) that "a Scheffé post hoc contrast indicated that the people who read the term 'cripple' evaluated the protagonist more negatively than the people who read a vignette using some other label, $F(1, 56) = 83.95$, $p < .001$." Other post hoc comparisons could also be calculated and compared to the same post hoc critical value.   ■

Orthogonality

Up until this point, we have been discussing comparisons one at a time. When you are data snooping, because of the stringent critical value used in the Scheffé post hoc procedure, it doesn't matter if you test only one comparison or as many as your inspiration and patience can generate. However, when you are testing a priori comparisons, the situation is not so clear. All researchers, as far as I am aware, feel that it is appropriate to test a single a priori comparison by using the a priori critical value. All, or almost all, researchers would probably feel that it is not appropriate to test an infinite number of comparisons with the a priori critical value. However, what to do when there are a limited number of comparisons that were indeed formulated before the data were gathered is not always obvious. Some researchers feel that, as long as a hypothesis was truly formulated before the data are gathered, it is appropriate to test it by the a priori criterion. Others feel that the a priori critical value should be used only when the researcher is testing a single hypothesis or a set of hypotheses that possess the property of orthogonality.

Orthogonality, which means independence, is a property of a relationship between comparisons rather than of a single comparison. Two comparisons are **orthogonal** to each other when they account for non-overlapping portions of the variation among the K means (Hancock & Klockars, 1996). More specifically, two comparisons are orthogonal to each other if the sum of the cross products for the corresponding coefficients of the two contrasts is zero. In other words, if the weight given to the first mean in the first contrast is multiplied by the weight given to the first mean in the second contrast, and this product is added to the product of the weights given to the second mean in the two contrasts, which sum in turn is added to the products of the coefficients associated with the subsequent means, the contrasts will be orthogonal if and only if this sum is equal to zero.

The formula for two orthogonal contrasts is, therefore

$$\Sigma C_{j1} C_{j2} = 0$$

where C_{j1} is equal to the coefficient given to mean j in the first contrast and C_{j2} is equal to the weight given to mean j in the second contrast. To use this formula to determine whether or not two contrasts are orthogonal, you need to perform the following steps.

Step 1: Multiply the weight given to the mean of the first group in the first contrast by the weight given to the first mean in the second contrast.

Step 2: Multiply the weight given to the mean of the second group in the first contrast by the weight given to the second mean in the second contrast.

Step 3: Repeat this process for each of the groups.

Step 4: Sum these products. If the sum equals zero, the contrasts are orthogonal; if it does not, they are not independent.

TIP ▬▬▬▬▬▬▬▬▬▬▬▬▬▬▬▬▬▬▬▬▬▬▬▬▬▬▬▬▬▬▬▬

Remember that you are multiplying the coefficients, not the group means. You do not need to have any actual data in order to decide whether or not two comparisons are orthogonal. Also remember that if either comparison assigns a coefficient of zero to a group mean, then the product of the weights for that mean will be zero. Finally, remember that this formula applies to only two comparisons at a time. If you want to know if several comparisons are orthogonal to each other, you have to check them pair by pair.

EXAMPLE

We can consider the a priori comparison calculated earlier for the labeling study, in which the weights were –1, –1, +1, and +1. Is this comparison orthogonal to a comparison testing the hypothesis that the C condition has a lower mean than the *HP* condition, which would have the weights –1, +1, 0, and 0?

Solution: To find out, we need to multiply the corresponding coefficients and sum the products. Doing so, we get

$$[(-1)(-1)] + [(-1)(+1)] + [(+1)(0)] + [(+1)(0)] = +1 + (-1) = 0$$

Therefore, we can conclude that the two comparisons are orthogonal. ■

Suppose we had wanted to know whether the a priori comparison in this example was orthogonal to the post hoc comparison we tested, which had coefficients –3, +1, +1, and +1? Multiplying the coefficients and summing them would give

$$(-1)(-3) + (-1)(+1) + (+1)(+1) + (+1)(+1) = +3 - 1 + 1 + 1 = 4$$

Since this sum does not equal zero, these two comparisons would not be orthogonal.

EXAMPLE

Suppose that you have one comparison with weights for groups 1 through 4 of –1, –1, +1, and +1. Let's call this contrast Q. Which of the following comparisons is orthogonal to it?

A:	–3	+1	+1	+1
B:	–1	+1	–1	+1
C:	–2	–1	+1	+2

Solution: To check whether comparison A is orthogonal to our original comparison Q, we would take

$$[(-3)(-1)] + [(+1)(-1)] + [(+1)(+1)] + [(+1)(+1)] = 3 - 1 + 1 + 1 = 4$$

Since the sum of the cross products is 4, not zero, these comparisons are not orthogonal.

Next, we can try comparison B:

$$[(-1)(-1)] + [(+1)(-1)] + [(-1)(+1)] + [(+1)(+1)] = 1 - 1 - 1 + 1 = 0$$

Since the sum of the cross products equaled zero, comparison Q and comparison B are orthogonal.

Finally, let's check comparison C:

$$[(-2)(-1)] + [(-1)(-1)] + [(+1)(+1)] + [(+2)(+1)] = 2 + 1 + 1 + 2 = 6$$

Comparison C is not orthogonal to comparison Q.   ■

Relationship to the Sum of Squares Between.   Although it is possible to formulate a large number of comparisons when the number of groups is large, there is only a limited number of comparisons that would be orthogonal to each other. If there are K groups, then $K - 1$ comparisons can be found to be orthogonal to each other. An entire set of comparisons is orthogonal only if each comparison is orthogonal to each other comparison. There may be many sets of orthogonal comparisons, but there will be no more than $K - 1$ orthogonal comparisons within each set.

EXAMPLE   ▬▬▬▬▬▬▬▬▬▬▬▬▬▬▬▬▬▬▬▬▬▬▬▬▬▬▬▬▬▬▬▬▬▬▬▬▬▬▬

A third comparison that is orthogonal to comparison Q (and comparison B) in the previous example is –1, +1, +1, and –1. To check that this comparison (which we can call Z) is orthogonal to comparison Q, we use the formula and see that

$$[(-1)(-1)] + [(+1)(-1)] + [(+1)(+1)] + [(-1)(+1)] = 1 - 1 + 1 - 1 = 0$$

Similarly, this comparison is also orthogonal to contrast B:

$$[(-1)(-1)] + [(+1)(+1)] + [(+1)(-1)] + [(-1)(+1)] = 1 + 1 - 1 - 1 = 0 \quad ■$$

In thinking about this example, you might have come up with a different-looking comparison that you thought was orthogonal to comparisons Q and B. If so, remember that two comparisons are identical if one of them is equivalent to the other multiplied by some constant. Thus +1/3, –1/3, –1/3, and +1/3 is identical to comparison Z because it is the same as –1, +1, +1, and –1 multiplied by –1/3. Thinking that you have formulated two comparisons when you have really tested only one is a minor mistake that is easily recognized when you try to put the comparisons into words. Another error that is easy to make is to come up with some weights that do not sum to zero and therefore do not represent a comparison.

If you were to calculate the sums of squares for all $K - 1$ orthogonal comparisons in a set, using the formula given earlier, you would find that these sums of squares would add up to the sum of squares between groups from the analysis of variance whenever the n's for the groups are equal. In other words, when all cell sizes are equal, the sum of squares between groups can be divided into exactly $K - 1$ independent parts, each reflecting a different portion of the variance of scores on the dependent measures. In fact, this is what is done in a factorial analysis of variance; the total variance is divided into a portion due to each independent variable plus a portion due to the interaction(s) in a fashion similar to the way in which it could be divided up by using orthogonal comparisons to reflect the independent variables.

Orthogonal comparisons thus have some very useful properties. Many researchers, but not all (Harris, 1994), feel that it is acceptable to use the a priori critical value whenever you have $K - 1$ or fewer a priori orthogonal hypotheses (comparisons) to test. Harris (1994) points out that, for a given number of contrasts, the inflation of Type I error rate is greatest when they are mutually orthogonal.

Regardless of whether your comparisons were a priori or post hoc, if they are orthogonal, they can be used to carve up the sum of squares between groups (reflecting the variance due to group differences, the independent variable in an experiment) into independent portions, making it possible to compare the relative importance of different factors. However, the most important aspect of comparisons is not that they be orthogonal to each other but that they make sense. If there are logical reasons for testing hypotheses that are not orthogonal to each other, do so; ignoring potentially interesting comparisons because they are not orthogonal to other ones would be a mistake. Remember that, as long as the post hoc critical values are used, you can legitimately test any and all comparisons of interest while keeping your chance of making a Type I error at alpha.

Advantages and Disadvantages of the Scheffé Procedure

Advantages.   There are four major advantages of the Scheffé comparison procedure.

1. It can be used to test a priori or post hoc hypotheses (although it is not usually called a Scheffé comparison in the former instance).
2. It can be used for nonpairwise contrasts, unlike other comparison procedures.
3. You can do all the data snooping that you wish by this procedure without inflating your error rate.
4. The procedure is a conservative one; no one will criticize you for using it, as might be done if you were to pick some other procedure, such as Duncan's multiple range test. In other words, you don't have to learn any other comparison procedure; you can always do a Scheffé contrast to appropriately follow up on a significant F from an analysis of variance.

Disadvantages.   I am aware of only two serious disadvantages to the use of the Scheffé procedure. The first is the same as the last advantage mentioned: It is a conservative technique. As is the case when you do a two-tailed test, your ethics are impeccable but you may miss some excitement. If all you want to do is some pairwise comparisons, then another test, such as the Tukey HSD procedure to be discussed next, would be more powerful and equally correct.

The second disadvantage is that the Scheffé procedure may appear difficult to someone not used to it; you have to think about what hypotheses you want to test and what the relevant weights would be, and you have to compute the critical value rather than just looking it up in a table.

Scheffé Comparison Procedure

Purpose: To compare means of groups, usually following an analysis of variance

Definition: A *comparison* or *contrast* is a weighted set of means, with the weights reflecting the research hypothesis to be tested.

Assumptions:

- The data are measured on an interval or ratio scale.
- The scores are randomly sampled.
- The distribution of the dependent measure is normal in the populations from which the data come.
- The populations have equal variances.

Formulas:

$$F = \frac{(\Sigma C_j \overline{X}_j)^2}{(MS_W)\left(\Sigma \dfrac{C_j^2}{n_j}\right)}$$

Critical value for post hoc contrast: $(K-1)[F_\alpha(K-1, N-K)]$
Critical value for a priori contrast: $F_\alpha(1, N-K)$

Advantages:

- It can be used to test a priori or post hoc hypotheses (although it may not be called a Scheffé comparison when it is used a priori).
- It can be used for nonpairwise contrasts.
- Any and all post hoc hypotheses can be tested without inflating the error rate.
- It is a conservative procedure.

What Is the Tukey HSD Procedure?

The **Tukey HSD** (Honestly Significant Difference) procedure is a procedure that permits any and all pairwise comparisons to be tested (Hancock & Klockars, 1996). It is most often used as a post hoc test to compare means after an analysis of variance has led to the rejection of the overall null hypothesis, although Harris (1994) feels that it should always be preceded by a studentized range test, rather than an analysis of variance. Unlike a Scheffé comparison, it involves only pairwise contrasts and does not permit comparing a combination of means with another mean or combination of means.

Formulas

The formula below is a general formula for a Tukey HSD statistic, which was modified by Kramer (1956) to make it applicable for samples that have either equal or unequal n's. The formula for HSD, which is sometimes called Q, is as follows:

$$HSD = \frac{\overline{X}_1 - \overline{X}_2}{\sqrt{\left(\dfrac{MS_W}{2}\right)\left(\dfrac{1}{n_1} + \dfrac{1}{n_2}\right)}}$$

The numerator of the formula consists of the difference in the two sample means. To compute the denominator, you proceed as follows.

Step 1: Compute the reciprocal of (i.e., 1 divided by) the number of scores making up the first mean. To do this, divide 1 by n_1.

Step 2: Compute the reciprocal of the number of scores making up the second mean (i.e., $1/n_2$).

Step 3: Sum these two values.

Step 4: Find the mean square within from the analysis of variance.

Step 5: Divide the MS_W by 2.

Step 6: Multiply this quotient by the sum in step 3.

Step 7: Take the square root of this quotient.

There is a simplified formula that can be used when the n's in the two groups are equal. If n is the number *per group* (not the overall N), then

$$HSD \text{ (or } Q) = \frac{\overline{X}_1 - \overline{X}_2}{\sqrt{\dfrac{MS_W}{n}}}$$

In other words, the numerator is the difference in the means and the denominator is the square root of the mean square within divided by the sample size. When $n_1 = n_2$, this formula is exactly equivalent to the general one, so either one can be used. If you prefer to always use the more general formula listed first, you will be correct whether the n's are equal or unequal.

Critical Value. Once a Tukey HSD has been computed, it needs to be compared with the appropriate critical value in order to determine whether or not the difference in the means is statistically significant. The critical value for a Tukey HSD is found in Appendix Table 7, which presents the critical values

TABLE 11.1   Sample Portion of Appendix Table 7: Critical Values for Tukey HSD Test

	Number of Means (K)								
df_{WG}	*2*	*3*	*4*	*5*	*6*	*7*	*8*	*9*	*10*
1	17.97	26.98	32.82	37.08	40.41	43.12	45.40	47.36	49.07
2	6.08	8.33	9.80	10.88	11.74	12.44	13.03	13.54	13.99
3	4.50	5.91	6.82	7.50	8.04	8.48	8.85	9.18	9.46
4	3.93	5.04	5.76	6.29	6.71	7.05	7.35	7.60	7.33
5	3.64	4.60	5.22	5.67	6.03	6.33	6.58	6.80	7.00
6	3.46	4.34	4.90	5.31	5.63	5.90	6.12	6.32	6.49
7	3.34	4.16	4.68	5.06	5.36	5.61	5.82	6.00	6.16
8	3.26	4.04	4.53	4.89	5.17	5.40	5.60	5.77	5.92

$\alpha = .05$

for a statistic called the *studentized range* (or sometimes the Q statistic). A portion of this table is reproduced in Table 11.1. To use this table, notice that two different types of information need to be considered along with the selected alpha level. First, the degrees of freedom within groups is used, which is $N - K$. Second, the number of means, or the number of levels of the independent variable, must be taken into account. Note that this number is *not* generally going to be 2, since you would not need to do a post hoc test if you had a significant F from an analysis of variance with only two groups. In that case, there would be only one possible conclusion: The larger mean was significantly higher than the smaller one. Even though you are always comparing only two means at a time, the number of means that you use to look up the critical value with which to compare your computed value of Tukey's HSD is always K.

Examples of Tukey's HSD

As a first example of a situation in which a Tukey HSD might be used, let's take the situation with male and female dentists used to illustrate the use of a Scheffé comparison.

EXAMPLE

Dentists and Leisure. Suppose that, instead of contrasting the two groups of experienced dentists with the inexperienced group, you decided to simply compare each group with each other.

Solution: You might begin by testing the largest difference in means, that between the novice female dentists, for whom $\overline{X} = 2$, and the experienced male dentists, for whom $\overline{X} = 8$:

$$HSD = \frac{\overline{X}_1 - \overline{X}_2}{\sqrt{\left(\frac{1.00}{2}\right)\left(\frac{1}{3} + \frac{1}{3}\right)}} = \frac{6}{\sqrt{(.5)\left(\frac{2}{3}\right)}} = \frac{6}{\sqrt{.333}} = \frac{6}{.5773} = 10.39$$

Alternatively, since the n's are each equal to 3, we could use the equal n formula:

$$HSD = \frac{6}{\sqrt{\frac{1.00}{3}}} = 10.39$$

To determine the critical value for this test, we need to use Appendix Table 7. With 3 means and 6 degrees of freedom for the mean square within, the critical values for the .05 and .01 α-levels are 4.34 and 6.33, respectively. The computed value of 10.39 far exceeds these, so we would conclude (in APA style) that "a Tukey HSD test revealed that the mean number of hours of leisure for experienced male dentists was significantly greater than the mean number of leisure hours for novice female dentists, $HSD = 10.39, p < .01$."

As a next step, we might compare the means for inexperienced male and female dentists. Using the general formula, we would have

$$HSD = \frac{5 - 2}{\sqrt{\left(\frac{1.00}{2}\right)\left(\frac{1}{3} + \frac{1}{3}\right)}} = \frac{3}{.5773} = 5.20$$

This difference, like the difference between experienced and novice male dentists (which I'll leave to you to calculate), reaches significance at the .05 but not the .01 critical value. ■

For a second example, we could revisit the study on the effects of labels on perceptions of people who have a disability.

EXAMPLE

Effects of Labels. In order to test the original hypothesis that the two "people who" groups would differ from the other two groups, we could compute four Tukey HSD tests.

Solution: The first one would be to compare the participants in the PWHD condition with those in the C condition. For this analysis,

$$HSD = \frac{\overline{X}_1 - \overline{X}_2}{\sqrt{\left(\frac{MS_W}{2}\right)\left(\frac{1}{n_1} + \frac{1}{n_2}\right)}} = \frac{17.33 - 7.33}{\sqrt{\left(\frac{10.06}{2}\left(\frac{1}{15} + \frac{1}{15}\right)\right)}}$$

$$= \frac{10.00}{\sqrt{(5.03)(.133)}} = \frac{10.00}{\sqrt{.671}} = \frac{10.00}{.819} = 12.21$$

The critical value for the Tukey HSD test can be found from Appendix Table 7 by looking for the value for four treatment groups and 60 degrees of freedom (or you could use 40 to be conservative): 3.74 and 4.59 at the .05 and .01 α-levels, respectively. Since the computed value for HSD exceeds the critical value, you could conclude that the mean for the $PWHD$ group is statistically significantly higher than the mean for the C group.

To compare the $PWHD$ and the HP groups,

$$HSD = \frac{17.33 - 11.27}{\sqrt{\left(\frac{10.06}{2}\right)\left(\frac{1}{15} + \frac{1}{15}\right)}} = \frac{6.06}{.819} = 8.06$$

which would also be statistically significant at the $p < .01$ level. On the other hand, a test comparing the $PWUW$ and the $PWHD$ groups would not lead to statistical significance:

$$HSD = \frac{19.40 - 17.33}{\sqrt{\left(\frac{10.06}{2}\right)\left(\frac{1}{15} + \frac{1}{15}\right)}} = \frac{2.07}{.819} = 2.53$$

which is less than the critical value for the studentized range statistic at the $p < .05$ level. Therefore, we would have to conclude that there was not a statistically significant difference in the reactions of people who read about "a person who has a disability" versus "a person who uses a wheelchair," $HSD = 2.53$, $p > .05$.

Advantages and Disadvantages of the Tukey HSD Procedure

Advantages.   There are two major advantages of the Tukey HSD procedure. First, it holds your error rate at α for as many pairwise comparisons as you care to do. If you wish to do only pairwise comparisons, then the Tukey HSD procedure is as correct as the Scheffé procedure but is more powerful. Second, it is relatively easy to compute, and the critical value is easy to look up in a table. The decisions about weights and the computation of the appropriate critical value, which are necessary for a Scheffé post hoc comparison, are not required for a Tukey HSD test.

Disadvantages.   The Tukey procedure, like all other comparison procedures except the Scheffé, cannot be used to test nonpairwise contrasts. Thus, it is less versatile than the Scheffé procedure. It is also less consistent with the analysis of variance procedure, since it is possible to have a statistically significant F from an ANOVA but no pairwise comparison that is significant by the HSD test.

Tukey HSD Procedure

Purpose: To compare means of pairs of scores following an analysis of variance procedure or a studentized range test

Assumptions:

- The data are measured on an interval or ratio scale.
- The scores are randomly sampled.
- The distribution of the dependent measure is normal in the populations from which the data came.
- The populations have equal variances.

Formula:

$$HSD = \frac{\overline{X}_1 - \overline{X}_2}{\sqrt{\left(\dfrac{MS_W}{2}\right)\left(\dfrac{1}{n_1} + \dfrac{1}{n_2}\right)}}$$

Advantages:

- It holds your error rate at alpha for as many pairwise comparisons as you care to do.
- If you wish to do only pairwise comparisons, it is more powerful than the Scheffé procedure.
- It is relatively easy to compute.
- It is easy to look up the critical value in a table.

What Are Some Other Comparison Procedures?

Although the Tukey HSD and the Scheffé procedures may be the most widely accepted post hoc tests, several other procedures are sometimes used (Hancock & Klockars, 1996). The *Newman–Keuls test* is a method of doing pairwise comparisons in which the critical values for the pairs of means being tested vary, depending on the relative position of the means in the distribution. Like the Tukey HSD procedure, it uses the studentized range or Q distribution. *Duncan's multiple range test* is another stepwise or layered procedure, which is considered less conservative and less desirable than the Tukey HSD test. Dunnett's procedure is a way of comparing the means of each of several experimental groups with the mean of a control group.

The *Bonferroni critical value procedure* is a very general approach to setting critical values that can be used when one is doing a limited number of comparisons but also when doing a limited number of t-tests, correlation coefficients, or any other statistical procedure. The use of this procedure involves dividing up the α-level into as many parts as tests, so that each of m (for example) statistical tests is done at the α/m level, leaving the overall chance of making a Type I error at alpha. To use the Bonferroni procedure for a set of a priori tests, just count the number of hypotheses you intend to test and divide your alpha level by that number. For example, if you intend to compute five t-tests or five correlation coefficients, use the .05/5 or .01 α-level for each test. Select your critical values to correspond to this new alpha level. This procedure will keep your chance of finding any significant difference or correlation at or below .05 (if H_0 is true). To use the Bonferroni procedure for a post hoc test, you need to consider all the comparisons that you *might* do, although you will actually compare only those means that look as though they reflect large differences. The Tukey HSD procedure is usually more powerful than the Bonferroni procedure as a post hoc test and is always more powerful if you want to test all pairwise comparisons.

How Do You Select the Appropriate Procedure?

There are a number of questions that researchers have to consider when they are trying to test their research hypotheses. The answers to these questions help them decide whether or not to do a comparison and, if so, which type of comparison to use.

Questions to Consider

- *What question are you asking?* In order to decide whether or not to perform a comparison, the first thing to consider is the question that you are asking. If it is a question about relationships or about proportions, or if it deals with scores on a qualitative variable, then a comparison is not the appropriate technique, since comparisons deal only with differences between or among means.

- *How many means are there?* The second thing to consider is whether or not the number of means in which you are ultimately interested is greater than 2. If it is not, then either a t-test or a one-way analysis of variance is sufficient to permit a definitive decision about whether or not to reject the null hypothesis that the means do not differ. A comparison is used in situations where you have a hypothesis about mean scores for a research study in which there were more than two groups.

- *Are your hypotheses a priori or post hoc?* If you want to test an a priori hypothesis about the means of two or more of the groups in the study, you would do an a priori comparison. If you want to test as many as $K-1$ orthogonal a priori hypotheses, most researchers feel that it is permissible to do up to $K-1$ orthogonal contrasts, testing each one by the a priori critical value. If you wish to do a number of nonorthogonal contrasts formulated before looking at the data, then there is not complete agreement about whether you should use the a priori critical value for each comparison, although many researchers feel that, as long as your hypotheses were really formulated before the data were gathered, it is acceptable to use the a priori critical value to test them. Other statisticians feel that you should either use the Scheffé post hoc critical value for each comparison or use the Bonferroni critical value procedure of correcting the α level to keep the chance of making a Type I error at α.

• *Should you do a Tukey HSD or a Scheffé comparison?* The most common use of a comparison is to draw inferences about differences in means following a significant analysis of variance, in other words as a post hoc procedure. In this case, you usually need to decide between the two most widely accepted techniques: the Scheffé procedure and the Tukey HSD test. One possibility is to always use the Scheffé procedure, regardless of the hypothesis that you are testing. The only disadvantage is that this approach is less powerful than the Tukey HSD test if all you want to do is pairwise comparisons (Hancock & Klockars, 1996). The alternative possibility is to use the Tukey HSD procedure when you wish to compare only two means at a time and to use the Scheffé procedure for comparisons involving more than two means.

Other Issues

There are three other points about comparisons that would be useful to keep in mind.

1. The major reason for using a post hoc critical value is to control the overall error rate, so that your chance of making any Type I error remains at alpha, no matter how many tests you do. Sometimes this approach is called controlling the *experimentwise error rate* (if you are holding your chance of finding a Type I error at alpha across all the statistical tests that you might run in the entire research study—which needn't be an experiment, by the way). Sometimes researchers refer to controlling the *familywise error rate*, when they are controlling the alpha level for an entire group or family of tests but not necessarily for all the statistical tests that might be done in the research study. For example, you could control the familywise error rate for all the tests done comparing the levels of one factor in a factorial design. Whenever you see (or use) the term *experimentwise error rate* or *familywise error rate*, you can assume that, instead of doing each individual test at the .05 level, the chance of finding *anything* significant was kept at .05 (or whatever alpha level was selected).

2. A second issue to consider is the relationship of the weights in the comparison to your hypotheses. A comparison is a numerical representation of a verbal hypothesis, with the numbers reflecting the size of the hypothesized means. For example, a comparison of two means uses weights of +1 for the larger mean and –1 for the smaller. It's a good idea to describe your comparison in words as well as simply presenting the numbers, both to be sure that the numbers are an accurate translation of your ideas and to express the finding in the form that someone without much statistical background can understand. So don't just say that the comparison +1, +1, and –2 was significant; say that the mean of the third group was significantly smaller than the average of the other two means.

3. A final issue to consider is the unusual situation in which the overall F for the analysis of variance is statistically significant but you cannot find any reasonable comparison that reaches significance by the post hoc criterion. Even more common is the instance when there is no significant pairwise comparison. For example, if the means of five groups are 5, 5, 5, 2, and 2, and an analysis of variance reveals an F that just exceeds the critical value at the .05 level, it may be the case that no two means differ significantly from each other but that the first three means differ from the latter two.

TIP

> An analysis of variance with a significant F implies that there will be some comparison that is significant. However, if the only significant comparison uses such a peculiar set of weights that its meaning is obscure, there is little point in reporting it. When something like this occurs, most researchers will simply report that no obvious comparison was statistically significant and suggest that future research, presumably with more accurate measures and/or a larger sample size and/or a design that better controls extraneous sources of variance, should reveal which groups differ significantly from which others.

CHAPTER SUMMARY

A comparison, or contrast, is a procedure that allows the researcher to test a particular hypothesis about how different means compare with each other. Unlike t-tests, a comparison can compare more than two means at once, uses an estimate of variance based on all the scores in the study, and controls the overall alpha level. Unlike an ANOVA with more than two groups, a comparison can lead to a conclusion about which particular means differ from which specific other means. Comparisons involve a set of weights that multiply the group means, with the weights reflecting the hypothesis being tested. The sum of the weights must equal zero, and larger weights represent larger hypothesized means.

Comparisons can be either a priori, formulated prior to gathering the data, or post hoc, following a significant analysis of variance. The critical values for post hoc comparisons are larger, to keep the chance of making a Type I error at alpha.

Two comparisons are orthogonal when the sum of the cross products of their coefficients equals zero. A set of $K - 1$ orthogonal comparisons uses up the entire between-groups sum of squares, so no more than $K - 1$ comparisons will be orthogonal to each other. Some researchers feel that it is appropriate to compare a priori orthogonal comparisons but not nonorthogonal ones to the a priori critical value.

A Scheffé post hoc comparison involves computing an F-value for a hypothesized contrast and comparing it with a critical value that depends on the degrees of freedom from the ANOVA and the number of groups in the study. Another kind of post hoc comparison is the Tukey HSD procedure. Unlike the Scheffé procedure, it compares only two means at a time; however, it is more powerful than the Scheffé technique when only pairwise comparisons are desired. The Bonferroni critical value procedure, although not a comparison, also shares the advantage of keeping the overall or experiment-wise alpha level at .05 (or whatever is desired) for an entire series of statistical tests.

CHAPTER REVIEW

Multiple-Choice Questions

1. When is a Tukey HSD test most likely to be preferable to a Scheffé test?
   a. when you want to test a priori hypotheses
   b. when you want to test all possible post hoc pairwise comparisons (and only pairwise comparisons)
   c. when you want to compare the means of two groups combined with the mean of a third group
   d. when you don't want to do an analysis of variance
   e. always

2. Which of the following contrasts is orthogonal to the comparison $-2, -1, 0, +3,$ and 0?
   a. $-1, -1, +1, +1, 0$ b. $-2, -1, 0, +1, +2$ c. $-1, +1, -1, -1, +2$
   d. $0, 0, -1, 0, +1$ e. all of the above   f. none of the above

3. A researcher who is "data snooping" is
   a. cheating
   b. testing an a priori hypothesis
   c. doing one or more post hoc tests
   d. trying a lot of different statistical tests to see if any of them reaches statistical significance
   e. looking at the results of a pilot study

4. If a Tukey HSD reaches statistical significance, what do you conclude?
   a. The population means are unlikely to be different.
   b. The population from which the larger sample mean comes is likely to have

a higher mean than the population from which the smaller sample mean was drawn.

c. There is no chance that the population means are the same.

d. Your analysis of variance must have been wrong.

e. You must have made a Type II error.

5. Suppose that you have found a nonsignificant difference among group means after computing a one-way analysis of variance. What should you do next?

   a. a Tukey HSD

   b. a Scheffé post hoc comparison

   c. a Scheffé a priori comparison

   d. a Pearson r

   e. none of the above

6. Suppose that you wanted to compare each of five means with each other mean by means of a t-test. How many individual tests would you have to do?

   a. 5   **b.** 9   **c.** 10   **d.** 20   **e.** 120

7. In a research study, you read that the researcher used a familywise alpha level of .05. What does that mean?

   a. Each individual significance test was done at the .05 level.

   b. The researcher did research on families.

   c. The chance of finding any statistically significant result for the entire group of statistical tests was .05.

   d. The power of the analyses was .05.

   e. Each significance test was done at .05 of its usual critical value.

8. Suppose you hypothesize that the mean weight of rats fed cereal A would be higher than the mean weights of rats fed cereals B and C, which would not differ from each other but would in turn be higher than the mean weight of rats fed cereal D. What would be the best weights for a Scheffé comparison to test this hypothesis?

   a. 4   3   2   1   **b.** 4   3   3   2   **c.** 4   2   0   –6

   d. 3   1   1   –1   **e.** 1   0   0   –1

9. Suppose you hypothesize that not all teachers are equally effective. You randomly assign 20 students to each of four teachers, have the teachers teach a lesson about social customs affecting business in Malaysia, and then test the students on their knowledge. Which kind of test do you need in order to test the hypothesis that the mean scores of the students from the four teachers will not all be equal?

   a. a Pearson r

   b. an independent-samples t-test

    c. a one-way analysis of variance

    d. a Scheffé post hoc comparison

    e. a Tukey HSD

    f. both c and d

    g. either d or e

10. (See if you can answer this one without looking at the book.) Which of the following is an a posteriori comparison procedure?

    a. Dunbar's test   **b.** Cool and Newman's test

    c. Ferrari's test   **d.** the Newman-Keuls test

    e. the orthogonality test

Problems

11. Which, if any, of the following comparisons are orthogonal to the comparison +2, +2, –1, and –3?

    a. +1, –1, +1, –1   **b.** +2, +1, –1, –2   **c.** +1, –1, 0, 0

    d. +3, +1, –2, –2   **e.** +1, +2, –2, –1

12. You have decided to compare four different textbooks for teaching introductory statistics. You randomly assign the students in the course to receive one of four different textbooks, which you provide to them at no cost (thus avoiding the ethical issue of forcing students to pay for a possibly worthless book). The students are all taught by the same instructor and given the same quizzes and assignments. At the end of the semester, all students are given a comprehensive final exam. The scores on the final are as follows:

Book	Exam Scores								
Sordid Statistics	70	40	80	20	80	80	70	40	50
Statistics for Simpletons	10	40	20	30	40	10	20	20	
Sex and Statistics	90	80	90	60	70	80	90	70	80	100
The Singing Statistician	50	60	70	40	40	70	60	50	

    a. Perform a one-way analysis of variance on these data and report your results in an analysis of variance summary table.

    b. What can you conclude from the results of this analysis?

    c. Perform a Scheffé post hoc comparison to test the hypothesis that *Sex and Statistics* led to a higher mean score than the average of the other three textbooks.

    d. Now do a Tukey HSD test of the hypothesis that *Statistics for Simpletons* led to poorer scores on the final than did *The Singing Statistician*.

13. For each of the following statements, identify whether it is true or false.

   a. If you have 7 groups with 10 participants in each, you could find no more than 6 comparisons that are orthogonal to each other.

   b. It is possible to do both a priori and post hoc comparisons in the same research project.

   c. A Scheffé post hoc comparison should be done whenever an analysis of variance leads to a significant F.

   d. It is possible to do an a priori comparison instead of computing an analysis of variance.

   e. If an analysis of variance leads to an F that just misses statistical significance, it is possible for a Tukey HSD to reveal a statistically significant difference in the means.

   f. To keep the familywise error rate at .05, you could do each of 20 tests at the .01 level.

14. For each of the following hypotheses, identify the coefficients for the comparison that will provide an appropriate test of the hypothesis.

   a. Group A will have higher scores than groups B and C, which will not differ. The control group, group D, will have the lowest score.

   b. Groups A, B, and C will have similar means which are higher than the mean for group D.

   c. Boys in group A (let's call them AB) will score higher than girls in group A (AG); girls in group C (CG) will score higher than boys in group C (CB). This is an example of an interaction between gender and group.

   d. Of all 5 groups, group 4 will have a mean higher than the average of the other four groups.

   e. Groups A, B, C, D, and E reflect doses of 1, 2, 3, 4, or 5 tablets of some miracle drug. Your hypothesis is that there is a direct linear relationship between amount of drug taken and the mean score on some measure; in other words, that the means will form an interval scale such that the distance between the means of groups A and B will be the same as the distance between the means of groups B and C, C and D, and D and E.

15. What are the correct critical values for each of the following tests?

   a. A comparison of five types of plant foods, each tested on 12 plants, to see whether the mean heights of the plants fed the different types of food differ or do not differ at the $p < .01$ level.

   b. A Tukey HSD test comparing two of five means, each of which is based on 12 scores, at the .01 level.

   c. A Scheffé post hoc comparison contrasting the means for two types of plant food with the means for three other types of plant food, each based on 12 scores, at the .01 level.

d. An a priori comparison contrasting the means for two types of plant food with the means for three other types of plant food, each based on 12 scores, at the .01 level.

e. An independent-samples t-test comparing the mean heights of plants fed one of two different kinds of plant food, with a total N of 57 at the .01 level.

16. You are interested in the effects of caffeine on academic performance. Accordingly, you randomly assign 14 individuals to drink one cup of either coffee, decaffeinated coffee, or tea at 8:00, 9:00, and 10:00 prior to a test at 10:30. The mean performance scores of the people on the test are as follows, with higher scores being better:

Beverage			*Raw Scores*			*Mean*	*n*
Coffee	10	10	9	9		9.5	4
Decaf	5	4	5	4	5	4.6	5
Tea	2	1	2	2	1	1.6	5

The mean square between from the analysis of variance was 69.764, the mean square within was 0.309, and the F was 225.70. (This is an enormous F, reflecting the large differences in the sample means and the small variances within each sample). You may want to work through the computations for the ANOVA. Then again, you may not.

a. Suppose that you had an a priori hypothesis that the people who drank coffee (regular or decaffeinated) would score higher on the test than the people who drank tea. Perform a test of this hypothesis.

b. Now perform a Scheffé post hoc comparison testing the hypothesis that the people who drank regular coffee scored higher on the test than the people who drank either tea or decaf. Report your conclusion in a sentence.

c. Finally, perform a Tukey HSD test of the hypothesis that the decaf group scored significantly higher than the tea-drinking group. Report your conclusions in a sentence.

17. A superintendent of schools had a belief that extra recess periods would cause children to concentrate better during the time that they are in the classroom. He therefore ordered the principals at three primary schools to provide an extra half-hour of recess per day. A question and answer test given to a sample of students at each school provided a measure of student concentration. At the end of the year, data were collected on seven schools, three with extra recess (schools $R1$, $R2$, and $R3$) and four with the normal recess periods (schools $C1$, $C2$, $C3$, and $C4$). The mean concentration scores (higher is better) and sample size for each school are presented below. The mean square within groups from a one-way analysis of variance on the seven groups was 24.50.

				School			
	R1	R2	R3	C1	C2	C3	C4
$\overline{X}$	10.5	13.2	9.8	10.0	7.7	8.7	7.2
n	20	32	19	26	19	22	18

a. Perform an a priori test of the superintendent's hypothesis that having extra recess will lead to higher mean concentration scores.

b. Report your conclusion in a sentence.

c. Suppose that the superintendent had not had any particular hypothesis and you had simply looked at the concentration test scores of students at these seven schools. If you had performed a contrast with the same weights as a post hoc test, what would you have concluded?

d. Perform a Tukey HSD test comparing the highest and the lowest means. What can you conclude from this test?

18. At a school in which you are working, two new programs have been developed to deal with high school students who are failing at least two classes. One program provides intensive remedial work with each student in an after-school program. The second program assigns these students to a separate, small, daylong class where all subjects are taught by a single teacher, the requirements are eased, and students are taught at their own pace. The 67 students who meet the criterion of failing at least two classes have been randomly assigned to either the after-school program, the single-class program, or a control group in which intervention is left up to individual teachers. You are interested in the relative effectiveness of these programs.

a. What are two orthogonal planned comparisons that it would make sense to make?

b. At the end of the fall semester, you have gathered data on the grade-point averages of the students in the three groups.

	Program		
	After School	Separate Class	Control
$\overline{X}$	1.98	2.22	1.56
n	23	22	22

The mean square within for a one-way analysis of variance on these data was .55. Perform a test of your first a priori comparison.

c. Report your conclusion in a sentence.

d. Now test your second a priori comparison.

e. Report your conclusion in a sentence.

f. Now perform a Tukey HSD test comparing the separate class with the control condition.

19. Do people from different areas of the United States speak at different speeds? To check this out, you get samples of people from four different cities, New York, Mobile, Des Moines, and Sacramento, and ask them to read aloud a standard passage, measuring the number of minutes it takes to complete it. An analysis of variance reveals a significant F, $MS_W = 2.86$, and the following means and n's from the different cities.

	City			
	New York	Mobile	Des Moines	Sacramento
$\overline{X}$	6.00	10.35	7.22	8.56
n	32	42	37	38

a. You want to compare the mean time to read the passage taken by people in each of the other cities with the mean time taken by New Yorkers. What is the most appropriate procedure to use and why?

b. Using this procedure, compare each of the other cities with New York. Based on this sample, do New Yorkers speak faster than others?

c. Looking at the data, it appears that the Southerners from Mobile speak more slowly than the people in the other cities. Carry out a post hoc comparison to test this inference.

20. A nutritionist has sampled the five most popular meals at each of four fast-food chains and has counted the caloric content of each. She conducted an analysis of variance in which she found that the mean caloric content of the different chains varied statistically significantly: $F(3, 16) = 4.07$, $p < .05$. Her $MS_W = 8004.58$. Her data looked like this:

	Chain			
	Burger Bar	Pizza Pub	Tamale Tom	China Carol
$\overline{X}$	736.20	810.00	777.22	583.38
n	5	5	5	5

a. Perform the post hoc Scheffé comparison that you think has the greatest chance of finding a statistically significant difference.

b. Report your conclusions in a sentence.

    c. Now perform the Tukey HSD test that you think has the greatest likelihood of finding a statistically significant difference.

    d. Report your conclusions in a sentence.

    e. Discuss the relationship between the results of the analysis of variance, the Scheffé comparison, and the Tukey HSD test. Look at the means to help you to do so.

Study Questions

1. Go to the library, look through some journals in your field, and try to find several articles that use comparison techniques. Look at the group means and standard deviations (or the MS_W from the analysis of variance) reported. In each case, can you see the relationship between the differences in the means and the value of the test statistic for the comparison technique? If the report presents enough information, try to carry out the comparison yourself, checking the work, to see the relationship between the numbers and the conclusions.

2. Suppose that you have the task of comparing the achievement level of tenth-grade male and female students in six schools, two of which are in a rural area, two of which are suburban, and two of which are urban. In addition, you have data indicating that the two rural schools and one of the urban schools have a policy of promoting all students regardless of performance or attendance, whereas the other three schools do not. You have tabulated your data separately by sex of student. First, think about how you could label the means representing the boys and girls at these six schools—maybe $\overline{X}_1$ to $\overline{X}_{12}$ or maybe something more descriptive. Then think about what contrasts you would use to test each of the following hypotheses: (a) that boys would score higher than girls; (b) that suburban schools would have the highest means, followed by rural and then urban schools; and (c) that schools that fail students who do not perform adequately or attend school will have higher means than schools that promote all students. What would be the weights for these contrasts?

3. It is possible to compare two means out of three groups of scores (perhaps mean number of hot dogs sold at baseball, football, and basketball games) by an independent-samples t-test, an analysis of variance, a Tukey HSD test, or a Scheffé post hoc comparison. What would be the advantages and disadvantages of each of these approaches, if you wanted to compare, for example, hot dog sales at baseball and football games? How would you describe the results of each kind of analysis in words?

4. Think about the question of how the sample size affects the results of your analyses. Imagine that you want to compare the means of several small groups with equal n's and that you have performed an analysis of variance of differences in group means followed by one or more comparisons on these

means. If you have the time, make up some data and carry out the computations. Now double the sample sizes, keeping the means and standard deviations constant. How would the results change? What if you doubled the n for one group and halved the n for another group? Notice that it is the n's for the groups actually being compared (but the MS_W based on all of the groups) that affect the value of the comparison. Can you adjust the values for means and n's so that a smaller absolute difference between two means is statistically significant but a larger absolute difference based on means with smaller n's is not quite significant? (You should be able to do so.) In other words, a mean based on a very small n may not differ significantly from other means, even though it is the most extreme mean and even though the ANOVA led to a significant F.

[handwritten notes in top margin: "1 dV 2 IV - w/ at least 2 levels or factors two way"]

Two-Way Analysis of Variance

What Is a Two-Way Analysis of Variance?

A two-way analysis of variance is a type of analysis used to compare mean scores on a dependent variable when there are two independent variables or *factors*, each with two or more levels or values. For example, suppose that you want to study the effects of instruction booklet and type of VCR on the time it takes to program a VCR to record a television show. Also suppose that there are three different instruction booklets (highly technical, moderately technical, and cookbook style), each used with two types of VCRs (basic and loaded with extra features). If the dependent variable is number of minutes until the VCR is programmed correctly, the design would be a 3 (booklet) by 2 (type of VCR) factorial design. It would be called a two-way design, because there are two independent variables: instruction booklet and type of VCR.

TIP

> This example assumes that each person reads only one booklet and learns to program only one VCR. In other words, each participant is at one level of the variable called booklet and at one level of the variable called VCR. Each person also gets measured on the dependent variable, the time needed to program the VCR.

A two-way analysis of variance is one of many different types of factorial designs. As discussed in Chapter 2, a factorial design is a way of controlling for extraneous variables and of investigating the effects of two or more independent variables in a single study. A factorial design always involves at least two independent variables and one dependent variable. Each combination of a particular level of one independent variable and a particular level of another independent variable is called a *cell*. Every individual score is located in some cell of a table that reflects the intersection of Variable *A* and Variable *B*.

Types of Factorial Designs

Within- Versus Between-Participants Designs. There are many types of factorial designs, only some of which will be considered in this chapter. First, as was mentioned in Chapter 2, there is a distinction between within-participants factors and between-participants factors. A within-participants factor or variable is one in which each person (or unit being measured) has a score at each level of the factor, such as scores on a pretest, posttest, and followup test. A between-participants factor is one in which each person has a score for only one level of the factor, such as male for the factor gender.

Recall from Chapter 9 that a within-participants design with only one factor, which has only two levels, is analyzed by a dependent-samples *t*-test. More complicated within-participants designs are analyzed by more complicated procedures, such as a repeated-measures ANOVA, a randomized-block ANOVA, and a split-plot ANOVA. Chapter 10 mentioned that a repeated-measures analysis of variance is a type of analysis of variance that can analyze more than two levels of a single variable when each person has a score on all levels. In other words, a repeated-measures analysis of variance is used when there is a single within-participants variable. A repeated-measures ANOVA is a special case of a randomized-block analysis of variance, a procedure used to analyze a factorial design in which there are two or more within-participants factors. A split-plot factorial analysis of variance is used to analyze even more complex designs that employ both within-participants and between-participants variables. All these procedures are covered in more advanced statistics textbooks. In this chapter, we will not discuss how to analyze any within-participants designs.

Fixed, Random, and Mixed Effects Designs. Another distinction relevant to the analysis of variance models is that between fixed effects and random effects. A *fixed effect* is a factor for which all the levels of interest have been included. Gender (for which male and female constitute the levels) or modality of presenting information (with auditory and visual, and combined auditory–visual as the levels) are examples of fixed effects. A *random effect* is one for which the levels in your study represent only a sample (theoretically a random one) of the possible levels to which you might want to generalize. For instance, if you are interested in the issue of whether teachers differ in their teaching ability, you might have four different teachers as four levels of the Teacher variable in your study. In this instance, Teacher would be considered a random effect (unless you were interested in only those four teachers).

A factorial design with at least one fixed factor and at least one random factor is called a *mixed-effects design*. The formulas for computing *F*-values are different, depending on whether the design is a fixed, random, or mixed-effects design. This book will cover only a two-way fixed-effects design, but more advanced textbooks cover random and mixed designs.

Fully Crossed and Nested Designs.   A fully crossed or complete factorial design is one in which at least one score represents each level of one variable associated with each level of every other variable. Another way of thinking of a fully crossed factorial design is to recognize that all combinations of the levels of the independent variables are included. A third way to visualize a complete factorial design is to recognize that, if you listed the levels of one independent variable horizontally and the levels of the other variable vertically, so as to form a matrix or table, every cell in the table would have at least one score in it. In the VCR example at the beginning of the chapter, each of the three booklets would be paired with each of the two VCRs, making a total of six experimental conditions. As another example, if you studied men and women readers, with half of the men and half of the women reading Dave Barry and half of each gender reading Erma Bombeck, to see how gender of the reader and gender of the humorist affected liking of humor, this would be a fully crossed or complete factorial design.

An incomplete design is one in which some of the possible combinations are missing. An example of an incomplete design is a nested design, in which each level of one variable is included or nested within a single level of another variable. For instance, you might sample children from eight classrooms, with four classrooms getting one curriculum and four getting another. In this case, classrooms are nested within curricula, since each classroom is paired with only one curriculum. As another example, you might have three research assistants working with participants in one location (Japan) and three different research assistants gathering data from participants in another location (Argentina). Research assistant is then nested within location. Formulas for analyzing designs with one or more nested factors can get very complicated. They will not be covered in this chapter.

Three-Way and Four-Way Factorial Designs.   Many research studies consider more than two independent variables. If there are a very large number of them, or if the variables are quantitative ones with more than a few levels, multiple regression rather than analysis of variance is almost always used to analyze them. However, sometimes factorial analyses of variance are conducted with three, four, or even more factors. The procedures for computing these analyses are not extremely difficult, but interpreting them can be, particularly if there are three-way or four-way interactions (Wilkinson, 1966). They, too, will not be covered in this chapter.

Designs in Which the Cells Do Not All Have the Same *n*.   When researchers are carrying out a true experiment, they usually have the opportunity to decide how many participants will be in each cell. Even if a few people drop out, they have the option of randomly discarding other potential participants to keep the numbers in the cells equal. On the other hand, much descriptive research, including research that compares people at different levels of a single variable, does not permit the researcher to have total control over the sample size and particularly the number of people in each condition.

To some extent, the types of statistical analyses that are appropriate are affected by the variability of the sample sizes, that is, by whether the groups being compared have equal n's. As you have learned in the last two chapters, independent samples t-tests and one-way analyses of variance can be conducted when the n's in the different groups are unequal. Only if the assumptions of homogeneity of variance and normality of distributions are violated and if the n's are very small and very unequal is there a major problem. However, with a factorial analysis of variance, equal sample sizes are more important. If the sample sizes are unequal, then more complex statistical procedures, such as an unweighted means analysis of variance or some type of least-squares analysis of variance, need to be done. A least-squares ANOVA, in particular, can be computationally complex and is almost always done via a computer. Therefore, in this book, as in most introductory statistics textbooks, we will discuss only the situation in which there are equal n's in each cell.

In short, this chapter will focus on two way fully crossed between-participants analyses of variance with equal n's in each cell, called two-way ANOVAs for short. However, the interpretation of the results of two-way ANOVAs can easily be extended to cover more complex designs, and the computations for more complex designs are almost always done by computer, anyway.

Assumptions of the Two-Way ANOVA

The assumptions for the two-way between-participants analysis of variance are essentially the same as the assumptions for the one-way analysis of variance.

1. The data are measured on an interval or ratio scale (or close enough to it for it to be reasonable to compute a mean),
2. The scores are randomly (or at least independently) sampled.
3. The distribution of the dependent measure is normal in the populations from which the data come, and
4. The populations have equal variances.
5. Finally, the type of two-way analysis of variance that we are discussing in this chapter assumes that we have a fixed-effects, fully crossed between-participants design with equal n's in each cell.

Like a one-way ANOVA, a two-way analysis of variance is generally robust to violations of the assumptions of normal distributions and equal variances.

Overview of the Two-Way ANOVA

Main Effects.   One reason to carry out a two-way ANOVA is that it allows you to consider the effects of two variables in one condensed study. Instead of doing one study to consider the effects of type of instruction booklet and one to study the effects of type of VCR, a factorial experiment followed by a two-way analysis of variance can measure the effects of both independent variables in one analysis. Such an approach to research can produce savings in both time expended and number of participants needed for the study.

In this type of analysis, the difference in scores on the dependent measure associated with the levels of a factor is called the *main effect* of that factor. For instance, if type of instruction booklet is strongly associated with speed of learning to program a VCR, but type of VCR is not, then the main effect of instruction booklet is likely to be statistically significant and the main effect of VCR type would not be.

TIP

> The word *effect* is used even when the study is not a true experiment and unequivocal inferences about cause and effect cannot be drawn. Yes, this can be misleading.

Interactions.   Although it is convenient to be able to measure two main effects in one study, a more important benefit of a factorial analysis of variance is its ability to measure interactions. As mentioned in Chapter 2, an interaction occurs when the effect of one variable depends on the level of the other variable. In other words, an interaction effect is a joint effect of the two variables. If there is an interaction between two independent variables, then when you change the level of one factor, you also change the relationship between the dependent variable and the other independent variable. If, for example, Booklet A (compared to Booklets B and C) led to faster learning regardless of type of VCR, there would be a main effect of booklet. If Booklet B (compared to Booklets A and C) led to much faster performance for participants who were using VCR A, but to much slower performance for participants who were using VCR B, this would almost certainly be reflected in a significant interaction between booklet and VCR. Many researchers consider testing an interaction term to be the most important reason for doing a two-way analysis of variance and feel that the primary difference between a one-way and a two-way analysis of variance is the potential for assessing the presence of an interaction.

Null Hypotheses.   In a one-way ANOVA, one null hypothesis is tested: that the means from the different levels of the independent variable represent random samples from the same population. In a two-way ANOVA, three different null hypotheses are tested: (1) that the means from the different levels of Variable A represent random samples from the same population, (2) that the means from the different levels of Variable B represent random samples from the same population, and (3) that there are no differences among the cells that cannot be explained by adding the separate effects of Variable A and Variable B. As you can see, these hypotheses correspond to the tests for the main effects and interaction.

What Are the Formulas for the Two-Way Analysis of Variance?

Notation

The formulas for a two-way analysis of variance use some familiar terms and some which are new. As for a one-way analysis of variance, there are sums of squares, degrees of freedom, mean squares, and F-values. However, a one-way analysis of variance has only one main effect for the independent variable, which is called the between-groups effect, reflected in the SS_B and MS_B. In a two-way analysis of variance, each of the two independent variables has its own main effect, as does the interaction. Each main effect and each interaction is tested by a separate F-test as well.

Following convention, we will call one of the main effects A and the other one B. The interaction between them is called the $A \times B$ or A by B interaction. Thus, in a two-way analysis of variance, we will have a SS_A, df_A, MS_A, and F_A; a SS_B, df_B, MS_B, and F_B; and a $SS_{A \times B}$, $df_{A \times B}$, $MS_{A \times B}$, and $F_{A \times B}$.

TIP

In a real study, researchers sometimes call the effects by the name of the variable that they represent and use initials that represent the names of the factors. For instance, in place of F_A and SS_A, they might use F_V and SS_V for the effect of VCR.

Another aspect of the notation system is the terminology used to indicate the number of levels of each factor. In a one-way analysis of variance, as you recall from Chapter 10, K stands for the number of levels of the between-participants variable. In a two-way analysis of variance, we will use a lowercase a to stand for the number of levels of Variable A and a lowercase b to stand for the number of levels of Variable B. The levels of Variable A will be labeled A_1, A_2, A_3, and so on, up until the last level, A_a. Similarly, the levels of Variable B will be labeled B_1, B_2, B_3, . . . , through B_b. Each cell in the table is labeled by the levels of Factor A and Factor B that it reflects. A diagram of a 2×2 ANOVA is shown in Figure 12.1.

FIGURE 12.1 Diagram of a 2×2 ANOVA

Factor A: Instruction Booklet

Factor B: VCR	A_1	A_2	A_3
Type 1 B_1	X	X	X
	X	X	X
	X	X	X
	X	X	X
	X	X	X
	X	X	X
	$\overline{X}_{A_1 B_1}$	$\overline{X}_{A_2 B_1}$	$\overline{X}_{A_3 B_1}$
Type 2 B_2	X	X	X
	X	X	X
	X	X	X
	X	X	X
	X	X	X
	X	X	X
	$\overline{X}_{A_1 B_2}$	$\overline{X}_{A_2 B_2}$	$\overline{X}_{A_3 B_2}$

Note that the number of cells in the table equals ab, or the number of columns times the number of rows. The total number of scores equals abn, the number of cells times the number of scores per cell. In other words, $N = abn$.

Partitioning of Sums of Squares

With a one-way ANOVA, we considered the sum of squares of the scores on the dependent measure as divided into two parts: one due to the differences between the group means, the SS_B, and one due to the differences of the individual scores from the means of their groups, the SS_W. In a two-way ANOVA, the SS_W remains as a measure of individual differences, but the SS_B is divided into three parts: the variability due to Factor A, SS_A, the variability due to Factor B, SS_B, and the variability due to the interaction between Factors A and B, $SS_{A \times B}$.

When computing the effect of Factor A, we ignore the level of Factor B; when computing the effect of Factor B, we ignore the level of Factor A. Computing the effect of the interaction is done by removing the main effects of Factor A and Factor B and seeing whether knowing the particular combination of levels adds anything to the accuracy of prediction. One way to envision the partitioning of the sums of squares is to look at Figure 12.2.

FIGURE 12.2   Partitioning of Sums in a Two-Way ANOVA

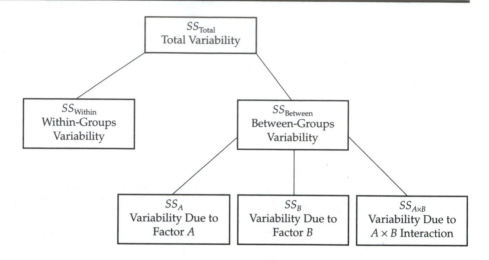

Logic of the Analysis

The logic of a two-way analysis of variance is similar to that of a one-way analysis, with some additional complications. As before, two estimates of variance are computed, with one reflecting only individual differences or random error (the MS_W) and one reflecting both individual differences and group differences (the $MS_{Between}$ in a one-way ANOVA and the MS_A, MS_B, or $MS_{A\times B}$ in a two-way ANOVA). If there are no differences in the means of the populations from which the different groups come, then both estimates of variance will be approximately equal, and their ratio, F, will be approximately 1.00. If the population means for the different levels of Factor A are different, then the MS for Factor A will generally be greater than the MS_W, and F_A will be > 1. If the population means for the different levels of Factor B are different, then the MS for Factor B will usually be greater than the MS_W, and F_B will be greater than 1. If the population means for the different subgroups or cells are different after the effects of Factor A and Factor B have been removed, then the MS for the $A \times B$ interaction will ordinarily be greater than the MS_W, and $F_{A\times B}$ will be greater than 1.

TIP

As is true for one-way ANOVAs, there are definitional as well as computational formulas for the sums of squares in a factorial analysis of variance. However, to save space, only the computational formulas will be provided here.

Computational Formulas

Formula for SS_T. The computational formula for the SS_T in a two-way ANOVA is exactly the same as that for a one-way ANOVA.

$$SS_T = \Sigma X^2 - \frac{T^2}{N}$$

where X equals each raw score and T equals the sum or total of all the raw scores.

What this formula tells you to do is the following:

1. Square each raw score.
2. Sum these squared raw scores. In practice, this is often done in two steps: first summing within each cell and then summing across cells.
3. Sum all the raw scores. This, too, is often done in two steps: first summing within each cell and then summing across cells.
4. Square this sum.
5. Divide this squared sum by N to get the correction factor.
6. Subtract this quotient from the sum of the squared raw scores.

Formula for SS_A. The computational formula for SS_A can be written as

$$\Sigma \left[\frac{(\Sigma A_1)^2}{bn} + \frac{(\Sigma A_2)^2}{bn} + \ldots + \frac{(\Sigma A_a)^2}{bn} \right] - \frac{T^2}{N}$$

This formula tells you to do the following:

1. Sum all the scores at level 1 of Factor A.
2. Square this sum.
3. Divide the squared sum by the number of scores at level 1 of Factor A (which equals the number of levels of Factor B times the number of scores per cell).
4. Repeat this procedure for each level of Factor A. There will be as many quotients as there are levels of Factor A.
5. Sum these quotients.
6. Add up all the scores in the study, square this sum, and divide this squared sum by N to get the correction factor.
7. Subtract the correction factor in step 6 from the sum in step 5.

Formula for SS_B. The computational formula for SS_B is analogous to that for SS_A. It can be written as

$$\Sigma \left[\frac{(\Sigma B_1)^2}{an} + \frac{(\Sigma B_2)^2}{an} + \ldots + \frac{(\Sigma B_b)^2}{an} \right] - \frac{T^2}{N}$$

This formula tells you to do the following:

1. Sum the scores at level 1 of Factor B.
2. Square this sum.

3. Divide the squared sum by the number of scores at level 1 of Factor B (which equals the number of levels of Factor A times the number of scores per cell).
4. Repeat this procedure for each level of Factor B. There will be as many quotients as there are levels of Factor B.
5. Sum these quotients.
6. Add up all the scores in the study, square this sum, and divide this squared sum by N to get the correction factor.
7. Subtract the correction factor in step 6 from the sum in step 5.

Formula for $SS_{A \times B}$. The formula for $SS_{A \times B}$ looks complicated (okay, horrendous), but the computations are really not bad. It can be written as

$$\Sigma \left[\begin{array}{l} \dfrac{(\Sigma X_{A1B1})^2}{n} + \dfrac{(\Sigma X_{A2B1})^2}{n} + \ldots + \dfrac{(\Sigma X_{AaB1})^2}{n} + \dfrac{(\Sigma X_{A1B2})^2}{n} + \\[3ex] \dfrac{(\Sigma X_{A2B2})^2}{n} + \ldots + \dfrac{(\Sigma X_{AaB2})^2}{n} + \ldots + \dfrac{(\Sigma X_{AaBb})^2}{n} \end{array} \right] - \dfrac{T^2}{N} - SS_A - SS_B$$

All it really says to do is this:

1. Take the total for the first cell (ΣX_{A1B1}) and square it.
2. Divide this total by n.
3. Repeat this process for every other cell in the table, that is, for every combination of levels of Factor A and Factor B.
4. Sum these quotients.
5. Add up all the scores in the study, square this sum, and divide this squared sum by N to get the correction factor.
6. Subtract the correction factor from the sum in step 4.
7. Subtract the SS_A from the number of step 6.
8. Subtract the SS_B from the number in step 7 to get the $SS_{A \times B}$.

TIP

The formula for $SS_{A \times B}$ is equivalent to the SS_{Between} computed as if this were a one-way ANOVA minus T^2/N minus SS_A minus SS_B.

Formula for SS_W. The formula for SS_W is

$$SS_W = \Sigma X^2 - \Sigma \left[\begin{array}{l} \dfrac{(\Sigma X_{A1B1})^2}{n} + \dfrac{(\Sigma X_{A2B1})^2}{n} + \ldots + \dfrac{(\Sigma X_{AaB1})^2}{n} + \dfrac{(\Sigma X_{A1B2})^2}{n} + \\[3ex] \dfrac{(\Sigma X_{A2B2})^2}{n} + \ldots + \dfrac{(\Sigma X_{AaB2})^2}{n} + \ldots + \dfrac{(\Sigma X_{AaBb})^2}{n} \end{array} \right]$$

If you have computed SS_T and $SS_{A \times B}$, computing SS_W is easy, because you have already computed the necessary summations. The steps are as follows:

1. Square each raw score and sum the squares.
2. Take the total for the first cell (ΣX_{A1B1}) and square it.
3. Divide this total by n.
4. Repeat this process for every other cell in the table, that is, for every combination of levels of Factor A and Factor B.
5. Sum these quotients.
6. Subtract this sum from the sum of the squared raw scores in step 1.
7. As a check on your work, SS_W should equal SS_T minus SS_A minus SS_B minus $SS_{A \times B}$.

Degrees of Freedom.   In order to compute the mean squares, you have to first calculate the degrees of freedom.

1. The degrees of freedom for the SS_T will be $N - 1$.
2. The degrees of freedom for SS_A equals $a - 1$, where a is the number of levels of Factor A.
3. The degrees of freedom for SS_B equals $b - 1$, where b is the number of levels of Factor B.
4. The degrees of freedom for $SS_{A \times B}$ equals $(a - 1)(b - 1)$.
5. The degrees of freedom for SS_W is $N - ab$. Or you could compute it as $ab(n - 1)$, where n = the number per cell.

TIP

> Since ab = the number of cells or groups, you could think of the degrees of freedom within as the number of scores minus the number of groups, just as it is in the one-way ANOVA.

Formulas for MS_A, MS_B, $MS_{A \times B}$, and MS_W.   In each case, the formula for the mean square is the sum of squares divided by the degrees of freedom. More specifically,

1. $MS_A = \dfrac{SS_A}{a - 1}$

2. $MS_B = \dfrac{SS_B}{b - 1}$

3. $MS_{A \times B} = \dfrac{SS_{A \times B}}{(a - 1)(b - 1)}$

418

4. $MS_W = \dfrac{SS_W}{N - ab}$

Formulas for F. In each case the formula for F equals the mean square for that effect divided by the mean square within.

1. $F_A = \dfrac{MS_A}{MS_W}$

2. $F_B = \dfrac{MS_B}{MS_W}$

3. $F_{A \times B} = \dfrac{MS_{A \times B}}{MS_W}$

How Is a Two-Way ANOVA Used?

Now that you have learned about what a two-way ANOVA is, you may be wondering how and why someone would choose to use one, when a one-way ANOVA appears to be much simpler. The reason that people use a two-way ANOVA is that factorial designs have certain advantages and can be interpreted to provide a great deal of information.

Advantages of a Factorial Design

As the above discussion implies, there are several advantages of a factorial design compared with a one-way ANOVA.

1. It permits the assessment of two (or more) rather than only one independent variable in a single study. A larger total sample size would be necessary to conduct a separate study of each variable. In other words, it is efficient.

2. It permits the assessment of interactions. When the effects of one variable depend on the level of another variable, a factorial analysis of variance makes it possible to recognize this, rather than to generalize inappropriately.

3. It permits greater confidence when you do generalize. Because you have studied the effects of Variable A at various levels of Variable B (and vice versa), you can have more confidence in saying that the conclusions you reach about Variable A are valid for all levels of Variable B (and vice versa).

4. It permits a more powerful and accurate assessment of the effect of Variable A than would be the case if Variable A were the only one investigated in a one-way study. The reason for this greater power is that the effects of Variable B would be part of the within-groups mean square (the error variance) in a one-way ANOVA of Variable A, leading to a larger value of MS_W and a smaller value for F. In a factorial ANOVA, the effect of Variable B will be removed from the MS_W, making the MS_W smaller, the value of F larger, and the *F*-test more powerful. Another way of thinking of this advantage is that it permits greater control over extraneous variables.

TIP

> A different way for controlling for the effect of Variable *B*, as discussed in Chapter 2, would be to hold Variable *B* constant. If that were done, the one-way ANOVA of Variable *A* would be as powerful as a factorial ANOVA of Variables *A* and *B* for detecting effects of Variable *A*, but it would be impossible to generalize to different levels of Variable *B*.

Interpreting Significant Main Effects and Interactions

In a one-way analysis of variance, a statistically significant main effect either leads to a definite conclusion about which of two levels of the variable has the higher mean (when the independent variable has only two levels) or leads to some kind of a priori or post hoc tests (when the independent variable has more than two levels). With a two-way analysis of variance, it is necessary to consider the effect of the interaction before interpreting the meaning of a significant main effect. If the interaction is not statistically significant, then it is appropriate to go ahead and interpret a significant main effect as reflecting a difference among the means of scores at different levels. However, if the interaction is statistically significant, then another step must be taken.

Remember that a statistically significant interaction really means a conclusion of "it all depends"; that is, the effect of Variable *B* depends on the level of Variable *A*, and the effect of Variable *A* depends on the level of Variable *B*. In order to decide what a significant interaction means, it is usually necessary to graph it. By convention, a line graph is drawn with the dependent measure represented on the ordinate and either Factor *A* or Factor *B* along the abscissa. Both (or all) levels of the other factor are represented by separate lines. Graphs of various possible patterns of main effects and interactions are provided in Figure 12.3.

When there is no interaction, as in graphs (a) and (b) of Figure 12.3, then the lines will be parallel, and it will be seen that the difference between the levels of *B* is the same distance for each value of *A*. When there is a significant noncrossover (or ordinal) interaction, as depicted in graphs (c) and (f), the lines are not parallel, but they do not intersect. Assuming that all the values of interest for Variables *A* and *B* have been represented in the study, it is possible to come to clear conclusions about the effects of Variables *A* and *B* by looking at the means of the groups formed by combining across levels of the other variable. It may be the case, for instance, as it is in graphs (c) and (f), that the mean for level B_1 is always higher than the mean for level B_2, but that the level of Factor *A* affects how much higher it is.

FIGURE 12.3 Line Graphs of Some Patterns of Main Effects and Interactions

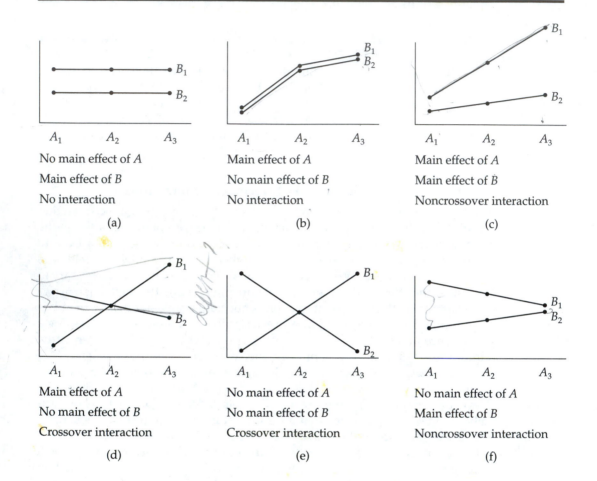

No main effect of A
Main effect of B
No interaction

(a)

Main effect of A
No main effect of B
No interaction

(b)

Main effect of A
Main effect of B
Noncrossover interaction

(c)

Main effect of A
No main effect of B
Crossover interaction

(d)

No main effect of A
No main effect of B
Crossover interaction

(e)

No main effect of A
Main effect of B
Noncrossover interaction

(f)

TIP

Statistical authorities are not in agreement about the best way of analyzing data when there appears to be an interaction. In 1996, *Psychological Science* published a debate on some of the technical issues involved (Abelson, 1996; Petty, Fabrigar, Wegener & Priester, 1996; Rosnow & Rosenthal, 1996). It is clear from the debate that there is no ideal way of analyzing an interaction that will be appropriate in all situations. It is also clear that having clear and specific predictions makes it easier to plan appropriate analyses. If you feel that you need help in deciding which type of analysis to do after identifying a significant interaction, you would be wise to seek out an expert.

When there is a significant crossover (or disordinal) intersection, in which the lines intersect, as illustrated in graph (d) of Figure 12.3, then, even though the overall mean scores on the dependent measure at levels A_1, A_2, and A_3 are not the same, which level is the highest depends partially on the level of Factor B. In such a case, drawing an inference about the overall main effect of Variable A, even though it is statistically significant, might be misleading. It would be more reasonable to compare the different levels of Variable A separately for people who are at each of the levels of Variable B.

Post Hoc Tests. Several different kinds of post hoc tests can be done after a significant main effect or interaction has been found. A post hoc Scheffé comparison is one common procedure (Diekholt, 1996; Shavelson, 1996). These post hoc comparisons can be done to test any hypothesis that looks reasonable from the pattern of means. To compute a post hoc Scheffé comparison after a two-way analysis of variance, be sure that means that are of no interest are given weights of 0 and that the weights sum to 0. To compute the critical value for the comparison, multiply the value for F with $ab - 1$ and $N - ab$ degrees of freedom by $ab - 1$ (i.e., by the number of groups in the analysis minus 1).

If a main effect is significant and the interaction is not, Tukey HSD tests can also be used (Diekholt, 1996; Evans, 1996; Shavelson, 1996). In this case, you can treat the analysis as if it were a one-way ANOVA, collapsing across the levels of the other variable. For example, if you are doing a Tukey HSD test comparing two levels of Variable A, you would compute the means for each level of A based on bn scores per cell.

Simple Main Effects. After a significant two-way interaction has been found, a procedure called a test of simple main effects or a test of simple effects can be used to compare the effects of one independent variable at a single level of the other variable. A test of simple main effects involves computing a sum of squares for each level of one of the variables (e.g., for level 1 and then for level 2 of Factor B). This sum of squares is then divided by the degrees of freedom for the effect to get a mean square for the effect (e.g., for Factor A at level 1 of Factor B). Finally, this mean square is divided by the mean square within from the overall analysis of variance to get a value of F for the effect of one factor at a particular level of the other factor. If a simple mean effect is significant for a variable that has more than two levels, then it is usually followed by a post hoc comparison in order to see which means are significantly different from which other means.

The formulas for computing a test of simple main effects for the effects of Factor A at different levels of Factor B are given below. To simplify matters, these formulas are for the instance when A has three levels, but it is easy to extend it to more levels, if needed. Parallel formulas would be used if you wanted to compute the simple main effects of Factor B at each level of Factor A.

$$SS_{A \text{ at } B1} = \frac{(\Sigma X_{A1B1})^2}{n} + \frac{(\Sigma X_{A2B1})^2}{n} + \frac{(\Sigma X_{A3B1})^2}{n} - \frac{(\Sigma X_{B1})^2}{an}$$

$$SS_{A \text{ at } B2} = \frac{(\Sigma X_{A1B2})^2}{n} + \frac{(\Sigma X_{A2B2})^2}{n} + \frac{(\Sigma X_{A3B2})^2}{n} - \frac{(\Sigma X_{B2})^2}{an}$$

$$MS_{A \text{ at } B1} = \frac{SS_{A \text{ at } B1}}{df_A}$$

$$MS_{A \text{ at } B2} = \frac{SS_{A \text{ at } B2}}{df_A}$$

$$F_{A \text{ at } B1} = \frac{MS_{A \text{ at } B1}}{MS_W}$$

$$F_{A \text{ at } B2} = \frac{MS_{A \text{ at } B2}}{MS_W}$$

What these formulas say to do is this:

1. Take the total for the first cell ($\Sigma X_{A_1 B_1}$) and square it.
2. Divide this total by n.
3. Repeat this process for every other level of Factor A at level 1 of Factor B.
4. Sum these quotients.
5. Sum all the scores at level 1 of Factor B.
6. Square this sum.
7. Divide this squared sum by the number of scores per cell times the number of levels of Factor A.
8. Subtract this quotient from the sum in step 4 to get $SS_{A \text{ at } B_1}$.
9. Divide by the number of levels of Factor A minus 1 to get $MS_{A \text{ at } B_1}$.
10. Divide by MS_W to get $F_{A \text{ at } B_1}$.
11. Repeat these procedures for level 2 of Factor B to get $F_{A \text{ at } B_2}$.
12. Repeat these procedures for the remaining levels of Factor B.

Further Interpretation of Significant F's.   As with a one-way analysis of variance, eta squared (η^2) can be used as a measure of the proportion of variance in the dependent measure that can be attributed to a particular independent variable in the sample. Omega squared (ω^2) can be used as an estimate of the proportion of variance in the dependent measure that can be attributed to a particular independent variable in the population. A separate eta squared and omega squared can be computed for each significant main and interaction effect.

Effect sizes for both independent variables can also be computed, and the power of an analysis to find a difference of any given size can also be estimated. However, some of these calculations are more complex than the corresponding ones for a one-way design. More advanced statistics books provide the formulas for the computations.

Computational Example of a 2×2 ANOVA

Suppose that you are interested in comparing the attitudes of special education and general education teachers toward inclusion or mainstreaming, the practice of educating all children as much as possible in the regular classroom. You are also interested in seeing how elementary and secondary school teachers feel about this issue. You have a suspicion that special education teachers will be more favorably inclined toward inclusion than general education teachers, because general education teachers may feel less qualified to handle children with special needs. You have no prediction about differences between elementary and secondary teachers or about an interaction between the two factors.

To study this issue, you pick a random sample of 24 teachers: 6 general educators and 6 special educators who are teaching at the elementary school level and 6 general educators and 6 special educators teaching at the secondary school level. Each teacher is given a test measuring attitudes toward inclusion, with 20 being a highly favorable attitude and 1 reflecting strong opposition to inclusion. The data look like this:

	Teaching Status (A)	
	Special Education	*General Education*
School Level (B)		
Elementary	A_1B_1	A_2B_1
	8	6
	10	8
	12	8
	10	10
	8	7
	12	9
Secondary	A_1B_2	A_2B_2
	7	6
	8	8
	10	3
	5	5
	12	8
	6	6

From these data you should be able to see that $a = 2$, $b = 2$, $n = 6$, and $N = 24$.

The first step in computing an analysis of variance will be to get the sums, means, and sums of squares for each cell of the table. When you do so, you will get a table like this:

	Teaching Status (A)		
	Special Education	General Education	
School Level (B)			
Elementary	A_1B_1	A_2B_1	
	$\Sigma X_{A_1B_1} = 60$	$\Sigma X_{A_2B_1} = 48$	$\Sigma X_{B_1} = 108$
	$\Sigma X_{A_1B_1}{}^2 = 616$	$\Sigma X_{A_2B_1}{}^2 = 394$	$\Sigma X_{B_1}{}^2 = 1010$
	$(\Sigma X_{A_1B_1})^2 = 3600$	$(\Sigma X_{A_2B_1})^2 = 2304$	
	$\overline{X}_{A_1B_1} = 10.00$	$\overline{X}_{A_2B_1} = 8.00$	
	$n_{A_1B_1} = 6$	$n_{A_2B_1} = 6$	
Secondary	A_1B_2	A_2B_2	
	$\Sigma X_{A_1B_2} = 48$	$\Sigma X_{A_2B_2} = 36$	$\Sigma X_{B_2} = 84$
	$\Sigma X_{A_1B_2}{}^2 = 418$	$\Sigma X_{A_2B_2}{}^2 = 234$	$\Sigma X_{B_2}{}^2 = 652$
	$(\Sigma X_{A_1B_2})^2 = 2304$	$(\Sigma X_{A_2B_2})^2 = 1296$	
	$\overline{X}_{A_1B_2} = 8.00$	$\overline{X}_{A_2B_2} = 6.00$	
	$n_{A_1B_2} = 6$	$n_{A_2B_2} = 6$	
	$\Sigma X_{A_1} = 108$	$\Sigma X_{A_2} = 84$	
	$\Sigma X_{A_1}{}^2 = 1034$	$\Sigma X_{A_2}{}^2 = 628$	

A few more sums are necessary before substituting into the formula.

$$\Sigma X^2 = 1010 + 652 = 1034 + 628 = 1662$$

$$\Sigma X = 108 + 84 = 192, \quad (\Sigma X)^2 = 36{,}864$$

$$\frac{(\Sigma X)^2}{N} = \frac{36{,}864}{24} = 1536.00$$

Using these data, you can now compute the sums of squares.

$$SS_T = \Sigma X^2 - \frac{T^2}{N} = 1662 - 1536 = 126.00$$

$$SS_A = \Sigma \left[\frac{(\Sigma A_1)^2}{bn} + \frac{(\Sigma A_2)^2}{bn} + \dots + \frac{(\Sigma A_a)^2}{bn} \right] - \frac{T^2}{N}$$

$$= \left[\frac{108^2}{(6)(2)} + \frac{84^2}{(6)(2)} \right] - 1536 = \left(\frac{11{,}664}{12} + \frac{7056}{12} \right) - 1536$$

$$= (972 + 588) - 1536 = 1560 - 1536 = 24.00$$

$$SS_B = \Sigma\left[\frac{(\Sigma B_1)^2}{an} + \frac{(\Sigma B_2)^2}{an} + \dots + \frac{(\Sigma B_b)^2}{an}\right] - \frac{T^2}{N}$$

$$= \left[\frac{108^2}{(6)(2)} + \frac{84^2}{(6)(2)}\right] - 1536 = \left(\frac{11,664}{12} + \frac{7056}{12}\right) - 1536$$

$$= (972 + 588) - 1536 = 1560 - 1536 = 24.00$$

TIP

> Whenever you square any total in any analysis of variance formula, divide that squared total by the number of scores that you added to obtain it.

$$SS_{A \times B} = \Sigma\left[\frac{(\Sigma X_{A1B1})^2}{n} + \dots + \frac{(\Sigma X_{AaBb})^2}{n}\right] - \frac{T^2}{N} - SS_A - SS_B$$

$$= \left(\frac{60^2}{6} + \frac{48^2}{6} + \frac{48^2}{6} + \frac{36^2}{6}\right) - 1536 - 24.00 - 24.00$$

$$= (600 + 384 + 384 + 216) - 1536 - 24.00 - 24.00$$

$$= 1584 - 1584 = 0$$

$$SS_W = \Sigma X^2 - \Sigma\left[\frac{(\Sigma X_{A1B1})^2}{n} + \dots + \frac{(\Sigma X_{AaBb})^2}{n}\right]$$

$$= 1662 - 1584 = 78$$

Check: SS_T should equal $SS_A + SS_B + SS_{A \times B} + SS_W$.

$$126 = 24 + 24 + 0 + 78$$

Next, we will calculate the mean squares.

$$MS_A = \frac{SS_A}{a-1} = \frac{24.00}{1} = 24.00$$

$$MS_B = \frac{SS_B}{b-1} = \frac{24.00}{1} = 24.00$$

$$MS_{A \times B} = \frac{SS_{A \times B}}{(a-1)(b-1)} = \frac{0}{1} = 0.00$$

$$MS_W = \frac{SS_W}{N - ab} = \frac{78}{24 - (2)(2)} = \frac{78}{20} = 3.90$$

The last calculations are the values for F.

$$F_A = \frac{MS_A}{MS_W} = \frac{24.00}{3.90} = 6.15$$

$$F_B = \frac{MS_B}{MS_W} = \frac{24.00}{3.90} = 6.15$$

$$F_{A\times B} = \frac{MS_{A\times B}}{MS_W} = \frac{0}{3.90} = 0.00$$

Finally, we want to see whether the F-values are statistically significant. To do so, we need to figure out the degrees of freedom and then look in Appendix Table 6.

df for $F_A = a - 1$ and $N - ab = 1$ and 20
df for $F_B = b - 1$ and $N - ab = 1$ and 20
df for $F_{A\times B} = (a - 1)(b - 1)$ and $N - ab = 1$ and 20
$df_{total} = N - 1 = 23$

Appendix Table 6 indicates that the critical values for F with 1 and 20 degrees of freedom are 4.35 at the .05 α level and 8.10 at the .01 α level.

Based on the computed values, we would conclude that the main effects of variables A and B were statistically significant at the .05 level and that the interaction effect was not. When we put the results into an ANOVA summary table, we get the following:

Source	SS	df	MS	F	p
Teaching status (A)	24.00	1	24.00	6.15	< .05
School level (B)	24.00	1	24.00	6.15	< .05
$A \times B$	0.00	1	0.00	0.00	> .05
Within	78.00	20	3.90		
Total	126.00	23			

TIP

When an independent variable has only two levels and there is a significant main effect of that variable and no significant interaction, as in the example above, you can come to a definite conclusion about which level of the variable was the higher one. If there are three or more levels, you will need to follow up a finding of a significant main effect with some type of post hoc comparison procedure.

In APA style, we might say something like "A 2 by 2 factorial analysis of variance revealed that the elementary school teachers ($\underline{M} = 9.00$) were significantly more favorable toward inclusion than the secondary school teachers ($\underline{M} = 7.00$), $\underline{MSE} = 3.90$, $\underline{F}$, $(1, 20) = 6.15$, $\underline{p} < .05$. Similarly, special education teachers ($\underline{M} = 9.00$) had significantly more positive attitudes toward inclusion than did general education teachers ($\underline{M} = 7.00$), $\underline{F}(1, 20) = 6.15$, $\underline{p} < .05$. However, there was no evidence of any interaction between school level and teaching status, $\underline{F}(1, 20) = 0.00$, $\underline{p} > .05$."

Computational Example of a 3×2 ANOVA

Suppose that you have been asked by a popcorn company to conduct a test of the overall popularity of three types of popcorn that they are considering manufacturing: movie popcorn, microwave popcorn, and pot-popped popcorn. Each type of popcorn will be rated by some people who are watching a movie and by some who are not watching a movie. The popcorn people are interested in which formula to sell to movie theater owners and to the general public. If there is no interaction with movie condition, then they might manufacture and sell only the most popular type of popcorn. If there is an interaction, they might try to sell one type of popcorn to theater owners and another type to the general public. You have a theoretical interest in the effect of context on taste and have developed a model saying that foods taste better when consumed in settings in which they have previously been eaten. This model leads you to predict an interaction: that movie popcorn will be preferred by people when they are watching a movie and the other two types by people who are not watching a movie.

You bring 48 people into the laboratory and randomly assign them to one of six groups in a fully crossed between-participants factorial design. After two hours of eating one type of popcorn, while watching a movie or not, the participants complete a series of ratings that are summed to produce an overall measure of liking for the popcorn from 0 (ugh!) to 100 (umm!). The data look like this:

	Movie Popcorn (A_1)	Microwave Popcorn (A_2)	Pot-Popped Popcorn (A_3)
See movie (B_1)	100	40	60
	90	60	70
	100	30	55
	85	60	80
	70	25	40
	60	35	45
	90	35	70
	65	50	60

	Movie Popcorn (A_1)	Microwave Popcorn (A_2)	Pot-Popped Popcorn (A_3)
No movie (B_2)	40	55	65
	70	35	70
	30	40	80
	55	50	60
	60	60	90
	45	75	65
	30	60	80
	50	50	50

As usual, to solve the problem, it is necessary to get the sums, means, sums of squares, and n for each cell of the table and for each level of the variables. They are in the table below.

	Movie Popcorn (A_1)	Microwave Popcorn (A_2)	Pot-Popped Popcorn (A_3)
See movie (B_1):	$\Sigma X_{A_1B_1} = 660$	$\Sigma X_{A_2B_1} = 335$	$\Sigma X_{A_3B_1} = 480$
	$\Sigma X_{A_1B_1}^2 = 56{,}150$	$\Sigma X_{A_2B_1}^2 = 15{,}275$	$\Sigma X_{A_3B_1}^2 = 30{,}050$
	$(\Sigma X_{A_1B_1})^2 = 435{,}600$	$(\Sigma X_{A_2B_1})^2 = 112{,}225$	$(\Sigma X_{A_3B_1})^2 = 230{,}400$
	$\overline{X}_{A_1B_1} = 82.50$	$\overline{X}_{A_2B_1} = 41.88$	$\overline{X}_{A_3B_1} = 60.00$
	$n_{A_1B_1} = 8$	$n_{A_2B_1} = 8$	$n_{A_3B_1} = 8$
No movie (B_2):	$\Sigma X_{A_1B_2} = 380$	$\Sigma X_{A_2B_2} = 425$	$\Sigma X_{A_3B_2} = 560$
	$\Sigma X_{A_1B_2}^2 = 19{,}450$	$\Sigma X_{A_2B_2}^2 = 23{,}675$	$\Sigma X_{A_3B_2}^2 = 40{,}350$
	$(\Sigma X_{A_1B_2})^2 = 144{,}400$	$(\Sigma X_{A_2B_2})^2 = 180{,}625$	$(\Sigma X_{A_3B_2})^2 = 313{,}600$
	$\overline{X}_{A_1B_2} = 47.50$	$\overline{X}_{A_2B_2} = 53.13$	$\overline{X}_{A_3B_2} = 70.00$
	$n_{A_1B_2} = 8$	$n_{A_2B_2} = 8$	$n_{A_3B_2} = 8$
	$\Sigma X_{A_1} = 1040$	$\Sigma X_{A_2} = 760$	$\Sigma X_{A_3} = 1040$
	$\overline{X}_{A_1} = 65.00$	$\overline{X}_{A_2} = 47.50$	$\overline{X}_{A_3} = 65.00$
	$\Sigma X_{A_1}^2 = 75{,}600$	$\Sigma X_{A_2}^2 = 38{,}950$	$\Sigma X_{A_3}^2 = 70{,}400$
	$\Sigma X_{B_1} = 1475$	$\Sigma X_{B_2} = 1365$	
	$\overline{X}_{B_1} = 61.46$	$\overline{X}_{B_2} = 56.88$	
	$\Sigma X_{B_1}^2 = 101{,}475$	$\Sigma X_{B_2}^2 = 83{,}475$	

$\Sigma X = 2840 \qquad \Sigma X^2 = 184{,}950 \qquad N = abn = (3)(2)(8) = 48$

$$\frac{(\Sigma X)^2}{N} = \frac{8{,}065{,}600}{48} = 168{,}033.33 = \frac{T^2}{N}$$

$nb = 16 \qquad na = 24$

Now we are ready to begin computing the sums of squares.

$$SS_T = \Sigma X^2 - \frac{T^2}{N} = 184{,}950 - 168{,}033.33 = 16{,}916.67$$

$$SS_A = \Sigma \left[\frac{(\Sigma A_1)^2}{bn} + \frac{(\Sigma A_2)^2}{bn} + \cdots + \frac{(\Sigma A_a)^2}{bn} \right] - \frac{T^2}{N}$$

$$= \left(\frac{1040^2}{16} + \frac{760^2}{16} + \frac{1040^2}{16} \right) - 168{,}033.33$$

$$= \left(\frac{1{,}081{,}600}{16} + \frac{577{,}600}{16} + \frac{1{,}081{,}600}{16} \right) - 168{,}033.33$$

$$= (67{,}600 + 36{,}100 + 67{,}600) - 168{,}033.33$$

$$= 171{,}300 - 168.033.33 = 3266.67$$

$$SS_B = \Sigma \left[\frac{(\Sigma B_1)^2}{an} + \frac{(\Sigma B_2)^2}{an} + \cdots + \frac{(\Sigma B_b)^2}{an} \right] - \frac{T^2}{N}$$

$$= \left(\frac{1475^2}{24} + \frac{1365^2}{24} \right) - 168{,}033.33$$

$$= \left(\frac{2{,}175{,}625}{24} + \frac{1{,}863{,}225}{24} \right) - 168{,}033.33$$

$$= 90{,}651.04 + 77{,}634.38 - 168{,}033.33$$

$$= 168{,}285.38 - 168{,}033.33 = 252.05$$

$$SS_{A \times B} = \Sigma \left[\frac{(\Sigma X_{A1B1})^2}{n} + \cdots + \frac{(\Sigma X_{AaBb})^2}{n} \right] - \frac{T^2}{N} - SS_A - SS_B$$

$$= \left(\frac{435{,}600}{8} + \frac{112{,}225}{8} + \frac{230{,}400}{8} + \frac{144{,}400}{8} + \frac{180{,}625}{8} + \frac{313{,}600}{8} \right)$$

$$- 168{,}033.33 - 3266.67 - 252.05$$

$$= (54{,}450.00 + 14{,}028.13 + 28{,}800.00 + 18{,}050.00 + 22{,}578.13 + 39{,}200.00)$$

$$- 168{,}033.33 - 3266.67 - 252.05$$

$$= 177{,}106.26 - 168{,}033.33 - 3266.67 - 252.05$$

$$= 5554.21$$

$$SS_W = \Sigma X^2 - \Sigma \left[\frac{(\Sigma X_{A1B1})^2}{n} + \cdots + \frac{(\Sigma X_{AaBb})^2}{n} \right]$$

$$= 184{,}950 - 177{,}106.26 = 7843.74$$

Check: $16{,}916.67 = 3266.67 + 252.05 + 5554.21 + 7843.74$

To get the mean squares, we divide each SS by its degrees of freedom.

$$MS_A = \frac{SS_A}{a-1} = \frac{3266.67}{2} = 1633.34$$

$$MS_B = \frac{SS_B}{b-1} = \frac{252.05}{1} = 252.05$$

$$MS_{A\times B} = \frac{SS_{A\times B}}{(a-1)(b-1)} = \frac{5554.21}{2} = 2777.11$$

$$MS_W = \frac{SS_W}{N-ab} = \frac{7843.74}{42} = 186.76$$

Next, calculate the values for F.

$$F_A = \frac{MS_A}{MS_W} = \frac{1633.34}{186.76} = 8.75$$

$$F_B = \frac{MS_B}{MS_W} = \frac{252.05}{186.76} = 1.35$$

$$F_{A\times B} = \frac{MS_{A\times B}}{MS_W} = \frac{2777.11}{186.67} = 14.88$$

In order to see whether the F-values are statistically significant, we need to figure out the degrees of freedom and then look in Appendix Table 6.

$$df \text{ for } F_A = a-1 \quad \text{and} \quad N-ab = 2 \text{ and } 42$$
$$df \text{ for } F_B = b-1 \quad \text{and} \quad N-ab = 1 \text{ and } 42$$
$$df \text{ for } F_{A\times B} = (a-1)(b-1) \quad \text{and} \quad N-ab = 2 \text{ and } 42$$
$$df_{\text{total}} = N-1 = 47$$

Appendix Table 6 indicates that the critical value for F with 2 and 40 degrees of freedom at the .001 α level is 8.25. The critical value for F with 1 and 40 degrees of freedom is 4.09 at the .05 α level. Thus, the main effect of A and the interaction are statistically significant at the .001 level, and the main effect of B is not significant at even the .05 level.

Finally, we will put the results in an ANOVA summary table:

Source	SS	df	MS	F	p
Popcorn (A)	3266.67	2	1633.34	8.75	< .001
Movie (B)	252.05	1	252.05	1.35	> .05
$A \times B$	5554.21	2	2777.11	14.88	< .001
Within	7843.74	42	186.76		
Total	16,916.67	47			

FIGURE 12.4   Results from Popcorn Study

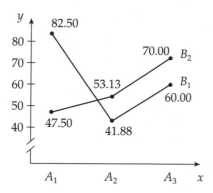

Interpretation.   Based on the above findings, we would say something like "A 3 by 2 factorial analysis of variance revealed a significant main effect of popcorn, $\underline{F}(2, 42) = 8.75$, $\underline{p} < .001$, and a significant interaction, $\underline{F}(2, 42) = 14.88$, $\underline{p} < .001$, but no significant main effect of attending a movie, $\underline{F}(1, 42) = 135$, $\underline{p} > .05$, on rated quality of the popcorn consumed." In order to further interpret the results of the study, we will need to look at the means of the six groups, which are represented in the line graph of Figure 12.4. From the pattern of results, it looks as if your theoretical model may be correct: that movie popcorn is preferred by people watching a movie and other types of popcorn by those who are not watching a movie. It also looks as if pot-popped popcorn (A_3) is always preferred to microwave popcorn (A_2). The use of Scheffé post hoc comparisons would be one way to test these post hoc hypotheses.

TIP

> You could argue that the hypothesis about the interaction that was based on a theoretical model should be considered a priori, rather than post hoc. An a priori hypothesis leads to the same computation of F as a post hoc comparison, but is compared to a critical value based on an F with 1 and $N - ab$ degrees of freedom.

The weights for the first comparison would be as follows:

$$\overline{X}_{A_1B_1} = 82.50 \qquad \overline{X}_{A_2B_1} = 41.88 \qquad \overline{X}_{A_3B_1} = 60.00$$
$$C_1 \quad +2 \qquad\qquad -1 \qquad\qquad\qquad -1$$

$$\overline{X}_{A_1B_2} = 47.50 \qquad \overline{X}_{A_2B_2} = 53.13 \qquad \overline{X}_{A_3B_2} = 70.00$$
$$C_1 \quad -2 \qquad\qquad +1 \qquad\qquad\qquad +1$$

Note that the sum of these weights is 0.
The formula for F for the comparison is

$$F = \frac{(\Sigma c_j \overline{X}_j)^2}{(MS_W)(\Sigma c_j^2 / n_j)}$$

Substituting into the formula, we get

$$F = \frac{[(2)(82.50) + (-1)(41.88) + (-1)(60.00) + (-2)(47.50) + (1)(53.13) + (1)(70.00)]^2}{[186.76][(-2)^2 / 8 + (-1)^2 / 8 + (-1)^2 / 8 + (-2)^2 / 8 + (1)^2 / 8 + (1)^2 / 8]}$$

$$= \frac{[165.00 - 41.88 - 60.00 - 95.00 + 53.13 + 70.00]^2}{[186.76][4 / 8 + 1 / 8 + 1 / 8 + 4 / 8 + 1 / 8 + 1 / 8]}$$

$$= \frac{91.25^2}{[186.76][1.5]}$$

$$= \frac{8326.56}{280.14} = 29.72$$

Since there are six groups in the study, we multiply the critical values for an F with 5 and 42 degrees of freedom by 5 to get the critical values for the post hoc comparisons. Since Appendix Table 6 has critical values for 40 but not 42 degrees of freedom in the denominator, we will use those. The critical value for the comparison would be $(5)(2.45) = 12.25$ at the .05 α level, $(5)(3.51) = 17.55$ at the .01 α level, and $(5)(5.13) = 26.65$ at the .001 α level. Since the computed value for F exceeds this critical value, we can conclude that the hypothesis appears to be correct and state that "A Scheffé post hoc comparison revealed that movie popcorn was preferred by people watching a movie and other types of popcorn by those who were not watching a movie, $F(1, 42) = 29.72$, p $< .001$."

TIP

> The above sentence is only an approximate description of the interaction. More precise (but perhaps less clear) would be a statement that the tendency for movie popcorn to be preferred to the other two types was greater for participants watching a movie than for those not watching a movie.

To see whether or not pot-popped popcorn is preferred to microwave popcorn, we would use weights of 0 for movie popcorn, -1 for microwave popcorn, and $+1$ for pot-popped popcorn. Substituting into the formula for F, we get

$$F = \frac{[(0)(82.50) + (-1)(41.88) + (1)(60.00) + (0)(47.50) + (-1)(53.13) + (1)(70.00)]^2}{[186.76][(0)^2 / 8 + (-1)^2 / 8 + (1)^2 / 8 + (0)^2 / 8 + (-1)^2 / 8 + (1)^2 / 8]}$$

$$= \frac{34.99^2}{[186.76][.5]} = \frac{1224.30}{93.38}$$

$$= 13.11$$

Since 13.11 exceeds the critical value of 12.25 at the .05 α level, we would conclude that "A post hoc Scheffé comparison indicated that pot-popped popcorn was rated significantly higher than microwave popcorn, $\underline{F}(1, 42) = 13.11$, $\underline{p} < .05$."

TIP ▬▬▬▬▬▬▬▬▬▬▬▬▬▬▬▬▬▬▬▬▬▬▬▬▬▬▬▬▬▬

These two comparisons are orthogonal to each other. You can check this by multiplying the weights for each mean from the two comparisons and seeing that the cross products sum to 0.

Simple Main Effects. An alternative to the post hoc Scheffé comparison in this study would be to do tests of simple main effects. In this situation, the tests that make sense would be to look at the effect of popcorn for people who are watching a movie (the effect of A at B_1) and for people who are not watching a movie (the effect of A at B_2). The sum of squares for A at B_1, $SS_{A \text{ at } B_1}$, would be

$$\frac{(\Sigma X_{A1B1})^2}{n} + \frac{(\Sigma X_{A2B1})^2}{n} + \frac{(\Sigma X_{A3B1})^2}{n} - \frac{(\Sigma X_{B1})^2}{an}$$

$$= \frac{435,600}{8} + \frac{112,225}{8} + \frac{230,400}{8} - \frac{2,175,625}{24}$$

$$= 54,450.00 + 14,028.13 + 28,800.00 - 90,651.04$$

$$= 97,278.13 - 90,651.04 = 6627.09$$

The sum of squares for A at B_2, $SS_{A \text{ at } B2}$, would be

$$\frac{(\Sigma X_{A1B2})^2}{n} + \frac{(\Sigma X_{A2B2})^2}{n} + \frac{(\Sigma X_{A3B2})^2}{n} - \frac{(\Sigma X_{B2})^2}{an}$$

$$= \frac{144,400}{8} + \frac{180,625}{8} + \frac{313,600}{8} - \frac{1,863,225}{24}$$

$$= 18,050.00 + 22,578.13 + 39,200.00 - 77,634.38$$

$$= 79,828.13 - 77,634.38 = 2193.75$$

TIP

The sum of the sums of squares for the simple main effects of all levels of a factor should equal the sum of squares for the factor plus the sum of squares for the interaction. In other words, for this example, $SS_{A \text{ at } B_1}$ + $SS_{A \text{ at } B_2}$ should equal $SS_A + SS_{A \times B}$.

Check: $6627.09 + 2193.75 = 8820.84 = 3266.67 + 5554.21$ (except for rounding error).

$$MS_{A \text{ at } B1} = \frac{SS_{A \text{ at } B1}}{df_A} = \frac{6627.09}{2} = 3313.55$$

$$MS_{A \text{ at } B2} = \frac{SS_{A \text{ at } B2}}{df_A} = \frac{2193.75}{2} = 1096.88$$

$$F_{A \text{ at } B1} = \frac{MS_{A \text{ at } B1}}{MS_W} = \frac{3313.55}{186.76} = 17.74$$

$$F_{A \text{ at } B2} = \frac{MS_{A \text{ at } B2}}{MS_W} = \frac{1096.88}{186.76} = 5.87$$

With 2 and 47 degrees of freedom, the critical values for F are approximately 3.20, 5.09, and 8.05. The $F_{A \text{ at } B1}$ is significant at the .01 level, and the $F_{A \text{ at } B2}$ is significant at the .001 level. We would therefore conclude that people seeing a movie do not like all three types of popcorn equally well, $F_{A \text{ at } B1}(2, 47) = 17.74$, $\underline{p} < .001$, and people not seeing a movie also differ in their preferences for popcorn, $F_{A \text{ at } B2}(2, 47) = 5.87$, $\underline{p} < .01$.

TIP

Some people (Hinkle et al., 1994) recommend that the critical values for tests of simple main effects should be adjusted for the number of tests that could be performed in order to more adequately control your chance of making a Type I error. In that case, you would divide the overall alpha level (e.g., .05) by the number of degrees of freedom (or the number of simple effects) for each factor. In other words, the two tests done above should each be compared with critical values for the .025, .005, and .0005 alpha levels in order to keep the family-wise error rate at .05, .01, or .001.

Next Steps

Although a two-way analysis of variance is not too difficult to compute by hand, especially if each variable has only two levels, more complex analyses can be extremely tedious to calculate. Many computer programs will compute factorial analyses of variance for you, saving substantial amounts of time, even if you have to enter the data yourself. However, computer programs cannot identify what the factors are, whether they are fixed or random, whether a particular factor is between-participants or within-participants, or whether the dependent variable is measured on an interval scale or is purely qualitative. You are the one who has to make decisions about what are the most reasonable hypotheses to test and analyses to do. More advanced statistics courses will consider a variety of analysis of variance models and teach you how to make some of the above decisions.

Two-Way Analysis of Variance

Purpose: To look at the effects of two independent variables and their interaction on mean scores on a dependent variable

Assumptions:

- The data are measured on an interval or ratio scale.
- The scores are randomly sampled.
- The distribution of the dependent measure is normal in each of the populations from which the data come.
- The populations have equal variances.
- You have a fixed-effect, fully crossed, between-participants design with equal n's in each cell (for the type of two-way ANOVA discussed in this chapter).

Advantages over a One-Way ANOVA:

- Evaluates two independent variables in a single study
- Evaluates interactions and avoids incorrect generalizations
- Permits greater confidence in generalizations
- Provides more powerful and accurate assessment of the effects of each independent variable

Formulas:

$$SS_T = \Sigma X^2 - \frac{T^2}{N}$$

$$SS_A = \Sigma \left[\frac{(\Sigma A_1)^2}{bn} + \frac{(\Sigma A_2)^2}{bn} + \dots + \frac{(\Sigma A_a)^2}{bn} \right] - \frac{T^2}{N}$$

$$SS_B = \Sigma \left[\frac{(\Sigma B_1)^2}{an} + \frac{(\Sigma B_2)^2}{an} + \dots + \frac{(\Sigma B_b)^2}{an} \right] - \frac{T^2}{N}$$

$$SS_{A \times B} = \Sigma \left[\frac{(\Sigma X_{A1B1})^2}{n} + \ldots + \frac{(\Sigma X_{AaBb})^2}{n} \right] - \frac{T^2}{N} - SS_A - SS_B$$

$$SS_W = \Sigma X^2 - \Sigma \left[\frac{(\Sigma X_{A1B1})^2}{n} + \ldots + \frac{(\Sigma X_{AaBb})^2}{n} \right]$$

$$MS_A = \frac{SS_A}{a - 1} \qquad\qquad F_A = \frac{MS_A}{MS_W}$$

$$MS_B = \frac{SS_B}{b - 1} \qquad\qquad F_B = \frac{MS_B}{MS_W}$$

$$MS_W = \frac{SS_W}{N - ab}$$

Degrees of Freedom:

$F_A = a - 1 \quad$ and $\quad N - ab$

$F_B = b - 1 \quad$ and $\quad N - ab$

$F_{A \times B} = (a - 1)(b - 1) \quad$ and $\quad N - ab$

$df_{\text{total}} = N - 1$

Follow-ups to Significant F:

- Graph interaction
- Post hoc comparisons
- Simple main effects
- Compute eta squared or omega squared
- Compute effect sizes
- Compute power

CHAPTER SUMMARY   A two-way analysis of variance is a type of factorial analysis used to compare mean scores on a dependent variable when there are two independent variables or factors. Factorial designs can have within-participants or between-participants variables; involve fixed, random, or mixed effects; be fully crossed or nested; incorporate two or more factors; and have equal or unequal n's in each cell. This chapter considered only between-participants, fixed-effects, fully crossed two-way designs with equal n's in each cell.

A two-way analysis of variance involves computing sums of squares, mean squares, and F's for main effects of each variable and for the interaction. As with a one-way ANOVA, the F-values are compared to critical values based on the F-distribution, and the findings are usually presented in a summary table. A two-way ANOVA permits the evaluation of two independent variables and the interaction between them in a single study, leading to more accurate generalizations and more powerful assessment of the effects of each independent variable.

When there is a significant interaction, it should be considered in interpreting the main effects of the study. Follow-up tests like Scheffé comparisons and Tukey HSDs should be used when a factor found to be statistically significant has more than two levels. Tests of simple main effects can also be used to assess the effects of one variable for scores at a particular level of another variable.

CHAPTER REVIEW

Multiple-Choice Questions

1. Reading a results section of an article, you encounter the sentence, "A two by two factorial analysis of variance revealed no significant effects of gender, $F(1, 44) = 2.33$, treatment, $F(1, 44) = 1.20$, or the interaction, $F(1, 44) = 2.05$, all ps $>$ .05." Which of the following statements is true?

   a. There was only one treatment.

   b. The N was 45.

   c. The N was 47.

   d. One treatment was significantly more effective than the other.

   e. The mean square for gender was larger than the mean square within.

   f. None of the above can be true.

2. The SS_A for a two-way ANOVA is 66, the MS_W is 11, the total degrees of freedom is 33, and there are three levels of Variable A. What is the value of F for the main effect of A?

   a. .50   b. 1.00   c. 2.00   d. 3.00   e. 6.00   f. None of the above

   g. It is impossible to determine from the above information.

3. The F for an interaction between Factor A and Factor B is 7.09 with 2 and 56 degrees of freedom. Factor A has four levels and Factor B has two levels. What can you conclude?

   a. Factor A had no effect on the dependent variable.

   b. The higher the score on Factor A, the lower the score on Factor B.

   c. The effect of Factor A was different for people at level 1 and level 2 of Factor B.

   d. People at level 1 of Factor B had different scores on the dependent variable than people at level 2 of Factor B.

   e. Factor B had a greater effect on the dependent variable than Factor A.

4. You have compared the mean scores for students randomly assigned to be taught via computer ($M = 90$ correct) or lecture ($M = 60$ correct), $F(1, 415) =$

32.05, $p < .001$. The effect for semester (fall, spring, summer) and the interaction were small and nonsignificant. What should you do next?

a. Conclude that the computer was more effective than lecture in this case.

b. Conduct a post hoc test to see whether the difference between the computer and lecture was statistically significant.

c. Decide that your results were inconclusive, since the interaction was non-significant.

d. Conclude that students learned less in the summer than in the fall or spring semester.

e. Recognize that you must have made a mistake in computation, as F cannot be that large.

5. After conducting a fully crossed two-way ANOVA, you find a significant main effect of Variable A, which has three levels, a significant main effect for Variable B, which has two levels, and a significant crossover interaction. What do you know for sure?

a. The scores for the three levels of Variable A represent random samples from the same population.

b. The scores for the two levels of Variable B represent random samples from the same population.

c. As level of Variable A increases, the level of Variable B decreases.

d. There were exactly five cells in the design.

e. The degrees of freedom for A is 2.

f. Both response (a) and response (b) are correct.

6. You have done a 2 by 2 factorial ANOVA and found significant effects of treatment and gender. Now you want to compare the size of the difference between the experimental group and the control group in your study with the size of the experimental/control difference in other studies that have also measured the effect of the experimental procedure, but used different dependent measures. You feel that adjusting for the standard deviation of the dependent measures would lead to values that you could compare. Which of the following measures would be the most appropriate?

a. F for treatment

b. F for the interaction

c. The effect size for treatment

d. Omega squared

e. Tukey HSD for treatment

7. Suppose that you have the following data from a 2×2 factorial design:

	A_1B_1	A_1B_2	A_2B_1	A_2B_2
$\overline{X}$	10.5	10.5	5.3	5.3
n	12	12	12	12

Which of the following is true?

a. There is a significant main effect of A.

b. There is a significant main effect of B.

c. There is no significant main effect of B.

d. The degrees of freedom within is 11.

e. The total degrees of freedom is 48.

8. A sentence from the results section of a journal article reads, "A two-way analysis of variance revealed a significant effect of gender, $F(1, 70) = 17.88$, $p < .001$, but no significant main effect of institution, $F(4, 70) = 1.18$, $p > .05$, and no significant interaction, $F(4, 70) = 1.23$, $p > .05$." Which of the following do you know to be true?

a. Males scored higher than females.

b. The gender difference was no larger than expected from random sampling from the same population.

c. There were four institutions in the study.

d. There were five institutions in the study.

e. The sample size was 70.

f. Since the interaction was not significant, you cannot tell anything about the gender difference.

9. You have conducted a study in which you concluded that gender of child, type of toy, and the interaction all affect liking for a toy. You now want to know what proportion of variance in liking for a toy in the population can be accounted for by the interaction between gender and type of toy. Which is the most appropriate procedure to answer your question?

a. Pearson r

b. The F for the interaction

c. Eta squared for the interaction

d. Omega squared for the interaction

e. The effect size for the interaction

f. None of the above would tell you anything about the proportion of variance liking for a toy in the population that can be accounted for by the interaction

10. Boys and girls were randomly assigned to watch the movies *Beethoven, Balto, Bingo,* or *Benji* and to rate how much they liked the movie. According to the results, "The main effect of gender and the interaction were not significant, both $Fs < 1$, but there was a significant main effect of movie, $F(3, 56) = 5.33$, $p < .01$." Which of the following is true?

a. The interaction had 5 degrees of freedom.

b. The sample size was 56.

c. The sample size was 63.

d. The N was 64.

e. *Beethoven* was preferred to the other movies.

f. The author must have made a mistake in computation.

Problems

11. For each of the following two-way designs, identify the two independent variables, the number of levels of each, the dependent variable, and the total N.

   a. Eighteen males and eighteen females from each of three schools are given a test of grip strength.

   b. Astronauts from the United States, Russia, and France who have or have not been in orbit are given a test of globalmindedness. There are 12 astronauts in each cell.

   c. Children who live in either two-parent families ($n = 15$), single-parent families ($n = 15$), or three-generation families (with one parent and grandparents) ($n = 15$) are randomly assigned to one of three educational conditions: cross-grade tutoring, outside mentoring, or no special treatment. After three months, they are asked how old they want to be before they become parents.

   d. Five healthy men and five healthy women in their 60s, in their 70s, in their 80s, and in their 90s are given a test of memory.

12. For each of the following two-way designs, identify the two independent variables, the dependent variable, and the number of degrees of freedom for testing each effect.

   a. Participants are asked to read a fictitious job application written by someone named Jordan, Kelly, Dale, or Mickey, later identified by "he" or "she." There were 12 people in each condition. They rated how likely they were to hire the person on a 9-point scale ranging from "no way" to "absolutely."

   b. Five cats, 5 dogs, and 5 rats were asked to run a maze for a water reward; 5 cats, 5 dogs, and 5 rats were asked to run the same maze to avoid electric shock. The number of seconds taken to run the maze on the second trial was measured for each animal.

   c. Three different approaches to purifying water were each tried out in 14 large cities, 14 small cities, and 14 towns. The amount of contaminants in each water supply was measured to the nearest 10 parts per million.

   d. A total of 60 children, one-third age 4, one-third age 5, and one-third age 6 years were randomly assigned to be taught articulation skills by one of four different methods. The proportion of mispronunciations in 5 minutes of free speech was then measured for each child.

13. Given the following ANOVA summary table:

Source	SS	df	MS	F	p
Drug (A)	256.67	2	128.34		
Dosage (B)	34.84	2	17.42	1.61	> .05
$A \times B$	346.99	4			
Within	877.77	81	10.83		
Total		89			

a. What is the SS_T?

b. How many cells were there in the study?

c. What is the N?

d. What is the critical value for the effect of dosage at the .05 α level?

e. What is the F for the effect of drug?

f. What is the mean square for the interaction?

g. Is the interaction statistically significant?

14. Complete the following ANOVA table.

Source	SS	df	MS	F	p
A		2	23.41	1.92	
B	32.12	1		2.62	> .05
$A \times B$	12.06	2	6.03		> .05
Within	662.84	54			
Total	753.84				

15. Draw a graph to represent each of the following sets of data.

a. $\overline{X}_{A_1B_1} = 20$ $\overline{X}_{A_2B_1} = 30$ $\overline{X}_{A_3B_1} = 40$

$\overline{X}_{A_1B_2} = 50$ $\overline{X}_{A_2B_2} = 40$ $\overline{X}_{A_3B_2} = 30$

b. $\overline{X}_{A_1B_1} = 20$ $\overline{X}_{A_2B_1} = 30$ $\overline{X}_{A_3B_1} = 40$ $\overline{X}_{A_4B_1} = 50$

$\overline{X}_{A_1B_2} = 25$ $\overline{X}_{A_2B_2} = 35$ $\overline{X}_{A_3B_2} = 45$ $\overline{X}_{A_4B_2} = 55$

c. $\overline{X}_{A_1B_1} = 20$ $\overline{X}_{A_2B_1} = 30$ $\overline{X}_{A_3B_1} = 40$

$\overline{X}_{A_1B_2} = 20$ $\overline{X}_{A_2B_2} = 20$ $\overline{X}_{A_3B_2} = 20$

$\overline{X}_{A_1B_3} = 50$ $\overline{X}_{A_2B_3} = 30$ $\overline{X}_{A_3B_3} = 10$

d. $\overline{X}_{A_1B_1} = 20$ $\overline{X}_{A_2B_1} = 30$ $\overline{X}_{A_3B_1} = 40$ $\overline{X}_{A_4B_1} = 50$

$\overline{X}_{A_1B_2} = 20$ $\overline{X}_{A_2B_2} = 40$ $\overline{X}_{A_3B_2} = 60$ $\overline{X}_{A_4B_2} = 80$

16. You are interested in the most effective means of studying. Therefore, you randomly assign 60 individuals to study one of two lessons (one dealing with chemistry and one with sociology) by one of three methods: just reading and rereading the lesson, reading and taking notes, or reading and underlining. You then measure the amount of time it takes until the person reports that he or she knows the content thoroughly. Your data are shown below, with the scores in minutes.

	Study type (A)		
	Reading (A₁)	Notetaking (A₂)	Underlining (A₃)
Lesson (B)			
Chemistry (B₁)	12	19	18
	19	17	15
	16	18	13
	17	21	18
	13	18	15
	17	15	17
	17	14	17
	15	15	20
	18	17	12
	20	16	19
Sociology (B₁)	10	15	16
	12	9	8
	16	12	10
	9	11	13
	11	14	8
	7	10	11
	12	11	15
	9	7	7
	10	13	11
	12	8	10

a. What is a major flaw in this study?

b. Perform an analysis of variance and present the summary table from it.

c. Describe your findings in a sentence or two.

17. You have collected data from a sample of male and female chief executive officers (CEOs) of small- to medium-sized companies and male and female chief financial officers (CFOs) of other companies of the same size. They are asked how many hours a week they spend at meetings. The data look like this:

	Gender (A)	
	Male	*Female*
Status (B)	A_1B_1	A_2B_1
CEO	28	26
	37	28
	12	18
	20	15
	26	35
	24	20
CFO	A_1B_2	A_2B_2
	17	8
	18	18
	10	13
	15	15
	12	18
	16	21

a. Perform an analysis of variance on the results.

b. Report your findings in an analysis of variance summary table.

c. Then describe your findings in words.

18. A friend of yours is just beginning college and is trying to decide whether to major in science education, bilingual education, or elementary education. This interest stimulates you to survey recent graduates of your college of education and to see what kinds of salaries they are being offered. You confine your study to people with degrees in elementary education, bilingual education, or science education. Their first year salaries (in thousands) look like this:

	Specialty (A)		
	Elementary (A_1)	*Bilingual* (A_2)	*Science* (A_3)
Gender (B)			
Males (B_1)	28	29	38
	19	27	38
	27	38	25
	24	32	27
	23	28	32
	19	25	23
	27	32	36
	25	36	34

	Specialty (A)		
	Elementary (A₁)	Bilingual (A₂)	Science (A₃)
Females (B₂)	18	22	36
	21	26	28
	24	27	30
	19	29	23
	18	28	28
	23	27	31
	24	23	25
	22	28	27

a. Report the results of an analysis of variance in an ANOVA summary table.

b. Describe your conclusions based on the ANOVA.

c. Are there any next steps that you need to take in order to come to more definite conclusions?

19. You are interested in how personal ties lead to possible biases in evaluation. At the conclusion of a Cubs/Cardinals baseball game, you have eight Cubs fans and eight Cardinals fans who have just watched the game rate the quality of the Cubs' fielding; you have eight other Cubs fans and eight other Cardinals fans rate the quality of the Cardinals' fielding. The ratings are made on a 7-point scale ranging from poor (1) to outstanding (7). The data look like this:

	Cubs Fans (A₁)	Cardinals Fans (A₂)
Team Rated (B)		
Cubs (B₁)	7	2
	7	4
	7	3
	6	5
	5	1
	7	3
	7	4
	5	4
Cardinals (B₂)	4	5
	3	6
	5	4
	4	6
	1	1
	3	7
	4	5
	4	6

a. Report the results of an analysis of variance in an ANOVA summary table.

b. Describe your conclusions based on the ANOVA.

c. Are there any next steps that you need to take in order to come to more definite conclusions?

20. In order to see whether participation in a drama class would have an effect on shy children's ability to make friends, you assign eight friendly children and eight shy children to take a half-hour drama class for 10 Saturdays. Eight friendly children and eight shy children were not assigned to the class. At the end of the 10 weeks, you ask each child to name all the children who are his or her friends. The numbers of friends named are as follows:

Drama Class (A)	Yes (A_1)	No (A_2)
Shy (B_1)	8	9
	9	7
	7	8
	6	5
	5	8
	9	5
	7	5
	5	4
Friendly (B_2)	6	2
	3	3
	5	4
	4	2
	7	1
	3	3
	4	5
	4	2

a. Report the results of an analysis of variance in an ANOVA summary table.

b. Describe your conclusions based on the ANOVA.

Study Questions

1. Suppose that you wish to study the question of whether practice in writing poetry leads elementary school students to enjoy reading and listening to poetry more. First, decide on (exactly) two independent variables that you could use if you were to conduct an experiment to answer this question. Second, identify a dependent variable that you might use in this potential experiment. Then design your imaginary study using these variables. Next, identify whether your study used a within-participants or between-participants design. Can you redesign it using the other approach? Are the factors

in your study both fixed or both random, or is there one of each? Could that be changed? Is your design a fully crossed design? Would it make sense to change it? If you were to actually carry out the study, would the cells all have the same n? Finally, are there other variables you might want to add to the design to make it a three-way or four-way design?

2. Go to the library and find a report of an article that uses a two-way analysis of variance. See if you can tell from the article whether the design involved between- or within-participants factors; had fixed, random, or mixed factors; was fully crossed or incomplete; and had equal or unequal n's in the different cells. Did the authors predict main effects, interactions, or both? Were these predictions supported by the analyses? How did they test any significant interactions?

3. Try to think of a situation in which you would do a two-way analysis of variance and predict only one statistically significant main effect and no significant interaction. Write your description and your prediction on separate pieces of paper. Try to think of a situation in which you would do a two-way analysis of variance and predict two significant main effects and no interaction. Write your description and your prediction on separate pieces of paper. Now, try to think of a situation in which you would do a two-way analysis of variance and predict no significant main effects and a significant interaction. Again, write your description and your prediction on separate pieces of paper. The last situation to imagine is one in which you would do a two-way analysis of variance and predict both a significant main effect and a significant interaction. Once more write your description and your predictions on separate pieces of paper.

   Now trade descriptions with someone else. Write out your predictions for each of the other person's four descriptions. Then compare your predictions. Were they all the same? If not, why not?

4. Suppose that you have done a study comparing the effects of caffeine consumption on fathers of children diagnosed with Attention Deficit Hyperactivity Disorder (ADHD) and fathers whose children do not have such a diagnosis. You measure the fathers' ability to concentrate on a boring task after being randomly assigned to drink an exceedingly high caffeine cola or a caffeine-free cola. You predict an interaction such that fathers of ADHD children who consume caffeine and fathers of non-ADHD children who do not consume caffeine will be relatively more able to concentrate on the task.

   Make up some data that you might obtain from such a study that you think would support this hypothesis. Conduct a two-way ANOVA on the data. Test the interaction appropriately and describe it in APA style.

CHAPTER

13

Chi-Square

What Is a Chi-Square Test?

Aside from Spearman's rho, the statistical procedures discussed in this book have all been parametric tests. This chapter deals with the most commonly used nonparametric tests, the chi-square goodness-of-fit test and the chi-square test of independence, both often referred to as *chi-square* (χ^2). As promised, the computation of the χ^2 statistic is noticeably easier than that of most parametric tests, and the procedure itself is a very versatile one.

A **chi-square test** is a test that looks at scores on one or more nominal-level variables and at the frequencies with which these scores occur. More specifically, a chi-square procedure is a test of the null hypothesis that the frequencies or numbers of scores falling into different categories do not differ from the frequencies or numbers that have been hypothesized based on some theory or data. Such a hypothesis might be worded in terms of proportions or percentages, but the actual χ^2 test is conducted using the numbers that are observed to fall into various categories and the numbers that would be expected to fall into these categories if the null hypothesis is true.

For example, suppose that you have developed a new product and want to know whether it is superior to the other products of its kind. Perhaps this product is a new insect repellent, which (you hope) smells less repellent to humans than the other two leading brands. You give each of 100 people a sample of each of the three brands to sniff and ask them which product they prefer. Since you are comparing the percentages of scores falling into each of several categories, a χ^2 goodness-of-fit-test would be the procedure you would use to see whether or not the participants show a preference for one of the participants three products that exceeds the chance level.

χ^2 Distribution

Similarity to Other Distributions. Like the *t*-distribution and the *F*-distribution, the chi-square distribution is really a series of distributions, each with its associated degrees of freedom. Like the t-distribution but unlike the F-distribution, the χ^2 distribution has only one degree of freedom parameter. It is related to the normal, t-, and F-distributions, as you can surmise from the fact that the critical value for the χ^2 distribution with 1 degree of freedom is equal to the critical value for the F-distribution with 1 and infinite degrees of freedom at the same alpha level and to the square of the critical value for t with infinite degrees of freedom. So, in the unlikely event that you have failed to get on intimate terms with that exciting number 3.84 and its square root, 1.96, you have yet another chance.

Critical Values.   Although there are some similarities between the χ^2 distribution and the t- and F-distributions, the differences between them are more important. One of these differences concerns the critical value for the χ^2 distribution. Unlike all the other statistical procedures that we have discussed, the degrees of freedom for χ^2 does not depend on the sample size. It is completely unrelated to the number of scores in the sample. The critical value for a χ^2 test depends on the degrees of freedom, but the degrees of freedom parameter is related to the number of categories or possible scores rather than to the sample size. Thus, a larger number of degrees of freedom for a χ^2 test is associated with a larger critical value, unlike the pattern with other statistical procedures, in which the critical value decreases as the number of degrees of freedom increases. Remember that the reason for this relationship is not that a larger sample size is associated with a larger critical value but rather that the degrees of freedom for the test is independent of the sample size.

Assumptions

Because the chi-square test is nonparametric, it requires far fewer assumptions than do the parametric tests that we have been discussing. Unlike parametric tests, it does not assume that the data have been measured on an interval or ratio scale or that the scores are normally distributed. Since a χ^2 test deals with frequencies rather than means, its use does not require that the data fit any particular shape but only that the scores be independently sampled. In fact, since the raw scores on the dependent measure consist of categories, usually with a limited number of alternative values, they are unlikely to have a shape anything like the normal distribution.

Like any statistical test, the results of a χ^2 test can be generalized with confidence only to the population from which the scores were randomly selected. Thus, if the scores are not representative of the population in which you are interested, generalization from the results of a χ^2 (or any other) analysis must be done with caution. If you ask people whom they support for senator, but your sample includes only Republicans, it is unlikely that your results will generalize to the entire sample of registered voters, no matter how honestly your respondents reply to your question.

What Is a χ^2 Goodness-of-Fit Test?

A **chi-square goodness-of-fit test** is used to test a theory about the proportions of scores that should fall into certain categories. Sometimes the theory is a formal one, based on reasoning that leads to the assumption that particular scores should occur certain proportions of the time. For example, a genetic theory about transmission of certain traits might predict that one-fourth of the offspring of a particular mating should have a certain observable characteristic and three-fourths of the offspring should not. More commonly, the theory is an informal one, based on assumptions that may need to be made explicit before the goodness-of-fit test can be conducted. For instance, if you want to know whether people have a preference among four alternatives, the informal theory that you are testing is that there is no preference, leading to the null hypothesis that each of the alternatives will be selected equally often (i.e., by one-fourth of the people).

Sometimes a χ^2 goodness-of-fit test is done to see whether or not the results of your study are similar to those someone else has found or assumed would be found. For example, if it has been reported that 20% of people fall into one category, 30% into another, and 50% into the remaining category, you may wish to compare the proportions of the individuals in your sample to these reported proportions, testing the null hypothesis (or informal theory) that the people in your study do not differ from those described in the report. Perhaps, for instance, you know from census data the relative distribution of individuals in your state into different counties and you want to see whether or not the people in your sample can be viewed as representative of those in the state with respect to county of residence. A χ^2 goodness-of-fit test would be the appropriate statistic to use.

Relationship of χ^2 to the Hypothesis.   With all of the statistical tests described so far—tests for the significance of r, ρ, t, and F—a large value of the test statistic allows you to reject the null hypothesis and conclude that there is a statistically significant difference between the groups or a significant relationship among the variables. Similarly, a large value of χ^2 allows you to reject the null hypothesis that the proportions in your sample are identical to the hypothesized proportions and to conclude that the frequencies observed in your sample differ significantly from those expected if the null hypothesis is true.

In other words, a large value of χ^2 means that the data are a poor fit to the theory. However, it must be remembered that the theory that led to the expected proportions may or may not be the research hypothesis. Sometimes a researcher will compare the data to the frequencies she truly expects, based on her sophisticated mathematical theory; sometimes the hypothesized proportions (such as equal numbers in each category) are not what the researcher expects to find.

For example, suppose that you wish to test the hypothesis that a particular employer discriminates against Hispanic applicants. What would you use as your null hypothesis? If all applicants are classified as African–American, Anglo–American, Asian–American, Hispanic–American, or "Other," you could test the null hypothesis that .2 of the employees for the company come from each ethnic group. If you are interested only in Hispanics versus other ethnic groups, you could test the null hypothesis that .2 of the employees are Hispanic and .8 come from other backgrounds. However, this seems inherently silly, since you have no reason to believe that .2 of the potential or actual applicants for employment were Hispanic.

TIP

> With most statistical procedures, the research hypothesis is usually different from the null hypothesis; with a χ^2 goodness-of-fit test, sometimes the research hypothesis is tested directly and is therefore equivalent to the null hypothesis. This is not a problem in terms of carrying out the procedures or interpreting the findings, but it does imply that you have to think carefully about exactly what you are testing.

As another possibility, you could look at the population of the metropolitan area from which the employees come and use the proportions of Hispanics and non-Hispanics as the basis for your null hypothesis, which assumes that people from all ethnic groups in the area are equally likely to apply for employment.

Alternatively, if you could get access to application forms, you could consider the proportion of applicants for employment who are Hispanic and non-Hispanic. To be more sophisticated, you could look at the applicant pool on a job-to-job basis, omitting all applicants who do not meet the minimum advertised qualifications for employment. You might even wish to consider the issue of whether or not there were qualified Hispanics who did not apply because the company did not have an affirmative action program designed to ensure that qualified potential employees from all ethnic groups were equally likely to hear about the job openings. Clearly, there is no single answer to the question of what the appropriate null hypothesis should be. The point here is that identifying the null hypothesis to be tested is not necessarily obvious, and it is often as much a design problem as a statistical one.

Formula

The formula for chi-square is a relatively simple one, as is true for most nonparametric tests:

$$\chi^2 = \Sigma \frac{(O - E)^2}{E}$$

where O stands for the number of scores observed in a category (the **observed frequency**) and E stands for the number of scores expected in a category based on the theory (the **expected frequency**). The formula states that, once the expected frequency has been computed for each category, it is subtracted from the observed frequency, the discrepancy is squared, the squared number is divided by the expected frequency, and this quotient is summed across all the categories.

Expected Frequencies Versus Proportions.   The most difficult aspect of the formula for a goodness-of-fit χ^2 test is figuring out the expected frequencies. The calculations are not the problem; the issue is keeping straight the distinctions among proportions, percentages, and frequencies. Ordinarily a theory would be worded in terms of percentages or proportions rather than frequencies. However, the formula for χ^2 deals with the numbers expected in each category, not with the expected proportions or percentages. To calculate the expected frequencies, it is necessary to multiply the hypothesized proportions by the total sample size, N.

Sample Size.   There are two useful things to keep in mind about the sample size in a χ^2 test. First of all, $N = \Sigma O$; or, in words, the sum of the observed or actual frequencies in each category equals the total sample size. Similarly, $N = \Sigma E$—that is, the sum of the expected frequencies also equals the total sample size. This equation provides a helpful check on the computation of the expected frequencies in the different categories. Second, remember that the larger the sample size, the more likely it is that a false null hypothesis will be rejected. A chi-square analysis with the same number of degrees of freedom is more likely to lead to a rejection of the null hypothesis if the sample size is large than if it is small. Although the power of all statistical procedures increases with an increase in the sample size, it may not be as obvious in the case of χ^2, where the sample size is unrelated to the degrees of freedom.

Degrees of Freedom.   The degrees of freedom parameter for a χ^2 goodness-of-fit test is equal to the number of categories minus the number of constraints on the expected frequencies, which is usually equal to the number of categories minus one (due to the constraint that $\Sigma E = N$). Thus, if there are 7 different values for the dependent variable, then the relevant χ^2 test would have 6 degrees of freedom. The degrees of freedom parameter, however, depends not upon the number of possible response categories that participants could conceivably have used but upon the number of categories that you are actually comparing.

For example, if you were asking people to name their favorite colors, and only five colors were named, the χ^2 goodness-of-fit test would have 4 degrees of freedom, even though there are more than five possible responses to the question "What is your favorite color?" Moreover, if you decided to look at only three categories (e.g., "red," "blue," and "other"), meaning that you put all responses such as "fuchsia" or "ecru" into the "other" category, a χ^2 goodness-of-fit test comparing the observed and actual frequencies of responses in these three categories would have only 2 degrees of freedom.

Examples of Goodness-of-Fit Tests

Let's consider two different examples of a χ^2 goodness-of-fit test, one in which the expected proportions are based on previously reported data and one in which they are based on a theory.

EXAMPLE

Leisure Activities. Suppose that you have read a newspaper article reporting that 40% of American men say that their favorite pastime is sports, 40% say that it is spending time with their family, and 20% name some other activity. You survey the men in your neighborhood and find that 10 reported a preference for sports, 15 chose being with their family, and 5 chose to do something else. Do your neighbors differ significantly from the American men described in the newspaper article in terms of how they choose to spend their leisure time?

Solution: In order to answer this question, you need first to recognize that it involves a hypothesis about the distribution of scores among the categories of a qualitative variable. This variable, preferred pastime, has three different levels: sports, family, and other, with hypothesized percentages of 40%, 40%, and 20%, respectively. These percentages translate into proportions of .40, .40, and .20. One way to set up the problem is given in the following table:

Category	O Frequency	E Proportion	EF	O − E	(O − E)²	(O − E)²/E
Sports	10	.40	12	−2	4	.333
Family	15	.40	12	3	9	.750
Other	5	.20	6	−1	1	.167

$$\chi^2 = \Sigma(O - E)^2/E = 1.250$$

Note that although the computations were carried out to three decimal places, it is customary to round off and report χ^2 and all other test statistics to two decimal places.

In order to decide whether or not a χ^2 value of 1.25 is statistically significant, you need to compare it with the relevant critical value from Appendix Table 8, a portion of which is reproduced in Table 13.1. Since there were three categories, χ^2 had 2 degrees of freedom. The table reveals that the critical value for a χ^2 test with 2 degrees of freedom at the .05 α-level is 5.991, and $\chi^2_{.01}(2) = 9.210$.

Since the obtained value of χ^2 was less than the critical value, we would retain H_0 and conclude that there was not a significant difference between

TABLE 13.1   Sample Portion of Appendix Table 8: Critical Values for Chi-Square

			Alpha			
df	*.10*	*.05*	*.02*	*.01*	*.002*	*.001*
1	2.706	3.841	5.412	6.635	9.550	10.828
2	4.605	5.991	7.824	9.210	12.430	13.816
3	6.251	7.815	9.837	11.345	14.796	16.267
4	7.779	9.488	11.668	13.277	16.924	18.468
5	9.236	11.071	13.388	15.086	18.908	20.516
6	10.645	12.592	15.033	16.812	20.792	22.459
7	12.017	14.067	16.622	18.475	22.601	24.323
8	13.362	15.507	18.168	20.090	24.353	26.124

our neighbors' preferred pastimes and those reported in the newspaper. In fact, if we had remembered that the critical value for χ^2 at the .05 α-level with 1 degree of freedom is 3.84 and recognized that no value for χ^2 that is less than 3.84 will ever be significant at the .05 level, we could have saved the step of referring to Appendix Table 8.   ■

EXAMPLE

Most Romantic City. Suppose that you work for the Paris Chamber of Commerce and want to see whether or not you can promote it as the World's Most Romantic City. You survey a group of travellers about what city they consider to be the most romantic and find that 158 pick Paris, 40 pick New York, and 2 pick Chicago. What should you conclude?

Solution: First, since you are a sophisticated statistician, you do not settle for the "eyeball test," which shows that more people picked Paris than either of the other two cities. The question of interest is whether or not this difference is statistically significant. More specifically, you would probably be interested in testing the hypothesis that the respondents had no preferences among the three cities—that is, that none of the cities deserves the title. Your null hypothesis would therefore be that .33 of the population would choose each of the cities. The following table shows your data and the relevant calculations:

City	*OF*	*EP*	*EF*	*O – E*	$(O - E)^2$	$(O - E)^2/E$
Chicago	2	.33	66.67	−64.67	4182.21	62.73
New York	40	.33	66.67	−26.67	711.29	10.67
Paris	158	.33	66.67	91.33	8341.17	125.11
					$\chi^2 = \Sigma(O - E)^2/E =$	198.51

In order to decide whether or not a χ^2 value of 198.51 is statistically significant, you need to compare it with the critical value for χ^2 with 2 degrees of freedom:

$$\chi^2_{.001}(2) = 13.82$$

which is much smaller than the actual value for χ^2. Accordingly, we would reject the null hypothesis that the cities are equally popular. However, this decision does not allow you to conclude that Paris was viewed as the most romantic, any more than a significant F from a one-way analysis of variance with more than two groups permits you to conclude that one particular mean was significantly higher than the other means. The fact that the numbers of people picking the various cities as most romantic differed from the hypothetical frequencies could have been due as much to the fact that only two discerning individuals selected Chicago as to the fact that 158 people chose Paris.

In order to directly test the hypothesis that Paris is preferred to the other two cities, you would have to reduce the data to a test with 1 degree of freedom and directly compare the number of people choosing Paris with the number choosing both other cities combined. Collapsing across categories, we would get:

City	OF	EP	EF	O – E	(O – E)²	(O – E)²/E
Paris	158	.33	66.67	91.33	8341.17	125.11
New York and Chicago	42	.67	133.33	–91.33	8341.17	62.56

$$\chi^2 = \Sigma(O - E)^2/E = 187.67$$

Since this χ^2 test has only two categories, it has only 1 degree of freedom. A χ^2 value of 187.67 far exceeds the critical value at the .001 α-level of 10.83, which permits you to conclude (in APA style) that "Paris was considered the most romantic city by a significantly higher proportion than that choosing New York or Chicago, $\chi^2(1, N = 200) = 187.67, p < .001$." ∎

Deciding on the Hypothesis to Test

Although the computations for a chi-square goodness-of-fit test are relatively simple, performing such a test is not as cut and dried as doing a one-way analysis of variance, for instance. In order to do a χ^2 goodness-of-fit test, you have to decide on the exact hypothesis that you are testing.

For example, if you want to see whether one of several alternatives is preferred, you would ordinarily test the hypothesis that each alternative is selected by the same proportion (and therefore the same number) of people. However, consider the instance in which you want to know whether boys are more likely than girls to take calculus courses in high school. What is the appropriate null hypothesis? Is it that .5 of the students taking calculus will be boys and .5 will be girls, or is it that the proportions of male and female students in calculus classes will be equal to the proportions of male and female students (perhaps .55 and .45) in the prerequisite courses? Either is a reasonable hypothesis to test, but it is important to decide which is the one of interest to you and to specify exactly what hypothesis is being tested when you describe your procedures.

As another example, imagine that you want to know whether fire engines painted red are more likely to be involved in traffic accidents (caused by people who don't see them in time to get out of their way) than fire engines painted chartreuse, yellow, or some other color. What is the relevant null hypothesis? You could presumably gather information about the colors of all fire engines involved in accidents, but with what would you compare this number? .5? $1/N$, where N is the number of different colors of fire engines involved in accidents? $1/N$, where N is the number of different colors that fire engines are painted? Probably the most sensible hypothetical proportion is the proportion of fire engines that are painted red—assuming that all fire engines are equally likely to be called out to fires. In short, whenever a goodness-of-fit χ^2 test is done, it is important to precisely specify the hypothesis against which your observed proportions are being compared.

χ^2 Goodness-of-Fit Test

Purpose: To test a theory about the proportions of scores that should fall into certain categories

Assumptions:

- Scores have been independently sampled.
- N is reasonably large (few expected frequencies < 5).
- Scores are representative of the population.

Formulas:

$$\chi^2 = \Sigma \frac{(O - E)^2}{E}$$

E in a category = (N) (expected proportion in the category)
df = number of categories – 1

Advantages:

- It does not assume normality or interval-level data.
- It is easy to compute.

Disadvantages:

- You must specify precisely what hypothesis you wish to test.
- Packaged statistical programs may not perform a chi-square goodness-of-fit test.

One caution to point out is that packaged statistical packages generally do not perform χ^2 goodness-of-fit tests. Therefore, you will probably have to perform these tests by hand, even if you are doing your other analyses by the computer. However, you can get the computer to print out the numbers and percentages of scores that fall into each category, so the computations should be quite simple.

What Is a χ^2 Test of Independence?

A **chi-square test of independence** is used to determine whether or not two variables measured on a nominal scale are associated or related. This purpose is achieved by comparing the actual frequencies obtained with those that would be expected if the two variables were independent. A χ^2 test of independence can therefore be viewed as similar to other measures of association like Pearson r and Spearman rho except that these latter measures cannot be used with qualitative variables.

On the other hand, a χ^2 test of independence also tests the null hypothesis that the proportions of responses in the categories representing different levels of one variable are the same for people at all levels of the other variable; for example, that the proportions of males and females who say "yes," "not sure," and "no" do not differ significantly. When viewed in this way, a χ^2 test of independence can be viewed as similar to an analysis of variance in that it compares the scores of two or more groups on a dependent measure. Thus a χ^2 test of independence can be viewed both as an indicator of association and as an indicator of difference, depending on how the question is worded.

Contingency Tables

The data for a χ^2 test of independence are usually placed in the form of a **contingency table**, which is an arrangement of scores in which the various levels of one variable form columns and the levels of another variable represent rows. Each category or cell in the table represents the union of a particular score on one variable with a particular score on the other. For example, consider the following simple table;

	"Yes"	"Not sure"	"No"
Male	7	3	8
Female	4	6	12

In this table, the number 12 represents the fact that there were 12 females who responded "no" (or, put another way, 12 of the people who said "no" were female). Based on the contingency table, you should be able to see that there were 11 "yes" responses, 9 "not sure" responses, and 20 "no" responses; similarly, there were 18 males and 22 females in the study. Remember, though, that the data do not arrive in the form of a contingency table. There is no score of "7" in your data, even though there is a "7" in the contingency table. The raw data are pairs of scores like "male, yes" from one person or "female, not sure" from another. As was the case for frequency distributions back in Chapter 3, you have to use these raw scores to construct the contingency table.

Formulas

The general formula for a chi-square test of independence is the same as the formula for a goodness-of-fit test:

$$\chi^2 = \Sigma \frac{(O - E)^2}{E}$$

where O stands for the observed frequency and E stands for the expected frequency of each cell in the contingency table. The number of cells in the table is equal to the number of rows times the number of columns; thus, a 3×2 contingency table will have 6 cells and therefore 6 numbers that will be summed to produce the value of χ^2.

Expected Values for Cells.   The expected frequencies for the cells in a contingency table are based on the theory that the variables are independent. If that is true, then the proportions of people scoring in the different categories of one variable should be the same regardless of a person's position on the other variable. For example, if occupation is unrelated to endorsement of a particular candidate, then the same percentage of plumbers, construction workers, and schoolteachers should endorse each of the candidates. Similarly, if one-third of the people supporting candidate A are plumbers, then one-third of the people supporting candidate B would also be expected to be plumbers. Since a χ^2 test of independence does test a theory—the theory that the variables are unrelated to each other—it can be viewed as a special case of a χ^2 goodness-of-fit test. However, in order to avoid confusion, most people describe and discuss these procedures as if they were separate ones.

Formula. The formula for computing the expected frequencies for a χ^2 test of independence is straightforward. The expected value for each cell in a contingency table is equal to the total frequency for the row in which the cell appears times the total frequency for the column in which the cell appears divided by the sample size. This formula can be represented as

$$EF = \frac{(\text{row} f)(\text{column} f)}{N}$$

TIP ▪▪

> Sometimes these frequencies are called *marginal frequencies,* as they may be computed and written in the margins of the contingency table.

Degrees of Freedom.   The degrees of freedom for a χ^2 test of independence is equal to one less than the number of rows in the contingency table times one less than the number of columns. More formally,

$$df = (R - 1)(C - 1)$$

A 2×3 contingency table therefore leads to a χ^2 test of independence with $(2-1)(3-1)$ or 2 degrees of freedom.

TIP ▪▪

> There are three rules of thumb that you can follow to identify some results that will not be statistically significant.
>
> - If $\chi^2 < 3.84$, it will not be significant.
> - If $\chi^2 < df$, it will not be significant.
> - With a χ^2 test of independence, the number of cells in the contingency table is a very rough approximation to the critical value.

Calculator Formula for 2×2 Table.   There is an additional formula for a 2×2 chi-square test that does not require the calculation of expected frequencies and can be done easily on a hand calculator. For a contingency table with 2×2 cells, such as the following,

A	B
C	D

the formula is

$$\chi^2 = \frac{N\left[((A)(D)) - ((B)(C))\right]^2}{(A + B)(C + D)(A + C)(B + D)}$$

It says to do the following steps.

Step 1: Multiply the frequency in the upper left-hand cell (*A*) by the frequency in the lower right-hand cell (*D*).

Step 2: Multiply the frequency in the upper right-hand cell (*B*) by the frequency in the lower left-hand cell (*C*).

Step 3: Subtract the product in step 2 from the product in step 1 and square the difference.

Step 4: Divide this value by each of the four marginal frequencies—that is, the totals for the two rows and for the two columns:

A	B	A + B
C	D	C + D
A + C	B + D	Total (N)

Step 5: Multiply this quotient by N.

TIP

> In theory, step 5 could precede step 4. In practice, with most hand calculators it is better to divide the squared difference obtained in step 3 by some or all of the marginal frequencies before multiplying by N. This usually keeps the numbers small enough so that even an inexpensive calculator does not become intimidated or overwhelmed.

Examples of χ^2 Tests

Let's see how these formulas apply to a research situation in which you want to see how members of two different professions differ in their opinions.

EXAMPLE

A 2 × 2 Chi-Square. Imagine that you are interested in the issue of whether physicians or nurses are more likely to support a bill pending in the state legislature that permits nurse practitioners to prescribe certain drugs. You sample individuals affiliated with two large hospitals and ask the physicians and nurses who agree to participate whether they support or oppose the bill. The data, including the totals, are shown in the following table:

	Support	Oppose	Total
Physician	16	34	50
Nurse	72	36	108
Total	88	70	158

Solution: To use the conventional formula, you would calculate the expected frequency for each cell:

For physicians supporting, $\dfrac{(50)(88)}{158} = 27.848$

For physicians opposing, $\dfrac{(50)(70)}{158} = 22.152$

For nurses supporting, $\dfrac{(108)(88)}{158} = 60.152$

For nurses opposing, $\dfrac{(108)(70)}{158} = 47.848$

Remember that these expected frequencies come from the null hypothesis that the proportions of supporters in the population are the same for nurses and physicians. Notice that in the sample these proportions were 88/158 or 56% supporters and 70/158 or 44% opponents. Thus, if the null hypothesis were true, 56% of the nurses and 56% of the doctors would support the act.

TIP

> As a check on your computations, you could add the expected frequencies in each row and column. Unless you have made a mistake in your computation, the expected frequency in each row will equal the observed frequency for that row, and the expected frequency in each column will equal the observed frequency for that column.

Checking, we see that

27.848 + 22.152 = 50	the number of physicians
60.152 + 47.848 = 108	the number of nurses
27.848 + 60.152 = 88	the number of supporters
22.152 + 47.848 = 70	the number of opponents

And, of course, the sum of all four expected values equals the sample size, 158.

After computing the expected frequencies the next step is to compute the value of χ^2. To do this, we take $\Sigma(O - E)^2/E$ for each of the four cells. We could put these computations in a table:

Category	O	E	O − E	$(O - E)^2$	$(O - E)^2/E$
P/S	16	27.848	−11.848	140.375	5.041
P/O	34	22.152	11.848	140.375	6.337
N/S	72	60.152	11.848	140.375	2.334
N/O	36	47.848	−11.848	140.375	2.934
					16.646

Chi-square, therefore, equals 16.65.   ■

Interpretation. In order to find out what this result means, we need to decide whether the value of χ^2 is or is not statistically significant. The degrees of freedom is equal to $(2 - 1)(2 - 1)$ or 1, and a look at Appendix Table 8 reveals that the critical values for χ^2 with 1 degree of freedom are 3.84, 6.64, and 10.83 at the .05, .01, and .001 α-levels, respectively. Since the actual value of χ^2 exceeds even $\chi^2_{.001}$, we can reject H_0 and conclude that there is a significant difference in the proportions of physicians and nurses who endorse the bill permitting nurse practitioners to prescribe certain drugs. Because this was a 1 degree of freedom χ^2 test with only one possible interpretation, we can even go beyond this general statement to draw a con-clusion about the direction of the difference. More precisely, we could state (in APA style) that "the percentage of nurses who supported the bill (67%) was significantly higher than the percentage of physicians who supported it (32%), $\chi^2(1, N = 158) = 16.65$, $p < .001$." Alternatively, we could say that there was a significant relationship between the variables of profession and atti-tude toward the bill, with supporters being more likely to be nurses than were opponents.

Calculator Formula. Instead of using the step-by-step approach to cal-culating the value of χ^2, we could have used the calculator formula

$$\chi^2 = \frac{N\left[((A)(D)) - ((B)(C))\right]^2}{(A+B)(C+D)(A+C)(B+D)} = \frac{158\left[((16)(36)) - ((34)(72))\right]^2}{(50)(108)(88)(70)}$$

$$= \frac{158(-1872)^2}{33,264,000} = \frac{553,692,672}{33,264,000} = 16.65$$

On my calculator, I was able to do this formula without having to copy down any intermediate values, which can save a lot of time.

TIP ▬▬▬▬▬▬▬▬▬▬▬▬▬▬▬▬▬▬▬▬▬▬▬▬▬▬▬▬▬▬▬▬

Using the first formula, you may have noticed that the absolute values of the discrepancies between the observed and expected frequencies for each cell were the same. This saves some time in computation, as the numera-tor for calculating the value of χ^2 for each cell will be the same when you have a 2×2 contingency table. However, you still have to calculate and divide by the expected frequencies for each cell, as they will not all be the same. Moreover, with a table with more than one degree of freedom, the discrepancies between O and E will generally all be different.

EXAMPLE

A 3 × 4 Chi-Square. Suppose that you are interested in the relationship between an individual's experiences in childhood and the kind of parenting which he or she provides (which is a more complicated situation than the previous example since there are more than two levels of each of the variables). You obtain a sample of children who have been brought to a community mental health center because they have been subject to physical abuse, sexual abuse, or neglect. You also have a sample of children who are attending the same school as the abused children and who have presumably not been abused.

Your actual interest is in the parents of these children, to see whether or not their own experiences as children are related to how they (mis)treat their own children. You manage to track down the mothers of all of these children and conduct a structured interview with each one about her experiences as a child. Based on these interviews, you classify each mother as Definitely Abused, Possibly Abused or Neglected, and Not Abused and arrange the data as in the following table:

Mother

Child	Definitely Abused	Possibly Abused	Not Abused
Physical Abuse	4	12	5
Sexual Abuse	10	8	6
Neglect	3	8	5
None	1	3	22

Solution: To answer the general question of whether or not a mother's history of being abused (definite, possible, or none) is related to child's experiences (physical abuse, sexual abuse, neglect, or no abuse), you would do a $3 \times 4 \; \chi^2$ test of independence. To do so, you first compute the row and column totals:

Mother

Child	Definitely Abused	Possibly Abused	Not Abused	Total
Physical Abuse	4	12	5	21
Sexual Abuse	10	8	6	24
Neglect	3	8	5	16
None	1	3	22	26
Total	18	31	38	87

TABLE 13.2   Computation of Expected Frequencies and Chi-Square Values

Cell	OF	(R)(C)/T	EF	O – E	(O – E)²	(O – E)²/E
DA/Ph	4	(21)(18)/87	4.345	–.345	.119	.027
PA/Ph	12	(21)(31)/87	7.483	4.517	20.403	2.727
NA/Ph	5	(21)(38)/87	9.172	–4.172	17.405	1.898
DA/S	10	(24)(18)/87	4.966	5.034	25.346	5.104
PA/S	8	(24)(31)/87	8.552	–.552	.304	.036
NA/S	6	(24)(38)/87	10.483	–4.483	20.095	1.917
DA/Ne	3	(16)(18)/87	3.310	–.310	.096	.029
PA/Ne	8	(16)(31)/87	5.701	2.299	5.285	.927
NA/Ne	5	(16)(38)/87	6.989	–1.989	3.954	.566
DA/No	1	(26)(18)/87	5.379	–4.379	19.178	3.565
PA/No	3	(26)(31)/87	9.264	–6.264	39.242	4.236
NA/No	22	(26)(38)/87	11.356	10.644	113.294	9.976
						31.464

You then compute the expected frequency for each cell, multiplying the row total by the corresponding column total and dividing the product by 87, the total N.

- For Definitely Abused mothers of Physically Abused children, the expected frequency would be 21(18)/87 or 4.345.
- Next, the discrepancy between that and the observed value of 4.00 is computed.
- This difference of –.345 is squared.
- This square of .119 is divided by the expected frequency of 4.345, yielding .027.

This process is repeated for each of the 12 cells and the totals are summed to obtain the data shown in Table 13.2. Summing all the numbers in the last column leads to 31.464 as the value for chi-square, which rounds off to 31.46.

Interpretation.   To calculate the degrees of freedom, we need to multiply the number of rows minus 1 (or 3) by the number of columns minus 1 (or 2) to get 6 degrees of freedom. Using Appendix Table 8, we can see that the critical values for 6 degrees of freedom are 12.59, 16.81, and 22.46 at the .05, .01, and .001 α-levels, respectively. We could therefore conclude (in APA style) that "there is a significant relationship between a mother's experience of abusive treatment and her child's status, $\chi^2(6, N = 87) = 31.46, p < .001$."

Collapsing Across Categories.   This conclusion is necessarily a somewhat general one. In order to come to a more definitive conclusion about how the variables are related, we would want to look at a 2 × 2 contingency table.

One way to do this would be to combine (or collapse) across categories and compare mothers who were abused as children and those who were not with respect to whether their children fit into the categories indicating abuse or not, ignoring those mothers whose interview could not be clearly classified as indicating a history of abuse or one of nonabuse. This means that the 31 women in the Possibly Abused category would not be included in this analysis. By combining the categories of Physical Abuse, Sexual Abuse, and Neglect, we can take the data presented above and put it into a new contingency table, as follows:

	Mother Abused	Mother Not Abused	Total
Child Abused	17	16	33
Child Not Abused	1	22	23
Total	18	38	56

Using the formula for χ^2, we get an expected value of $(33)(18)/56$ or 10.607 for the MA/CA cell and a contribution to the total χ^2 of $(17 - 10.607)^2/10.607$ or 3.858. The other cells lead to expected values of

$$\frac{(33)(38)}{56} = 22.393 \qquad \frac{(18)(23)}{56} = 7.393 \qquad \frac{(23)(38)}{56} = 15.607$$

contributing 1.825, 5.528, and 2.619, respectively, to χ^2. Note that in each case the discrepancy between the observed and the expected value is 6.393, which yields a square of 40.870. Since the expected values are all different, however, each cell contributes a different amount to the value of χ^2.

In this case, the total value of $\chi^2 = 13.83$, which exceeds the critical value of 10.83 at the .001 α-level. We would therefore conclude that abused children were more likely to have mothers who had been abused (52% of them did) than were nonabused children (4%), $\chi^2(1, N = 56) = 13.83, p < .001$.

TIP

Of course, this kind of correlational research study does not prove that being abused causes abuse or tolerance of abuse (some of the children may have been abused by people other than their mother), as contributory factors such as poverty, stress, cultural traditions, differences in reporting of abuse, and other factors may be influencing the apparent relationship. However, it does allow you to conclude that the variables are clearly associated with each other.

χ^2 Test of Independence

Purpose: To determine whether or not two variables measured on a nominal scale are associated or related *and* to test hypotheses about differences in proportions or percentages between groups

Assumptions:

- Scores have been independently sampled.
- N is reasonably large (few expected frequencies < 5).
- Scores are representative of the population.
- Each participant contributes data to one and only one cell.

Formulas:

$$\chi^2 = \Sigma \frac{(O - E)^2}{E}$$

$$E = \frac{(\text{row } f)(\text{column } f)}{N}$$

$$df = (R - 1)(C - 1)$$

$$\chi^2 = \frac{N\big[((A)(D) - (B)(C))\big]^2}{(A + B)(C + D)(A + C)(B + D)} \quad \text{for a } 2 \times 2 \text{ contingency table}$$

Advantages:

- It does not assume normality or interval-level data.
- It can test hypotheses about both differences and relationships.

Disadvantages:

- For more than a 2×2 design, you cannot draw conclusions about the precise relationship between the variables without additional tests on 2×2 subtables or collapsed tables.

Strength of the Relationship

Although a chi-square test tells you whether the relationship between two variables is statistically significant, a chi-square test does not provide a direct measure of the strength of that relationship. There are two measures that can be used to describe the strength of the relationship more directly. The **phi coefficient** is equivalent to a Pearson r computed on two dichotomous variables. Whenever you have a 2×2 contingency table, you can compute phi (ϕ) using the following formula:

$$\phi = \sqrt{\frac{\chi^2}{N}}$$

When you have a two-variable contingency table that is larger than 2×2, you can compute **Cramer's** V statistic, which is also a measure of the strength of the relationship. The formula for Cramer's V is

$$V = \sqrt{\frac{\chi^2}{N(n-1)}}$$

where n is the number of rows or the number of columns in the contingency table, whichever is smaller.

Both phi and Cramer's V can range from 0 to 1, with a larger value indicating a stronger relationship between the two variables. As is true for Pearson r, a value of 0 indicates that the variables are unrelated and a value of 1 indicates a perfect relationship. However, neither phi not Cramer's V would ordinarily be calculated unless χ^2 is significant (Diekhoff, 1996; Evans, 1996).

How Can You Correct for Small Expected Frequencies?

Although the chi-square procedure has fewer assumptions than do parametric tests, it cannot be used when the sample size is too small. More specifically, it is not the sample size but the expected frequencies in the cells that limit the use of χ^2, although it has been suggested that the χ^2 distribution can be used whenever the sample size divided by the number of cells exceeds 5 (Kenny, 1987, p. 299). While it used to be suggested that an ordinary χ^2 test not be used whenever any of the expected frequencies fell below 5 (e.g., Gravetter & Wallnau, 1988), it is now recognized that this warning is too rigid. The exact instance in which the use of the χ^2 procedure is no longer appropriate is still a matter of debate (Comrey, Bott & Lee, 1989). However, if a majority of the expected values fall below 5 or if any of the expected values fall below 3, then one of the following alternative procedures should be considered.

Collapse Across Categories

As was done in the child-abuse example, it is possible to combine one or more cells in a table in order to create a new table composed of fewer cells with larger frequencies. If a particular combination makes logical sense, then this is the most appropriate approach to use. However, you have to realize that the research hypothesis being tested will be a somewhat different one if your new variables are somewhat different. For example, if you were comparing Catholics, Protestants, and Jews, in terms of whether or not they supported singing Christmas carols in school, it might make sense to combine the Catholics and Protestants into the new category of Christian. Combining the categories of Catholic and Jewish might make less logical sense for this purpose, even though it would be possible to do so statistically.

It is also possible to omit a level of one variable that has a small sample size, if it is not one that is of major importance. In the child-abuse example, if there had been few neglected children, they could have been excluded entirely. Again, this changes the precise hypothesis being tested. Of course, if it is possible to increase the sample size so as to ensure that there will be no cells with small expected frequencies, this is an even better approach to take.

Yates' Correction

Another approach to dealing with small expected frequencies is to use a procedure called *Yates' correction* (Yates, 1934). In this procedure, .5 is subtracted from the *absolute value* of the difference between the observed and expected frequencies for *every cell*, not just those with small expected frequencies, before squaring the difference and dividing by the expected frequency to get χ^2. This procedure has the effect of making the value of each of the terms smaller and thus of reducing the value of χ^2. Although this procedure used to be widely recommended (e.g., Comrey, Bott, & Lee, 1989), it is now recognized that it is probably too conservative in most cases, leading to a reduction in power (Hinkle, Wiersma, & Jurs, 1994; Howell, 1987). However, it has the advantage of being easy to compute, and you know that a result that is statistically significant with Yates' correction would also have been significant without it.

Fisher's Exact Probability Test

The last procedure that should be considered when the expected frequencies in a distribution are very small is one called *Fisher's exact probability test*. Although a description of the formula for the test is outside the scope of this book, it can be found in books focusing on nonparametric statistics and is included in a number of statistical packages for computers.

How Are Results of χ^2 Tests Reported?

APA Style

As with most statistical tests, the APA style for reporting chi-square results uses a standard format that includes the name of the test, the degrees of freedom, the value of the test statistic, and the corresponding significance level. However, unlike other statistical tests, χ^2 requires reporting of the sample size as well as the degrees of freedom, since the two are not closely related to each other. Thus the results of a χ^2 test comparing the frequencies of purchases of six different brands of breakfast cereals with those expected under the null hypothesis that all cereals were equally preferred might be reported thus: "A chi-square goodness-of-fit test indicated that there was no significant preference for any of the six cereals, $\chi^2(5, N = 124) = 4.98, p > .05$."

TIP

> Note that it is always necessary to indicate the type of χ^2 test performed, as it may not always be obvious to a casual reader whether you did a χ^2 goodness-of-fit test or a χ^2 test of independence.

Describing the Finding

After a χ^2 test has been performed, it would be very unusual for the actual contingency table or the calculations to be reported in a journal article. Instead, a table of percentages or proportions is commonly presented, although sometimes the proportions or percentages of the scores falling into each of the various categories are reported in a sentence rather than in a table. When a χ^2 goodness-of-fit test is performed, the finding is usually described in terms of differences between observed and expected proportions or percentages. However, for a χ^2 test of independence, the results are sometimes described in terms of differences in proportions or percentages (e.g., "A significantly higher percentage of cancer patients (54%) than of orthopedic patients (32%) said that they dreaded coming to the hospital for checkups") and sometimes described in terms of relationships (e.g., "The patient's diagnostic category was significantly related to his reporting that he dreaded coming to the hospital for checkups"). Of course, both of these descriptions assume that subjects' responses could be scored as dreading or not dreading a checkup. The way you choose to describe the results depends primarily on the wording of your research question and hypothesis.

When Should χ^2 Tests Be Used?

There are several factors that should be considered in deciding whether or not to use a χ^2 test and, if so, which type to use. The first thing to consider is whether or not the assumptions for the use of a χ^2 test have been met.

In general, a chi-square test is used when the researcher (1) has nominal data, (2) has a reasonable sample size (large enough to have expected values close to or greater than 5 in most of the cells), and (3) wishes to see whether or not the frequencies observed for the various values on the variable(s) differ from those expected based on some theory (such as the theory that the two nominal variables in a contingency table are independent or unrelated to each other). The use of a chi-square test also implies that each participant contributes data to only one cell.

Goodness of Fit Versus Test of Independence

The major distinction between these two procedures is that a χ^2 goodness-of-fit test can be used when you have scores on only one variable while a test of independence is used only when you have scores on two variables. In social science research, unless it is highly theoretical, the latter situation is more common. However, sometimes it is not immediately obvious that there are really two variables, particularly if one of them has only two levels.

For instance, if the percentage of men is reported for each of seven different professions, it may take a moment of reflection to recognize that the sex of the individual is a second variable (profession is, of course, the first), with everyone who is not scored as a man being scored as a woman. A χ^2 test of independence would therefore be used to see whether or not the percentages of men and women differed across the different professions.

TIP

> The distinction between a goodness-of-fit χ^2 test and a χ^2 test of independence is similar to that between a single-sample t-test and an independent-samples t-test.

χ^2 Versus r or ρ

Several of the techniques discussed in this book are appropriately used when the researcher is interested in the relationship between two variables. If both of these variables are measured on an interval or ratio scale (and if assumptions of linearity and homoscedasticity have not been too badly violated), then Pearson r or one of its closely related procedures like the point biserial correlation coefficient (discussed in Chapter 6) is ordinarily the correct statistic to use. If both of these variables have been measured on ordinal scales (e.g., if the basic data are ranks), then Spearman's rho is an appropriate technique. When both of the variables are measured on nominal scales, a χ^2 test of independence will give you an indication of whether or not the variables are significantly related. The phi coefficient for 2×2 tables and Cramer's V for larger contingency tables can be used to assess the actual degree of association in a manner parallel to the Pearson and Spearman correlation coefficients.

χ^2 Versus t or ANOVA

When a problem is worded in terms of differences between or among groups, a t-test or analysis of variance would be used to assess differences in means. However, if the hypothesis deals with differences in proportions or percentages between groups, then a χ^2 test is the appropriate technique to use. The issue to keep in mind is the nature of the data; if the scores are measured at a nominal level, then a χ^2 test would ordinarily be used to assess the significance of group differences.

CHAPTER SUMMARY

A chi-square test is a nonparametric technique that assesses whether or not the frequencies of scores obtained on one or more nominal-level variables differ significantly from those to be expected based on some theory. A goodness-of-fit χ^2 test can be used to measure the differences between the frequencies observed at the different levels of a single variable and those expected based on some theory. A χ^2 test of independence assesses whether or not two nominal-level variables are significantly associated—that is, whether or not the proportions in the categories of one variable differ depending upon the level of the other variable. For such a test, scores are arranged in a contingency table, with each category or cell in the table representing a combination of scores on the two variables.

The formula for χ^2 is equal to the square of the observed frequency minus the theoretically expected frequency divided by the expected frequency for each cell, summed across all cells. The larger the value of χ^2, the more likely it is to be statistically significant—that is, to represent a non-chance difference from the expected distribution. The degrees of freedom parameter for χ^2 depends only upon the number of cells (or of rows and columns in a contingency table), not upon the sample size. However, a χ^2 test may be inappropriate when the sample size is too small, requiring you to combine across categories, use Yates' correction to the formula, or use an alternative procedure.

CHAPTER REVIEW

Multiple-Choice Questions

1. As the degrees of freedom increases, the critical value gets larger for which of the following tests?

   a. analysis of variance

   b. chi-square

   c. dependent-samples t-test

   d. single-sample t-test

   e. all of the above

   f. none of the above

2. When doing a χ^2 test, the number of observations or participants is equivalent to

   a. the sum of the observed frequencies

b. the sum of the expected frequencies

c. the degrees of freedom

d. the degrees of freedom plus 1

e. Both a and b are correct.

f. a, b, and d are all correct.

3. When doing a χ^2 goodness-of-fit test, a high value of χ^2 means

    a. a good fit to the null hypothesis

    b. that the observed frequencies are different from the expected frequencies

    c. that you have made a type I error

    d. that you have made a type II error

    e. that you should have done a test of independence instead

4. What is the correct critical value for a 3×4 χ^2 test with a total of 30 participants at the $p < .001$ level?

    a. 12.59   **b.** 16.81   **c.** 22.46   **d.** 26.22

    e. 32.91   **f.** 58.30   **g.** 59.70

5. With a χ^2 test, as the sample size increases (say from 10 to 100),

    a. the critical value increases

    b. the critical value decreases

    c. the power decreases

    d. the chance of making a type I error increases

    e. the chance of making a type II error increases

    f. the sum of the observed frequencies increases

6. Which of the following characteristics is most important to consider when doing a χ^2 test?

    a. linearity

    b. interval/ratio scale data

    c. normality of distribution

    d. adequately large expected values

    e. equal numbers of subjects in each condition

7. Suppose that you calculate that the value for a χ^2 test relating occupation (3 levels) to attitude (2 levels) is -12.35 for a sample of 50 people. What do you conclude?

    a. Attitude and occupation are not significantly related.

    b. Attitude and occupation are significantly related at the .01 level but not at the .001 level.

    c. People from certain occupations have different attitudes from people in other occupations.

d. Both b and c are correct.

e. none of the above

8. Which of the following tests involve scores on only one variable?

a. independent-samples t-test

b. analysis of variance

c. Pearson r

d. paired-samples t-test

e. single-sample t-test

f. χ^2 goodness-of-fit test

g. χ^2 test of independence

h. both e and f

i. e, f, and g

j. all of the above

9. The null hypothesis for χ^2 states that

a. the group means are all equal to each other

b. the observed and expected frequencies are the same

c. the distributions are all normal

d. the frequencies in each category are the same

e. the degrees of freedom are a chance deviation from zero

10. The χ^2 distribution

a. is normal

b. is a family of distributions

c. has two associated degrees of freedom

d. is the square root of the F-distribution

e. is the t-distribution divided by its degrees of freedom

Problems

11. You are interested in knowing whether or not the composition of a family is related to the type of vacations they like to take. Accordingly, you collect the following data from a survey of preferred vacations:

	Family Type		
	---	---	---
Vacation	*No Children*	*Children < 10*	*Children 10–18*
Visit relatives	0	15	5
Beach	5	5	10
Urban sightseeing	15	0	5

a. What can you conclude about the relationship between family composition and type of vacation preferred? Are they significantly related?

b. Suppose that you were interested in the issue of whether families with children differ from families without children in whether they prefer to visit relatives versus some other type of vacation. Conduct an appropriate statistical significance test and report your conclusions.

12. You are planning a menu for a banquet for a convention and want to have a popular dessert. You sample a group of people as they are leaving another convention and ask them which kind of pie they prefer. (Note that this problem is similar to an example from Chapter 9 but uses a different measure and thus requires a different analysis.) You have gathered the following data:

Pumpkin	10
Apple	12
Cherry	8
Lemon	14
Pecan	20

a. Perform the appropriate test of the hypothesis that all flavors of pie are equally well liked.

b. Report your conclusion in a sentence.

c. Now perform the correct test of the hypothesis that pecan pie is preferred to all other flavors. Report your conclusion in a sentence.

13. What are the degrees of freedom for each of the following?

a. a goodness-of-fit χ^2 test with 4 categories and 27 observations

b. a goodness-of-fit χ^2 test with 27 categories and 4 observations

c. a test of independence relating gender of subject to preference for a male or female principal (3 levels, including "no preference")

d. a test of the null hypothesis that season of the year is unrelated to whether people are wearing sandals, bare feet, or ordinary shoes, based on a sample of 150 people

e. a test of the null hypothesis that freshmen, sophomores, juniors, and seniors are equally likely to say "yes" when asked if they like school, based on 74 respondents

f. a test of the null hypothesis that freshmen, sophomores, juniors, and seniors have equal numbers of absences over a four-month span, based on 74 respondents

14. As the Head Honcho in charge of selecting a speaker for your club's weekly meetings, you have surveyed the attendees to find out their preferences.

When given a choice among four potential speakers, 30 chose Tom, 20 chose Tim, 20 chose Jim, and 60 chose Mortimer.

a. Perform the appropriate statistical significance test of the null hypothesis that people have no particular preferences for these four speakers—that is, that all four speakers were equally likely to be chosen. Report your conclusions in a sentence.

b. Now perform a statistical test of the hypothesis that Mortimer is significantly more popular than the other three potential speakers. Report your conclusions.

15. You are interested in whether or not male and female doctoral students are equally represented in various programs at your university. A survey reveals that the College of Education has 50 male and 150 female doctoral students, the College of Engineering has 100 male and 20 female doctoral students, and the College of Arts and Sciences has 200 male and 200 female doctoral students.

a. What is the appropriate statistical procedure to use to test the research hypothesis that gender is related to field of study for doctoral students based on these data. Why?

b. Carry out the appropriate test and report your conclusions in a sentence.

c. Suppose that you wanted to test whether or not men are underrepresented in the College of Education compared to Engineering and Arts and Sciences combined. Carry out the correct test and report your conclusions.

16. Assume that a nationwide survey of contributions to charity has shown that 50% of all contributions go to religious organizations, 20% to medical organizations, 15% to educational institutions, 10% to social service organizations, and 5% to other causes. In a survey of 80 people from Middleville, participants were asked about the last donation that they had made to charity. In response, 45 people said that they had given to a church or other religious organization, 20 had given to a medical organization, 5 had given to an educational institution, 8 had given to a social service organization, and 2 had given to another cause.

a. Perform a test of the null hypothesis that people in Middleville do not differ from those nationwide in terms of the type of charitable institution to which they donate. Report your conclusions in a sentence.

b. Now perform a test of the hypothesis that a smaller proportion of charitable donations in Middleville go to educational institutions (and thus a larger proportion to all other causes) compared with national norms. Report your conclusions.

17. The fifth-grade students at Appleby, Bandelier, and Coronado Elementary schools have all been asked to indicate whether they prefer alligators, bears, or cougars as their school mascot. The data look like this:

	Appleby	Bandelier	Coronado
Alligator	120	20	40
Bear	90	200	80
Cougar	10	10	100

a. Perform the appropriate test to see whether school attended is related to preference for school mascot.

b. Report your conclusions in a sentence.

c. Now test the research hypothesis that people at Bandelier prefer bears more than do people at Appleby and Coronado.

d. Report your conclusions in a sentence.

e. Now test the null hypothesis that all three mascots are equally popular, ignoring the school attended by the students.

f. Report your conclusions in a sentence.

18. You are interested in testing your hypothesis that men and women are diagnosed differently, even when they have the same symptoms. Therefore, you write an ambiguous case history that has symptoms of depression, dependent personality disorder, and antisocial personality disorder. You ask 50 beginning counseling psychology students to read a case history and try to diagnose the person described. Half of the respondents read about "Paul" and half read about "Paula." The data look like this:

	Diagnosis		
	Depression	Dependent	Antisocial
"Paul"	5	0	20
"Paula"	18	7	0

a. Perform an appropriate test of the null hypothesis that diagnosis is unrelated to whether the person is described as "Paul" or "Paula."

b. Report your conclusions in a sentence.

c. Now perform an appropriate test of the null hypothesis that, when the person described in the case history is female, all three diagnoses are equally likely.

d. Report your conclusions in a sentence.

19. A researcher is interested in whether people prefer to look at material that confirms their expectations or at material that disconfirms them. Her theory is that confident people choose to view material that contradicts their expectations; insecure people prefer to look at material that confirms them. To test this theory, she classifies people into Secure and Insecure categories, based on an interview, and then gives them the choice of watching a video that is described as confirming or one described as contradicting their beliefs about health (measured on a previous day). The data look like this:

	Insecure	Secure
Confirming	35	20
Contradicting	5	20

a. Using the formula in which you calculate expected frequencies, conduct a chi-square test of independence on these data.

b. Now conduct a chi-square test of independence on the same data using the calculator formula.

c. Now calculate the phi coefficient for these data.

d. Report your conclusion in a sentence.

20. Evolutionary psychologists believe that genes predisposing to behaviors that lead to the production and survival of more offspring are likely to continue in a species. One derivation of this theory is the prediction that people should be more likely to kill those who are not biologically related to them than to kill their biological offspring. To test this prediction, you have collected murder statistics and census data from a major city. The census data for the city show that, of the 10,000 children aged 0 to 14 years who are living with a man in their house, 6500 live with a biological mother and father, 1000 live with a biological father but not a biological mother, and 2500 live with a biological mother and an unrelated adult male (mother's boyfriend or second husband). The data on children aged 0 to 14 years who were murdered in their homes show that there were 30 murders of children by their biological fathers, 20 murders of children by their mother's boyfriend or their stepfather, and 2 murders by mothers.

a. Perform an analysis to test the hypothesis that a father is less likely to kill his child than a stepfather or unrelated adult male is to kill a child living with him.

b. Report your conclusion in a sentence.

c. Are these results consistent with the evolutionary hypothesis?

Study Questions

1. See if you can list at least five demographic characteristics that are measured on a nominal scale. Select a pair of them (e.g., nationality and religion) and imagine a study in which you would code people's score on both of them, probably including a large category labeled "other" for each variable. Try to formulate a hypothesis about the relationship between these two variables

(e.g., that people from a particular nationality would be more likely to identify with a particular religion and less likely to identify with another). Then make up some data, based on a sample size of 100, which would be consistent with your hypothesis. Arrange these data in a contingency table, perform a χ^2 test on them, and report your conclusion. If necessary, collapse across categories to perform a second χ^2 test that gets at a more precise hypothesis and report the conclusion from that test.

2. Go to the library, locate a recent issue of a journal in a field of interest to you, and look for articles using a χ^2 test. For each test, identify whether it was a test of independence or a goodness-of-fit test and try to justify why that particular test was used. See if you can find any articles in which a variable that was or could have been measured on an interval scale (e.g., age) was treated as if it were nominal and analyzed by a χ^2 test.

3. As long as you're in the library, find another article that presents a table of data in terms of percentages but that includes the total sample size. The authors may report only the percentages saying "yes" to certain questions, for example, and present the results of a χ^2 test relating the answers to some other variable, such as political affiliation. See if you can reconstruct the contingency table from the information given and can replicate the calculations to arrive at the value for χ^2.

4. Imagine that you have been asked to investigate the question of whether or not people from various minority groups are underrepresented on juries. You can get data on the numbers (or percentages) of people from different ethnic groups in the county who are registered to vote, of different ages, or classified in various ways. Make up these data. Then think of the various possible specific hypotheses that you could test (presumably via a χ^2 goodness-of-fit test). Which one or ones would be most relevant to answering the question that you have been asked to investigate?

Selecting Appropriate Statistical Tests

If you've reached this point in the book, you not only have demonstrated patience and perseverance but you should know quite a lot about a number of statistical procedures. You now can put numbers into a formula and arrive at another number; even better, you can describe the results of a Scheffé post hoc comparison or a Pearson r in terms of the variables that you were studying. This chapter focuses on a question that involves a synthesis of all the discrete bits of information presented in the earlier chapters: How do you select the appropriate test to answer your research question? Once you're a wealthy and funded researcher, you can hire someone else to actually carry out your statistical analyses or you can purchase a computer and statistical package that will do most of the computations for you. However, it's usually up to you to decide on what procedures you want the research assistant or the computer to carry out. In selecting a statistical test, there are a number of issues that you need to consider.

What Is the Nature of Your Data?

Perhaps the first thing that a researcher should think about before selecting a statistical test is the nature of the dependent measure or measures. It is possible that two people using two different measures to study exactly the same problem might find it necessary to use two different statistical procedures.

Scale of Measurement

Perhaps the most important aspect of your data to consider is the level of measurement used. If your scores reflect an interval or ratio scale, then any of the procedures described in this book could conceivably be used, although the data would need to be converted to ranks before using Spearman's rho and to a reasonably small number of categories before using chi-square.

Categorized Variables. Sometimes people take a variable that could be measured on an interval scale but form questions for respondents that are based on categories rather than specific data points. For example, people could be asked to check off the category that represents their age, with 60+ as the highest category. In such a case, it is impossible to carry out precise analyses that depend on the mean age or that attempt to correlate age with something else. An even more common example is the case in which people are asked to indicate the category in which their income falls. Although there may be valid reasons for using broad categories, primarily a fear that people will be less likely to respond if bluntly asked to indicate their income or age, it should be recognized that analyses based on such categories will be less powerful than those based on more accurate raw data.

Likert Scales. As was mentioned in Chapter 2, attitude measures commonly use scales that ask people to indicate the extent of their agreement or disagreement with various statements using five- or seven-point scales. Ordinarily the responses to a number of items are summed to produce an overall score, after reversing the coding of negatively worded items (Kidder & Judd, 1986). Although these scales may not truly have interval properties, they are usually constructed so that the apparent distances between the categories seem similar and are almost always analyzed by parametric tests.

Shape, Variance, and Other Characteristics

Besides the level of measurement, which you can usually determine before the data are collected, you also need to consider the distribution of the data, the actual scores themselves. If, for example, people give only two of 17 possible responses, you may wish to consider the dependent measure as having only two values, rather than 17.

Parametric Tests. If you wish to do parametric tests, you should check to see whether or not the data greatly violate the assumptions of such tests. For example, if 95% of the scores on a test are zero, the distribution is very far from normal; it might make sense to reclassify scores as "zero" or "other" and do a nonparametric test. Similarly, if scores in different groups have greatly unequal variances, have very different sample sizes, and look far from normally distributed, you may wish to consider a nonparametric test instead of an analysis of variance or *t*-test. Although parametric tests are generally robust to violations of their assumptions, instances may arise when substitution of a nonparametric test for a planned parametric one may make sense. In such cases, you need to recognize that the nonparametric and parametric tests may be testing somewhat different hypotheses.

Sample Size. Sometimes, you are unable to get as many people in your sample as you would like. In such a case, the sample size may be too small to permit you to do the kinds of analyses you had originally planned. For example, if you had planned to compare people from seven different cities, but you had only three or four respondents from some of the cities, it might be necessary to combine the data into only two categories (cities 1–3 versus cities 4–7, if that distinction makes some theoretical sense) and to do a *t*-test instead of an analysis of variance with seven groups.

What Is Your Purpose?

In addition to the nature of the data, the other essential issue to consider in deciding upon the appropriate statistical technique is the purpose of the analysis. What is it that you want to do, or what question do you want to answer?

Describing Data

Suppose that your purpose is to describe an array of data that you have collected. A first thing to consider is the degree of detail that you want to present.

Detailed Information.   Sometimes you want to present enough detail so that the reader can see or reconstruct the entire distribution of raw scores. In that case, you may want to present a frequency distribution in either tabular or graphic form. Either the absolute frequency or the percentages of each raw score would be given. If a somewhat lesser degree of precision is desired, a grouped frequency distribution can be graphed or presented in a table. You could even construct a percentile distribution if others will be comparing their scores to the scores of those in your sample.

Summary Numbers.   Instead of all the scores, you may prefer to provide only a few summary numbers. Most commonly, a measure of central tendency will be provided, along with a measure of variability if the data are not nominal. Sometimes more than one measure of central tendency will be provided, particularly if the data are skewed. Sometimes the mean (or median) and standard deviation (or range) will be provided for each subgroup or each level of the independent variable. In deciding what descriptive statistics to present, think about the potential reader and what he or she would find most useful.

Predicting Scores

Besides simply describing scores, sometimes you will want to predict scores on one variable from known scores on another.

Regression.   When both variables are measured on at least an interval scale, the procedure for doing so is to compute a regression equation. A regression equation can be considered a descriptive statistic, as it is simply the formula that best describes the linear relationship between score on one variable and score on the other variable for the data in your sample. However, it is generally used for prediction rather than merely as a description.

Bivariate Versus Multiple Regression.   When you wish to predict score on one I/R variable from score on another, then ordinary linear regression or bivariate regression is used. Even more common (but more complicated computationally) is the instance in which several predictor variables are used to predict score on a single dependent measure. This procedure, called *multiple regression*, is typically conducted by computer. It is covered in more advanced statistics courses.

Although they can be considered descriptive techniques, both bivariate and multiple regression have inferential aspects. It is possible, for instance, to test the significance of the associated r and R^2 and of the increment to R^2 caused by adding a new predictor, in order to see whether or not the new variable contributes significantly to the regression equation.

Relating Variables

Measures of Association.   Sometimes the purpose of a research study is to assess whether or not two variables are significantly related and to measure the degree of relationship between them. When the variables have been measured on at least an interval scale, then a Pearson product-moment correlation coefficient is the technique to use. If the variables are measured on an ordinal scale, then Spearman rho would be the correct technique. If the variables are qualitative or categorized, then a chi-square test of independence would be used to assess the significance of the association between them. A phi coefficient or Cramer's V could be used to describe the magnitude of the association.

Depending on the nature of the data, it is sometimes necessary to use other correlational techniques that are essentially variants on Pearson r. Such techniques include the point biserial or biserial coefficient, used when one of the two variables has only two values. However, it is important to think about the meaning of the hypothesis that you are testing in deciding whether or not a measure of association or correlation is really what is intended. For example, if the hypothesis is that "gender is related to income," it might make more sense to reword it as "the mean incomes of males and females differ" and to do a t-test comparing the means of the two groups. In other words, consider whether the hypothesis of interest is really one about association or if, in fact, it deals with a difference in central tendency. If the latter, then different techniques are used. Of course, it is possible to compute both t and r, if you wish to know both the difference in the means and the proportion of variance in one variable that is predictable from the other.

Comparing Means

Many of the hypotheses that researchers want to test concern differences in means.

One Actual Mean. If the hypothesis concerns how a single mean differs from some hypothesized value, then a single-sample t-test or z-test is used. Remember that the hypothesized value may come from previously collected data, such as a normative sample, as well as from a theory. Since such data are subject to sampling error, an independent-samples t-test would be better if the mean, standard deviation, and sample size are known for the previous sample as well as for the current data.

Two Means. If the hypothesis concerns a difference between two sample means, then several possible analyses could be used. If the means are paired in some way, then a dependent-samples t-test is commonly used, although a repeated-measures analysis of variance, Hotelling's T^2, and multivariate analysis of variance are alternative procedures. If the means are not paired, then there are three possible procedures: an independent-samples t-test, a one-way analysis of variance, and an a priori comparison. These procedures will lead to identical conclusions if there are only two levels of the independent variable or two means to be considered. However, if there are three or more groups but the particular hypothesis to be tested concerns only two of them, then an a priori comparison is the procedure to be used.

Three or More Means. If you want to compare the means of three or more groups and are interested in all possible comparisons among them, then an analysis of variance is the correct approach. If you are interested in only certain comparisons, then the use of t-tests with Bonferroni adjusted critical values or the studentized range test may be more powerful. Harris (1994) feels that if only pairwise comparisons are of interest, then a studentized range test followed by Tukey HSDs should be used, rather than an analysis of variance. However, most introductory textbooks recommend the use of an analysis of variance followed by Tukey HSD tests or Scheffé post hoc comparisons.

Two Independent Variables. If you wish to compare means for a study with two independent variables or factors, then a two-way ANOVA is the procedure to use. This procedure can be used to test hypotheses about interactions as well as main effects. Tests of simple main effects, post hoc comparisons, or Tukey HSD tests can be used to follow up on significant interactions or main effects for factors with more than two levels.

If the design is more complex, then more complicated analysis of variance techniques would be used.

Comparing Medians

Sometimes a hypothesis will directly deal with medians rather than with means; for instance, a prediction that the median age of students at a community college will be higher than the median age of students at a four-year residential college. Sometimes the raw data are ranks; for example, you might want to compare the rankings or seedings of tennis players attending different schools. Sometimes, the original hypothesis was formulated in terms of means, but the data are so skewed and the variances so different that a parametric test is clearly inappropriate. In all of these cases, you may wish to perform a test comparing medians of two groups. The Mann–Whitney U test, sometimes called the *rank sum test* (Brase & Brase, 1991), is used to compare the medians of two groups of unpaired scores, and the Kruskal–Wallis one-way ANOVA compares the medians of three or more groups. Textbooks on nonparametric statistics provide information about how to compute these and other nonparametric tests.

Differences in Frequencies or Proportions

Sometimes a hypothesis concerns differences in the frequencies or proportions of scores falling into several categories, rather than in some measure of central tendency. If the hypothesis concerns a difference between actual and hypothesized proportions, a chi-square goodness-of-fit test is used. If the hypothesis concerns differences in the proportions receiving certain scores for people who differ with respect to their position on some other variable, then a chi-square test of independence is the appropriate procedure.

Multiple Independent and Dependent Variables

Multiple Independent Variables.   Sometimes you wish to examine the effects of more than one independent (manipulated or classification) variable. In this instance, the research design is usually called a factorial design. When the data fit the assumptions for parametric tests, the procedure that would usually be used is a factorial analysis of variance. If one of the variables is an I/R one used to reduce error variance, then it can be treated as a covariate in an analysis of covariance. If the variables studied are all nominal-level ones, then chi-square tests of independence or the closely related log-linear procedure would be used (Harris, 1994).

Multiple Dependent Measures.   When there is more than one score for each individual, or if there are individuals paired with each other, then the design is usually a multivariate one. The very simplest case would be the one in which there are two scores on the same variable for each individual or pair of individuals, a paired-samples design. With only two paired scores, a correlated-samples t-test is acceptable. If there are more than two means that are associated, such as pretest, posttest, and follow-up scores on each individual, then more sophisticated procedures such as a repeated measures analysis of variance, Hotelling's T^2, or multivariate analysis of variance must be used.

Multiple Significance Tests

An assumption underlying the use of a statistical significance test is that you know the probability of obtaining results as extreme as the actual ones when the null hypothesis is true. Clearly, if you do more significance tests, your likelihood of making at least one Type I error will increase, unless you do something about it. When more than one significance test is being conducted, it is important to adjust the critical values to account for the fact that multiple tests are being done.

The easiest way to approximate the correct critical value is to divide your intended α-level (e.g., .05) by the number of significance tests (e.g., tests for the significance of a correlation coefficient) you intend to compute. However, you have to keep in mind that it is not the number of actual tests which you perform but the number of possible ones which you might perform that must be considered. Thus, if you are computing ten correlation coefficients, you divide your alpha level by ten, even if you don't bother looking up the critical values for those having small absolute values and small sample sizes.

This approach to adjusting your significance level is the Bonferroni critical value procedure, and people using it talk about adjusting the experiment-wise or familywise error rate. It is applicable to any type of statistical significance test, not just correlation coefficients or t-tests.

Alternative procedures to correct for multiple significance tests are the use of other multiple comparison procedures, like the Scheffé post hoc and Tukey HSD tests, or the use of multivariate statistical tests.

How Do Your Questions and Hypotheses Influence the Choice of Analysis?

If your purpose is to describe your data, you need to decide whether to present your data in the form of tables, graphs, and/or summary statistics. If you are unsure as to which mode of presentation or which summary statistics to use, remember that you should first consider the nature of your data, which may limit the possibilities. Second, you should look at other similar research studies to see what kind of information other people have presented. Third, imagine yourself as the person reading your study. What would such a person want to know? What would be most useful and meaningful to him or her? Fourth, you might try putting the data into several forms—a graph, a table, and a sentence summarizing a measure of central tendency and one of variability—and showing it to someone else, asking for that other person's opinion. Remember that, unless you make an error in computation or graphing, deciding how to present descriptive data is not an issue of right or wrong but rather a choice between more and less informative and interesting.

Questions and Hypotheses

In contrast to descriptive statistics, selecting the wrong analysis to answer your question or test your hypothesis can indeed lead to incorrect conclusions, even if your arithmetic is perfect. If your hypothesis is worded in terms of differences, then you will usually be comparing either *proportions*, via a type of chi-square test, or *means*, via some kind of t-test or analysis of variance. If your hypothesis is worded in terms of relationships, you will be computing some kind of correlation coefficient or possibly testing the significance of an association between variables by a chi-square test of independence.

Besides the issue of whether you are dealing with differences or relationships, it is useful to consider whether or not particular scores are paired or matched with particular other scores, like pretest and posttest values for each individual. Computation of correlation coefficients always requires pairs of scores, but hypotheses about pairs of scores could also involve comparisons of means that are matched in various ways. The only analysis for comparing mean differences between paired scores that is covered in this book is the correlated samples t-test. However, there are other analyses that can be used to compare means if the scores are not independent. Consult an expert if that is the case in your research.

If it is not clear to you what analysis to perform when you are designing a study, it may be helpful to think in terms of the numbers that you will be collecting and the scores that you expect to get. By making up a few imaginary raw scores, you can often recognize the nature of your data and realize, for example, that each person is being measured on two nominal variables. Similarly, by looking at the distribution of your actual data, you may be able to recognize, for example, that the scores are so far from normal that the use of parametric techniques would be problematic.

Examples of Research Situations

In case the above descriptions sound somewhat abstract, let's take some concrete examples of research situations in which you might have to select an appropriate statistical procedure. We can even go beyond naming the procedure to consider the appropriate degrees of freedom to use.

1. You are interested in assessing the relationship between people's preferences for desserts (pies, cookies, or fruit) and their preferences for main dishes (meats, seafood, or casseroles), based on a sample of 30 people. Assume that each person is asked to indicate both a favorite dessert and a favorite main dish. In this case, you are looking for a relationship between two variables, each of which is measured on a nominal scale. The appropriate test would be a chi-square test of independence, with the degrees of freedom equal to the number of rows (3) minus 1 times the number of columns (also 3) minus 1 or 4.

2. You wish to compare the mean number of cookies eaten by 15 middle-aged fathers with the mean number eaten by their teen-aged sons. In this case you are comparing the mean scores of two groups that are paired, each father belonging with his own son. The only appropriate procedure that you know how to do is a correlated-samples t-test, although a repeated measures analysis of variance, a Hotelling's T^2, or a MANOVA could also be used. In this case the degrees of freedom would be the number of pairs of scores minus 1, which would equal 14.

3. Next, you want to know whether or not students taking five sections of the same introductory biology class have significantly different scores on the final. If they do, one thing you want to do is to compare the mean scores on the final of the students in the two sections taught by Thelma Toad with the mean scores of the students in the other three sections, which were taught by Freddy Frog. There were 31 students in each of the five sections.

In order to compare the mean scores of the five sections of the course, you need to do an analysis of variance. Since there are 31(5) or 155 participants and 5 groups, the ANOVA would have 4 and 150 degrees of freedom. In general, if the results of an ANOVA are statistically significant, you could follow it up either by a Scheffé post hoc comparison or by a Tukey HSD test. However, in this case, you want to compare the means of two groups with the means of three other groups. This can be done via a single Scheffé comparison, whereas you would have to do six Tukey HSDs to approximate the same test. (Why six? Because each of the two sections taught by Thelma would have to be compared with each of the three sections taught by Freddy.) Since the particular comparison was formulated prior to gathering and analyzing the data, it is an a priori one and can legitimately be compared to the a priori critical value. The degrees of freedom for this comparison would be 1 and $N - K$ or 1 and 150.

4. In a follow-up study, you are interested in the issue of whether the mean number of frog's legs eaten by the 31 students in one of Thelma's sections of biology at the postexam party was significantly higher than the mean number of frog's legs eaten by the 30 students in her other section (one student croaked in the meantime). In this case, you are comparing the means of two groups of unpaired scores. Either an independent-samples t-test or an analysis of variance would be correct. In the first instance, the degrees of freedom would be $n_1 + n_2 - 2$, or 59. For an analysis of variance, the degrees of freedom would be $K - 1$ and $N - K$, or 1 and 59.

5. Next you are interested in the relationship between the number of frog's legs eaten and the number of cookies eaten at the party for a sample of 21 students. This example, like the first one, involves a relationship between variables. However, it deals with variables that are measured on a ratio scale. (Fourteen cookies is twice as many as seven.) Therefore, you would calculate a Pearson product-moment correlation coefficient between the two pairs of scores, with $N - 2$ or 19 degrees of freedom.

6. After the party, you want to predict the number of frog's legs eaten from the number of cookies eaten, thinking that you can use this information in planning your next party. In this case, you would want to compute a regression equation, with cookies as the predictor (probably labeled X) and frog's legs as the variable to be predicted (probably labeled Y).

7. Some weeks later, you find an article by some nutritionists who have calculated the ideal number of frog's legs to be eaten per party in order to insure the optimal physical and mental health of partying biology students. You want to know whether or not the amount eaten by your sample differed significantly from this value. This is an instance where a single-sample t-test would be appropriate, since you wish to compare your sample mean with a theoretical value. You would have $N-1$ degrees of freedom, with N being the number of students for whom you have measured frog leg consumption.

8. Suppose that you want to know how Fernando's feasting compares with the national norm for frog's legs eaten. (Fernando is inordinately fond of frog's legs.) If the mean and standard deviation for a national sample were given, you could consider this as a normal curve problem, based on the assumption that the number of frog's legs eaten is likely to be normally distributed.

9. Finally, imagine that you want to know how the mean amount of frog's legs eaten for your sample of partygoers differs from that of a national sample. You could perform an independent-samples t-test comparing the two groups, even though the sample sizes would be vastly different, if you know the mean and standard deviation of the national sample.

Statistical Procedures Discussed in This Book

To show the entire distribution of raw scores on one variable:

1. Simple frequency distribution*
2. Relative frequency distribution*
3. Grouped frequency distribution
4. Percentile distribution
5. Stem-and-leaf diagram
6. Cumulative frequency distribution
7. Bar graph*
8. Pie graph*
9. Frequency polygon
10. Frequency histogram
11. Box-and-whisker plot

To show the entire distribution of raw scores on two variables:

1. Scattergram
2. Line graph

To summarize a distribution of scores:

1. Measures of central tendency
   - Mean
   - Median
   - Mode[*]
2. Measures of variability
   - Range
   - Standard deviation
   - Variance

To find frequencies, values, or proportions of scores within certain parameters:

1. Normal curve table

To describe the relationship between two variables:

1. Pearson r
2. Spearman rho
3. Chi-square test of independence[*] (to see if they're independent or not)
4. Phi coefficient*
5. Cramer's V*

To predict scores on Y from scores on X:

1. Regression

To compare a single mean with a hypothesized value:

1. Single-sample t-test
2. z-test (if σ is known)

To compare two sample means:

1. If paired,
   - dependent-samples t-test
2. If independent,
   - Independent-samples t-test
   - One-way analysis of variance
   - A priori comparison
3. After a significant analysis of variance,
   - Tukey HSD
   - Scheffé post hoc comparison

To estimate a population mean or a difference in means from a sample mean or difference in means with a certain probability of being wrong:

1. Confidence interval

To compare three or more means simultaneously:

1. One-way analysis of variance
2. Scheffé comparisons

To compare means when there are two or more independent variables:

1. Two-way analysis of variance
2. Follow-up tests
   - Tests of simple main effects
   - Scheffé post hoc comparison
   - Tukey HSD

To compare actual with hypothesized proportions:

1. Chi-square goodness-of-fit test*

To compare proportions with certain scores on one variable for persons who differ in their scores on another variable:

1. Chi-square test of independence*

---

*Denotes that a procedure can be used with nominal-level data

What Are Some Issues in Reporting Research Results?

Perhaps the most important issue to consider when reporting the results of a research study is what to include and what to omit. Generally, the purpose of a results section is to present all information, analyses, and conclusions directly relevant to your hypotheses and any statistically significant findings that were not hypothesized but that might conceivably be of interest to the reader. In achieving this noble goal, you want to be clear, concise, comprehensible, and maximally informative—aims that may seem somewhat contradictory.

What to Omit

Generally, no raw data are reported as part of the statistical section of a manuscript, although they may be summarized in tables or graphs. Similarly, the original calculations are not reported, although tables may present some of the intermediate information, such as the sums of squares in an analysis of variance summary table.

What to Include

As a rule of thumb, you always include the name of the statistic, the degrees of freedom, the value of the statistic, and the associated probability level. However, in order to save space, when a number of similar analyses have been done, it is acceptable to list all the measures that led to statistically significant results but to report only the numerical value of the *least* statistically significant analysis, saying that this was the smallest computed value of the statistic. Similarly, for findings that were not statistically significant, it is acceptable to list only the largest numerical value of a nonsignificant statistic and to say that the other results were even farther from statistical significance. However, it is essential to identify all the tests that you conducted, even if you do not report their numerical results, so as not to give the false impression that the tests that were statistically significant were the only ones done (Kromrey, 1993).

APA Style

The style used by the American Psychological Association to report the results of statistical findings is outlined in the *APA Publication Manual* (1994). In general, this style requires that you report the name of the statistic, the degrees of freedom (in parentheses), the value of the statistic to two decimal places, and the probability level; for example, $F(2, 35) = 2.36, p > .05$. For a chi-square test, the N is also reported; for example, $\chi^2(1, N = 50) = 16.88, p < .001$. Usually the p-value is given as $>.05$, $<.05$, $<.01$, or $<.001$, unless there is a good reason for reporting something else. Values of physical quantities are given in metric units (e.g., kilograms rather than pounds), and tables and graphs must be fully labeled. Further details can be found in the manual.

Significance

In discussing the meaning of the results of a research study, it is important to consider the significance of the results, in both senses of the word. Ordinarily, results that do not reach conventional statistical significance levels will be reported but not discussed further. However, if the findings are in the expected direction but not statistically significant due to small sample sizes, it is acceptable to mention this and to recommend that future research be done utilizing a larger sample and perhaps a more adequate design (Cohen, 1992a; Thompson, 1989b). Similarly, it is acceptable to indicate that a statistically significant finding is of such a small magnitude (e.g., a correlation of .1 or a difference in means of a tenth of a standard deviation) that it has almost no practical significance or useful application. Again, it is up to the researcher to identify what aspects of the results are considered important and meaningful, rather than to blithely equate importance with significance at the .05 α-level (Cohen, 1990; Kromrey, 1993; Shaver, 1985, 1993; Thompson, 1989a, 1993).

What Next?

Is there life after introductory statistics? Is there life *during* introductory statistics? Some of you may have been wondering all semester whether or not leading a normal life is compatible with taking an introductory statistics course. However, now that you are near the end of the course (or, at least, of the book), you may be considering even more of the same. For those of you who are completely burned out, I urge you to enjoy yourself, take time to smell the flowers and experience the other pleasures of life, and return to this section if and when you find yourself missing statistics after all. For those of you who are eager for more, I have a few suggestions.

Take More Statistics Courses

I would say that what you have learned from this book is not the tip of the iceberg but rather its base. The principles identified in this book are generally applicable to all statistical procedures, and the particular procedures discussed here are widely used and widely understood. However, there are so many statistical methods that have been developed that a single course can serve as only an introduction.

Usually, the second statistics class that students take focuses on analysis of variance techniques, including factorial designs, repeated measures analyses, analysis of covariance, and even more complicated procedures. A third statistics course might concentrate on multiple regression and multivariate procedures. Still more advanced courses could involve such sophisticated procedures as path analysis, LISREL analysis, structural equation modeling, and other approaches to causal modeling that allow you to test a theory about the quantitative relationships among variables. Courses in biostatistics or medical statistics may include techniques for predicting who will drop out (die) at various times or for comparing the likelihood of contracting a condition under certain circumstances via odds ratios. A course in nonparametric statistics will focus on procedures for analyzing data that do not meet the assumptions for the use of parametric techniques. Those who like mathematics and probability can even take a course in probability theory or matrix algebra.

Learn About Computers

Almost all of the procedures that have been discussed in this book can be easily (usually, more easily) done with the use of a computer program or package. (The exceptions are a chi-square goodness-of-fit test and a Scheffé comparison used to contrast the mean of a combination of groups with a different combination of means.) Depending on your resources, you may wish to use a mainframe computer package available at your university or workplace, such as SPSS or SAS. These mainframe packages have the advantage of being extremely powerful and able to deal with large data sets. Alternatively, you may have access to a microcomputer and a statistical package used with that microcomputer, like SPSS-PC or SYSTAT.

Sometimes a formal course is the best way to learn how to use a particular computer and statistical package; sometimes informal tutoring is more effective. Ask around to see what resources are available to you and what statistical packages other people use. Remember that it is more important to use correct analyses that you can understand than to produce sophisticated computer output that neither you nor the people who will be reading your results can fully comprehend (Cohen, 1990). If you are not comfortable with the use of a computer, there may be a big advantage to selecting a program used by someone who is willing to help you. And that leads to my next suggestion.

Know When and How to Seek Help

In this book, I have tried to point out some of the ambiguous situations in which it is not always clear which is the appropriate test to use. If your dependent measure is somewhere between an ordinal and an interval scale, if your expected values in a contingency table are around 3 or so in a number of the cells, if the variances and sample sizes in your two independent samples seem very different to you, it's probably time to consult an expert. Similarly, if you have a complicated design, with classrooms nested within schools and schools nested within communities, you may need the advice of a statistician. However, when you ask for advice, do so wisely. Be sure to describe the relevant aspects of your situation, such as the way in which your dependent variable is measured, the distribution of the scores, and the hypothesis you are trying to test. Even better is the situation in which you can describe the possible tests you are considering and ask for advice on which one would be preferable. Few unpaid consultants are happy with strangers who come to them with questions like "How do I analyze the results of my questionnaire?" or "Now that I've collected my data, what do I do with them?" The more specific you can make your question, and the more knowledge you can demonstrate in asking it, the more likely it is that you will be given helpful and understandable advice.

Get Involved in Research

My last piece of advice is that you use the statistical procedures you have learned, not just as a diversion to put you to sleep (or keep you up worrying) but as a tool to help you understand the results of research. It's a big first step to be able to read the research of others and to question magazine advertisements; for example, by asking whether toothpaste A really led to significantly fewer cavities than toothpaste B. An even bigger step is to conduct your own research, whether studying toothpaste, solid waste, how foods taste, or marrying in haste.

There are a lot of ways to learn how to do research. You can begin by reviewing Chapter 2 of this book. Next you might want to take a course in research methodology, take content courses that focus heavily on research methodology, read a lot of research studies in an area of interest to you, and/or talk to faculty members and ask if you can get involved with some of their research. Being able to ask and answer your own research questions can be much more exciting than just reading about what other people have done. If you think that statistics was fun, wait until you try research!

CHAPTER SUMMARY

One of the most important things to learn from this book is how to select an appropriate statistical test to analyze your data. In order to do so, you need to consider the nature of your data, especially the level of measurement of the dependent variable; your purpose (e.g., describing a distribution, predicting scores, assessing the relationship between two variables, or comparing differences in means or proportions); and whether or not you have multiple variables and are performing multiple significance tests.

In reporting research results it is important to include the relevant information in a concise and informative matter, to use APA or another consistent style, and not to confuse the statistical significance of a finding with its importance. For those who wish to continue increasing their knowledge in this area, I suggest taking more statistics courses, learning about computers, seeking help when needed, and getting involved in research.

CHAPTER REVIEW

Multiple-Choice Questions

1. For which of the following statistical tests does the degrees of freedom equal $N - 2$?

   a. a χ^2 goodness-of-fit test with 3 groups

   b. a 2×2 χ^2 test of independence

   c. a Pearson r

   d. a paired-samples t-test

   e. an analysis of variance with 6 people in each of 2 groups

   f. a, b, and c

   g. b and c

   h. a and c

   i. all of the above

   j. none of the above

2. Which of the following is a possible value?

   a. $r = -1$

   b. $F = -1$

   c. $s = -1$

   d. $s^2 = -1$

   e. $\chi^2 = -1$

   f. All of the above are possible values.

   g. None of the above is a possible value.

3. Suppose that you are doing a χ^2 test of independence and conclude that the observed and expected frequencies differ when, in fact, the null hypothesis is true. Which of the following have you definitely done?

   a. made a type I error

   b. made a type II error

   c. made a correct decision

   d. used the wrong statistical test (You should have used a goodness-of-fit test.)

   e. used the wrong statistical test (You should have used an analysis of variance.)

   f. made a computational error

4. As the sample size increases, the critical value decreases for which of the following procedures?

   a. analysis of variance

   b. Pearson r

   c. dependent-samples t-test

   d. χ^2

   e. a, b, and c are correct.

   f. all of the above

   g. none of the above

5. "The mean difference in the pretest and posttest scores of individuals who participate in this program is zero" is a null hypothesis for which kind of test?

   a. a Pearson r

   b. a Spearman rho

   c. a single sample t-test

   d. a correlated-samples t-test

   e. a one-way ANOVA

   f. a χ^2 goodness-of-fit test

   g. a χ^2 test of independence

6. "People who take hot showers will have dryer skin than people who take lukewarm baths" is a research hypothesis for which kind of test?

   a. a Pearson r

   b. a Spearman rho

   c. a single-sample t-test

   d. a correlated-samples t-test

   e. a one-way ANOVA

   f. a χ^2 goodness-of-fit test

   g. a χ^2 test of independence

Problems

7. For each of the situations described, indicate a statistical procedure that could be appropriately used to analyze the data. Usually there will be only one correct answer, but for some of these situations there may be more than one correct way to analyze the data.

Procedures

χ^2 goodness-of-fit test	χ^2 test of independence
one-way ANOVA	Tukey HSD test
two-way ANOVA	Scheffé post hoc comparison
Scheffé a priori comparison	Spearman rho
Pearson r	single-sample t-test
normal curve problem	independent-samples t-test
dependent-samples t-test	F-test (not part of ANOVA)
confidence interval	regression
z-test	

Research Situations

a. You want to know what the relationship is between how twenty people do in a debate tournament (first place to twentieth place) and how they do in a drama meet (also ordered from first to last).

b. You want to know whether the variance of the scores on a test of self-esteem is higher for a group of people who have been through psychotherapy as compared with a group of people who have not had psychotherapy.

c. You want to know what proportion of people in the normative sample could do fewer than three push-ups on the President's National Fitness Test.

d. You want to compare the mean numbers of push-ups done by 42 boys versus 34 girls in your school on the President's National Fitness Test.

e. After an analysis of variance revealed that the means of the students from three first-grade classes at school A and two first-grade classes at school B were unlikely to represent five random samples from the same population, you want to test the hypothesis that the combined mean of the classes at school A is higher than the combined mean of the classes at school B.

f. You want to see whether the choice of jogging, bicycling, or swimming as a favorite activity is related to which one of three summer fitness camps people attended.

g. You want to predict how many push-ups students will be able to do after participating in a fitness program from the number of push-ups they could do before the program began.

h. You want to compare the mean numbers of push-ups done by children who have attended one of three different fitness camps in order to see which fitness program is better.

i. You want to see what the relationship is between the number of sit-ups children can do in an hour and the number of push-ups they can do in an hour.

j. You want to compare the mean numbers of push-ups done by 66 children in your class before and after having been through a fitness training program.

k. You want to discover whether mothers or their teenage daughters own more pairs of shoes.

l. You want to know whether the variance in number of books read per year is greater for a sample of women or for a sample of men.

m. You want to see whether people's preferences for caffeinated or decaffeinated cola (they must choose one or the other) are related to their preferences for regular or decaf coffee (again, a choice).

n. After discovering from an analysis of variance that freshmen, sophomores, juniors, seniors, and graduate students differ in the mean number of hours they are taking this semester, you wish to compare the mean number of hours taken by graduate students with the mean number of hours taken by all undergraduates.

o. You want to see whether the number of letters that people mail is related to the number of letters that they receive per week.

p. To test Carlos Colorblind's theory that people have no preference among four different colors, you ask 100 people to select among red, green, blue, and black paint samples.

q. You want to compare the mean weights of football players at UNM and NMSU.

r. You want to see what proportion of people in Albuquerque are over seventy years old, based on your knowledge of the mean age and standard deviation of the ages of Albuquerque residents.

s. You want to predict a person's high school grade point average from that person's GPA in middle school.

t. You want to see whether or not the mean age of a sample of 2000 Albuquerque residents is significantly higher than the national norm of 38 years.

u. You want to estimate the mean number of bedrooms in an Albuquerque house, based on a sample of 500 houses, with no more than a 1% chance of your estimate being wrong.

v. You want to find out how similar the rankings of 10 colleges by *US News and World Report* are to the way these have been ranked by the Organization of University Presidents.

w. You want to know whether the mean family sizes of students at three different elementary schools differ significantly from each other.

x. After rejecting the null hypothesis that the means of groups A, B, and C are all equal, by finding a significant F from an analysis of variance comparing groups A, B, and C, you now want to compare the mean of group C to the mean of group B.

y. You want to see whether or not there is a relationship between how well people did on the first statistics test in a course and how well they did on their final exam.

z. You want to see whether religion and political party affiliation interact to affect amount of money donated to organizations in a year for a sample of 200 taxpayers.

8. For each of the situations below, name a statistical procedure that you could use to analyze the data and answer your research question.

a. You have read that 38% of all college students own computers. Based on a sample of students from your college who were asked whether they owned a computer, you want to conclude whether the proportion of students owning a computer in your college differs significantly from the national norm.

b. You decide to compare the mean grade-point averages of students in your college who do and who do not own a computer, in order to test your hypothesis that students who own a computer will make higher grades.

c. Funded by a grant, you decide to give computers to 15 randomly chosen students to test whether their grade-point averages improve after they are given a computer.

d. You are interested in the issue of whether time spent playing computer games is related to time spent reading. Therefore, you sample 40 students and, for each, measure how many hours per week they spend playing computer games and how many hours per week they spend reading. You want to see whether those who spend more time playing computer games tend to spend more or less time reading.

e. You have collected data from a sample of 400 college students, revealing that they spend a mean of 16.5 hours per week ($s = 4$ hours) interacting with a computer. Since a new study has just revealed that spending more than 3 hours a day bent over the computer is bad for your posture (just kidding!), you want to know what proportion of the students spent more than 21 hours per week at the computer (assuming that your dependent measure is approximately normally distributed).

f. The 20 students in the Technology and the Arts program have just completed two contests in which their artistic productions were ranked for creativity: one dealing with computer-assisted graphics and one on computer-created music. You want to know whether students who ranked high in one contest tended to rank similarly high (or possibly low) in the other contest.

g. You believe that boys will show greater variance than girls in the amount of time that they spend with computers. In other words, some boys will spend no time and others will spend large amounts of time at the computer, whereas girls will all spend a small amount of time using the computer. Therefore, you sample 50 boys and 50 girls and measure how much time each person spends interacting with the computer in the course of a week.

h. An analysis of variance comparing the amount of time spent in computer lab by 60 children from three different schools has revealed a significant F. Now you want to see whether the 20 children at school C spend significantly more time in computer lab than the 20 children in school B.

i. You want to test your hypothesis that 50-year-olds will learn a new concept relatively faster if it is presented in a booklet, whereas 20-year-olds will learn it relatively faster if it is presented via computer, based on a sample of thirty 50-year-olds and thirty 20-year-olds attending a trade fair.

j. You want to test your hypothesis that both 50-year-olds and 20-year-olds will learn a new concept faster if it is presented via computer rather than in written form, based on a sample of thirty 50-year-olds and thirty 20-year-olds attending a trade fair.

k. You want to predict students' grade-point averages from the amount of time that they spend using computers.

l. You want to know whether the proportions of student who do and do not own computers are different for students majoring in fine arts, engineering, and education.

9. For each of the following situations, identify the appropriate test and the degrees of freedom for the test. Then indicate the *critical value* of the appropriate test. You do not need to (indeed you can't) compute the test statistic.

a. You are interested in deciding whether or not the mean math test scores of ten sophomores, ten juniors, and ten seniors differ significantly across grade levels at the $p < .01$ level.

b. You are interested in seeing what the relationship is between the number of years a person has studied math and his or her attitude toward math as measured by a fifty-point attitude test at the $p < .001$ level. Your sample consists of 19 adults.

c. After concluding that dogs, cats, and rabbits differ in their mean size of litter, you have decided to do a post hoc test of the hypothesis that rabbits have larger litters than either dogs or cats. Your sample size is 68 animals, and you want to use the $p < .05$ significance level.

d. You are interested in seeing whether husbands have more or less positive attitudes toward mathematics than their wives, based on a study of 26 married couples, using the $p < .001$ level.

e. You are interested in seeing whether the sex of an individual is related to whether that person prefers to eat string beans, lima beans, or bean soup, based on a sample of 15 men and 14 women and using the $p < .01$ significance level.

f. After doing an analysis of variance on three groups with a total of 20 participants, you decide to do a Tukey HSD test to compare groups 2 and 3 at the $p < .01$ level.

g. You are interested in seeing whether 12 people from each of four different European countries differ significantly in the minutes per day that they spend walking at the $p < .01$ level.

h. You are interested in the relationship between a person's political affiliation (Republican, Democrat, or neither) and whether that person would vote "yes" or "no" on a bill to make all state universities charge the same tuition. You have a sample of 28 people and wish to use the .01 significance level.

i. You are interested in the relationship between how two members of a search committee rank the same 18 applicants for a position at the $p < .05$ level.

j. You are interested in comparing the mean number of cigarettes smoked by 16 people before and after participating in a "Just Say No" program at the $p < .001$ level.

10. For each of the following research situations based on the upcoming Olympics, identify the test that you would use to analyze the data, the degrees of freedom for the test, and the critical value for it at the .05 α-level.

a. You want to know whether the 24 Olympic divers are ranked the same by the American and Chinese judges.

b. You want to see whether the mean time of the 12 African runners in the 1500 meters is higher than the mean time of the 18 European runners in the same race.

c. You want to see whether the 28 females and 24 males competing in the equestrian events is a proportion that differs from the expected proportion of .5 females and .5 males.

d. You want to see whether the mean time for the 28 women in the marathon is significantly lower than the mean time for men from the years before 1950. (You don't have individual scores for these men, just an overall mean.)

e. For the seven people competing in both the 100-meter and the 200-meter races, you want to see if those who are fastest in the 100-meter race are also fastest in the 200-meter race.

f. There are 30 people from East Africa entering the summer Olympic events and 4 people from East Africa entering the winter Olympic events. There are 10 people from Scandinavia entering the summer Olympics and 35 Scandinavians entering the winter Olympics. You want to see whether Scandinavians and East Africans differ in the types of events (classified as "summer" versus "winter") that they choose to enter.

g. You want to compare the mean scores in archery of 13 North Americans, 12 Asians, and 16 Europeans.

h. After finding a significant F from the analysis of variance, you want to compare the mean score of the 13 North Americans with the mean of the 12 Asians and 16 Europeans combined.

Study Questions

1. For each of the following techniques, describe at least two situations in which each of the following procedures would be used. For each situation, provide enough information (design, groups, sample size) so that you could select the correct statistical procedure to use.

a. χ^2 goodness-of-fit test

b. χ^2 test of independence

c. one-way ANOVA

d. Tukey HSD test

e. Scheffé a priori comparison

f. Scheffé post hoc comparison

g. Pearson r

h. Spearman rho

i. normal curve problem

j. single-sample t-test

k. dependent-samples t-test

l. independent-samples t-test

m. confidence interval

      n. *F*-test (not part of ANOVA)

      o. *z*-test

      p. regression

2. Find someone else in the class who has done Study Question 1. Trade your list of situations with this person. See if each of you can identify the test to use in each of the situations. Discuss any discrepancies in your interpretations.

3. Try to find ten research articles that use statistical analyses. It's fine to consider ones you're using in writing a paper. Make up three lists: "Analyses I Know How to Do" (like one-way ANOVA), "Analyses I Can More-or-Less Get the Point Of" (like multiple regression), and "Analyses I Have Never Heard Of" (if I gave an example, you'd then have heard of it, so you're on your own with this one).

4. In case you're tired of reading, relax in front of the television set; if you prefer reading, curl up with a newspaper or magazine. As you watch or read each commercial or advertisement, try to think what kind of statistical test could have been done (or should have been done) to allow the advertisers to make their claims. Imagine that you are considering suing the advertisers for false advertising. What kinds of questions would you ask in order to discover whether or not their assertions are valid?

5. Find the "Results" section of the journal article that you photocopied in response to Study Question 2 of Chapter 1. Read it over again. How much of the material that confused you is clear to you now? Are there still aspects of the analyses that you don't understand? If so, you may want to sign up for another statistics class next semester.

References

Abelson, R.P. (1995). *Statistics as principled argument.* Hillsdale, NJ: Lawrence Erlbaum Associates.

Abelson, R.P. (1996). Vulnerability of contrast tests to simpler interpretations: An addendum to Rosnow and Rosenthal. *Psychological Science, 7,* 242–246.

Abelson, R.P. (1997). On the surprising longevity of flogged horses: Why there is a case for the significance test. *Psychological Science, 8,* 12–15.

American Psychological Association (1994). *Publication Manual of the American Psychological Association* (4th ed.). Washington, DC: APA.

Anderson, C.A., & Anderson, K.B. (1996). Violent crime rate studies in philosophical context: A destructive testing approach to heat and Southern culture of violence effects. *Journal of Personality and Social Psychology, 70,* 740–756.

Aron, A., & Aron, E.N. (1997). *Statistics for the behavioral and social sciences: A brief course.* Upper Saddle River, NJ: Prentice Hall.

Barry, D. (1992, June 20). Watch out for falling goats, snakes in toilet. *Albuquerque Journal,* p. B1.

Begley, S. (1993, March 22). The meaning of junk. *Newsweek, 121(12),* 62–64.

Benjafield, J.G. (1994). *Thinking critically about research methods.* Boston: Allyn & Bacon.

Berkowitz, L. (1992). Some thoughts about conservative evaluations of replications. *Personality and Social Psychology Bulletin, 18(3),* 319–324.

Brase, C.H., & Brase, C.P. (1991). *Understandable statistics: Concepts and methods* (4th ed.). Lexington, MA: D.C. Heath and Company.

Braver, S.L. (1975). On splitting the tails unequally. *Educational and Psychological Measurement, 35,* 283–301.

Campbell, D.T., & Erlebacher, A. (1975). How regression artifacts in quasi-experimental evaluations can mistakenly make compensatory education look harmful. In E.L. Struening & M. Guttentag (Eds). *Handbook of evaluation research* (Volume 1), pp. 597–617. Beverly Hills, CA: Sage Publications.

Campbell, D.T., & Stanley, J.C. (1963). *Experimental and quasi-experimental designs for research.* Chicago: Rand McNally.

Carver, R.P. (1978). The case against statistical significance testing. *Harvard Educational Review, 48,* 378–399.

Carver, R.P. (1993). The case against statistical significance testing, revisited. *Journal of Experimental Education, 61(4)*, 287–292.

Cohen, J. (1988). *Statistical power analysis for the behavioral sciences* (2nd ed.). Hillsdale, NJ: Erlbaum.

Cohen, J. (1990). Things I have learned (so far). *American Psychologist, 45(12)*, 1304–1312.

Cohen, J. (1992a). Statistical power analysis. *Current Directions in Psychological Science, 1(3)*, 98–101.

Cohen, J. (1992b). A power primer. *Psychological Bulletin, 112(1)*, 155–159.

Cohen, J., & Cohen, C. (1983). *Applied multiple regression/correlation analysis for the behavioral sciences* (2nd ed.). Hillsdale, NJ: Lawrence Erlbaum Associates.

Comrey, A.L., Bott, P.A., & Lee, H.B. (1989). *Elementary statistics: A problem-solving approach.* Dubuque, IA: Wm. C. Brown.

Coombs, W.T., Algina, J., & Oltman, D.O. (1996). Univariate and multivariate omnibus hypothesis tests selected to control Type I error rates when population variances are not necessarily equal. *Review of Educational Research, 66*, 137–179.

Craig, J.R., Eison, C.L., & Metze, L.P. (1976). Significance tests and their interpretation: An example utilizing published research and omega-squared. *Bulletin of the Psychonomic Society, 7(3)*, 280–282.

Devaney, B. (1991). The special supplemental food program for Women, Infants and Children (WIC). *Contemporary Nutrition, 16(7)*, 1–2.

Diekhoff, G.M. (1996). *Basic statistics for the social and behavioral sciences.* Upper Saddle River, NJ: Prentice Hall.

Estes, W.P. (1997). Significance testing in psychological research: Some persisting issues. *Psychological Science, 8*, 18–20.

Evans, J.D. (1996). *Straightforward statistics for the behavioral sciences.* Pacific Grove, CA: Brooks/Cole.

Freund, J.E., & Simon, G.A. (1991). *Statistics: A first course* (5th ed). Englewood Cliffs, NJ: Prentice Hall.

Gravetter, F.J., & Wallnau, L.B. (1988). *Statistics for the behavioral sciences* (2nd ed.). St Paul, MN: West.

Greenwald, A.G. (1975). Consequences of prejudice against the null hypothesis. *Psychological Bulletin, 82(1)*, 1–20.

Hancock, G.R., & Klockars, A.J. (1996). The quest for α: Developments in multiple comparison procedures in the quarter century since Games (1971). *Review of Educational Research, 66*, 269–306.

Harlow, L. (1997). Significance testing introduction and overview. In L. Harlow & S. Mulaik (Eds.), *What if there were no significance tests?* Mahwah, NJ: Erlbaum.

Harris, M.B. (1991). Sex differences in stereotypes of spectacles. *Journal of Applied Social Psychology, 21(20)*, 1659–1680.

Harris, M.B. (1995). Waiters, customers, and service: Some tips about tipping. *Journal of Applied Social Psychology, 25*, 725–744.

Harris, M.B. (1996). Aggressive experiences and aggressiveness: Relationship to ethnicity, gender, and age. *Journal of Applied Social Psychology, 26*, 843–870.

Harris, R.J. (1994). *ANOVA: An analysis of variance primer.* Itasca, IL: Peacock.

Harris, R.J. (1997). Significance tests have their place. *Psychological Science, 8*, 8–11.

Hartley, J. (1992). A postscript to Wainer's "Understanding Graphs and Tables." *Educational Researcher, 21(5)*, 25–26.

Hinkle, D.E., Wiersma, W., & Jurs, S.G. (1994). *Applied statistics for the behavioral sciences*. Boston: Houghton Mifflin.

Howell, D.C. (1987). *Statistical methods for psychology* (2nd ed.). Boston: Duxbury Press.

Huberty, C.J. (1987). On statistical testing. *Educational Researcher, 16(8)*, 4–9.

Hunter, J. (1997). Needed: A ban on the significance test. *Psychological Science, 8*, 3–7.

Hyde, J.S., Fennema, E., & Lamon, S.J. (1990). Gender differences in mathematics performance: A meta-analysis. *Psychological Bulletin, 107(2)*, 139–155.

Hyde, J.S., & Linn, M.C. (1988). Gender differences in verbal ability: A meta-analysis. *Psychological Bulletin, 104(1)*, 53–69.

Ito, T.A., Miller, N., & Pollock, V.E. (1996). Alcohol and aggression: A meta-analysis on the moderating effects of inhibitory cues, triggering events, and self-focused attention. *Psychological Bulletin, 120*, 60–82.

Kenny, D.A. (1987). *Statistics for the social and behavioral sciences*. Boston: Little, Brown & Co.

Kidder, L.H., & Judd, C.M. (1986). *Research methods in social relations* (5th ed.). New York: Holt, Rinehart & Winston.

Kramer, C.Y. (1956). Extension of multiple range test to group means with unequal number of replications. *Biometrics, 57*, 649–655.

Kromrey, J.D. (1993). Ethics and data analysis. *Educational Researcher, 22(4)*, 24–27.

Kupfersmid, J. (1988). Improving what is published: A model in search of an editor. *American Psychologist, 43(8)*, 635–642.

Leventhal, L., & Huynh, C-L. (1966). Directional decisions for two-tailed tests: Power, error rates, and sample size. *Psychological Methods, 1*, 278–292.

Lind, M. (1996, August 11). A 'crisis' of illegitimacy? Try hoax instead. *Boston Sunday Globe*, pp. D1–D2.

Meehl, P.E. (1978). Theoretical risks and tabular asterisks: Sir Karl, Sir Ronald, and the slow progress of soft psychology. *Journal of Consulting and Clinical Psychology, 46*, 806–834.

O'Grady, K.E. (1981). Probabilities and critical values for z, chi-square, r, t and F. *Behavior Research Methods & Instrumentation, 13*, 55–56.

Petty, R.E., Fabrigar, L.R., Wegener, D.T., & Priester, J.R. (1996). Understanding data when interactions are present or hypothesized. *Psychological Science, 7*, 247–252.

Pillemer, D.B. (1991). One-tailed vs. two-tailed hypothesis tests in contemporary educational research. *Educational Researcher, 20(9)*, 13–17.

Prentice, D.A., & Miller, D.T. (1992). When small effects are impressive. *Psychological Bulletin, 112(1)*, 160–164.

Rosenthal, R. (1979). The "file drawer" problem and tolerance for null results. *Psychological Bulletin, 86(3)*, 638–641.

Rosnow, R.L., & Rosenthal, R. (1989). Statistical procedures and the justification of knowledge in psychological science. *American Psychologist, 44(10)*, 1276–1284.

Rosnow, R.L., & Rosenthal, R. (1996). Contrasts and interactions redux: Five easy pieces. *Psychological Science, 7*, 253–257.

Scarr, S. (1997). Rules of evidence: A larger context for the statistical debate. *Psychological Science, 8*,

Schaller, M., Asp, C.H., Rosell, M.C., and Heim, S.J. (1996). Training in statistical reasoning inhibits the formation of erroneous group stereotypes. *Personality and Social Psychology Bulletin, 22*, 829–844.

Schneider, A.L., & Darcy, R.E. (1984). Policy implications of using significance tests in evaluation research. *Evaluation Review, 8(4)*, 573–582.

Shavelson, R.J. (1996). *Statistical reasoning for the behavioral sciences.* Boston: Allyn & Bacon.

Shaver J.P. (1985). Chance and nonsense: A conversation about interpreting tests of statistical significance, part 1. *Phi Delta Kappan, 67(1),* 57–60.

Shaver, J.P. (1993). What statistical significance testing is, and what it is not. *Journal of Experimental Education, 61(4),* 293–316.

Shrout, P.E. (1997). Should significance tests be banned? Introduction to a symposium exploring the pros and cons. *Psychological Science, 8,* 1–2.

Snyder, M. (1993). Basic research and practical problems: The promise of a "functional" personality and social psychology. *Personality and Social Psychology Bulletin, 19(3),* 251–264.

Spatz, C., & Johnston, J.O. (1989). *Basic statistics: Tales of distributions* (4th ed.). Pacific Grove, CA: Brooks/Cole.

Thompson, B. (1989a). Statistical significance, result importance, and result generalizability: Three noteworthy but somewhat different issues. *Measurement and Evaluation in Counseling and Development, 22,* 2–6.

Thompson, B. (1989b). Asking "what if" questions about significance tests. *Measurement and Evaluation in Counseling and Development, 22,* 66–68.

Thompson, B. (1992). Misuse of ANCOVA and related "statistical control" procedures. *Reading Psychology: An International Quarterly, 13,* iii–xviii.

Thompson, B. (1993). The use of statistical significance tests in research: Bootstrap and other alternatives. *Journal of Experimental Education, 61(4),* 361–377.

Wainer, H. (1992). Understanding graphs and tables. *Educational Researcher, 21(1),* 14–23.

Wang, M.C., Haertel, G.D., & Walberg, H.J. (1993). Toward a knowledge base for school learning. *Review of Educational Research, 63(3),* 249–294.

Wilcox, R.R. (1992). Why can methods for comparing means have relatively low power, and what can you do to correct the problem? *Current Directions in Psychological Science, 1(3),* 101–105.

Wilkinson, L. (1996, August). Alternatives to significance tests. In P.E. Shrout (chair), *Significance tests—Should they be banned from APA journals?* Symposium conducted at the American Psychological Association convention, Toronto, Canada.

Willig, A.C. (1985). A meta-analysis of selected studies on the effectiveness of bilingual education. *Review of Educational Research, 55(3),* 269–317.

Yates, F. (1934). Contingency tables involving small numbers and the χ^2 test. *Supplemental Journal of the Royal Statistical Society, 1,* 217–235.

Zuckerman, M., Hodgins, H.S., Zuckerman, A., & Rosenthal, R. (1993). Contemporary issues in the analysis of data: A survey of 551 psychologists. *Psychological Science, 4(1),* 49–53.

Appendix

Table 1   Areas Under Unit Normal Curve

Table 2   Critical Values for Pearson r

Table 3   Critical Values of Spearman rho

Table 4   Three-Digit Random Numbers

Table 5   Critical Values for t

Table 6   Critical Values for F

Table 7   Critical Values for Tukey HSD Test

Table 8   Critical Values for Chi-Square

Acknowledgments: Tables 1, 2, 4, 5, 6, and 8 were generated by Richard J. Harris using driver programs and subroutines adapted from Kevin E. O'Grady's (1981) PROB program.

Table 3 was adapted from E. G. Olds (1938), "Distributions of Sums of Squares of Rank Differences for Small Numbers of Individuals," *Annals of Mathematical Statistics, 9,* 133–148, and E. G. Olds (1949), "The 5 Percent Significance Levels of Sums of Squares of Rank Differences and a Correction," *Annals of Mathematical Statistics, 20,* 117–118. Reprinted by permission of the Institute of Mathematical Statistics.

Table 7 was adapted from H. L. Harter (1960), "Tables of the range and the studentized range," *Annals of Mathematical Statistics, 31,* 1123–1147. Reprinted by permission of the Institute of Mathematical Statistics.

TABLE 1   Areas Under Unit Normal Curve

z	Area Between z and Mean	Area Beyond z	z	Area Between z and Mean	Area Beyond z	z	Area Between z and Mean	Area Beyond z
0.00	0.0000	0.5000	0.40	0.1554	0.3446	0.80	0.2881	0.2119
0.01	0.0040	0.4960	0.41	0.1591	0.3409	0.81	0.2910	0.2090
0.02	0.0080	0.4920	0.42	0.1628	0.3372	0.82	0.2939	0.2061
0.03	0.0120	0.4880	0.43	0.1664	0.3336	0.83	0.2967	0.2033
0.04	0.0160	0.4840	0.44	0.1700	0.3300	0.84	0.2995	0.2005
0.05	0.0199	0.4801	0.45	0.1736	0.3264	0.85	0.3023	0.1977
0.06	0.0239	0.4761	0.46	0.1772	0.3228	0.86	0.3051	0.1949
0.07	0.0279	0.4721	0.47	0.1808	0.3192	0.87	0.3078	0.1922
0.08	0.0319	0.4681	0.48	0.1844	0.3156	0.88	0.3106	0.1894
0.09	0.0359	0.4641	0.49	0.1879	0.3121	0.89	0.3133	0.1867
0.10	0.0398	0.4602	0.50	0.1915	0.3085	0.90	0.3159	0.1841
0.11	0.0438	0.4562	0.51	0.1950	0.3050	0.91	0.3186	0.1814
0.12	0.0478	0.4522	0.52	0.1985	0.3015	0.92	0.3212	0.1788
0.13	0.0517	0.4483	0.53	0.2019	0.2981	0.93	0.3238	0.1762
0.14	0.0557	0.4443	0.54	0.2054	0.2946	0.94	0.3264	0.1736
0.15	0.0596	0.4404	0.55	0.2088	0.2912	0.95	0.3289	0.1711
0.16	0.0636	0.4364	0.56	0.2123	0.2877	0.96	0.3315	0.1685
0.17	0.0675	0.4325	0.57	0.2157	0.2843	0.97	0.3340	0.1660
0.18	0.0714	0.4286	0.58	0.2190	0.2810	0.98	0.3365	0.1635
0.19	0.0753	0.4247	0.59	0.2224	0.2776	0.99	0.3389	0.1611
0.20	0.0793	0.4207	0.60	0.2257	0.2743	1.00	0.3413	0.1587
0.21	0.0832	0.4168	0.61	0.2291	0.2709	1.01	0.3438	0.1562
0.22	0.0871	0.4129	0.62	0.2324	0.2676	1.02	0.3461	0.1539
0.23	0.0910	0.4090	0.63	0.2357	0.2643	1.03	0.3485	0.1515
0.24	0.0948	0.4052	0.64	0.2389	0.2611	1.04	0.3508	0.1492
0.25	0.0987	0.4013	0.65	0.2422	0.2578	1.05	0.3531	0.1469
0.26	0.1026	0.3974	0.66	0.2454	0.2546	1.06	0.3554	0.1446
0.27	0.1064	0.3936	0.67	0.2486	0.2514	1.07	0.3577	0.1423
0.28	0.1103	0.3897	0.68	0.2517	0.2483	1.08	0.3599	0.1401
0.29	0.1141	0.3859	0.69	0.2549	0.2451	1.09	0.3621	0.1379
0.30	0.1179	0.3821	0.70	0.2580	0.2420	1.10	0.3643	0.1357
0.31	0.1217	0.3783	0.71	0.2611	0.2389	1.11	0.3665	0.1335
0.32	0.1255	0.3745	0.72	0.2642	0.2358	1.12	0.3686	0.1314
0.33	0.1293	0.3707	0.73	0.2673	0.2327	1.13	0.3708	0.1292
0.34	0.1331	0.3669	0.74	0.2704	0.2296	1.14	0.3729	0.1271
0.35	0.1368	0.3632	0.75	0.2734	0.2266	1.15	0.3749	0.1251
0.36	0.1406	0.3594	0.76	0.2764	0.2236	1.16	0.3770	0.1230
0.37	0.1443	0.3557	0.77	0.2794	0.2206	1.17	0.3790	0.1210
0.38	0.1480	0.3520	0.78	0.2823	0.2177	1.18	0.3810	0.1190
0.39	0.1517	0.3483	0.79	0.2852	0.2148	1.19	0.3830	0.1170

TABLE 1   *Continued*

z	Area Between z and Mean	Area Beyond z	z	Area Between z and Mean	Area Beyond z	z	Area Between z and Mean	Area Beyond z
1.20	0.3849	0.1151	1.60	0.4452	0.0548	2.00	0.4772	0.0228
1.21	0.3869	0.1131	1.61	0.4463	0.0537	2.01	0.4778	0.0222
1.22	0.3888	0.1112	1.62	0.4474	0.0526	2.02	0.4783	0.0217
1.23	0.3907	0.1093	1.63	0.4484	0.0516	2.03	0.4788	0.0212
1.24	0.3925	0.1075	1.64	0.4495	0.0505	2.04	0.4793	0.0207
1.25	0.3944	0.1056	1.65	0.4505	0.0495	2.05	0.4798	0.0202
1.26	0.3962	0.1038	1.66	0.4515	0.0485	2.06	0.4803	0.0197
1.27	0.3980	0.1020	1.67	0.4525	0.0475	2.07	0.4808	0.0192
1.28	0.3997	0.1003	1.68	0.4535	0.0465	2.08	0.4812	0.0188
1.29	0.4015	0.0985	1.69	0.4545	0.0455	2.09	0.4817	0.0183
1.30	0.4032	0.0968	1.70	0.4554	0.0446	2.10	0.4821	0.0179
1.31	0.4049	0.0951	1.71	0.4564	0.0436	2.11	0.4826	0.0174
1.32	0.4066	0.0934	1.72	0.4573	0.0427	2.12	0.4830	0.0170
1.33	0.4082	0.0918	1.73	0.4582	0.0418	2.13	0.4834	0.0166
1.34	0.4099	0.0901	1.74	0.4591	0.0409	2.14	0.4838	0.0162
1.35	0.4115	0.0885	1.75	0.4599	0.0401	2.15	0.4842	0.0158
1.36	0.4131	0.0869	1.76	0.4608	0.0392	2.16	0.4846	0.0154
1.37	0.4147	0.0853	1.77	0.4616	0.0384	2.17	0.4850	0.0150
1.38	0.4162	0.0838	1.78	0.4625	0.0375	2.18	0.4854	0.0146
1.39	0.4177	0.0823	1.79	0.4633	0.0367	2.19	0.4857	0.0143
1.40	0.4192	0.0808	1.80	0.4641	0.0359	2.20	0.4861	0.0139
1.41	0.4207	0.0793	1.81	0.4649	0.0351	2.21	0.4864	0.0136
1.42	0.4222	0.0778	1.82	0.4656	0.0344	2.22	0.4868	0.0132
1.43	0.4236	0.0764	1.83	0.4664	0.0336	2.23	0.4871	0.0129
1.44	0.4251	0.0749	1.84	0.4671	0.0329	2.24	0.4875	0.0125
1.45	0.4265	0.0735	1.85	0.4678	0.0322	2.25	0.4878	0.0122
1.46	0.4279	0.0721	1.86	0.4686	0.0314	2.26	0.4881	0.0119
1.47	0.4292	0.0708	1.87	0.4693	0.0307	2.27	0.4884	0.0116
1.48	0.4306	0.0694	1.88	0.4699	0.0301	2.28	0.4887	0.0113
1.49	0.4319	0.0681	1.89	0.4706	0.0294	2.29	0.4890	0.0110
1.50	0.4332	0.0668	1.90	0.4713	0.0287	2.30	0.4893	0.0107
1.51	0.4345	0.0655	1.91	0.4719	0.0281	2.31	0.4896	0.0104
1.52	0.4357	0.0643	1.92	0.4726	0.0274	2.32	0.4898	0.0102
1.53	0.4370	0.0630	1.93	0.4732	0.0268	2.33	0.4901	0.0099
1.54	0.4382	0.0618	1.94	0.4738	0.0262	2.34	0.4904	0.0096
1.55	0.4394	0.0606	1.95	0.4744	0.0256	2.35	0.4906	0.0094
1.56	0.4406	0.0594	1.96	0.4750	0.0250	2.36	0.4909	0.0091
1.57	0.4418	0.0582	1.97	0.4756	0.0244	2.37	0.4911	0.0089
1.58	0.4429	0.0571	1.98	0.4761	0.0239	2.38	0.4913	0.0087
1.59	0.4441	0.0559	1.99	0.4767	0.0233	2.39	0.4916	0.0084

(continues)

TABLE 1 *Continued*

z	Area Between z and Mean	Area Beyond z	z	Area Between z and Mean	Area Beyond z	z	Area Between z and Mean	Area Beyond z
2.40	0.4918	0.0082	2.80	0.4974	0.0026	3.20	0.4993	0.0007
2.41	0.4920	0.0080	2.81	0.4975	0.0025	3.21	0.4993	0.0007
2.42	0.4922	0.0078	2.82	0.4976	0.0024	3.22	0.4994	0.0006
2.43	0.4925	0.0075	2.83	0.4977	0.0023	3.23	0.4994	0.0006
2.44	0.4927	0.0073	2.84	0.4977	0.0023	3.24	0.4994	0.0006
2.45	0.4929	0.0071	2.85	0.4978	0.0022	3.25	0.4994	0.0006
2.46	0.4931	0.0069	2.86	0.4979	0.0021	3.26	0.4994	0.0006
2.47	0.4932	0.0068	2.87	0.4979	0.0021	3.27	0.4995	0.0005
2.48	0.4934	0.0066	2.88	0.4980	0.0020	3.28	0.4995	0.0005
2.49	0.4936	0.0064	2.89	0.4981	0.0019	3.29	0.4995	0.0005
2.50	0.4938	0.0062	2.90	0.4981	0.0019	3.30	0.4995	0.0005
2.51	0.4940	0.0060	2.91	0.4982	0.0018	3.31	0.4995	0.0005
2.52	0.4941	0.0059	2.92	0.4982	0.0018	3.32	0.4995	0.0005
2.53	0.4943	0.0057	2.93	0.4983	0.0017	3.33	0.4996	0.0004
2.54	0.4945	0.0055	2.94	0.4984	0.0016	3.34	0.4996	0.0004
2.55	0.4946	0.0054	2.95	0.4984	0.0016	3.35	0.4996	0.0004
2.56	0.4948	0.0052	2.96	0.4985	0.0015	3.36	0.4996	0.0004
2.57	0.4949	0.0051	2.97	0.4985	0.0015	3.37	0.4996	0.0004
2.58	0.4951	0.0049	2.98	0.4986	0.0014	3.38	0.4996	0.0004
2.59	0.4952	0.0048	2.99	0.4986	0.0014	3.39	0.4997	0.0003
2.60	0.4953	0.0047	3.00	0.4987	0.0013	3.40	0.4997	0.0003
2.61	0.4955	0.0045	3.01	0.4987	0.0013	3.41	0.4997	0.0003
2.62	0.4956	0.0044	3.02	0.4987	0.0013	3.42	0.4997	0.0003
2.63	0.4957	0.0043	3.03	0.4988	0.0012	3.43	0.4997	0.0003
2.64	0.4959	0.0041	3.04	0.4988	0.0012	3.44	0.4997	0.0003
2.65	0.4960	0.0040	3.05	0.4989	0.0011	3.45	0.4997	0.0003
2.66	0.4961	0.0039	3.06	0.4989	0.0011	3.46	0.4997	0.0003
2.67	0.4962	0.0038	3.07	0.4989	0.0011	3.47	0.4997	0.0003
2.68	0.4963	0.0037	3.08	0.4990	0.0010	3.48	0.4997	0.0003
2.69	0.4964	0.0036	3.09	0.4990	0.0010	3.49	0.4998	0.0002
2.70	0.4965	0.0035	3.10	0.4990	0.0010	3.50	0.4998	0.0002
2.71	0.4966	0.0034	3.11	0.4991	0.0009	3.51	0.4998	0.0002
2.72	0.4967	0.0033	3.12	0.4991	0.0009	3.52	0.4998	0.0002
2.73	0.4968	0.0032	3.13	0.4991	0.0009	3.53	0.4998	0.0002
2.74	0.4969	0.0031	3.14	0.4992	0.0008	3.54	0.4998	0.0002
2.75	0.4970	0.0030	3.15	0.4992	0.0008	3.55	0.4998	0.0002
2.76	0.4971	0.0029	3.16	0.4992	0.0008	3.56	0.4998	0.0002
2.77	0.4972	0.0028	3.17	0.4992	0.0008	3.57	0.4998	0.0002
2.78	0.4973	0.0027	3.18	0.4993	0.0007	3.58	0.4998	0.0002
2.79	0.4974	0.0026	3.19	0.4993	0.0007	3.59	0.4998	0.0002

TABLE 1   *Continued*

z	Area Between z and Mean	Area Beyond z	z	Area Between z and Mean	Area Beyond z	z	Area Between z and Mean	Area Beyond z
3.60	0.4998	0.0002	3.74	0.4999	0.0001	3.88	0.4999	0.0001
3.61	0.4998	0.0002	3.75	0.4999	0.0001	3.89	0.4999	0.0001
3.62	0.4999	0.0001	3.76	0.4999	0.0001	3.90	0.5000	0.0000
3.63	0.4999	0.0001	3.77	0.4999	0.0001	3.91	0.5000	0.0000
3.64	0.4999	0.0001	3.78	0.4999	0.0001	3.92	0.5000	0.0000
3.65	0.4999	0.0001	3.79	0.4999	0.0001	3.93	0.5000	0.0000
3.66	0.4999	0.0001	3.80	0.4999	0.0001	3.94	0.5000	0.0000
3.67	0.4999	0.0001	3.81	0.4999	0.0001	3.95	0.5000	0.0000
3.68	0.4999	0.0001	3.82	0.4999	0.0001	3.96	0.5000	0.0000
3.69	0.4999	0.0001	3.83	0.4999	0.0001	3.97	0.5000	0.0000
3.70	0.4999	0.0001	3.84	0.4999	0.0001	3.98	0.5000	0.0000
3.71	0.4999	0.0001	3.85	0.4999	0.0001	3.99	0.5000	0.0000
3.72	0.4999	0.0001	3.86	0.4999	0.0001	4.00	0.5000	0.0000
3.73	0.4999	0.0001	3.87	0.4999	0.0001			

Two-Tailed Critical Values for z-ratios

alpha = .10: 1.645   alpha = .05: 1.960   alpha = .02: 2.326   alpha = .01: 2.576   alpha = .002: 3.090
alpha = .001: 3.291

TABLE 2   Critical Values for Pearson *r*

	Level of Significance for One-Tailed Test					
	.05	*.025*	*.01*	*.005*	*.001*	*.0005*
	Level of Significance for Two-Tailed Test					
df	*.10*	*.05*	*.02*	*.01*	*.002*	*.001*
1	0.988	0.997	1.000	1.000	1.000	1.000
2	0.900	0.950	0.980	0.990	0.998	0.999
3	0.805	0.878	0.934	0.959	0.986	0.991
4	0.729	0.811	0.882	0.917	0.963	0.974
5	0.669	0.754	0.833	0.875	0.935	0.951
6	0.621	0.707	0.789	0.834	0.905	0.925
7	0.582	0.666	0.750	0.798	0.875	0.898
8	0.549	0.632	0.715	0.765	0.847	0.872
9	0.521	0.602	0.685	0.735	0.820	0.847
10	0.497	0.576	0.658	0.708	0.795	0.823
11	0.476	0.553	0.634	0.684	0.772	0.801
12	0.458	0.532	0.612	0.661	0.750	0.780
13	0.441	0.514	0.592	0.641	0.730	0.760
14	0.426	0.497	0.574	0.623	0.711	0.742
15	0.412	0.482	0.558	0.606	0.694	0.725
16	0.400	0.468	0.543	0.590	0.678	0.708
17	0.389	0.456	0.529	0.575	0.662	0.693
18	0.378	0.444	0.516	0.561	0.648	0.679
19	0.369	0.433	0.503	0.549	0.635	0.665
20	0.360	0.423	0.492	0.537	0.622	0.652
21	0.352	0.413	0.482	0.526	0.610	0.640
22	0.344	0.404	0.472	0.515	0.599	0.629
23	0.337	0.396	0.462	0.505	0.588	0.618
24	0.330	0.388	0.453	0.496	0.578	0.607
25	0.323	0.381	0.445	0.487	0.568	0.597
26	0.317	0.374	0.437	0.479	0.559	0.588
27	0.311	0.367	0.430	0.471	0.550	0.579
28	0.306	0.361	0.423	0.463	0.541	0.570
30	0.296	0.349	0.409	0.449	0.526	0.554
40	0.257	0.304	0.358	0.393	0.463	0.490
50	0.231	0.273	0.322	0.354	0.419	0.443
60	0.211	0.250	0.295	0.325	0.385	0.408
80	0.183	0.217	0.257	0.283	0.336	0.357
100	0.164	0.195	0.230	0.254	0.303	0.321
200	0.116	0.138	0.164	0.181	0.216	0.230
500	0.073	0.088	0.104	0.115	0.138	0.146

TABLE 3   Critical Values of Spearman rho

		Level of Significance for One-Tailed Test			
		.05	.025	.01	.005
		Level of Significance for Two-Tailed Test			
N	df	.10	.05	.02	.01
5	3	.900	1.000	1.000	—
6	4	.829	.886	.943	1.000
7	5	.714	.786	.893	.929
8	6	.643	.738	.833	.881
9	7	.600	.683	.783	.833
10	8	.564	.648	.746	.794
12	10	.506	.591	.712	.777
14	12	.456	.544	.645	.715
16	14	.425	.506	.601	.665
18	16	.399	.475	.564	.625
20	18	.377	.450	.534	.591
22	20	.359	.428	.508	.562
24	22	.343	.409	.485	.537
26	24	.329	.392	.465	.515
28	26	.317	.377	.448	.496
30	28	.306	.364	.432	.478

N = number of pairs

TABLE 4   Three-Digit Random Numbers

Row	1–3	4–6	7–9	10–12	13–15	16–18	19–21	22–24	25–27	28–30	31–33	34–36	37–39
						Columns							
1	318	627	204	014	302	833	519	776	969	017	220	314	648
2	989	953	621	950	703	395	318	887	920	450	663	537	904
3	292	001	125	919	351	167	872	447	257	508	742	597	090
4	572	080	091	638	502	966	876	692	455	253	102	098	593
5	804	305	226	990	758	928	618	782	321	929	986	019	570
6	741	026	148	109	433	053	130	719	520	310	387	654	579
7	550	696	174	503	107	625	729	244	977	353	777	458	758
8	373	374	252	896	781	701	886	378	562	369	366	496	994
9	254	035	974	487	089	846	373	333	532	866	802	169	515
10	866	893	607	299	995	325	608	436	136	294	280	924	347
11	473	910	087	319	422	903	153	794	837	835	977	615	070
12	574	686	899	104	236	483	288	356	588	463	753	214	319
13	654	914	798	555	039	730	604	080	591	436	067	560	449
14	486	590	291	534	191	900	561	883	985	417	030	824	826
15	432	165	832	016	516	035	930	062	897	423	548	397	158
16	153	822	663	466	118	739	074	879	293	758	476	858	320
17	195	078	225	126	748	695	997	990	067	156	731	741	107
18	870	878	106	893	158	129	100	411	807	294	311	773	343
19	879	392	433	495	882	404	580	705	674	871	123	262	796
20	105	683	663	628	884	931	411	083	831	445	608	345	332
21	028	444	707	759	498	577	849	097	861	205	048	768	741
22	179	988	322	273	113	771	387	625	609	884	534	879	678
23	097	685	709	661	033	491	114	820	891	970	510	546	155
24	196	019	258	425	951	306	392	729	501	440	838	664	023
25	008	465	374	393	467	687	819	250	956	173	317	947	876
26	220	375	324	137	106	749	384	134	418	245	600	693	821
27	952	047	034	174	249	622	780	698	229	294	442	217	549
28	710	177	794	634	438	645	787	960	497	132	217	617	141
29	449	882	780	095	477	559	682	866	169	807	643	590	054
30	194	467	356	266	768	892	605	300	032	284	650	959	719
31	644	139	081	197	331	724	816	567	075	953	330	619	187
32	203	853	355	725	927	016	790	047	655	132	910	574	267
33	871	468	653	813	746	698	075	678	895	766	680	763	588
34	447	413	280	504	065	692	862	989	766	504	809	359	024
35	452	034	574	148	348	069	196	352	275	343	007	225	922
36	248	838	513	607	203	520	772	139	209	023	944	219	564
37	753	783	650	121	633	331	249	483	866	370	381	036	309
38	218	836	318	513	040	049	021	322	207	757	944	270	847
39	489	967	037	446	392	029	383	414	879	894	487	389	003
40	189	774	081	384	008	046	028	014	535	113	961	306	527
41	278	920	103	973	396	160	816	898	891	347	752	231	320
42	393	582	806	524	574	024	747	423	959	990	409	507	506
43	448	080	547	268	321	821	079	309	897	821	705	092	821
44	890	898	856	097	794	015	532	830	905	178	964	402	734

TABLE 4   *Continued*

						Columns							
Row	1–3	4–6	7–9	10–12	13–15	16–18	19–21	22–24	25–27	28–30	31–33	34–36	37–39
45	088	260	768	454	934	108	505	104	615	587	599	176	741
46	251	468	944	080	124	590	257	170	398	002	796	078	273
47	356	176	480	292	515	263	975	533	044	875	275	695	665
48	484	796	377	481	467	136	681	873	235	223	071	643	594
49	031	217	579	524	542	072	906	600	263	890	279	453	462
50	215	036	545	794	483	377	067	946	418	186	686	934	132
51	321	470	263	452	620	517	497	274	493	092	234	687	465
52	121	151	669	713	141	151	048	309	835	220	263	480	097
53	914	991	395	776	660	670	221	951	393	715	450	147	895
54	605	299	786	093	525	428	746	385	184	284	396	714	520
55	284	334	124	682	307	845	563	161	624	543	798	436	547
56	726	494	997	159	888	588	134	931	160	867	135	431	567
57	248	317	750	178	621	994	018	536	644	932	820	596	718
58	382	493	955	971	957	943	661	128	879	135	335	501	083
59	767	053	841	675	010	357	328	015	773	084	105	940	383
60	737	953	612	129	486	511	113	913	560	333	644	830	409
61	004	216	604	830	405	358	977	305	489	570	899	144	631
62	904	826	206	740	065	036	733	569	455	427	748	569	424
63	625	571	495	625	689	758	933	596	985	106	973	575	338
64	868	006	506	623	171	267	586	557	028	010	860	577	860
65	358	742	094	709	383	049	641	520	979	571	746	887	102
66	672	230	305	776	471	478	181	605	386	445	467	133	851
67	794	241	215	981	569	104	262	359	761	286	643	846	420
68	847	226	158	082	384	241	331	043	954	264	718	890	739
69	444	737	281	423	074	075	167	512	502	534	721	426	120
70	085	109	380	273	876	452	276	388	413	821	666	098	131
71	042	579	933	193	897	545	682	199	809	335	532	137	035
72	175	034	284	139	524	601	049	181	871	183	765	053	199
73	102	575	904	956	889	921	075	428	525	470	238	616	942
74	181	089	675	990	814	299	091	073	299	285	605	813	239
75	720	009	131	470	687	083	802	201	792	751	983	460	731
76	871	449	590	368	699	050	119	160	206	325	911	163	472
77	631	918	125	423	886	289	998	980	348	549	508	315	845
78	397	770	295	005	402	273	247	570	573	415	781	818	103
79	511	615	590	521	475	315	219	393	084	564	016	209	952
80	225	839	521	036	472	578	346	298	031	475	180	889	623
81	535	461	285	818	515	858	433	198	852	852	293	137	877
82	314	474	960	460	088	287	668	292	289	387	682	592	363
83	179	892	145	309	066	184	266	494	514	093	074	902	785
84	545	669	007	850	613	209	709	790	814	388	460	212	301
85	276	687	648	762	372	027	490	179	252	120	659	197	604
86	404	995	752	315	401	663	328	905	764	723	532	309	113
87	321	495	430	804	284	735	767	664	117	689	780	940	712
88	909	249	220	708	849	752	113	462	165	541	251	182	483

(continues)

TABLE 4   *Continued*

Row	1–3	4–6	7–9	10–12	13–15	16–18	19–21	22–24	25–27	28–30	31–33	34–36	37–39
						Columns							
89	024	610	155	257	946	670	641	833	842	504	719	865	862
90	788	351	867	093	705	885	001	082	340	045	046	580	654
91	115	990	630	726	722	857	781	255	887	490	678	352	361
92	914	491	318	451	616	551	141	519	590	887	417	663	233
93	403	533	173	433	374	881	473	641	752	315	390	516	505
94	979	531	363	639	942	345	014	247	125	821	174	212	246
95	073	601	231	302	494	038	360	560	524	168	991	544	253
96	428	651	197	609	805	237	800	294	240	598	934	089	443
97	247	792	244	298	184	730	436	397	690	775	137	278	160
98	635	249	914	860	391	097	993	329	748	116	857	950	853
99	786	965	768	011	982	115	289	564	185	681	368	054	554
100	337	086	244	155	513	473	272	999	659	820	642	206	589
101	345	509	837	492	049	006	592	962	699	765	728	783	970
102	309	689	554	480	409	606	615	511	109	346	772	232	899
103	680	876	580	337	589	019	845	693	234	022	631	295	824
104	298	996	082	255	798	710	667	474	537	423	997	830	478
105	196	341	094	030	538	972	367	016	903	577	979	917	349
106	198	259	433	792	186	493	358	980	123	021	086	938	014
107	761	040	555	518	487	533	542	563	992	969	530	314	769
108	486	184	321	013	421	932	769	940	458	748	813	592	000
109	752	230	587	058	864	116	302	800	258	663	511	570	732
110	894	340	562	403	495	294	250	675	480	500	204	137	785
111	368	823	881	294	366	034	882	735	488	835	491	531	988
112	346	797	314	226	602	410	788	746	651	358	022	689	877
113	176	154	061	600	635	895	799	878	302	385	492	385	320
114	133	035	568	986	440	202	621	042	386	740	519	842	504
115	922	002	799	661	189	250	106	457	207	218	363	500	725
116	344	082	896	133	768	450	111	119	737	792	417	635	412
117	584	873	186	311	602	492	875	875	905	764	392	511	838
118	546	920	439	032	208	822	853	780	317	045	161	756	924
119	676	513	348	619	934	004	943	422	842	752	175	652	618
120	714	130	147	165	303	142	049	916	485	308	404	010	242
121	803	687	311	223	411	559	907	236	018	233	733	347	276
122	408	793	276	598	817	917	124	589	770	818	752	024	002
123	465	201	120	920	353	967	360	512	041	856	879	045	451
124	208	634	129	691	297	110	591	372	557	638	754	211	083
125	114	177	207	497	354	973	389	969	427	386	836	301	646
126	389	426	046	058	868	163	168	928	010	308	148	981	653
127	456	574	007	821	714	409	313	553	160	483	103	119	902
128	852	633	647	776	298	268	150	852	259	738	349	201	485
129	006	963	824	173	116	585	678	403	496	723	573	532	730
130	304	312	326	850	293	894	018	755	823	362	195	906	500
131	897	548	951	834	556	946	496	059	015	872	901	441	292
132	687	262	991	922	061	559	314	599	293	534	936	260	580

TABLE 5   Critical Values for *t*

	Level of Significance for One-Tailed Test					
	.05	*.025*	*.01*	*.005*	*.001*	*.0005*
	Level of Significance for Two-Tailed Test					
df	*.10*	*.05*	*.02*	*.01*	*.002*	*.001*
1	6.314	12.706	31.820	63.657	318.309	636.619
2	2.920	4.303	6.965	9.925	22.327	31.599
3	2.353	3.182	4.541	5.841	10.215	12.924
4	2.132	2.776	3.747	4.604	7.173	8.610
5	2.015	2.571	3.365	4.032	5.893	6.869
6	1.943	2.447	3.143	3.707	5.208	5.959
7	1.895	2.365	2.998	3.499	4.785	5.408
8	1.860	2.306	2.896	3.355	4.501	5.041
9	1.833	2.262	2.821	3.250	4.297	4.781
10	1.812	2.228	2.764	3.169	4.144	4.587
11	1.796	2.201	2.718	3.106	4.025	4.437
12	1.782	2.179	2.681	3.055	3.930	4.318
13	1.771	2.160	2.650	3.012	3.852	4.221
14	1.761	2.145	2.624	2.977	3.787	4.140
15	1.753	2.131	2.602	2.947	3.733	4.073
16	1.746	2.120	2.583	2.921	3.686	4.015
17	1.740	2.110	2.567	2.898	3.646	3.965
18	1.734	2.101	2.552	2.878	3.610	3.922
19	1.729	2.093	2.539	2.861	3.579	3.883
20	1.725	2.086	2.528	2.845	3.552	3.850
21	1.721	2.080	2.518	2.831	3.527	3.819
22	1.717	2.074	2.508	2.819	3.505	3.792
23	1.714	2.069	2.500	2.807	3.485	3.768
24	1.711	2.064	2.492	2.797	3.467	3.745
25	1.708	2.060	2.485	2.787	3.450	3.725
26	1.706	2.056	2.479	2.779	3.435	3.707
27	1.703	2.052	2.473	2.771	3.421	3.690
28	1.701	2.048	2.467	2.763	3.408	3.674
29	1.699	2.045	2.462	2.756	3.396	3.659
30	1.697	2.042	2.457	2.750	3.385	3.646
50	1.676	2.009	2.403	2.678	3.261	3.496
100	1.660	1.984	2.364	2.626	3.174	3.390
∞	1.645	1.960	2.326	2.576	3.090	3.291

TABLE 6   Critical Values for F

		df for Numerator				
df^*	p	1	2	3	4	5
1	.05	161.447	199.500	215.707	224.583	230.162
	.01	4052.176	4999.492	5403.344	5624.574	5763.641
2	.05	18.513	19.000	19.164	19.247	19.296
	.01	98.502	99.000	99.166	99.249	99.299
	.001	998.500	999.000	999.166	999.250	999.299
3	.05	10.128	9.552	9.277	9.117	9.013
	.01	34.116	30.816	29.457	28.710	28.237
	.001	167.029	148.500	141.108	137.100	134.580
4	.05	7.709	6.944	6.591	6.388	6.256
	.01	21.198	18.000	16.694	15.977	15.522
	.001	74.137	61.246	56.177	53.436	51.712
5	.05	6.608	5.786	5.409	5.192	5.056
	.01	16.258	13.274	12.060	11.392	10.967
	.001	47.181	37.122	33.202	31.085	29.752
6	.05	5.987	5.143	4.757	4.534	4.387
	.01	13.745	10.925	9.780	9.148	8.746
	.001	35.507	27.000	23.703	21.924	20.803
7	.05	5.591	4.737	4.347	4.120	3.972
	.01	12.246	9.547	8.451	7.847	7.460
	.001	29.245	21.689	18.772	17.198	16.206
8	.05	5.318	4.459	4.066	3.838	3.687
	.01	11.259	8.649	7.591	7.006	6.632
	.001	25.415	18.494	15.829	14.392	13.485
9	.05	5.117	4.256	3.863	3.633	3.482
	.01	10.561	8.022	6.992	6.422	6.057
	.001	22.857	16.387	13.902	12.560	11.714
10	.05	4.965	4.103	3.708	3.478	3.326
	.01	10.044	7.559	6.552	5.994	5.636
	.001	21.040	14.905	12.553	11.283	10.481
11	.05	4.844	3.982	3.587	3.357	3.204
	.01	9.646	7.206	6.217	5.668	5.316
	.001	19.687	13.812	11.561	10.346	9.578
12	.05	4.747	3.885	3.490	3.259	3.106
	.01	9.330	6.927	5.953	5.412	5.064
	.001	18.643	12.974	10.804	9.633	8.892
13	.05	4.667	3.806	3.411	3.179	3.025
	.01	9.074	6.701	5.739	5.205	4.862
	.001	17.815	12.313	10.209	9.073	8.354
14	.05	4.600	3.739	3.344	3.112	2.958
	.01	8.862	6.515	5.564	5.035	4.695
	.001	17.143	11.779	9.729	8.622	7.922
15	.05	4.543	3.682	3.287	3.056	2.901
	.01	8.683	6.359	5.417	4.893	4.556
	.001	16.587	11.339	9.335	8.253	7.567

*For denominator.

		df for Numerator					
df*	*p*	6	7	8	10	15	20
1	.05	233.986	236.768	238.882	241.882	245.950	248.013
	.01	5858.977	5928.348	5981.062	6055.836	6157.273	6208.719
2	.05	19.330	19.353	19.371	19.396	19.429	19.446
	.01	99.333	99.356	99.374	99.399	99.432	99.449
	.001	999.333	999.356	999.375	999.399	999.433	999.449
3	.05	8.941	8.887	8.845	8.786	8.703	8.660
	.01	27.911	27.672	27.489	27.229	26.872	26.690
	.001	132.847	131.583	130.619	129.247	127.374	126.418
4	.05	6.163	6.094	6.041	5.964	5.858	5.803
	.01	15.207	14.976	14.799	14.546	14.198	14.020
	.001	50.525	49.648	48.996	48.053	46.761	46.100
5	.05	4.950	4.876	4.818	4.735	4.619	4.558
	.01	10.672	10.456	10.289	10.051	9.722	9.553
	.001	28.834	28.163	27.649	26.917	25.911	25.395
6	.05	4.284	4.207	4.147	4.060	3.938	3.874
	.01	8.466	8.260	8.102	7.874	7.559	7.396
	.001	20.030	19.463	19.030	18.411	17.559	17.120
7	.05	3.866	3.787	3.726	3.637	3.511	3.445
	.01	7.191	6.993	6.840	6.620	6.314	6.155
	.001	15.521	15.019	14.634	14.083	13.324	12.292
8	.05	3.581	3.500	3.438	3.347	3.218	3.150
	.01	6.371	6.178	6.029	5.814	5.515	5.359
	.001	12.858	12.398	12.046	11.540	10.841	10.480
9	.05	3.374	3.293	3.230	3.137	3.006	2.936
	.01	5.802	5.613	5.467	5.257	4.962	4.808
	.001	11.128	10.698	10.368	9.894	9.238	8.898
10	.05	3.217	3.135	3.072	2.978	2.845	2.774
	.01	5.386	5.200	5.057	4.849	4.558	4.405
	.001	9.926	9.517	9.204	8.754	8.129	7.804
11	.05	3.095	3.012	2.948	2.854	2.719	2.646
	.01	5.069	4.886	4.744	4.539	4.251	4.099
	.001	9.047	8.655	8.355	7.922	7.321	7.008
12	.05	2.996	2.913	2.849	2.753	2.617	2.544
	.01	4.821	4.640	4.499	4.296	4.010	3.858
	.001	8.379	8.001	7.710	7.292	6.709	6.405
13	.05	2.915	2.832	2.767	2.671	2.533	2.459
	.01	4.620	4.441	4.302	4.100	3.815	3.665
	.001	7.856	7.489	7.206	6.799	6.231	5.934
14	.05	2.848	2.764	2.699	2.602	2.463	2.388
	.01	4.456	4.278	4.140	3.939	3.656	3.505
	.001	7.436	7.077	6.802	6.404	5.848	5.557
15	.05	2.790	2.707	2.641	2.544	2.403	2.328
	.01	4.318	4.142	4.004	3.805	3.522	3.372
	.001	7.092	6.741	6.471	6.081	5.535	5.248

(continues)

df between

TABLE 6   *Continued*

df*	p	df for Numerator				
		1	2	3	4	5
16	.05	4.494	3.634	3.239	3.007	2.852
	.01	8.531	6.226	5.292	4.773	4.437
	.001	16.120	10.971	9.006	7.944	7.272
17	.05	4.451	3.592	3.197	2.965	2.810
	.01	8.400	6.112	5.185	4.669	4.336
	.001	15.722	10.658	8.727	7.683	7.022
18	.05	4.414	3.555	3.160	2.928	2.773
	.01	8.285	6.013	5.092	4.579	4.248
	.001	15.379	10.390	8.487	7.459	6.808
19	.05	4.381	3.522	3.127	2.895	2.740
	.01	8.185	5.926	5.010	4.500	4.171
	.001	15.081	10.157	8.280	7.265	6.622
20	.05	4.351	3.493	3.098	2.866	2.711
	.01	8.096	5.849	4.938	4.431	4.103
	.001	14.819	9.953	8.098	7.096	6.461
21	.05	4.325	3.467	3.072	2.840	2.685
	.01	8.017	5.780	4.874	4.369	4.042
	.001	14.587	9.772	7.938	6.947	6.318
22	.05	4.301	3.443	3.049	2.817	2.661
	.01	7.945	5.719	4.817	4.313	3.988
	.001	14.380	9.612	7.796	6.814	6.191
23	.05	4.279	3.422	3.028	2.796	2.640
	.01	7.881	5.664	4.765	4.264	3.939
	.001	14.195	9.469	7.669	6.696	6.078
24	.05	4.260	3.403	3.009	2.776	2.621
	.01	7.823	5.614	4.718	4.218	3.895
	.001	14.028	9.339	7.554	6.589	5.977
25	.05	4.242	3.385	2.991	2.759	2.603
	.01	7.770	5.568	4.675	4.177	3.855
	.001	13.877	9.223	7.451	6.493	5.885
26	.05	4.225	3.369	2.975	2.743	2.587
	.01	7.721	5.526	4.637	4.140	3.818
	.001	13.739	9.116	7.357	6.406	5.802
27	.05	4.210	3.354	2.960	2.728	2.572
	.01	7.677	5.488	4.601	4.106	3.785
	.001	13.613	9.019	7.272	6.326	5.726
28	.05	4.196	3.340	2.947	2.714	2.558
	.01	7.636	5.453	4.568	4.074	3.754
	.001	13.498	8.931	7.193	6.253	5.656
29	.05	4.183	3.328	2.934	2.701	2.545
	.01	7.598	5.420	4.538	4.045	3.725
	.001	13.391	8.849	7.121	6.186	5.593
30	.05	4.171	3.316	2.922	2.690	2.534
	.01	7.562	5.390	4.510	4.018	3.699
	.001	13.293	8.773	7.054	6.125	5.534

*For denominator.

df (within)

		df for Numerator					
df*	p	6	7	8	10	15	20
16	.05	2.741	2.657	2.591	2.494	2.352	2.276
	.01	4.202	4.026	3.890	3.691	3.409	3.259
	.001	6.805	6.460	6.195	5.812	5.274	4.992
17	.05	2.699	2.614	2.548	2.450	2.308	2.230
	.01	4.102	3.927	3.791	3.593	3.312	3.162
	.001	6.562	6.223	5.962	5.584	5.054	4.775
18	.05	2.661	2.577	2.510	2.412	2.269	2.191
	.01	4.015	3.841	3.705	3.508	3.227	3.077
	.001	6.355	6.021	5.763	5.390	4.866	4.590
19	.05	2.628	2.544	2.477	2.378	2.234	2.155
	.01	3.939	3.765	3.631	3.434	3.153	3.003
	.001	6.175	5.845	5.590	5.222	4.704	4.430
20	.05	2.599	2.514	2.447	2.348	2.203	2.124
	.01	3.871	3.699	3.564	3.368	3.088	2.938
	.001	6.019	5.692	5.440	5.075	4.562	4.290
21	.05	2.573	2.488	2.420	2.321	2.176	2.096
	.01	3.812	3.640	3.506	3.310	3.030	2.880
	.001	5.881	5.557	5.308	4.946	4.437	4.167
22	.05	2.549	2.464	2.397	2.297	2.151	2.071
	.01	3.758	3.587	3.453	3.258	2.978	2.827
	.001	5.758	5.438	5.190	4.832	4.326	4.058
23	.05	2.528	2.442	2.375	2.275	2.128	2.048
	.01	3.710	3.539	3.406	3.211	2.931	2.781
	.001	5.649	5.331	5.085	4.730	4.227	3.961
24	.05	2.508	2.423	2.355	2.255	2.108	2.027
	.01	3.667	3.496	3.363	3.168	2.889	2.738
	.001	5.550	5.235	4.991	4.638	4.139	3.873
25	.05	2.490	2.405	2.337	2.236	2.089	2.007
	.01	3.627	3.457	3.324	3.129	2.850	2.699
	.001	5.462	5.148	4.906	4.555	4.059	3.794
26	.05	2.474	2.388	2.321	2.220	2.072	1.990
	.01	3.591	3.421	3.288	3.094	2.815	2.664
	.001	5.381	5.070	4.829	4.480	3.986	3.723
27	.05	2.459	2.373	2.305	2.204	2.056	1.974
	.01	3.558	3.388	3.256	3.062	2.783	2.632
	.001	5.308	4.998	4.759	4.412	3.920	3.658
28	.05	2.445	2.359	2.291	2.190	2.041	1.959
	.01	3.528	3.358	3.226	3.032	2.753	2.602
	.001	5.241	4.933	4.695	4.349	3.859	3.598
29	.05	2.432	2.346	2.278	2.177	2.027	1.945
	.01	3.499	3.330	3.198	3.005	2.726	2.574
	.001	5.179	4.873	4.636	4.292	3.804	3.543
30	.05	2.421	2.334	2.266	2.165	2.015	1.932
	.01	3.473	3.304	3.173	2.979	2.700	2.549
	.001	5.122	4.817	4.581	4.239	3.753	3.493

(continues)

TABLE 6 *Continued*

df*	p			df for Numerator		
		1	2	3	4	5
40	.05	4.085	3.232	2.839	2.606	2.449
	.01	7.314	5.179	4.313	3.828	3.514
	.001	12.609	8.251	6.595	5.698	5.128
50	.05	4.034	3.183	2.790	2.557	2.400
	.01	7.171	5.057	4.199	3.720	3.408
	.001	12.222	7.956	6.336	5.459	4.901
60	.05	4.001	3.150	2.758	2.525	2.368
	.01	7.077	4.977	4.126	3.649	3.339
	.001	11.973	7.768	6.171	5.307	4.757
70	.05	3.978	3.128	2.736	2.503	2.346
	.01	7.011	4.922	4.074	3.600	3.291
	.001	11.799	7.637	6.057	5.201	4.656
80	.05	3.960	3.111	2.719	2.486	2.329
	.01	6.963	4.881	4.036	3.563	3.255
	.001	11.671	7.540	5.972	5.123	4.582
90	.05	3.947	3.098	2.706	2.473	2.316
	.01	6.925	4.849	4.007	3.535	3.228
	.001	11.573	7.466	5.908	5.064	4.526
100	.05	3.936	3.087	2.696	2.463	2.305
	.01	6.895	4.824	3.984	3.513	3.206
	.001	11.495	7.408	5.857	5.017	4.482
120	.05	3.920	3.072	2.680	2.447	2.290
	.01	6.851	4.787	3.949	3.480	3.174
	.001	11.380	7.321	5.781	4.947	4.416
150	.05	3.904	3.056	2.665	2.432	2.274
	.01	6.807	4.749	3.915	3.447	3.142
	.001	11.267	7.236	5.707	4.879	4.351
200	.05	3.888	3.041	2.650	2.417	2.259
	.01	6.763	4.713	3.881	3.414	3.110
	.001	11.154	7.152	5.634	4.812	4.287
300	.05	3.073	3.026	2.635	2.402	2.244
	.01	6.720	4.677	3.848	3.382	3.079
	.001	11.044	7.069	5.562	4.746	4.225
400	.05	3.865	3.018	2.627	2.394	2.237
	.01	6.699	4.659	3.831	3.366	3.063
	.001	10.989	7.028	5.527	4.713	4.194
500	.05	3.860	3.014	2.623	2.390	2.232
	.01	6.686	4.648	3.821	3.357	3.054
	.001	10.957	7.004	5.506	4.693	4.176
1000	.05	3.851	3.005	2.614	2.381	2.223
	.01	6.660	4.626	3.801	3.338	3.036
	.001	10.892	6.956	5.464	4.655	4.139
∞	.05	3.841	2.996	2.605	2.372	2.214
	.01	6.635	4.605	3.782	3.319	3.017
	.001	10.828	6.908	5.422	4.617	4.103

*For denominator.

df*	p	df for Numerator					
		6	7	8	10	15	20
40	.05	2.336	2.249	2.180	2.077	1.924	1.839
	.01	3.291	3.124	2.993	2.801	2.522	2.369
	.001	4.731	4.436	4.207	3.874	3.400	3.145
50	.05	2.286	2.199	2.130	2.026	1.871	1.784
	.01	3.186	3.020	2.890	2.698	2.419	2.265
	.001	4.512	4.222	3.998	3.671	3.204	2.951
60	.05	2.254	2.167	2.097	1.993	1.836	1.748
	.01	3.119	2.953	2.823	2.632	2.352	2.198
	.001	4.372	4.086	3.865	3.541	3.078	2.827
70	.05	2.231	2.143	2.074	1.969	1.812	1.722
	.01	3.071	2.906	2.777	2.585	2.306	2.150
	.001	4.275	3.992	3.773	3.452	2.991	2.741
80	.05	2.214	2.126	2.056	1.951	1.793	1.703
	.01	3.036	2.871	2.742	2.551	2.271	2.115
	.001	4.204	3.923	3.705	3.386	2.927	2.677
90	.05	2.201	2.113	2.043	1.938	1.779	1.688
	.01	3.009	2.845	2.715	2.524	2.244	2.088
	.001	4.150	3.870	3.653	3.336	2.879	2.629
100	.05	2.191	2.103	2.032	1.927	1.768	1.676
	.01	2.988	2.823	2.694	2.503	2.223	2.067
	.001	4.107	3.829	3.612	3.296	2.840	2.591
120	.05	2.175	2.087	2.016	1.910	1.750	1.659
	.01	2.956	2.792	2.663	2.472	2.192	2.035
	.001	4.044	3.767	3.552	3.237	2.783	2.534
150	.05	2.160	2.071	2.001	1.894	1.734	1.641
	.01	2.924	2.761	2.632	2.441	2.160	2.003
	.001	3.981	3.706	3.493	3.179	2.727	2.479
200	.05	2.144	2.056	1.985	1.878	1.717	1.623
	.01	2.893	2.730	2.601	2.411	2.129	1.971
	.001	3.920	3.647	3.434	3.123	2.672	2.424
300	.05	2.129	2.040	1.969	1.862	1.700	1.606
	.01	2.862	2.699	2.571	2.380	2.099	1.940
	.001	3.860	3.588	3.377	3.067	2.618	2.371
400	.05	2.121	2.032	1.962	1.854	1.691	1.597
	.01	2.847	2.684	2.556	2.365	2.084	1.925
	.001	3.830	3.560	3.349	3.040	2.592	2.344
500	.05	2.177	2.028	1.957	1.850	1.686	1.592
	.01	2.838	2.675	2.547	2.356	2.075	1.915
	.001	3.813	3.542	3.332	3.023	2.576	2.328
1000	.05	2.108	2.019	1.948	1.840	1.676	1.581
	.01	2.820	2.657	2.529	2.339	2.056	1.897
	.001	3.778	3.508	3.299	2.991	2.544	2.297
∞	.05	2.099	2.010	1.938	1.880	1.831	1.752
	.01	2.802	2.639	2.511	2.407	2.321	2.185
	.001	3.743	3.475	3.266	3.097	2.959	2.742

TABLE 7 Critical Values for Tukey HSD Test

$\alpha = .05$; Number of Means (K)

df_{WG}	2	3	4	5	6	7	8	9	10	11	12	13	14	15
1	17.97	26.98	32.82	37.08	40.41	43.12	45.40	47.36	49.07	50.59	51.96	53.20	54.33	55.36
2	6.08	8.33	9.80	10.88	11.74	12.44	13.03	13.54	13.99	14.39	14.75	15.08	15.38	15.65
3	4.50	5.91	6.82	7.50	8.04	8.48	8.85	9.18	9.46	9.72	9.95	10.15	10.35	10.53
4	3.93	5.04	5.76	6.29	6.71	7.05	7.35	7.60	7.33	8.03	8.21	8.37	8.52	8.66
5	3.64	4.60	5.22	5.67	6.03	6.33	6.58	6.80	7.00	7.17	7.32	7.47	7.60	7.72
6	3.46	4.34	4.90	5.31	5.63	5.90	6.12	6.32	6.49	6.65	6.79	6.92	7.03	7.14
7	3.34	4.16	4.68	5.06	5.36	5.61	5.82	6.00	6.16	6.30	6.43	6.55	6.66	6.76
8	3.26	4.04	(4.53)	4.89	5.17	5.40	5.60	5.77	5.92	6.05	6.18	6.29	6.39	6.48
9	3.20	3.95	4.42	4.76	5.02	5.24	5.43	5.60	5.74	5.87	5.98	6.09	6.19	6.28
10	3.15	3.88	4.33	4.65	4.91	5.12	5.30	5.46	5.60	5.72	5.83	5.94	6.03	6.11
11	3.11	3.82	4.26	4.57	4.82	5.03	5.20	5.35	5.49	5.60	5.71	5.81	5.90	5.98
12	3.08	3.77	4.20	4.51	4.75	4.95	5.12	5.26	5.40	5.51	5.62	5.71	5.79	5.88
13	3.06	3.74	4.15	4.45	4.69	4.88	5.05	5.19	5.32	5.43	5.53	5.63	5.71	5.79
14	3.03	3.70	4.11	4.41	4.64	4.83	4.99	5.13	5.25	5.36	5.46	5.55	5.64	5.71
15	3.01	3.67	4.08	4.37	4.60	4.78	4.94	5.08	5.20	5.31	5.40	5.49	5.57	5.65
16	3.00	3.65	4.05	4.33	4.56	4.74	4.90	5.03	5.15	5.26	5.35	5.44	5.52	5.59
17	2.98	3.63	4.02	4.30	4.52	4.70	4.86	4.99	5.11	5.21	5.31	5.39	5.47	5.54
18	2.97	3.61	4.00	4.28	4.50	4.67	4.82	4.96	5.07	5.17	5.27	5.35	5.43	5.50
19	2.96	3.59	3.98	4.25	4.47	4.64	4.79	4.92	5.04	5.14	5.23	5.32	5.39	5.46
20	2.95	3.58	3.96	4.23	4.44	4.62	4.77	4.90	5.01	5.11	5.20	5.28	5.36	5.43
24	2.92	3.53	3.90	4.17	4.37	4.54	4.68	4.81	4.92	5.01	5.10	5.18	5.25	5.32
30	2.89	3.49	3.84	4.10	4.30	4.46	4.60	4.72	4.82	4.92	5.00	5.08	5.15	5.21
40	2.86	3.44	3.79	4.04	4.23	4.39	4.52	4.64	4.74	4.82	4.90	4.98	5.04	5.11
60	2.83	3.40	3.74	3.98	4.16	4.31	4.44	4.55	4.65	4.73	4.81	4.88	4.94	5.00
120	2.80	3.36	3.69	3.92	4.10	4.24	4.36	4.47	4.56	4.64	4.71	4.78	4.84	4.90
∞	2.77	3.31	3.63	3.86	4.03	4.17	4.29	4.39	4.47	4.55	4.62	4.68	4.74	4.80

$\alpha = .01$; Number of Means (K)

df_{WG}	2	3	4	5	6	7	8	9	10	11	12	13	14	15
1	90.03	135.0	164.3	185.6	202.2	215.8	227.2	237.0	245.6	253.2	260.0	266.2	271.8	277.0
2	14.04	19.02	22.29	24.72	26.63	28.20	29.53	30.68	31.69	32.59	33.40	34.13	34.81	35.43
3	8.26	10.62	12.17	13.33	14.24	15.00	15.64	12.60	16.69	17.13	17.53	17.89	18.22	18.52
4	6.51	8.12	9.17	9.96	10.58	11.10	11.55	11.93	12.27	12.57	12.84	13.09	13.32	13.53
5	5.70	6.98	7.80	8.42	8.91	9.32	9.67	9.97	10.24	10.48	10.70	10.89	11.08	11.24
6	5.24	6.33	7.03	7.56	7.97	8.32	8.62	8.87	9.10	9.30	9.48	9.65	9.81	9.95
7	4.95	5.92	6.54	7.00	7.37	7.68	7.94	8.17	8.37	8.55	8.71	8.86	9.00	9.12
8	4.75	5.64	6.20	6.62	6.96	7.24	7.47	7.68	7.86	8.03	8.18	8.31	8.44	8.55
9	4.60	5.43	5.96	6.35	6.66	6.92	7.13	7.32	7.50	7.65	7.78	7.91	8.02	8.13
10	4.48	5.27	5.77	6.14	6.43	6.67	6.88	7.06	7.21	7.36	7.48	7.60	7.71	7.81
11	4.39	5.15	5.62	5.97	6.25	6.48	6.67	6.84	6.99	7.13	7.25	7.36	7.46	7.56
12	4.32	5.05	5.50	5.84	6.10	6.32	6.51	6.67	6.81	6.94	7.06	7.17	7.26	7.36
13	4.26	4.96	5.40	5.73	5.98	6.19	6.37	6.53	6.67	6.79	6.90	7.01	7.10	7.19
14	4.21	4.90	5.32	5.63	5.88	6.08	6.26	6.41	6.54	6.66	6.77	6.87	6.96	7.05
15	4.17	4.84	5.25	5.56	5.80	5.99	6.16	6.31	6.44	6.56	6.66	6.76	6.84	6.93
16	4.13	4.79	5.19	5.49	5.72	5.92	6.08	6.22	6.35	6.46	6.56	6.66	6.74	6.82
17	4.10	4.74	5.14	5.43	5.66	5.85	6.01	6.15	6.27	6.38	6.48	6.57	6.66	6.73
18	4.07	4.70	5.09	5.38	5.60	5.79	5.94	6.08	6.20	6.31	6.41	6.50	6.58	6.66
19	4.05	4.67	5.05	5.33	5.55	5.74	5.89	6.02	6.14	6.25	6.34	6.43	6.51	6.58
20	4.02	4.64	5.02	5.29	5.51	5.69	5.84	5.97	6.09	6.19	6.28	6.37	6.45	6.52
24	3.96	4.55	4.91	5.17	5.37	5.54	5.69	5.81	5.92	6.02	6.11	6.19	6.26	6.33
30	3.89	4.46	4.80	5.05	5.24	5.40	5.54	5.65	5.76	5.85	5.93	6.01	6.08	6.14
40	3.82	4.37	4.70	4.93	5.11	5.26	5.39	5.50	5.60	5.69	5.76	5.84	5.90	5.96
60	3.76	4.28	4.60	4.82	4.99	5.13	5.25	5.36	5.45	5.53	5.60	5.67	5.73	5.78
120	3.70	4.20	4.50	4.71	4.87	5.0	5.12	5.21	5.30	5.38	5.44	5.51	5.56	5.61
∞	3.64	4.12	4.40	4.60	4.76	4.88	4.99	5.08	5.16	5.23	5.29	5.35	5.40	5.45

TABLE 8   Critical Values for Chi-Square

			Alpha			
df	.10	.05	.02	.01	.002	.001
1	2.706	3.841	5.412	6.635	9.550	10.828
2	4.605	5.991	7.824	9.210	12.430	13.816
3	6.251	7.815	9.837	11.345	14.796	16.267
4	7.779	9.488	11.668	13.277	16.924	18.468
5	9.236	11.071	13.388	15.086	18.908	20.516
6	10.645	12.592	15.033	16.812	20.792	22.459
7	12.017	14.067	16.622	18.475	22.601	24.323
8	13.362	15.507	18.168	20.090	24.353	26.124
9	14.684	16.919	19.679	21.666	26.056	27.877
10	15.987	18.307	21.161	23.209	27.722	29.588
11	17.275	19.675	22.618	24.725	29.354	31.264
12	18.549	21.026	24.054	26.217	30.957	32.909
13	19.812	22.362	25.472	27.688	32.535	34.528
14	21.064	23.685	26.873	29.141	34.091	36.123
15	22.307	24.996	28.259	30.578	35.628	37.697
16	23.542	26.296	29.633	32.000	37.146	39.252
17	24.769	27.587	30.995	33.409	38.648	40.790
18	25.989	28.869	32.346	34.805	40.136	42.312
19	27.204	30.144	33.687	36.191	41.610	43.820
20	28.412	31.410	35.020	37.566	43.072	45.315
21	29.615	32.671	36.343	38.932	44.522	46.797
22	30.813	33.924	37.659	40.289	45.962	48.268
23	32.007	35.172	38.968	41.638	47.391	49.728
24	33.196	36.415	40.270	42.980	48.812	51.179
25	34.382	37.652	41.566	44.314	50.223	52.620
26	35.563	38.885	42.856	45.642	51.627	54.052
27	36.741	40.113	44.140	46.963	53.023	55.476
28	37.916	41.337	45.419	48.278	54.411	56.892
29	39.087	42.557	46.693	49.588	55.792	58.301
30	40.256	43.773	47.962	50.892	57.167	59.703
50	63.167	67.505	72.613	76.154	83.657	86.661
100	118.498	124.342	131.142	135.807	145.577	149.449
500	540.930	553.127	567.070	576.493	595.882	603.446

Glossary

A priori comparisons   Planned tests of the statistical significance of differences among means based on hypotheses formulated before collecting the data

A priori tests   Statistical tests used to compare means based on hypotheses formulated before the data were collected

Abscissa   The horizontal or x-axis of a graph

Absolute value   The value of a number without regard to its sign

Alpha level (α)   The criterion p-value for rejecting the null hypothesis; the probability of rejecting the null hypothesis when it is true (i.e., of making a Type I error)

Alternative hypothesis   A statistical hypothesis indicating that the value of the population parameter specified in the null hypothesis is incorrect

Analysis of covariance   A type of analysis of variance procedure that attempts to control for scores on a pretest or other measure

Analysis of variance (ANOVA)   The parametric statistical procedure for determining the statistical significance of differences among two or more means; involves the use of the F-test

Applied research   Research designed to solve a practical problem or to answer an immediate question

Bar graph   A graph used to illustrate scores on nominal or qualitative data by centering a bar over each score on the x-axis, with the height of the bar representing the frequency of that score

Basic research   Research designed to test and evaluate theories or to contribute to a body of knowledge

Between-participants variable   An independent variable in which each participant receives (or is at) only one level of the variable

Bias   Systematic error in sampling, measurement, or other aspects of a research study

Biased sample   A sample that clearly is not representative of the population

Bimodal distribution   A frequency distribution that has two modes

Binomial distribution   A distribution of events that can have only two possible outcomes, like the flip of a coin

Bivariate distribution   A distribution of scores of units or individuals on two variables

Bonferroni critical value procedure   A procedure for adjusting the significance level of each individual test so as to keep the chance of finding anything significant at or below the desired α-level

Box-and-whisker plot   A graphical representation of a frequency distribution that presents the median, the range of scores, and the 25th and 75th percentiles

Case study   A research project that involves the intensive investigation of a single individual or group

Causal–comparative research   Correlational research that attempts to draw inferences about cause and effect by looking at differences between groups of people who have and have not been exposed to some experience or other variable

Cell   A category in a table reflecting an intersection of levels of two variables; used in factorial analysis of variance and in the chi-square test of independence

Census   A sample that includes each unit or score in the population

Central Limit Theorem   The theorem stating that, as the sample size increases, the shape of the sampling distribution approaches a normal distribution with a mean equal to μ and a standard deviation equal to $\sigma / \sqrt{N}$

Central tendency   A measure of a typical or average score in a distribution, usually the mean, median, or mode

Change score   A difference in two scores for an individual; a posttest score minus a pretest score

Chi-square (χ^2) goodness-of-fit test   A nonparametric procedure for testing whether the observed frequencies of scores in different categories of a variable differ from the theoretically predicted frequencies

Chi-square (χ^2) test of independence   A nonparametric statistical procedure for testing whether two qualitative variables are independent or related

Class interval   A range of scores grouped together in a grouped frequency distribution

Cluster sampling   A sampling procedure in which entire groups of scores are sampled and each member in the group then serves in the sample

Coefficient of determination   The proportion of variance that two variables have in common, computed by squaring the correlation coefficient

Comparison   A procedure for comparing two or more sample means, to see whether or not they are likely to come from populations with the same mean; also called a contrast

Confidence interval   An interval or range of scores within which there is a certain confidence that the population parameter will lie

Confidence level   The confidence that an interval contains a parameter, which $= 1 - \alpha$

Constant   A value that does not change (at least within a particular research study)

Contingency table An arrangement of scores in which the various levels of one variable form columns, the levels of another variable represent rows, and the data in the table are frequencies; used in the chi-square test of independence

Continuous quantitative variable A variable that can assume an infinite number of values

Contrast A procedure for comparing two or more sample means, to see whether or not they are likely to come from populations with the same mean; also called a comparison

Control group The group in an experiment that is randomly assigned to receive the ordinary or traditional treatment (or none)

Convenience sampling A sampling process in which the researcher selects a sample primarily because it is accessible and reasonably representative of the population of interest

Correlated-samples *t*-test A statistical procedure used to compare the means of two variables when scores on the variables are paired; also called a dependent-samples *t*-test and a paired-samples *t*-test

Correlation coefficient A number that represents the intensity and direction of a relationship between two quantitative variables

Correlational research A type of research in which two or more variables are measured but not manipulated and the relationship between the variables is assessed

Cramer's *V* A measure of the strength of the relationship between two variables in a contingency table that is larger than 2×2

Critical region The region of the sampling distribution that includes the values of the statistic that would lead to rejection of the null hypothesis; also called the region of rejection

Critical value The value against which a test statistic is compared in order to determine whether or not the result is statistically significant; the minimum value that a statistic must reach in order to be considered statistically significant

Cross-sectional research A type of developmental research that involves studying people who differ in age at the same point in time

Cumulative frequency distribution A distribution of scores that shows the frequency of scores below the upper limit of each class interval

Cumulative relative frequency distribution A distribution of scores that shows the proportion or percentage below the upper limit of each class interval

Curvilinear relationship A nonlinear relationship between scores on two variables

Data Observations or scores; the basic information used to compute statistics

Degrees of freedom The number of scores in a sample that are free to vary; the number of observations minus the number of constraints on those observations

Dependent-samples *t*-test A correlated-samples *t*-test

Dependent variable A variable that is measured but not manipulated in a research study; also called a dependent measure

Descriptive research Research in which the purpose is to describe or report scores on some variables

Descriptive statistics   The use of statistics to summarize and describe a group of scores or a set of data

Deviation score   A raw score minus the mean of the distribution from which it came

Developmental research   Research dealing with changes that occur as a result of maturation or development

Dichotomous variable   A variable that can have only two values

Direct relationship   A relationship between two variables in which high scores on one variable are associated with high scores on the other and low scores with low; a positive correlation

Directional hypothesis   A hypothesis that specifies the direction of a difference in means or of a relationship between variables

Discrete quantitative variable   A quantitative variable that can take on only a limited number of values

Effect size   A measure of the amount of difference between the experimental and control groups in standard deviation units; or the proportion of variance in the dependent variable due to the differences in the independent variable

Empirical   Based on data or observations

Empirical frequency distribution   A distribution of observed frequencies of actual scores

Eta (η)   A correlation coefficient used to describe a relationship between two variables that may not be linear; eta squared is a measure of effect size that equals the proportion of variance in the dependent variable due to levels of the independent variable in the sample

Expected frequency   The number of scores expected in a particular category under a particular null hypothesis

Expected value   The mean of the scores in a sampling distribution

Experimental group   Those individuals in an experiment who are randomly assigned to receive the special manipulation, procedure, or experience that is usually called the experimental treatment

Experimental research   Research in which participants are randomly assigned to experimental and control groups, an independent variable is manipulated, and scores on a dependent variable are measured, leading to conclusions about the effect of the independent variable upon the dependent variable

Experimentwise error rate   The probability of incorrectly rejecting at least one true null hypothesis in an entire research study

External validity   The ability to correctly generalize the results of a research study to other settings and participants

Extraneous variable   A variable not of interest to the researcher that might affect the results of a study

F-test   A statistical procedure that involves computing the ratio of two sample variances, testing the null hypothesis that the population variances do not differ

Factor   An independent or manipulated variable in a research study

Factorial design   A research design that contains more than one independent variable

Field research   Research conducted in the real world or a natural setting

Fixed effect   In a factorial ANOVA, an independent variable for which all the levels of interest have been measured

Frequency   The number of times that a score or event occurs

Frequency distribution   A list of all the scores for a sample or population indicating the number of times that each score occurs

Frequency histogram   A graph of a frequency distribution in which interval- or ratio-level scores are represented on the x-axis and frequencies on the y-axis; a bar extends from the lower to the upper limit of each class interval

Frequency polygon   A graph of a frequency distribution in which interval or ratio level scores are represented on the x-axis and frequencies on the y-axis; a line connects the frequencies of the midpoints of the class intervals

Fully crossed factorial design   A factorial design in which all combinations of the levels of the independent variables are included

Grand mean   The mean of all the scores in a research study

Grouped frequency distribution   A list of all the scores for a sample or population, with scores grouped into class intervals and the number of scores in each class interval reported

Heteroscedasticity   An unequal spread of Y-scores around the regression line for different values of X

Historical research   Research designed to explain or interpret a particular event that happened in the past

Homogeneity of variance   Equal variances for the populations from which the samples come

Homoscedasticity   An equal spread of Y-scores around the regression line for each value of X

Hypothesis   A statement about the value of a population parameter; a prediction

Hypothesis testing   The type of inferential statistics in which hypotheses about values of population parameters are tested

Inclusive range   The distance between the upper limit of the highest score in a distribution and the lower limit of the lowest score

Incomplete factorial design   A factorial design in which some of the possible combinations of levels of the independent variables are missing

Independent events   Events that have nothing to do with each other; the probability of one does not depend on the occurrence of the other

Independent samples t-test   A test used to compare the means of two groups in which the scores in one group are not paired with scores in the other group

Independent variable   A variable that is manipulated in an experiment

Inferential statistics   The use of statistics to test hypotheses or draw conclusions about a population based upon data collected from a sample

Interaction   A situation in which the effect of one independent variable upon a dependent variable depends upon the level of a second independent variable

Internal validity   The ability to correctly conclude that a result is indeed due to the variable that is believed to be its cause

Interpolation   A method for determining a value that lies between two other values

Interval scale   A scale of measurement for which equal differences in scores represent equal differences in amount of the property measured, but with an arbitrary zero point

Interview research   A type of survey research in which people are asked questions orally and their responses are recorded by the researcher

Inverse relationship   A relationship between two variables in which high scores on one variable are associated with low scores on the other and vice versa; a negative correlation

Kurtosis   The relative peakedness or flatness of a distribution

Laboratory research   Research conducted in a setting specifically designed for research

Least-squares estimate   An estimate based on minimizing the sum of squared deviations about the number estimated

Level   A value of the independent variable

Line graph   A graph presenting scores on two variables, usually with class intervals for scores on one variable along the x-axis and mean scores on the other variable for each class interval along the y-axis

Linear   Referring to a straight line, the formula for which can be written as $Y = a + bX$

Longitudinal research   A type of developmental research that involves measuring the same individuals at various times as they grow older

Lower limit   The lower boundary of a category

Main effect   In a factorial ANOVA, the variation among scores on the dependent measure associated with the levels of an independent variable

Mean   The sum of the scores divided by the number of scores; also called the arithmetic average

Mean square   An estimate of variance; a sum of squares divided by its degrees of freedom

Mean square between groups   An estimate of variance based on the deviations of the group means from the grand mean

Mean square within groups   An estimate of variance based on the deviations of the raw scores from the means of their groups

Measurement   The process of assigning numbers to events or objects according to predetermined rules

Measure of central tendency   A measure of a central point in a distribution of scores

Measure of dispersion or variability   A measure of the extent to which the scores in a distribution differ from each other

Median   The score below which 50% of the scores in a distribution fall; also called the 50th percentile

Mode   The score in a distribution that occurs most often

Monotonic   Constantly increasing or constantly decreasing, but not necessarily by any consistent amount

Multiple comparison tests   Procedures used to compare group means or combinations of means, usually following an analysis of variance

Multiple correlation   A correlation coefficient between one variable and a linear combination of predictor variables, symbolized by R

Multiple regression   An equation predicting score on one variable from a linear combination of predictor variables

Multivariate analysis of variance   An extension of the analysis of variance procedure to deal with two or more dependent measures simultaneously

Multivariate statistical techniques   A group of statistical techniques used for analyzing more than one dependent measure and/or more than one independent variable at a time

Mutually exclusive events   Events that cannot both occur

Negative correlation   A statistical relationship between two quantitative variables in which higher scores on one variable are associated with lower scores on the other variable and vice versa

Negatively skewed distribution   A frequency distribution with its tail on the left side of the distribution, reflecting a preponderance of high scores

Nested design   A design in which each level of one variable is included within a single level of another variable

Nominal scale   A scale or level of measurement in which scores represent names only but not differences in amount

Nonpairwise comparison   A procedure for comparing more than two sample means at a time, to determine the probability that they represent samples from populations with the same mean

Nonparametric statistical tests   Statistical tests that do not make many assumptions about the nature of the populations from which the samples come and that can be used with nominal- and ordinal-level data

Normal curve table   A table giving the proportion of the total area falling between the mean and various z-scores for a normal distribution

Normal distribution   A theoretical frequency distribution that is bell shaped and symmetrical and in which the mean, median, and mode coincide; also called the normal curve

Notation system   A way of representing the terms in an equation and the associated mathematical procedures

Null hypothesis   The hypothesis that specifies a particular population parameter or parameters and that is tested directly by most statistical significance tests; usually the hypothesis that any relationships or differences are due to chance

Observed frequency   The actual number of scores in a particular category

Omega squared   In ANOVA, an estimate of the proportion of variance in the dependent variable in the population that can be explained by the independent variable

One-tailed test   A directional statistical significance test that has the critical region entirely in one tail of the distribution

One-way ANOVA   An analysis of variance with only one independent variable; it compares the means of several groups to determine whether or not they are likely to come from the same population

Operational   Stated specifically and precisely, in terms of what is to be done or measured

Ordinal scale   A measurement scale in which scores indicate only relative amounts or rank order

Ordinate   The vertical or y-axis of a graph

Paired-samples t-test   A correlated-samples t-test

Pairwise comparison   A procedure for comparing two sample means at a time, to determine the probability that they represent samples from populations with the same mean

Parameter   A number that describes a characteristic of a population; symbolized by a Greek letter

Parameter estimation   A type of inferential statistics in which a statistic is calculated from a sample and an estimate of the corresponding parameter is formulated based on the statistic

Parametric statistical tests   Statistical tests that make assumptions about population parameters and that can be used with variables measured on interval or ratio scales

Partial correlation   A procedure that makes it possible to examine the relationship between two variables while controlling for scores on a third variable

Participants   The people who provide data in a research study; sometimes called subjects

Pearson product-moment correlation coefficient   A measure of the linear relationship between two interval or ratio level variables; symbolized by r

Percentage   A proportion times 100; the number of scores in a class interval multiplied by 100 and divided by the total number of scores

Percentile or percentile point   The score below which a certain percentage of the scores in a frequency distribution lie

Percentile rank   The percentage of cases that lie below a given score; each score in a frequency distribution has an associated percentile rank

Phi coefficient   A measure of the strength of the relationship between two dichotomous variables

Pie graph   A circular graph of a frequency distribution with the segments of the circle representing the frequencies of different scores

Point estimate   An estimate of a specific value for a population parameter based on a sample

Pooled estimate of variance   An estimate of variance based on all the scores in the entire sample

Population All scores or members of a group that are of interest to a researcher; the group to which the researcher wishes to generalize

Positive correlation A relationship in which high scores on one variable are associated with high scores on another variable

Positively skewed distribution A distribution of scores in which the tail is on the right side of the distribution, with relatively few high scores

Post hoc tests Statistical tests used to compare means after the data have been examined to determine which comparisons to make; also called a posteriori tests

Power The likelihood that a statistical test will reject the null hypothesis when it is false; the likelihood of recognizing a relationship or difference in the population

Primary sources Records made by a witness or participant in the event

Probability The likelihood that an event will occur; the relative frequency of an event

Proportion A part of a whole; the frequency in a category divided by the total frequency

Qualitative research Research that does not follow the scientific model and that focuses on the collection and subjective interpretation of data rather than on the testing of theory

Qualitative variable A nominal-scale variable; a variable for which different scores represent differences in kind or quality, not in amount

Quantitative variable An ordinal-, interval-, or ratio-scale variable; a variable for which different scores represent different amounts of the property being measured

Quasi-experimental research A loosely defined type of research that is intended to draw inferences about causality and that has some built in methodological controls; it usually involves a manipulated independent variable but nonrandom assignment to levels of the independent variable

Questionnaire research A type of survey research in which people are asked written questions and respond to them in writing

Quota sampling A sampling procedure that involves stratifying on a large number of demographic variables to end up with target numbers of respondents from very precisely specified subgroups

Random assignment An unbiased procedure in which participants are put into groups such that each participant has an equal chance of being assigned to any particular group

Random effect In a factorial ANOVA, an independent variable for which a random sample of the levels has been measured

Random sampling An unbiased procedure in which all members of a population have an equal chance of being selected and all samples of a given size have the same chance of being selected

Range The distance between the upper limit of the highest score in a sample or population and the lower limit of the lowest score

Ratio scale A scale in which a given distance between two scores represents the same difference in the underlying characteristic and in which zero indicates a total absence of the quality being measured; a scale in which statements about ratios of scores are meaningful

Raw score   A score as it is obtained in a research study

Region of rejection   The region of the sampling distribution that includes the values of the statistic that would lead to rejection of the null hypothesis; also called the critical region

Region of retention   The region of the sampling distribution that would lead to retention of the null hypothesis

Regression   Prediction

Regression equation   An equation used to predict scores on one variable from scores on one or more other variables

Regression line   The straight line that is described by the regression equation and that best fits the data points of a scattergram

Regression toward the mean   The tendency for individuals selected because of extreme scores on one variable to have less extreme scores on any other variable

Relative frequency distribution   A list of the proportions or percentages of the total number of cases in a distribution falling into each class interval

Repeated measures design   A design in which each individual is measured more than once

Research hypothesis   The hypothesis that the researcher formulates based on both theory and a knowledge of the subject matter

Robust   A procedure that estimates the probability of a Type I error accurately even if the assumptions of the procedure are not completely met

Sample   The group of scores that the researcher has or the people providing the scores; ordinarily, a subset of a population, although a census is a sample that is identical to the population

Sampling distribution   A frequency distribution of a statistic calculated from all possible samples of the same size

Sampling with replacement   A sampling procedure in which a sampled element or individual is returned to the distribution before the next score is selected, meaning that the same element can be sampled twice

Sampling without replacement   A sampling procedure in which an individual element or person cannot be sampled more than once

Scale of measurement   A set of rules for assigning scores to observations that depends on the nature of the variable and on the measurement procedure; also called level of measurement (Nominal, ordinal, interval, and ratio scales are the major scales of measurement.)

Scattergram, scattergraph, or scatterplot   A graph of the individual data points from a set of pairs of scores

Scheffé test   A multiple comparison procedure that can be used to compare all possible combinations of means

Scientific method   A method of testing a theory that involves formulating hypotheses, gathering empirical data, and using analyses to draw inferences about the theory

Scientific research Research that uses the scientific method to investigate a problem or answer a question

Secondary sources Records written after an event by someone who did not experience it directly; secondhand reports or summaries

Significance level The likelihood of obtaining results as extreme as those observed for the sample, when the null hypothesis is true

Simple frequency distribution A frequency distribution that lists the number of times that each score occurs

Single-sample *t*-test A test for comparing the mean of a sample to a hypothetical value for μ

Slope of a regression line for predicting *Y* from *X* Amount of change in Y expected for a one unit change in X

Spearman correlation coefficient A nonparametric correlation coefficient measuring the relationship between two sets of ranks; symbolized by ρ (rho)

Standard deviation A measure of variability that is equal to the square root of the average squared deviation from the mean of a set of scores; the square root of the variance

Standard error The standard deviation of a sampling distribution

Standard error of estimate The standard deviation of the differences between predicted scores and actual scores

Standard score A transformed score that relates a raw score to the mean and standard deviation of the distribution from which it comes

Statistic A number that describes a characteristic of a sample; characterized by a Roman letter

Statistically significant A term used to describe an observed difference or relationship among variables that is unlikely to be due to chance

Statistical tests Procedures designed to answer certain questions or to draw inferences from data

Stem-and-leaf diagram A table of a frequency distribution that provides a visual picture of the distribution

Stratified sampling A sampling procedure in which participants are drawn from each of a number of mutually exclusive subgroups; stratified random sampling is the most desirable type

Subjects Participants in a research study who provide the data

Sum of squares The sum of the squared deviations of scores from the mean

Survey research Research in which people are asked questions and their answers are analyzed

Systematic sampling A sampling procedure in which every nth score or person is sampled

t-test A statistical significance test used to test hypotheses about one or two means when the population standard deviation is unknown

Test statistic A computed value for an inferential statistic, based on actual data; contrasted with a critical value

Theoretical frequency distribution   A mathematical distribution based on a theoretical model of the relative frequencies of different scores in a population

Theory   A network of propositions about relationships among variables, with the purpose of explaining and predicting phenomena

Total sum of squares   The sum of the squared deviations of all scores from the grand mean

Transformed score   A score corresponding to a raw score that has been subjected to some particular mathematical procedure; standard scores and deviation scores are examples

Treatment   A level of the independent variable in which participants are exposed to some manipulation or experience

Two-tailed significance test   A statistical significance test in which the critical region is divided equally between two tails

Two-way analysis of variance   An analysis of variance with two independent variables; it compares mean scores to see whether they are associated with levels of either variable and whether an interaction exists

Type I error   Rejection of the null hypothesis when it is true

Type II error   Retention of the null hypothesis when it is false

Upper limit   The upper boundary of a category

Variable   A characteristic or event that takes on more than one value or score

Variance   A measure of the variability of scores in a distribution equal to the average of the squared deviations of the scores around the mean; the square of the standard deviation

Within-participants variable   An independent variable in which each participant receives more than one level of the variable

Y-intercept   The predicted value of Y when $X = 0$

z-score   A type of standard score equal to the raw score minus the mean divided by the standard deviation

z-test   A statistical test used to test hypotheses about one or two means when the population standard deviation is known

Answers and Solutions

To Odd-Numbered Questions and Problems

Note that numerical answers may differ slightly from those you compute due to rounding off and interpolation.

Chapter 1

Multiple-Choice Questions

1. e is the correct answer. a and b are constants, c is a discrete quantitative variable, and d is a qualitative variable.

3. b is the correct answer.

5. g is the correct answer, since all but nominal level variables are quantitative.

7. f is correct, since species is a qualitative variable, assessed on a nominal scale.

Problems

9.a. No. This is a question that relates to moral and ethical views rather than to data. There are no potential observations that could be made that would lead to a definitive conclusion.

b. Yes. Although you would have to define "better," as well as describe the methods and the samples, this question is potentially answerable by research. If one method consistently led to clearly superior reading performance, everyone would agree that it is better.

c. Yes. Data on population size and crime rates could be gathered from a number of cities, and the degree of association (correlation) between these two variables could be calculated.

d. No, presumably. Even if it were ethical to attempt to rear children without human contact, which it is not, it would not be possible, given our present state of knowledge. Some case studies have been done, however, with children raised with minimal contact with other people.

e. As worded, the answer is "no"; research can compare only a limited number of methods, and it is possible that the best method is not among them. If it were worded to ask which of several specified methods of teaching statistics produces the highest score on a statistics test, the answer would be "yes."

11.a. This is a constant: It is always 9.

b. This is a continuous quantitative variable; it varies from room to room, and any measure is an approximation.

c. This is a discrete quantitative variable; the number of houses will vary from block to block, but it will always be a whole number (unless you count those in the process of being built).

d. This is almost surely a qualitative variable, unless you intend to rank the occupations on some sort of scale related to income or prestige.

e. This is a qualitative variable.

f. This would be a discrete quantitative variable; you can count the shirts.

g. This is clearly a quantitative variable; a larger score represents more of something (presumably knowledge) than a smaller score. You might think that it is discrete, since a score would be reported as 76 or 77, not 76.77, but in fact it is usually considered to be continuous, as the underlying quality which the score measures does not come in units.

h. Age is a continuous quantitative variable. Even if we start at birth rather than conception, we cannot measure age precisely to fractions of a microsecond.

i. This is tricky. If there is only one species of cockroach in all the houses measured, it is a constant. If there is more than one species, then species is a qualitative variable.

13. Nonparametric tests make fewer assumptions about the data and so can be used, for example, with ordinal and sometimes nominal scale variables; they are also easier to compute. However, parametric tests are more powerful, more versatile, and robust enough so that they can be used even when the assumptions for their use aren't fully met.

15.a. This answer could be correct; the sum of squared numbers would be positive.

b. This answer must be wrong; a squared number cannot be negative.

c. This expression must be wrong; in statistics, you cannot take the square root of a negative number.

d. This cannot be correct if each person is in only one category; the sum of the proportions in all the categories = 1.00.

e. This is correct; the sum of the numbers in the categories is the same as the sum of the frequencies in the categories, as f and n refer to the same thing.

17. To answer these questions, since the numbers are large, let's keep them in a table.

X	X^2
466	217,156
321	103,041
87	7,569
502	252,004
100	10,000
56	3,136
612	374,544
2144	967,450

a. $\Sigma X = 2144$

b. $N = 7$

c. $(\Sigma X)^2 = (2144)(2144)$
$= 4,596,736$

d. X^2 for the first score is $(466)(466) = 217,156$.

e. $\Sigma X^2 = 967,450$

f. $\Sigma X^2/N = 967,450/7 = 138,207.14$ to 2 decimal places.

19.a. In this example, school is a qualitative variable. Number of classes and number of teachers are both discrete quantitative variables.

b. Number of teachers is measured on a ratio scale. Two teachers is twice one teacher. (We'll ignore parttime teachers.)

c. $\Sigma X = 27 + 15 + 18 = 60$ classes

d. $\Sigma Y = 32 + 15 + 22$ or 69; $(\Sigma Y)^2 = (69)(69) = 4761$

e. No, $\Sigma Y > \Sigma X$, since 69 is greater than 60.

f. $\Sigma XY = (27)(32) + (15)(15) + (18)(22) = 864 + 225 + 396 = 1485$

g. $\Sigma X \Sigma Y = (60)(69) = 4140$. 4140 is greater than 1485, so the answer is no. $\Sigma X \Sigma Y > \Sigma XY$, not $< \Sigma XY$.

Chapter 2

Multiple-Choice Questions

1. Since each person was measured twice, this would be considered a within-participants design and **a** is the correct answer.

3. **b** is correct; research with two or more dependent variables is called multivariate. I don't know what a "negatively skewed design" would be.

5. c is correct.

7. The correct answer is **e**, since the independent variable must have more than one level or it would not be a variable. Many experiments have only one independent variable, one dependent variable, one experimental group, and one control group.

9. a is correct.

Problems

11.a. This is clearly a developmental study as it is focusing on the life span. Moreover, it must be longitudinal, since the word "consistency" implies that individuals' scores at one point in time are related to their scores at a later time.

b. If this title truly refers to effects, then it should be describing an experimental study, with participants randomly assigned to conditions. However, if the author is using the term loosely, it could even be a case study of one person who took steroids or a correlational study comparing people who do and do not use steroids.

c. Unless this study randomly assigned people to engage in sexual activity or not, it must be a correlational study, since people cannot be assigned to be male or female. A much better title would be "Sex differences in spatial rotation ability," since this study might provide information about the relationship between the two variables but would not identify the cause of such a relationship.

d. This sounds like a historical study of a particular event.

e. If this project is not apocryphal, it must be a case study.

f. This is probably a qualitative research study, but it's difficult to tell in the absence of more information about what was actually done.

13.a. Hold the variable constant. For example, use only registered nurses in the study, to keep occupation and education constant; or spend exactly three hours counseling the people in each condition, to keep time spent with the counselor constant.

b. Incorporate the factor into a factorial design. For example, consider the effects of the treatment variable separately for males and females, treating sex as a factor; or classify people into the top, middle, and bottom thirds on a pretest, using pretest score as a factor.

c. Randomly assign participants to conditions and/or randomly select the participants for the research project. For example, you could flip a coin for each person to see whether he or she would be given 20 minutes or an hour of study time; or you could randomly select participants from the list of registered voters.

15.a. This sounds like an applied, decision-oriented study, which is done in the field, not in a laboratory setting.

b. This is a basic research study conducted in a field setting.

c. This is a basic research study done in the laboratory.

d. This is clearly an applied study; because the participants were brought to a special place to participate in the study, it would probably be called a laboratory study.

e. As described, this would be considered basic research, although it might well lead to practical applications. It is taking place in a field setting.

f. This is a basic research study in a laboratory setting.

17.a. Ability to hear high-pitched tones is not related to age.

b. The proportions of Americans and Venezuelans who vote in national elections do not differ. Or you could say that Americans and Venezuelans are equally likely to vote in national elections.

c. Eating a vegetarian (or nonvegetarian) diet is unrelated to health.

d. Men and women who enter medical school are equally likely to finish in 4 years. In this case the research hypothesis is the null hypothesis.

e. People who floss their teeth daily and people who do not use dental floss do not differ in amount of gum disease.

19.a. This was apparently a true experimental study, since participants were randomly assigned to groups. It has a longitudinal component, since people are measured a number of times, but it goes beyond being a purely developmental study.

b. A physician's office would be considered a field setting.

c. This is clearly applied research, but it is probably basic research as well, since she is interested in the operation of the drug.

d. At first glance, this does not appear to be a factorial design, since there is only one factor mentioned in the description: treatment, which has three levels (drug, placebo/injection of water, and no drug/no injection). However, statistically, we would consider time of measurement a second factor, since individuals are being repeatedly measured.

e. Presence or absence of the symptoms of AIDS is a dependent measure. Time until the first symptom appears could be considered another dependent measure.

Chapter 3

Multiple-Choice Questions

1. In a simple frequency distribution, the sum of all the frequencies is equal to the sample size, which is symbolized by N. Thus **e** is the correct response.

3. **a** is the only correct alternative.

5. The correct response is **b**.

7. You could always reconstruct the distribution of raw scores perfectly from a simple frequency distribution or from a stem and leaf diagram but not necessarily from the other types of frequency distributions. The correct response is **f**.

9. As there are only three different scores (easy, difficult, and slow-to-warm-up), you will need three segments for the pie chart. Alternative **a** is correct.

Problems

11.a. This turns out to be a difficult problem, as it is very hard to think of class intervals that convey the information in adequate detail to include both the large number of $0 and $1 donations and the entire range of scores. One possible solution is to use $0–$0.99, $1–$1.99, $2–$2.99, etc., as the class intervals, in order to put the donations of $0 and of $1 in separate categories. However, that has the disadvantage of having 41 class intervals. If you take the approach of having larger class intervals then you lose the information about the number of nondonors, as they would be combined with others who gave small amounts. Another possibility is to violate the rule of using equal category widths and to use an open-ended category, perhaps of >$1. Probably the best solutions would be either to present a table of a simple frequency distribution, or to graph the pattern by a frequency polygon or frequency histogram.

b. This kind of distribution would be called positively skewed, as most of the donations were at the low end with fewer and fewer people donating as the amounts grew larger. You could say that it is also bimodal, as it is true that there were large frequencies for donations of $0 and $1, with fewer donations in between, but the positive skew seems more noticeable.

13.a. percentile (not percentile rank); percentiles (or percentile points) can have any value similar to the raw scores for a distribution, while percentile ranks have values ranging from 1 to 99 (or perhaps 99.9).

b. cumulative frequency; the fourth score from the bottom of a distribution has a rank and a cumulative frequency of 4.

c. qualitative variable; it would also be correct to say a nominal scale variable.

d. y-axis

e. f or frequency in an interval; capital N stands for the entire sample size.

f. scattergraph or scatterplot

15.a.

Score	f	Score	f	Score	f
65	1	26	1	7	5
39	1	22	2	6	5
37	1	17	1	5	3
36	1	15	1	4	3
34	1	13	1	3	1
32	1	12	1	2	1
31	1	10	1		
29	1	9	2		
27	1	8	2		

b.

Interval	f	c. %	d. cum f	cum %
61–65	1	2.6%	39	100.1%
56–60	0	0%	38	97.5%
51–55	0	0%	38	97.5%
46–50	0	0%	38	97.5%
41–45	0	0%	38	97.5%
36–40	3	7.7%	38	97.5%
31–35	3	7.7%	35	89.8%
26–30	3	7.7%	32	82.1%
21–25	2	5.1%	29	74.4%
16–20	1	2.6%	27	69.3%
11–15	3	7.7%	26	66.7%
6–10	15	38.5%	23	59.0%
1–5	8	20.5%	8	20.5%

These class intervals were chosen to have an interval width of 5, an odd number. The intervals begin with 1 and end with 5, so that the score of 65 can be in the last interval, without necessitating another class interval with a frequency of 0. The number of intervals, 13, is a manageable one, and the interval width is small enough to pick up some of the distinctions at the lower end. This is an instance in which it would be tempting to have an open-ended interval at the high end, perhaps called "41+," and a case might be made for doing so. If that were done, the interval width might be made even smaller—perhaps 3.

e.

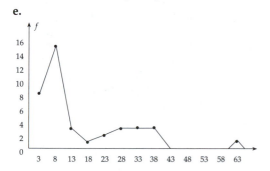

17.a. and b.

Month	a. Frequency	b. Cum. f
January	10	10
February	6	16
March	6	22
April	8	30
May	9	39
June	10	49
July	12	61
August	10	71
September	8	79
October	6	85
November	7	92
December	15	107

c. Month of the year can be viewed as an ordinal-level variable. Therefore, it is reasonable to put the results in a frequency polygon. If month were not at least an ordinal-level variable, it would not have been reasonable to construct a cumulative frequency distribution.

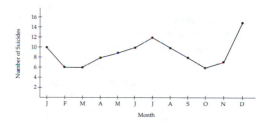

d. I think it would be reasonable to say that the summer months, along with December and January, seem to have the highest suicide rates. Spring and fall seem to have somewhat lower rates.

19.a. The number of men in the study was 20 who chose reasons related to intimacy + 40 who chose reasons related to shared activities + 30 who chose reasons related to proximity = 90 men.

b. Intimacy reasons were chosen by more women than were reasons related to proximity or shared activities.

c. Overall, 60 people chose intimacy, 60 chose shared activities, and 60 chose proximity. No type of reason was chosen overall.

d. 20 of 90 women or .22 of the women chose shared activities.

e. This is a bar graph of two frequency distributions. It provides frequencies separately for men and women.

Chapter 4

Multiple-Choice Questions

1. Although alternative e might sound like a good noncontroversial response, in fact response c is correct. Since the data are qualitative, it does not make sense to compute a mean or harmonic mean, nor can they be ordered in any sensible way to compute a median.

3. Don's score was 2 standard deviations above the mean, reflecting a z-score of 2. Response e is correct.

5. Since the square of a number larger than 1 is larger than the number, response d must be true and response b must be false. The standard deviation of a distribution is almost never larger than the range and is rarely larger than the mean; the range may or may not be larger than the variance.

7. With a normal distribution and hundreds of scores, the standard deviation is likely to be approximately 1/6th of the range. With an inclusive range of 301, the only one of the alternatives which seems reasonable is 50, alternative a.

9. If the range goes from 56 to 92, the lowest score in the distribution is 56, and 54 is not included in the distribution. However, unless the distribution is symmetric, there is no assurance that the median (or mean) is halfway between the lowest and the highest score, so a is the only correct response.

Problems

11.a. The mean could be a negative number if some of the raw scores are negative. For example, the mean number of dollars won by some-

one in 20 visits to the racetrack would be negative if he lost more dollars than he won.

b. The mode could also be negative; it will be negative whenever the most frequent score is a negative number.

c. The variance can never be negative, as it is based on the quotient of a sum of squares (always positive) divided by a positive N. (If N were 0 there would be no data and no variance.)

d. The range cannot be negative, as it is defined as the upper limit of the highest score minus the lower limit of the lowest score. It will be positive unless all the scores are identical, in which case the inclusive range will be 1.

e, f. Like the variance, both σ and s depend on a sum of squares divided by a positive number. If $N = 1$, no standard deviation can be computed, so $N - 1$ will always be a positive number. The positive square root of a positive number is, of course, positive.

13.a. In order to calculate the mean, you have to calculate N, which is 15, and ΣX, which is 45. Assuming that the scores constitute a population, $\mu = 45/15 = 3.00$.

b. In order to calculate the median, you have to put the scores in order from smallest to largest (or vice versa): 0, 0, 1, 1, 2, 2, 3, 3, 3, 3, 4, 5, 6, 6, 6. As there are 15 scores, an odd number, the median is the $(15 + 1)/2$ or 8th score from the top or the bottom. The median is therefore 3.

c. The mode is that score that occurs most often, which also happens to be 3. The fact that the mean, median, and mode are all equal to 3 is a coincidence, as the scores are not normally distributed.

d. To compute σ^2, let's use the deviation score formula and do the calculations from the ordered distribution of raw scores presented in part b above. The deviation scores from the mean of 3.00 are –3, –3, –2, –2, –1, –1, 0, 0, 0, 0, 1, 2, 3, 3, and 3. These values sum to 0, as they should. The squared deviation scores are 9, 9, 4, 4, 1, 1, 0, 0, 0, 0, 1, 4, 9, 9, and 9, which sum to 60. $\Sigma(X - \mu)/N = 60/15 = 4.00 = \sigma^2$.

e. This time, let's try the raw score formula but again work from the ordered distribution in part b above. $\Sigma X^2 = 0 + 0 + 1 + 1 + 4 + 4 + 9 + 9 + 9 + 9 + 16 + 25 + 36 + 36 + 36 = 195$. $\Sigma X = 45$; $45^2 = 2025$; $2025/15 = 135$. $(195 - 135)/(15 - 1) = 60/14 = 4.286 = s^2$.

15.a. This is false. Don's raw score $(18 + 44)$ was 62, but his T-score was 65.

b. This is false. Don's z-score was $18/12 = 1.5$.

c. This is true. 18 is 1.5 times the standard deviation of 12.

d. This is possible, but without knowing the sample (or population) size, it is impossible to know how many scores Don exceeded.

e. This is very unlikely to be true, unless the distribution is very negatively skewed. If there were one very low score, bringing the mean way, way down, it is barely possible that the median (or 50th percentile) could be 1.5 standard deviations above the mean, but this is extremely unlikely.

17. In order to solve the problem, it would be a good idea to add a column for X^2 next to the raw scores and a column for the deviations.

X	X^2	x
15	225	0
25	625	10
5	25	−10
15	225	0
10	100	−5
20	400	5
25	625	10
30	900	15
15	225	0
5	25	−10
0	0	−15
165	3375	0

a. The mean $= 165/11 = 15$

b. To get the median, it is necessary to order the scores: 0, 5, 5, 10, 15, 15, 15, 20, 25, 25, 30. The middle score is 15, so the median is 15.

c. Because there are three scores of 15, more than any other score, the mode $= 15$.

d. The inclusive range goes from 0 to 30; it could be viewed as 30.5 or 31, depending on whether it makes sense to think of a negative score.

e. To get the mean absolute deviation, you have to sum the absolute values of the deviation scores and divide by 11.

$0 + 10 + 10 + 0 + 5 + 5 + 10 + 15 + 0 + 10 + 15 = 80$
$80/11 = 7.27$, the mean absolute deviation.

f. Since this is a sample,

$$\text{variance} = \frac{\Sigma X^2 - (\Sigma X)^2/N}{N-1}$$

$$= \frac{3375 - (165)(165)/11}{11-1} = \frac{3375 - 27,225/11}{10}$$

$$= \frac{3375 - 2475}{10} = \frac{900}{10} = 90$$

g. The standard deviation is the square root of the variance. $\sqrt{90} = 9.49$.

19.a. The range was from 10 to 100.

b. The 75th percentile was 80.

c. The median was 70.

d. The mean cannot be determined from this box-and-whisker plot. It was definitely between 10 and 100 and probably between 50 and 80.

e. The distribution is not symmetric, since the median is not halfway between the 25th and 75th percentiles. It appears as if it was negatively skewed, since the distance from the lowest score to the median is much greater than the distance from the highest score to the median.

f. You can say that John scored somewhere between the 25th and the 50th percentile on the test, probably closer to the 50th percentile.

Chapter 5

Multiple-Choice Questions

1. Looking at the normal curve table, you should be able to see that .4505 or approximately 45% of the scores lie between the mean and a z-score of 1.65. Adding to this the 50% of scores that lie below the mean, you get the correct answer of 95%, alternative **g**.

3. This is just like question 1. Using a normal curve table, you can see that .1915 of the scores lie between the mean and a z-score of .5. When these are added to the .5 of scores that lie below the mean, you get .6915 or 69.15%, alternative **e**.

5. If you think about it, you should be able to eliminate a number of the alternatives. Response a cannot be correct, since there is no such thing as a negative percentage of the scores. Responses d through g are way too large; very few scores will fall below a z-score of –1.8. Looking in the table, you should see that .0359 of the scores fall below this value. Pick response **c**.

7. Only **b** is correct.

9. Since a normal distribution is symmetric, you know that the cutoff points will be equidistant from the mean: 15% of the scores lie between the mean and the 35th percentile; 15% of the scores lie between the mean and the 65th percentile. So alternative **a** must be correct. You can use the normal curve table to see that z-scores of –.39 and +.39 correspond to these percentiles. Therefore, none of the other responses is correct.

11.a. To solve this problem, you should draw a picture of what is asked for. The diagrams will be different for parts a, b, and c. Using column 2 of the table, we can see that .4332 of the scores lie between a z-score of –1.5 and the mean.

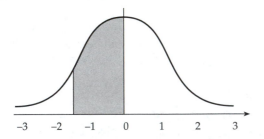

b. Using column 2, we can see that .0987 of the scores lie between the mean and a z-score of .25. Adding those scores to the .4332 of the

scores between a z of –.5 and the mean reveals that .5319 of the scores lie between a z-score of –1.5 and a z-score of .25

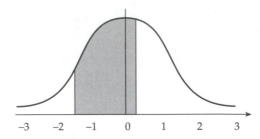

c. The proportion of scores between a z-score of –1.5 and a z-score of –.25 is equal to .4332 – .0987 or .3345. Alternatively, you could take the proportion of scores below a z-score of –.25, which is .4013, and subtract from that the proportion of scores below a z-score of –1.5, which is .0668, to get .3345, the same answer.

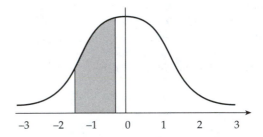

13.a. To get Alberta's z-score, subtract the mean of the normative sample from her raw score and divide by the standard deviation of the normative sample. $z = (80 – 50)/20 = 1.5$.

b. Her z-score compared to the other people in her program was $(80 – 85)/15 = –.33$.

c. Since her z-score was positive compared to the normative sample, you need the percentage of scores which are more extreme than Alberta's. Using column 3 of the table, you can see that .0668 of the scores lie beyond a z of 1.5. Multiplying by 100 gives 6.68% of the scores beyond Alberta's. Subtracting this from 100% and rounding to the nearest whole percent reveals that Alberta was at the 93rd percentile compared to the normative distribution.

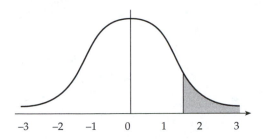

d. The number of people who were more depressed is equal to the sample size times the proportion of people who were more depressed or (1000)(.0668), which is 67 people.

e. To get the number of people in her program who were more depressed, you first need to find the proportion of people who scored between Alberta's score and the mean and add this to the proportion of people who scored above the mean. Column 2 of the table indicates that .1293 of all scores fall between a z-score of −.33 and the mean. Adding that to the .5000 of scores that exceed the mean gives .6293 of the scores that are higher than Alberta's. To get the actual number of scores, multiply the sample size of 100 by .6293 to get 62.93. Rounding it off to the nearest whole person, we would say that 63 of the 100 people in the program were more depressed than Alberta.

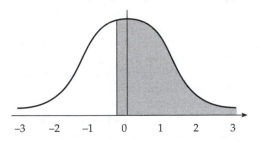

f. I think that it would be fair to conclude that Alberta was depressed. She scored substantially above the average on depression compared with a group of normal individuals and was in the 37th percentile compared with a group of people seeking treatment for depression. Of course, this conclusion is based on the assumption that the DEPR test is a valid measure of depression.

15.a. Four out of the 52 cards are aces, making a 1/13 or .0769 chance of getting an ace. Similarly, the chance of getting a king is .0769. To get the probability of either of these two mutually exclusive events occurring, you have to add these probabilities, getting .1538. Alternatively, you could have divided 8 (the number of events leading to the desired outcome) by 52 to get .1538.

b. Since .25 of the cards are spades and .25 of the cards are clubs, the chance of getting one or the other is .50.

c. Since .25 of the cards are clubs and .0769 of the cards are kings, the chance of getting a card that is both a club and a king is (.25)(.0769), which is .0192. Alternatively, you could say that one of the 52 outcomes is the desired one: 1/52 = .0192.

17.a. To answer this, you need to calculate the total number of children in the population, which is 40 + 45 + 60 + 60 + 65 + 60 + 70 + 70 = 470. You also need to know the number of boys, which is 45 + 60 + 60 + 70 = 235. The probability of picking a boy at random is 235/470 = .500.

b. The probability that a child picked at random will be a kindergarten boy is 45/470 = .0957.

c. Assuming sampling with replacement for parts c, d, and e, the probability that two children picked at random will both be boys is (.5)(.5) = .25.

d. The probability that two children picked at random will both be first graders is (120/470)(120/470) = (.2553)(.2553) = .065.

e. The probability that at least one will be a boy is the probability that the first child will be a boy plus the probability that the second child will be a boy minus the probability that both will be boys, or .5 + .5 − .25 = .75. Another way to think about it is that it is 1.00 minus the probability that both will be girls, which is 1 − .25 = .75.

19.a. To answer this question, we'll assume that the lengths are normally distributed. First, draw a picture and then compute the z-score. (3 − 3.01)/.100 = .01/.100 = −.1. Looking in

Appendix Table 1, we can see that .0398 of the scores lies between a z-score of –.1 and the mean. Adding .0398 to the .5000 of all scores above the mean means that .5398 of the rubber bands is longer than 3 inches.

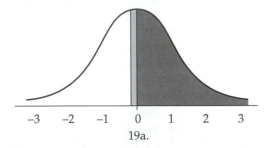

19a.

b. Again, we need to draw a picture and compute a z-score. $(2.85 - 3.01)/.100 = -.16/.100 = -1.60$. From Appendix Table 1, we can see that .0548 of the scores is lower than a z-score of –1.60. Multiplying .0548 by 500 gives 27.4. Either 27 or 28 of the rubber bands are shorter than 2.85 inches.

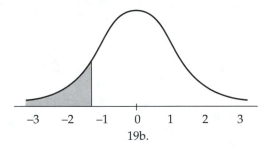

19b.

c. Drawing another picture, we can recognize that we already know the proportion of scores below 2.85 inches, which is .0548. To find the proportion of scores above 3.15 inches, we need to calculate the z-score, which is $(3.15 - 3.01)/.100 = .15/.100 = 1.50$. Appendix Table 1 shows that .0668 of the scores in a normal distribution lies above a z-score of 1.50. Adding that to the proportion below 2.85 inches gives $.0548 + .0668 = .1216$.

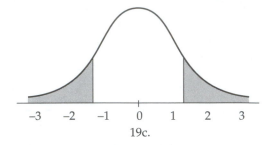

19c.

d. If .1216 of the rubber bands will be discarded, $1 - .1216$ or .8784 of them will be kept. Multiplying this proportion by 500 gives 439.2, rounded to 439 rubber bands.

Chapter 6

Multiple-Choice Questions

1. The correct answer is **f**, since r cannot exceed 1.00.

3. The table shows that a correlation coefficient with 30 degrees of freedom must exceed .349 to be statistically significant at the .05 level. Since the correlation is less than that, you should not conclude anything about the direction of the relationship, and **e** is the correct answer. In addition, you should realize that even if r were statistically significant, you could not conclude that a or b was true, because you would not know the causal relationship between the variables. Response c is not correct, since the correlation of –.20 is not statistically significant with 30 degrees of freedom. Alternative d refers to a question about a proportion, not a relationship between variables, so is not relevant to a correlation coefficient.

5. With 10 pairs of ranks and 8 degrees of freedom, the critical value for rho at the .05 level is .648. Since the computed value is less than that, you should conclude that the two sets of ranks are not significantly correlated and choose alternative **a**.

7. Looking at the table, going down the column for two-tailed critical values at the .05 level, you should see that a sample with 9 degrees of freedom would require an r of .602 for significance and a sample with 10 degrees of freedom would require an r of .576 to be statistically significant. Therefore, you must have a sample with 10 degrees of freedom and 12 pairs of scores, making **f** the correct response.

Problems

9. I like this problem because it's one that a number of smart people get wrong. It's hard to think of a sensible reason to expect the correlation coefficient to be negative, unless you think that women (a) have smaller toes than men, which is probably true and (b) score higher on reading achievement tests than men, which is probably false. Many people assume that the value of r must be 0, which is almost surely false, because they can see no way in which toe length can affect reading achievement or vice versa. Nor can I. However, there is a third variable, namely age, which can affect both toe length and reading. Babies have small toes and can't read; both toe length and reading achievement probably increase in most people over the school years. Thus, there is probably a weak but statistically significant positive correlation between the two variables in a large sample of people who vary in age. To be honest, though, I don't have any empirical data to prove this.

11.a. The correct test to use is Spearman rho, because you want to look at the degree of correlation between two ordinal-level variables— your evaluations and Mr. Fierce's evaluations.

b. First, you have to order the scores:

Person	Your Ranking	FF's Ranking	D	D²
Perry	1	1	0	0
Parry	2	3	−1	1
Peter	3	2	1	1
Paul	4	4	0	0
Percival	5	5.5	−.5	.25
Popeye	6	5.5	.5	.25

Since Percival and Popeye are tied for fifth and sixth places in Mr. Fierce's ratings, they each get the average rank of 5.5. The sum of the

squared differences in ranks is 2.5, so $\rho = 1 - 6(2.5)/(6)(36 - 1)$ or $1 - 15/(6)(35)$ or $1 - .071$ or $.929$.

c. To decide whether or not the value of .929 is statistically significant, you have to look in the table for the .05 significance level with 6 pairs of scores and 4 degrees of freedom. Since .929 exceeds the critical value of .886, it is significant at the .05 level; however, it does not reach the critical value of 1.000 which would be needed for significance at the .01 level.

d. You could say that there is a statistically significant positive correlation between your rankings and those of Mr. Fierce, indicating that you tended to rank the actors similarly, $\rho(4) = .93, p < .05$. This relationship accounted for 86% of the variance in the rankings.

13.a. This conclusion is incorrect; the relationship is statistically significant, as you can see from the table.

b. This conclusion is wrong, as the correlation was negative. People who read more watch less television, and people who watch less television read more, according to these data.

c. This is true. A significant correlation implies this.

d. Although this is possible, you cannot conclude it from correlational data. You don't know what the causal relationships are.

e. This is no more valid a conclusion than the one in part d, even if it sounds more persuasive. You don't know from a significant r what is causing what. Maybe there are individual differences in people who choose to read or to watch television.

15.a. This is not a correct conclusion from the data. You don't know what the correlation between the two tests is, so you don't know what the coefficient of determination is.

b. This is not a conclusion that you can draw, since you have no information on the relationship between scores on the two tests. The correlation could even be negative.

c. This is false. Test A accounts for $.3^2$ or .09, which is 9% of the variance in grades, not 30%.

d. This is false. Test A accounts for .09 of the variance in grades, whereas Test B accounts for $.6^2$ or .36 of the variance in grades.

e. Since the correlation between test scores and grades is statistically significant, this is true.

17.a. In order to answer part a, we have to find the means and standard deviations of X and Y. To begin, let's set up columns for X^2, Y^2, and XY and calculate the sums of all the columns.

X	X^2	Y	Y^2	XY
8	64	4	16	32
6	36	5	25	30
4	16	3	9	12
3	9	5	25	15
1	1	6	36	6
0	0	10	100	0
22	126	33	211	95

To calculate σ_x, we'll first compute the variance, using the raw score formula.

$$\frac{\Sigma X^2 - (\Sigma X)^2/N}{N} = \frac{126 - (22)(22)/6}{6} = \frac{126 - 484/6}{6}$$

$$= \frac{126 - 80.67}{6} = \frac{45.33}{6} = 7.56$$

Next, we'll take the square root of the variance to get 2.75 as σ_x. Using similar procedures to calculate σ_y, we have

$$\frac{211 - (33)(33)/6}{6} = \frac{211 - 1089/6}{6}$$

$$= \frac{211 - 181.50}{6} = \frac{29.50}{6} = 4.92$$

$\sqrt{4.92} = 2.22$, which is σ_y. We also need to calculate a mean for each variable. The mean for $X = \Sigma X/N = 22/6 - 3.67$. The mean for $Y = \Sigma Y/N = 33/6 = 5.50$. The next step in the z-score formula is to calculate a z-score for each person on each variable. For each person, $z_x = (X - \mu_x)/\sigma_x$ and $z_y = (Y - \mu_y)/\sigma_y$. To make it clearer, let's put together a table with the deviation scores and z-scores on each variable.

X	Y	$X - \mu_x$	$Y - \mu_y$	z_x	z_y	$z_x z_y$
8	4	4.33	-1.50	1.57	-0.68	-1.07
6	5	2.33	-0.50	0.85	-0.23	-0.20
4	3	0.33	-2.50	0.12	-1.13	-0.14
3	5	-0.67	-0.50	-0.24	-0.23	0.06
1	6	-2.67	0.50	-0.97	0.23	-0.22
0	10	-3.67	4.50	-1.33	2.03	-2.70
		0.02	0.00	0.00	-0.01	-4.27

Note that the sums of the deviation scores and the z-scores are very close to 0. They would be exactly 0 if we had not rounded off the values in the table.

The final steps in calculating r are to take the cross products of the z-scores, sum them, and divide this sum by N. In this case, we have $-4.27/6 = -.7117$ as our value of r.

b. To use the formula with means, we need to get $\Sigma XY/N$, which is $95/6 = 15.833$. From this we subtract the product of the means, which is $(3.67)(5.50) = 20.185$. This difference, -4.352, is then divided by the product of the standard deviations, $(2.75)(2.22)$, which equals 6.105. $-6.018/6.105 = -.7129$.

c. To use the raw score formula, we need to substitute into the formula.

$$\frac{N\Sigma XY - \Sigma X \Sigma Y}{\sqrt{[N\Sigma X^2 - (\Sigma X)^2][N\Sigma Y^2 - (\Sigma Y)^2]}}$$

The numerator will be $6(95) - (22)(33)$, or $570 - 726 = -156$. The first term under the square root sign in the denominator will be $(6)(126) - (22)(22) = 756 - 484 = 272$. The second term under the square root sign is $(6)(211) - (33)(33) = 1266 - 1089 = 177$. The product of these two terms is $(272)(177) = 48,144$. The denominator of the formula will be the square root of 48,144, which is 219.42. As the final step, we divide -156 by 219.42 and get .7110. Note that the values from all three formulas are .71 to two decimal places. The differences in the third and fourth decimal place are due to rounding off in our calculations.

19.a. Appendix Table 2 shows that with 200 degrees of freedom a Pearson r of .230 would be statistically significant at the .001 level. Since .32 is larger than .23, this relationship is statistically significant.

b. $.32^2$ or .1024 of the variance in these men's earnings can be predicted from knowing their height. Whether 10% of the variance is important depends on your theoretical and practical interests, but most researchers would probably consider this size correlation with this large a sample to be reasonably important.

c. A scattergram of a correlation of this magnitude would show a general tendency for the points to cluster in the center, the lower-left corner, and the upper-right corner.

d. You can be almost sure that having a high income does not increase height in adult men. It is certainly possible that men who are taller get offered higher-paying jobs (basketball player; movie star) or get raises more easily because of their height. It is also possible that some other factor, such as childhood nutrition or malnutrition could affect both height and other variables, such as intelligence and physical fitness, which could in turn influence salaries. In short, we do not know for sure what the causal pathway is in this instance.

Chapter 7

Multiple-Choice Questions

1. Alice's predicted shoe size is 1.2(5) + 1 or 6 + 1 or 7, making **d** the correct answer. The information about the means is irrelevant. Don't assume that if you have information it must be used in the solution of a problem.

3. **b** is the correct response.

5. **e** is correct. Think about the z-score regression equation. When $r = -1$, the predicted z-score on Y is -1 times the z-score on X.

7. In this case, the slope will be (.4)(10/8) or (.4)(1.25) or .5. The correct response is **c**.

9. The correct answer is **a**.

Problems

11.a. Let's begin by getting the sums of X^2, Y^2, and XY:

Worker	ALAT Score (X)	X^2	Errors (Y)	Y^2	XY
Fran	14	196	0	0	0
Frank	8	64	2	4	16
Frances	6	36	4	16	24
Frieda	4	16	6	36	24
Fred	1	1	10	100	10
Σ	33	313	22	156	74

Based on the above data, $\overline{X} = 6.6$ and $\overline{Y} = 4.4$. To calculate b,

$$\frac{5(74) - 33(22)}{5(313) - 33^2} = \frac{370 - 726}{1565 - 1089} = \frac{-356}{476} = -.7479$$

To compute a, $\overline{Y} - b\overline{X} = 4.4 - (-.7479)(6.6) = 9.3361$. The regression equation is therefore $Y' = 9.3361 - .7479X$.

b. Fay would be predicted to make 9.3361 − .7479(12) errors per day, which = 9.3361 − 8.9748 or approximately .36 errors per day.

c. Based on the above data, the ALAT does seem to do a good job of predicting number of errors. It does make sense to use it. As a check, you could compute Pearson r, which = −.95, significant at the .05 level.

13.a. Yes, a correlation coefficient of .4 with 36 degrees of freedom is statistically significant at the .05 level.

b. $s_{N \cdot C} = S_N \sqrt{1 - r^2} = 2\sqrt{1 - .16} = 2\sqrt{.84}$

$= 2(.917) = 1.83$

c. $b_C = r(s_C/s_N) = .4(4/2) = .8$; $a_C = \overline{C} - b\overline{N} = 30 - .8(20) = 30 - 16 = 14$. So the regression equation is $C' = 14 + .8N$.

d. Goofy's predicted creativity score is 14 + .8(25) = 14 + 20 = 34.

15.a. $b_{H \cdot P} = (-.5)(6/8) = -.375$

b. $b_{P \cdot H} = (-.5)(8/6) = -.667$

c. $s_{H \cdot P} = 6\sqrt{1 - .25} = 6\sqrt{.75} = 6(.866) = 5.20$

d. $r^2 = (-.5)^2 = .25$

e. 25%; for those who wondered why I provided the means: No, you didn't need to know the means on variables H and P to answer the questions. Outside of textbooks you don't always get just the relevant information; you have to figure out what's needed.

17.a. To compute the correlation coefficient, we need to compute the squares, cross products, and their sums. Let's consider books read in October as X and those read in January as Y.

	X	X^2	Y	Y^2	XY
Linda	0	0	0	0	0
Larry	2	4	1	1	2
Laurie	3	9	4	16	12
Landra	5	25	6	36	30
Louis	6	36	8	64	48
Lionel	3	9	4	16	12
Luisa	3	9	3	9	9
Lola	1	1	1	1	1
Σ	23	93	27	143	114

The numerator of the raw score formula is $(8)(114) - (23)(27) = 912 - 621 = 291$. The first part of the denominator is $(8)(93) - (23)(23) = 744 - 529 = 215$. The second part is $(8)(143) - (27)(27) = 1144 - 729 = 415$. Multiplying these terms together gives $(215)(415) = 89,225$; the square root of 89,225 is 298.706. Dividing the numerator by the denominator yields $291/298.706 = .97$, which is the value for r.

b. Since r is positive, b will be positive. To compute b, we take

$$\frac{N\Sigma XY - \Sigma X\Sigma Y}{N\Sigma X^2 - (\Sigma X)^2} = \frac{(8)(114) - (23)(27)}{(8)(93) - (23)(23)} = \frac{291}{215} = 1.3535$$

c. To get the entire regression equation, we need to compute a, which equals $\overline{Y} - b\overline{X}$. $\overline{Y} = 27/8 = 3.375$, and $\overline{X} = 23/8 = 2.875$. The value of a is $3.375 - (1.3535)(2.875) = 3.375 - 3.8913 = -.5163$. The regression equation thus is $Y' = 1.3535X - .5163$.

d. Lulu would be predicted to read $(1.3535)(4) - .5163 = 5.4140 - .5163 = 4.8977$, or approximately 5 books in January.

19.a. In this case you are predicting a numerical variable from another numerical variable and should use bivariate (linear) regression.

b. In this case, you want to predict scores on one variable from scores on three other variables. You need to use multiple regression.

c. In this case, you want the relationship between two variables, each of which is presumably measured on an interval scale. Use Pearson r. If you are concerned that the Masculinity and Femininity scales might be only ordinal, you could use Spearman rho instead.

d. In this case, you would use a partial correlation procedure.

e. You are asking for the slope of the regression line.

f. To know how much error you will have in prediction, you need to calculate the standard error of estimate.

Chapter 8

Multiple-Choice Questions

1. Since power $= (1 - \beta)$, it is $1 - .10$ or $.90$; **c** is correct.

3. By failing to reject the null hypothesis when it is true, Sally has made a correct decision. If you picked alternative **e**, then you have, too.

5. The correct response is **b**.

7. In this case you would reject the null hypothesis and conclude that there is a significant difference in the means, alternative **c**.

9. Since 0 is not contained in the confidence interval, you know that there is less than a 1% chance (really, less than a .05% chance) that the real difference in the population means is less than 2 and an even smaller chance that it is in the opposite direction. Therefore, you can conclude that the means differ significantly at the .01 α-level and select response **c**. The difference in the sample means, by the way, is the midpoint of the confidence interval, or 4.5.

Problems

11.a. This is an example of cluster sampling, with classroom as the cluster.

b. If all students in high school in the city are the population of interest, then this is a census. If all students in the city are the intended population, then this would be a clearly biased sample, as younger students are not represented.

c. This is a clearly biased sample, as students who belong to such an organization are going to have identifiable and presumably relatively extreme opinions on the topic of drugs.

d. This is an example of systematic sampling from the population of high school students.

e. This is an example of stratified random sampling. The sample is stratified on the variable of school and randomly selected within each stratum.

f. This is an example of stratified sampling that may or may not be random. It is stratified on the variable of school but, without information on the sampling procedure at each school, you don't know whether or not the selection was random.

13. In order to answer this question, you can do a z-test, since you want to compare your sample mean to a hypothetical value of 48 and you know the standard deviation in the population. Your formula for z would be

$$\frac{50 \text{ (the statistic)} - 48 \text{ (the hypothetical parameter)}}{12 / \sqrt{400} \text{ (the standard error of the mean)}}$$

$$= \frac{2}{(12/20)} = \frac{2}{.6} = 3.33$$

There are two ways to decide whether or not this value of z is statistically significant. One is to look it up in the table. Since slightly fewer than .0005 of the scores lie beyond $z = 3.33$, slightly fewer than .001 of the scores lie beyond a z of either −3.33 or +3.33. Therefore, the difference in the means is significant at the $p < .001$ level. The other alternative is to remember the critical values for the normal curve: 1.96 for the .05 α-level, 2.58 for the .01 level, and 3.30 for the .001 level. Note that I used a two-tailed test. (Even though the question was stated in a directional form, presumably you would have been interested in knowing if the mean for the new employees had been lower than the national norm as well.)

15.a. This is generally false. It is true only if the sample is drawn from a normal distribution.

As N gets large, the shape of the sampling distribution gets closer and closer to a normal distribution.

b. This is false. As N gets larger, the standard error of the mean gets smaller. It approximates $\sigma / \sqrt{N}$, not σ.

c. This is true. The larger the N, the closer the sample mean will be to μ.

d. The Central Limit Theorem says nothing about this. However, it must logically be true. N could be as large as (in which case you'd have a census) but no larger than the number of scores in the population.

17.a. A clearly biased procedure would be to go to a private university and sample the women students.

b. A type of cluster sampling would be to go to five PTA meetings and sample the women attending each.

c. To do a census, it would be necessary to do such things as go to every building on every street in the city; check hospitals, colleges, prisons, and other institutions; look for homeless individuals; make many return calls where no one was at home; and recognize that it is still highly unlikely that all women would be found.

d. A convenience sample might be people shopping at a shopping center that draws from a reasonably wide geographic and socioeconomic area.

e. Quota sampling might involve getting the previous census data, estimating how many women from different age, occupational, and ethnic groups live in each neighborhood, deciding how many women from each age/ethnic/occupational category to sample from each neighborhood, and knocking on doors to find the right number of women.

f. There is no list of all women in Kansas City, so you could not randomly sample from the population of all women in Kansas City. It might be possible to do simple random sampling from the voter registration list, for example. Number all the female names on the list, and use a table of random numbers to select as many as you want for the sample.

g. As stated before, you cannot randomly sample from the population of all women in Kansas City. However, you could probably get a list of all telephone prefixes (exchanges) in the Kansas City area and randomly sample 10 numbers from each exchange. After calling the numbers, you could exclude any men who answered the phone from your sample. (In fact, this technique of random digit dialing is becoming quite popular with pollsters.)

h. You could go to every residential block in the city and sample one woman living on that block.

i. Since there is no list of all women in Kansas City, you could not use systematic sampling from the entire population. However, you could systematically sample from the list of registered voters by picking every 100th female name on the list.

19.a. Assuming that we are interested in means, we first need to compute the standard error of the mean for each group. For group P, it is $15/\sqrt{100} = 1.5000$. For group T, it is $12/\sqrt{81} = 12/9 = 1.3333$. Next, let's compute the standard error of the difference in the means, which is $\sqrt{1.5000^2 + 1.3333^2} = \sqrt{2.25 + 1.78} = \sqrt{4.03} = 2.01$ Substituting into the formula for z gives $z = (80 - 75)/2.01 = 5/2.01 = 2.49$.

Appendix Table 1 shows that only .0064 of the scores in a normal distribution lies above a z of 2.49. Adding the .0064 of the scores below a z of –2.49 still gives only .013 of the scores as far away as this z-value. We can conclude that it is unlikely that the students in the schools represent random samples from the same population.

b. We cannot conclude from this information that the difference in the scores was due to the curriculum. Students at the two schools may have differed on the test for other reasons—different teachers, different exposure to science outside the classroom, different motivation, different patterns of attendance, different abilities, and a host of other potential variables. Correlational research of this type is not nearly

as useful as experimental research when your purpose is to draw causal inferences.

Chapter 9

Multiple-Choice Questions

1. Since you did a one-tailed test and the results came out in the opposite direction from what you predicted, all you can do is retain the null hypothesis and select response **d**. If this seems wrong to you, given that the value for t was $(3 - 6)/.5$ or –6, then you shouldn't do one-tailed tests.

3. The correct response is **c**.

5. In this case, since you are comparing the means of two separate random samples, not paired in any way, you should do an independent-samples t-test; **d** is correct.

7. The correct answer is **c**, a single-sample t-test, since you are comparing the mean of one sample with a hypothetical value. The only alternative might be a z-test, if you know σ, but this was not listed as a response.

9. The 95% confidence interval must be smaller than the 99% confidence interval, since you are less confident that it contains the mean (and since the .05 critical value is a smaller number than the .01 critical value). It also must be symmetric around the midpoint of the 99% confidence interval, which is 4.5. The only alternative that fits these criteria is response **a**.

Problems

11.a. In this case, we have two separate groups of individuals randomly assigned to conditions. An independent-samples t-test is therefore the appropriate procedure to use. If we consider the 7 A.M. group as X_1 and the 2 P.M. group as X_2, then $\Sigma X_1 = 330$, $\overline{X}_1 = 66$, $(\Sigma X_1)^2 = 108,900$, and $\Sigma X_1^2 = 24,100$. $\Sigma X_2 = 125$, $\overline{X}_2 = 25$, $(\Sigma X_2)^2 = 15,625$, and $\Sigma X_2^2 = 4625$.

Substituting into the formula for t, we get

$$t = \frac{66 - 25}{\sqrt{\frac{[(24,100 - 108,900/5) + (4625 - 15,625/5)](1/5 + 1/5)}{8}}}$$

$$= \frac{41}{\sqrt{[(2320 + 1500)(.4)]/8}} = \frac{41}{\sqrt{191}} = \frac{41}{13.82} = 2.97$$

With $n_1 = 5$ and $n_2 = 5$, $df = 8$, and the critical value at the .05 α-level is 2.306. Therefore, you would conclude that the students taught at 7 A.M. had significantly higher vocabulary test scores at the $p < .05$ level than those taught at 2 P.M.

b. To answer this question, you have to recognize that Bertha used a pretest–posttest design with five pairs of scores. Subtracting the 2:00 scores from the 7:00 scores, we get difference scores of 50, 40, 40, 40, and 35 and D^2 scores of 2500, 1600, 1600, 1600, and 1225. $\Sigma D = 205$ and $\Sigma D^2 = 8525$. $(\Sigma D)^2 = 42{,}025$. The standard deviation of the difference scores is

$$\sqrt{(8525 - 205^2 / 5)/4} = \sqrt{(8525 - 8405)/4} =$$

$$\sqrt{120/4} = \quad \sqrt{30} = 5.48$$

The standard error of the mean difference = $5.48/\sqrt{5} = 2.45$. $t = (66 - 25)/2.45 = 41/2.45 = 16.73$. This is a very large value for t, so large that it exceeds the critical value of 8.61 with 4 degrees of freedom at the $p < .001$ level. So you could conclude that the students learned significantly better at 7 A.M. than they did at 2 P.M. (If you are curious as to why this within-participants design produced results that are so much more significant than the between-participants design with the same numerical scores, look at the pairs of scores. The rank order of the scores on the pretest and posttest would be identical; clearly there are large individual differences, which are taken into account in a within-participants design. The paired-samples t-test assesses the consistency of the pretest–posttest difference from participant to participant, which an independent-samples t-test does not.)

c. The mean difference for Bertha's data was 41, the standard error of the mean difference was 2.45, and the critical value at the .05 α-level with 4 df is 2.776. The lower limit of the confidence interval is therefore $41 - (2.776)(2.45)$ or $41 - 6.801$ or 34.199. The upper limit is $41 + 6.801$ or 47.801. Rounding off to two decimal places, we find that the 95% confidence interval for the difference between the mean vocabulary scores for material learned at 7 A.M. and material learned at 2 P.M. is from 34.20 to 47.80. Note that this interval does not include 0, consistent with the significant value of t.

13.a. Linear regression is the correct answer; the word "predict" is a giveaway.

b. You need an independent-samples t-test as you want to compare the means of two groups of scores that are not paired in any apparent way.

c. You want a correlated-samples t-test, as each child's score in May is paired with his or her score in June. You do not want a correlation coefficient, because you are comparing means, not relating the variables of May and June running speeds.

d. In this case you need to calculate Pearson r, as you are looking for a relationship between variables, not a difference in means.

e. You need to construct a 99% confidence interval for the mean, since you want to estimate the mean for a population with a certain probability of being correct. Only a range of scores could have such a probability of being correct; any particular point estimate is almost certain to be wrong.

f. This question is really asking for Spearman ρ, since it is looking for the relationship between two ordinal variables, rank in the boys' race and rank in the girls' race, with sibling pair as the unit.

15.a. It will be easier to compute t if we copy the data:

Person	Pretest	Posttest	D	D²
Barney	10	15	5	25
Bobby	8	12	4	16
Billy	6	7	1	1
Brandy	8	10	2	4
Betty	7	8	1	1
Σ	39	52	13	47

The mean on the pretest is 7.8, the posttest mean is 10.40, and the mean gain was 2.6 points. To calculate s_D,

$$\sqrt{(47 - 169/5)/4} = \sqrt{(47 - 33.8)/4}$$

$$= \sqrt{13.2/4} = \sqrt{3.3} = 1.817$$

The standard error of the difference in the means is $s_D/\sqrt{N}$ or $1.817/\sqrt{5} = .81$. The value for t is therefore $2.6/.81$ or 3.20.

b. To decide if the mean change of 2.6 points is statistically significant, we need to compare the computed value of t with the critical value with 4 degrees of freedom. The test statistic exceeds the value of 2.776 needed for significance at the .05 α-level but is less than the critical value of 4.604 at the .01 level. We would therefore conclude that "the posttest scores on the critical thinking test were significantly higher than the pretest scores, $t(4) = 3.20$, $p < .05$." However, it would be incorrect to conclude that the critical thinking program caused the change in the scores, since this was not an experimental design.

c. Other possible influences on the scores include practice on the test, maturation of the participants, other experiences they had between the pretest and posttest, a reduction in test anxiety, various environmental factors such as the time of day and noise in the room, and perhaps regression toward the mean, if the participants were picked because their pretest scores were low.

17.a. The correct procedure would be a paired samples t-test, since each person rated both bars of soap.

b. To carry out this test, we will have to calculate a difference score for each rater, get the mean score for each soap bar or the mean of the differences, square the difference scores, and get the sum of the squared difference scores. This can be done in a table.

	A	B	D	D²
Stinky	0	3	-3	9
Scruffy	5	5	0	0
Smelly	2	3	-1	1
Snoozy	6	7	-1	1
Snoopy	4	3	1	1
Spotty	5	6	-1	1
	22	27	-5	13

Next, we have to calculate the mean difference score. We can calculate the mean for bar A,

$22/6 = 3.67$, and the mean for bar B, $27/6 = 4.5$, and subtract to get the difference, $-.83$. Alternatively, we can take the mean of the differences, $-5/6$, which also is $-.83$. Next, we need to find the standard deviation of the differences and then the standard error of the mean difference.

$$s_D = \sqrt{\frac{13 - (-5)(-5)/6}{5}} = \sqrt{\frac{13 - 25/6}{5}}$$

$$= \sqrt{\frac{13 - 4.167}{5}} = \sqrt{\frac{8.83}{5}} = \sqrt{1.767}$$

$$= 1.329 = s_D$$

To get the standard error of the mean difference, we need to divide s_D by $\sqrt{6}$.

$1.329/2.449 = 0.54$

The value of t is simply $\overline{D}/s_D = -.83/.54 = -1.54$.

c. A dependent-samples t-test has $N - 1$ degrees of freedom, which in this case is 5.

d. The difference in the means is not statistically significant, since 1.54 is lower than the critical value of 2.571 at the .05 α-level with 5 degrees of freedom. All you can conclude is that there was not a statistically significant difference in preference for the two bars of soap. However, it is possible that with a larger sample size, and therefore greater power, the difference would be statistically significant.

19. First, I would want to do a single-sample t-test to see whether the mean score was significantly higher than the neutral point of 4.00. The value of t would be

$$\frac{4.32 - 4}{2.11/\sqrt{225}} = \frac{.32}{2.11/15} = \frac{.32}{.14} = 2.27$$

As can be seen from Appendix Table 5, this value of t is statistically significant, so you could conclude that there was a statistically significant tendency for parents to favor having a curfew for teens, $t(224) = 2.27$, $p < .05$. On the other hand, the mean score of 4.32 is closer to "neutral" than to "slightly in favor," suggesting that support for a curfew is quite weak. As a practical issue, this may be one of those examples where "statistically significant" does not mean "important."

Chapter 10

Multiple-Choice Questions

1. The correct answer is **b**. The within-groups sum of squares (and mean square) depends upon differences in the scores within each group but says nothing about whether the means for each group differ from each other.

3. **c** is the correct response.

5. The correct response is **a**.

7. With 14 people in each of 2 groups, your F-test has 1 and 26 degrees of freedom. The critical value would be 4.225, so the difference is not significant, so alternatives a, b, c, and e are false. There is no reason to think that response f is correct, but response **d** is clearly right, since the value for an F-test will always be the square of the value for a t-test computed on the same data.

9. Since there are 4 groups of 12 people each, $N = 48$, and the degrees of freedom within is $48 - 4$ or 44. The MS_{within} is .25. The $MS_{between}$ is $9/(4 - 1) = 3$. $F = 3/.25$ or 12.00, alternative **f**.

Problems

11.a. The first thing to be done is to regroup the data so that you can easily calculate the sums, sums of squares, and means for each group. You may wonder why the data weren't organized that way to begin with (Has watching too many movies damaged my brain?), but remember that when you are gathering the data they often arrive piece by piece and that you are the one who has to do the organizing. So let's regroup:

	Comedy (X_1)	X_1^2	Action (X_2)	X_2^2
	600	360,000	1,200	1,440,000
	800	640,000	1,000	1,000,000
	900	810,000	1,100	1,210,000
	1000	1,000,000	1,500	2,250,000
Σ	3300	2,810,000	4,800	5,900,000
n	4		4	
$\overline{X}$	825		1,200	

Before going further, I should acknowledge that some of you may be worrying that your

calculators can't deal with such large numbers. If this is the case, you can easily convert the scores to hundreds of tickets sold by simply dividing the raw scores by 100. The results of the analysis of variance and of the t-test will be exactly the same. However, if you are going to report means, it is important to convert your data back into actual numbers of tickets sold, so as not to give a misleading impression and get you arrested for purloining box office receipts. Let's look at the data for ticket sales in hundreds:

$$\Sigma X_1 = 33.00 \quad \Sigma X_2 = 48.00 \quad n_1 = 4 \quad n_2 = 4$$
$$\overline{X}_1 = 8.25 \quad \overline{X}_2 = 12.00$$
$$(\Sigma X_1)^2/n_1 = 1089/4 = 272.25$$
$$(\Sigma X_2)^2/n_2 = 2304/4 = 576.00$$
$$\Sigma X_1^2 = 281 \quad \Sigma X_2^2 = 590$$
$$\Sigma X = 81.00 \quad \Sigma X^2 = 871$$

Now, let's compute the sums of squares for the analysis of variance:

$$SS_T = 871 - 81^2/8 = 871 - 6561/8$$
$$= 871 - 820.125 = 50.875$$
$$SS_B = 272.25 + 576.00 - 820.125 = 28.125$$
$$SS_W = (281 - 272.25) + (590 - 576) = 8.75 + 14$$
$$= 22.75$$

To check, $50.875 = 28.125 + 22.75$. Since $N = 8$ and $K = 2$, the df total $= 7$, the df between $= 1$, and the df within $= 6$. The analysis of variance summary table would read:

Source	SS	df	MS	F(1, 6)	p
Between	28.125	1	28.125	7.42	<.05
Within	22.75	6	3.792		
Total	50.875	7			

b. Since $F_{.05}(1, 6) = 5.987$, this F exceeds the critical value of F at the .05 α-level. With only two means to be considered, you could conclude, for example, "The mean number of tickets sold per week for the action movies ($\overline{M} = 1200$) was significantly higher than the mean number of tickets sold per week for the comedies ($\overline{M} = 825$), $F(1, 6) = 7.42, p < .05$."

c.

$$t = \frac{8.25 - 12.00}{\sqrt{\left(\frac{(281 - 272.25) + (590 - 576)}{4 + 4 - 2}\right)\left(\frac{1}{4} + \frac{1}{4}\right)}}$$

$$= -3.75 / \sqrt{(8.75 + 14)(.5)/6}$$

$$= -3.75 / \sqrt{(22.75)(.5)/6}$$

$$= -3.75 / \sqrt{11.375/6} = -3.75 / \sqrt{1.896}$$

$$= -3.75 / 1.377 = -2.72$$

Note that this value of –2.72 is the square root of 7.42, the F-value from the analysis of variance. Note, too, that the critical value for $t_{.05}(6)$, 2.447, is the square root of the critical value for $F_{.05}(1, 6)$, 5.99. You can also see that a number of terms in the equations for t and F are the same. However, the analysis of variance need not involve computing the means of the two groups, as the t-test does.

13.a. To perform this test, we'll need to get some summary statistics for the data. In order to preserve our calculators and our sanity, let's consider income in thousands of dollars (number of thousand dollar bills, if you prefer). The salaries are (in 1000s):

Engineering Ph.D (X_1)	Humanities Ph.D (X_2)	Education Ph.D (X_3)	J.D. (X_4)	M.D. (X_5)
$40	$22	$25	$40	$50
$28	$24	$27	$35	$43
$32	$28	$31	$33	$33
$36	$24	$24	$36	$39
$30		$27	$38	$50
			$32	

$\Sigma X_1 = 166 \qquad \Sigma X_2 = 98 \qquad \Sigma X_3 = 134$

$\Sigma X_4 = 214 \qquad \Sigma X_5 = 215$

$\Sigma X_1^2 = 5604 \qquad \Sigma X_2^2 = 2420 \qquad \Sigma X_3^2 = 3620$

$\Sigma X_4^2 = 7678 \qquad \Sigma X_5^2 = 9459$

$\overline{X}_1 = 33.20 \qquad \overline{X}_2 = 24.50 \qquad \overline{X}_3 = 26.80$

$\overline{X}_4 = 35.67 \qquad \overline{X}_4 = 43.00$

$n_1 = 5 \qquad n_2 = 4 \qquad n_3 = 5 \qquad n_4 = 6 \qquad n_5 = 5$

$\Sigma X_T = 166 + 98 + 134 + 214 + 215 = 827$

$\Sigma X_{T2}^2 = 5604 + 2420 + 3620 + 7678 + 9459$

$\qquad = 28{,}781$

$n_T = 5 + 4 + 5 + 6 + 5 = 25$

$SS_T = 28{,}781 - 827^2/25 = 28{,}781 - 683{,}929/25$

$\qquad = 28{,}781 - 27{,}357.16 = 1423.84$

$SS_B = 166^2/5 + 98^2/4 + 134^2/5 + 214^2/6 + 215^2/5 -$
$27{,}357.16 = 28{,}381.07 - 27{,}357.16 = 1023.91$

$SS_W = 28{,}781.00 - 28{,}381.07 = 399.93$

$df_T = 25 - 1 = 24 \qquad df_B = 5 - 1 = 4$
$df_W = 25 - 5 = 20$

$MS_B = 1023.91/4 = 255.98$
$MS_W = 399.93/20 = 20.00$

$F(4, 20) = 255.98/20.00 = 12.80$
$F_{.001}(4, 20) = 7.096$

Reject H_0

b. First, we can look at the ANOVA summary table:

Source	SS	df	MS	F(4, 20)	p
Between	1023.91	4	255.98	12.80	<.001
Within	399.93	20	20.00		
Total	1423.84				

Since the obtained value of F exceeds the critical value at the $p < .001$ level, we would reject the null hypothesis and conclude that the five different types of degree holders do not all have the same income levels, $F(4, 20) = 12.80$, $p < .001$.

c. Looking at the data, it appears that the incomes of the humanities and education Ph.D's are lower than the incomes of the engineering Ph.D's, J.D.'s and M.D.'s. I would want to test a comparison which reflects this hypothesis.

15.a. Either an independent-samples t-test or a one-way analysis of variance would be appropriate.

b. In this case, you need a factorial analysis of variance.

c. Because these scores are paired, you could either do a dependent-samples t-test or you could do a repeated measures analysis of variance.

d. Since you are asking a question about differences in the variances of two groups, you would do an F-test.

e. Because this hypothesis involves only one group, you would do a single-sample t-test or (if you know σ for adults in the community) a z-test. You could not do an analysis of variance, as there is only one sample mean.

f. The answer to this question depends on whether the bedtime experience was a between participants or a within participants factor. If each person experienced only one bedtime ritual, then this design is appropriately analyzed by a one-way ANOVA. However, if bedtime ritual was a within participants factor, with each person experiencing all four possibilities on four different nights, then a repeated measures analysis of variance would be necessary.

17.a. To solve this problem, we need to do a number of preliminary calculations. Let's call the ratings of the thin photo X_1, the ratings of the normal photo X_2, and the ratings of the fat photo X_3. We will need the squares and sums of squares.

X_1	X_1^2	X_2	X_2^2	X_3	X_3^2	
5	25	8	64	3	9	$n_2 = 7$
4	16	10	100	2	4	$n_2 = 7$
5	25	7	49	4	16	
7	49	7	49	5	25	$n_3 = 6$
3	9	6	36	0	0	
5	25	9	81	1	1	$N = 20$
4	16	10	100	15	55	
33	165	57	479			

$\Sigma X = 33 + 57 + 15 = 105 = T$
$\Sigma X^2 = 165 + 479 + 55 = 699$

$T^2 = (105)(105) = 11{,}025$
$T^2/N = 11{,}025/20 = 551.25$

$SS_T = \Sigma X^2 - T^2/N = 699 - 551.25 = \mathbf{147.75}$
$SS_B = \Sigma(T_j^2/N_j) - T^2/N$
$\quad = (33^2/7 + 57^2/7 + 15^2/7) - 551.25$
$\quad = (155.57 + 464.14 + 32.14) - 551.25$
$\quad = 651.85 - 551.25 = \mathbf{100.60}$

$SS_W = \Sigma X^2 - \Sigma(T_j^2/N_j) = 699 - 651.85 = \mathbf{47.15}$
$MS_B = SS_B/(K-1) = 100.60/2 = \mathbf{50.30}$
$MS_W = SS_W/(N-K) = 47.15/17 = \mathbf{2.77}$
$F = MS_B/MS_W = 50.30/2.77 = \mathbf{18.16}$

The critical value for F with 2 and 17 degrees of freedom is 10.66 at the .001 α-level.

b.

Source	*SS*	*df*	*MS*	*F*	*p*
Between	100.60	2	50.30	18.16	< .001
Within	47.15	17	2.77		
Total	147.75	19			

c. A one-way analysis of variance revealed that respondents had significantly different attitudes toward the three photographs: $F(2, 17) = 18.16$, $p < .001$.

19.a. You are interested in comparing mean scores on a ratio-level variable. However, you cannot be sure whether the scores in the populations are normally distributed, and the data suggest that the variance of the population of insured people may be lower than the variance of the population of noninsured people. Nevertheless, the test is reasonably robust to violations of these assumptions, so it would probably be acceptable to perform an analysis of variance. A nonparametric test might be better, however, and the study would be improved with a larger sample.

b. Let's call insured X_1 and noninsured X_2. As usual, we need to get squares and sums of squares.

X_1	X_1^2	X_2	X_2^2	
0	0	4	16	$n_1 = 8$, 4/8 = 0.5
0	0	5	25	
1	1	2	4	$n_2 = 5$, 17/5 = 3.4
2	4	0	0	
1	1	6	36	$N = 13$
0	0	17	81	
0	0			
0	0			
4	6			

$\Sigma X = 4 + 17 = 21 = T \qquad \Sigma X^2 = 6 + 81 = 87$

$T^2 = (21)(21) = 441 \qquad T^2/N = 441/13 = 33.92$

$SS_T = \Sigma X^2 - T^2/N = 87 - 33.92 = \mathbf{53.08}$

$SS_B = \Sigma(T_j^2/N_j) - T^2/N = (6^2/8 + 17^2/5 - 33.92$

$\qquad = (4.5 + 57.8) - 33.92 = 62.30 - 33.92 = \mathbf{28.38}$

$SS_W = \Sigma X^2 - \Sigma(T_j^2/N_j) = 87 - 62.30 = \mathbf{24.70}$

$MS_B = SS_B/(K-1) = 28.38/1 = \mathbf{28.38}$

$MS_W = SS_W/(N-K) = 24.70/11 = \mathbf{2.25}$

$F = MS_B/MS_W = 28.38/2.25 = \mathbf{12.61}$

Appendix Table 6 shows that the critical values for F with 1 and 11 degrees of freedom are 9.65 at the .01 α-level and 19.69 at the .001 α-level.

c.

Source	SS	df	MS	F	p
Between	28.38	1	28.38	12.61	< .01
Within	24.70	11	2.25		
Total	53.08	12			

d. From these data, you can conclude that people standing in line to get a New Mexico driver's license who do not have insurance say that they made more emergency room visits in the last year ($M = 3.4$ visits) than people with medical insurance ($M = .5$ visits), $F(1, 11) = 12.61$, $MS_W = 2.25$, $p < .01$.

Chapter 11

Multiple-Choice Questions

1. The correct answer is **b**. Tukey HSD is not an a priori test, and it cannot be used to compare the mean of two groups with the mean of another group in a single comparison.

3. c is correct.

5. e; if your analysis of variance is not significant, unless you had planned to do a priori comparisons, you should stop. Redesign your research study, perhaps with a larger sample and a more sensitive measure.

7. The correct alternative is **c**.

9. Since your hypothesis does not concern any particular means, a one-way ANOVA alone is adequate to test it. You don't need a comparison in this case, so pick alternative **c**.

Problems

11. To check whether the comparisons are orthogonal to +2, +2, –1, –3, multiply the cross products and sum them.

a. $1(2) + (-1)(2) + 1(-1) + (-1)(-3) = 2 - 2 - 1 + 3 = 2$

b. $2(2) + 1(2) + (-1)(-1) - 2(-3) = 4 + 2 + 1 + 6 = 13$

c. $1(2) + (-1)(2) + 0(-1) + 0(-3) = 2 - 2 + 0 + 0 = 0$

d. $3(2) + 1(2) + (-2)(-1) + (-2)(-3) = 6 + 2 + 2 + 6 = 16$

e. $1(2) + 2(2) + (-2)(-1) + (-1)(-3) = 2 + 4 + 2 + 3 = 11$

Only the third comparison is orthogonal to 2, +2, –1, –3.

13.a. This statement is true; you can do as many as but no more than $K - 1$ orthogonal contrasts in any particular set.

b. true; it is possible to do both *a priori* and *post hoc* comparisons in the same research project if you have made some predictions but also want to test some unexpected findings. Of course, your critical values for the latter will be more stringent.

c. false; If there are only two groups (levels of the independent variable), there is no reason to do any comparison, as a significant F means that the larger mean is statistically significantly larger than the smaller mean. Also, if there are more than two groups but you are interested in only pairwise comparisons, you may prefer to use the more powerful Tukey HSD procedure.

d. This is true if all you want to test is a specific hypothesis and you are not interested in the overall null hypothesis that the means of the groups do not differ.

e. It might be possible, if the two means being compared have much larger n's than the other means and are also the most extreme. This would be an unusual situation.

f. false; the idea of altering your α-level to keep your overall chance of making a Type I error at α is a good one, but you would have to do each test at the .05/20 or the .0025 level to keep your familywise α-level at .05.

15.a. Even though this sentence uses the word "comparison," the description sounds as if what is needed is simply an analysis of variance (Aha! and you thought this chapter dealt only with comparisons), with a total N of 60 and $K = 5$. Thus it has 4 and 55 degrees of freedom, leading to a critical value of 3.68 at the .01 level. You could use the critical value of 3.72, for 4 and 50 degrees of freedom, if you prefer not to interpolate.

b. In this case, you need to use the table and find the critical value of the studentized range for 5 groups and 55 degrees of freedom for the error term. This turns out to be a little more than 4.82 (which is the critical value for 60 df) at the .01 level; interpolating, we might say 4.84.

c. Again $K = 5$ and $N - K = 55$. The critical value with 4 and 55 degrees of freedom is still 3.68 at the .01 level; multiplying it by 4 yields 14.72, the critical value for a Scheffé comparison.

d. For this comparison, K still $= 5$ and $N - K$ still $= 55$. However, the critical value is the critical value for 1 and 55 degrees of freedom, which is 7.12.

e. The degrees of freedom for such a test is $N - 2$ or 55. The critical value at the .01 level is 2.678 for 50 degrees of freedom. Amazingly (not really; you knew it would be, didn't you?), this is the square root of the critical value for F with 1 and 50 degrees of freedom.

17.a. To test this hypothesis, the obvious weights are

School:	R1	R2	R3	C1	C2	C3	C4
C_1	4	4	4	−3	−3	−3	−3

Adding the means and n's, we get

School:	R1	R2	R3	C1	C2	C3	C4
$\overline{X}$	10.5	13.2	9.8	10.0	7.7	8.7	7.2
n	20	32	19	26	19	22	18
C_1	4	4	4	−3	−3	−3	−3

The formula for F for the comparison is

$$F = \frac{(\Sigma c_j \overline{X}_j)^2}{(MS_W)(\Sigma c_j^2 / n_j)}$$

The numerator is therefore $[(4)(10.5) + (4)(13.2) + (4)(9.8) + (-3)(10.0) + (-3)(7.7) + (-3)(8.7) + (-3)(7.2)]^2 = (42.0 + 52.8 + 39.2 - 30.0 - 23.1 - 26.1 - 21.6)^2 = 33.2^2 = 1102.24$. The denominator is $(24.50)(16/20 + 16/32 + 16/19 + 9/26 + 9/19 + 9/22 + 9/18) = (24.50)(.80 + .50 + .84 + .35 + .47 + .41 + .50) = (24.50)(3.87) = 94.815$. The value of F is therefore $1102.24/94.82 = 11.62$.

Since this is an a priori test, the critical value will be the critical value for F with 1 and $N - K$ degrees of freedom. In this case, $N = 156$ and $K = 7$, so $N - K = 149$. The critical values for $F(1, 150)$ are 3.90, 6.81, and 11.27 at the .05, .01, and .001 α-levels, respectively, so the computed value for F is significant at the .01 α-level.

b. An a priori comparison revealed that the mean concentration scores for students at the three schools with extra recess were significantly higher than the mean concentration scores at the four schools with no extra recess: $F(1, 149) = 11.62, p < .01$.

c. The critical value for a post hoc comparison would be $(K - 1)[F_\alpha(K - 1, N - K)] = (6)[F_\alpha(6, 149) = (6)(2.16)] = 12.96$ at the .05 α-level. Since the test statistic is less than the critical value, we would have to conclude that students at the three R schools did not differ significantly from students at the four C schools in concentration test scores.

d. Using the formula, we get

$$HSD = \frac{13.2 - 7.2}{\sqrt{(24.50/2)(1/32 + 1/18)}}$$

$$= \frac{6}{\sqrt{(12.25)(.0868)}} = \frac{6}{\sqrt{1.0633}}$$

$$= \frac{6}{1.031} = 5.82$$

Looking at Appendix Table 7 for 7 means and 120 df_W, the critical value at the .05 level is 4.24, and the critical value at the .01 level is 5.00. We could conclude that the mean concentration test score at school $R2$ was significantly higher than the mean concentration test score at school $C4$.

19.a. Since you will be doing pairwise comparisons, a Tukey HSD procedure would be the best. Just doing t-tests would inflate the error rate, and Scheffé comparisons are not as powerful when you want to do only pairwise comparisons (although post hoc Scheffé contrasts would not be *wrong*, just not as good a choice).

b. First, let's copy the basic data. $MS_W = 2.86$.

City	New York	Mobile	Des Moines	Sacramento
$\overline{X}$	6.00	10.35	7.22	8.56
n	32	42	37	38

Then we'll compare New York with Mobile.

$$HSD = \frac{10.35 - 6.00}{\sqrt{(2.86)(1/42 + 1/32)}}$$

$$= \frac{4.35}{\sqrt{(2.86)(.055)}} = \frac{4.35}{\sqrt{.157}} = \frac{4.35}{.397}$$

$$= 10.96$$

The degrees of freedom within equal $(32 + 42 + 37 + 38) - 4 = 149 - 4 = 145$. The critical values for HSD with four means and $df = 120$ are 3.69 at the .05 α-level and 4.20 at the .01 level. The difference between New York and Mobile is significant at the .01 level.

Next, we'll compare New York with Des Moines.

$$HSD = \frac{7.22 - 6.00}{\sqrt{(2.86)(1/37 + 1/32)}}$$

$$= \frac{1.22}{\sqrt{(2.86)(.058)}} = \frac{1.22}{\sqrt{.166}} = \frac{1.22}{.407} = 3.00$$

This difference is not statistically significant.

Last, we'll compare New York with Sacramento.

$$HSD = \frac{8.56 - 6.00}{\sqrt{(2.86)(1/38 + 1/32)}}$$

$$= \frac{2.56}{\sqrt{(2.86)(.058)}} = \frac{2.56}{\sqrt{.166}} = \frac{2.56}{.407} = 6.29$$

This difference is significant at the .01 level. We could conclude from this sample that New Yorkers speak significantly faster than people from Mobile, $HSD = 10.96$, and Sacramento, $HSD = 6.29$, both $ps < .01$, but not than people from Des Moines, $HSD = 3.00$, $p > .05$.

c. The weights for that comparison would be $-1 +3 -1 -1$.

$$F = \frac{[(-1)(6.00) + (3)(10.35) + (-1)(7.22) + (-1)(8.56)]^2}{(2.86)(1/32 + 9/42 + 1/37 + 1/38)}$$

$$= \frac{9.27^2}{(2.86)(.299)} = \frac{85.93}{.855} = 100.51$$

The critical value for F at the .001 level is $(3)(5.707) = 17.121$. We can therefore conclude that people from Mobile spoke significantly more slowly than people from New York, Des Moines, and Sacramento, $F(1, 145) = 100.51$, $p < .001$.

Chapter 12

Multiple-Choice Questions

1. The correct answer is **e**. Since the F for gender was greater than 1, the mean square for the numerator (MS_{gender}) must be larger than the mean square for the denominator (MS_W). We know that answer a is wrong, since treatment would not be a variable if it had only one level. In fact, it had two levels, since the degrees of freedom for the effect was 1. Alternatives b and c are wrong, since the total degrees of freedom must be $44 + 1 + 1 + 1$, making the total $N = 48$, not 45 or 47. Response d is wrong, since the treatment effect was nonsignificant. Response f is wrong, since e is correct.

3. Response **c** correctly describes what a significant interaction means. Since you do not know whether the main effects of factors A and B are significant, you do not know anything about the correctness of alternatives a, c, and e. Alternative b refers to a relationship between the two independent variables, which would be measured by an index of association such as a correlation coefficient.

5. Responses a, b, and f are false, since the main effects of A and B are statistically significant. Response c doesn't make sense; you don't know that A and B are quantitative variables. Response d is wrong; there are (2)(3) or 6 groups. Response **e** is correct; the degrees of freedom for A is $3 - 1$ or 2.

7. You cannot know whether there is a statistically significant main effect or interaction without doing an appropriate statistical analysis, in this case a two-way analysis of variance. However, you can be positive that there is not a significant main effect of A in this example. Both means for B at level A_1 are identical, and both means for B at level A_2 are identical. The degrees of freedom within will be $N - ab = 48 - 4$; the total degrees of freedom will be $N - 1 = 47$.

9. The correct answer is **d**. Omega squared is an estimate of the proportion of variance in the dependent measure that can be attributed to a particular independent variable in the population. Eta squared is an estimate of the proportion of variance in the dependent measure attributed to a particular independent variable in the *sample*, and the other responses are even less relevant.

11.a. The independent variables are gender, with two levels, and school, with three levels. The dependent variable is grip strength. The total N is $(18)(2)(3) = 108$.

b. The independent variables are country, with three levels, and orbit/no orbit, with two levels. The dependent variable is globalmindedness, and the N is $(12)(2)(3) = 72$.

c. The independent variables are family structure, with three levels, and educational condition, with three levels. The dependent variable is age at which they wish to become parents, and the total N is 45.

d. The independent variables are gender, with two levels, and age, with four levels. The dependent measure is memory test score, and the N is $(5)(2)(4) = 40$.

13. The easiest way to see the answers to the questions is to fill in the relevant parts of the summary table:

Source	SS	df	MS	F	p
Drug (A)	256.67	2	128.34	11.85	< .001
Dosage (B)	34.84	2	17.42	1.61	> .05
$A \times B$	346.99	4	86.75	8.01	< .001
Within	877.77	81	10.83		
Total	1516.27	89			

a. 1516.27

b. Since there were 2 degrees of freedom for A and for B, there were three levels of A and three levels of B, leading to nine cells.

c. The N is $89 + 1$ or 90.

d. With 2 and 81 degrees of freedom, the critical value at the .05 level is 3.11.

e. The F for the effect of drug is $128.34/10.83 = 11.85$.

f. The mean square for the interaction is 86.75.

g. With 4 and 81 degrees of freedom, the interaction is significant at the .001 level. The critical value is 5.12.

15.

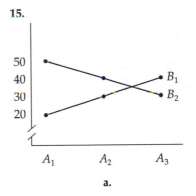

a.

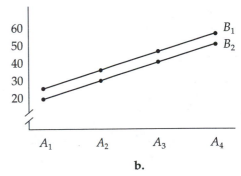

b.

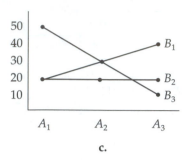

c.

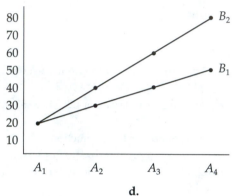

d.

17.a. First, compute some sums, squares, and sums of squares.

$\Sigma X_{A1B1} = 147 \quad \Sigma X_{A1B1}^2 = 3949$
$(\Sigma X_{A1B1})^2 = 21,609 \quad (\Sigma X_{A1B1})^2/n = 3601.5$
$\Sigma X_{A1B1}/n = \overline{X}_{A1B1} = 24.50$

$\Sigma X_{A2B1} = 142 \quad \Sigma X_{A2B1}^2 = 3634$
$(\Sigma X_{A2B1})^2 = 20,164 \quad (\Sigma X_{A2B1})^2/n = 3360.67$
$\Sigma X_{A2B1}^2/n = \overline{X}_{A2B1} = 23.67$

$\Sigma X_{A1B2} = 88 \quad \Sigma X_{A1B2}^2 = 1338 \quad (\Sigma X_{A1B2})^2 = 7744$
$(\Sigma X_{A1B2})^2/n = 1290.67$
$\Sigma X_{A1B2}/n = \overline{X}_{A1B2} = 14.67$

$\Sigma X_{A2B2} = 93 \quad \Sigma X_{A2B2}^2 = 1547$
$(\Sigma X_{A2B2})^2 = 8649$
$(\Sigma X_{A2B2})^2/n = 1441.50$
$\Sigma X_{A2B2}/n = \overline{X}_{A2B2} = 15.50$

$\Sigma X_{A1} = 235 \quad \Sigma X_{A1}^2 = 5287 \quad (\Sigma X_{A1})^2 = 55,225$

$\Sigma X_{A2} = 235 \quad \Sigma X_{A2}^2 = 5181 \quad (\Sigma X_{A2})^2 = 55,225$

$\Sigma X_{B1} = 289 \quad \Sigma X_{B1}^2 = 7583 \quad (\Sigma X_{B1})^2 = 83,521$

$\Sigma X_{B2} = 181 \quad \Sigma X_{B2}^2 = 2885 \quad (\Sigma X_{B2})^2 = 32,761$

$\overline{X}_{A1} = 19.58 \quad \overline{X}_{A2} = 19.58 \quad \overline{X}_{B1} = 24.08$
$\overline{X}_{B2} = 15.08$

$\Sigma X^2 = 10,468 \quad \Sigma X = 470 \quad (\Sigma X)^2 = 220,900$

$(\Sigma X)^2/N = 220,900/24 = 9204.17 = T^2/N$

$$
\begin{aligned}
SS_T &= \Sigma X^2 - T^2/N = 10,468 - 9204.17 \\
&= 1263.83
\end{aligned}
$$

$$
\begin{aligned}
SS_A &= \Sigma[(\Sigma A_1)^2/bn + (\Sigma A_2)^2/bn + \ldots + \\
&\quad (\Sigma A_a)^2/bn] - T^2/N \\
&= [(55,225/12) + (55,225/12)] - 9204.17 \\
&= 4602.08 + 4602.08 - 9204.17 = 0.01
\end{aligned}
$$

$$
\begin{aligned}
SS_B &= \Sigma[(\Sigma B_1)^2/an + (\Sigma B_2)^2/an + \ldots + \\
&\quad (\Sigma B_b)^2/an] - T^2/N \\
&= [(83,521/12) + 32,761/12)] - 9204.17 \\
&= (6960.08 + 2730.08) - 9204.17 = 485.99
\end{aligned}
$$

$$
\begin{aligned}
SS_{A \times B} &= \Sigma[(\Sigma X_{A1B1})^2/n + \ldots + (\Sigma X_{AaBb})^2/n] \\
&\quad - T^2/N - SS_A - SS_B \\
&= (3601.50 + 3360.67 + 1290.67 + 1441.50) \\
&\quad - 9204.17 - .01 - 485.99 \\
&= 9694.34 - 9204.17 - .01 - 485.99 = 4.17
\end{aligned}
$$

$$
\begin{aligned}
SS_W &= \Sigma X^2 - \Sigma[(\Sigma X_{A1B1})^2/n + \ldots + (\Sigma X_{AaBb})^2/n] \\
&= 10,468 - 9694.34 = 773.66
\end{aligned}
$$

Check: SS_T should equal $SS_A + SS_B + SS_{A \times B} + SS_W$.

$1263.83 = 0.01 + 485.99 + 4.17 + 773.66$

$MS_A = SS_A/(a-1) = 0.01$

$MS_B = SS_B/(b-1) = 485.99$

$MS_{A \times B} = SS_{A \times B}/(a-1)(b-1) = 4.17$

$MS_W = SS_W/(N-ab) = 773.66/(24-4)$
$\quad\quad = 38.68$

$F_A = MS_A/MS_W = 0.01/38.68 = 0$

$F_B = MS_B/MS_W = 485.99/38.68 = 12.56$

$F_{A \times B} = MS_{A \times B} / MS_W = 4.17 / 38.68 = 12.56$

df for $F_A = a - 1$ and $N - ab = 1$ and 20

df for $F_B = b - 1$ and $N - ab = 1$ and 20

df for $F_{A \times B} = (a-1)(b-1)$ and $N - ab$
$= 1$ and 20

$df_{total} = N - 1 = 23$

The critical values for F with 1 and 20 degrees of freedom are 4.35 at the .05 α-level, 8.10 at the .01 α-level, and 14.82 at the .001 α-level.

b.

Source	SS	df	MS	F	p
Gender (A)	0.01	1	0.01	0.00	> .05
Status (B)	485.99	1	485.99	12.56	< .01
A × B	4.17	1	4.17	0.11	> .05
Within	773.66	20	38.68		
Total	1263.83	23			

c. A 2×2 factorial analysis of variance revealed that CEOs spent significantly more hours per week in meetings ($M = 24.08$ hours) than did CFOs ($M = 15.08$ hours), $F(1, 20) = 12.56$, $MS_W = 38.68$, $p < .01$, but that there was no significant difference between male and female executives in the number of hours spent at meetings, $F(1, 20) = 0.00$, $p > .05$, and no significant interaction, $F(1, 20) = 0.11$, $p > .05$.

19.a.

Source	SS	df	MS	F	p
Team Supported (A)	5.28	1	5.28	2.88	> .05
Team Rated (B)	2.53	1	2.53	1.38	> .05
A × B	42.78	1	42.78	23.32	< .001
Within	51.38	28	1.84		
Total	101.97	31			

b. An analysis of variance on the rated quality of fielding revealed no significant main effects of team for which the rater rooted, $F(1, 28) = 2.88$, $p > .05$, or team that was being rated, $F(1, 28) = 1.38$, $p > .05$. However, there was a significant interaction between the two variables, $F(1, 28) = 23.32$, $MS_W = 1.84$, $p < .001$, indicating that Cubs fans rating Cubs ($M = 6.38$) and Cardinals fans rating Cardinals ($M = 5.00$) gave significantly higher ratings than did Cubs fans rating Cardinals ($M = 3.50$) and Cardinals fans rating Cubs ($M = 3.25$).

c. Because this is a crossover interaction with one degree of freedom and a clear pattern of results, it is not necessary to do post hoc comparisons, although you could do some Tukey HSD tests if you want to make pairwise comparisons.

Chapter 13

Multiple-Choice Questions

1. The only correct answer is **b**. The critical values get smaller with increasing degrees of freedom for the other tests.

3. For either kind of chi-square test, a high value of χ^2 means that the observed and expected frequencies differ. The correct answer is **b**.

5. Only **f** is correct. The critical value does not change, nor does the chance of making a Type I error. The power increases and the chance of making a Type II error decreases.

7. Since it is impossible to get a negative value for χ^2, you must have made an error in computation. Answer **e** is the only possible one.

9. Only alternative **b** is always correct. In some specific situations, d may be true as well, but not necessarily.

Problems

11.a. In order to answer this question, we need to conduct a chi-square test of independence on the data. To do so we need to compute the marginal frequencies and then compute the expected values. As it turns out, the marginal frequencies for these data are all the same, 20. For the first cell, families with no children visiting relatives, the expected value equals $(20)(20)/60$ or 6.667. Indeed, the expected value for each cell in this example turns out to be 6.67. However, the observed values differ, and so do the discrepancies, making the overall value for $\chi^2 = 37.50$.

Cell	O	E	(O – E)	(O – E)²	(O – E)²/E
NoC/Rel	0	6.667	–6.667	44.449	6.667
NoC/Bea	5	6.667	–1.667	2.779	.417
NoC/Urb	15	6.667	8.333	69.439	10.415
C<10/Rel	15	6.667	8.333	69.439	10.415
C<10/Bea	5	6.667	–1.667	2.779	.417
C<10/Urb	0	6.667	–6.667	44.449	6.667
C10-18/Rel	5	6.667	–1.667	2.779	.417
C10-18/Bea	10	6.667	3.333	11.109	1.667
C10-18/Urb	5	6.667	–1.667	2.779	.417

Since there are three rows to the table and three columns, there are $(3 - 1)(3 - 1)$ or 4 degrees of freedom for the χ^2 test. Since the observed value of 37.50 exceeds the critical value at even the .001 α-level, we reject the null hypothesis of independence and conclude that family structure is related to the type of vacation preferred.

b. In order to investigate this issue, we have to set up a new contingency table formed by collapsing categories. The table will look like this:

	No Children	Children	Total
Visit Relatives	0	20	20
Other Vacation	20	20	40
Total	20	40	60

After calculating the expected values, the data look like this:

Cell	O	E	(O – E)	(O – E)²	(O – E)²/E
NoC/Rel	0	6.667	–6.667	44.449	6.667
NoC/Other	20	13.333	6.667	44.449	3.333
C/Rel	20	13.333	6.667	44.449	3.333
C/Other	20	26.667	–6.667	44.449	1.667

The value of $\chi^2 = 15$, which is significant at beyond the .001 level. It is therefore possible to conclude not only that having children is related to the type of vacation preferred but that people with children are significantly more likely to choose a vacation visiting relatives (50%) than are people without children (0%), $\chi^2(1, N = 60) = 15$, $p < .001$. (Note, by the way, that for both parts a and b, the sum of the expected values for each row and column equals the sum of the observed values for the corresponding row and column.)

13.a. Since there are four categories, $df = 3$. The number of observations is irrelevant.

b. In theory such a test would have 26 degrees of freedom. In fact, you could not do that test or any chi-square test with a sample size of only 4, since the expected frequencies would be far too small.

c. Since one variable has 2 levels and one has 3, there are $(1)(2)$ or 2 degrees of freedom.

d. Presumably there are four seasons and three types of footwear, leading to $(4 - 1)(3 - 1)$ or 6 degrees of freedom.

e. It is necessary to recognize that there are really two variables here: class standing, with four levels, and attitude toward school, presumably with two levels ("yes" and "no"). Therefore a chi-square test of independence with $(3)(1)$ or 3 degrees of freedom is needed.

f. In this case, although the variable of class standing is a nominal one, the variable of number of absences is a ratio scale variable. The question is really asking about differences in the mean numbers of absences among the four groups. The proper analysis is not a chi-square but an analysis of variance, with $K - 1$ and $N - K$ degrees of freedom. In this case, $df = 3$ and 70.

15.a. The appropriate procedure is a chi-square test of independence, as you want to assess whether or not there is a significant relationship between two nominal level variables (gender and program or college).

b. The first step would be to put the data into a contingency table and to compute the marginal totals, as follows:

	Male	*Female*	*Total*
Education	50	150	200
Engineering	100	20	120
Arts & Sciences	200	200	400
Total	350	370	720 = N

The next step is to compute the expected values. For the cell of males in Engineering, the expected value would be $(200)(350)/720 = 97.222$. Using the observed and expected values to compute χ^2 gives:

	O	*E*	*(O − E)*	*(O − E)²*	*(O − E)²/E*
Ed/M	50	97.222	−47.222	2229.917	22.936
Ed/F	150	102.778	47.222	2229.917	21.696
Eng/M	100	58.333	41.667	1736.111	29.762
Eng/F	20	61.667	−41.667	1736.111	28.153
A&S/M	200	194.444	5.556	30.864	.159
A&S/F	200	205.556	5.556	30.864	.150

The value of χ^2, 102.856, clearly exceeds the critical value of 13.82 for $(2 − 1)(3 − 1) = 2$ degrees of freedom. Therefore, you can conclude that males and females are not equally distributed among the three colleges or that gender and college are not independent, $\chi^2(2, N = 720) = 102.86, p < .001$.

c. To do this test, you need to combine across the categories of Engineering and Arts & Sciences. The contingency table and totals look like this:

	Male	*Female*	*Total*
Education	50	150	200
Eng/A&S	300	220	520
Total	350	370	720

Using the calculator formula for χ^2, we get

$$\chi^2 = \frac{N[(A)(D) - (B)(C)]^2}{(A + B)(C + D)(A + C)(B + D)}$$

$$= \frac{720[(50)(220) - (150)(300)]^2}{(200)(520)(350)(370)} = 61.80$$

Since this value for χ^2 has only 1 degree of freedom, it is highly statistically significant, leading to the conclusion that the percentage of students in the College of Education who were men (25%) is significantly less than the percentage of males in the other two colleges (58%), $\chi^2(1, N = 720) = 61.80, p < .001$.

17.a. The correct test is a 3×3 chi-square test of independence. We'll begin by calculating the row and column totals for the data.

	Appleby	*Bandelier*	*Coronado*	*Total*
Alligator	120	20	40	180
Bear	90	200	80	370
Cougar	10	10	100	120
Total	220	230	220	670 = N

Next we'll calculate the expected frequencies.

Appleby Alligator = $(220)(180)/670 = 59.10$
Appleby Bear = $(220)(370)/670 = 121.49$
Appleby Cougar = $(220)(120)/670 = 39.40$
Bandelier Alligator = $(230)(180)/670 = 61.79$
Bandelier Bear = $(230)(370)/670 = 127.01$
Bandelier Cougar = $(230)(120)/670 = 41.19$
Coronado Alligator = $(220)(180)/670 = 59.10$
Coronado Bear = $(220)(370)/670 = 121.49$
Coronado Cougar = $(220)(120)/670 = 39.40$

Next, we'll put together a table.

	O	*E*	*(O − E)*	*(O − E)²*	*(O − E)²/E*
Ap/Al	120	59.10	60.90	3708.81	62.75
Ap/Be	90	121.49	−31.49	991.62	8.16
Ap/Co	10	39.40	−29.40	864.36	21.94
Ba/Al	20	61.79	−41.79	1746.40	28.26
Ba/Be	200	127.01	72.99	5327.54	41.95
Ba/Co	10	41.19	−31.19	972.82	23.62
Co/Al	40	59.10	−19.10	364.81	6.17
Co/Be	80	121.49	−41.49	1721.42	14.17
Co/Co	100	39.40	60.60	3672.36	93.21
					300.23 = χ^2

$df = (3 − 1)(3 − 1) = 4$
$\chi^2_{.001}(4) = 18.47$

b. A chi-square test of independence shows that there is a highly significant relationship between school attended and preference for a school mascot, $\chi^2(4, N = 670) = 300.23, p < .001$. If you are wondering why this value of chi-square is so large, good for you! In fact, there are two reasons. First, I made up the data based on my knowledge that Bandelier is a real school with the Bandabear as the mascot. I assumed that students at each school would prefer to have the mascot that they already have. Second, the N is very large. Significant results are much more likely when Ns are large.

c. To do this test, we have to collapse across categories.

	Bandelier	*Appleby + Coronado*	*Total*
Bears	200	170	370
Alligators + Cougars	30	270	300
Total	230	440	

Next, we calculate expected values.

$$\text{Banda/Bears} = (230)(370)/670 = 127.01$$
$$\text{Banda/Al + Co} = (230)(300)/670 = 102.99$$
$$\text{Ap + Co/Bears} = (440)(370)/670 = 242.99$$
$$\text{Ap + Co/Al + Co} = (440)(300)/670 = 197.01$$

Then we calculate chi-square.

O	E	$(O - E)$	$(O - E)^2$	$(O - E)^2/E$
200	127.01	72.99	5327.54	41.95
30	102.99	−72.99	5327.54	51.73
170	242.99	−72.99	5327.54	21.93
270	197.01	72.99	5327.54	27.04
				$142.65 = \chi^2$

This analysis has 1 degree of freedom. Appendix Table 8 shows that $\chi^2_{.001}(1) = 10.83$

d. From this analysis we can conclude that students at Bandelier prefer bears as mascots more than do students at Appleby and Coronado, $\chi^2(1, N = 670) = 142.65, p < .001$.

e. We would need to do a goodness-of-fit test, comparing our data with the theoretical proportion of .3333 of the 670 students choosing each mascot.

	OF	*EP*	*EF*	$(O - E)$	$(O - E)^2$	$(O - E)^2/E$
Alligators	180	.3333	223.33	−43.33	1877.49	8.41
Bears	370	.3333	223.33	146.67	21512.09	96.32
Cougars	120	.3333	223.33	−103.33	10677.97	47.81
						$152.54 = \chi^2$

This analysis has 2 degrees of freedom. $\chi^2_{.001}(2) = 13.82$.

f. A chi-square goodness-of-fit test revealed that Alligators, Bears, and Cougars were not equally preferred as mascots, $\chi^2(2, N = 670) = 152.54, p < .001$.

19.a. As usual, we begin by calculating the row and column totals.

	Insecure	*Secure*	*Total*
Confirming	35	20	55
Contradicting	5	20	25
Total	40	40	80

Next we need to calculate the expected frequencies.

$$\text{Insecure/Confirming: } (40)(55)/80 = 27.5$$
$$\text{Insecure/Contradicting: } (40)(25)/80 = 12.5$$
$$\text{Secure/Confirming: } (40)(55)/80 = 27.5$$
$$\text{Secure/Contradicting: } (40)(25)/80 = 12.5$$

O	E	$(O - E)$	$(O - E)^2$	$(O - E)^2/E$
35	27.5	7.5	56.25	2.05
5	12.5	−7.5	56.25	4.50
20	27.5	−7.5	56.25	2.05
20	12.5	7.5	56.25	4.50
				$13.10 = \chi^2$

b. Using the calculator formula, we have

$$\chi^2 = \frac{(80)[(35)(20)-(20)(5)]^2}{(55)(25)(40)(40)} = \frac{(80)(600)^2}{2,200,000}$$

$$= \frac{(80)(360,000)}{2,200,000} = 13.09$$

(The difference in the two values is due to rounding.)

c. phi $= \sqrt{\dfrac{\chi^2}{N}} = \sqrt{\dfrac{13.09}{80}} = \sqrt{.1636} = .40$

d. Since $\chi^2_{.001}(1) = 10.83$, I would conclude that a significantly higher percentage of people who felt secure chose to view videos described as contradicting their expectations (50%) than did people who were insecure (12.5%): $\chi^2(1, N = 80) = 13.09, p < .001$.

Chapter 14

Multiple-Choice Questions

1. The correct answer is **c.**

3. In this case, you have mistakenly concluded that there is a relationship between variables, which is a Type I error. Answer **a** is correct.

5. This is a hypothesis about differences in the means of paired scores. Alternative **d** is correct.

Problems

7.a. The correct answer is Spearman rho, since you are relating scores on two ordinal variables.

b. In this case, you are testing a hypothesis about variances, so you would perform an *F*-test.

c. In order to answer this question, you would have to use the normal curve table. This presumes that the number of pushups is normally distributed.

d. This is a case of either an independent-samples *t*-test or a one-way analysis of variance.

e. In this case you would have to perform a Scheffé post hoc comparison.

f. You are relating two nominal level variables, so you should use a chi-square test of independence.

g. Since you wish to predict score on one interval level variable from score on the other, regression is the correct choice.

h. To compare three means, use an analysis of variance.

i. To relate two interval scale variables, do a Pearson *r*.

j. Since you are comparing the means of pairs of scores, do a paired-samples *t*-test.

k. A dependent-samples *t*-test, since each mother is paired with her daughter.

l. You need to do an *F*-test.

m. You need to do a chi-square test of independence.

n. You should do a Scheffé post hoc comparison. You could do four Tukey HSD's instead, but it would be less efficient.

o. Do a Pearson *r*. A Spearman rho could also be computed, after transforming the data to ranks, but since the number of letters is a ratio scale variable, Pearson *r* would be preferable.

p. Since you have only one (nominal level) variable, you would do a chi-square goodness-of-fit test.

q. You could do either a one-way analysis of variance or an independent-samples *t*-test.

r. This is a normal curve problem.

s. Since you wish to predict, you need regression.

t. In this case, you could use either a single-sample *t*-test or a *z*-test if you know the standard deviation.

u. To estimate the mean, you need to construct a confidence interval. (The point estimate provided by the sample mean is almost surely wrong.)

v. Since you are relating two sets of rankings, Spearman rho is the correct answer.

w. You need a one-way ANOVA.

x. You could use either a Tukey HSD or a Scheffé post hoc comparison procedure.

y. Since test scores are presumably interval level variables, you would use Pearson r.

z. Since you are interested in an interaction between two factors, you would use a two-way ANOVA.

9.a. You need to do a one-way analysis of variance, with 2 and 27 degrees of freedom, leading to a critical value of 5.49.

b. You need to compute a Pearson r with 17 degrees of freedom, leading to a critical value of .693.

c. Since you have already done a one-way analysis of variance, you should do a Scheffé post hoc test of your hypothesis. The critical value will be twice the critical value for F with 2 and 65 degrees of freedom or 2(3.14), which = 6.28.

d. You need to do a paired-samples t-test to compare the mean scores of husbands and wives. With 25 degrees of freedom, the critical value is 3.725.

e. Since both variables are nominal, you should do a chi-square test of independence. With 2 degrees of freedom, the critical value is 9.21.

f. In this case, you have 3 means and 17 degrees of freedom within groups. The critical value is 4.74.

g. You need to do a one-way analysis of variance with 3 and 44 degrees of freedom. The critical value is 4.26. Or, use the value for 3 and 40 df, which = 4.31.

h. In this case, the correct test is a chi-square test of independence with 2 degrees of freedom, leading to a critical value of 9.21.

i. Since you are relating ranks, use a Spearman rho with 16 degrees of freedom and a critical value of .475.

j. This is an example of a correlated samples t test, with 15 degrees of freedom and a critical value of 4.073.

Index

Abscissa (*x*-axis), 84–85, 527
Absolute value, 26, 527
  of *t*, 295–296
Action research, 56. *See also*
  Research, applied
Alpha (α) level, 196, 197, 277, 278,
  372, 527
Alternate hypothesis, 274–276, 527.
  See also Hypotheses;
  Hypothesis testing
Analysis of covariance
  (ANCOVA), 62, 359, 527
Analysis of variance (ANOVA),
  341–361. *See also* *F*-test
  a priori vs. post hoc
    comparisons and, 374–375
  vs. chi-square or *t*-test, 469–470
  employing *F*-test, 340, 342
  F-distribution and, 334
  formulas for, 344–349
  interpretation of *F* from, 356–357
  Kruskal–Wallis one-way, 483
  vs. multiple regression, 359–361
  vs. multiple *t*-tests, 343–344
  multivariate, 358–359
  one-way, 341–357, 360, 534
  one-way vs. *t*-test, 357
  repeated measures, 358, 536
  summary table, 349
  sum of squares, 344–345
  3 × 3, 427–434
  2 × 2, 423–427
  two-way, 407–446
APA (American Psychological
  Association) style, 115, 131,
  203, 427, 467–468, 490
A posteriori test. *See* Post hoc
  comparison
Applied research, 54, 56–57, 527.
  See also Research
A priori comparison, 66, 373–375,
  377, 378, 380, 395–396, 397, 527
Asymptote, 88

Bar graph, 85–86, 90–91, 92–93,
  527. *See also* Graphs
Basic research, 54, 56–57, 527. *See
  also* Research
Beta (β), 280. *See also* Null
  hypothesis; Type II (β) error
Between-participants variable,
  60–61, 408, 527. *See also*
  Variables
Bimodal distribution, 89–90, 528.
  See also Distributions
Binomial distribution, 145,

151–154, 528. *See also*
  Distributions
Bivariate distribution, 180–181,
  528. *See also* Distributions
Bonferroni critical value
  procedure, 278, 394–395, 528
Box-and-whisker plot, 118, 528

Calculators, 32–33
  formula for 2 × 2 chi-square
    table, 458–459
Case study, 48, 54, 528. *See also*
  Research
Causal–comparative research, 51,
  54, 528. *See also* Research
Census, 249, 258, 528
Central Limit Theorem, 260–263,
  528
Central tendency, measures of,
  106–115, 528, 532
  estimating from grouped data,
    115
  level of measurement, 113
  mean, 109–111, 112
  median, 107–109, 112
  mode, 106–107, 112
  reporting in APA style, 115
Change scores, 62, 528
Chi-square (χ^2), 22, 145, 447–477.
  See also Distributions
  contingency tables for, 456–457
  critical values for, 448, 452–453,
    526
  distribution, 447–448
  formula for, 450–452, 455, 457,
    465
  goodness-of-fit test, 449–456,
    469, 528
  goodness-of-fit vs. test of
    independence, 469
  reporting in APA style, 467–468
  vs. *r* or rho, 469
  test of independence, 186, 209,
    456–466, 528
  3 × 4 test, 462–463
  vs. *t* or ANOVA, 469–470
  2 × 2 test, 459–461
Class interval, 76, 84, 95, 97, 528
  limits, 14, 76
Clearly biased sampling method,
  257, 286
Cluster sampling, 256–257, 258,
  286, 528
Coefficient of determination (r^2),
  202, 528
Comparison of means, 371–406,

528. *See also* Scheffé
  comparison; Tukey HSD
  procedure
  advantages of, 372–373
  a priori vs. post hoc, 373–375
Computers, 32–33, 491–492
Confidence intervals, 271–272,
  316–322, 528
  formulas for, 317–322
  vs. *t*-test, 324
Constant, holding variables, 58
Constants, 12, 15, 528
Contingency table, 456–457, 529
Continuous quantitative variable,
  13–14, 15, 529. *See also*
  Variables
Contrast, 529. *See also* Comparison
  of means
Convenience sampling method,
  257, 258, 286, 529. *See also*
  Sampling
Correlated-samples *t*-test. *See*
  Dependent-samples *t*-test
Correlation, 180–216, 218–219. *See
  also* Pearson *r*; Spearman rho
  (ρ)
  coefficient, 91–92, 181, 208–209,
    529
  curvilinear relationship,
    182–183, 529
  direction, 181–183
  Kendall's tau, 204
  multiple, 207–208, 239, 533
  near-zero relationship, 183
  negative, 181, 182, 184, 533
  partial, 62, 207, 534
  Pearson *r*, 184–203
  positive, 181, 182, 184, 535
  ratio, eta (η), 186, 208, 530
  regression and, 184, 218–219
  reporting in APA style, 203
  Spearman rho, 204–207
  strength of, 183–184
  zero, 184
Correlational research, 50–52, 529.
  See also Research
Cramer's *V*, 466, 529
Critical region, 277, 529
Critical values, 196–198, 277–278,
  529
  for a priori comparison, 380
  for Bonferroni procedure, 278,
    394–395
  for chi-square, 452–453, 526
  for chi-square distribution, 448
  for *F*-ratios, 338–340, 518–523

for normal distribution, 277
for Pearson r, 196–198, 512
for Scheffé post hoc comparison,
    378–379
for Spearman rho, 513
test statistic, 300
for t-ratios, 299–300, 305, 312, 517
for Tukey HSD test, 390–391,
    524–525
Cross-sectional research, 49–50, 54,
    529. *See also* Research
Cumulative frequency
    distribution, 78–79, 84, 529.
    See also Frequency
    distributions
Cumulative frequency polygon, 94
Cumulative relative frequency
    distributions, 81, 84, 529
Curvilinear relationship, 529. *See
    also* Correlation

Data, 1, 2, 529
    describing, 106–144, 480
    in graphs, 85–88, 91–94, 96–97.
        See also Graphs
    measurement level of, 128
    nature of, 478–480
    original, 73
    qualitative, 13, 15, 85–86, 128,
        137
    quantitative, 13, 15, 16, 87–88
    summarizing, 484
    in tables, 74–81, 95–96. *See also*
        Frequency distributions
Data snooping. *See* Post hoc
    comparison
Degrees of freedom, 196, 529
    for chi-square goodness-of-fit
        test, 451–452
    for chi-square test of
        independence, 458
    for comparisons, 380
    for F-test, 338
    for Pearson r, 196
    for sum of squares, 344, 345
    for t-distribution, 298
    two-way ANOVA, 417, 436
Dependent measures, 52. *See also*
    Variables, dependent
Dependent-samples t-test,
    309–315, 316, 323–324, 529. *See
    also* t-test
Dependent variable, 52, 529. *See
    also* Variables
Descriptive research, 48, 54, 529.
    See also Research
Descriptive statistics, 6–8. *See also*
    Statistics
Developmental research, 49–50, 55,
    530. *See also* Research

Deviation. *See* Standard deviation;
    z-scores
Deviation score, 23, 530. *See also*
    Transformed scores
Discrete quantitative variable,
    13–14, 15, 530. *See also*
    Variables
Distributions, 84. *See also*
    Frequency distributions;
    Normal curve
    bimodal, 107, 528
    binomial, 145, 151–154, 528
    bivariate, 180–181, 528
    chi-square, 145, 447–448
    F-distribution, 145, 334–335,
        341–342
    multimodal, 107
    normal, 89–90, 107, 145, 154–157,
        187, 277, 533
    shape of, 88–89, 113–114
    skewness, 88–91, 112, 533, 535
    t-distribution, 145
Duncan's multiple range test, 394

Effect size, 282, 422, 530
Empirical frequency distribution,
    145, 530
Error. *See* Standard error; Type I
    (α) error; Type II (β) error
Error variance, 310
Eta (η), 186, 208, 530
Eta squared (η^2), 356–357, 533
Ethnographic research, 47. *See also*
    Research, qualitative
Expected frequency, 451, 457–458,
    530
    collapsing, 463–464, 466–467
    correcting, 466–467
    Fisher's exact probability test of,
        467
    marginal, 458
    vs. proportions, 451
    Yates' correction of, 467
Expected value, 260, 530. *See also*
    Sampling distribution
Experimental research, 52–56, 530.
    See also Research
    control groups in, 53
    effect size of mean in, 282
    experimental groups in, 53
    quasi-, 52, 55
    validity of, 63
Experimentwise error rate, 278,
    396, 530
Ex post facto research, 51. *See also*
    Research, causal-comparative
External validity of research, 63, 530

Factor, 52. *See also* Variables,
    independent

Factorial design, 53, 59–61, 358,
    408–419, 531. *See also* Analysis
    of variance (ANOVA); Two-
    way ANOVA; Variables,
    control of
Familywise error rate, 396
F-distribution, 145, 334–335,
    341–342. *See also*
    Distributions
Field research, 55, 57, 531. *See also*
    Research
Fisher, Sir Ronald, 334
Fixed effect, 408, 531
F-ratio, 335, 338–340, 518–523
Frequency distributions, 74–81,
    84–94, 531. *See also*
    Distributions
    cumulative, 78–79, 84, 529
    cumulative relative, 81, 84
    empirical, 145, 530
    grouped, 75–77, 84, 531
    percentile, 81–83, 84, 534
    relative, 80–81, 84, 536
    simple, 74–75, 84, 537
    stem-and-leaf display of, 78, 84,
        537
    in tabular form, 95–96
    theoretical, 145–146, 537
Frequency histogram, 87–88, 94,
    96, 531. *See also* Graphs
Frequency polygon, 87, 88, 94, 96,
    97, 531. *See also* Graphs
F-test, 334–340, 530. *See also*
    Analysis of variance
    (ANOVA)
Fully crossed factorial design, 409,
    531

Goodness-of-fit test, chi-square,
    449–456, 469, 528
Grand mean, 344–345, 531
Graphs, 84–94, 96–97, 172. *See also*
    Frequency distributions
    bar, 85–86, 91, 94, 97, 528
    frequency histogram, 87–88, 94,
        96, 531
    frequency polygon, 87, 88, 94,
        96, 97, 531
    line, 91, 94, 97, 532
    pie, 86, 94, 534
    scattergraph, 92, 94, 97, 181–182,
        183, 536
Grouped frequency distributions,
    75–77, 84, 531

H_0, 273–274. *See also* Null
    hypothesis
H_a, 274–276. *See also* Alternate
    hypothesis
Haphazard sampling method, 257,

258, 286, 529. *See also*
   Sampling
Heteroscedasticity, 237, 238, 531
Historical research. *See* Research
Homoscedasticity, 228, 237, 238, 531
Honestly significant difference. *See*
   Tukey HSD procedure
Hotelling's T^2, 482
Hypotheses, 4, 43–45, 273–276,
   484–485, 531
   alternate, 274–276, 527
   directional, 44
   null, 44–45, 273–274, 275, 277,
     279–280, 287, 411–412, 533
   role in research, 43–45
   theoretical vs. operational, 44
Hypothesis testing, 272–273, 531.
    See also F-test; t-test; z-tests
   effect size of mean in, 282
   errors in, 279–280
   about means, t-tests for, 294–298
   null vs. alternative hypotheses,
     273–276
   power of, 281–282
   significance levels in, 276–278
   significance tests in, 282–285

Inclusive range, 116, 531. *See also*
   Range
Incomplete factorial design, 409,
   531
Independent events, 149–150, 151,
   531. *See also* Probability (P)
Independent-samples t-test,
   303–309, 316, 323–324, 531. *See*
   also t-test
Independent variable, 52, 531. *See*
   also Variables
Inferential statistics, 8, 10–11, 20,
   249–293, 531
   Central Limit Theorem and,
     260–263
   hypothesis testing and, 272–273,
     275
   parameter estimation and,
     270–272, 275
Interaction, 60, 411, 419–423, 532
Internal validity of research, 63,
   532
Interpolation, 29–30, 171, 532
Interquartile range, 118, 127, 129.
   See also Range
Interval scale, 17, 19, 20, 87–88,
   129, 137, 184–185, 296, 532
   equal-appearing interval scales,
     19
   vs. ordinal scale, 18–19
   vs. ratio scale, 19
Interview research, 50, 55. *See also*
   Research, survey

Kruskal–Wallis. *See* Analysis of
   variance (ANOVA)

Laboratory research, 55, 57, 532.
   See also Research
Least-squares estimate, 110, 532
Level of measurement, 15–20,
   478–479. *See also*
   Measurement, scale; Variables
   measures of central tendency
     and, 113
   measures of variability and,
     128–130
Level of variables, 52, 341, 532. *See*
   also Measurement, scale;
   Variables
Likert scales, 18, 129, 479
Linear model, 345
Linear regression. *See* Regression
Line graph, 91–92, 94, 97, 532. *See*
   also Graphs
Longitudinal research, 49–50, 55,
   532. *See also* Research

Main effect, 411, 419–423, 433–434,
   532
Mann–Whitney U test, 483
Mathematical procedures
   formulas and equations,
     guidelines for, 31–32
   fractions, 28–29
   interpolation, 29–30
   proportions and percentages,
     27–28
   rounding off, 29
   significant digits and decimal
     places, 30–31
   symbols for, 24–31
Mean, 24, 109–111, 112, 485, 532.
    See also Central tendency,
    measures of
   comparison of, 482
   confidence intervals for,
     317–322
   differences in, 267–270, 282,
     294–296, 318–322, 325, 341,
     357, 359
   expected value of, 260
   formula for, 24, 109, 110
   formula for Pearson r, 189–190,
     194–195
   regression toward the, 230–235
   sampling distribution of the, 259
   symbol for, 24
   testing hypotheses about,
     264–265, 294–298, 340
   weighted, 375–376
Mean absolute deviation, 118–119,
   127, 129. *See also* Variability,
   measures of

Mean square. *See* Analysis of
   variance (ANOVA); Sum of
   squares
Measurement, 12, 532
   dependent measure, 52
   multiple dependent measures,
     483
   scale of, 15–20, 478–479, 536
Measures of central tendency. *See*
   Central tendency, measures
   of
Measures of variability. *See*
   Variability, measures of
Median, 107–109, 112, 533. *See also*
   Central tendency, measures
   of
   comparison of, 482–483
Mixed effects design, 408–409
Mode, 106–107, 112, 533. *See also*
   Central tendency, measures of
Monotonic scale, 18, 533
Multimodal distribution, 107. *See*
   also Distributions
Multivariate analysis of covariance
   (MANCOVA), 358–359, 533.
    See also Analysis of covariance
   (ANCOVA)
Mutually exclusive events,
   148–149, 151, 152, 533

Negative correlation, 181, 182, 184,
   533. *See also* Correlation
Negatively skewed distribution,
   90–91, 112, 533. *See also*
   Distributions
Negative numbers, 26–27
Nested designs, 409, 533
Newman–Keuls test, 394
Nominal scale, 16, 19, 85–86, 128,
   533
Nonparametric tests, 20, 21, 22,
   479, 533. *See also* Chi-square
   (χ^2); Spearman rho (ρ)
Normal curve, 22, 88–89, 145,
   154–174
   areas under unit, 508–511
   cutoff scores, 165–170
   dividing area under, 156–157
   graphing, 154–155, 172
   mutually exclusive areas of, 156
   probability and, 155–156,
     158–160
   problem-solving guidelines,
     172–174
   table, 157–160, 533
   types of problems, 160–171
   z-scores and, 156–157
Normal distribution, 88–89, 145,
   154–157, 186, 277, 533. *See also*
   Distributions; Normal curve

Null hypothesis, 44–45, 273–274, 275, 287, 533
    errors in retaining or rejecting, 279–280
    region of rejection, 277, 536
    region of retention, 277, 536
    in two-way ANOVA, 411–412

Observed frequency, 451, 533
Omega squared, 357, 422, 534
One-tailed significance test, 282–285, 534. *See also* Hypothesis testing
    decision rules for, 283–285
One-way ANOVA, 341–357, 360, 534. *See also* Analysis of variance (ANOVA)
Ordinal scale, 16, 19–20, 87–88, 534
    vs. interval scale, 18–19
    Spearman rho and, 204
Ordinate (*y*-axis), 84, 534
Orthogonality, of comparisons, 384–388, 395, 397–398

P. See Probability (*P*)
Paired-samples *t*-test. *See* Dependent-samples *t*-test
Parameter, 10–11, 534
Parameter estimation, 270–272, 275, 534
    confidence intervals and, 271–272
    point estimation and, 271
Parametric tests, 20–22, 479, 534
Partial correlation, 62, 207, 534. *See also* Correlation
Pearson, Karl, 184
Pearson *r*, 184–203, 208, 534
    causality and, 200–201
    vs. chi-square or rho, 469
    critical values for, 512
    degrees of freedom and, 196
    formula for, using means, 195–203
    formula for, using raw scores, 190, 192
    formula for regression line, 222
    formula for standard error of estimate, 236
    linearity of, 188–189
    range of values of, 185
    reporting in APA style, 203
    significance of, 195–203
    slope formula using, 223–225
    vs. Spearman rho, 207
    vs. *t*-test, 322–323
    two-tailed critical values for, 196
    variation in, 201–202
    z-score formula for, 189–190

Percentage, 28
Percentile, 81–83, 84, 534. *See also* Distributions
    computing, guidelines for, 83
Phi coefficient, 465–466, 534
Pie graph, 86, 94, 534. *See also* Graphs
p-level, 196, 203, 490. *See also* Significance
Point estimation, 271, 534
Population, 8–9, 119–121, 534
    equal *n*'s, 254–255
    generalizing to, 258–259
    proportional *n*'s, 254
Positive correlation, 181, 182, 184, 535. *See also* Correlation
Positively skewed distribution, 90–91, 112, 535. *See also* Distributions
Positive numbers, 26–27
Post hoc comparison, 66, 373–375, 378–379, 395–396, 397, 421, 535. *See also* Scheffé comparison
Power, 535
    of tests, 21, 22, 281–282
Predicted scores, notation, 217–218
Prediction, 217, 240. *See also* Regression
Probability (*P*), 146–151, 535
    binomial distribution and, 151–154
    formulas for, 146–151
    independent events, 149–150, 151, 531
    mutually exclusive events, 148–149, 151, 152, 533
    nonindependent events, 150–151
    normal curve and, 155–156, 158–160, 508–511
    normal distribution and, 155–156
Product-moment correlation coefficient. *See* Pearson *r*
Proportion, 27–28, 146, 485, 535
    differences in proportions, 483
    vs. expected frequencies, 451
    proportional *n*'s, 254

Qualitative data, 128, 137. *See also* Nominal scale
    graphing, 96
Qualitative research, 47–48, 55, 535. *See also* Research
Quantitative data. *See also* Interval scale; Ordinal scale; Ratio scale
    graphing, 96
Quasi-experimental research, 52, 55, 535. *See also* Research

Questionnaire research, 50, 55. *See also* Research, survey
Quota sampling method, 255, 258, 286, 535. *See also* Sampling

r. See Pearson *r*
Random assignment, 53, 59. *See also* Random sampling
Random effect, 408, 535
Random number table, 250–252, 514–516
Random sampling, 59, 186, 250–253, 258, 286, 535. *See also* Sampling
    methods of, 250–252
    random selection vs. assignment, 252–253
    stratified, 253–254
Range, 116–118, 535
    inclusive, 116, 531
    interquartile, 118, 127, 129
Rank. *See* Spearman rho (*ρ*); Variables
Rank sum test. *See* Mann–Whitney *U* test
Ratio scale, 17–18, 19, 20, 87–88, 184–185, 296, 341, 535
Raw scores, 23, 535
    converting from *z*-score, 132
    converting to *z*-score, 132, 160
    corresponding percentile rank, 82–83
    formula for Pearson *r*, 192–195
    formula for slope of regression line, 222–227
    formula for standard deviation of population, 120–121, 124
    formula for standard deviation of sample, 125
    formula for variance, 127
    symbols for, 23
Region of rejection, 277, 536. *See also* Null hypothesis
Region of retention, 277, 536. *See also* Null hypothesis
Regression, 217–248, 480–481, 536
    bivariate, 217, 481
    coefficients of, 220–221
    computational formula for, 220–227, 228
    correlation and, 218–219
    equation, 183, 217, 223–227, 536
    linear, 184, 217
    toward the mean, 230–235, 536
    multiple, 238–240, 359–361, 481, 533
    vs. multiple ANOVA, 359–361
    multiple regression, 238–240, 481
    predicted values for, 217–218

standard error of estimate and, 236–238
Y-intercept and, 221, 223, 228, 230
z-score formula for, 219–220
Regression line, 184, 217, 228, 536
least-squares estimate of Y, 217
plotting, 228
slope formula, using raw scores, 222–223
slope formulas, using r, 222
slope of, 201, 221
using, 229–230
Relative frequency distribution, 80–81, 84, 536. *See also* Frequency distributions
Repeated measures, 358, 536. *See also* Analysis of variance (ANOVA)
Research, 42–72, 492–493
applied, 54, 56–57, 527
basic, 54, 56–57, 527
case study, 48, 54, 528
causal–comparative, 51, 54, 528
control methods for, 58–63
correlational, 50–52, 529
cross-sectional, 49–50, 54, 529
descriptive, 48, 54, 529
developmental, 49–50, 55, 530
estimating results in, 65–66
experimental, 52–56, 530
field, 55, 57, 531
generalizing results of, 258–259
historical, 46–47, 55, 531
interview, 55
laboratory, 55, 57, 531
longitudinal, 49–50, 55, 532
meaning of numbers in, 64
meeting assumptions of, 65
purposes of, 56–57
qualitative, 47–48, 55, 535
quasi-experimental, 52, 55, 535
scientific, 42–46
survey, 50, 55, 537
types of, 54–55
validity of, 63
Research design, 58–63, 232
Research hypothesis, 44, 273, 275, 536. *See also* Hypotheses
Robust, 21, 22, 297, 342, 536

Sample, 9, 124–126, 536
census, 9
formulas for standard deviation, 124–126
formulas for variance, 127
generalizing to population, 258–259
in inferential statistics, 10–11, 249–259
mean, 317

size, 451, 479–480
types of, 258
Sampling. *See also* Distributions; Sampling distribution
biased, 250, 258
clearly biased, 257, 286
cluster, 256–257, 258, 286, 528
convenience, or haphazard, 257, 258, 286, 529
quota, 255, 258, 286, 535
random, 59, 186, 250–253, 258, 286, 535
without replacement, 536
stratified, 253–255, 258, 286, 537
systematic, 255–256, 258, 286, 537
types of, 258
with replacement, 150, 536
without replacement, 150, 536
Sampling distribution, 259–263, 536. *See also* Distributions
Central Limit Theorem and, 260–263
expected values of, 260
of the mean, 259
standard error of, 260
Scattergraph, 92–93, 94, 97, 181–182, 183, 536. *See also* Graphs
Scheffé comparison, 376–389, 396, 398, 421, 431, 432, 536
advantages and disadvantages, 388–389
critical values for, 378–380
formulas, 377–378
orthogonality, 384–388
procedure, 389
Scientific research, 42–46. *See also* Research
hypotheses in, 43–45
observation in, 43
Scores. *See also* z-scores; T-score
class intervals for, 76, 84, 95, 97
organizing, 73
predicting, 480–481
raw. *See* Raw scores
standard, 131–136
transformed. *See* Transformed scores
Significance, 490, 537
correlation and, 195–203
F-test and, 338–340
levels of, 196–197, 203, 276–278, 374, 490
vs. meaningfulness, 285–286
Pearson r and, 195–203
t-test, 190, 299–300, 305, 312
Significance tests, 282–285
decision rules for, 283–285
multiple, 484
one-tailed vs. two-tailed, 282–285

Simple frequency distribution, 74–75, 84, 537. *See also* Frequency distributions
Simple random sampling, 253–254. *See also* Random sampling
Single-sample t-test, 298–303, 316, 537
Skewness, 90–91, 112, 533, 535
Slope, 221, 537. *See also* Regression line
Spearman rho (ρ), 22, 204–207, 208, 537
vs. chi-square or Pearson r, 469
critical values of, 513
formula for, 204
vs. Pearson r, 207
Standard deviation, 119–126, 129, 537
definitional (deviation score) formula for a population, 119–123
definitional (deviation score) formula for a sample, 125–126
pooled error term, 344
raw score formula for a population, 120–121, 124
raw score formula for a sample, 125–126
Standard error, 537
of the difference in means, 267–269
of estimate, 236–238, 537
of the mean, 268
of a sampling distribution, 260
Standard scores, 131–136. *See also* z-scores
SAT scores, 135–136
standardized tests, 134, 135–136
T-scores, 134–135, 136
Statistic, 10–11
Statistical relationship, 180, 181–184. *See also* Correlation
Statistical test, 20. *See also* Nonparametric tests; Parametric tests
selecting appropriate, 478–501
Statistics, 1, 10–11, 487–489, 537
descriptive, 6–8
guidelines for using, 64–66
inferential, 8, 10–11, 20, 249–293, 531
vs. parameters, 10–11. *See also* Parameter estimation
research and, 1–6, 492–493. *See also* Research
research issues, 489–490
study of, 33–35, 491
uses of, 6–12

Stem-and-leaf display, 78, 84, 537.
    See also Frequency
    distributions
Stratified sampling method,
    253–255, 258, 286, 537. *See also*
    Frequency distributions;
    Sampling
    equal *n*'s, 254–255
    proportional *n*'s, 254
    vs. simple random sampling,
       253–254
    stratified random, 253–254
Student's *t*-test. *See t*-test
Subscripts, 27
Sum of squares, 120, 344–345, 537
    between groups, 344, 345, 347,
       387–388
    grand mean, 344–345, 531
    mean square, 344, 532
    notation system for formulas of,
       346
    partitioning of, in two-way
       ANOVA, 413–414
    partitioning of variance, 346
    total, 344, 345
    within groups, 344–345, 347, 348
Survey research, 50, 55, 537. *See
    also* Research
Symbols
    multiplication, 24
    parameters, 10
    positive and negative numbers,
       26–27
    proportions and percentages,
       27–28
    for scores, 23
    squares and square roots, 25
    statistics, 10
    subscripts, 27
    summation, 23
Systematic sampling, 255–256, 258,
    286, 537. *See also* Sampling

t-distribution, 145. *See also*
    Distributions; *t*-test
    family of, 298
    relationship of *F*-distribution
       and, 341–342
Test statistic, 300, 537
Theoretical distribution, 145, 259,
    537. *See also* Frequency
    distributions
    types of, 145–146
Transformed scores, 538
    deviation score, 23
    standard score, 131–136
    symbols for, 23

z-score, 131–134, 156–157. *See
    also z*-scores
T-score, 134–135, 136
t-test, 264, 294–316, 537
    assumptions of, 296–298
    vs. chi-square or ANOVA,
       469–470
    vs. confidence interval, 324
    critical values for *t*-ratios, 305, 517
    degrees of freedom and, 298
    dependent-samples *t*-test,
       309–315, 316, 323–324, 529
    one-tailed vs. two-tailed,
       305–306
    vs. one-way ANOVA, 357
    vs. Pearson *r*, 322–323
    single-sample *t*-test, 298–303,
       316, 537
    types of, 298, 316
    vs. *z*-tests, 294–295
Tukey HSD procedure, 389–394,
    396, 482
    critical values for, 390–391,
       524–525
Two-tailed significance test,
    282–285, 538
    decision rules for, 283–285
Two-way ANOVA, 407–446, 538
    assumptions of, 410, 435
    formulas for, 412–418, 435
    logic of, 414
    notation, 412–413
    overview of, 411–412
    uses of, 418–436
Type I (α) error, 279, 538
    experimentwise error rate, 278,
       396, 530
    familywise error rate, 396
Type II (β) error, 279–280, 538

Validity, regression toward mean
    as, 232, 233
Variability, measures of, 115–131.
    See also Mean absolute
    deviation; Range; Standard
    deviation; Variance
    estimating from grouped data,
       130–131
    level of measurement, 128–130
    reporting in APA style, 131
    types of, 127–128
Variables, 12–15, 538
    between-participants, 60–61,
       527
    categorized, 479
    continuous, 13–14, 15, 529
    dependent, 52, 483, 529

discrete, 13–14, 15, 530
    extraneous, control of, 58–63
    independent, 52, 60–61, 341, 484,
       531
    interval-level, 17
    nominal-level, 16, 74
    ordinal-level, 16–17
    qualitative, 13, 15, 535
    quantitative, 13, 15, 16, 535
    ratio-level, 17–18
    relationship between, 481
    within-participants, 60–61, 408,
       538
Variance, 126–127, 128, 538
    error, 310
    formulas for, 126–127
    pooled error term, 344
    pooled estimate of, 373, 534
    proportion of common, in
       Pearson *r*, 202–203
    testing hypotheses about,
       335–340

Weights, 375–376, 396–397
Within-participants variable,
    60–61, 408, 538. *See also*
    Variables

X. See also Raw scores
    axis, 84
    symbol for scores, 23

Y-intercept, 221, 223, 228, 230, 538.
    See also Regression;
    Regression line

Zero correlation, 184
z-scores, 131–134
    converting from raw scores, 132,
       160
    converting to raw scores, 132
    formula for Pearson *r*, 188–189,
       192–194
    formula for regression, 219–220
    formulas for, 131–132, 136, 160
    and normal curve, 156–157. *See
       also* Normal curve
z-tests, 263–270, 286–287, 538. *See
    also* Central Limit Theorem
    general procedure for, 264–265
    with single sample, 266–267
    standard error of the difference
       in means, 267–269
    standard error of the mean, 268
    vs. *t*-test, 294–295
    with two sample means,
       267–269

List of Formulas

1. **Chi-square:** $\chi^2 = \Sigma\left[(O - E)^2 / E\right]$ Expected frequencies for a contingency table: $EF = \left[(\text{row } f)(\text{column } f)\right] / N$

   Calculator formula for 2×2 contingency table: $\chi^2 = \dfrac{N\left[(A)(D) - (B)(C)\right]^2}{(A + B)(C + D)(A + C)(B + D)}$

2. **Confidence interval:** For one sample mean: $\overline{X} \pm \left[t_\alpha(N - 1)\right](S_{\overline{X}})$

   For the difference in means of two independent samples: $\left(\overline{X}_1 - \overline{X}_2\right) \pm \left[t_\alpha(N - 2)\right]\left(s_{\overline{X}_1 - \overline{X}_2}\right)$

   For the difference in means of two paired samples: $\left(\overline{X}_1 - \overline{X}_2\right) \pm \left[t_\alpha(N - 1)\right](s_{\overline{D}})$

3. **Deviation score:** $X - \overline{X}$

4. **F-test:** $F = \dfrac{s_1^2}{s_2^2}$ F from analysis of variance: $\dfrac{MS_B}{MS_W}$

5. **Mean:** $\dfrac{\Sigma X}{N}$ Group mean computed from subgroup means: $\overline{X}_T = \dfrac{\Sigma f_i \overline{X}_i}{N}$

6. **Median:** Middle score when scores are arranged in rank order

7. **Mode:** Most frequent score

8. **One-way analysis of variance:**

   $$SS_T = \Sigma X^2 - \dfrac{T^2}{N} \qquad SS_B = \Sigma \dfrac{T_j^2}{n_j} - \dfrac{T^2}{N} \qquad SS_W = \Sigma X^2 - \Sigma \dfrac{T_j^2}{n_j}$$

   $$SS_W = \left(\Sigma X_1^2 - \dfrac{(\Sigma X_1)^2}{n_1}\right) + \left(\Sigma X_2^2 - \dfrac{(\Sigma X_2)^2}{n_2}\right) + \ldots \quad MS_B = \dfrac{\Sigma(T_j^2/n_j) - T^2/N}{(K - 1)} \quad MS_W = \dfrac{\Sigma X^2 - \Sigma\left(T_j^2/n_j\right)}{N - K}$$

   $$F = \dfrac{MS_B}{MS_W}$$

9. **Probability:** Event A: $P_A = \dfrac{n_A}{t}$ One or the other of two events: $P_{A \text{ or } B} = P_A + P_B - P_{A+B}$

   Both of two independent events: $P_{A+B} = (P_A)(P_B)$

10. **Pearson r:** z-score formula: $r = \dfrac{\Sigma z_X z_Y}{N}$, where z-scores have been calculated using σ_X and σ_Y

    Raw score formula: $r = \dfrac{N\Sigma\,XY - \Sigma X \Sigma Y}{\sqrt{\left(N\Sigma X^2 - (\Sigma X)^2\right)\left(N\Sigma Y^2 - (\Sigma Y)^2\right)}}$ Formula using means: $r = \dfrac{(\Sigma XY/N) - (\overline{X})(\overline{Y})}{\sigma_X \sigma_Y}$

11. **Range (inclusive):** Upper limit of highest score – lower limit of lowest score

12. **Regression:** z-score formula: $z_y' = r_{XY} z_X$ Raw score formula: $Y' = a + bX$

    Slope of the regression line using r: $b = r(\sigma_Y/\sigma_X)$ and $b = r(s_Y/s_X)$

    Raw score formula for slope: $b = \dfrac{N\Sigma XY - (\Sigma X)(\Sigma Y)}{N\Sigma X^2 - (\Sigma X)^2}$ Formula for Y-intercept: $a = \overline{Y} - b\overline{X}$

13. **Scheffé comparison:** $F = \dfrac{\left(\Sigma C_j \overline{X}_j\right)^2}{(MS_W)\left[\Sigma(C_j^2/n_j)\right]}$ Two comparisons are orthogonal if $\Sigma C_{j1} C_{j2} = 0$

    Critical value for a priori comparison: $F_{\text{com}} = F_\alpha(1, N - K)$

    Critical value for post hoc comparison: $F_{\text{com}} = (K - 1)[F_\alpha(K - 1, N - K)]$

14. **Spearman rho:** $\rho = 1 - \dfrac{6\Sigma D^2}{N(N^2 - 1)}$

15. **Standard deviation:** Deviation score formula for a population: $\sigma = \sqrt{\dfrac{\Sigma(X - \mu)^2}{N}}$

    Raw score formula for a population: $\sigma = \sqrt{\dfrac{\Sigma X^2 - (\Sigma X)^2/N}{N}}$